Emerging Technologies of Text Mining:
Techniques and Applications

Hércules Antonio do Prado
Catholic University of Brasilia, Brazil
Embrapa Food Technology, Brazil

Edilson Ferneda
Catholic University of Brasilia, Brazil

INFORMATION SCIENCE REFERENCE

Hershey • New York

Acquisitions Editor:	Kristin Klinger
Development Editor:	Kristin Roth
Senior Managing Editor:	Jennifer Neidig
Managing Editor:	Sara Reed
Assistant Managing Editor:	Carole Coulson
Copy Editor:	April Schmidt, Jeannie Porter
Typesetter:	Michael Brehm
Cover Design:	Lisa Tosheff
Printed at:	Yurchak Printing Inc.

Published in the United States of America by
Information Science Reference (an imprint of IGI Global)
701 E. Chocolate Avenue, Suite 200
Hershey PA 17033
Tel: 717-533-8845
Fax: 717-533-8661
E-mail: cust@igi-global.com
Web site: http://www.igi-global.com/reference

and in the United Kingdom by
Information Science Reference (an imprint of IGI Global)
3 Henrietta Street
Covent Garden
London WC2E 8LU
Tel: 44 20 7240 0856
Fax: 44 20 7379 0609
Web site: http://www.eurospanonline.com

Library of Congress Cataloging-in-Publication Data

Emerging technologies of text mining : techniques and applications / Hercules Antonio do Prado & Edilson Ferneda, editors.

p. cm.

Summary: "This book provides the most recent technical information related to the computational models of the text mining process, discussing techniques within the realms of classification, association analysis, information extraction, and clustering. Offering an innovative approach to the utilization of textual information mining to maximize competitive advantage, it will provide libraries with the defining reference on this topic"--Provided by publisher.

Includes bibliographical references and index.

ISBN 978-1-59904-373-9 (hardcover) -- ISBN 978-1-59904-375-3 (ebook)

1. Data mining. 2. Web databases. I. Prado, Hercules Antonio do. II. Ferneda, Edilson.

QA76.9.D343E53 2007

005.74--dc22

2007022229

British Cataloguing in Publication Data
A Cataloguing in Publication record for this book is available from the British Library.

All work contributed to this book set is new, previously-unpublished material. The views expressed in this book are those of the authors, but not necessarily of the publisher.

"To my sweetheart Adriana and my children Elisa and Daniel that have made my life a very pleasant and exciting experience!"

Hércules Prado

"To Lúcia, my beloved wife"

Edilson Ferneda

Table of Contents

Detailed Table of Contents

Chapter I

This chapter discusses information extraction related problems and provides an overview on the existing methodologies facing these problems. Rule learning based, classification based, and sequential labeling based methods are explained in detail. This discussion, along with some extraction applications experienced by the authors and examples of well-known applications in this field, makes this chapter an excellent reference for a tutorial program.

Chapter II

Departing from a sound point of view about the importance of information treatment and analysis as the most critical organizational competence for the information society, the authors bring an interesting discussion regarding the use of strategic information in Competitive Intelligence. They also present a comprehensive review on the methodologies tuned to the French school of Information Science and discuss the necessary integration of information for analysis and the data and text mining processes, presenting examples of real-world applications.

The integration of Natural Language Processing (NLP), Information Retrieval, Data Mining, and Text Mining to support competitive intelligence is the focus of this chapter. The authors hold with a disclosure tendency that leads companies to be more transparent as demanded by apprehensive shareholders in the face of unexpected crises in big companies. The chapter discusses NLP techniques applied to analyze the increasing amount of organizational information published in that scenario, looking for competitive advantages.

Natural Language Processing (NLP) technology for mining textual resources and extracting knowledge are the core of this chapter. An overview on the NLP techniques involved, beyond a brief explanation on the application of these techniques, is provided along with two case studies. The case studies focus on finding definitions in vast text collections and obtaining a short multi-document summary of a cluster to respond to a relevant question posed by an analyst.

Here the authors describe an approach for deriving a taxonomy from a set of documents by using semantic information generated at the document sentence level. This information is obtained from a document profile model built by applying a frequent word sequence method. The agglomerative hierarchical method is applied to create a clustering configuration from what the taxonomy is derived. Experimental results show that the derived taxonomy can demonstrate how the information is interwoven in a comprehensive and concise form.

An original approach to knowledge discovery from textual data based on a fuzzy decision tree is presented in this chapter. The methods involved in the rule extraction process are described, including the inductive learning method and the inference method involved. Two applications, one for analyzing daily business reports and another for rule discovering from e-mails, are presented in detail in order to make evident the effectiveness of the proposal.

This chapter extends the semi-supervised multi-view learning techniques for Text Mining. Semi-supervised learning is usually applied to build classification models over labeled and unlabeled data. The authors describe some algorithms related to this task, present a review of applications found in literature, including Web page classification and e-mail classification, and show experimental results found by analyzing academic and newsgroup related texts.

The authors of this chapter propose a multi-neural-network-agent-based Web text mining system for decision support by processing Web pages. The system comprises the processes of Web document searching, Web text processing, text feature conversion, and the neural model building. The scalability of this system is assured by the learning process implemented in a multi-agent structure. For performance evaluation, the authors describe a practical application for the crude oil price movement direction prediction.

The focus of this text is a problem usually experienced by millions of Web users when searching for information: how to analyze hundreds or thousands of ranked documents. Research results have shown that, if nothing interesting appears in the two or three top ranked documents, users prefer to reformulate their query instead of sifting through the numerous pages of search results that can hide relevant information. In this chapter an innovative approach based on the Suffix Tree Clustering algorithm to sift the search results is proposed. Also, a review on other text mining techniques used in exploratory search solutions, a discussion on some advantages and disadvantages of contextualized clustering, and experimental results are presented.

This chapter presents a study on the application of the Ant Colony Optimization model to improve Web navigation. Considering the existing similarities in behavior between Web users' navigation and ant colonies, the authors describe a system able to shorten the paths to a target page by applying information related to previous navigation. Although unable to have global vision due to their physical characteristics, ants at foraging use a curious marking system, in which any ant can leave a pheromone mark for others. The specific trails with stronger concentration of pheromone can guide the ants in finding shorter paths between their nest and the food source. AntWeb, the system resulting from the application of this metaphor, is described along with experimental results that demonstrate its benefits for users navigating in the Web and also its capacity to modify the Web structure adaptively.

Aiming to overcome the semantic mistakes that arise when applying the traditional word-based documents clustering techniques, an alternative to cluster textual documents using concepts is presented in this chapter. The use of concepts instead of simple words adds semantics to the document clustering process, leading to a better understanding of large document collections, easing the summarization of each cluster and the identification of its contents. A useful methodology for document clustering and some practical experiments in a case study are shown in detail to demonstrate the effectiveness of the proposed alternative.

Text Categorization (TC) techniques applied to the patent categorization problem are studied in this chapter. The patent categorization problem presents specific characteristics, like the existence of many vague or general terms, acronyms, and new terms, that make the traditional TC methods insufficient for an adequate categorization. Taking into account the application domain particularities and an important drawback in the existing TC solutions, the authors propose their method. An evaluation of this method on two English patent databases is presented and compared with other text categorization methods, showing how the proposed method outperforms the latter.

This chapter presents an application of Text Mining in the health management field. Nominal data related to patient medical conditions are used to define a patient severity index to model the quality of healthcare providers. A clustering analysis to rank groups of levels in the nominal data is carried out, issuing results that can help improving the healthcare system.

The interpretation process of patterns involved in any knowledge discovery task, particularly in clustering analysis, is approached in this chapter. In order to deal with the hard burden of subjectivity of this task, the authors built from the Ontology of Language a method to help the specialists in searching for a consensus when analyzing a given clustering configuration. This method, grounded in speech acts like affirmations, declarations, assessments, and so on, fits naturally as a pathway for the interpretation phase of Text Mining.

Foreword

All around modern society, an enormous amount of strategic information is spread in many different presentation forms, like e-mail, formal and informal documents, historical reports, personal notes, Web pages, and so on. The access and transformation of this information in knowledge as a basis for decision making in the corporate world have become crucial in the face of global competitiveness. Since the mid-1990s, much research has been devoted to creating techniques, methods, and tools to support organizations in discovering useful knowledge from those sources. An important challenge has been brought into the scene for the next 10 years: how can we prepare a real David's Army in order to take advantage from this exponentially generated information in favor of a society with more wisdom, justice, and equal opportunities for all citizens? For this purpose, it is necessary intelligence and technology.

In this context of information-drowning fields as data, text, and Web mining have developed many solutions by extending techniques from artificial intelligence, statistic, data bases, and information retrieval aiming to scale them to the new problems. Also, new techniques to extract knowledge from corporate databases have been proposed crossing those areas. Text mining (TM), in particular, has presented a significant evolution from simple word processing, around 1997, until now, when the adequate processing of concepts or even the extraction of knowledge from linguistic structures has been made possible. In this way, the complexity involved in processing the huge amount of texts available in the organizations can be effectively approached.

Drs. Edilson Ferneda and Hércules Prado, since 2002, have carried out methodological and applied research in data and text mining fields in the context of competitive and organizational intelligence. Particularly, on the TM side, their effort was focused first in covering the gap existing between the technology and its effective application in organizations. Next, they stressed the application of TM in solving problems in governmental research and development (R&D) and strategic management.

The book *Emerging Technologies of Text Mining: Techniques and Applications* brings some of the most significant research results achieved recently in the TM field, and represents a reference for researchers and practitioners.

Cláudio Chauke Nehme, DSc
Catholic University of Brasilia
Head of the Development and Innovation Directorate

Cláudio Chauke Nehme is a mathematician by the Federal Fluminense University (1986), MSc in systems and computing by the Military Engineering Institute (1989), and DSc in systems engineering and computing by the Federal University of Rio de Janeiro (1996). He is specialized in ontological coaching by a joint initiative of the Newfield Group and the Technological and High Studies Institute of Monterrey, Mexico (1999). He is head of the development and innovation directorate in the Catholic University of Brasilia (UCB) and full professor in the graduate program of knowledge and information management in that university. Previous to his work at UCB, Dr. Nehme held many positions as researcher, supervisor in ontological coaching programs, coordinator of many research projects in artificial and military intelligence, and consultant in some of the most important Brazilian research agencies. His main research interests are organizational intelligence, innovation, social technologies, foresight and complex Systems.

Since its creation in 2001, the graduate program in knowledge and information technology management of the Catholic University of Brasilia, has contributed significantly to the knowledge management field by means of MSc dissertations and scientific publications concerning to real world problems. Methodologies and techniques have been proposed, beyond their application, in public and private organizations, for competitive and organizational intelligence.

Preface

Text mining (TM) has evolved from the simple word processing at the end of the 1990s to now, when the concepts processing or even the knowledge extraction from linguistic structures are possible due to the most recent advances in its realm. The complexity inherent to the enormous and increasing amount of textual data can now be effectively approached, what enables the discovery of interesting relations in documents, e-mails, Web pages, and other nonstructured information sources. The need for effective TM approaches becomes more important if we consider that, according to the experts, most of the organizational information available in the modern enterprises comes in textual format.

TM can be defined as the application of computational methods and techniques over textual data in order to find relevant and intrinsic information and previously unknown knowledge. TM techniques can be organized into four categories: classification, association analysis, information extraction, and clustering. Classification techniques consist of the allocation of objects into predefined classes or categories. Association analysis can be applied to help the identification of words or concepts that occur together and to understand the content of a document or a set of documents. Information extraction techniques are able to find relevant data or expressions inside documents. Clustering is applied to discover underlying structures in a set of documents.

This book aims to provide researchers, graduate students, and practitioners the most recent advances in the TM process. The topics approached include: methodological issues, techniques, and models, successful experiences in applying this technology to real world problems, and new trends in this field. By offering this book to researcher and developer audiences, the editors aim to provide some start points for new developments in TM, and its correlated fields and bring to practitioners the newest information for building and deploying applications in the organizational context. Due to the meticulous process for selecting chapters,based on a strict peer-to-peer blind review, scholars can find interesting research results in the state of the art of Text Mining.

Critical applications can be developed in the fields of organizational and competitive intelligence, environmental scanning, prospective scenarios analysis, and business intelligence, among others, allowing the organizations to have a much more competitive position in the modern economy, while also obtaining a self knowledge with respect to their structure and dynamics. By applying the methods described in this book, one can transform textual patterns into valuable knowledge. This book goes beyond simply showing techniques to generate patterns from texts; it gives the road map to guide the subjective task of patterns interpretation.

Chapter I discusses information extraction related problems and provides an overview on the existing methodologies facing these problems. Rule learning based, classification based, and sequential labeling based methods are explained in detail. This discussion, along with some extraction applications experienced by the authors and examples of well-known applications in this field makes this chapter an excellent reference for a tutorial program.

Departing from a sound point of view about the importance of the information treatment and analysis as the most critical organizational competence for the information society, **Chapter II** brings an interesting discussion regarding the use of strategic information in competitive intelligence. Authors present a comprehensive review on the methodologies tuned to the French School of Information Science and discuss the necessary integration of information for analysis and the data and text mining processes, presenting examples of real-world applications.

Chapter III takes into account the competitive intelligence needs of gathering information related to external environment, analyzing, and disseminating the results to the board of a company. The authors hold with a disclosure tendency that leads companies to be more transparent as a demand posed by apprehensive shareholders in the face of unexpected crises in big companies. The chapter discusses natural language processing (NLP) techniques applied to analyze the increasing amount of organizational information published in that scenario, looking for competitive advantages.

NLP technology for mining textual resources and extracting knowledge are also the focus of **Chapter IV**. An overview on the NLP techniques involved, beyond a brief explanation on the application of these techniques, is provided along with two case studies. The case studies focus on finding definitions in vast text collections and obtaining a short multidocument summary of a cluster to respond to a relevant question posed by an analyst.

Chapter V describes an approach for deriving a taxonomy from a set of documents by using semantic information generated at the document sentence level. This information is obtained from a document profile model built by applying a frequent word sequence method. The agglomerative hierarchical method is applied to create a clustering configuration from which the taxonomy is derived. Experimental results show that the derived taxonomy can demonstrate how the information is interwoven in a comprehensive and concise form.

Chapter VI brings an original approach to knowledge discovery from textual data based on a fuzzy decision tree. The methods involved in the rule extraction process are described, including the inductive learning method, and the inference method involved. Two applications, one for analyzing daily business reports and other for rule discovering from e-mails, are presented in detail in order to make evident the effectiveness of the proposal.

Chapter VII extends the semisupervised multiview learning techniques for TM. Semisupervised learning is usually applied to build classification models over labeled and unlabeled data. The chapter contains the description of some algorithms related to this task, a review of applications found in literature, including Web page classification and e-mail classification, and experimental results found by analyzing academic and newsgroup related texts.

Chapter VIII proposes a multi-neural-network-agent-based Web text mining system for decision support by processing Web pages. The system comprises the processes of Web document searching, Web text processing, text feature conversion, and the neural model building. The scalability of this system is assured by the learning process implemented in a multi-agent structure. For performance evaluation, the authors describe a practical application for the crude oil price movement direction prediction.

Chapter IX focuses on a problem usually experienced by millions of Web users when searching for information: how to analyze hundreds or thousands of ranked documents. Research results have shown that if nothing interesting appears in the two or three top ranked documents, users prefer to reformulate their query instead of sifting through the numerous pages of search results that can hide relevant information. In this chapter an innovative approach based on the suffix tree clustering algorithm to sift the search results is proposed. Also, a review on other text mining techniques used in exploratory search solutions, a discussion on some advantages and disadvantages of contextualized clustering, and experimental results are presented.

Still in the Web search domain, **Chapter X** presents a study on the application of the ant colony optimization model to improve Web navigation. Considering the existing similarities in behavior between Web users' navigation and ant colonies, the chapter describes a system able to shorten the paths to a target page by applying information related to previous navigation. Although unable to have global vision due to their physical characteristics, ants at foraging use a curious marking system, in which any ant can leave a pheromone mark for others. The specific trails with stronger concentration of pheromone can guide the ants in finding shorter paths between their nest and the food source. AntWeb, the system resulting from the application of this metaphor, is described along with experimental results that demonstrate its benefits for users navigating in the Web and also its capacity to modify the Web structure adaptively.

Aiming to overcome the semantic mistakes that arise when applying the traditional word-based documents clustering techniques, **Chapter XI** introduces an alternative to cluster textual documents using concepts. The use of concepts instead of simple words adds semantics to the document clustering process, leading to a better understanding of large document collections, easing the summarization of each cluster and the identification of its contents. A useful methodology for document clustering and some practical experiments in a case study are shown in detail to demonstrate the effectiveness of the proposed alternative.

Chapter XII studies the text categorization (TC) techniques applied to the patent categorization problem. The patent categorization problem presents specific characteristics like the existence of many vague or general terms, acronyms, and new terms that make the traditional TC methods insufficient for an adequate categorization. Taking into account the application domain particularities and an important drawback in the existing TC solutions, the authors propose their method. An evaluation of this method on two English patent databases is presented and compared with other text categorization methods, showing how the proposed method outperforms the latter.

Chapter XIII presents an application of TM in the healthy management field. Nominal data related to patient medical conditions are used to define a patient severity index to model the quality of healthcare providers. A clustering analysis to rank groups of levels in the nominal data is carried out, issuing results that can help improving the healthcare system.

Finally, **Chapter XIV** enlightens an important problem of both data and text mining that usually remains unsolved due to their strong subjective nature: the clustering interpretation process. In order to deal with this inevitable characteristic of clustering analysis, that is, the hard burden of subjectivity, the authors built from the ontology of language a method to help the specialists in searching for a consensus when analyzing a given clustering configuration. This method, grounded in speech acts like affirmations, declarations, assessments, and so on, fits naturally as a pathway for the interpretation phase of Text Mining.

Hércules Antonio do Prado, DSc, Catholic University of Brasilia & Embrapa Food Technology
Edilson Ferneda, DSc, Catholic University of Brasilia
Editors
June 2007

Acknowledgment

We would like to express our gratitude to the many people that helped us in developing this project. From the book proposal to the distribution to libraries and scholars, an endeavor like this involves so complex set of activities that, without the support from those people, it would not have been possible to carry out.

First, we want to thank the authors that submitted their contributions, accepted or not, by putting their efforts and commitment in this project. At this point, it is important to say that, in face of the competitiveness and space limitations, some good chapters could not be included in the final manuscript. We also wish to thank the research colleagues that spent their time and effort by reviewing and evaluating the contributions, offering an important and invaluable feedback for improving the final versions of the chapters. Yet, we would like to thank the colleagues that helped us in reviewing the subsidiary texts. We are especially grateful to the team at IGI Global that during the entire process offered a worthwhile support and infrastructure that were fundamental for conducting the project. Finally, we are grateful to our families by their patience and care during the time that we had involved with the many activities necessary to accomplish our objectives.

Hércules Antonio do Prado and Edilson Ferneda

Chapter I
Information Extraction:
Methodologies and Applications

Jie Tang
Tsinghua University, China

Mingcai Hong
Tsinghua University, China

Duo Zhang
Tsinghua University, China

Bangyong Liang
NEC Labs, China

Juanzi Li
Tsinghua University, China

ABSTRACT

This chapter is concerned with the methodologies and applications of information extraction. Information is hidden in the large volume of Web pages and thus it is necessary to extract useful information from the Web content, called information extraction. In information extraction, given a sequence of instances, we identify and pull out a subsequence of the input that represents information we are interested in. In the past years, there was a rapid expansion of activities in the information extraction area. Many methods have been proposed for automating the process of extraction. However, due to the heterogeneity and the lack of structure of Web data, automated discovery of targeted or unexpected knowledge information still presents many challenging research problems. In this chapter, we will investigate the problems of information extraction and survey existing methodologies for solving these problems. Several real-world applications of information extraction will be introduced. Emerging challenges will be discussed.

INTRODUCTION

Information extraction (IE), identifying and pulling out a subsequence from a given sequence of instances that represents information we are interested in, is an important task with many practical applications. Information extraction benefits many text/Web applications, for example, integration of product information from various Web sites, question answering, contact information search, finding the proteins mentioned in a biomedical journal article, and removal of the noisy data.

We will focus on methodologies of automatic information extraction from various types of documents (including plain texts, Web pages, e-mails, etc.). Specifically, we will discuss three of the most popular methods: rule learning based method, classification model based method, and sequential labeling based method. All these methods can be viewed as supervised machine learning approaches. They all consist of two stages: extraction and training.

In extraction, the subsequences that we are interested in are identified and extracted from given data using learned model(s) by different methods. The extracted data are then annotated as specific information on the basis of the pre-defined metadata.

In training, the model(s) are constructed to detect the subsequence. In the models, the input data is viewed as a sequence of instances. For example, a document can be viewed as either a sequence of words or a sequence of text lines (it depends on the specific application).

All these methodologies have immediate real-life applications. Information extraction has been applied, for instance, to part-of-speech tagging (Ratnaparkhi, 1998), named entity recognition (Zhang, Pan & Zhang, 2004), shallow parsing (Sha & Pereira, 2003), table extraction (Ng, Lim, & Koo, 1999; Pinto, McCallum, Wang, & Hu, 2002; Wei & Croft, 2003), and contact information extraction (Kristjansson, Culotta, Viola, & McCallum, 2004).

In the rest of the chapter, we will describe the three types of the state-of-the-art methods for information extraction. This is followed by presenting several applications to better understand how the methods can be utilized to help businesses. The chapter will have a mix of research and industry flavor, addressing research concepts and looking at the technologies from an industry perspective. After that, we will discuss the challenges the information extraction community has faced. Finally, we will give concluding remarks.

METHODOLOGIES

Information extraction is an important research area, and many research efforts have been made so far. Among these research works, rule learning based method, classification based method, and sequential labeling based method are the three state-of-the-art methods.

Rule Learning-Based Extraction Methods

In this section, we review the rule based algorithms for information extraction. Numerous information systems have been developed based on the method, including: AutoSlog (Riloff, 1993), Crystal (Soderland, Fisher, Aseltine, & Lehnert, 1995), (LP)2 (Ciravegna, 2001), iASA (Tang, Li, & Lu, 2005), Whisk (Soderland, 1999), Rapier (Califf & Mooney, 1998), SRV (Freitag, 1998), WIEN (Kushmerick, Weld, & Doorenbos, 1997), Stalker (Muslea, Minton, & Knoblock, 1998, 1999), BWI (Freitag & Kushmerick, 2000), and so forth. See Muslea (1999), Siefkes and Siniakov (2005), and Peng (2001) for an overview. In general, the methods can be grouped into three categories: dictionary based method, rule based method, and wrapper induction.

Dictionary-Based Method

Traditional information extraction systems first construct a pattern (template) dictionary, and then use the dictionary to extract needed information from the new untagged text. These extraction systems are called as dictionary based systems (also called pattern based systems) including: AutoSlog (Riloff, 1993), AutoSlog-TS (Riloff, 1996), and CRYSTAL (Soderland et al., 1995). The key point in the systems is how to learn the dictionary of patterns that can be used to identify the relevant information from a text.

AutoSlog (Riloff, 1993) was the first system to learn text extraction dictionary from training examples. AutoSlog builds a dictionary of extraction patterns that are called concept nodes. Each AutoSlog concept node has a conceptual anchor that activates it and a linguistic pattern, which, together with a set of enabling conditions, guarantees its applicability. The conceptual anchor is a triggering word, while the enabling conditions represent constraints on the components of the linguistic pattern.

For instance, in order to extract the target of the terrorist attack from the sentence "The Parliament was bombed by the guerrillas," one can use a concept that consists of the triggering word bombed together with the linguistic pattern <subject> passive-verb. Applying such an extraction pattern is straightforward: first, the concept is activated because the sentence contains the triggering word "bombed", then the linguistic pattern is matched against the sentence and the subject is extracted as the target of the terrorist attack.

AutoSlog uses a predefined set of 13 linguistic patterns. The information to be extracted can be one of the following syntactic categories: subject, direct object, or noun phrase. In general, the triggering word is a verb, but if the information to be extracted is a noun phrase, the triggering word may also be a noun.

In Figure 1, we show a sample concept node. The slot "Name" is a concise, human readable

Figure 1. Example of AutoSlog concept node

```
Concept Node:
   Name:     target-subject-passive-verb-bombed
   Trigger:   bombed
   Variable Slots:  (target (*S *1))
   Constraints:   (class phys-target *S*)
   Constant Slots:  (type bombing)
   Enabling Conditions: ((passive))
```

description of the concept. The slot "Trigger" defines the conceptual anchor, while the slot "Variable Slots" represents that the information to be extracted is the subject of the sentence. Finally, the subject must be a physical target (see "Constraints"), and the enabling conditions require the verb to be used in its passive form.

AutoSlog needs to parse the natural language sentence using a linguistic parser. The parser is used to generate syntax elements of a sentence (such as subject, verb, preposition phrase). Then the output syntax elements are matched against the linguistic pattern and fire the best matched pattern as the result pattern to construct a pattern dictionary.

AutoSlog need tag the text before extracting patterns. This disadvantage has been improved by AutoSlog-TS (Riloff, 1996). In AutoSlog-TS, one does not need to make a full tag for the input data and only needs to tag the data whether it is relevant to the domain or not. The procedure of AutoSlog-TS is divided into two stages. In the first stage, the sentence analyzer produces a syntactic analysis for each sentence and identifies the noun phrases using heuristic rules. In the second stage, the preclassified text is inputted to the sentence analyzer again with the pattern dictionary generated in the first stage. The sentence analyzer activates all the patterns that are applicable in each sentence. The system then computes relevance statistics for each pattern and uses a rank function to rank the patterns. In the end, only the top patterns are kept in the dictionary.

Riloff and Jones (1999) propose using bootstrapping to generate the dictionary with a few tagged texts (called seed words). The basic idea is to use a mutual bootstrapping technique to learn extraction patterns based on the seed words and then exploit the learned extraction patterns to identify more seed words that belong to the same category. In this way, the pattern dictionary can be learned incrementally as the process continues. See also Crystal (Soderland et al., 1995).

Rule-Based Method

Different from the dictionary based method, the rule based method uses general rules instead of dictionary to extract information from text. The rule based systems have been mostly used in information extraction from semi structured Web pages.

A usual method is to learn syntactic/semantic constraints with delimiters that bound the text to be extracted, that is, to learn rules for boundaries of the target text. Two main rule learning algorithms of these systems are: bottom-up method, which learns rules from special cases to general ones, and top-down method, which learns rules from general cases to special ones. There are many algorithms proposed, such as (LP)2 (Ciravegna, 2001), iASA (Tang, Li, Lu et al., 2005), Whisk (Soderland, 1999), Rapier (Califf, 1998), and SRV (Freitag, 1998). Here we will take (LP)2 and iASA as examples in our explanation.

$(LP)^2$

$(LP)^2$ (Ciravegna, 2001) is one of the typical bottom-up methods. It learns two types of rules that respectively identify the start boundary and the end boundary of the text to be extracted. The learning is performed from examples in a user-defined corpus (training data set). Training is performed in two steps: initially a set of tagging rules is learned and then additional rules are induced to correct mistakes and imprecision in extraction.

Three types of rules are defined in $(LP)^2$: tagging rules, contextual rules, and correction rules.

A tagging rule is composed of a pattern of conditions on a connected sequence of words and an action of determining whether or not the current position is a boundary of an instance. Table 1 shows an example of the tagging rule. The first column represents a sequence of words. The second to the fifth columns represent Part-Of-Speech, Word type, Lookup in a dictionary, and Name Entity Recognition results of the word sequence respectively. The last column represents the action. In the example of Table 1, the action "<Speaker>" indicates that if the text match the pattern, the word "Patrick" will be identified as the start boundary of a speaker.

Table 1. Example of initial tagging rule

Pattern					Action
Word	**POS**	**Kind**	**Lookup**	**Name Entity**	
;	;	Punctuation			
Patrick	NNP	Word	Person's first name	Person	<Speaker>
Stroh	NNP	Word			
,	,	Punctuation			
assistant	NN	Word	Job title		
professor	NN	Word			
,	,	Punctuation			
SDS	NNP	Word			

The tagging rules are induced as follows: First, a tag in the training corpus is selected, and a window of w words to the left and w words to the right is extracted as constraints in the initial rule pattern. Second, all the initial rules are generalized. The generalization algorithm could be various. For example, based on NLP knowledge, the two rules (at 4 pm) and (at 5 pm) can be generalized to be (at DIGIT pm). Each generalized rule is tested on the training corpus and an error score E=wrong/matched is calculated. Finally, the k best generalizations for each initial rule are kept in a so called best rule pool. This induction algorithm is also used for the other two types of rules discussed below. Table 2 indicates a generalized tagging rule for the start boundary identification of the Speaker.

Another type of rules, contextual rules, is applied to improve the effectiveness of the system. The basic idea is that <tagx> might be used as an indicator of the occurrence of <tagy>. For example, consider a rule recognizing an end boundary between a capitalized word and a lowercase word. This rule does not belong to the best rule pool as its low precision on the corpus, but it is reliable if used only when closing to a tag <speaker>. Consequently, some nonbest rules are recovered,

and the ones which result in acceptable error rate will be preserved as the contextual rules.

The correction rules are used to reduce the imprecision of the tagging rules. For example, a correction rule shown in Table 3 is used to correct the tagging mistake "at <time> 4 </time> pm" since "pm" should have been part of the time expression. So, correction rules are actions that shift misplaced tags rather than adding new tags.

After all types of rules are induced, information extraction is carried out in the following steps:

- The learned tagging rules are used to tag the texts.
- Contextual rules are applied in the context of introduced tags in the first step.
- Correction rules are used to correct mistaken extractions.
- All the identified boundaries are to be validated, for example, a start tag (e.g., <time>) without its corresponding close tag will be removed, and vice versa.

See also Rapier (Califf & Mooney, 1998, 2003) for another IE system which adopts the bottom-up learning strategy.

Table 2. Example of generalized tagging rule

Pattern					Action
Word	**POS**	**Kind**	**Lookup**	**Name Entity**	
;	:	Punctuation			
		Word	Person's first name	Person	<Speaker>
		Word			
		Punctuation			
assistant	NN	Word	Jobtitle		
professor	NN	Word			

Table 3. Example of correction rule

Pattern		Action
Word	Wrong tag	Move tag to
At		
4	</stime>	
pm		</stime>

iASA

Tang, Li, Lu et al. (2005) propose an algorithm for learning rules for information extraction. The key idea of iASA is that it tries to induce the "similar" rules first. In iASA, each rule consists of three patterns: body pattern, left pattern, and right pattern, respectively representing the text fragment to be extracted (called target instance), the w words previous to the target instance, and w words next to the target instance. Thus, the rule learning tries to find patterns not only in the context of a target instance, but also in the target instance itself. Tang, Li, Lu et al. define similarity between tokens (it can be word, punctuation, and name entity), similarity between patterns, and similarity between rules. In learning, iASA creates an initial rule set from the training data set. Then it searches for the most similar rules from the rule set and generalizes a new rule using the found rules. The new rule is evaluated on the training corpus and a score of the rule is calculated. If its score exceeds a threshold, it would be put back to the rule set. The processing continues until no new rules can be generalized.

The other type of strategy for learning extraction rules is the top-down fashion. The method starts with the most generalized patterns and then gradually adds constraints into the patterns in the learning processing. SRV (Freitag, 1998) and Whisk (Soderland, 1999) are examples.

Wrapper Induction

Wrapper induction is another type of rule based method which is aimed at structured and semi-structured documents such as Web pages. A wrapper is an extraction procedure, which consists of a set of extraction rules and also program codes required to apply these rules. Wrapper induction is a technique for automatically learning the wrappers. Given a training data set, the induction algorithm learns a wrapper for extracting the target information. Several research works have been studied. The typical wrapper systems include WIEN (Kushmerick et al., 1997), Stalker (Muslea et al., 1998), and BWI (Freitag & Kushmerick, 2000). Here, we use WIEN and BWI as examples in explaining the principle of wrapper induction.

WIEN

WIEN (Kushmerick et al., 1997) is the first wrapper induction system. An example of the wrapper defined in WIEN is shown in Figure 2, which aims to extract "Country" and "Area Code" from the two HTML pages: D1 and D2.

The rule in Figure 2 has the following meaning: ignore all characters until you find the first occurrence of <B> and extract the country name as the string that ends at the first </B>. Then ignore all characters until <I> is found and extract the string that ends at </I>. In order to extract the information about the other country names and area codes, the rule is applied repeatedly until it fails to match. In the example of Figure 2, we can see that the WIEN rule can be successfully to be applied to both documents D1 and D2.

Figure 2. Example of wrapper induction

```
D1: <B>Congo</B> <I>242</I><BR>
D2: <B>Egypt</B> <I>20</I><BR>

Rule: *'<B>'(*)'</B>'*'<I>'(*)'</I>'
Output: Country_Code {Country@1}{AreaCode@2}
```

The rule defined above is an instance of the so called LR class. An LR wrapper is defined as a vector $<l_1, r_1, ..., l_k, r_k>$ of $2K$ delimiters, with each pair $<l_i, r_i>$ corresponding to one type of information. The LR wrapper requires that resources format their pages in a very simple manner. Specifically, there must exist delimiters that reliably indicate the left- and right-hand boundaries of the fragments to be extracted. The classes HLRT, OCLR, and HOCLRT are extensions of LR that use document head and tail delimiters, tuple delimiters, and both of them, respectively. The algorithm for learning LR wrappers (i.e., learnLR) is shown in Figure 3.

In Figure 3, E represents the example set; notation $cands_l(k, E)$ represent the candidates for delimiter l_k given the example set E. The candidates are generated by enumerating the suffixes of the shortest string occurring to the left of each instance of attribute k in each example; $valid_l(u, k, E)$ refers to the constraints to validate a candidate u for delimiter l_k.

LR wrapper class is the simplest wrapper class. See Kushmerick (2000) for variant wrapper classes.

Stalker (Muslea et al., 1998, 1999) is another wrapper induction system that performs hierarchical information extraction. It can be used to extract data from such documents with multiple levels. In Stalker, rules are induced by a covering algorithm which tries to generate rules until all instances of an item are covered and returns

Figure 3. The learnLR algorithm

```
procedure learn_LR(examples E)
{
    for each 1≤k≤K
        for each u∈cands_l(k, E)
    if valid_l(u, k, E) then l_k u and terminate this loop
        for each 1≤k≤K
            for each u∈candsr(k, E)
    if valid_r(u, k, E) then r_k u and terminate this loop
    return LR wrapper <l_1, r_1, ..., l_k, r_k>
}
```

a disjunction of the found rules. A Co-Testing approach has been also proposed to support active learning in Stalker. See Muslea, Minton, and Knoblock (2003) for details.

BWI

The boosted wrapper induction (BWI) system (Freitag & Kushmerick, 2000) targets at making wrapper induction techniques suitable for free text, which uses boosting to generate and combine the predictions from numerous extraction patterns.

In BWI, a document is treated as a sequence of tokens, and the IE task is to identify the boundaries of different type of information. Let indices i and j denote the boundaries, we can use $<i, j>$ to represent an instance.

A wrapper $W = <F, A, H>$ learned by BWI consists of two sets of patterns that are used respectively to detect the start and the end boundaries of an instance. Here $F = \{F_1, F_2, ..., F_T\}$ identifies the start boundaries and $A = \{A_1, A_2, ..., A_T\}$ identifies the end boundaries; and a length function $H(k)$ estimates the maximum-likelihood probability that the field has length k.

To perform extraction using the wrapper W, every boundary i in a document is first given a "start" score $F(i) = \sum_k C_{F_k} F_k(i)$ and an "end" score $A(i) = \sum_k C_{A_k} A_k(i)$. Here, C_{F_k} is the weight for F_k, and $F_k(i) = 1$ if i matches F_k, otherwise $F_k(i) = 0$. For $A(i)$, the definition is similar. W then classifies text fragment $<i, j>$ as follows:

$$W(i, j) = \begin{cases} 1 & \text{if } F(i)A(j)H(j-i) > \tau \\ 0 & \text{otherwise} \end{cases} \quad (1)$$

where τ is a numeric threshold.

Learning a wrapper W involves determining F, A, and H.

The function H reflects the prior probability of various field lengths. BWI estimates these probabilities by constructing a frequency histogram $H(k)$ recording the number of fields of length k occurring in the training set. To learn F and A, BWI

Figure 4. The BWI algorithm

```
procedure BWI (example sets S and E)
{
    F ←AdaBoost(LearnDetector, S)
    A ←AdaBoost(LearnDetector, E)
    H ←field length histogram from S and E
    return wrapper W = <F, A, H>

}
```

boosts *LearnDetector*, an algorithm for learning a single detector. Figure 4 shows the learning algorithm in BWI.

In BWI, AdaBoost algorithm runs in iterations. In each iteration, it outputs a weak learner (called hypotheses) from the training data and also a weight for the learner representing the percentage of the correctly classified instances by applying the weak learner to the training data. AdaBoost simply repeats this learn-update cycle *T* times, and then returns a list of the learned weak hypotheses with their weights. BWI invokes LearnDetector (indirectly through AdaBoost) to learn the "fore" detectors *F*, and then *T* more times to learn the "aft" detectors *A*. LearnDetector iteratively builds from an empty detector. At each step, LearnDetector searches for the best extension of length L (a lookahead parameter) or less to the prefix and suffix of the current detector. The procedure returns when no extension yields a better score than the current detector. More detailed experiments and results analysis about BWI is discussed in Kauchak, Smarr, and Elkan (2004).

Classification-Based Extraction Methods

In this section, we introduce another principled approach to information extraction using supervised machine learning. The basic idea is to cast information extraction problem as that of classification. In this section, we will describe the method in detail. We will also introduce several improving efforts to the approach.

Classification Model

Let us first consider a two class classification problem. Let $\{(x_1, y_1), \ldots, (x_n, y_n)\}$ be a training data set, in which x_i denotes an instance (a feature vector) and $y_i \in \{-1, +1\}$ denotes a classification label. A classification model usually consists of two stages: learning and prediction. In learning, one attempts to find a model from the labeled data that can separate the training data, while in prediction the learned model is used to identify whether an unlabeled instance should be classified as +1 or -1. In some cases, the prediction results may be numeric values, for example, ranging from 0 to 1. Then an instance can be classified using some rules, for example, classified as +1 when the prediction value is larger than 0.5.

Support Vector Machines (SVMs) is one of the most popular methods for classification. Now, we use SVM as example to introduce the classification model (Vapnik, 1998).

Support vector machines (SVMs) are linear functions of the form $f(x) = w^T x + b$, where $w^T x$ is the inner product between the weight vector w and the input vector x. The main idea of SVM is to find an optimal separating hyper-plane that maximally separates the two classes of training instances (more precisely, maximizes the margin between the two classes of instances). The hyper-plane then corresponds to a classifier (linear SVM). The problem of finding the hyper-plane can be stated as the following optimization problem:

$$Minimize: \frac{1}{2} w^T w$$
$$s.t.: y_i(w^T x_i + b) \geq 1, i = 1, 2, \ldots, n \qquad (2)$$

To deal with cases where there may be no separating hyper-plane due to noisy labels of both positive and negative training instances, the soft margin SVM is proposed, which is formulated as:

$$Minimize: \frac{1}{2}w^T w + C\sum_{i=1}^{n} x_i$$
$$s.t.: y_i(w^T x_i + b) \geq 1 - x_i, i = 1, 2, \ldots, n \qquad (3)$$

where $C \geq 0$ is the cost parameter that controls the amount of training errors allowed.

It is theoretically guaranteed that the linear classifier obtained in this way has small generalization errors. Linear SVM can be further extended into nonlinear SVMs by using kernel functions such as Gaussian and polynomial kernels (Boser, Guyon, & Vapnik, 1992; Schölkopf, Burges, & Smith, 1999; Vapnik, 1999). When there are more than two classes, we can adopt the "one class vs. all others" approach, that is, take one class as positive and the other classes as negative.

Boundary Detection Using Classification Model

We are using a supervised machine learning approach to IE, so our system consists of two distinct phases: learning and extracting. In the learning phase our system uses a set of labeled documents to generate models which we can use for future predictions. The extraction phase takes the learned models and applies them to new unlabelled documents using the learned models to generate extractions.

The method formalizes the IE problem as a classification problem. It is aimed at detecting the boundaries (start boundary and end boundary) of a specific type of information. For IE from text, the basic unit that we are dealing with can be tokens or text-lines in the text. (Hereafter, we will use token as the basic unit in our explanation.) We then try to learn two classifiers that are respectively used to identify the boundaries. The instances are all tokens in the document. All tokens that begin with a start-label are positive instances for the start classifier, while all the other tokens become negative instances for this classifier. Similarly, the positive instances for the end classifier are the last tokens of each end-label, and the other tokens are negative instances.

Figure 5 gives an example of IE as classification. There are two classifiers—one to identify starts of target text fragments and the other to identify ends of text fragments. Here, the classifiers are based on tokens only (however other patterns, e.g., syntax, can also be incorporated into). Each token is classified as being a start or nonstart and an end or non-end. When we classify a token as a start, and also classify one of the closely following token as an end, we view the tokens between these two tokens as a target instance.

In the example, the tokens "Dr. Trinkle's" is annotated as a "speaker" and thus the token "Dr." is a positive instance and the other tokens are as negative instances in the speaker-start classifier. Similarly, the token "Trinkle's" is a positive in-

Figure 5. Example of information extraction as classification

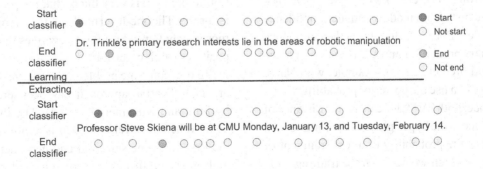

stance and the other tokens are negative instances in the speaker-end classifier. The annotated data is used to train two classifiers in advance. In the extracting stage, the two classifiers are applied to identify the start token and the end token of the speaker. In the example, the tokens "Professor", "Steve", and "Skiena" are identified as two start tokens by the start classifier and one end token by the end classifier. Then, we combine the identified results and view tokens between the start token and the end token as a speaker. (i.e., "Professor Steve Skiena" is outputted as a speaker)

In the extracting stage, we apply the two classifiers to each token to identify whether the token is a "start", "end", neither, or both. After the extracting stage, we need to combine the starts and the ends predicted by the two classifiers. We need to decide which of the starts (if there exist more than one starts) to match with which of the ends (if there exist more than one ends). For the combination, a simple method is to search for an end from a start and then view the tokens between the two tokens as the target. If there exist two starts and only one end (as the example in Figure 5), then we start the search progress from the first start and view the tokens between the first token and the end token (i.e., "Professor Steve Skiena") as the target. However, in some applications, the simple combination method may not yield good results.

Several works have been conducted to enhance the combination. For example, Finn and Kushmerick (2004) propose a histogram model (Finn, 2006). In Figure 5, there are two possible extractions: "Professor Steve Skiena" and "Steve Skiena". The histogram model estimates confidence as $Cs * Ce * P(|e - s|)$. Here Cs is the confidence of the start prediction and Ce is the confidence of the end prediction. (For example, with Naïve Bayes, we can use the posterior probability as the confidence; with SVM, we can use the distance of the instance to the hyper-plane as the confidence.) $P(|e - s|)$ is the probability of a text fragment of that length which we get from the training data.

Finally, the method selects the text fragment with the highest confidence as output.

To summarize, this IE classification approach simply learns to detect the start and the end of text fragments to be extracted. It treats IE as a standard classification task, augmented with a simple mechanism to combine the predicted start and end tags. Experiments indicate that this approach generally has high precision but low recall. This approach can be viewed as that of one-level boundary classification (Finn & Kushmerick, 2004).

Many approaches can be used to train the classification models, for example, support vector machines (Vapnik, 1998), maximum entropy (Berger, Della Pietra, & Della Pietra, 1996), adaboost (Shapire, 1999), and voted perceptron (Collins, 2002).

Enhancing IE by a Two-Level Boundary Classification Model

Experiments on many data sets and in several real-world applications show that the one-level boundary classification approach can competitive with the start-of-the-art rule learning based IE systems. However, as the classifiers are built on a very large number of negative instances and a small number of positive instances, the prior probability that an arbitrary instance is a boundary is very small. This gives a model that has very high precision. Because the prior probability of predicting a tag is so low, and because the data is highly imbalanced, when we actually do prediction for a tag, it is very likely that the prediction is correct. The one-level model is, therefore, much more likely to produce false negatives than false positives (high precision).

To overcome the problem, a two-level boundary classification approach has been proposed by Finn and Kushmerick (2004). The intuition behind the two-level approach is as follows. At the first level, the start and end classifiers have high precision. To make a prediction, both the start

Figure 6. Example of information extraction by the two-level classification models

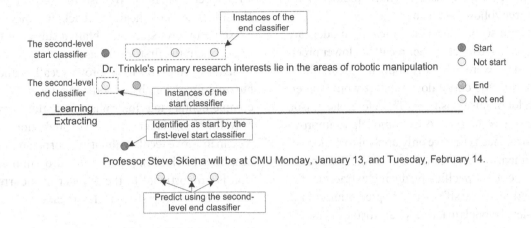

classifier and the end classifier have to predict the start and end respectively. In many cases where we fail to extract a fragment, one of these classifiers made a prediction, but not the other. The second level assumes that these predictions by the first level are correct and is designed to identify the starts and ends that we failed to identify at the first level.

The second-level models are learned from training data in which the prior probability that a given instance is a boundary is much higher than for the one-level learner. This "focused" training data is constructed as follows. When building the second-level start model, we take only the instances that occur in a fixed distance before an end tag. Similarly, for the second-level end model, we use only instances that occur in a fixed distance after a start tag. For example, an second-level window of size 10 means that the second-level start model is built using only 10 instances that occur before an end-tag in the training data, while the second-level end model is built using only those instances that occur in the 10 instances after a start tag in the training data. Note that these second-level instances are encoded in the same way as for the first-level; the difference is simply that the second-level learner is only allowed to look at a small subset of the available training data. Figure 6 shows an

example of the IE using the two-level classification models.

In the example of Figure 6, there are also two stages: learning and extracting. In learning, the tokens "Dr." and "Trinkle's" are the start and the end boundaries of a speaker respectively. For training the second-level start and end classifiers. We use window size as three and thus three instances after the start are used to train the end classifier and three instances before the end are used to train the start classifier. In the example, the three tokens "Trinkle's", "primary", and "research" are instances of the second-level end classifier and the token "Dr." is an instance of the second-level start classifier. Note, in this way, the instances used for training the second-level classifiers are only a subset of the instances for training the first-level classifiers. These second-level instances are encoded in the same way as for the first-level. When extracting, the second-level end classifier is only applied to the three tokens following the token which the first-level classifier predicted as a start and the token itself. Similarly the second-level start classifier is only applied to instances predicted as an end by the first-level classifier and the three preceding tokens.

In the exacting stage of the example, the token "Professor" is predicted as a start by the first-level start classifier and no token is predicted as the end in the first-level model. Then we can use the second-level end classifier to make prediction for the three following tokens.

These second-level classification models are likely to have much higher recall but lower precision. If we were to blindly apply the second-level models to the entire document, it would generate a lot of false positives. Therefore, the reason we can use the second-level models to improve performance is that we only apply it to regions of documents where the first-level models have made a prediction. Specifically, during extraction, the second-level classifiers use the predictions of the first-level models to identify parts of the document that are predicted to contain targets.

Figure 7 shows the extracting processing flow in the two-level classification approach. Given a set of documents that we want to extract from, we convert these documents into a set of instances and then apply the first-level models for start and end to the instances and generate a set of predictions for starts and ends. The first-level predictions are then used to guide which instances we need to apply the second-level classifiers. We use the predictions of the first-level end model to decide which instances to apply the second-level start model to, and we use the predictions of the first-level start model to decide which instances to apply the second-level end model to. Applying the second-level models to the selected instances gives us a set of predictions which we pass to the combination to output our extracted results.

The intuition behind the two-level approach is that we use the unmatched first-level predictions (i.e., when we identify either the start or the end but not the other) as a guide to areas of text that we should look more closely at. We use more focused classifiers that are more likely to make a prediction on areas of text where it is highly likely that an unidentified fragment exists. These classifiers are more likely to make predictions due to a much lower data imbalance so they are only applied to instances where we have high probability of a fragment existing. As the level

of imbalance falls, the recall of the model rises while precision falls. We use the second-level classifiers to lookahead/lookback instances in a fixed windows size and obtain a subset of the instances in the first-level classifier.

This enables us to improve recall without hurting precision by identifying the missing complementary tags for orphan predictions. If we have 100% precision at first-level prediction then we can improve recall without any corresponding drop in precision. In practice, the drop in precision is proportional to the number of incorrect prediction at the first-level classification.

Enhancing IE by Unbalance Classification Model

Besides the two-level boundary classification approach, we introduce another approach to deal with the problem so as to improve performance of the classification based method.

Figure 7. Extracting processing flow in the two-level classification approach

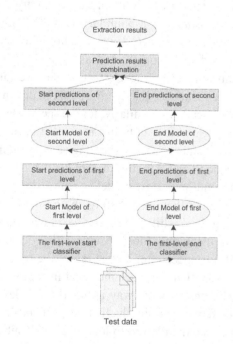

As the classifiers are built on a very large number of negative instances and a small number of positive instances, the prior probability that an arbitrary instance is a boundary is very small. This gives a model that has very high precision but low recall. In this section, we introduce an approach to the problem using an unbalanced classification model. The basic idea of the approach is to design a specific classification method that is able to learn a better classifier on the unbalanced data.

We have investigated the unbalanced classification model of SVMs (Support Vector Machines). Using the same notations in section Classification Model, we have the unbalanced classification model:

$$Minimize: \frac{1}{2} w^T w + C_1 \sum_{i=1}^{n_1} \xi_i + C_2 \sum_{i=1}^{n} \xi_i \qquad (4)$$
$$s.t.: y_i(w^T x_i + b) \geq 1 - \xi_i, i = 1, 2, \ldots, n$$

Here, C_1 and C_2 are two cost parameters used to control the training errors of positive examples and negative examples respectively. For example, with a large C_1 and a small C_2, we can obtain a classification model that attempts to penalize false positive examples more than false negative examples. The model can actually increase the probability of examples to be predicted as positive, so that we can improve the recall while likely hurting the precision, which is consistent with the method of two-level classification. Intuition shows that in this way we can control the trade-off between the problem of high precision and low recall and the training errors of the classification model. The model obtained by this formulation can perform better than the classical SVM model in the case of a large number of negative instances and a small number of positive instances. To distinguish this formulation from the classical SVM, we call the special formulation of SVM as Unbalanced-SVM. See Morik, Brockhausen, and Joachims (1999) and Li and Liu (2003) for details.

Unbalanced-SVM enables us to improve the recall by adjusting the two parameters. We need to note that the special case of SVM might hurt the precision while improving the recall. The most advantage of the model is that it can achieve a better trade-off between precision and recall.

Sequential Labeling-Based Extraction Methods

Information extraction can be cast as a task of sequential labeling. In sequential labeling, a document is viewed as a sequence of tokens, and a sequence of labels are assigned to each token to indicate the property of the token. For example, consider the nature language processing task of labeling words of a sentence with their corresponding Part-Of-Speech (POS). In this task, each word is labeled with a tag indicating its appropriate POS. Thus the inputting sentence "Pierre Vinken will join the board as a nonexecutive director Nov. 29." will result in an output as:

[NNP Pierre] [NNP Vinken] [MD will] [VB join] [DT the] [NN board] [IN as] [DT a] [JJ nonexecutive] [NN director] [NNP Nov.] [CD 29] [. .]

Formally, given an observation sequence $x = (x_1, x_2, \ldots, x_n)$, the information extraction task as sequential labeling is to find a label sequence $y^* = (y_1, y_2, \ldots, y_n)$ that maximizes the conditional probability $p(y|x)$, that is,

$$y^* = \text{argmax}_y \, p(y|x) \qquad (5)$$

Different from the rule learning and the classification based methods, sequential labeling enables describing the dependencies between target information. The dependencies can be utilized to improve the accuracy of the extraction. Hidden Markov Model (Ghahramani & Jordan, 1997), Maximum Entropy Markov Model (McCallum, Freitag & Pereira, 2000), and Conditional Random Field (Lafferty, McCallum & Pereira, 2001) are widely used sequential labeling models.

For example, a discrete hidden Markov model is defined by a set of output symbols **X** (e.g., a set of words in the above example), a set of states **Y** (e.g., a set of POS in the above example), a set of probabilities for transitions between the states $p(y_i|y_j)$, and a probability distribution on output symbols for each state $p(x_i|y_i)$. An observed sampling of the process (i.e., the sequence of output symbols, e.g., "Pierre Vinken will join the board as a nonexecutive director Nov. 29." in the above example) is produced by starting from some initial state, transitioning from it to another state, sampling from the output distribution at that state, and then repeating these latter two steps. The best label sequence can be found using Viterbi algorithm.

Generative Model

Generative models define a joint probability distribution $p(\mathbf{X}, \mathbf{Y})$ where **X** and **Y** are random variables respectively ranging over observation sequences and their corresponding label sequences. In order to calculate the conditional probability $p(\mathbf{y}|\mathbf{x})$, Bayesian rule is employed:

$$y^* = \arg\max_y p(y \mid x) = \arg\max_y \frac{p(x, y)}{p(x)} \quad (6)$$

Hidden Markov Models (HMMs) (Ghahramani & Jordan, 1997) are one of the most common generative models currently used. In HMMs, each observation sequence is considered to have been generated by a sequence of state transitions, beginning in some start state and ending when some pre-designated final state is reached. At each state an element of the observation sequence is stochastically generated, before moving to the next state. In the case of POS tagging, each state of the HMM is associated with a POS tag. Although POS tags do not generate words, the tag associated with any given word can be considered to account for that word in some fashion. It is,

therefore, possible to find the sequence of POS tags that best accounts for any given sentence by identifying the sequence of states most likely to have been traversed when "generating" that sequence of words.

The states in an HMM are considered to be hidden because of the doubly stochastic nature of the process described by the model. For any observation sequence, the sequence of states that best accounts for that observation sequence is essentially hidden from an observer and can only be viewed through the set of stochastic processes that generate an observation sequence. The principle of identifying the most state sequence that best accounts for an observation sequence forms the foundation underlying the use of finite-state models for labeling sequential data.

Formally, an HMM is fully defined by

- A finite set of states Y.
- A finite output alphabet X.
- A conditional distribution $p(y'|y)$ representing the probability of moving from state y to state y', where $y, y' \in Y$.
- An observation probability distribution $p(x|y)$ representing the probability of emitting observation x when in state y, where $x \in X, y \in Y$.
- An initial state distribution $p(y)$, $y \in Y$.

From the definition of HMMs, we can see that the probability of the state at time t depends only on the state at time t-1, and the observation generated at time t only depends on the state of the model at time t. Figure 8 shows the structure of a HMM.

These conditional independence relations, combined with the probability chain rule, can be used to factorize the joint distribution over a state sequence y and observation sequence x into the product of a set of conditional probabilities:

$$p(y, x) = p(y_1)p(x_1 \mid y_1)\prod_{t=2}^{n} p(y_t \mid y_{t-1})p(x_t \mid y_t) \quad (7)$$

Figure 8. Graphic structure of first-order HMMs

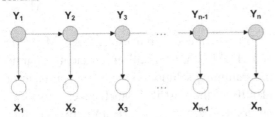

In supervised learning, the conditional probability distribution $p(y_t|y_{t-1})$ and observation probability distribution $p(x|y)$ can be gained with maximum likelihood while in unsupervised learning, there is no analytic method to gain the distributions directly. Instead, Expectation Maximization (EM) algorithm is employed to estimate the distributions.

Finding the optimal state sequence can be efficiently performed using a dynamic programming such as Viterbi algorithm.

Limitations of Generative Models

Generative models define a joint probability distribution $p(\mathbf{X}, \mathbf{Y})$ over observation and label sequences. This is useful if the trained model is to be used to generate data. However, to define a joint probability over observation and label sequences, a generative model needs to enumerate all possible observation sequences, typically requiring a representation in which observations are task-appropriate atomic entities, such as words or nucleotides. In particular, it is not practical to represent multiple interacting features or long-range dependencies of the observations, since the inference problem for such models is intractable. Therefore, generative models must make strict independence assumptions in order to make inference tractable. In the case of an HMM, the observation at time t is assumed to depend only on the state at time t, ensuring that each observation element is treated as an isolated unit, independent from all other elements in the sequence (Wallach, 2002).

In fact, most sequential data cannot be accurately represented as a set of isolated elements. Such data contain long-distance dependencies between observation elements and benefit from being represented in by a model that allows such dependencies and enables observation sequences to be represented by non-independent overlapping features. For example, in the POS task, when tagging a word, information such as the words surrounding the current word, the previous tag, and whether the word begins with a capital character, can be used as complex features and help to improve the tagging performance.

Discriminative models provide a convenient way to overcome the strong independence assumption of generative models.

Discriminative Models

Instead of modeling joint probability distribution over observation and label sequences, discriminative models define a conditional distribution $p(y|x)$ over observation and label sequences. This means that when identifying the most likely label sequence for a given observation sequence, discriminative models use the conditional distribution directly, without bothering to make any dependence assumption on observations or enumerate all the possible observation sequences to calculate the marginal probability $p(x)$.

Maximum Entropy Markov Models (MEMMs)

MEMMs (McCallum et al., 2000) are a form of discriminative models for labeling sequential data. MEMMs consider observation sequences to be conditioned upon rather than generated by the label sequence. Therefore, instead of defining two types of distribution, a MEMM has only a single set of separately trained distributions of the form:

$$p(y'\,|\,x) = p(y'\,|\,y, x) \qquad (8)$$

Figure 9. Graphic structure of first-order MEMMs

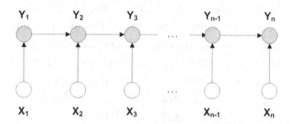

which represent the probability of moving from state y to y' on observation x. The fact the each of these functions is specific to a given state means that the choice of possible states at any given instant in time $t+1$ depends only on the state of the model at time t. Figure 9 show the graphic structure of MEMMs.

Given an observation sequence x, the conditional probability over label sequence y is given by

$$p(y \mid x) = p(y_1 \mid x_1) \prod_{t=2}^{n} p(y_t \mid y_{t-1}, x_{t-1}) \quad (9)$$

Treating observations as events to be conditioned upon rather than generated means that the probability of each transition may depend on non-independent, interacting features of the observation sequence. Making use of maximum entropy frame work and defining each state-observation transition function to be a log-linear model, equation (8) can be calculated as:

$$p(y' \mid x) = \frac{1}{Z(y,x)} \exp(\sum_{k} \lambda_k f_k(y', x)) \quad (10)$$

where $Z(y, x)$ is a normalization factor; λ_k are parameters to be estimated and f_k are feature functions. The parameters can be estimated using Generalized Iterative Scaling (GIS) (McCallum et al., 2000). Each feature function can be represented as a binary feature. For example:

$$f(y', x) = \begin{cases} 1 & \text{if } b(x) \text{ is true and } y = y' \\ 0 & \text{otherwise} \end{cases} \quad (11)$$

Despite the differences between MEMMs and HMMs, there is still an efficient dynamic programming solution to the classic problem of identifying the most likely label sequence given an observation sequence. A variant Viterbi algorithm is given by McCallum et al. (2000).

Label Bias Problem

Maximum Entropy Markov Models define a set of separately trained per-state probability distributions. This leads to an undesirable behavior in some situations, named label bias problem (Lafferty et al., 2001). Here we use an example to describe the label bias problem. The MEMM in Figure 10 is designed to shallow parse the sentences:

1.   The robot wheels Fred round.
2.   The robot wheels are round.

Consider when shallow parsing the sentence (1). Because there is only one outgoing transition from state 3 and 6, the per-state normalization requires that $p(4 \mid 3, \text{Fred}) = p(7 \mid 6, \text{are}) = 1$. Also it's easy to obtain that $p(8 \mid 7, \text{round}) = p(5 \mid 4, \text{round}) = p(2 \mid 1, \text{robot}) = p(1 \mid 0, \text{The}) = 1$, and so forth. Now, given $p(3 \mid 2, \text{wheels}) = p(6 \mid 2, \text{wheels}) = 0.5$, by combining all these factors, we obtain:

Figure 10. MEMM designed for shallow parsing

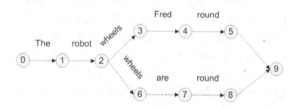

p(0123459|The robot wheels Fred round.) = 0.5,

p(0126789|The robot wheels Fred round.) = 0.5.

Thus the MEMM ends up with two possible state sequences 0123459 and 0126789 with the same probability independently of the observation sequence. It is impossible for the MEMM to tell which one is the most likely state sequence over the given sentence.

Likewise, given p(3|2, wheels) < p(6|2, wheels), MEMM will always choose the bottom path despite what the preceding words and the following words are in the observation sequence.

The label bias problem occurs because a MEMM uses per-state exponential model for the conditional probability of the next states given the current state.

Conditional Random Fields (CRFs)
CRFs are undirected graphical model trained to maximize a conditional probability. CRFs can be defined as follows:

Let G = (V, E) be a graph such that Y=(Y$_v$)$_{v∈V}$, so that Y is indexed by the vertices of G. Then (X, Y) is a conditional random field in case, when conditioned on X, the random variable Y$_v$ obey the Markov property with respect to the graph: p(Y$_v$|X, Y$_w$, w≠v) = p(Y$_v$|X, Y$_w$, w∞v), where w∞v means that w and v are neighbors in G.

A CRF is a random field globally conditioned on the observation X. Linear-chain CRFs were first introduced by Lafferty et al. (2001). Figure 11 shows the graphic structure of the linear-chain CRFs.

By the fundamental theorem of random fields (Hammersley & Clifford, 1971), the conditional distribution of the labels y given the observations data x has the form:

$$p_\lambda(y\,|\,x) = \frac{1}{Z_\lambda(x)} \exp(\sum_{t=1}^{T} \sum_k \lambda_k \cdot f_k(y_{t-1}, y_t, x, t)) \quad (12)$$

Figure 11. Graphic structure of linear-chain CRFs

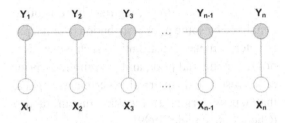

where $Z_\lambda(x)$ is the normalization factor, also known as partition function, which has the form

$$Z_\lambda(x) = \sum_y \exp(\sum_{t=1}^{T} \sum_k \lambda_k \cdot f_k(y_{t-1}, y_t, x, t)) \quad (13)$$

where $f_k(y_{t-1}, y_t, x, t)$ is a feature function which can be both real-valued and binary-valued. The feature functions can measure any aspect of a state transition, $y_{t-1} \rightarrow y_t$, and the observation sequence, x, centered at the current time step t. λ_k corresponds to the weight of the feature f_k.

The most probable labeling sequence for an input x:

$$y^* = \arg\max_y p_\lambda(y\,|\,x) \quad (14)$$

can be efficiently calculated by dynamic programming using Viterbi algorithm.

We can train the parameters $\lambda=(\lambda_1, \lambda_2, ...)$ by maximizing the likelihood of a given training set $T = \{(x_k, y_k)\}_{k=1}^N$:

$$L_\lambda = \sum_{i=1}^{N} (\sum_{t=1}^{T} \sum_k \lambda_k \cdot f_k(y_{t-1}, y_t, x_i, t) - \log Z_\lambda(x_i)) \quad (15)$$

Many methods can be used to do the parameter estimation. The traditional maximum entropy learning algorithms, such as GIS, IIS can be used to train CRFs (Darroch & Ratcliff, 1972). In addition to the traditional methods, preconditioned conjugate-gradient (CG) (Shewchuk, 1994) or limited-memory quasi-Newton (L-BFGS) (Nocedal & Wright, 1999) have been found to perform better than the traditional methods (Sha

& Pereira, 2004). The voted perceptron algorithm (Collins, 2002) can also be utilized to train the models efficiently and effectively.

To avoid overfitting[1] , log-likelihood is often penalized by some prior distribution over the parameters. Empirical distributions such as Gaussian prior, exponential prior, and hyperbolic-L_1 prior can be used, and empirical experiments suggest that Gaussian prior is a safer prior to use in practice (Chen & Rosenfeld, 1999).

CRF avoids the label bias problem because it has a single exponential model for the conditional probability of the entire sequence of labels given the observation sequence. Therefore, the weights of different features at different states can be traded off against each other.

Sequential Labeling-Based Extraction Methods

By casting information extraction as sequential labeling, a set of labels need to be defined first according to the extraction task. For example, in metadata extraction from research papers (Peng & McCallum, 2004), labels such as TITLE, AUTHOR, E-MAIL, and ABSTRACT are defined. A document is viewed as an observation sequence x. The observation unit can be a word, a text line, or any other unit. Then the task is to find a label sequence y that maximize the conditional probability $p(y|x)$ using the models described above.

In generative models, there are no other features that can be utilized except the observation itself. Due to the conditional nature, discriminative models provide the flexibility of incorporating non-independent, arbitrary features as input to improve the performance. For example, in the task of metadata extraction from research papers, with CRFs we can use as features not only text content, but also layout and external lexicon. Empirical experiments show that the ability to incorporate non-independent, arbitrary features can significantly improve the performance.

On the other hand, the ability to incorporate

non-independent, arbitrary features of discriminative models may sometimes lead to too many features and some of the features are of little contributions to the model. A feature induction can be performed when training the model to obtain the features that are most useful for the model (McCallum, 2003).

NonLinear Conditional Random Fields

Conditional random fields (CRFs) are the state-of-the-art approaches in information extraction taking advantage of the dependencies to do better extraction, compared with HMMs (Ghahramani & Jordan, 1997) and MEMMs (McCallum et al., 2000). However, the previous linear-chain CRFs only model the linear-dependencies in a sequence of information, and is not able to model the other kinds of dependencies (e.g., nonlinear dependencies) (Lafferty et al., 2001; Zhu, Nie, Wen, Zhang, & Ma, 2005). In this section, we will discuss several nonlinear conditional random field models.

Condition Random Fields for Relational Learning

HMMs, MEMMs and linear-chain CRFs can only model dependencies between neighboring labels. But sometimes it is important to model certain kinds of long-range dependencies between entities. One important kind of dependency within information extraction occurs on repeated mentions of the same field. For example, when the same entity is mentioned more than once in a document, such as a person name Robert Booth, in many cases, all mentions have the same label, such as SEMINAR-SPEAKER. An IE system can take advantage of this fact by favoring labelings that treat repeated words identically, and by combining feature from all occurrences so that the extraction decision can be made based on global information. Furthermore, identifying all mentions of an entity can be useful in itself, because each mention might contain different useful information. The skip-chain CRF is proposed to address this (Bunescu & Mooney, 2005; Sutton & McCallum, 2005).

The skip-chain CRF is essentially a linear-chain CRF with additional long-distance edges between similar words. These additional edges are called skip edges. The features on skip edges can incorporate information from the context of both endpoints, so that strong evidence at one endpoint can influence the label at the other endpoint.

Formally, the skip-chain CRF is defined as a general CRF with two clique templates: one for the linear-chain portion, and one for the skip edges. For an input x, let it be the set of all pairs of sequence positions for which there are skip edges. The probability of a label sequence y given an x is modeled as:

$$p_\lambda(y \mid x) = \frac{1}{Z(x)} \exp(\sum_{t=1}^{T} \sum_k \lambda_k \cdot f_k(y_{t-1}, y_t, x, t)$$
$$+ \sum_{(u,v) \in C} \sum_l \lambda_l \cdot f_l(y_u, y_v, x, u, v)) \qquad (16)$$

where $Z(x)$ is the normalization factor, f_k is the feature function similar to that in equation (12) and f_l is the feature function of the skip edges. λ_k and λ_l are weights of the two kinds of feature functions.

Because the loops in a skip-chain CRF can be long and overlapping, exact inference is intractable for the data considered. The running time required by exact inference is exponential in the size of the largest clique in the graph's junction tree. Instead, approximate inference using loopy belief propagation is performed, such as TRP (Wainwright, Jaakkola, & Willsky, 2001).

Richer kinds of long-distance factors than just over pairs of words can be considered to augment the skip-chain model. These factors are useful for modeling exceptions to the assumption that similar words tend to have similar labels. For example, in named entity recognition, the word China is as a place name when it appears alone,

but when it occurs within the phrase The China Daily, it should be labeled as an organization (Finkel, Grenager, & Manning, 2005).

2D CRFs for Web Information Extraction

Zhu et al. (2005) propose 2D conditional random fields (2D CRFs). 2D CRFs are also a particular case of CRFs. They are aimed at extracting object information from two-dimensionally laid-out Web pages. The graphic structure of a 2D CRF is a 2D grid, and it is natural to model the 2D laid-out information. If viewing the state sequence on diagonal as a single state, a 2D CRF can be mapped to a linear-chain CRF, and thus the conditional distribution has the same form as a linear-chain CRF.

Dynamic CRFs

Sutton et al. (2004) propose dynamic conditional random fields (DCRFs). As a particular case, a factorial CRF (FCRF) was used to jointly solve two NLP tasks (noun phrase chunking and part-of-speech tagging) on the same observation sequence. Improved accuracy was obtained by modeling the dependencies between the two tasks.

Tree-Structure CRFs for Information Extraction

We have investigated the problem of hierarchical information extraction and propose tree-structured conditional random fields (TCRFs). TCRFs can incorporate dependencies across the hierarchically laid-out information.

We here use an example to introduce the problem of hierarchical information extraction. Figure 12 (a) gives an example document in which the underlined text is what we want to extract including two telephone numbers and two addresses. The information can be organized as a tree structure (ref. Figure 12 (b)). In this case, the existing linear-chain CRFs cannot model the hierarchical dependencies and thus cannot distinguish the office telephone number and the home telephone number from each other. Likewise for the office address and home address.

To better incorporate dependencies across hierarchically laid-out information, we propose a tree-structured conditional random field (TCRF) model. We present the graphical structure of the TCRF model as a tree and reformulate the conditional distribution by defining three kinds of edge features respectively representing the parent-child dependency, child-parent dependency, and sibling dependency. As the tree structure can be cyclable, exact inference in TCRFs is expensive. We propose to use the tree-based reparameterization (TRP) algorithm (Wainwright et al., 2001) to compute the approximate marginal probabilities for edges and vertices. We conducted experiments on company annual reports collected from the Shanghai Stock Exchange. On the annual reports we defined ten extraction tasks. Experimental results indicate that the TCRFs can significantly outperform the existing linear-chain CRF model (+7.67% in terms of F1-measure) for hierarchical information extraction. See Tang, Hong, Li, and Liang (2006) for details.

APPLICATIONS

In this section, we introduce several extraction applications that we experienced. We will also introduce some well-known applications in this area.

Information Extraction in Digital Libraries

In digital libraries (DL), "metadata" is structured data for helping users find and process documents and images. With the metadata information, search engines can retrieve required documents more accurately. Scientists and librarians need use great manual efforts and a lot of time to create metadata for the documents. To alleviate the hard labor, many efforts have been made toward the automatic metadata generation based on information extraction. Here we take Citeseer, a popular scientific literature digital library, as an example in our explanation.

Citeseer is a public specialty scientific and academic DL that was created in NEC Labs, which is hosted on the World Wide Web at the College of Information Sciences and Technology, The Pennsylvania State University, and has over 700,000 documents, primarily in the fields of computer and information science and engineering (Han, Giles, Manavoglu, Zha, Zhang, & Fox, 2003; Lawrence, Giles, & Bollacker, 1999). Citeseer crawls and harvests documents on the Web, extracts documents metadata automatically, and indexes the metadata to permit querying by metadata.

By extending Dublin Core metadata standard, Citeseer defines 15 different metatags for the

Figure 12. Example of tree-structured laid-out information

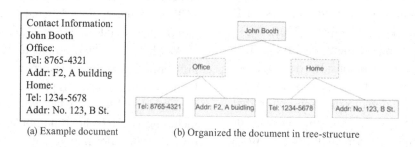

(a) Example document   (b) Organized the document in tree-structure

document header, including Title, Author, Affiliation, and so on. They view the task of automatic document metadata generation as that of labeling the text with the corresponding metatags. Each meta-tag corresponds to a metadata class. The extraction task is cast as a classification problem and SVM is employed to perform the classification. They show that classifying each text line into one or more classes is more efficient for metatagging than classifying each word, and decompose the metadata extraction problem into two subproblems: (1) line classification and (2) chunk identification of multiclass lines.

In line classification, both word and line-specific features are used. Each line is represented by a set of word and line-specific features. A rule-based, context-dependent word clustering method is developed to overcome the problem of word sparseness. For example, an author line "Chungki Lee James E. Burns" is represented as "CapNonDictWord: :MayName: :MayName: : SingleCap: :MayName:", after word clustering. The weight of a word-specific feature is the number of times this feature appears in the line. And line-specific features are features such as "Number of the words in the line," "The position of the line," "The percentage of dictionary words in the line," and so on. The classification process is performed in two steps, an independent line classification followed by an iterative contextual line classification. Independent line classification uses the features described above to assign one or more classes to each text line. After that, by making use of the sequential information among lines output by the first step, an iterative contextual line classification is performed. In each iteration, each line uses the previous N and next N lines' class information as features, concatenates them to the feature vector used in step one, and updates its class label. The procedure converges when the percentage of line with new class labels is lower than a threshold. The principle of the classification based method is the two-level boundary classification approach as described in section 2.2.3. After classifying each

line into one or more classes, meta-tag can be assigned to lines that have only one class label. For those that have more than one class label, a further identification is employed to extract metadata from each line. The task is cast as a chunk identification task. Punctuation marks and spaces between words are considered candidate chunk boundaries. A two-class chunk identification algorithm for this task was developed and it yields an accuracy of 75.5%. For lines that have more than two class labels, they are simplified to two-class chunk identification tasks by detecting natural chunk boundary. For instance, using the positions of e-mail and URL in the line, the three-class chunk identification can be simplified as two-class chunk identification task. The position of the e-mail address in the following three-class line "International Computer Science Institute, Berkeley, CA94704. E-mail: aberer@ icsi.berkeley.edu." is a natural chunk boundary between the other two classes. The method obtains an overall accuracy of 92.9%. It's adopted in the DL Citeseer and EbizSearch for automatic metadata extraction. It can be also generalized to other DL. See Lawrence et al. (1999) and Han et al. (2003) for details.

Information Extraction from E-Mails

We also make use of information extraction methods to e-mail data (Tang, Li, Cao, & Tang, 2005). e-mail is one of the commonest means for communication via text. It is estimated that an average computer user receives 40 to 50 e-mails per day (Ducheneaut & Bellotti, 2001). Many text mining applications need take e-mails as inputs, for example, e-mail analysis, e-mail routing, e-mail filtering, information extraction from e-mail, and newsgroup analysis.

Unfortunately, information extraction from e-mail has received little attention in the research community. E-mail data can contain different types of information. Specifically, it may contain headers, signatures, quotations, and text content. Furthermore, the text content may have program codes, lists, and paragraphs; the header may have metadata information such as sender, receiver, subject, and so forth; and the signature may have metadata information such as author name, author's position, author's address, and so forth.

In this work, we formalize information extraction from e-mail as that of text-block detection and block-metadata detection. Specifically, the problem is defined as a process of detection of different types of informative blocks (it includes header, signature, quotation, program code, list, and paragraph detections) and detection of block-metadata (it includes metadata detection of header and metadata detection of signature). We propose to conduct e-mail extraction in a "cascaded" fashion. In the approach, we perform the extraction on an e-mail by running several passes of processing on it: first at e-mail body level (text-block detection), next at text-content level (paragraph detection), and then at block levels (header-metadata detection and signature-metadata detection). We view the tasks as classification and propose a unified statistical learning approach to the tasks, based on SVMs (Support Vector Machines). Features used in the models have also been defined. See Tang, Li, Cao et al. (2005) for details.

Figure 13 shows an example of e-mail that includes much typical information. Lines from 1 to 3 are a header; lines from 18 to 20 are a signature; and a forwarded message lies from line 21 to line 24. Lines from 4 to 8 are the actual text content, which should be two paragraphs, but is mistakenly separated by extra line breaks. Moreover, the header has a sender (line 1), a sent time (line 2), and a subject (line 3); the signature has an author name (line 18), a telephone (line 19), and a homepage (line 20).

Figure 14 shows an ideal result of information extraction on the e-mail in Figure 13. Within it, the text-blocks (the header, signature and the forwarded message) have been identified. The actual text content has been detected. In the text content, extra line breaks have been detected and the text has been annotated as two paragraphs. Metadata

Figure 13. Example of e-mail message

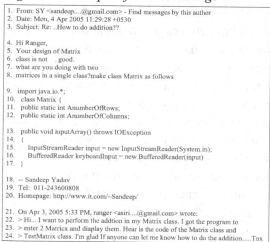

Figure 14. Annotation results of the e-mail message

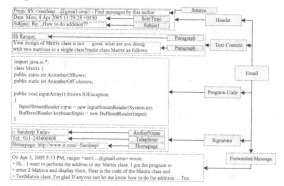

information is recognized in the identified header and the identified signature.

We propose a cascaded approach for information extraction from e-mail and cast the extraction tasks as detection tasks of different types of information blocks. We employ a unified machine learning approach in the detection tasks.

The input is an e-mail message. The implementation carries out extraction in the following steps. The identified text-blocks and other extraction results in each step will be saved for use in the later steps.

1. **Preprocessing:** It uses patterns to recognize "special words," including e-mail address, IP address, URL, date, file directory, number (e.g., 5.42), money (e.g., $100), percentage

(e.g., 92.86%), words containing special symbols (e.g., C#, .NET, .doc).

2. **Forwarded message detection:** It identifies forwarded messages using hard-coded rules. It views lines starting with special characters (e.g., >, |, >>) as forwarded messages. It then eliminates the identified forwarded messages for later processing.

3. **Header and signature detection:** It detects the header and signature (if there exist) in the e-mail by using a classification model. It next eliminates the identified blocks (headers and signatures).

4. **Metadata detection in header and signature:** It uses the identified headers and signatures as input and then detects the metadata information from the headers and signatures, respectively.

5. **List and program code detection:** It detects list and program code (if there exist) in the e-mail with the same approach as that in header and signature detection and removes them from the text content. After that, only natural language text remains.

6. **Paragraph annotation:** It identifies whether or not each line break is a paragraph ending by using a classification model. If not, it removes the line break. As a result, the text is segmented into paragraphs. The step is based on paragraph ending detection.

We make use of support vector machines (SVM) as the classification model (Vapnik, 1998). We use SVM-light, which is available at http://svmlight.joachims.org/. We obtain high performances in all detection tasks. (The F1-measuer scores range from 89.83% to 97.17%.)

The extracted information from e-mail is applied to applications of e-mail data cleaning (Tang, Li & Cao et al., 2005) and e-mail classification.

In e-mail data cleaning, we try to remove noisy (irrelevant) blocks for a specific application (e.g., term extraction, a task in which base noun phrases are extracted from documents) and transform relevant text into a canonical form as that in a newspaper article. For term extraction, we identify and remove the header, signature, program code, and forwarded message. We view the remaining text as the relevant text. In the relevant text, we identify and remove extra line breaks, remove extra punctuations, and restore badly cased words. Experimental results show that the extraction based e-mail cleaning can significantly improve the accuracy of term extraction. The improvements on precision range from +49.90% to +71.15%. See Tang, Li, and Cao et al. (2005) for details.

In e-mail classification, we are aimed at taking advantage of the extracted information to improve the performance of e-mail classification. We evaluated the classification results on Enron e-mail Dataset, which is available at http://www.cs.umass.edu/~ronb/enron_dataset.html. Experimental results show that the classification performance can be significantly improved (averagely +49.02% in terms of F1-measure) by making use of the extraction results from e-mails. The related issues are what we are currently researching, and will be reported elsewhere.

Person Profile Extraction

Person information management is an important topic in both the academic and industrial communities. A person can have different types of information: person profile (including portrait, homepage, position, affiliation, publications, and documents), contact information (including address, e-mail, telephone, and fax number), and social network information (including person or professional relationships between persons, e.g., friend relationship). However, the information is usually hidden in heterogeneous and distributed Web pages.

We have investigated the problem of person information extraction. We have found that the person information is mainly hidden in person homepage, person introduction page (Web pages that introduces the person), person list (e.g., a faculty list), and e-mail message (e.g., in signature). We employed the classification based method to extract the person information from the different types of Web pages.

More specifically, in extraction we convert a Web page into a token sequence (the token can be word, punctuation, and space). Then we view each token as a candidate and define features for each candidate. Due to space limitation, we omit the details of the feature definition. After that, we use two classification models to respectively identify whether a token is the start position and whether the token is the end position for each type of information. We next view the tokens between the start token and the end token as the target. We can also use the text-line as candidate in extraction.

For learning the classification models, we have human annotators conduct annotation on the Web pages. We also convert the Web page into a token sequence and view each token as the candidate. Features are defined for each candidate. Finally, we learn two classification models respectively for the start position identification and the end position identification for each type of information.

As models, we use SVMs (support vector machines) (Vapnik, 1998). Features are defined in the SVM models respectively for each type of the information. The average F1-measure obtained in extraction is 91.18%.

We have developed a system based on the extracted person information, which is called academic research social networking mining system (Arnetminer, available at http://www.arnetminer.org). In Arnetminer, the user inputs a person name, and the system returns the information of the person. Given a person name, we first utilize Google API to get a list of relevant documents. Then a classification model is employed to identify whether or not a document in the list is really "related" to the person. Next, we extract person information from the identified documents using the classification based method as described above.

Figure 15 shows the snapshots of the Arnetminer system. In Figure 15 (a), the user types a

Figure 15. Arnetminer system

(a)

(b)

person name, and he gets a detailed description of the person. Figure 15 (b) shows the list of gathered persons in our current system. See Tang, Hong, Zhang, Liang, and Li (2006) for details.

Table Extraction Using Conditional Random Fields

Tables, textual tokens laid out in tabular form, are often used to compactly communicate information in fields and records. They have been described as "databases designed for human eyes." Tables appear in the earliest writing on clay tablets, and in the most modern Web pages. Some make use of line-art, while others rely on white space only. They sometimes consist merely of two simple columns, other times of extremely baroque collections of headings, embedded subheadings, and varying cell sizes. They are used in everything from government reports, to magazine articles, to academic publications.

Pinto et al. (2003) propose a model of table extraction that richly integrates evidence from both content and layout by using conditional random fields (CRFs). They describe a method that simultaneously locates tables in plain-text government statistical reports, and labels each of their constituent lines with tags such as header, subheader, data, separator, and so forth. The features measure aspects of the input stream such as the percentage of alphabetic characters, the presence of regular expression matching months or years, and the degree to which white space in the current line aligns with white space in the previous line. In experiments on government reports, tables are located with 92% in terms of F1-measure, and lines are labeled with 94% accuracy—reducing error by 80% over a similarly configured hidden Markov model with the same features. See Pinto et al. for details. See also Wang and Hu (2002).

Shallow Parsing with Conditional Random Fields

Shallow parsing identifies the nonrecursive cores of various phrase types in text, possibly as a precursor to full parsing or information extraction (Abney, 1991). The paradigmatic shallow parsing problem is NP chunking, which finds the nonrecursive cores of noun phrases called base NPs. The pioneering work of Ramshaw and Marcus (1995) introduced NP chunking as a machine-learning problem, with standard datasets and evaluation metrics. The task was extended to additional phrase types for the CoNLL-2000 shared task (Tjong Kim Sang & Buchholz, 2000), which is now the standard evaluation task for shallow parsing.

Sha and Pereira (2003) employ conditional random fields (CRFs) into shallow parsing. They have carried out an empirical study on different sequential labeling approaches in shallow parsing. Their experimental results show that CRFs outperform all reported single-model NP chunking results on the standard evaluation dataset. They also compared different kinds of parameter estimation methods for training CRF models that confirm and strengthen previous results on shallow parsing and training methods for maximum entropy models.

FUTURE RESEARCH DIRECTIONS

There are a variety of promising directions for future research in applying supervised machine learning to information extraction. On the machine-learning side, it would be interesting to generalize the ideas of large-margin classification to sequence models, strengthening the results of (Collins, 2002) and leading to new optimal training algorithms with stronger guarantees against overfitting. For example, Taskar, Guestrin, and Koller (2003) propose a maximal Markov model for sequential labeling task using the maximal margin theory.

In information extraction, in addition to identifying entities, an important problem is extracting specific types of relations between entities. For example, in newspaper text, one can identify that an organization is located in a particular city or that a person is affiliated with a specific organization (Zelenko, Aone, & Richardella, 2003). In biomedical text, one can identify that a protein interacts with another protein or that a protein is located in a particular part of the cell (Bunescu, Ge, Kate, Marcotte, Mooney & Ramani et al., 2005; Craven & Kumlien, 1999). The entities may occur in different parts of a sentence or paragraph. New principled methods are needed to such problems to identify both the entities while identifying their relations. Bunescu and Mooney (2005) propose to use a Statistical Relational Learning (SRL) method for the complex problem. They are trying to integrate decision at different levels (e.g., different kinds of entity identification and different kinds of relations identification) into the SRL model. Moreover, several recent projects have taken the first steps in this direction. For example, Sutton, Rohanimanesch, and McCallum (2004) present a dynamic version of CRF that integrates part-of-speech tagging and noun-phrase chunking into one coherent process. Roth and Yih (2004) present an information extraction approach based on linear-programming that integrates recognition of entities with the identification of relations between these entities.

As another future work, more applications, especially practical applications, need to be investigated. The new applications can provide rich data sources for conducting information extraction, at the same time bring big challenges to the field. This is because different applications have different characteristics, needing to use different methods to deal with.

CONCLUSION

Aiming to apply methods and technologies from practical computer science such as compiler construction and artificial intelligence to the problem of processing unstructured textual data automatically, information extraction has become an important subdiscipline of language engineering, a branch of computer science. Today, the significance of information extraction is determined by the growing amount of information available in unstructured (i.e., without metadata) form, for instance Web pages on the Internet.

In this chapter, we have reviewed the information extraction methods. Specifically, we focus on the three state-of-the-art methods: rule learning based method, classification based method, and sequential labeling base method. We have explained the principle of the three methods by using several developed systems as examples. We have also introduced our research work on the information extraction methods and their applications. We have introduced several practical applications of information extraction, ranging from natural language processing to information extraction from Web pages and plain texts.

The rule learning based method tries to exploit the regularity in language expressions of certain information to find common linguistic patterns that match these expressions. It is easy to understand by an average user. The method can obtain good performance when processing some semi-structured documents (e.g., template-based Web page). Its disadvantage lies in that its rudimentary learning mechanisms cannot provide enough generalization capabilities. This makes it difficult to obtain good performance in complicated situations (e.g., extraction from natural language text).

The classification based method casts the IE task as a classification problem in terms of the statistical theory. It can incorporate different types of information (including words, syntax, a prior knowledge, etc.). Thus it has more generalization capabilities than the rule based method. In several real-world applications, it can outperform the rule based method. Its drawback is that its model is usually complex and it is difficult for the general user to understand (e.g., the feature definition). Thus the performances of extraction differ from application to application.

The sequential labeling based method can make use of dependencies between information to improve the extraction performance. It is also based on the statistical theory and thus has strong generalization capabilities. In many applications, in particular natural language processing, it can outperform the rule based method and the classification based method. As for the disadvantage, similar to the classification based method, it is not easily understood by a general user.

Information extraction suffers from uncertainty and implication of the natural language. Both of the two problems are difficult for machine to automatic extraction, sometimes even for human. For example, "It is likely that ...". In such a sentence, it is difficult to determine the reliability degree of the information. Consider another example: "After a furious fight, enemy raised the white flag." Here the white flag means a defeat. However, it would, of course, be difficult for computers to conclude the implication.

Another interesting and important issue is how to make use of the prior knowledge in information extraction. So far, a usual method for incorporating the prior knowledge is to use some domain-specific dictionaries, thesauri in the extraction. The question is whether the simple method still works well when dealing with more complex extraction tasks. A further question asks whether we can incorporate the different types of prior knowledge into a unified model for extraction.

In future work, the research community has to face the rising challenges and focus on how to enhance the practical usefulness of IE methods.

ACKNOWLEDGMENT

The work is funded by the Natural Science Foundation of China under Grant No. 90604025. Thanks to the anonymous reviewers for their constructive suggestions.

REFERENCES

Abney, S. (1991). Parsing by chunks. In R. Berwick, S. Abney, & C. Tenny (Eds.), *Principle-based parsing: Computation and psycholinguistics* (pp. 257-278). Boston: Kluwer Academic Publishers.

Berger, A. L., Della Pietra, S. A., & Della Pietra, V. J. (1996). A maximum entropy approach to natural language processing. *Computational Linguistics, 22*, 39-71.

Boser, B. E., Guyon, I. M., & Vapnik, V. N. (1992). A training algorithm for optimal margin classifiers. In D. Haussler (Ed.), *5th Annual ACM Workshop on COLT* (pp. 144-152). Pittsburgh, PA: ACM Press.

Bunescu, R., Ge, R., Kate, R. J., Marcotte, E. M., Mooney, R. J., Ramani, A. K., et al. (2005). Comparative experiments on learning information extractors for proteins and their interactions. *Artificial Intelligence in Medicine [special issue on Summarization and Information Extraction from Medical Documents], 33*(2), 139-155.

Bunescu, R., & Mooney, R. J. (2005). Statistical relational learning for natural language information extraction. In L. Getoor & B. Taskar (Eds.), *Statistical relational learning*, forthcoming.

Califf, M. E., & Mooney, R. J. (1998). Relational learning of pattern-match rules for information extraction. In *Working Notes of AAAI Spring Symposium on Applying Machine Learning to Discourse Processing* (pp. 6-11).

Califf, M. E., & Mooney, R. J. (2003). Bottom-up relational learning of pattern matching rules for information extraction. *Journal of Machine Learning Research, 4,* 177-210.

Chen, S. F., & Rosenfeld, R. (1999). *A Gaussian prior for smoothing maximum entropy models* (Tech. Rep. No. CMU-CS-99-108). Carnegie Mellon University.

Ciravegna, F. (2001). (LP)2 An adaptive algorithm for information extraction from Web-related texts. In *Proceedings of the IJCAI-2001 Workshop on Adaptive Text Extraction and Mining held in conjunction with 17th International Joint Conference on Artificial Intelligence (IJCAI),* Seattle, Washington.

Collins, M. (2002). Discriminative training methods for hidden Markov models: Theory and experiments with perceptron algorithms. In *Proceedings of the Conference on Empirical Methods in NLP (EMNLP'02)* (pp. 1-8).

Craven, M., & Kumlien, J. (1999). Constructing biological knowledge bases by extracting information from text sources. In *Proceedings of the 7th International Conference on Intelligent Systems for Molecular Biology (ISMB-1999)* (pp. 77-86).

Darroch, J. N., & Ratcliff, D. (1972). Generalized iterative scaling for log-linear models. *The Annals of Mathematical Statistics, 43*(5), 1470-1480.

Ducheneaut, N., & Bellotti, V. (2001). E-mail as habitat: An exploration of embedded personal information management. *Interactions, 8,* 30-38.

Finkel, J. R., Grenager, T., & Manning, C. D. (2005). Incorporating nonlocal information into information extraction systems by Gibbs sampling. In *Proceedings of the 43rd Annual Meeting of the Association for Computational Linguistics (ACL-2005)* (pp. 363-370).

Finn, A., & Kushmerick, N. (2004). Information extraction by convergent boundary classification. In *AAAI-04 Workshop on Adaptive Text Extraction and Mining* (pp. 1-6). San Jose, CA.

Finn, A. (2006). *A multi-level boundary classification approach to information extraction.* Doctoral thesis, University College Dublin.

Freitag, D. (1998). Information extraction from HTML: Application of a general machine learning approach. In *Proceedings of the 15th Conference on Artificial Intelligence (AAAI'98)* (pp. 517-523).

Freitag, D., & Kushmerick, N. (2000). Boosted wrapper induction. In *Proceedings of 17th National Conference on Artificial Intelligence* (pp. 577-583).

Ghahramani, Z., & Jordan, M. I. (1997). Factorial hidden Markov models. *Machine Learning, 29,* 245-273.

Hammersley, J., & Clifford, P. (1971). *Markov fields on finite graphs and lattices.* Unpublished manuscript.

Han, H., Giles, L., Manavoglu, E., Zha, H., Zhang, Z., & Fox, E.A. (2003). Automatic document metadata extraction using support vector machines. In *Proceedings of 2003 Joint Conference on Digital Libraries (JCDL'03)* (pp. 37-48).

Kauchak, D., Smarr, J., & Elkan, C. (2004). Sources of success for boosted wrapper induction. *The Journal of Machine Learning Research, 5,* 499-527.

Kristjansson, T. T., Culotta, A., Viola, P. A., & McCallum, A. (2004). Interactive information extraction with constrained conditional random fields. In *Proceedings of AAAI'04* (pp. 412-418).

Kushmerick, N., Weld, D. S., & Doorenbos, R. (1997). Wrapper induction for information extraction. In *Proceedings of the International Joint Conference on Artificial Intelligence (IJCAI'97)* (pp. 729-737).

Kushmerick, N. (2000). Wrapper induction: Efficiency and expressiveness. *Artificial Intelligence, 118,* 15-68.

Lafferty, J., McCallum, A., & Pereira, F. (2001). Conditional random fields: Probabilistic models for segmenting and labeling sequence data. In *Proceedings of the 18th International Conference on Machine Learning (ICML'01)* (pp. 282-289).

Lawrence, S., Giles, C. L., & Bollacker K. (1999). Digital libraries and autonomous citation indexing. *IEEE Computer, 32*(6), 67-71.

Li, X., & Liu, B. (2003). Learning to classify texts using positive and unlabeled data. In *Proceedings of International Joint Conference on Artificial Intelligence (IJCAI'2003)* (pp. 587-592).

McCallum, A., Freitag, D., & Pereira, F. (2000). Maximum entropy Markov models for information extraction and segmentation. In *Proceedings of the 17th International Conference on Machine Learning (ICML'00)* (pp. 591-598).

McCallum, A. (2003). Efficiently inducing features of conditional random fields. In *Proceedings of the 19th Conference in Uncertainty in Artificial Intelligence* (pp. 403-410).

Morik, K., Brockhausen, P., & Joachims, T. (1999). Combining statistical learning with a knowledge-based approach: A case study in intensive care monitoring. In *Proceedings of International Conference on Machine Learning (ICML'99)* (pp. 268-277).

Muslea, I., Minton, S., & Knoblock, C. (1998). STALKER: Learning extraction rules for semistructured, Web-based information sources. In *the AAAI Workshop on AI and Information Integration* (pp. 74-81).

Muslea, I., Minton, S., & Knoblock, C. (1999). Hierarchical wrapper induction for semistructured information sources. *Autonomous Agents and Multi-Agent Systems, 4,* 93-114.

Muslea, I. (1999). Extraction patterns for information extraction tasks: A survey. In *Proceedings of AAAI-99: Workshop on Machine Learning for Information Extraction.*

Muslea, I., Minton, S., & Knoblock, C. A. (2003). Active learning with strong and weak views: A case study on wrapper induction. In *Proceedings of the International Joint Conference on Artificial Intelligence (IJCAI)* (pp. 415-420).

Ng, H. T., Lim, C. Y., & Koo, J. L. T. (1999). Learning to recognize tables in free text. In *Proceedings of the 37th Annual Meeting of the Association for Computational Linguistics on Computational Linguistics (ACL'99)* (pp. 443-450).

Nocedal, J., & Wright, S. J. (1999). *Numerical optimization.* New York: Springer Press.

Peng, F. (2001). *Models for information extraction* (Technique Report).

Peng, F., & McCallum, A. (2004). Accurate information extraction from research papers using conditional random fields. In *Proceedings of HLT-NAACL* (pp. 329-336).

Pinto, D., McCallum, A., Wei, X., & Croft, W. B. (2003). Table extraction using conditional random fields. In *Proceedings of the 26th Annual International ACM SIGIR Conference on Research and Development in Information Retrieval (SIGIR'03)* (pp. 235-242).

Ramshaw, L. A., & Marcus, M. P. (1995). Text chunking using transformation-based learning. In *Proceedings of Third Workshop on Very Large Corpora, ACL* (pp. 67-73).

Ratnaparkhi, A. (1998). Unsupervised statistical models for prepositional phrase attachment. In *Proceedings of COLING ACL'98* (pp. 1079-1085). Montreal, Canada.

Riloff, E. (1993). Automatically constructing a dictionary for information extraction tasks. In *Proceedings of the Eleventh National Conference on Artificial Intelligence* (pp. 811-816).

Riloff, E. (1996). Automatically generating extraction patterns from untagged text. In *Proceedings of the Thirteenth National Conference on Artificial Intelligence* (pp. 1044-1049).

Riloff, E., & Jones, R. (1999). Learning dictionaries for information extraction by multi-level bootstrapping. In *Proceedings of the Sixteenth National Conference on Artificial Intelligence* (pp. 474-479).

Roth, D., & Yih, W. (2004). A linear programming formulation for global inference in natural language tasks. In *Proceedings of the Eighth Conference on Computational Natural Language Learning (CoNLL-2004)* (pp. 1-8). Boston.

Schölkopf B., Burges, C. J. C., & Smola A. J. (1999). *Advances in kernel methods: Support vector learning*. MA: MIT Press.

Sha, F., & Pereira, F. (2003). Shallow parsing with conditional random fields. In *Proceedings of Human Language Technology, NAACL* (pp. 188-191).

Shapire, R. E. (1999). A brief introduction to boosting. In *Proceedings of the 16th International Joint Conference on Artificial Intelligence (IJCAI-1999)* (pp. 1401-1405).

Shewchuk, J. R. (1994). *An introduction to the conjugate gradient method without the agonizing pain*. Retrieved March 22, 2007, from http://www-2.cs.cmu.edu/.jrs/jrspapers.html#cg

Siefkes, C., & Siniakov, P. (2005). An overview and classification of adaptive approaches to information extraction. *Journal on Data Semantics, 4,* 172-212.

Soderland, S., Fisher, D., Aseltine, J., & Lehnert, W. (1995). CRYSTAL: Inducing a conceptual dictionary. In *Proceedings of the Fourteenth International Joint Conference on Artificial Intelligence (IJCAI'95)* (pp. 1314-1319).

Soderland, S. (1999). Learning information extraction rules for semi-structured and free text. *Machine Learning, 34*(1-3), 299-272.

Sutton, C., Rohanimanesh, K., & McCallum, A. (2004). Dynamic conditional random fields: Factorized probabilistic models for labeling and segmenting sequence data. In *Proceedings of ICML'2004* (pp. 783-790).

Sutton, C., & McCallum, A. (2005). An introduction to conditional random fields for relational learning. In L. Getoor & B. Taskar (Eds.), *Statistical relational learning*, forthcoming.

Tang, J., Li, H., Cao, Y., & Tang, Z. (2005). E-mail data cleaning. In *Proceedings of SIGKDD'2005* (pp. 489-499). Chicago.

Tang, J., Li, J., Lu, H., Liang, B., & Wang, K. (2005). iASA: Learning to annotate the semantic Web. *Journal on Data Semantic, 4,* 110-145.

Tang. J., Hong, M., Zhang, J., Liang, B., & Li, J. (2006). A new approach to personal network search based on information extraction. In *Proceedings of the first International Conference of Asian Semantic Web (ASWC)*. To appear.

Tang, J., Hong, M., Li, J., & Liang, B. (2006). Tree-structured conditional random fields for semantic annotation. In *Proceedings of 5th International Conference of Semantic Web (ISWC'2006)* (pp. 640-653).

Taskar, B., Guestrin, C., & Koller, D. (2003). Max-margin markov networks. In Proceedings of Advances in *Neural Information Processing Systems* (NIPS'03) . Cambridge, MA: MIT Press.

Tetko, I.V., Livingstone, D.J., & Luik, A.I. (1995). Neural network studies. 1. Comparison of overfitting and overtraining. *Journal of Chemical Information and Computer Sciences, 35,* 826-833.

Tjong Kim Sang, E. F., & Buchholz, S. (2000). Introduction to the CoNLL-2000 shared task: Chunking. In *Proceedings of CoNLL-2000* (pp. 127-132).

Vapnik, V. (1998). *Statistical learning theory.* NY: Springer-Verlag.

Vapnik V. (1999). *The nature of statistical learning theory.* NY: Springer-Verlag.

Wallach, H. (2002). *Efficient training of conditional random fields.* Unpublished master's thesis, University of Edinburgh, USA.

Wang, Y., & Hu, J. (2002). A machine learning based approach for table detection on the Web. In *Proceedings of the 11th International World Wide Web Conference (WWW'02)* (pp. 242-250). Honolulu, Hawaii.

Wainwright, M., Jaakkola, T., & Willsky, A. (2001). Tree-based reparameterization for approximate estimation on graphs with cycles. In *Proceedings of Advances in Neural Information Processing Systems (NIPS'2001)* (pp. 1001-1008).

Zelenko, D., Aone, C., & Richardella, A. (2003). Kernel methods for relation extraction. *Journal of Machine Learning Research, 3,* 1083-1106.

Zhang, L., Pan, Y., & Zhang, T. (2004). Recognizing and using named entities: Focused named entity recognition using machine learning. In *Proceedings of the 27th Annual International ACM SIGIR Conference on Research and Development in Information Retrieval (SIGIR'04)* (pp. 281-288).

Zhu, J., Nie, Z., Wen, J., Zhang, B., & Ma, W. (2005). 2D conditional random fields for Web information extraction. In *Proceedings of 22nd International Conference on Machine Learning (ICML2005)* (pp. 1044-1051). Bonn, Germany.

Additional Reading

Adwait, R. (1996). Maximum entropy model for POS tagging. In *Proceedings of the Conference on Empirical Methods in Natural Language Processing* (pp. 133-142). Somerset, NJ.

Ahn, D. (2006). The stages of event extraction. In *Proceedings of the Workshop on Annotating and Reasoning about Time and Events* (pp. 1-8).

Allen, J. (1994). *Natural language understanding* (2nd ed.). Addison-Wesley.

Altun, Y., Tsochantaridis, I., & Hofmann, T. (2003). Hidden Markov support vector machines. In *Proceedings of the 20th International Conference on Machine Learning (ICML 2003)* (pp. 3-10).

Appelt, D. & Israel, D. (1999). Introduction to information extraction technology. In *Proceedings of IJCAI'99 Tutorial* (pp. 1-41).

Baum, L. E., & Petrie, T. (1966). Statistical inference for probabilistic functions of finite state Markov chains. *Annual of Mathematical Statistics, 37,* 1554-1563.

Borthwick, A., Sterling, J., Agichtein, E., & Grishman, R. (1998). Exploiting diverse knowledge sources via maximum entropy in named entity recognition. In *Proceedings of the Sixth Workshop on Very Large Corpora* (pp. 152-160). New Brunswick.

Bunescu, R. C., & Mooney, R. J. (2004). Collective information extraction with relational Markov networks. In *Proceedings of the 42nd Annual Meeting fo the association for Computational Linguistics (ACL'2004)* (pp. 439-446). Barcelona, Spain.

Cafarella, M. J., Downey, D., Soderland, S., & Etzioni, O. (2005). KnowItNow: Fast, scalable information extraction from the Web. In *Proceedings of the Conference on Human Language Technology and Empirical Methods in Natural Language Processing (HLT/EMNLP'2005)* (pp 563-570). Vancouver: British Columbia.

Chieu, H. L. (2002). A maximum entropy approach to information extraction from semi-structured and free text. In *Proceedings of the Eighteenth National Conference on Artificial Intelligence (AAAI'2002)* (pp. 786-791).

Collins, M. (2002, July 6). Discriminative training methods for hidden Markov models: Theory and experiments with perceptron algorithms. In *Proceedings of the Conference on Empirical Methods in Natural Language Processing (EMNLP'2002)* (pp. 1-8).

Dietterich, T. (2002). Machine learning for sequential data: A review. In *Proceedings of the Joint IAPR International Workshop on Structural, Syntactic, and Statistical Pattern Recognition* (pp. 15-30).

Downey, D., Etzioni, O., & Soderland, S. (2005). A probabilistic model of redundancy in information extraction. In *Proceedings of 22th International Joint Conference on Artificial Intelligence (IJCAI'2005)* (pp. 1034-1041).

Durbin, R., Eddy, S., Krogh, A., & Mitchison, G. (1998). *Biological sequence analysis: Probabilistic models of proteins and nucleic acids.* Cambridge University Press.

Eikvil, L. (1999, July). *Information extraction from World Wide Web: A survey* (Report No. 945).

Embley, D. W. (2004). Toward semantic understanding: An approach based on information extraction. In *Proceedings of the Fifteenth Australasian Database Conference* (pp. 3-12). Dunedin, New Zealand.

Freitag, D. (1998). *Machine learning for information extraction from online documents.* Doctoral thesis, Carnegie Mellon University, School of Computer Science.

Freitag, D., & McCallum, A. (2000). Information extraction with HMM structures learned by stochastic optimization. In *Proceedings of the Sixteenth National Conference on Artificial Intelligence (AAAI'2000)* (pp. 584-589).

Grishman, R., & Sundheim, B. (1996, June). Message understanding conference 6: A brief history. In *Proceedings of the 16th International Conference on Computational Linguistics* (pp. 466-471). Copenhagen, Denmark.

Hu, Y., Li, H., Cao, Y., Meyerzon, D., Teng, L., & Zheng, Q. (2006). Automatic extraction of titles from general documents using machine learning. *Information Processing and Management, 42*(5), 1276-1293.

Huffman, S. B. (1995). Learning information extraction patterns from examples. In *Proceedings of Learning for Natural Language Processing'1995* (pp. 246-260).

Jackson, P., & Moulinier, I. (2002). *Natural language processing for online applications.* John Benjamins.

Klein, D., & Manning, C. (2002). Conditional structure versus conditional estimation in NLP models. In *Proceedings of the Conference on Empirical Methods in Natural Language Processing (EMNLP'2002)* (pp 9-16). Morristown, NJ.

Laender, A. H. F., Ribeiro-Neto, B. A., da Silva, A. S., & Teixeira, J. S. (2002). A brief survey of Web data extraction tools. *Journal of ACM SIGMOD Record, 31*(2), 84-93.

Leek, T. B. (1997). *Information extraction using hidden Markov models.* Master's thesis.

Li, Y., Bontcheva, K., & Cunningham, H. (2005). Using uneven-margins SVM and perceptron for information extraction. In *Proceedings of the Ninth Conference on Computational Natural Language Learning (CoNLL-2005)* (pp. 72-79).

Manning, C., & Schutze, H. (1999). Markov models. In C. Manning & H. Schutze (Eds.), *Foundations of statistical natural language processing.* The MIT Press.

Moens, M. (2006). *Information extraction: Algorithms and prospects in a retrieval context.* Springer Press.

Pazienza, M. T. (1999). *Information extraction: Towards scalable, adaptable systems.* Springer Press.

Punyakanok, V., & Roth, D. (2001). The use of classifiers in sequential inference. In *Proceedings of NIPS'01* (pp. 995-1001).

Rabiner, L. A. (1990). Tutorial on hidden Markov models and selected applications in speech recognition. In A. Waibel & K. F. Lee (Eds.) *Readings in speech recognition.* San Francisco: Morgan Kaufmann Publishers Inc.

Shawe-Taylor, J., & Cristianini, N. (2000). *Introduction to support vector machines.* Cambridge University Press.

Skounakis, M., Craven, M., & Ray, S. (2003). Hierarchical hidden Markov models for information extraction. In *Proceedings of the 18th International Joint Conference on Artificial Intelligence* (pp. 427-433). Acapulco, Mexico.

Zhang, Z. (2004). Weakly-supervised relation classification for information extraction. In *Proceedings of the Thirteenth ACM International Conference on Information and Knowledge Management (CIKM'2004)* (pp. 581-588).

ENDNOTE

[1] In machine learning, usually a learning algorithm is trained using some set of training examples. The learner is assumed to reach a state where it will also be able to predict the correct output for other examples. However, especially in cases where learning was performed too long or where training examples are rare, the learner may adjust to very specific random features of the training data, that have no causal relation to the target function. In this process of overfitting, the performance on the training examples still increases while the performance on unseen data becomes worse (Tetko, 1995).

Chapter II
Creating Strategic Information for Organizations with Structured Text

Roberto Penteado
Brazilian Agricultural Research Corporation, Brazil

Eric Boutin
University du Sud Toulon-Var, France

ABSTRACT

The information overload demands that organizations set up new capabilities concerning the analysis of data and texts to create the necessary information. This chapter presents a bibliometrical approach for mining on structured text and data tuned to the French school of information science. These methodologies and techniques allow organizations to identify the valuable information that will generate better decisions, enabling and capacitating them to accomplish their mission and attain competitive advantages over the competition. The authors think that information treatment and analysis is the most critical organizational competence on our information society and that organizations and universities should take measures to develop this new field of research.

INTRODUCTION

There is a universal tendency for an "information overload." Naisbitt (1996) best summarized this situation: "we are drowned in information but thirsty for knowledge." Human knowledge more than duplicates each year. This quantita-tive evolution is due to the convergence of several phenomena: technological development, the emergence of the Web, and the widening of the economic actors action capacity.

Fayyad and Stolorz (1997, p.101) indicated that since "the rates of growth of datasets are exceeding by far any rates that traditional 'manual' analysis techniques can cope with," the option available to organizations is to leave most of the data unused. Thus, they state that such a scenario is not realistic in any competitive environment where others who do utilize data resources better will gain a distinct advantage," and that all kinds of organizations, "spanning from business, to science, to government" are concerned by this sort of pressure (Fayyad & Stolorz, p. 101).

Added to this quantitative increase in information available is a qualitative problem corresponding to the shift that exists between supply of information available and demand of information expressed by the economic actors.

"While available information is abundant, incomplete, doubtful, public and confused, *necessary information* is synthetic, complete, reliable, confidential and precise" (Boutin, 1999), the use of available information is limited. The more unrefined the information, the slower it takes to the decision maker to act on it. While making sense of raw information can take more than one day, the strategic information that is processed and validated could be understood and adapted for action by the decision maker in just one minute. Quoniam (2001) affirms that it should be "the right information, provided at the right time, in the right form, to the right person and should result in the right decision." The usage determines the true value of the information. If it cannot be used, it has zero value. This shift between supply and demand in the market of information requires new capabilities, which ask for the development of analysis and mining of texts and data inside the organizations. In order to remain viable and robust, organizations should dominate methodologies and techniques with human and material resources, able to accomplish the operations demanded to create intelligence, in other words, the *necessary information*.

Levet (2001) affirms that "it is no longer access to information that provides the wheel for economic growth and employment but the actor's aptitude to transform, understand, interpret and use information" (p. 38). This was recognized by the international community in the environmental management standards known as the ISO 14.000 family of international standards. They enforce a system of environmental administration. It requires, among other relevant environment aspects, to register and to analyze information on legislation, processes, products, sub-contractors, suppliers, management, prevention of crises and response capacity.

Dou (2003) recognizes that organizations need to anticipate on competitors' actions. They need present or near future information and should use it as soon as possible. What is at stake is the organization capacity to analyze, in real time, the maximum possible amount of information and to establish a significant number of economic, financial, juridical, diplomatic, cultural, social, scientific, and political intelligences. To perceive, before the competitors, some week signs, indicating a business opportunity or a new technology, and to act in this sense can result in competitive advantages.

These methodologies and techniques to "create, associate, treat and use information to answer specific questions concerning current operations, research, product improvement or commercial conquest" (Dou, 2003) are the main objectives of this chapter. They refer to a well-defined process that has its productivity expanded by new data storage technologies that have emerged over the last decades, and does not spare data preparation and reformatting before analysis. First, we will provide a synthetic vision of the different stages of the information process that are becoming vital to every organization; then we will describe some ways on accomplishing the information analysis generating information ready for action. We make two restrictions on the many techniques available for *data mining* and *text mining*: first, we favor those methodologies that are tuned to the French School of Information Science and second, we use a bibliometrical approach for mining on structured text and data.

INTELLIGENCE VS. ESPIONAGE

A safeguard is fundamental: all this information originates from personal sources, from public domain sources (the Web, for example) or can be bought from public databases. Many scholars (Rouach, 1999; Masson, 2001; Dedijer, 2003; Dou, 2003; Steele, 2005) say that more than 95% of all strategic information is accessible, legally and ethically available. Those organizations that are able to collect, analyze, separate, and manage this information attain competitive advantages over the competition.

Thus, we use the term *competitive intelligence.* It concerns an innovative activity that has nothing to do with "espionage." The legality is exactly the dividing line between competitive intelligence and espionage. When it concerns obtaining information in an illegal and unethical way, this is the spy's domain. When it works in an ethical way, with legal and public information and manages to extract relevant and strategic information, this is the domain of *competitive intelligence.* Today going after non-public information illegally—espionage—is becoming less and less worthwhile. Especially when one knows how to use the ample stock of public information to extract the *necessary information.* However, as espionage equipment and methods are increasingly powerful, sophisticated, and extensive, protection of knowledge is also getting desirable and necessary for intelligent organizations.

A SYSTEMIC APPROACH

We provide a graphic description of the *data mining* and the *text mining* process to generate the *necessary information.* It is known as the "snail scheme." See Figure 1.

This process consists of eight stages: *diagnosis, planning, collection and storage, treatment and preparation, analysis and synthesis, diffusion, application, evaluation and updating.* This

Figure 1. Stages of the information cycle

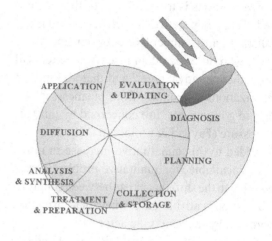

chapter will not provide a detailed explanation of all these stages because the denominations are self-explanatory. We emphasize mostly on four stages: *collection and storage, treatment and preparation, analysis and synthesis, and diffusion for decision makers.* However, the reader should know that this is a general process, used in each mining operation on data and/or texts.

COLLECTION AND STORAGE: DATA WAREHOUSE

Quoniam (1996) cautions that, in the quest for *necessary information,* one of the first precautions would be the integration of all information in a unique system of "information for intelligence." This need to integrate information was one of the factors that contributed to the development of a new concept of data organization known as data warehouse (DW). It originated from the United States' great department stores. In order to always be a step ahead of the competition, they set up DWs, which gather financial, juridical, political, administrative, human resources, commercial, technical, scientific, and other databases. In technical terms, the *data warehouse* represents a computational space where information gathered in the operating systems become available for on-line access. Two environments are created separately in different computers: the operational on-line systems and the analytical on-line systems.

Data storage or *data warehouse* is guided towards decision-making through a friendly and thoroughly available interface. The "keyword" is democratization of data access. As Nobrega (2001, p. 286) explained, DW means "granting autonomy to the user so that he/she could obtain his/her reports, without the need to get them from the IT personnel."

This chapter emphasizes on a semi-automated methodology of bibliometric type that can be used by analysts for competitive technical intelligence for treating and analyzing various databases, internal and external. We note however that when organizations integrate their information resources in a DW, a superior stage of information analysis and exploration is achieved with multiplied potential benefits. Many analyses can then be performed on an automated scheme, especially those that depend on internal data.

TREATMENT AND PREPARATION: CONDITION OF QUALITY

The golden rule is that mining garbage generates more garbage. Therefore, the stage of treatment, preparation, cleaning and, as some will add, data enrichment, is essential.

The data preparation stage is in direct connection with the DW. The creation of two environments, the operational and the analytical, allows the automation of the usually slow process of data cleaning and preparation. This is called extraction, transformation, and load (ETL) in the DW literature. It increases analysis speed, productivity, and the whole process of intelligence creation.

The data and text *treatment and preparation* phase has a direct influence on the analysis quality and reliability. Jambu (2000) pointed out

that the high or low degree of insufficient data (which should have been informed but were not) or incoherent data determines the outcome quality. Any analysis that incorporates a great amount of "insufficient data" produces "erroneous results in chain and, at the end of this chain, the decision maker will not be able to identify whom it should trust" (p. 68).

In general, databases were not created to allow analyses. The emphasis in most of them is to allow for a fast recovery of information. There are rare cases in that data recovered from a database can be used directly by the analysis softwares (Quoniam, Hassanaly, Baldit, Rostaing, & Dou, 1993; Mogee, 1997). More often, the structure of recovered information is not compatible with the required standards for loading information in the softwares. Sometimes external data need to be incorporated. Then, before analyzing, it is necessary to integrate data of different origins and bases, standardize names, gather concepts and reorganize fields, among other things.

As for names standardization of authors and organizations, Penteado (2006, pp. 168-170) found, among others, 90 different denominations of one of the *Brazilian Agricultural Research Corporation* (Embrapa) research centers, "Embrapa Genetic Resources and Biotechnology," in a sample of Web of Science database articles published between 1998 and 2002. He also found (2006, pp. 144-151) in Embrapa's Agricultural Research Database (BDPA), 43 different entries for IICA. Programa Cooperativo para el Desarrollo Tecnologico Agropecuario del Cono Sur, 39 for SAS Institute, 10 for HERRMANN JUNIOR, P. S. de P., and 17 for REIFSCHNEIDER, F. J. B., two Embrapa researchers. Data imprecision has many causes (O'Neill & Vizine-Goetz, 1988; Pao, 1989; O'Neill, Rogers, & Oskins, 1993; Jacsó, 1993a; Jacsó, 1993b; Medawar, 1995; Jacsó, 1997; Hood & Wilson, 2003; Penteado, 2006). They are common in most databases. Therefore, before any analyses that focus on counts of such values/words can occur, it is necessary to standardize them.

There are specific software tools for this. See more details in the commented example and in Appendix 1. As a rule, data treatment, cleaning, and preparation demand time spent in a semi-automated process of information reformatting. Leeds (2000) estimates that 60% of the entire effort undertaken in the information cycle is allocated only for data preparation and treatment. Before it, about 20% of total time would be dedicated to identify the information needs, the Diagnosis and Planning stages. After the preparation, 10% of the time goes to the Analysis and Synthesis stage and another 10% for the knowledge assimilation, the Diffusion to Decision Makers, Application, Evaluation and Updating stages.

The data *treatment and preparation* stage is intertwined with the analysis stage since information's final value will depend on its weakest link. It is only after having reliable and validated information that one can focus on analyses. In the next topics, we consider the stage of Analysis and Synthesis. For that we describe some methods and give some examples on data mining and text mining.

DATA MINING

For Jambu (2000, p. 8) *data mining* is a process that combines several mathematical, statistical or algorithm methods, to determine a solution for a problem in a decisional universe. Porter (2003, p. 3) describes another characteristic of the process: in general, when mining data, we extract useful information from any type of data. However, the most common is to use numeric and so, quantitative data. It requires a good knowledge of statistics. These general characteristics affect the choice of tools to mine data. They are oriented towards the quantitative treatment. More details are provided in Appendix 1. Sulaiman and Souza (2001, p. 267) mentioned five forms for generating results through *data mining*: associative rules, classifica-

tion hierarchies, sequential patterns, patterns of temporary series, clustering and segmentation.

1. **Associative rules:** To seek to "find items in a transaction that can determine the presence of other items in the same transaction." Example: a consumer who buys milk and bread also buys butter.

2. **Classification hierarchies:** To create "a model based on known data" and help to explain the reason of a given classification. This model allows to "classify new data with an existing classification." Example: to create limits for credit concession based on the transaction report of previous loans (Sulaiman & Souza, 2001, p. 267).

3. **Sequential patterns:** To indicate behaviors or a sequence of behaviors. Example: "whenever a young woman buys leather shoes, she will also buy belts and bags in the next thirty days" (Sulaiman & Souza, 2001, p. 268).

4. **Patterns in temporary series:** To show similar occurrences in a space of time. To the above data, seasons are added—such as, in the winter, young women buy leather shoes, bags and belts. In the summer, this pattern is inverted to sandals, bags and hats.

5. **Clustering and segmentation:** To gather occurrences with similar characteristics. Example: based on their buying expenses, a group of consumers can be classified as "small buyers," "average buyers," or "big buyers" of a certain product.

In general, *data mining* seeks to identify the different types of user or customer profiles and their several patterns of consumption or behavior. This is followed by work on the segments, identifying the best user/customer profile, products, and services consumed or the characteristics of each segment of customers, and patterns of product consumption: when two or more products or characteristics associate or if they are grouped in a single purchase/event, to determine the pattern of consumption/behavior of an area, neighborhood, age, or sex. Jambu (2000, p. 93) lists the typical fields of application for *data mining*: case studies, quality improvement and business efficiency, customer's satisfaction, employees' satisfaction, customer relations, sales and markets monitoring, local marketing, business indicators, forecasts, tendencies, competition monitoring, purchases, information technology, expenditures control, revenues and administrative processes. Fayyad and Stolorz (1997, pp. 106-112) indicated other fields of application "in the scientific realm": sky survey cataloging, finding volcanoes on Venus, Earth geophysics, earthquake photography from space, atmospheric science, and scalable decomposition for RNA folding.

SOME INTELLIGENT APPLICATIONS

Relationship with Clients

Telemar, one of the major Latin American telecommunication companies, covering 64% of the Brazilian territory in 16 of the 27 states, offering services for fixed, cellular, Internet, broadband, corporate data, long distance calls and call centers, implemented a *data warehouse* to integrate its 25 million clients database (Balaj, 2005a). Balaj (2005b, pp. 24-27) states that the system enabled sales to increase and to cut back client loss and costs. Between 2003 and 2005, the company's participation in the broadband market increased from 7% to 25%. The company was also able to "anticipate the cellular telephone market growth and maintain the customers base expansion" (p.26). Participation of new services (cellular, data, broadband and long distance) compared to traditional services (fixed telephone, network of public telephones) increased from 30% in 2003 to 39% in 2005, even with a real growth of 9% in 2004 (p.27).

Credit and Insolvency

Mathematical models were created to calculate probabilities of financial operations and were fed on the variables that explained insolvency. These models were applied to clients database of financial institutions. Pereira (2005, pp. 15-18) reported that clients who are at risk of not paying could be identified (p.15), avoiding the difficult recovery of credits conceded. A simulation running on a list of 252 cases of insolvency identified 196 (78%) of the clients as potential bad creditors.

Wal-Mart "Beer and Diapers"

This is a classic case in the U.S. It was discovered that the profile of beer consumers was similar to that of diapers consumers: married men, in the age bracket of 25-30 years who bought both products on Fridays, in the afternoon or at night. Wal-Mart stores decided to put diapers next to beer. Sales of diapers and beer increased 30% on Fridays.

Procter & Gamble Sales Data

Reynolds (1992, p. 344) notes that this multinational company of consumer products employed a Nielsen market research company service. It collects data from all products scanned at cash registers of associated supermarkets. These data enabled to estimate consumption and verify prices in each geographical area of the United States. Using them, Procter & Gamble (P&G) monitored competition and compared the data with their sales reports. It extracted indicators such as its participation in the market by product and by area. Result details are magnified since a 1% change in a large market could mean plus or minus millions of dollars in sales volume.

Sky Survey Cataloging

Fayyad and Stolorz (1997) report the development of the Sky Image Cataloging and Analysis Tool (SKICAT) to identify the class of a celestial object (star or galaxy) with 94% accuracy using decision tree learning algorithms over "3 terabytes of image data containing an estimated two billion sky objects" (p. 107). When they know a celestial object class, astronomers can conduct all sorts of scientific analyses such as probing Galactic structure from star/galaxy counts, model evolution of galaxies, or study the formation of large structures in the universe. SKICAT is also "learning" the data to create clusters. Unusual or unexpected clusters are shown to astronomers that can look further and search for technical explanations for the phenomena.

TEXT MINING

The study of texts to count scientific publication activity emerged and developed from the efforts of some forerunners such as Derek de Solla Price, Henry Small, Antony van Raan, Donald Swanson, Henry Dou, and Alan Porter. Their first results where in working with "structured texts" in opposition to "unstructured texts" and "free texts" that where developed in areas such as natural processing language, knowledge discovery in databases and computational linguistics.

The main commercial interest over *text mining* is that 85% of all data stored is held in an unstructured format and it doubles every three months (White, 2005). Other interests very strong on "unstructured texts" and "free texts" are those of the intelligence and security community. Powerful softwares monitor the Web, radio, cellular, and telephone waves looking for certain keywords. When found, results are recorded, downloaded, and analyzed. This is the main principle over the classified Echelon surveillance system developed by the United States National Security Agency

(NSA) in partnership with the United Kingdom, Canada, Australia, and New Zealand. Europe created in response an Echelon equivalent, the Enfopol Project. Its emphasis is on monitoring "hot areas" of the world and on prediction of crises.

This book provides information over *text mining* on many different domains. The focus of this chapter is *text mining* in "structured texts." In other words, to use organizational (internal) or external databases, such as Web of Science, Derwent, Pascal, and Francis, with a structure of data fields indicating, for instance, "author," "title," "publication date," "keyword," as a way to extract information on the evolution and "development of scientific activities to administrate, evaluate and measure productivity of SC&T activities, to build indicators, networks (communities) and to monitor innovations, technologies, and competitors (Dou, 1989; Quoniam et al., 1993; Dou, 1995; Mogee, 1997; Porter, 2003; Porter & Cunningham, 2005).

Text mining in structured texts is found in fields such as *bibliometry*, scientometry, informetry, mediametry, museometry, and webmetry. They deal with many different aspects of information and its quality, their main raw material being words. A word can represent between many other things, a concept or theme, an individual, an organization or even a group of themes, individuals, or organizations. The methods of analysis involve one-dimensional statistics (sum and meaning of the values/words), two-dimensional statistics (how it is and how much measures the relationship among two values/words), multidimensional statistics (how they are and to measure relationships between several variables/values/words) and, finally, probabilistic (to detect emerging or atypical behaviors, or even to determine how these variables/values/words will behave).

The singularity of *text mining* is that, as words are the raw materials, the traditional statistical laws and softwares that abide by the "normal distribution," the mean and the standard deviation are not applied comfortably. Texts and words have

Figure 2. A comparison between hyperbolic and normal distributions

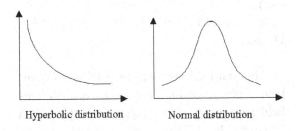

Hyperbolic distribution   Normal distribution

other kind of properties that are better described by the "hyperbolic distribution." This particular distribution results from the fact that to a variable increasing in an arithmetic way, there corresponds a variable increasing in a geometrical way (Le Coadic, 2003). It is characterized by the fact that a small number of observations are very common and a big number of observations are present only a small number of times. Such distributions were observed in various fields. In the 1930s, Zipf become interested in the frequency of words in a text. He observed a hyperbolic relation between word ranks and frequencies. See in Figure 2 the distribution shapes.

Several softwares accomplish analyses such as exploring, positioning, structuring, and searching structured texts. Many were created in the last decade and originated from MS-DOS (Microsoft Corp.) operating system (Dataview). For MS-Windows (Microsoft Corp.) operating systems, there are at least three softwares—VantagePoint (Search Technology Inc.), Matheo Analyzer (Matheo Software) and WinIDAMS (Unesco). The first two allow for the integration of bibliometric treatment, statistical treatment and graphic representation functions within a single space. The third is a hybrid between statistical and bibliometrical analysis software and is part of a family of free softwares developed by Unesco—IsisAscII/WinISIS/GenIsisWeb/WinIDAMS. They allow, respectively, to import, to generate, to dispose and to access on the Internet and to analyze data and text databases.

Practical Examples

The next examples involve the following stages of structured text analysis: (a) treatment and preparation by database fusion and reformatting and (b) analysis and synthesis by the construction of one-dimensional, or two-dimensional indicators and networks (multidimensional). The softwares used are Infotrans (IuK Gmbh)), Dataview, Matrisme (U.Marseilles, CRRM) and Excel (Microsoft Corp.).

The first example was extracted from the article "From the Creation of Databases to the Development of Intelligence Systems for the Organization" (Penteado, Dou, Boutin, & Quoniam, 2003), a case study data of the *Brazilian Agricultural Research Corporation* (Embrapa). Created on April 26, 1973, Embrapa is today one of the largest institutions of agricultural research in the tropical world. It has 8,619 employees, of which 2,221 are researchers, 45% of these with a Masters degree and 53% with Doctorate degree. It operates a budget of US$500 million per annum, 38 research centers and 3 service units. It is present in almost all the States of the Brazilian Federation and under the most different ecological conditions. Its mission is to provide feasible solutions for the sustainable development of the Brazilian rural areas, with focus on agribusiness, through the generation, adaptation and transfer of knowledge and technologies, to benefit the Brazilian society. Thanks to its agricultural research, Brazil can increase at least three times its actual grain production going from 120 million tons to 350 million tons, using 90 million hectares of land yet not cultivated in its cerrados (savannas) region, a place that until 30 years ago was only suitable for cattle breeding. It is becoming today a major grain production region. Gasques et al. (2003, p.42) wrote that "technology had a decisive role" in the agribusiness success and "*Embrapa* has had a leadership role in the generation and diffusion of innovations to this sector."

In this case, we will deal with some aspects of knowledge management, such as competency management (formation and age), technology transfer capacity and the organization's products and themes. Considering that *Embrapa* is now aged more than three decades, we consider the following research questions:

- What would be the effect of researchers retirement on *Embrapa's* research programs?
- What are the research units and competencies of research teams most affected by this situation?
- Who is doing what in the organization?
- How competencies are distributed within the organization?

To answer them, two *Embrapa* researchers' databases were combined. We emphasize each time that it is possible the necessary treatment at the database level and, after that, the results that can be obtained with text analysis with specialized bibliometric software (see Appendix 1).

The Corpus of Data to be Treated

The analysis combines an internal database of *Embrapa* personnel and a public database, available on the Internet, of *Embrapa* researchers competencies called the "Guia de Fontes." The database combination is as follows:

NOME (name): JOSE IVO BALDANI
DATN (date of birth): 12/2/1953
FORM (education): AGRONOMY, 1976; MASTERS DEGREE: SOIL SCIENCE, UNIVERSIDADE FEDERAL RURAL DO RIO DE JANEIRO, 1984; DOCTORATE: SOIL SCIENCE, UNIVERSITY OF TEXAS A&M—UNITED STATES, 1990.
APSQ (research area): MOLECULAR BIOLOGY; NITROGEN-FIXING BACTERIA; GENOMICS; BIOLOGICAL CONTROL; GRASSES
PROD (products and themes of work): BIOIN-

PROD (products and themes of work): BIOINSETICIDES, BIOFERTILIZERS, BIOTECNOLOGY
UNID (research center): EMBRAPA AGROBIOLOGY

The first treatment was the COOR—Cohort field creation, starting from the date of birth. This field was regrouped in 5 Cohorts: N.º 1, less than 25 years—N.º 2, 25 to 34 years—N.º 3, 35 to 44 years—N.º 4, 45 to 54 years—N.º 5, 55 years and above. Each researcher year of birth was also separated in the ANON field.

A second reformatting was done in the FORM—Education field. The FORM field was broken into various ones such as, among others: year and field of first degree; field and year of Master Degree; University of Master Degree; country of Doctorate. The reformatted base looks like this:

NOME (name): JOSE IVO BALDANI
DATN (date of birth): 12/2/1953
COOR (cohort): 4
ANON (year of birth): 1953
FORM (first superior degree): AGRONOMY
QDFORM (year of first superior degree):1976
MASTER (field of master degree): SOIL SCIENCE
DMEST (year of master degree):1984
UNIVMEST (university of master degree): UNIVERSIDADE FEDERAL RURAL DO RIO DE JANEIRO
DOCTORATE (field of PHD degree): SOIL SCIENCE
DDOU (year of PHD degree): 1990
UNIVDOU (university of PHD degree): UNIVERSITY OF TEXAS A&M
PAISDOU (country of PHD degree): UNITED STATES
APSQ (research area): MOLECULAR BIOLOGY; NITROGEN-FIXING BACTERIA; GENOMICS; BIOLOGICAL CONTROL; GRASSES
PROD (products and themes of work): BIOIN-

SETICIDES, BIOFERTILIZERS, BIOTECNOL-OGY

UNID (research center): EMBRAPA AGROBI-OLOGY

The Analyses Performed

To answer the first two research questions based on these initial data, several analyses were executed in a single field, for instance, ANON—Year of Birth which generated the age pyramid of *Embrapa*. We also made matrices with fields Cohort and Unit, to analyze and identify the researcher's age profile at each different research center.

See in Figure 3 *Embrapa* researchers age pyramid.

The largest number of researchers (the summit of the pyramid) is aged between 53 and 57 years. They were born between 1953 and 1949.

Cohort 2 (25 to 34 years)

As for the second research question, in four research centers, the number of young researchers is above the mean:

EMBRAPA UVA E VINHO

EMBRAPA INFORMATICA AGROPECU-ARIA

EMBRAPA RORAIMA

EMBRAPA ACRE

Our interest next will focus on the left slope of the pyramid. The researchers born between 1927 and 1949.

Cohort 5 (55 years and above)

In three research centers the number of senior researchers is above the mean:

EMBRAPA AMAZONIA ORIENTAL

EMBRAPA CLIMA TEMPERADO

EMBRAPA SEDE

This analysis indicates the spots where it is necessary to preview the need to hire more researchers in the medium run. Each unit is then analyzed thoroughly concerning their competencies pool.

Figure 3. Embrapa researchers age pyramid

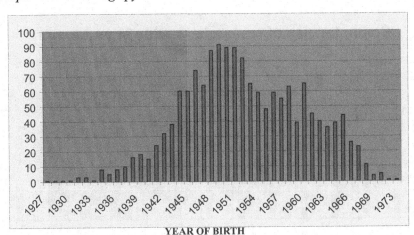

YEAR OF BIRTH

Competences at Risk

A matrix crossing Cohort 5 (more experienced Researchers) with the PROD field (Figure 4) indicates which competences the company is at risk of losing, because of future retirement of their holders. In that case, we can readily identify areas where more experienced researchers are far more numerous than younger ones. Such analysis allows for a finer administration of research teams (Penteado & Quoniam, 2001).

Development of Products (Technology Transfer, Businesses)

Every organization seeks better interaction conditions with its environment in order to add value to its products and services and to attain the best possible conditions for their deals and negotiations. For this, it must know its resources and, when needed, be able to make use of them.

To answer the third research question, it was executed a bibliometric treatment by pairs, associating the NAME field to the PROD field.

This matrix reveals products or activities that can be transferred by researchers and what are their competencies. In other words, what is the general capacity of *Embrapa's* technology transfer, prime information for managers concerned with technology transfer. Table 1 demonstrates Embrapa technological transfer response capacity at the specialist level.

This list can be also classified by alphabetical order in the COMPETENCE column (this will show all researchers working on a single competency) and allows for a fast access to the organization multicompetences. Other dimensions can also be added, such as the research unit or the geographic region). This information helps Decision makers to define who participates in a negotiation or heads a technology transfer operation.

Specialists Networks

As for the remaining question, about the distribution of competencies, a square matrix gathering all pairs

Figure 4. Competences at risk at Embrapa. Categories: 25 to 34, 34 to 44; 45 to 54; 55 and above (Penteado & Quoniam, 2001)

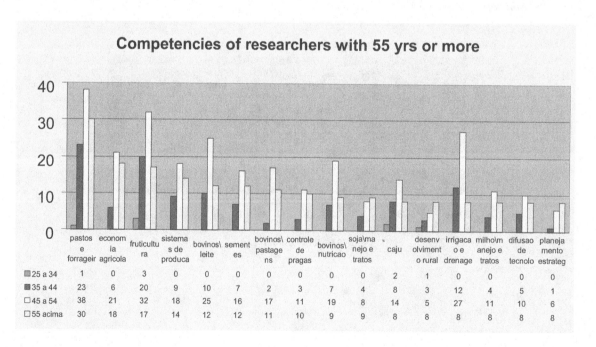

	pastos e forrageir	econom ia agricola	fruticultu ra	sistema s de produca	bovinos\ leite	sement es	bovinos\ pastage ns	controle de pragas	bovinos\ nutricao	soja\ma nejo e tratos	caju	desenv olviment o rural	irrigaca o e drenage	milho\m anejo e tratos	difusao de tecnolo	planeja mento estrateg
■ 25 a 34	1	0	3	0	0	0	0	0	0	0	2	1	0	0	0	0
■ 35 a 44	23	6	20	9	10	7	2	3	7	4	8	3	12	4	5	1
□ 45 a 54	38	21	32	18	25	16	17	11	19	8	14	5	27	11	10	6
□ 55 acima	30	18	17	14	12	12	11	10	9	9	8	8	8	8	8	8

Table 1. Specialists ordered by name and alphabetical

NAME	COMPETENCE
ADRIANO VENTURIERI	ZONING
ADRIANO VENTURIERI	REMOTE SENSING
ADRIANO VENTURIERI	FOREST STATISTICS
ADRIANO VENTURIERI	ENVIRONMENTAL ANALYSIS
ALFREDO KINGO OYAMA HOMMA	AGRO-FOREST SYSTEMS
ALFREDO KINGO OYAMA HOMMA	SILVICULTURE
ALFREDO KINGO OYAMA HOMMA	PEPPER
ALFREDO KINGO OYAMA HOMMA	ECOLOGY
ALFREDO KINGO OYAMA HOMMA	AGRO-FOREST
ALTEVIR DA SILVA LOPES	RICE GENETIC RESOURCES
ALTEVIR DA SILVA LOPES	RICE IMPROVEMENT
ANGELA MARIA LEITE NUNES	PEPPER
ANGELA MARIA LEITE NUNES	FRUIT CULTURE PESTS
ANGELA MARIA LEITE NUNES	CUPUACU
ANGELA MARIA LEITE NUNES	PESTS CONTROL

of terms contained in the PROD field was created to represent *Embrapa*'s network of economical and technological competencies by products and themes. Such a matrix came from specialized bibliometrical software called Matrisme, which transformed it into a map (Figure 5).

This map may be interpreted at the macro, medium (one or more groups) and micro (net nodes in each group) levels. It is possible to analyze the configuration of a group, its density, the connectivity of an individual/product, the centrality of a net node, the intensity of group's links and isthmuses between two or more groups. The fact that both domains are linked means that there is at least one researcher dominating that competency. For instance, pepper [pimenta-do-reino, see the arrow] is the isthmus between a group of Amazonian fruits and products and another group of systems of agro-forest and ecology products. This can indicate that fruit culture in the Amazonian region is becoming a more technical and systematic activity, preserving the vegetation with viable economic practices and that is good for forest conservation.

Such maps are useful not only for knowledge transfer but also to answer to questions like the evolution of a subject, a theme, or a scientific field. When associated with time series they indicate the evolution of that variable along decades, and when competencies or research areas are crossed with work location, it identifies organizations working with a particular area and so on (Polity & Rostaing, 1997).

The same technique can be used in the analysis of patents and technological databases. Eric Boutin (2001) describes, for instance, how inventors (IN-) were extracted from a selected universe of 400 patents in a public database. They were then related in the square matrix of collaborations that resulted, at the end, in a network of inventors. See Figure 6.

INFORMATION DIFFUSION TO THE DECISION MAKER

Intelligence creation is not an end in itself. It answers an expressed need by a decision maker and must nourish a process of strategic deci-

Figure 5. General representation: Network of economical competencies by products and themes researched at Embrapa Amazonia Oriental

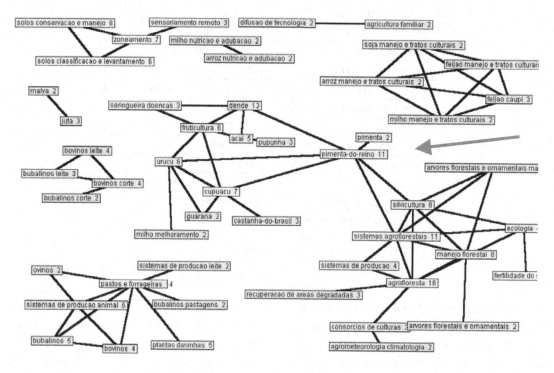

Figure 6. General representation of the necessary information creation process. In this case, the inventors of gas turbines for Rolls Royce (Boutin, 2001)

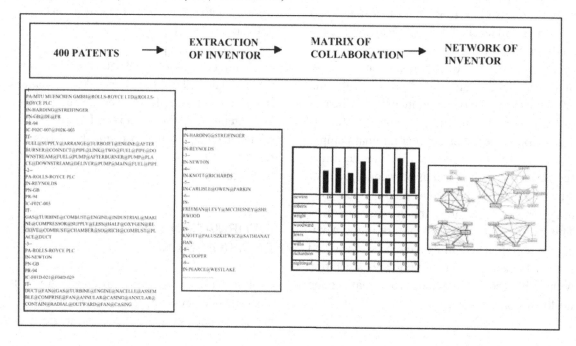

sion-making. To facilitate managers' intelligence appropriation some criteria must be present: First, information analyzed must be traceable. If necessary, one should be able to navigate up and down the information chain so that errors, misinterpretations, or manipulations are identified. Information must also be presented in at least two depth levels. The Decision maker can choose to access only synthetic information or he may decide to access the complete information. He must have the possibility to access the complete file that originated graphics and tables that he sees first.

In the competencies example the main topics matrices and graphics (personnel profiles and competencies at risk) were the synthetic information. The complete information consists of personnel profiles and competencies at risk analysis for each research unit. With the FORM field reformatting, we can look for the Doctorates repartition by country and by universities. One can avoid for example, too much expert's consanguinity in research groups and indicate other locations for expert's education. The APSQ—Research Area field was also studied. The research areas were classified by strategic importance. Personnel profiles of each research area and the many research lines inside those strategic areas were produced. Research and Development managers have if they choose to explore, a complete personnel profile analysis on every organization critical area.

When possible, technical artifacts that allow for an easy information appropriation by the Decision maker should also be used. The automatic representation of networks for example is a tempting tool in reducing information and still keeping explanation power.

Necessary information must be formatted and presented with tools familiar to the Decision makers. So that they can manipulate and explore texts and data at theirs wants and needs. Production of regular and systematic dashboards built around the same logic compel to the acquisition of refer-

ence marks and automatisms that will contribute positively on the next stage, the application of the information.

FUTURE TRENDS

The current evolution in this field set forth a double change in the data processing sequence previously defined. On one hand, there is a huge development on treatments for unstructured and semi-structured corpuses. The raw material (raw data) for such treatments has its origins in the Internet. This imposes also an analytical tool renewal. On the other hand, there is a downstream change on data processing sequence, concerning the passage from retrospective to prospective analyses and leading to the search for potential innovations.

Web mining emerged with three sub-fields of research: (1) Web content; (2) Web structures; (3) Web use. The first sub-field signifies carrying out a more or less elaborate textual analysis by integrating, for example, page semantic structure. The second sub-field deals with the analysis of hypertext link structures existing between corpuses of Web pages. The third sub-field seeks to establish navigation behaviors of net surfers as they can be apprehended through sources of information such as the log files.

The methods described in this chapter are also useful to detect weak signals (Boutin & Quoniam, 2006). The idea is no longer to present past tendencies in a synthetic way and to do states-of-the-art for a field or a domain but to seek emergent information. In the economic intelligence field, the detection of weak signals in the organizational environment is essential. Locating emergent information, the more upstream possible, provides the organization with the capacity to act on its environment. The tardier the signal is detected, the more the organization will have to undergo exogenous constraints.

Another field of interest is the method developed by Swanson (Swanson, 2001, Pierret & Boutin, 2004) for knowledge discovery in databases. It has a direct impact in the medical field where R&D investments are usually counted with 10 figures and 5 to 10 years of maturing time. Often, it concerns a question of proposing drugs that already exist in the market and are associated to a particular therapeutic treatment, to treat another disease. The method lies on non-Boolean logics, allowing the generation of unsuspected latent connections. These models propose to seek latent connections between disciplines that become segregated. Innovation no longer consists of discovering something that does not exist but to transfer to another field knowledge already validated in another situation.

Its logic is based on the transitivity property. It is possible to identify (Swanson, 1986) three dimensions that allow this transitive action in the medical field:

- The dimension of the disease;
- The dimension of the physiological effects of the disease;
- The dimension of the drugs for a given disease.

The transitive mechanism can be described as follows:

- **Stage 1:** It is possible to know the physiological effects of a given disease. This operation can be carried out by recovering from a biomedical database a corpus associated with a given disease and to seek in this corpus to find which are the physiological effects associated with this disease.
- **Stage 2:** It is possible to know by a given physiological effect the name of the active chemical compound that treats this disease. With this intention, one carries out a search on a biomedical database relating the physiological effect studied and one retains the most frequent drugs recommended.

- **Stage 3:** If a disease is characterized by a physiological effect and if this physiological effect is associated with a treatment by a specific drug, then, by transitivity, it is possible to put forth an hypothesis according to which that specific treatment drug can be a substance to treat that particular disease.

In most cases, the supposed transitive relation is confirmed by the direct relation, the drug being already known to fight that disease. In some other cases, the drug is not used or was never used. It acts then as a potential innovation, which must be submitted and validated by an expert.

This transitive mechanism was largely exercised in the biomedical literature. Swanson (1986) showed first that such a transitive mechanism made it possible to recommend using fish oil to treat Raynaud disease. Such works open very rich prospects in the field of *Text mining* to nourish the economic intelligence process. New patents have been deposed in France based on this methodology of discovering knowledge (Pierret & Boutin, 2004, Pierret, 2006).

CONCLUSION

This chapter treats concisely and didactically the different forms which intelligent organizations are adopting, to create the *necessary information* for its employees and Decision makers. These are methodologies, techniques, and tools of *text mining* and *data mining* used to process the bulk of information available and to create intelligence. The examples above show how some very simple and common databases in organizations can be structured and analyzed, to become strategic tools. We emphasized on *text mining* techniques on structured data to identify the valuable information that will enable and capacitate organizations to accomplish their mission.

The semi-automated methodology of bibliometric type here described allows for an immediate start on intelligence activities. Thus, it is not necessary to wait for the arrival of data warehouses and a sophisticated information structure to start the process of intelligence creation by the analysis of internal and external databases.

We agree with Dedijer (2003, p. 10) that "intelligence of a social system depends on the analysis of the gathered information." Normally organizations would not privilege this competence over many others. We think that information treatment and analysis is the most critical organizational competence on our information society. Moreover, the most important, always, is the formation of personnel able to perform these analyses. Organizational structures and even universities have been slow in identifying this demand and to materialize it on their academic programs. As Penteado et al. (2003) mentioned, "stocking data and using only 10 or 20% of their potential is to lose time and can lead to a weakening of the organization."

REFERENCES

Balaj, S. T. (2005a, September). Telemar boots sales and satisfaction with powerful performance if informatica powercenter. *DM Review Magazine*. Retrieved March 25, 2007, from http://www.dmreview.com/article_sub.cfm?articleID=1035576

Balaj, S. T. (2005b, October). *Telemar Projeto Business Intelligence em DW*. Paper presented at the Symposium Inteligência Organizacional 2005 Rio de Janeiro. Rio de Janeiro, RJ.

Boutin, E. (1999). *Le traitement d'une information massive par l'analyse réseau: Méthode, outils et applications*. Unpublished doctoral dissertation, Université Aix-Marseille III. Marseilles.

Boutin, E. (2001, December). *A cadeia de tratamento da informação do CRRM*. Paper presented at the Seminar Tecnologias para Tratamento da Informação na Embrapa. Brasilia, DF.

Boutin, E., & Quoniam, L. (2006, May—June). *Thésaurus et clusterisation automatique de données Web: Deux outils au service de la détection de signaux faibles*. Paper presented at the 3rd CONTECSI International Conference on Information Systems and Technology Management. São Paulo, SP.

Dedijer, S. (2003, September). *Development & intelligence 2003-2053*. Paper presented at the Infoforum Business Intelligence Conference, Zagreb (Working Paper Series 10, Kund: Lund Institute of Economic Research).

Dou, H. (1989). Quelques indicateurs bibliométriques en science et technique. *La Tribune des Mémoires et Thèses, 3*, 25-28.

Dou, H. (1995). *Veille technologique et compétitivité*. Paris: Dunod.

Dou, H. (2003, September—October). *Competitive intelligence, trends, methodologies and tools*. Paper presented at the I Seminario Internacional Ferramentas para Inteligencia Competitiva. Brasília, DF.

Hood, W. W., & Wilson, C. S. (2003). Informetric studies using databases: Opportunities and challenges. *Scientometrics, 58*(3), 587-608.

Jacsó, P. (1993a). Searching for skeletons in the database cupboard Part I; Errors of omission. *Database, 16*(1), 38-49.

Jacsó, P. (1993b). Searching for skeletons in the database cupboard Part II; Errors of comission. *Database, 16*(2), 38-49.

Jacsó, P. (1997). Content evaluation of databases. In M. E. Williams (Ed.), *Annual review of information science and technology (ARIST), 32*, (pp. 231-267). Medford, NJ: American Society for Information Science (ASIS).

Jambu, M. (2000). *Introduction au data mining: Analyse intelligente des donnees*. Paris: Editions Eyrolles.

Le Coadic, Y. F. (2003). Mathématique et statistique en science de l'information: Infométrie mathématique et infométrie statistique. *Information Sciences for Decision Making, 6*(03).

Leeds, S. (2000, January). Data mining: Beware of the shaft. *Direct Marketing.* Retrieved March 25, 2007, from http://www.tmiassoc.com/articles/shaft.htm

Levet, J. L. (2001). *L'Intelligence Economique—Mode de pensée, mode d'action.* Paris: Economica.

Masson, H. (2001). *Les fondements politiques de l'intelligence économique.* Unpublished doctoral dissertation, Faculté Jean Monnet à Sceaux, Droit, Economie, Gestion—Université Paris Sud XI. Paris.

Medawar, K. (1995). Database quality: A literature review of the past and a plan for the future. *News of Computers in Libraries, 29*(3), 257-272.

Mogee, M. E. (1997). Patents and technology intelligence. In W. B. Ashton & R. A. Klavans (Eds.), *Keeping abreast of science and technology: Technical intelligence for business.* New York: Battelle Press.

Naisbitt, J. (1996). *Megatrends 2000.* New York: Smithmark Publishers.

Nobrega, R. G. (2001). Data warehousing. In K. Tarapanoff (Ed.), *Inteligência organizacional e competitiva* (pp. 285-302). Brasília: Editora Universidade de Brasília.

O'Neill, E. T., Rogers, S. A., & Oskins, M. W. (1993). Characteristics of duplicate records in OCLC's online union catalog. *Library Resources and Technical Services, 37*(1), 59-71.

O'Neill, E. T., & Vizine-Goetz, D. (1988). Quality control in online databases. In M. E. Williams (Ed.), *Annual review of information science and technology (ARIST), 23,* (pp. 125-156). Amsterdam: Elsevier Science Publishers, American Society for Information Science (ASIS).

Pao, M. L. (1989, May). Importance of quality data for bibliometric research. In M. E. Williams (Ed.), *Proceedings of the 10th national online meeting* (pp. 321-327). Medford, NY: Learned Information Inc.

Penteado, R. (2006). *Création de systèmes d'intelligence dans une organisation de recherche et développement avec la scientométrie et la médiamétrie.* Unpublished doctoral dissertation, Université du Sud Toulon Var, Toulon.

Penteado, R., Dou, H., Boutin, E., & Quoniam, L. (2003). De la création des bases de données au développement de systèmes d'intelligence pour l'entreprise. *Information Sciences for Decision Making, 8,* 67-105. Retrieved March 25, 2007, from http://isdm.univ-tln.fr/articles/num_archives.htm#isdm8

Penteado, R., & Quoniam, L. (2001, October). Aplicação da bibliometria na análise estratégica das competências da Embrapa. In *Proceedings of the 2° Workshop Brasileiro de Inteligência Competitiva e Gestão do Conhecimento.* Florianópolis, SC.

Pereira, J. J. de O. (2005, June). *Data mining—Trazendo poder ao business intelligence.* Paper presented at the Symposium Inteligência Organizacional 2005 Brasília. Brasília, DF.

Pierret, J. D. (2006). *Méthodologie et structuration d'un outil de découverte de connaissances basé sur la littérature biomédicale: Une application basée sur l'exploitation du MeSH.* Unpublished doctoral dissertation, Université du Sud Toulon Var, Toulon.

Pierret, J. D., & Boutin, E. (2004). Découverte de connaissances dans les bases de données bibliographiques. Le travail de Don Swanson: de l'idée au modèle. *Information Sciences for Decision Making, 12,* 109. Retrieved March 25, 2007, from http://isdm.univ-tln.fr/PDF/isdm12/isdm12a109_pierret.pdf

Polity, Y., & Rostaing, H. (1997, June). Cartographie d'un champ de recherche à partir du corpus des thèses de doctorat soutenues pendant 20 ans: Les sciences de l'information et de la communication en France: 1974-94. *Actes du Colloque: Les systèmes d'informations élaborées (SFBA)*. Ile Rousse.

Porter, A. L. (2003). Text mining for technology foresight. In *Futures Research Methodology-V2.0, The Millennium Project*. New York: American Council for the United Nations University.

Porter, A. L., & Cunningham, S. W. (2005). *Tech mining: Exploiting new technologies for competitive advantage*. New Jersey: John Wiley and Sons.

Quoniam, L. (1996). *Les productions scientifiques en bibliométrie*. Unpublished Habilitation à diriger des recherches, Université Aix Marseille III, Marseilles.

Quoniam, L. (2001, December). *Data mining, teoria e prática*. Paper presented at the Seminar Tecnologias para Tratamento da Informação na Embrapa. Brasilia, DF.

Quoniam, L., Hassanaly, P., Baldit. P., Rostaing, H., & Dou, H. (1993). Bibliometric analysis of patent documents for R&D management. *Research Evaluation*, *3*(1), 13-18.

Reynolds, G. W. (1992). *Information systems for managers*. St. Paul, MN: West Publishing Co.

Rouach, D. (1999). *La veille technologique et l'intelligence économique*. Paris: Collection Que sais-je? PUF.

Steele, R. D. (2005, August). The future of intelligence: Not federal, not secret, not expensive. In *Speech to DHS Intelligence*, Washington. Retrieved March 25, 2007, from http://www.oss.net/extra/news/?module_instance=1&id=2633

Sulaiman, A., & Souza, J. M. (2001). Data mining mineração de dados. In K. Tarapanoff (Ed.), *Inteligência Organizacional e Competitiva* (pp. 265-278). Brasília: Editora Universidade de Brasília.

Swanson, D. R. (1986). Fish oil, Raynaud's syndrome, and undiscovered public knowledge. *Perspectives in Biology and Medicine*, *30*(1), 7-18.

Swanson, D. R. (2001). ASIST award of merit acceptance speech: On fragmentation of knowledge, the connection explosion, and assembling other people's ideas. *Bulletin of the American Society for Information Science and Technology*, *27*(3).

White, C. (2005). Consolidating, accessing and analyzing unstructured data. *B-eye Business Intelligence Network*. Retrieved March 25, 2007, from http://www.b-eye-network.com/view/2098

Additional Reading

Association Française de Normalisation-AFNOR. (1998, April). XP X 50-053: Prestations de veille: Prestations de veille et prestations de mise en place d'un système de veille. Paris: AFNOR.

Basch, R. (1990). Measuring the quality of the data: Report on the fourth annual SCOUG retreat. *Database Searcher*, *6*(8) 18-23.

Bateson, G. (1979). *Mind and nature: A necessary unity*. New York, NY: Bantam Books.

Baumard, P. (1991). *Stratégie et surveillance des environnements concurrentiels*. Paris: Masson.

Bell, D. (1973). *The coming shape of post-industrial society, a venture in social forecasting*. New York: Basic Books.

Besson, B., & Poussim, J. C. (2001). *Du renseignement à l'intelligence économique*. Paris: Dunod.

Blakeslee, D. M., & Rumble, J. Jr. (2003). The essentials of a database quality process. *Data Science Journal*, *12*, 35-46.

Callon, M., Courtial, J. P., & Penan, H. (1993). *La Scientometrie*. Paris: Collection Que sais-je? PUF.

Cobb, P. (2003). Competitive intelligence through data mining. *Journal of Competitive Intelligence and Management, 1*(3), 80-89. Retrieved March 25, 2007, from http://www.scip.org/jcim.asp

Colby, W. (1978). *Honorable men: My life in the CIA*. New York: Simon & Schuster.

Courtial, J. P. (1990). *Introduction à la scientométrie: De la bibliométrie à la veille technologique*. Paris: Collection Sociologies, Anthropos.

Cronin, B., & Davenport, E. (1993). Social Intelligence. *Annual Review of Information Science and Technology (ARIST), 28*(1), 3-44.

Dedijer, S. (1994). Governments, business intelligence, a pioneering report from France. *Competitive Intelligence Review, 5*(3), 45-47.

Dedijer, S. (1984). The 1984 global system: Intelligent systems, development stability and international security. *Futures*, 18-37.

Dedijer, S., & Jequier, N. (1987). *Intelligence for economic development: An inquiry into the role of knowledge industry*. Oxford: Bergamon.

Faucompré, P., Quoniam, L., & Dou, H. (1997). The function-application relation through a link between classification and indexing. *World Patent Information, 19*(3), 167-174.

Federal Partners in Technology Transfer. (2001). *Links of Resources for Competitive Intelligence*.

Retrieved March 25, 2007, from http://www.fptt-pftt.gc.ca/news/2001/compintel_e.shtml

Gannon, J. C. (2000). *Intelligence challenges through 2015*. Speech presented at the Columbus Council on World Affairs, Washington. Retrieved March 25, 2007, from http://www.cia.gov/cia/public_affairs/speeches/2000/gannon_speech

Hood, W. W., & Wilson, C. S. (2003). Informetric studies using databases: Opportunities and challenges. *Scientometrics, 58*(3), 587-608.

Hunt, C., & Zartarian, V. (1990). *Le renseignement stratégique au service de votre entreprise*. Paris: Editions First.

Jakobiak, F. (1991). *Pratique de la veille technologique*. Paris: Les Editions d'Organisation.

Lafouge, T., Le Coadic, Y. F., & Michel, C. (2003). *Eléments de statistique et de mathématique de l'Information: Infométrie, bibliométrie, médiamétrie, scientométrie, wuséométrie, webométrie*. Villeurbanne: Collection Les Cahiers de l'Enssib, Presses de l'Enssib.

Quoniam, L., Balme, F., Rostaing, H., Giraud, E., & Dou, J. M. (1998). Bibliometric law used for information retrieval. *Scientometrics, 41*(1-2), 83-91.

Rockart, J. F. (1979, March). Chief executives define their own data needs. *Harvard Business Review*, 81-93.

Wright, R. (2000). *Nonzero: The logic of human destiny*. New York: Pantheon Books.

APPENDIX 1

SOME TOOLS FOR DATA MINING AND TEXT MINING	
Data Reformating	Infotrans—http://www.ever-germany.de/start.aspx Folio Search and Replace- http://www.nextpage.com/publishing/folio/ Textpipe—http://www.datamystic.com/
Text Mining	Dataview—http://crrm.u-3mrs.fr/commercial/software/dataview/dataview.html Matheo Anayzer, Matheo Patent—http://www.matheo-software.com VantagePoint—http://thevantagepoint.com WinIDAMS—http://www.unesco.org/webworld/idams/ Neotia—http://www.neotia.com/ Temis—http://www.temis.com/ Datops—http://www.datops.com/ Matrisme—http://lepont.univ-tln.fr/page_perso/boutin.htm NetDraw—http://www.analytictech.com/downloadnd.htm KartOO—http://www.kartoo.com/
Data Mining	SAS Enterprise Miner—http://www.sas.com/ SPSS Clementine—http://www.spss.com/ Microstrategy—http://www.microstrategy.com/ Oracle Mining Suite—http://www.oracle.com/ Gomining—http://www.godigital.com.br Weka—http://www.cs.waikato.ac.nz/~ml/weka/

Chapter III
Automatic NLP for Competitive Intelligence

Christian Aranha
Pontifical Catholic University of Rio de Janeiro, Brazil

Emmanuel Passos
Pontifical Catholic University of Rio de Janeiro, Brazil

ABSTRACT

This chapter integrates elements from natural language processing, information retrieval, data mining and text mining to support competitive intelligence. It shows how text mining algorithms can attend to three important functionalities of CI: filtering, event alerts and search. Each of them can be mapped as a different pipeline of NLP tasks. The chapter goes in-depth in NLP techniques like spelling correction, stemming, augmenting, normalization, entity recognition, entity classification, acronyms and co-reference process. Each of them must be used in a specific moment to do a specific job. All these jobs will be integrated in a whole system. These will be 'assembled' in a manner specific to each application. The reader's better understanding of the theories of NLP provided herein will result in a better 'assembly'.

COMPETITIVE INTELLIGENCE

There has been a huge computer technology development and an accelerated growth in information quantity produced in the last two decades of the 20th Century. But how do companies use these published data, mainly in the digital media? What do they use to increase their competitive advantages? It is true that most companies recognize information as an asset and believe in its value for strategic planning. The big difficulty however is to deal with information in a changing environment. To plan on an annual basis seems not to be sufficient anymore. The dynamism of the environment is faster. The temporal character of information is becoming more and more critical. Information valid today may not be valid tomorrow anymore. Data are not static blocks to become a building block of a temporal reality. Information analysis is no longer an action, it has become a process.

If in the past there was an information tap that could be opened and closed, today there is a river of information whose flow never ends.

Leaders can go out of business in a matter of months and challengers can assume their thrones. So companies wanting to succeed need to adopt a continuous and systematic approach in order to stay ahead of competition and be prepared for up comers, technological changes or economic turmoil. That is exactly the role that competitive intelligence (CI) promises to play. By definition, competitive intelligence is a continuous and systematic process of gathering information regarding the external environment, analyzing, and disseminating it to the top management . In thesis, the more systematic the approach, the more responsive the company will be to potential outside changes. What is the value of implementing a formalized CI process? It's hard to quantify, but quantification is probably unnecessary. How much is it worth if your company launches a new product before your main competitor? What about anticipating a major technological change and acting ahead of the industry to take advantage?

Furthermore, facts such as the Enron and WorldCom scandals have made shareholders more apprehensive about administrating a company. That is why, nowadays, we can observe a *disclosure trend*, i.e., investors and market regulation agencies pressure companies, more and more, to operate with increased transparency. If the tendency is a bigger amount of published information, those who handle it better will be the most competitive, heightening the importance of the CI technology market.

Additionally, the volume of information also grows day by day, calling for more analysts to process all the available content. Meanwhile, CI departments tend to be too small when compared to the volume of information that needs to be processed. This increases the demand a technology that would allow for a reduced number of high quality analysts to handle the big volume of information present inside, in the company, and outside, in the environment.

In this chapter we will cover natural language processing (NLP) techniques for text mining (TM) in order to make information analysis more efficient.

SUPPORTING FUNCTIONALITIES TO CI

A CI analyst should basically be aware of information surrounding him/her in order to be able to evaluate its importance and to prepare reports for decision making. As most data are presented in the form of texts, we will consider, in this chapter, three text mining functionalities to help this process. We should have in mind that the central objective is to keep the analyst informed. Besides TM, we should add CI network management, discussion forum and business intelligence as other examples of supporting functionalities to CI.

The first supporting functionality to the analyst comes from the limited daily reading capacity of a human being. The *Filtering* functionality has been created with the purpose of allowing pre-selection of reading contents, assuming that the important information is, very likely, within the filtered subset. These data are read progressively by the analyst in order to extract relevant facts.

This reading process, however, can still be time consuming. When dealing with information, timing is a crucial factor. The technological *Event Alert* functionality was developed with the objective of advising the analyst as soon as possible of some pre-specified events as being important to his business.

The third and last functionality refers to a *Semantic Search* tool that becomes necessary for ad-hoc demanded information. This demand comes from the fact that both *Filtering* and *Event Alert* are planned and predefined. The objective of this tool is, therefore, to allow the analyst to reach the information required in a particular instance, as soon as possible. Finally, the intersection of three sets of information, resulting from three functionalities of text mining, minimizes the information myopia problem, inasmuch as the sets do not present dependency among themselves. In this way, if important information was not filtered, it can be caught by the alert. Even if it could not be caught, the analyst can search for information.

TEXT MINING

Text mining attempts to discover new, previously unknown information by applying techniques from information retrieval, NLP and data mining. We will focus here on how NLP techniques can add to the text mining process.

In general, text mining is a process that contains four macro steps: gathering, preprocessing, indexing and mining (Figure 1). The objective of the initial step is to collect data that will compose the textual database (corpus), i.e., it will determine and select the domain in which TM techniques will be acting. After collecting the documents it is necessary to transform them into an appropriate format so as to be submitted to automatic knowledge extraction algorithms. The second step, called preprocessing, is responsible for obtaining a document's structured representation, generally in the form of an attribute-value table.

The attribute-value table represents the document, and its characteristics are sparse values of data and high dimensionality. These characteristics constitute some of the problems related to the TM process. Each word in the documents may potentially be an element of this attribute-value table. Although expensive, a careful preprocessing of documents is absolutely necessary for the success of the whole TM process.

The third step, indexing, is characterized by information retrieval (IR) methods, such as inverted-indexing, and is applied to increase the performance of the processes. This is a key step on the text mining process and there are many open source implementations for that (Perez, 2006). Finally, the last step is to find useful and unknown information or patterns present in documents. For patterns extraction, similar techniques to the traditional Data Mining (DM) process, like clustering, classification and machine learning, are used.

For each CI function, a specific form of preprocessing, indexing and data mining are demanded. According to the functionality the steps' customization grows from left to right, as shown in Figure 1.

The fifth and extra step is the human analysis. It may work by validation of mined information

Figure 1. Steps of text mining process

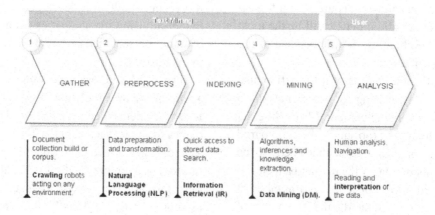

to build a report or for navigation. In the navigation process, human analysis drives the mining tools in order to reach desired information. In some cases, a collaborative validation may be recommended. This validation includes impact settings, adding relevant facts, report building and dissemination: all very important to TM and consequently to CI.

To know more about statistical methods for text mining take a look at Konchady (2006), to know more about the linking of NLP, IR and TM see Weiss et al (2005) and, finally, to know more about TM for CI see Zanasi (2005).

IMPORTANCE OF LINGUISTIC KNOWLEDGE

Without linguistic knowledge, a text, in a multi-disciplinary and multilingual collection of documents, is no more than a set of chained characters associated to their frequency measurement. In this kind of scene, the possibilities of automatic comprehension of contents are limited, which makes the performance of a textual recovery system yet unsatisfactory, from both the precision and recall points of view. The linguistic knowledge allows the text customization in two fundamental ways: the language in which the text is written and its syntactic-lexical structures. Both propose a bigger discriminatory potential.

The text's preprocessing depends greatly on availability of computer lexical resources. Such resources include electronic dictionaries, thesauri and lexical databases. Naturally, lexical repositories are a conjunction of computer and linguistic knowledge and are specifically built for each language.

Lexical repositories are big and dynamic. New lexical items can be obtained frequently, so, it is necessary for the NLP process to do lexical management automatically. To accomplish this task manually, as it has been done for example

in WorldNet, is expensive time-wise. Automatic strategies are, in general, corpus based.

Some open source machine learning tools like GATE[1] and OpenNLP[2] have a static corpus. Others, like Cortex Intelligence use a dynamic corpus approach. The difference is that Cortex is incremental and doesn't use rollback, while GATE and OpenNLP are done in batch and allow rollback. In a later section we will explain the NLP techniques that may be applied in both approaches.

Other approaches exist in the private domain. Some TM and CI players are Megaputer Intelligence, Cortex Intelligence, Temis Text Intelligence and ClearForest companies. Megaputer has a patented Neural Network to estimate a Semantic Network from texts. Temis is focused on Data Mining through statistical techniques, Cortex won the HAREM[3] 2006 competition for Names Entity Recognition (NER) and ClearForest won the ACE[4] 2002 competition also for NER.

NATURAL LANGUAGE PROCESSING

Natural language processing (NLP) is the science field that involves a set of formal methods to analyze texts and generate sentences in a human language. Methods to analyze texts can be used in the preprocessing step, in order to better represent the text and extract more from its content. The main objective of the preprocessing step is applying NLP for recognizing and classifying named entities. Although this is only one part of NLP, to do it efficiently is necessary at the same time to solve other NLP tasks that will be described in section **NLP Techniques**. In this case, the concurrent execution of many tasks is necessary, in order to obtain better performance for each task and as a whole. Figure 2 illustrates the graphics of cooperative necessity of NLP tasks. Imagine three NLP tasks T1, T2 and T3 connected

Figure 2. Graphics of cooperative necessity of NLP tasks

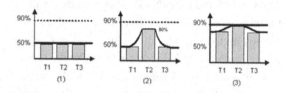

on their top by a rubber band. One task T2 can easily increase by itself until it achieves values near 90% of efficiency (see section **Precision and Recall**). Each percentage point is now harder to be achieved alone because the rubber band pulls it down. So T2 can reach 90% more easily if the other tasks, T1 and T3 are improved.

When applying a single task (e.g., single NLP technique), given the complexity of the algorithm, the difficulty in extracting entities grows exponentially. With simple heuristics we easily reach 80% of efficiency, the difficulty is reaching values above 90%, and 100% is practically impossible.

NLP MODEL

The NLP model used in the preprocessing step described in this chapter is based on a lexicon, which contains attributes relative to a primitive ontology and is updated in automatic form. The acquisition algorithms as well as text mining algorithms used in the updating are evaluated according to precision and recall measures. Some concepts about the orientation and proposal model used will be presented in later sections.

Automatic Acquisition

The automatic acquisition of entities (basic knowledge) through NLP techniques, works in bidirectional form. In order to know the objects in a text it is necessary to have a basic knowledge of the objects. This base comes from the knowledge

of previous objects. So, if there is a rule that uses knowledge of objects in order to recognize and extract them, another stronger (less ambiguous) rule is necessary to point out, in a dictatorial form, the object occurrence. These two rules can act on different parts of the corpus.

For example, in an occurrence in one text: "The presentation of Microsoft CEO Bill Gates will be in the morning." The lexicon (rule of force 2) will indicate "Bill Gates" is a person and will treat this entity separately. But to acquire "Bill Gates" as a person, it may occur, in another text, a stronger pattern. For example, "The richest man in the world is Bill Gates" which activates rule of force 1 (less ambiguous). The lexical acquisition of the lexeme "Bill Gates" classified as a person has been done to be used in rule of force 2 above.

The Lexicon

The NLP system described in this chapter includes a lexicon that stores the language's linguistic information. The lexicon is a table where each registry presents a lexeme and its attributes. The idea is that each registry presents a lexeme that has a specific meaning. A lexeme is a sequence of characters that contains any character including space (White space), e.g., "heavy metal".

Table 1 presents the representation of lexicon table. LexemId is a unique lexeme representation. There may exist as many entries of the same lexeme as there are possible meanings, e.g. Plant with LexemId = 12 and Plant with LexemId = 14. Thus, each entry corresponds to a different meaning and its morphological representation.

On other hand, two different sequences may point to the same meaning. This problem can be avoided using a different value to MeaningId, joining the previous identifiers, e.g. MeaningId = 356 and LexemeId = 12 and LexemeId = 13.

The other fields in the table are "Keylexem" that represents the lexeme character sequence, "POS", Part-Of-Speech, "Freq", the lexeme linear frequency, and "Lang" the language in which the lexeme was stored.

Table 1. Table of specification and occurrences of lexicon registry

MeaningId	LexemeId	Keylexem	POS	Freq	Lang
356	12	Plant	S	3500	E
356	13	Vegetal	S	56768	E
432	14	Plant	S	270	E
432	15	industrial plant	S	1390	E

In the transition step between preprocessing and indexing, the key lexemes generated by the NLP step and stored in the lexicon are now technically called an inverted index. This means the indexing system that will be used may contain an extended index, with all lexical attributes, differently from a traditional one, with just a keyword and frequency.

About the Delimitation of a Lexical Unit

This section will discuss how lexical items, constituents of a lexicon, are stored, as a language's words, into the lexicon (section **The Lexicon**). This study is necessary and essential in this point, because the use of terms whose concepts are not satisfactory will produce doubtful results.

The boundaries and characteristics of the lexical unit, which will be an object to be handled, will be established. Normally, the term used for this object is 'keyword'. The concept of a keyword usually only entails an uninterrupted sequence of alphabetical characters and hyphens. This definition, although simple enough, can bring us some difficulties in the composition of meanings.

The models described in this chapter are strongly based on a meaning-oriented lexicon, and we will define keylexem, as a concept analogous to keyword, which is a sequence of stored characters in a lexical registry. A keylexem can either be "ball" or "ahead of time", "One on One", "Michael J. Fox" or even "My Best Friend's Wedding".

The concept of a keylexem is used hereafter in the preprocessing steps in reference to a linguistic object formed by a sequence composed of any character.

Ontology

Ontology is a set of concept patterns, terms and definitions accepted by a specific community. It includes a definition of these concepts, its properties and restrictions. The most frequent ontology definition is given by Gruber "an ontology is a specification of a conceptualization". Its use has been growing in the Web Semantics environment.

An ontology can also be understood as a logical model of representing the world . As it is based on logic, it facilitates the computational implementation. However, as with all representations, an ontology expresses only one vision, a part, a world projection. It does not intend to cover it entirely.

Precision and Recall

Precision and recall are basic measures used to evaluate systems' efficiency, not only for its ability to search but for learning as well. Precision Search is adequate when it knows exactly what it wants. Recall Search is adequate when it does not know what is required or looked for and an exploration to get an overview of a domain is necessary to decide what it wants (Jizba, 2000). After obtains results about what is required or looked for, it is time to find the desired items, so increasing precision value.

A Precision Search tends to retrieve few documents and a Recall Search retrieves many documents. For learning purposes the measures work in an analogous way, except the items returned are lexemes. Instead of retrieving documents in a search, it selects lexemes for acquisition. A precision-oriented system hardly makes mistakes but it spends much time to learn. A recall-oriented system absorbs more knowledge in fewer texts, but makes many mistakes.

In practice there is a tradeoff between precision and recall. If one maximizes precision, one loses recall. If one maximizes recall one loses precision. But the main goal is to keep both up together, by reinforcing one or another depending on the application functionality. To retrieve all documents, maximize recall and minimize precision and to retrieve only one sought document, maximize precision and minimize recall getting a narrow view of the collection. In the first step of investigation, one may reinforce recall. If you already know what you want you may reinforce precision.

Each NLP technique described below (in section **NLP Techniques**) has impacts on these measures, making the system more precision or recall oriented. The calculations for these measures are described in depth in .

NLP Techniques

The techniques presented below are NLP independent modules that act in a cooperative way, establishing a NLP pipeline which is constructed by applying techniques in sequence, the posterior stage acting on the result of the previous stage, as shown in Figure 3. Observe that although modules are independent, it is strongly recommended that some techniques should come before others.

The presentation sequence is already a clue as to how they should be linked and are presented in further detail below. Finally, it is not necessary to use all of them in the construction of a pipeline.

Figure 3. Action of NLP pipeline as a text preprocessing

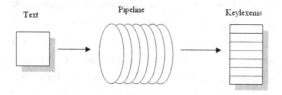

Tokenization

Tokenization is normally the first step of text preprocessing. The text is represented by a sequence of characters, delimited by primitive characters such as space (white space), comma, dot, etc. This process must keep exactly the same original sequence.

Each group of characters formed in the first level is called a *token*. A sequence of *tokens* forms a *tokenstream*. Both the character groups and the delimiters form a new sequence of tokens. The only discarded character is space, as it is usually the most frequent one. The symbols "[" and "]" shown below mark the first level groups.

The man, who worked a lot, is going on holiday on Sunday.
[The][man][,][who][worked][a][lot][,][is][going][on][holiday][on] [Sunday][.]

This process results, in English or Portuguese languages, in a sequence of words, separated by delimiter symbols. After that, it is already possible to activate an indexing process to retrieve information. If this approach is used, not only valid but invalid tokens, such as "(-):,/", will be stored, but it is also possible to find an excess of precision problems. Verbs and nominalizations may appear exactly in the typed form, without generalization, which will make the search more difficult. This also includes words typed with capital and small letters, so when the user looks for "dictionaries" it may return "Dictionaries" or not.

In the first run, one may feel that the delimiting characters have been stored in an excessive and unnecessary form and may be discarded (as done with blank spaces); however, in some moments they may assume critical roles for search purposes. A dot, for example, may take the role of the end of a sentence, URL, date, number, etc. Although dots generally indicate the end of a sentence, an efficient system can resolve other cases beyond that.

Normalization

Normalization is used to increase recall due to the fact that one concept may have many representations. The idea is to avoid that many forms of a word be associated with the same concept. For example, the concept of "book" is "physical objects consisting of a number of pages bound together" and can be represented by "book" and "books". The normalization process proposes that these two forms must be grouped in just one that has the same meaning. The central point of normalization is the approximation of concepts, i.e., they do not have the same meaning but a high level of redundancy in their meaning which, for a recall strategy, can be interesting.

In practice we see that by increasing the recall as above, we will group up many words that present different meanings, thus greatly decreasing the precision of the system. However, by reducing the size of the lexicon, a strategy such as recall will normally show a better performance when the objective is navigation.

According to the way the concept instances (words) are joined, the normalization process may be of many types. Some of them are:

- **Inflectional stemming:** Only takes into consideration the verb tenses. This proceeding truncates the words, which usually makes the words difficult to be understood. However, it can be automated more easily. Examples: "rule", "rules", "ruling" is substituted by a fourth form "rul".
- **Lemmatization:** The many ways of representing a word are substituted by its primitive form. The forms "analyse", "analyzer" and "analysed", all point to the lexeme "analysis". This strategy has the advantage of capturing the user's search intentions, since the form "analysis" is easier to understand.
- **Stemming to a root:** Is the most aggressive kind of normalization. It takes into account all forms of suffixes as well as prefixes.

- **Synonyms:** In common knowledge, synonyms are quite different words that hold the same meaning or refer to the same object. If both occurrences are grouped together by a sole identifier, we will also have a normalization process.

However, some linguists state that there are no exact synonyms i.e. there are no words that have really the same meaning. Thus, the more adequate relationship of synonyms would be similarity, or redundancy of information. So, if meanings are just similar it means that there is a different part. Furthermore, this different part can vary in each case, still maintaining the synonymy relationship.

For each different part, as indicated in Figure 4, we can state a type of synonymy relation. To exemplify, these relations allow for a real semantics stroll, where each word presents an intersection of meanings with another. One may demonstrate this with the word "plant". "Plant" may be a "factory", a "bush", a "flower", a "vegetable" or, finally even the verb "to cultivate". But none of these can be exactly equal to a plant, because, otherwise, it would naturally imply they are exactly equal amongst themselves and definitely a "bush" is neither a "flower", nor a "factory".

Figure 4. (a), (b) and (c) illustrate three different relations of synonymy.

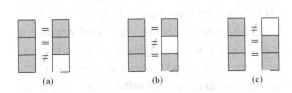

Multiword Expression

In general, lexical items are single words resulting from tokenization (Sag, 2002). But there are many cases where it is necessary to consider a group of words as an item. In linguistic literature there are some groups of words that are such: collocations, fixed expressions and idioms.

According to Saeed , the difference between collocations, fixed expressions and idioms relates to the dynamism of the language. So, collocations are more dynamic combinations, as they suffer a fossilization process and become fixed expressions. From this point of view, idioms would be the most fossilized kind of combinations, since individual words have ceased to have independent meanings. In other words, the distinction between these terms would be related to their use. Examples of these dynamics are "up to date", "up-to-date" and "update" or even "key word", "key-word" and "keyword". Frequent use during a considerable amount of time would be responsible for the status change from word to multiword expressions. That is why statistical approaches have stood out quite a bit in the solutions to these problems.

Once a multiword is detected, it is inserted into the lexicon, becoming a *keylexem*. The multi-word expressions renew the importance of the blank space. Furthermore, by analyzing a set of words with similar meanings this procedure can be regarded as a move in the direction of non-ambiguity, for their meaning is dissociated when an aggregated word occurs.

Sentence Boundary

Although intuitively it appears simple to consider everything that is enclosed within the delimiters (.!?), this approach is not very good because it reaches a percentage of right around 85% (test corpus) which is not good. In order to overcome a 95% barrier one must make delimiters non-ambiguous, i.e., classify them as delimiters or non-delimiters. This is one of the most difficult procedures and

in a way they are resolved gradually during the other NLP pipeline steps. So, a better approach to a certain sentence is to leave this step to the end, after solving others. Most delimiters, such as dot, will have already been grouped in names, URLs and dates. The remaining dots will provide much better classification accuracy.

Furthermore, on the ambiguity of delimiters problem, there are other challenges in defining sentence boundaries. First, the problem of the occurrence of "" (double quotes) and () (parentheses) operators, e.g. in sentences that contain phrases within them in a recursive way so that a dot does not promote the end of the sentence anymore. For example:

"I'm not going with you. Call me when you get there." said Jorge.

It is necessary to implement tree structures to represent sentences inside a sent.ence, paragraph, chapter and document. See Ide

Part-of-Speech Tagging

Part of speech (POS) can be considered a primitive ontology classification, a basic representation structure present in almost all languages. This primitive ontology starts with the division of words/lexemes in two main categories:

- **Function words:** Refers to prepositions, articles, pronouns, etc. This set is static, as a new functional word will rarely appear in a language; conversely, these words appear more frequently in a text. It is very rare to find a text where the lexeme "of" does not occur.
- **Content words:** Refers to names, verbs, adjectives, etc. This set is dynamic as at any given moment a new word of content may appear in a language. On the other hand, these words appear less frequently in a text. It is rare to find in a generic corpus many texts with the word "ontology".

As *function words* are static, they can be catalogued in a lexicon manually whereas *content words* must be constantly learned and/or inserted, this therefore should preferably be done in an automatic way. This does not mean discarding a dictionary of words for mapping associated POS. Dictionaries are useful but not sufficient. For example, the word "rule" can be a noun or a verb. The function of POS tagging is precisely to classify this kind of occurrence correctly.

Thus, for *content words* it is necessary to use an automatic acquisition of lexicon entries approach, as well as its respective class. In literature, machine learning algorithms that learn through annotated corpora such as hidden Markov models (HMM) and transformation based learning (TBL) have been used.

A good approach to acquire a classification of content words is to start by making a major distinction between noun and verb. Nouns, in general, name the objects while verbs specify actions and relationships. For some Latin languages this problem is easier since verbs present sophisticated suffixes that in most cases indicate the word's classification, whereas in the English language this task is not so easy. The noun word or verb normally appears in the same form, which demands a previous word sense disambiguation task.

Rule-based strategies are adequate if the neighbor word's class is considered to obtain a better classification. For this strategy it is necessary to use a dictionary giving an initial class condition to the system, and thus generating inputs to apply these rules. In the first application the rules change some classes. The new sequence of classes is used as a springboard for a new application of the same rules and so on. An example of this method can be found in.

Phrase Recognition

Phrase recognition technique can be understood as a pattern recognition that chunks sentences in non overlapping phrases. In general, this technique searches for strong syntactic patterns that play an important role in the parsing procedure (section **Parsing**). Traditionally chunks are noun phrases (NP) and verb phrases (VP) as an example:

- **Noun phrase (NP):** David Drummond evaluates [new strategic business opportunities]
- **Verb phrase (VP):** Yahoo Inc. [has purchased] Inktomi Corp. for about $235 million

Although NP and VP are more frequent, another phrase is still more special, the prepositional phrase (PP). This specialty refers to the fact that most of the time it deserves to be a lexeme unit so that parsing may be parsimonious. Examples of PP are "because of", "in favor of" and "what if". All of these can be recognized by Naïve Bayesian algorithms from POS sequences. Some other pieces that may be understood as phrases and so as lexemes are sequences of separator characters, patterns such as "'s" and "--" must be considered.

Named Entity Recognition

Named entity recognition is one of the main NLP tasks for competitive intelligence since it names objects of the real business world. Furthermore, a large fraction of information from a new article is filled by new nouns or new noun combination relationships. In IC domains, approximately 90% of new lexemes learned by an automatic system are proper nouns. Thus, it is interesting to give special attention to this entity recognition task.

The process starts by the evaluation of candidates to become named entities. In a macro form this evaluation consists of a sequence of filters. The candidates that persist will be grouped by proximity and considered entity names. These filters sometimes use semantic dependency of near words, behaving as a finite automaton.

A capital letter is a good marker that is used and usually gives a good list of initial candidates. Sentence boundaries are now critical because they force any word at the beginning of a sentence to be capitalized. These cases will be treated separately.

A good start is to know if a word is a verb or a noun before transforming the token into a candidate, since verbs aren't named entities. One should also consider that a proper noun token is found quite frequently with another proper noun token.

"John Marshall", "United States of America", "Manhattan Connection"

Tokens in sequence usually represent only one lexeme and must be grouped. It is important to keep in mind the prepositions as well, even though they are not marked by a Capital letter.

Another frequent problem is the existence of peripheral tokens, responsible for qualifying the entities which are also marked by the Capital letter, as shown below.

"Barcelona's Brazilian Ronaldinho celebrates their Spanish League title..."

Dots used in abbreviations cause big complications for recognition, mainly in the middle name as an abbreviation. To know whether "Michael J. Fox" is a name or "Michael J." is one sentence with "Fox" starting another may be seem trivial to the human being. Computers must have rules that will help in this rare grouping: a sentence ending with an initial, especially if preceded by a person's name. In this case, using the first option is preferable.

Finally, the last filter deals with dates, religions and geographical locations, and labels them as entity names. These names should be catalogued and learned periodically in order to help NLP tasks.

Named Entity Classification

Named Entity Classification is applied to known entities, that is, entities that were recognized by the Named Entity Recognition. The objective is to classify names, the main objects of CI, according to the ontology. Figure 5 shows classes used in recognition processes and named entity classification. The arrows indicate support given by knowledge from one to another. For example, date classification rules use questions about num-

Figure 5. Pre-requisites scheme among ontology classes

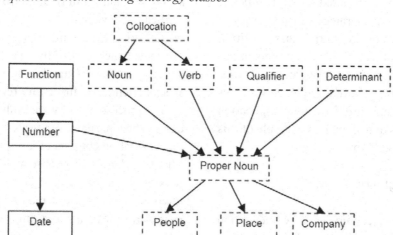

ber classification. Classes found in the lower part of the tree tend to be more independent of the language, like persons or organizations names, followed by geographic location names and finally date formats.

The Classification process can be done by following the same logic of the recognition process, but at a higher abstraction level. Most rules contain questions on the result of the recognition process. Furthermore, there are rules which use adjacent words to circumscribe the name classification, called meta-information:

"It happens near the west coast of Sumatra Island"

In this example, "west coast" and "Island" dictate a geographic location's classification for "Sumatra".

Parsing

Until now, techniques shown above describe processes that consider words individually in order to improve and transform them into a lexeme with self-meaning. The parser acts on the result generated by previous steps by linking words, establishing a relationship among them specified by the text itself. If the text is written correctly and refers to one same subject, no word will be left loose and all of them will have a specific position in a single graph, the edges representing the relationships. More precisely, each word has a role in the sentence. Each sentence may be represented in a syntactic tree structure; trees are connected between them through anaphora, hyperonyms, synonymies, etc., relating to form a final graph. Texts that result in two graphs which are not connected may refer to two different stories.

In Grune many parser types are presented as well as some approaches to solve this problem. One kind of representation cited is called the DCG (Definite Clause Grammar) structure: it combines a list of tree formation rules based on components. For example:

DCG	S = sentence
S → NP VP	class NP = Noun-Phrase
NP → DET N	class VP = Verb-Phrase
NP → Pronoun	class N = Noun
VP → V NP	class V = Verb

These rules operate with classes attributed to the lexemes in previous steps. They are stored in an inference base. One problem of this approach is that the number of rules can grow indefinitely trying to attend the biggest number of syntactic forms possible in a given language, which may be infinite. Furthermore it is necessary to maintain an inferences engine, to verify the integrity of the rules each time a new rule is added, as this rule may be in contradiction with another one or a logical combination of others.

In face of these problems, the parsing procedure is only used for specific cases and domains with some restrictions. Even with limitation, this procedure covers well the functionality of *information extraction*, since it has linguistics' objects and pre-specified relationships, leaving the parser to solely detect syntactic variations.

Under lexical acquisition we can use the frequency of each rule in order to estimate its performance strength. If a rule of type DET + S occurs a lot in a language, and if one finds a DET and the next word was evaluated as V (verb), this class can be relabeled as S. However, attention must be paid, for re-labeling rules increases the problem's computational complexity significantly.

Coreference

Considering a text as a graph structured by interconnected trees, where each tree represents a parsed relationship, most coreferences are forms of connection between trees. They occur when two terms in the text have the same reference, i.e., they refer to the same object/entity. They also frequently occur using an ontology relationship of a superior hierarchy. Coreferences are used when the object definition has a conceptual dependency relationship with another already instanced object.

Solution approaches to some of the more frequent types of coreferences can be found below.

Acronyms, Initials and Abbreviations

Acronyms are words formed by parts of extensive names like "United States of America" and "Federal Express" whose acronyms are USA and Fedex, respectively. They constitute two keylexems that are distinct and refer to the same exact entity which, in the first example, is a country with a determined number of inhabitants and a certain culture. In a text, an acronym is usually marked by parentheses.

- **Pattern 1:** Voice over Internet Protocol (VoIP) or
- **Pattern 2:** VoIP (Voice over Internet Protocol)

In this way, to learn connections between the keylexems is automatic, however, there are many cases in which parentheses appear and do not indicate acronyms. It is necessary to investigate other clues that might strengthen the rule. First one must find out if the possible acronym can be found in pattern 1 or in pattern 2 (shown above). Since names are always bigger than acronyms, the idea is to match the acronym candidate with the initials of the name.

This comparison should generate a probability score to show the existence of a connection.

Initials are different from acronyms by intercalation of dots (e.g.: "U.S."), and normally appear in names such as "Michael J. Fox". When it is otherwise, they can be compared to entities present in texts or very frequent ones.

Finally abbreviations are names truncated by dots. Most of them, such as "Dr.", "Inc." and "Corp.", are very frequent and can be catalogued. Some that appear rarely may be compared to long words and often used words to suggest an option for automatic learning.

Truncated Names

Truncated names are the most explicit coreferences, mainly in the competitive intelligence domain. Occurrence of this phenomenon comes from a principle of economy in communication. If the entity has already been presented with its entire name, it is not necessary to repeat the whole information. For person names, once the name "Tom Cruise" has been presented previously in the text, it can be referenced as "Cruise" or "Tom". This connection has an additional characteristic; it is valid only in the context (locally). The unique keylexem generated is "Tom Cruise", linked to all truncated names that will be normalized to the entire name.

Special attention should be given to this process due to the information value to CI present in people's names and the frequency they occur. After all the text entities have been recognized and classified, only people's names should be left, to directly compare all pair combinations. Names that fit perfectly (excluding misspelling for simplification) are candidates for coreference. In a second step, distance between positions of two names (in text) gauged in number of words should be considered. If the distance is very long, it may be a spurious co-relation due to the fact that even a reader would have much difficulty in remembering the mentioned name. Distance between words may also solve double reference problems when people have the same first or family name. Finally, it is very usual that the entire name sequence appears followed by the truncated one, getting then a stronger weight, although the opposite may happen as well.

Pronominal Anaphora

Pronominal anaphors are coreferences formed by *function words*, frequently by pronouns. These coreferences serve to append information to a linguistic object. As an anaphora does not contain any entity contents in their representation, they are in close proximity to the referenced object. However, even being close, to find the correct destination object is a hard task. This decision has to compare the linguistic attributes of the object, for example: the pronoun "She" refers to a female singular person object while "They" refers to a plural person object and so on.

The advantage is that pronouns are finite and can be catalogued, thus allowing the construction of a matrix of comparison attributes for each one. In the classification step we can also apply these characteristics. In order to solve this problem, some works like Lappin and Ge present algorithms for treating these cases.

Synonyms

Refer to the exact same object, assuming a coreference relationship, although their meanings are not identical in essence. In general, relationships between synonyms are special and present a certain hierarchical level of knowledge organization in the information redundancy such as "type of" or "part of".

The uses of horizontal synonyms, i.e. words that substitute others with similar meaning are also found. This coreference type in documents is often presented in order not to repeat the same word. An example is the word "research" that coreferences "work", "paper" or "development".

A common example in the CI domain is to reference "company" as "agency", "corporation", "organization", etc. Hierarchal relationships may be acquired in an automatic way through rules acting on patterns such as "gasoline and other fuels" indicates "gasoline" as a type of fuel.

Other linguistic patterns can be found in Hearst. After knowledge extraction, it is necessary to build a database which contains a relationship graph in order to assist in new texts coreferences' solutions.

Misspelling

An important algorithm for automatic spell checking, (Damerau, 1964), was the one that introduced the minimum edit idea. Briefly speaking, the edit distance concept quantifies if one string is "close" to another or not, by counting characters in editing operations (insertions, deletions or substitutions), needed to transform one string into another. Using this metric, best candidates for a misspelling are those which have the minimum edit distance.

The second approach is the similarity key technique, in which words are transformed into keys and similar spelled and misspelled words have the same key. Misspelling correction involves creating the key for misspelling and looking up keylexems with the same list of candidate keys. Soundex is the best-known similarity key for English language, and it is often used for phonetic applications. The combination of Minimum Edit Distance and similarity keys (metaphone) are at the heart of the successful strategy used by Aspell, an open source spell checker, available at http://aspell.net.

There is a third approach using an indexing technique called n-gram letter model. An n-gram letter is an n-letter sequence in a word. For instance, the word "modern" can be divided into four 3-grams, also known as trigrams: "mod", "ode", "der", and "ern". The idea is that misspellings typically affect a few of constituent n-grams, so we can recognize the intended word only by looking through correctly spelled words for those that share a high proportion of n-grams with the misspelled word.

In the normal indexing process, documents are indexed by words contained therein. In the misspelling process, documents are a set of words and the words are formed by n-grams that will constitute the index. When the word is searched, n-grams are processed and looked up in the index, the word that presents the biggest number of n-grams will be more relevant.

In practice, the n-gram approach executes well for keylexems bigger than 10 characters. For keylexems up to 10 characters, the results are better if one executes the n-gram and edit distance algorithms sequentially.

The misspelling problem is quite useful in NLP and has already presented works with good results in literature, that is why it is worthwhile to see other approaches .

Word Sense Discrimination

The discrimination of meaning is one of the most sophisticated problems in NLP mainly due to its algorithmic difficulty. In spite of substantial work over a long period of time, there are no algorithms that can completely discriminate a word's sense. The problem consists of determining which word meaning fits in the context. This problem exists due to the polysemy phenomenon existing in natural languages, i.e., the same sequence of characters may generate different meanings.

Under a certain point of view, most words are polysemous so a discrimination process to eliminate this ambiguity in each word in the text is necessary.

While most words have more than one meaning, due to their frequency of use, words generally have one strongest (the most frequent) meaning. This is why NLP can generate positive results in certain instances, without sophisticated Word Sense Discrimination procedures.

A larger version of the word sense discrimination problem is the word sense disambiguation problem. Most disambiguation algorithms perform labeling in addition to discrimination. However, discrimination algorithms using word meanings have the advantage of being oriented to automatic acquisition as they follow children's cognitive learning models, which, on other hand, generally, don't have access to the meaning labels.

A quite well known approach is described in Manning, where a context vector definition is developed based on occurrences. These vectors are plotted in an n-dimensional space and grouped by clustering algorithms. Each group indicates a discriminated context.

Automatic Detection of Synonyms

A rule-based approach of this problem has already been mentioned in section **Coreference** - Synonyms. In this section we will cover a statistical approach by trying to solve horizontal synonym problems (without hierarchy). The problem of automatic detection of synonyms is a mirror of Word Sense Discrimination. In a didactic way, discrimination of meanings starts off by the same word with two different meanings - synonyms are two distinct words with the same meaning. In the first case we have a "split" movement and in the second a "merge" movement.

Technically, a context vector for each occurrence is computed. After the clustering algorithm, groups of similar contexts are detected. In the discrimination task, two uses fall in different groups and present different meanings. Soon, if two different words generate context vectors of the same group (or very close) then one can infer a synonym relationship. Statistic proximity measures used in algorithms will indicate how close two meanings are. Normally, a limit factor (threshold) can be stipulated for the minimum similarity level that will be considered as a synonym.

CI Functionalities

CI functionalities, as shown below, have as their objective helping CI analysts to complete a CI processing cycle (Figure 6) of a large volume of information. Once the CI process is complete, it will attend to the needs of monitoring, collecting, analyzing and disseminating the environment's information.

Below, the three functionalities mentioned in section **Supporting Functionalities to CI** —Filtering, Event Alert and Investigation—using NLP and the Text Mining techniques seen in section **NLP Techniques** will be approached in more depth.

Figure 6. The CI processing cycle

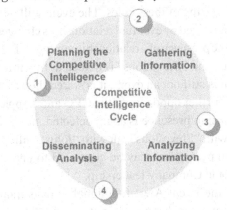

Filtering

Filtering is one of the most traditional functionalities, having been used for a long time in the form of clipping services (such as searching for a keyword). Since then, the technologies pertaining to this process have become more sophisticated, involving classification and contextualization, while the basic idea has remained the same—string matching. However, using Machine Learning (ML) techniques we may extract words pertinent to the subject automatically, without the need to insert keywords manually. This approach is done often and is called the *bag-of-words* approach. The objective is to build a *bag-of-words* of discriminating keywords during the classification algorithm's training. Adding NLP techniques seen in section **NLP Techniques**, these same algorithms will form a *bag-of-lexemes* of context discrimination lexemes.

A document collection is represented as a table as follows: each line indicates a term-document relationship $term_k$—$document_j$. To each relationship is associated a weight a_{jk}, as shown in Figure 7.

Additionally to the capacity of managing keylexems of a context, a statistical method that is used is the vector space model, in which, beyond the selection of words, a weight is associated to each word according to its importance level. An often used weight calculation is TFIDF (term frequency

Figure 7. Attributes conversion table

	$Term_1$	...	...	$Term_k$
d1	a_{11}	...	...	a_{1k}
...	...	...	...	...
dj	a_{j1}	...	...	a_{jk}

- inverse document frequency), which considers the word's linear frequency in the document, the quantity of documents wherein the word appears and the total quantity of documents. After this document's projection in an n-dimensional space, a classical data mining algorithm may be used, as Neural Nets or K-means.

Because filtering functionalities only work with discriminating keylexems, words used frequently may be discarded for indexing purposes—a procedure known as removing stop words—which increases the system performance. This procedure reduces the index length. This also allows the use of compound queries utilizing logic operators like AND, NOT and OR. The use of the OR operator without the loss of performance is the most important gain for this approach. Then weights associated to keylexems are based on linear frequency, and the document relevance takes into account the criteria of diversity (number of different keylexems). This means that not all the keylexems can be found in the text but the more found the better.

The inverted index structure should be done based on keylexems of the last stage of the NLP pipeline as this will favor the disambiguation of words. Another important technique is using misspelling correction in order to increase system precision.

For example, if we look for "California Pizza Kitchen" we may have a high score for the State California texts with many occurrences to "pizza" and "kitchen" jeopardizing the classification system. According to the keylexems approach, "California Pizza Kitchen" is different from "pizza kitchen California". In the first query, California is a kind of pizza while in the second California is a state. If we wish to increase the recall of the classification while "pizza" AND "kitchen" keylexems, with their respective weights have to be added, forming a meaning-oriented approach. Consequently, the better the disambiguation capacity of the procedure, the better will be its classification capacity.

The Support Vector Machine (SVM) is an example of a text mining technique that is being used recently, achieving good results for Text Classification (Burges, 1998; Joachims, 2002). This technique is specifically useful for this kind of filtering functionality.

Event Alert

The Event Alert function can evaluate a bigger base than the classification function, although this process is only focused on some relationships defined in advance. This is why it uses Information Extraction techniques such as HMM (Rabiner, 1989) or TBL (Brill, 1992) to detect the presence of some relationships among entities. For example: the dismissal of some executive, the hiring of a new executive, a joint-venture, the acquisition of a company, winning some award, etc. But what makes a certain piece of information an event beyond a simple Q&A is the changing of the answer or a relationship between entities.

A relationship is detected by the occurrence of some patterns such as, for example, found in the Apple Company site, "Steve Jobs is the CEO of Apple". The processing by NLP must finds the following keylexems: "Steve Jobs" as a person name, "is" as a verb, "the" as a determinant, "CEO" as an acronym of "Chief Executive Officer", "of" as a preposition and "Apple" as a company name. HMM and TBL algorithms could contain the rule "Person + is + the + Position + of + Company" and its relationship variants "Apple-CEO-Steve Jobs" generated by parsing.

However, the event is not characterized only by the triggering of these rules. The event will only be concretized by eventual relationships changes. Once the presence of a relationship among "CEO", "Apple" and "Steve Jobs" is detected, this information is still not an event; it is stored, however. If in a further opportunity the CEO and "Apple" relationship presence is again detected, not anymore with "Steve Jobs" but with "John Sculley", then an event alert may be generated to change the Apple Company leadership.

As the Event Alert functionality pays much importance to the syntactic structure, *function words* are fundamental to the indexing process, none of the keylexems can be eliminated from indexing. With this, the inverted index structure is bigger, jeopardizing the performance. On the other hand, not only is the word frequency not relevant to the process, all terms of the rule ("Apple", "of" etc.) must be present, which means that the query will not be done by an OR operator like in *Filtering* but by an AND operator instead, where joins are executed much quicker.

AND queries are used to select documents that are strong candidates to present syntactic pattern activation to a relationship rule. After this selection, the documents are submitted to a NLP criterion where keylexems will be processed in more detail and then applied to HMM and NLP techniques in order to detect patterns. As the indexing process only works to select candidate documents, another interesting option to increase the performance is to use a simple indexing, maintaining only a distinction of lower-case and Capital letters (Case Sensitive) in order to identify names easier, without applying all the NLP techniques.

Semantic Search

The method using semantic search consists of finding information in an even a bigger volume of documents. The required information in this case does not need any previous definition or specification. For this purpose the most commonly used tool is search engines that index a great part of the Internet or a company's content and allows a succession of quick searches by keywords and Boolean operators through manual input.

However it is not so easy to know the right word in order to find the desired information. With the aim of helping finding the keyword the concept of Semantic Navigation may be used. One form of this concept is a method that suggests new navigation modes and facilitates the identification of the most adequate keyword—which will result in search engine ranking better the document desired.

In a practical way, semantic navigation is not only worried about searching relevant documents of a given word but also pointing out different uses of the word (see polysemy in section **Word Sense Discrimination**) and some synonyms in a manner as to increase the recall. According to suggestions, the user chooses what direction to follow and moves in an interactive exploration until he or she finds the desired information.

In Figure 8 we show an investigation tool in-terface, where the user is looking for "petroleum". And the tool has returned documents about this subject with their associated links.

Another use is when we want to search for information about text mining, and in this case we should be informed that it is also good to look for "NLP", "computational linguistics", "KDT" and even "corpus"; and depending on the search level, "artificial intelligence", "indexing", "IR" and "crawler" and so on.

Some algorithms already offer some results to this problem, such as Latent Semantic Analysis (Landauer, 1998), association by co-occurrence, multifaceted navigation, and dynamic taxonomy by bisecting clustering (Steinbach, 2000). From the results obtained by the execution of these algorithms, another index on the original index will be generated, that can be explored in real time (online) and it can be treated through OLAP (Keith et al., 2005) techniques for terms indexing.

In the index structure, it is advisable to increase the recall. The best strategy to accomplish this is to use all normalization techniques, such as stemming, lowercase, misspelling. Keylexems are not necessary, since keywords are sufficient. For the

Figure 8. Example of Semantic Search

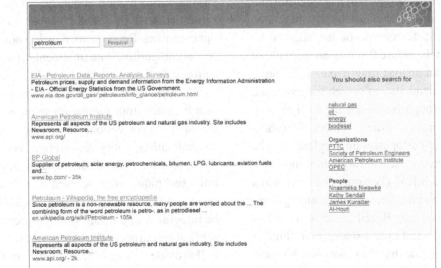

suggestions of alternative navigation, a parallel index (using keylexems) could be used in such a manner that it keeps permanently indexing new associations of synonyms and only use correlated keylexems in order to increase the precision of the association.

Finally, the initial manual query must be carried out on the document index as well as on the associated keylexems parallel index and both results returned to the user simultaneously, allowing an interactive semantic navigation just by clicking keylexems in texts, resulting in the suggested searches.

CASE STUDY

Without question, the age of cheap petroleum has come to an end. However, it is still the world's main source of energy, particularly for transportation; and oil consumption continues to grow.

Now suppose a player on the energy market wants to stay aware of information about fuels.

First the player starts to create an information filter about fuels by selecting news and training an SVM algorithm to classify news about fuel. As analysts read information about fuels, schemas of the market are created in the form of reports. In many cases these schemas will have an information gap. This information is what we call ad-hoc information and deserves to be investigated by Semantic Search. Figure 9 shows an example of a search that an analyst may make. The search results recommend also to search for biodiesel. Navigating through biodiesel, the analyst may reach the soybeans, Brazil (Place), Petrobras (Company) and "castor oil plant" keylexems. The result also suggests to search for ethanol and "Luiz Inácio Lula da Silva" (Person). The keylexems with meaning in parentheses are disambiguated by type. For example, Brazil could be a kind of wood (like Oak) and Lula a sea animal ('lula' is Portuguese for squid) but if an index was built us-

ing the NLP techniques described in section **NLP Techniques**, those things would not occur.

The new found content may improve the filtering by retraining the SVM algorithm. Important relationships like "soybeans—produce—biodiesel" and "Luiz Inácio Lula da Silva—president—Brazil" may be monitored by the Event Alert functionality. If "Luiz Inácio Lula da Silva" loses the election, the system would alert the analyst or if the new plant could produce biodiesel, another alert must be triggered. So the analyst will consume quality information and get a broader view when necessary.

CONCLUSION

This chapter integrates elements from content analysis techniques, text mining, artificial intelligence, and natural language processing (NLP) on a competitive intelligence application. The methods used in NLP must be adapted to take care of the rules and mainly of the existing exceptions in the written language.

Some of these methods are already used to analyze the information, regarding Competitive Intelligence, and the results show that techniques based on NLP theory can help managers to get strategic information about the competitive environment in digital data. It provides a variety of opportunities for systems development focused on the competitive data treatment in many digital sources.

The description of NLP techniques description includes implementation in many subjects, like spelling correction, stemming, augmenting, normalization, entity recognition, entity classification, acronyms and the co-reference process. Each technique must be used in a specific moment to execute a specific job. These jobs will be integrated in a whole system, oriented by the application purpose. The usage of these techniques will provide a more accurate text mining result.

It is important to realize that a great amount of people's tasks is accomplished through human language, and therein lies the growth of NLP applications associated to the CI process.

FUTURE RESEARCH DIRECTIONS

The main upcoming challenge for Competitive Intelligence is to join its data with internal Business Intelligence systems so that one may, for example, generate reports across sales and acquisitions.

The likely trend is one of hybridization; where BI may begin to make use of CI tools to augment its reporting facilities with textual data and CI may begin to produce calculations based on information extracted from text. It remains unclear which will be able to provide the best integrated tools to streamline simplify and increase the quality of an analyst's work. One may idealize a system flexible enough to provide the facilities of both, given the customer or analyst's need.

The most important challenge for text mining is to optimize calculation so that one must only calculate what is new, thus minimizing or, ideally, eliminating costly recalculations. One possible solution is to develop an OLAP-like technique to store pre-calculated and frequent jobs.

Given the current push for the development of semantic content in the web, the implementation of a link between NLP and Semantic Web tools and languages should prove of terrific use and strength. The potential automation of Web-Ontology construction is no longer wild imagination. Indeed it is already very much within the realm of possibility. More concretely, the growing popularity of a standard for metadata representation like the RDF may allow a mapping between the ontology and the NLP. This could provide a vast field for machine learning, and may prove a crucial part in taking the step from a word as a sequence of characters and the idea it represents.

While SPARQL promises to be a powerful tool for ontology search, a similar tool must be developed for natural language search. This tool ought to take into account syntactic/semantic ambiguity and context, providing better results than a simple keyword search.

REFERENCES

Baeza-Yates, B. & Ribeiro Neto, B. (1999). *Modern information retrieval.* Addison Wesley.

Brill, E. (1992) A simple rule-based part of speech tagger. In *Proceedings of the Third ACL Applied NLP*, Trento, Italy.

Brill, E. (1995, December). Transformation-Based error-driven learning and natural language processing: A case study in part of speech tagging. *Computational Linguistics, 21*(4), 543-565.

Burges, C.J.C. (1998). A tutorial on support vector machines for pattern recognition. *Data Mining and Knowledge Discovery, 2*(2)955-974.

Cucerzan, S. & Brill, E. (2004). Spelling correction as an iterative process that exploits the collective knowledge of web users. *Proceedings of EMNLP 2004* (pp. 293-300).

Damerau, F.J., (1964) Technique for computer detection and correction of spelling errors. *Communications of the ACM, 7*(3), 171-176.

Fuld, L. M. (1995). *The new competitor intelligence: the complete resource for finding, analyzing and using information about competitors.* New York: Wiley & Sons.

Ge, N., Hale, J., & Charniak, E. (1998). A statistical approach to anaphora resolution. In *Proceedings of the Sixth Workshop on Very Large Corpora.* (pp. 161-170). Montreal, Canada.

Gruber, T. R. (1993). A translation approach to portable ontologies. *Knowledge Acquisition, 5*(2), 199-220.

Grune, D. & Jacobs, C. J. H. (1991). *Parsing techniques: A practical guide*. Ellis Horwood Ltd.

Guarino, N. (1998). Formal ontology and information systems. In N. Guarino (Ed), *Proceedings of the 1st International Conference on Formal Ontology and Information Systems, (FOIS'98)* (pp. 3-15). Trento, Italy: IOS Press.

Hearst, M. A. (1992). Automatic acquisition of hyponyms from large text corpora. In *Proceedings of the Fourteenth International Conference on Computational Linguistics*. Nantes, France.

Ide, N. & Véronis, J. (1995). *Corpus encoding standard*. Document MUL/EAG CES1 Annex 10.Retrieved from http://www.lpl.univ-aix.fr/projects/multext/CES/CES1.html

Jizba, R., (2000). *Measuring search effectiveness*, Retrieved March 9, 2006 from http://www.hsl.creighton.edu/hsl/Searching/Recall-Precision.html

Joachims, T. (2002), *Learning to classify text using support vector machines, methods, theory and algorithms*, Kluwer Academic Publishers.

Kantrowitz, M., Mohit, B., & Mittal, V. O. (2000). Stemming and its effects on TFIDF ranking. In *Proceedings of SIGIR 2000* (pp. 357-359).

Keith, S., Kaser, O. & Lemire, D. (2005). *Analyzing large collections of electronic text using OLAP*. arXiv:cs.DB/0605127 v1.

Konchady M., (2006), *Text mining applications programming*, Boston: Charles River Media.

Landauer, T. K., Foltz, P. W., & Laham, D. (1998) Introduction to latent semantic analysis. *Discourse Processes, 25*, 259-284.

Lappin, S. & Leass, H. (1995). An algorithm for pronominal anaphora resolution. *Computational Linguistics, 20*(4), 535-561

Manning, C. & Schütze, H. (1999). *Foundations of statistical natural language processing*. Cambridge, MA: MIT Press.

Martins, B. & Silva, M. J. (2004). Spelling correction for search engine queries. *EsTAL—España for Natural Language Processing* (pp. 372-383). Alicante, Spain.

Perez, C. (2006). Open source full text search engines written in java. *Manageability Blog*. Retrieved January 9, 2007, from www.manageability.org/blog/stuff/full-text-lucene-jxta-search-engine-java-xml

Rabiner L. R., (1989, February). A tutorial on hidden markov models and selected applications in speech recognition. In *Proceedings of the IEEE, 77* (2), 257-286.

Saeed, J. L. (1997). *Semantics*. Oxford: Blackwell

Sag, I.A., Baldwin, T., Bond, F., Copestake, A. & Flickinger, D. (2002). Multiword expressions: A pain in the neck for NLP, In *Proceedings of the Third International Conference on Intelligent Text Processing and Computational Linguistics (CICLING 2002)*, Mexico City, Mexico.

Shapiro, C. & Varian, H. R. (1998). *Information rules: a strategic guide to the network economy*. Boston: Harvard Business School Press.

Steinbach, M., Karypis, G., & Kumar, V. (2000). A comparison of document clustering techniques. In *KDD Workshop on Text Mining*. Boston.

Weiss, S.M., Indurkhya, N., Zhang, T., Damerau, F. (2005). *Text mining: Predictive methods for analyzing unstructured information*.

Zanasi, A. (2005). Text mining and its applications to intelligence, CRM and knowledge management *Advances in management information, 2*, 131-143.

Additional Reading

Aranha, C. & Passos, E. (2006). A statistical approach for identifying collocations in Portuguese texts. In *Proceedings of the II Workshop em Algoritmos e Aplicações de Mineração de Dados (II WAAMD)*, Florianópolis.

Basu, A., Watters, C. & Shepherd, M. (2002). Support vector machines for text categorization. In *Proceedings of the 36th Hawaii International Conference on System Sciences (HICSS'03)*.

Biggs, M. (2000). Resurgent text-mining technology can greatly increase your firm's 'intelligence' factor. *InfoWorld, 11*(2), 52.

Borguraev, B. & Pustejovsky, J. (1996). *Corpus Processing for Lexical Acquisition*. The MIT Press.

Bouthillier, K., & Shearer (2003). Assessing competitive intelligence software: A guide to evaluating CI technology. *Information Today*. Medford, NJ.

Carreras, X., Chao, I., Padró, L., & Padró, M. (2004). FreeLing: An open-source suite of language analyzers *Proceedings of the 4th International Conference on Language Resources and Evaluation (LREC'04)*. Lisbon, Portugal.

Carpenter, B. (2004). Phrasal queries with LingPipe and Lucene. In *Proceedings of the 13th Meeting of the Text Retrieval Conference (TREC)*. Gaithersburg, Maryland

Chomsky, N. (1993). *Language and thought*. Wakefield: Rhode Islands & Londres.

Dumais, S. T., Platt, J., Heckerman, D. & Sahami, M. (1998). Inductive learning algorithms and representations for text categorization. In *Proceedings of ACM-CIKM98,* (pp. 148-155).

Ettorre, B. (1995). Managing competitive intelligence. *Management Review.*

Gib, A. G.; Marguiles, R. A. (1991). Making competitive intelligence relevant to the user. *Planning Review.*

Herring, J. P. (1999). Key intelligence topics: a process to identify and define intelligence needs. *Competitive Intelligence Review.*

Kahaner, L. (1998). *Competitive Intelligence: how to gather, analyze and use information to move your business to the top.* New York: Touchstone Books.

Konchady, M. (2006). *Text mining application programmimg.* Charles River Media.

Pérez, J., Arenas, M. & Gutierrez, C. (2006). Semantics and complexity of SPARQL. *The Semantic Web—ISWC*, Springer.

Pinker, S. (2000). *The language instinct: how the mind creates language.* New York: HarperCollins.

Prescott, J. E. & Miller, S. H. (2001). *Proven strategies in competitive intelligence: lessons from the trenches.* New York: Wiley.

Prud'hommeaux, E., Seaborne, A. (2005). SPARQL query language for RDF. *Technical report, World Wide Web Consortium.* http://www.w3.org/TR/rdf-sparql-query/

Seymore, K., McCallum, A., & Rosenfeld, R. (1999). Learning hidden Markov model structure for information extraction. In *AAAI 99 Workshop on Machine Learning for Information Extraction.*

Sullivan, D. (2000, December). The need for text mining in business intelligence. *DM Review.* Retrieved from http://www.dmreview.com/master.cfm

Tyson, K. (1998). *The complete guide to competitive intelligence.* Kirk Tyson International.

Wittgenstein, L. (1979). T*he philosophical investigations.* (3rd edition). Blackwell Publishing.

ENDNOTES

1 http://gate.ac.uk/
2 http://opennlp.sourceforge.net/

3 Portuguese Competition for Named Entity Recognition
4 English Competition for Automatic Content Extraction

Chapter IV
Mining Profiles and Definitions with Natural Language Processing

Horacio Saggion
University of Sheffield, UK

ABSTRACT

Free text is a main repository of human knowledge; therefore, methods and techniques to access this unstructured source of knowledge are of paramount importance. In this chapter we describe natural language processing technology for the development of question answering and text summarisation systems. We focus on applications aiming at mining textual resources to extract knowledge for the automatic creation of definitions and person profiles.

INTRODUCTION

Extracting relevant information from massive amounts of free text about people, companies, organisations, locations, and common terms in order to create definitions or profiles is a very challenging problem not only because it is very difficult to elucidate in a precise way what type of information about these entities is relevant for a definition/profile, but also because even if some types of information were known to be relevant, there are many ways of expressing them in natural language texts. As free text is by far the main

repository of human knowledge, solutions to the problem of extracting definitional information have many applications in areas of knowledge management and intelligence:

- **In intelligence analysis activities:** there is a need for access to personal information in order to create briefings for meetings and for tracking activities of individuals in time and space;

- **In journalism, broadcasting, and news reporting activities:** there is a need to find relevant information for writing backgrounds for the main actors of a breaking news story, but also term definitions need to be provided to non-specialist audiences (e.g., *What is bird flu?*);

- **In publishing:** Encyclopaedias and dictionaries need to be updated with new information about people and other entities found in text repositories;

- **In knowledge engineering:** ontologies and other knowledge repositories need to be populated with instances such as persons and their attributes extracted from text, but also new terms together with their definitions need to be identified in texts in order to make informed decisions about their inclusion in these knowledge repositories;

- **In business intelligence:** information about companies and their key company officers is of great relevance for decision making processes such as whether or not to give credit to a company given the profile of a key company director.

Recent natural language processing challenges such as the document understanding conferences (DUC) (*http://www-nlpir.nist.gov/projects/duc/*) and the text retrieval conferences question answering track (TREC/QA) evaluations (*http://trec.nist.gov/data/qa.html*) have focused on this particular problem and are creating useful language resources to study the problem and measure technical advances. For example, in task 5 in the recent DUC 2004 system participants had to create summaries from sets of documents answering the question *Who is X?*, and from 2003 onward, the TREC/QA evaluations have a specific task which consists of finding relevant information about a person, an organisation, an event, or a common term in a massive text repository (e.g., *What is X?*).

In the Natural Language Processing Group at the University of Sheffield we have been working on these problems for many years, and we have developed effective tools to address them using the general architecture for text engineering (GATE). The main purpose of this chapter is to study the problem of mining textual sources in order to find definitions, profiles, and biographies. This chapter provides first an overview of generic techniques in natural language processing to then present two case studies of the use of natural language technology in DUC and TREC/QA.

NATURAL LANGUAGE PROCESSING TOOLS

The General Architecture for Text Engineering (GATE) is a framework for the development and deployment of language processing technology in large scale (Cunningham, Maynard, Bontcheva, & Tablan, 2002). It provides three types of resources: language resources (LRs) which collectively refer to data; processing resources (PRs) which are used to refer to algorithms; and visualisation resources (VRs) which represent visualisation and editing components.

GATE can be used to process documents in different formats including plain text, HTML, XML, RTF, and SGML. When a document is loaded or opened in GATE, a document structure analyser is called upon which is in charge of creating a GATE document, an LR which will contain the text of the original document and one or more sets of annotations, one of which will contain the document markups (for example, html).

Annotations are generally updated by PRs during text analysis, but they can also be created during annotation editing in the GATE GUI (see Figure 1 for the GATE GUI). Each annotation belongs to an annotation set and has a type, a pair of offsets (the span of text one wants to annotate), and a set of features and values that are used to encode the information. Features (or attribute names) are strings, and values can be any Java object. Attributes and values can be specified in an annotation schema which facilitates validation and input during manual annotation. In Figure

Figure 1. GATE graphical user interface: A document has been annotated with semantic information

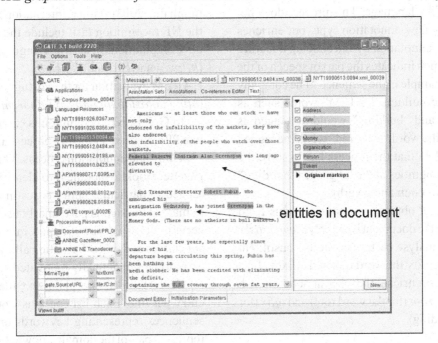

1 we show the GATE user interface. Programmatic access to the annotation sets, annotations, features, and values is possible not only through the GATE application program interface but also in the JAPE language (see Figure 1).

Text Processing Tools

After documents are uploaded or opened with GATE, one of the first steps in text processing is *document tokenisation* which is the process of segmenting the text of the document in units representing words, punctuation, and other elements. Two kinds of annotation are produced: "Token" —for words, numbers, symbols, and punctuation, and "SpaceToken"—for spaces and control characters. Features computed during this process are the type of tokens (word, punctuation, number, space, control character, etc.), their lengths, and their orthographic characteristics (all capitals, all lowercase, capital initial, etc). The process of tokenisation can be modified by changing the tokenisation rules of the system.

One important step after tokenisation is *sentence identification,* which is the process of segmenting the text into sentences. In GATE this is implemented through a cascade of finite state transducers which are created from a grammar file which can be customised. The process is language and domain dependent and makes use of the annotations produced by the tokenisation process (i.e., presence of punctuation marks, control characters, and abbreviations in the input document). This process produces a "Sentence" type of annotation and a default feature computed is an indication of whether or not the sentence is a quoted expression.

In text processing a *part of speech* (POS) *tagging* process is usually required. This is the process of associating to each word form or symbol a tag representing its part of speech. In GATE, it is implemented with a modified version of the Brill tagger (Brill, 1995). The process is dependent on the language and relies (as the Brill tagger does) on two resources—a lexicon and a set of transformation rules—which are trained over corpora. The default POS tagger in GATE is already trained for the English language. This process does not produce any new annotation type, but enriches the "Token" annotation by introducing a feature *category* which indicates the part of speech of the word. For example in the sentence "The company acquired the building for £2M" words such as "company" and "building" would be tagged as nouns, and the word "acquired" would be tagged as a verb. Note that the process has to solve the inherent ambiguities of the language ("building" can be both a noun and a verb).

One way of obtaining canonical forms from each word in the document is to apply a *lemmatiser* which will analyse each word in its constituent parts and identify the word root and affixes. This GATE process enriches the token annotation with two features *root* (for the word root) and *affix* (for the word ending).

Semantic Annotation

A process of *semantic annotation* consists of recognising and classifying a set of entities in the document, commonly referred as to a named entity (NE) recognition task. NE recognition is a key enabler of information extraction—the identification and extraction of key facts from text in specific domains. Today NE recognition is a mature technology which achieves performance levels of precision and recall above 90% for newswire texts where entities of interest are for example people, locations, times, organisations, and so forth.

Much research on NE recognition has been carried out in the context of the U.S. sponsored message understanding conferences (MUC) from 1987 until 1997 for research and development of information extraction systems. The ACE program was an extension of MUC but where the NE recognition task became more complex in the sense of being replaced by an *entity detection and tracking* task which involved, in addition to recognition, the identification of all mentions of a given entity (Maynard, Bontcheva & Cunningham, 2003). Other international efforts in the NE recognition task include the Conference on Computational Natural Language Learning (*http://www.cnts.ua.ac.be/conll2003*) and the HAREM evaluation for the Portuguese language (*http://poloxldb.linguateca.pt/harem.php*).

In GATE, NE recognition is carried out with two PRs, a *gazetteer lookup* process and a *pattern matching* and annotation process. The goal of the gazetteer lookup module is to identify key words related to particular entity types in a particular domain. This step is particularly useful because certain words can be grouped into classes and subclasses and this information allows the grammars to be semantically motivated and flexible.

Gazetteer lists are plain text files with one entry per line. Each list contains words or word sequences representing keywords or terms that represent part of the domain knowledge. An index file is used to tell the system which lists to use in a particular application. In order to classify terms into categories, for each list, a *major type* is specified and, optionally, a *minor type* using the following format:

Terms.lst : Class : SubClass

where *Term.lst* is the name of the list, and *Class* and *SubClass* are strings. The index file is used to create an automaton (which, in order to be efficient, operates on strings instead of on annotations) which recognises and classifies the keywords.

When the finite state automaton matches any strings with a term belonging to Terms.lst, a Lookup annotation is produced that spans the matched sequence; the features added to the annotation are majorType with value Class and minorType with value SubClass (note that when the minorType is omitted no minorType feature will be produced). Grammars use the information about the lookup process in their rules, to produce meaningful annotations.

In order to identify and classify sequences of tokens in the source document, we rely on the Java annotation pattern engine (JAPE) which is a pattern-matching engine implemented in Java. JAPE uses a compiler that translates grammar rules into Java objects that target the GATE API and a library of regular expressions. JAPE can be used to develop cascades of finite state transducers.

A JAPE grammar consists of a set of rules with the following format:

Rule: RuleName
Priority: Integer
LHS → RHS

The priority is used to control how rules that match at the same text offset should be fired. The left-hand side (LHS) is a regular expression over annotations, and the right-hand side (RHS), describes the annotation to be assigned to the piece of text matching the LHS or contains Java we want to execute when the regular expression is found in the text. The LHS is specified in terms of annotations already produced by any previous processing stage, including JAPE semantic tagging. The elements used to specify the pattern are groups of constraints specified as annotation types or as feature-values of annotation types in the following way:

({AnnotationType.AttributeName == Value, ...})
({AnnotationType})

These elements can be combined to form regular expressions using the regular operators: |, *. ?, +, and the sequence constructor. For example, the following is a valid pattern that will match a numeric token:

({Token.string == number})

and the following pattern over sequences of Tokens:

((({Token.string = "$")) ({Token.kind == number}))

matches a dollar sign followed by a number.

Labels can be associated to these constraint elements in the following way:

(Constraint):label

These labels are used in the RHS to specify how to annotate the text span(s) that matches the pattern. The following syntax is used to specify the annotation to be produced:

:label.AnnotationType = {feature=value, ...}

If Java code is used in the RHS of the rule, then the labels associated with constraints in the LHS can be referenced giving the possibility of performing operations on the annotations matched by the rule.

A grammar can also be a set of sub-grammars (called phases) from which a finite state transducer is created. The phases run sequentially and constitute a cascade of finite state transducers over annotations.

GATE comes with a full information extraction system called ANNIE which can be used to detect and extract named entities of different types in English documents.

Coreference Resolution

Coreference resolution, the identification of the referent of anaphoric expressions such as pronouns or definite expressions, is of major importance for natural language applications. It is particularly important in order to identify information about people as well as other types of entities. The MUC evaluations also contributed to fuel research in this area. The current trend in coreference resolution systems is the use of knowledge-poor techniques and corpora informed methods (Mitkov, 1999). For example, current systems use gender, number, and some semantic information together with heuristics for restricting the number of candidates to examine.

In GATE, two processes enable the identification of coreference in text: an *orthographical name matcher* and a *pronominal coreferencer* algorithm (Dimitrov, Bontcheva, Cunningham & Maynard, 2004). The orthographical name matcher associates *names* in text based on a set of rules, typically the full name of a person is associated with a condensed version of the same name (e.g., R. Rubin and Robert Rubin). The pronominal coreferencer used in this work uses simple heuristics identified from the analysis of a corpus of newspaper articles and broadcast news, and so it is well adapted for our task. The method assigns salience values to the antecedent (in a three sentence window) based on the rules induced from the analysis and then chooses as antecedent of an anaphoric expression, the candidate with the best value.

SYNTACTIC AND SEMANTIC ANALYSIS

Syntactic and semantic analysis are carried out with SUPPLE, a freely available, general purpose parser that produces both syntactic and semantic representations for input sentences (Gaizauskas, Hepple, Saggion, Greenwood & Humpreys, 2005). The parser is implemented in Prolog while a Java wrapper acts as a bridge between GATE and the parser, providing the input required by SUPPLE and reading back into the documents syntactic and semantic information. Access to SUPPLE functionalities in GATE is done though a plug-in.

The syntactic output of the parser consists of an analysis of the sentence according to a general purpose grammar of the English language distributed with the parser. The grammar is an attribute-valued *context-free* grammar which makes possible the treatment of long distance syntactic phenomena which can not be dealt with in a regular formalism such as JAPE.

Figure 2. Parse tree obtained from SUPPLE

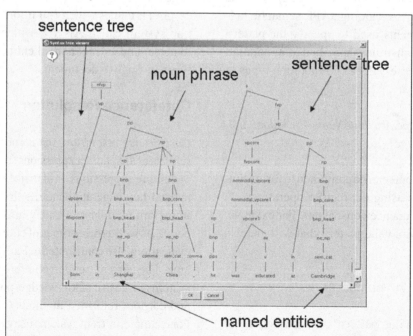

The semantic output of the parser is a quasi logical form (QLF)—a set of first order terms constructed from the interpretation of each syntactic rule applied to the final parse: each rule specifies how its semantics should be constructed from the semantics of constituents mentioned in the syntactic rule.

SUPPLE intends to create a full analysis and representation of the input sentence; however, this is not always possible, in which case it will not fail the analysis, instead it will provide a partial syntactic and semantic analysis of the input, which can be completed by other components such as a discourse interpreter (see Figure 2).

As an example the sentence from a profile:

Born in Shanghai, China, he was educated at Cambridge.

This sentence is analysed as two chunks of information "Born in Shanghai, China" and "he was educated at Cambridge". The analysis of the first fragment is as follows:

(nfvp (vp (vpcore (nfvpcore (av (v "Born"))))) (pp (in "in") (np (bnp (bnp_core (premods (premod (ne_np (sem_cat "Shanghai")))) (bnp_head (ne_np (sem_cat "China"))))))))

Note that the analysis of the sentence is correct. The phrase "Born…" is interpreted as a non finite verb phrase—because of the verb "Born" and the parser correctly attached the prepositional phrase "in Shanghai…" to the verb "Born". The names "China" and "Shanghai" have been interpreted as named entities and shown in the parse as "sem_cat" which is used to wrap named entities during parsing. The semantic interpretation of the fragment produces the following QLF:

bear(e1), time(e1,none), aspect(e1,simple), voice(e1,passive), in(e1,e2), name(e2,'China'), location(e2), country(e2), name(e3,'Shanghai'),

location(e3), city(e3), realisation(e3,offsets(9,17)), qual(e2,e3), realisation(e2,offsets(9,24)), realisation(e1,offsets(1,24)), realisation(e1,offsets(1,24))

where the verb "Born" has been mapped into the unary predicate bear(e1), the named entities "China" and "Shanghai" are represented as country(e2) and city(e3) respectively—being in addition linked together by the predicate qual(e2,e3)—for qualifier. Finally the predicate in(e1,e2) is used to represent the attachment between the main verb "Born" and the city "Shanghai". The constants e_n are used to represent entities and events in the text. Other predicates are also used to represent information such as aspectual information from the verb, name of the named entity, and where in the text (offsets) the particular entities are realised.

The analysis of the second fragment is:

(s (np (bnp (pps "he"))) (fvp (vp (vpcore (fvpcore (nonmodal_vpcore (nonmodal_vpcore1 (vpcore1 (v "was")) (av (v "educated"))))))) (pp (in "at") (np (bnp (bnp_core (bnp_head (ne_np (sem_cat "Cambridge"))))))))))

with semantic representation:

pronoun(e5,he), realisation(e5,offsets(26,28)), educate(e4), time(e4,past), aspect(e4,simple), voice(e4,passive), at(e4,e6), name(e6,'Cambridge'), location(e6), city(e6), realisation(e6,offsets(45,54)), realisation(e4, offsets(29,54)), realisation(e4,offsets(29,54)), lobj(e4,e5)

Syntactic and semantic information is particularly relevant for information extraction and question answering. In fact, suppose that we wanted to extract information on family relations from text: given a sentence such as "David is married to Victoria" we would like to extract a semantic relation *is_spouse_of*, and state that "David" *is_spouse_of* "Victoria" and "Victoria" *is_spouse_of* "David". Because "David" and "Victoria" are respectively the logical subject and the logical object of the verb "to marry" in the sentence, they can be used to extract this particular type of family relation. Note that the same relation should be extracted for a sentence such as "David is Victoria's husband", and in this case again syntactic information is very handy. The same applies for question answering; use of relations from text can be used as evidence for preferring an answer over a set of possible answer candidates.

In relational extraction syntactic and semantic information have been shown to play a significant role in machine learning approaches to relation extraction (Wang, Li, Bontcheva, Cunningham, & Wang, 2006).

SUMMARISATION TOOLKIT

A number of domain independent general purpose summarisation components are available in GATE through a plug-in.[1] The components are designed to create sentence extracts. Following the GATE philosophy, the objective is not to provide the best possible summarisation system, but an adaptable tool for the development, testing, and deployment of customisable summarisation solutions (Saggion, 2002). The core of the toolkit is a set of summarisation modules which compute numeric features for each sentence in the input document—the value of the feature indicates how relevant the information in the sentence is for the feature. The computed values—which are normalised yielding numbers in the interval [0..1]—are combined in a linear formula to obtain a score for each sentence which is used as the basis for sentence selection. Sentences are ranked based on their score and top ranked sentences selected to produce an extract. Many features implemented in this tool have been suggested in past research as valuable for the task of identifying sentences for creating summaries. See Mani (2001), for example. An example summary obtained with the tool can be seen in Figure 3.

Figure 3. Single document summary

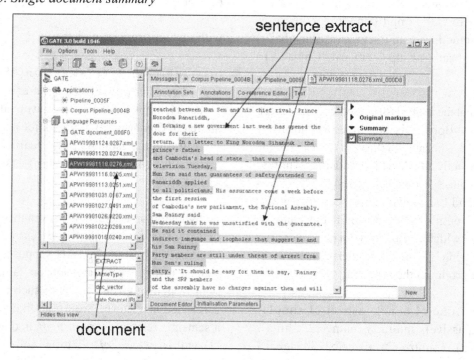

Figure 4. Centroid-based multi-document summary

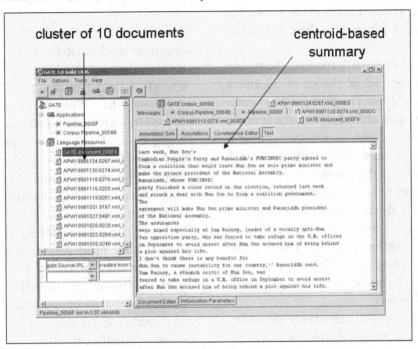

A corpus statistic module computes token statistics including term frequency—the number of times each term occurs in the document (tf). The vector space model has been implemented and it is used to create vector representations of different text fragments—usually sentences but also the full document. Each vector contains for each term occurring in the text fragment, the value tf*idf (term frequency * inverted document frequency). The inverted document frequency of a given term is the number of documents in a collection containing the term. These values can be loaded into the system from a table or can be computed on the fly by the summarisation tool. With the latter option the values can be then be saved for future use.

The term frequency module computes the sum of the tf*idf of all terms in each sentence—note that because frequent terms such as "the" have close to zero idf value, then their contribution to the term frequency feature is minimal. These values are normalised to yield numbers between 0 and 1. In a similar way, a named entity scorer module computes the frequency of each named entity in the sentence. This process is not based on the frequency of named entities in a corpus but on the frequency of named entities in the input document. A named entity occurring less frequently is more valuable than a named entity observed across different sentences.

A content analysis module is used to compute the similarity between two text fragments in the document represented in the vector space—for example between a sentence and the title of the document or between a sentence and the full document. The measure of similarity is the cosine of the angle between the two vectors. These values can be stored as sentence features and used in the scoring formula.

The sentence position module computes two features for each sentence: the absolute position of the sentence in the document and the relative position of the sentence in the paragraph. The absolute position of sentence i receives value i^{-1}

while the paragraph feature receives a value which depends on the sentence being in the beginning, middle or end of paragraph—these values are parameters of the system.

For a cluster of related documents, the system computes the centroid of the set of document vectors in the cluster. The centroid is a vector of terms and values which is in the center of the cluster. The value of each term in the centroid is the average of the values of the terms in the vectors created for each document.

The similarity of each sentence in the cluster to the centroid is also computed using the cosine metric. This value is stored as a sentence feature and used during sentence scoring in multi-document summarisation tasks (Saggion & Gaiza-uskas, 2004b). A multidocument summary is presented in Figure 4.

In order to support redundancy detection, resources for computing n-grams are also available. A metric for redundancy detection has been implemented which computes how close two text fragments are according to the proportion of n-grams they share.

Summarisation is a very important topic in natural language processing and it would be impossible to describe here all existent approaches and tools. Probably close to our approach is the MEAD toolkit (Radev, Allison, Blair-Gold-ensohn, Blitzer, Celebi, Dimitrov et al., 2004) which provides methods to compute features such as position, centroid similarity, and so forth, and to combine them with appropriate weights.

CASE STUDIES

GATE and summarisation components have been used to solve two problems identified by the natural language processing community: definitional question answering and profile-based text summarisation. Here we give an overview of how the tools we have described have been used to create practical and effective solutions.

Definitional Question Answering

The problem of finding definitions in vast text collections is related to the TREC QA definition subtask, where given a huge text collection like AQUAINT (over 1 million texts from the *New York Times*, the AP newswire, and the English portion of the Xinhua newswire and totaling about 3.2 gigabytes of data) and a definition question like *What is Goth?* or *Who is Aaron Copland?*, an automatic system has to find text fragments that convey essential and non-essential characteristics of the main question term (e.g., *Goth* or *Aaron Copland*). This is a challenging problem not only because of the many ways in which definitions can be conveyed in natural language texts but also because the definiendum (i.e., the thing to be defined) has not, on its own, enough discriminative power to allow selection of definition-bearing passages from the collection.

In the TREC 2003 QA definition subtask evaluation, participants used various techniques similar to those we are going to present here. Top ranked groups report on the use of some form of lexical resource like WordNet, the Web for answer redundancy, patterns for definition identification, and sophisticated linguistic tools (Harabagiu, Moldovan, Clark, Bowden, Williams, & Bensley, 2003; Kouylekov, Magnini, Negri, & Tanev, 2003).

BBN's definitional system (Xu, Licuanan, & Weischedel, 2003) that obtained the best performance in TREC QA 2003 relies on the identification, extraction, and ranking of *kernel facts* about the question target (i.e., definiendum) followed by a redundancy removal step. The system uses sophisticated linguistic analysis components such as parsing and coreference resolution. First, sentences containing the question target in the top 1000 documents retrieved by an information retrieval system are identified; then, kernel facts are identified in those sentences using criteria such as the presence of copula or appositive constructions involving the question target, or matching of a number of structural patterns (e.g., *TERM is a NP*), or containing special predicate-argument structures (e.g., *PERSON was born on DATE*), or presence of specific relations (e.g., *spouse of, staff of*); finally, kernel facts are ranked by a metric that takes into account their type and their similarity (using tf*idf metric) to a question profile constructed from online sources or from the set of identified kernel facts.

QUALIFIER (Yang, Cui, Maslennikov, Qiu, Kan, & Chua, 2003) obtained the second best performance using a data-driven approach to definitional QA. The system uses linguistic tools such as fine-grained named entity recognition and coreference resolution. WordNet and the Web are used to expand the original definition question to bridge the semantic gap between query space and document space. Given a set of documents retrieved from AQUAINT after query expansion, extractive techniques similar to those used in text summarisation are applied. The basic measure used to score sentences is a logarithmic sum of a variant of the tf*idf measure for each word. This metric scores a word proportional to the number of times it appears in sentences containing the definiendum and inversely proportional to the number of times it appears in sentences that do not contain the definiendum. Scores for words are computed from two sources: AQUAINT sentences and Web sentences. Sentence scores are first computed using word scores obtained from AQUAINT and Web and then these scores are combined in a linear way to obtain the sentence final value. Once all sentences have been evaluated and ranked, an iterative redundancy removal technique is applied to discard definitional sentences already in the answer set.

The DefScriber system (Blair-Goldensohn, McKeown, & Schlaikjer, 2003) combines world knowledge in the form of definitional predicates (genus, species, and nonspecific) and data-driven statistical techniques. World knowledge about the predicates is created relying on machine learning over annotated data. Data driven techniques in-

cluding the vector space model and cosine distance are used to exploit the redundancy of information about the definiendum in nondefinitional Web texts. Fleischman, Hovy, and Echihabi (2003) create pairs of concept instances such as "Bill Clinton-president" mining newspaper articles and Web documents. These pairs constitute pre-available knowledge that can be used to answer "Who is?" questions. They use lexico-syntactic patterns learnt from annotated data to identify such pairs. The knowledge acquired can be used to answer two different types of definition questions "Who" and "What".

Our Approach

In order to find good definitions, it is useful to have a collection of metalanguage statements (i.e., *DEFINIENDUM is a, DEFINIENDUM consists of*, etc.) which implement patterns for identification and extraction of "definiens"' (the statement of the meaning of the definiendum). Unfortunately there are so many ways in which definitions are conveyed in natural language that it is difficult to come up with a full set of linguistic patterns to solve the problem. To make matters more complex, patterns are usually ambiguous, matching nondefinitional contexts as well definitional ones. For example, a pattern like *Goth is a* to find definitions of *Goth*, will match *Becoming a goth is a process that demands lots of effort* as well as *Goth is a subculture*.

We will describe a method that uses external sources to mine knowledge which consists of terms that co-occur with the *definiendum* before trying to define it using the given text collection. This knowledge is used for definition identification and extraction. There are two sources of knowledge we rely on for finding definitions: linguistic patterns, which represent general knowledge about how definitions are expressed in language, and secondary terms, which represent specific knowledge about the definiendum outside the target collection.

Linguistic Patterns

Definition patterns or metalanguage statements containing lexical, syntactic, and sometimes semantic information have been used in the past in research in terminology (Pearson, 1998), ontology induction (Hearst, 1992), and text summarisation (Saggion & Lapalme, 2002) among others.

When a corpus for specific purposes is available, then patterns can be combined with well formed terms or specific words to restrict their inherent ambiguity. One simple formal defining expositive proposed by Pearson (1998) is $X = Y$ + *distinguishing characteristics* where possible fillers for X are well formed terms (those word sequences following specific patterns), fillers for Y are terms or specific words from a particular word list (e.g., method, technique, etc.), and fillers for = are connective verbs such as to *be, consist* or *know*. The use of predefined word lists or term formation criteria is, however, not possible in our case because we are dealing with a heterogeneous text collection where the notion of term is less precise than in a corpus of a particular domain.

Dictionaries are good sources for the extraction of definition knowledge. Recent research in classification and automatic analysis of dictionary entries (Barnbrook, 2002) has shown that a limited number of strategies for expressing meaning in those sources exists and that automatic analysis can be carried out on those sources to extract lexical knowledge for natural language processing tasks. Barnbrook (2002) identified 16 types of definitions in the Cobuild student's dictionary and extraction patterns used to parse them (e.g., *A/an/The TERM is/are a/an/the* ...). The question remains as to whether this typology of definition sentences (and associated extraction patterns) is sufficient to identify definition statements in less structured textual sources.

We have collected, through corpus analysis and linguistic intuition, a useful set of lexical patterns to locate definition-bearing passages. The purpose of these patterns is on the one hand

Table 1. Definition/profile patterns

General patterns	Person patterns
define TERM as	PERSON known for
TERM and others	PERSON who was
TERM consists of	PERSON a member of

to obtain definition contexts for the definiendum outside the target collection in order to mine knowledge from them, and on the other hand to use them for extracting definiens from the target collection. 36 patterns for general terms and 33 patterns for person profiles have been identified, a sample can be seen in Table 1, patterns used in this work contain only lexical information.

In this case, we have implemented the pattern matching process in GATE gazetteers instead of with JAPE grammars. This has the advantage of speeding up the matching process. The gazetteer lists are generated on-the-fly, for each term or person of interest we instantiate all the patterns and write them to gazeteer lists. For example if "Aaron Copland" is the person to be profiled (which is extracted from the question by performing syntactic analysis using SUPPLE) then the strings *Aaron Copland known for, Aaron Copland who was* and *Aaron Copland a member of* are all stored in the gazetteer lists files for the entity *Aaron Copland* and uploaded into the system to carry out linguistic analysis.

Secondary Terms

Terms that co-occur with the definiendum (outside the target collection) in definition-bearing passages seem to play an important role for the identification of definitions in the target collection. For example, in the AQUAINT collection there are 217 sentences referring to *Goth*, but only a few of them provide useful definitional contexts. We note that the term *subculture* usually occurs with *Goth* in definitional contexts on the Web, and there are only 6 sentences in AQUAINT which contain both terms. These six sentences provide useful descriptions of the term *Goth* such as *the Goth subculture* and *the gloomy subculture known as Goth*. So, the automatic identification of specific knowledge about the definiendum seems crucial in this task.

Our method considers nouns, verbs, and adjectives as candidate secondary terms (so a process of part-of-speech tagging is essential). Sources for obtaining definition-passages outside AQUAINT for mining secondary terms are the WordNet lexical database (Miller, 1995), the site of Encyclopaedia Britannica, and general pages on the Web (in further experiments we have used Wikipedia instead of Britannica as a trusted source for containing definitional contexts). The passages are obtained automatically from the Web by using the Google API exact search facility for each definition pattern (e.g., *Aaron Copland who was*).

Terms that co-occur with the definiendum are obtained following three different methods: (i) words appearing in WordNet glosses and hypernyms of the definiendum are extracted; (ii) words from Britannica sentences are extracted only if the sentence contains an explicit reference to the definiendum; (iii) words from other Web sentences are extracted only if the sentences match any definition pattern. Extracted terms are scored based on their frequency of occurrence. Table 2 shows top ranked terms mined from on-line sources for *Aaron Copland* (famous American musician who composed the ballet *Appalachian Spring*)

Table 2. Tems that co-occur with the definiendum in definition bearing passages

DEFINIENDUM	SECONDARY TERMS
Aaron Copland	music, american, composer, classical, appalachian, spring, brooklyn, and so forth
golden parachutes	plans, stock, executive, compensation, millions, generous, top, and so forth

and *golden parachutes* (compensation given to top executives that is very generous).

Identifying Definitions in Texts

In order to select text passages from the target text collection we relied on a document retrieval system which returns relevant text paragraphs. It is worth noting that GATE integrates the Lucene information retrieval system (*http://lucene. apache.org*) which is appropriate in this task (we have used it in further experiments). Different strategies can be used to select good passages from the collection. One strategy we have used consisted of an iterative process which uses the target term and if too many passages are returned and then secondary terms are used in conjunction with the target term to narrow the search.

We perform a linguistic analysis of each returned passage which consists of the following steps provided by GATE: tokenisation, sentence splitting, matching using the definiendum and any of the definiendum's secondary terms, and pattern matching using the definition patterns (this is a GATE gazetteer lookup process). We restrict our analysis of definitions to the sentence level. A sentence is considered a definition-bearing sentence if it matches a definition pattern or if it contains the definiendum and at least three secondary terms.

We perform sentence compression extracting a sentence fragment that is a sentence suffix and contains main and all secondary terms appearing in the sentence. This is done in order to avoid the inclusion of unnecessary information the sentence may contain. For example, the definition of *Anthony Blunt* extracted from the sentence.

A. *The narrator of this antic hall-of-mirrors novel, which explores the compulsive appeal of communism for Britain's upper classes in the 1930s, is based on the distinguished art historian Anthony Blunt, who was named as a Soviet spy during the Thatcher years.*

is

B. *art historian Anthony Blunt, who was named as a Soviet spy during the Thatcher years.*

All candidate definitions are proposed as answers unless they are too similar to any of the previous extracted answers. We measure similarity of a candidate definition to a previously extracted definition from the collection using *tf*idf* and the cosine similarity measure taken from the summarisation toolkit.

The method described here was used in the recent TREC QA 2003 competition in the definition task. This task required finding answers for 50 definition questions. The set consisted of 30 "Who" definition questions and 20 "What" definition questions. TREC assessors created for each question a list of acceptable information nuggets (pieces of text) from all returned system answers and information discovered during question development. Some nuggets are considered essential (i.e., a piece of information that should be part of the definition) while others are considered non-essential. During evaluation, the assessor takes each system response and marks all essential and non-essential nuggets contained in it. A score for each question consists of nugget-recall (NR) and nugget-precision (NP) based on length. These scores are combined in the F-score measure with recall five times as important as precision. We obtained a combined F-score of 0.236. The F-score of the systems that participated in the competition is 0.555 (best), 0.192 (median), 0.000 (worst). Our method was considered among the top 10 out of 25 participants. The method was improved with the incorporation of automatically induced definition patterns which are used in addition to the manually collected patterns and with a considerable increase in the number of documents retrieved for analysis (Gaizauskas, Greenwood, Hepple, Saggion, & Sargaison, 2004).

Profile-Based Summarisation

The National Institute of Standards and Technology (NIST), with support from the Defence Advanced Research Projects Agency (DARPA), is conducting a series of evaluations in the area of text summarisation, the Document Understanding Conferences (DUC), providing the appropriate framework for system-independent evaluation of text summarisation systems. In DUC 2004, one multi-document summarisation task consisted of the following: Given a document cluster and a question of the form *Who is X?* where X is the name of a person, create a short multi-document summary of the cluster that responds to the question. This task seems less complicated than the previously described task in that the process of finding the input passages for profiling is not necessary.

One of the first multidocument summarisation systems to produce summaries from templates was SUMMONS (Radev & McKeown, 1998). One of the key components of the system, which is relevant to research on profile creation, is a knowledge base of person profiles which support the summariser in a process of generation of descriptions during summary generation. The database is populated from online sources by identifying descriptions using a set of linguistic patterns which represent premodifiers or appositions. Schiffman, Mani, and Concepcion (2001) use corpus statistics together with linguistic knowledge to identify and weight descriptions of people to be included in a biography. Syntactic information is used to identify appositives describing people as well as sentences where the target person is the subject of the sentence. The mutual information statistic computed between verbs and subjects in a corpus is used to score and rank descriptions of the sought entity. Zhou, Ticrea, and Hovy (2004) use content reduction techniques as proposed by (Marcu, 1999); however the initial content of the summary is identified by a sentence classifier trained over a corpus of annotated biographies. The classifier identifies in-text sentences referring to different aspects of a person's life.

Many multidocument summarisation algorithms take advantage of the redundancy of information to measure relevance in order to decide which sentences in the cluster to select. However, one of the best performing systems in the profile-based summarisation task at DUC 2004 used syntactic criteria alone to select sentences in order to create a profile. Only two types of construction were used in that work: appositive and copula constructions, which both rely on syntactic analysis (Lacatusu, Hick, Harabagiu, & Nezd, 2004).

We follow a pattern-based shallow approach to the identification of profile information combined with a greedy search algorithm informed by corpus statistics. We will show that our proposed solution is ranked consistently high on the DUC 2004 data.

Sentence Extraction System

Here, we focus on the problem of extracting from a document cluster the necessary information to create the person's profile; the problem of synthesis—the production of a coherent and cohesive biography—will not be discussed. In order to select the content for a profile, we have developed a sentence selection mechanism which, given a target person and a cluster of documents referring to the target, extracts relevant content from the cluster and produces a summary which will contain information such as the person's age and profession (e.g., *"Hawking, 56, is the Lucasian Professor of Mathematics..."*), and life events (*e.g., "Hawking, 56, suffers from Lou Gehrig's Disease, which affects his motor skills..."*). The summary is created with sentence fragments from the documents, which have been analysed by a number of natural language processing components. The main steps in the process are:

- First, a pool of relevant sentences is identified as candidates in the input documents using a pattern-matching algorithm;
- Second, redundancy removal is carried out to eliminate from the pool of sentences repeated information
- Finally, the set of candidate sentences is reduced to match the required compression rate by a greedy sentence rejection mechanism;

Two pieces of information are key in the process: the GATE coreference resolution algorithm and a pattern matching mechanism, implemented in JAPE, which targets specific contexts in which a person is mentioned.

Preprocessing

We carry out document analysis using GATE tools discussed above. Modifications to the sentence identification module have been carried out to deal with the format of the input documents, the named entity recogniser has been adapted in the following way: we have created, on-the-fly and for each target, gazetteer lists needed to identify the target entity in the text. These lists contain the full name of the target person and the person's last name. We also provide gender information to the named entity recogniser by identifying the gender of the target in the input set. Using the distribution of male and female pronouns in the person cluster, the system guesses the gender of the target entity (the most frequent gender). This information is key for the coreference algorithm which uses information provided by the named entity recogniser to decide upon coreferent pronouns with the target. GATE part-of-speech tagging is also used as is a noun phrase chunker available in GATE as a plug-in; however, no syntactic or semantic analysis were necessary for the experiments reported here. After coreference resolution a step identifies a coreference chain—expressions referring to the same entity or the target entity— and marks each member of the chain so that a pattern matching mechanism can be applied.

Content Selection

In order to select sentence candidates to create an extract we rely on a number of patterns that have been proposed in the past to identify *descriptive phrases* in text collections. A list of patterns used in the system is given in Table 1 and have been proposed by Joho and Sanderson (2000). In this specification, DP is a *descriptive phrase* which is taken to be a noun phrase.

Our implementation of the patterns makes use of coreference information so that *target* is any expression in text which is coreferent with the sought person. We have implemented the patterns in JAPE. In order to implement the DP element in the patterns we use the information provided by the noun phrase chunker

For example a variation of the first pattern is implemented in JAPE as follows:

Rule: KeyPhrase1

```
({KeyPerson}
({ Token.string == "is" } |
{Token.string == "was" })
{NounChunk}):annotate -->
:annotate.KeyPhrase = {}
```

Note that because the NounChunk annotation produced by the noun chunker covers initial determiners, there is no need to make determiners explicit in the JAPE rule.

The process of content selection is simple: a sentence is considered a candidate for the extract if it matches a pattern (i.e., has an annotation of type "KeyPhrase"). We perform sentence compression by removing from the candidate sentence the longest suffix which does not match a pattern. The selected sentences are sorted according to their similarity to the centroid of the cluster (using the

Table 3. Set of patterns for identifying profile information

Pattern	Example
TARGET (is | was) (a|the|an|...) DP	Gen. Clark is a superv commandant...
TARGET (who|whose|...)	Glass, who has written...
TARGET, (a|the|one|...) DP	Sonia Ghandi, the Italian born widow
TARGET, DP	Hawkings, 56...
TARGET's	Darforth's law offices...
TARGET and other	Reno and other officials...

tools from the summarisation toolkit). In order to filter out redundant information, we use our n-gram similarity detection metric in the following way: a pattern-matched sentence is included in a list of candidate sentences if it is *different* from all other candidates in the list. In order to implement such a procedure, a threshold for our n-gram similarity metric has to be established so that one can decide whether two sentences contain different information. Such a threshold can be obtained if one has a corpus annotated with sentences known to be different. As such, a corpus is not available to us. We make the hypothesis that in a given document all sentences will report different information; therefore, we can use the n-gram similarity values between them to help estimate a similarity threshold. We computed pair wise n-gram similarity values between sentences in documents and have estimated a threshold for dissimilarity as the average of the pair wise similarity values.

Greedy Sentence Removal

Most sentence extraction algorithms work in a constructive way: given a document and a sentence scoring mechanism, the algorithm ranks sentences by score, and then chooses sentences from the ranked list until a compression rate is reached. We take a different approach which consists in removing sentences from a pool of candidate sentences until the desired compression is achieved. The question is, given that an exhaustive search is implausible, how to reduce the given candidate set so that the content is optimal. It follows a similar approach to Marcu's (1999) algorithm for the creation of extracts from pairs of *(document, abstracts)*. In his approach clauses from the document are greedily deleted in order to obtain an extract which is maximally similar to the abstract. In our case, as we do not have an oracle which gives us the ideal abstract we want to construct, we assume that the candidate list of sentences which refer to the person target is the ideal content to include in the final summary.

Given a set of sentences *C* which cover *essential* information about a person, the algorithm creates an extract which is close in content to C but which is reduced in form. The measure of proximity between documents is taken as the cosine between two vectors of term representations of the documents (as in an information retrieval context). At each step, the algorithm greedily rejects a sentence from the extract. The rejected sentence is one which if removed from the extract produces a pseudodocument which is closer to C among all other possible pseudodocuments. The algorithm is first called with a vector of terms created from the candidate list of sentences—obtained using the sentence selection and redundancy removal step, the candidate list of sentences, and a given compression rate. Note that summarisation by sentence rejection has a long history in text summarisation: it has been used in the ADAM system (Pollock & Zamora, 1975) to reject sentences based on a cue-word list, and also in the British Library Automatic Abstracting Project (BLAB) in order to exclude sentences with dangling anaphora which cannot be resolved in context (Johnson, Paice, Black & Neal, 1993).

Evaluation

The data used in the experiments reported here is the DUC 2004 Task 5 data which consists of 50 *Who is X?* questions and 50 document clusters (one per question): each cluster contained around 10 documents from news agencies. For each of the clusters in the data set, human analysts have created ideal or referent summaries against which the peer (system) summaries are compared. In order to take advantage of the document markup, we have transformed the original documents into XML in such a way that the processing components can concentrate on the textual information of the document alone. Given the question target and the document cluster we have created 665-byte long summaries following the method described below. We have followed the method used in DUC 2004 to evaluate the content of the automatic summaries and have compared our system against other algorithms.

Since human evaluation requires human judgements and these are expensive to obtain, automatic evaluation metrics for summary quality have been the focus of research in recent years (Saggion, Radev, Teufel, & Lam, 2002). In particular, the Document Understanding Conferences have adopted ROUGE (Lin, 2004), a statistic for automatic evaluation of summaries. ROUGE allows the computation of recall-based metrics using n-gram matching between a *candidate summary* and a *reference set of summaries*. The official DUC 2004 evaluation is based on six metrics ROUGE-N (N=1,2,3,4) based on n-gram matches, ROUGE-L, a recall metric based on the longest common subsequence match between peer and ideal summary, and ROUGE-W which is a weighted longest common subsequence that takes into account distances when applying the longest common subsequence. When multiple references are available in an evaluation, the ROUGE statistic is defined as the best score obtained by the summary when compared to each reference. Recent experiments have shown that some ROUGE scores correlate with rankings produced by humans. According to ROUGE scores, our pattern-based summariser consistently obtains the highest scores for all ROUGE metrics. The other algorithms we compared our system to are generally less consistent in ranking. A system from Columbia University is also rather consistent obtaining the second score for all metrics but ROUGE-4.

While evaluations using humans are desirable because they measure how helpful summaries are in a given tasks, automatic evaluation based on multiple reference summaries makes it possible comparison across sites. Task-based evaluation of summaries was the focus of SUMMAC—the first large scale task-based evaluation of text summarisation systems (Mani, Klein, House, Hirschman, Firmin, & Sundheim, 2002).

CONCLUSION

With the development of the Internet and the ever increasing availability of online textual information, automating the process of extracting relevant information about real entities or common terms has become increasingly important for intelligence gathering activities and knowledge management among others. In this chapter we have described two specific text mining tasks: creating profiles from a cluster of relevant documents and finding definitions in massive open text collections. We have described robust yet adaptable tools used as the analytical apparatus for implementation. The methods proposed for both tasks have been proved very effective as demonstrated by results obtained in international evaluations in natural language processing.

In spite of the success, considering how far automatic systems are from human performance in the same tasks, much needs to be done. An issue that needed to be tackled when extracting and combining information from multiple documents is that of cross-document coreference. In fact, the systems described here rely on identification of the name of the entity to be targeted, but they do not identify the referent of the entity or whether or not the same mention refers to the same entity in the real world. Some work has been carried out in the past few years in this subject and it is a problem which forms part of our research agenda. We have made little use of syntactic and semantic information here, it should be noted, however, that a great deal can be learned from the semantic analysis of the text: for example syntactic and semantic analysis of a corpus of profiles can bring to bear a number of predicates and arguments typically used to express core biographical facts which in turn could be used to detect that information in new texts.

Another issue we have not addressed here is that of presentation of information: how a coherent well formed profile or answer to a definition question is to be presented. Problems to be addressed here are sentence ordering, sentence reduction, and sentence combination.

Approaches described here are largely unsupervised: the patterns used are inspired by corpus analysis. But, with the increasing interest of corpus-based, statistical techniques in natural language processing it remains an open question whether better performance could be obtained by exploring machine learning approaches in all or some parts of the applications described here.

FUTURE RESEARCH DIRECTIONS

Recent years have witnessed an explosion of textual information online making human language technology and in particular text summarisation and question answering important for helping humans make informed decisions about the content of particular sources of information.

On the issue of text analysis, future directions in profile and definition mining have to address the problems of cross-document event and entity coreference, which arises when the same event or entity is described in multiple documents. In this context important research issues have to be investigated: identification of similar information in different sources and identification of complementary and contradictory information across sources. In order to develop solutions in this area, it is important the creation of standard data sets for development, testing, and evaluation, so that the research community can replicate experiments and compare results. Approaches relying on superficial features are likely to produce rapid and robust solutions; however attention has to be paid to knowledge-based approaches which can be made portable from one domain to another by the application of machine learning techniques.

On the issue of information presentation, techniques are required for producing good quality summaries and complicated answers. With the availability of massive text collections, progress is expected in the area of trainable language generation for profile generation.

It is important to note that human language technology faces new challenges with the adoption of Web 2.0 technology because of its multisource and multilingual nature. Intelligent access to information in collaborative environments with summarisation and question answering technology will certainly be a target of current and future applications.

ACKNOWLEDGMENT

The work described in this chapter was produced while the author was working for the Cubreporter Project (EPSRC Grant R91465). The writing of the chapter was produced while the author was working for the EU Musing Project (IST-2004-027097).

REFERENCES

Barnbrook, G. (2002). *Defining language. A local grammar of definition sentences.* John Benjamins Publishing Company.

Blair-Goldensohn, S., McKeown, K., & Schlaikjer, A. H. (2004). Answering definitional questions: A hybrid approach. In M. T. Maybury (Ed.) *New directions in question answering* (pp 47-58). MIT Press.

Brill, E. (1995). Transformation-based error-driven learning and natural language processing: A case study in part-of-speech tagging. *Computational Linguistics, 21*(4), 543-565.

Cunningham, H., Maynard, D., Bontcheva, K., & Tablan, V. (2002). GATE: A framework and graphical development environment for robust NLP tools and applications. In *ACL 2002*.

Dimitrov, M., Bontcheva, K., Cunningham, H., & Maynard, D. (2004). A light-weight approach to coreference resolution for named entities in text. In A. Branco, T.M., & R. Mitkov (Eds.), *Anaphora processing: Linguistic, cognitive and computational modelling.* John Benjamins Publishing Company.

Fleischman, Hovy, & Echihabi. (2003). Offline strategies for online question answering: Answering questions before they are asked. In *Proceedings of the ACL 2003* (pp. 1-7).

Gaizauskas, R, Greenwood, M., Hepple, M, Roberts, T, Saggion, H., & Sargaison, M. (2004). In *Proceedings of TREC 2004*. The University of Sheffield's TREC 2004 Q&A.

Gaizauskas, R., Hepple, M., Saggion, H., Greenwood, M., & Humpreys, K. (2005). SUPPLE: A practical parser for natural language engineering applications. In *Proceedings of the International Workshop on Parsing Technologies.*

Harabagiu, S., Moldovan, D., Clark, M., Bowden, J., Williams, & Bensley, J. (2003). Answer mining by combining extraction techniques with abductive reasoning. In *Proceedings of TREC-2003* (pp. 375-382).

Hearst, M.A. (1992). Automatic acquisition of hyponyms from large text corpora. In *Proceedings of COLING'92*, Nantes.

Johnson, F.C., Paice, C.D., Black, W.J., & Neal, A. (1993). The application of linguistic processing to automatic abstract generation. *Journal of Document & Text Management, 1*, 215-241.

Joho, H., & Sanderson, M. (2000). Retrieving descriptive phrases from large amounts of free text. In *Proceedings of Conference on Information and Knowledge Management* (pp. 180-186). ACM.

Kouylekov, M., Magnini, B., Negri, M., & Tanev, H (2003). ITC-irst at TREC-2003: The DIOGENE QA system. In *Proceedings of TREC-2003*.

Lacatusu, F., Hick, L., Harabagiu, S., & Nezd, L. (2004). Lite-GISTexter at DUC2004. In *Proceedings of DUC 2004*. NIST.

Lin, C.-Y. (2004). ROUGE: A package for automatic evaluation of summaries. In *Proceedings of the Workshop on Text Summarization*. Barcelona, ACL.

Mani, I. (2001). *Automatic text summarization*. John Benjamins Publishing Company.

Mani, I., Klein, G., House, D., Hirschman, L., Firmin, T., & Sundheim, B. (2002). SUMMAC: A text summarization evaluation. *Nat. Lang. Eng., 8*(1), 43-68.

Marcu, D. (1999). The automatic construction of large-scale corpora for summarization research. In M. Hearst, F., G., Tong, R. (Eds.), *Proceedings of SIGIR'99 22nd International Conference on Research and Development in Information Retrieval* (pp. 137-144). University of California, Berkeley.

Maynard, D., Bontcheva, K., & Cunningham, H. (2003). Towards a semantic extraction of named entities. In *Proceedings Recent Advances in Natural*, Borovets, Bulgaria.

Miller, G.A. (1995, November). WordNet: A lexical database. *Communications of the ACM, 38*(11), 39-41.

Mitkov, R. (1999). *Anaphora resolution: The state of the art*. University of Wolverhampton, Wolverhampton.

Pearson, J. (1998). Terms in context. *Studies in corpus linguistics: Vol. 1*. John Benjamins Publishing Company.

Pollock, J., & Zamora, A. (1975). Automatic abstracting research at chemical abstracts service. *Journal of Chemical Information and Computer Sciences, 15*(4), 226-232.

Radev, D., Allison, T., Blair-Goldensohn, S., Blitzer, S., Çelebi, A., Dimitrov, S., et al. (2004, May). MEAD: A platform for multidocument multilingual text summarization. In *Proceedings of LREC 2004*, Lisbon, Portugal.

Radev, D.R., & McKeown, K.R. (1998). Generating natural language summaries from multiple on-line sources. *Computational Linguistics, 24*, 469-500.

Saggion, H. (2002). Shallow-based robust summarization. In *ATALA Workshop*, Paris.

Saggion, H., & Gaizauskas, R. (2004a). Mining on-line sources for defnition knowledge. In *Proceedings of the 17th FLAIRS 2004*, Miami Beach, Florida. AAAI.

Saggion, H., & Gaizauskas, R. (2004b). Multidocument summarization by cluster/profile relevance and redundancy removal. In *Proceedings of the Document Understanding Conference 2004*. NIST.

Saggion, H., & Lapalme, G. (2002). Generating indicative-informative summaries with SumUM. *Computational Linguistics, 28*(4), 497-526.

Saggion, H., Radev, D., Teufel, S., & Lam, W. (2002). Meta-evaluation of summaries in a cross-lingual environment using content-based metrics. In *Proceedings of COLING 2002* (pp. 849-855). Taipei, Taiwan.

Schiffman, B., Mani, I., & Concepcion, K. (2001). Producing biographical summaries: Combining linguistic knowledge with corpus statistics. In *Proceedings of EACL/ACL*.

Wang, T., Li, Y., Bontcheva, K., Cunningham, H., & Wang, J. (2006). Automatic extraction of hierarchical relations from text. In *Proceedings of the Third European Semantic Web Conference (ESWC 2006)*. Lecture Notes in Computer Science 4011. Springer.

Xu, J., Licuanan, A., & Weischedel, R. (2003). TREC2003 QA at BBN: Answering definitional questions. In *Proceedings of TREC-2003*.

Yang, H., Cui, H., Maslennikov, M., Qiu, L., Kan, M.-Y., & Chua, T.-S. (2003). QUALIFIER in TREC-12 QA main task. In *Proceedings of TREC-2003*.

Zhou, L., Ticrea, M., & Hovy, E. (2004). Multi-document biography summarization. In *Proceedings of Empirical Methods in Natural Language Processing*.

Additional Reading

Bagga, A., & Baldwin, B. (1998). Entity-based cross-document coreferencing using the vector space model. In *Proceedings of the 36th Annual Meeting of the Association for Computational Linguistics and the 17th International Conference on Computational Linguistics (COLING-ACL'98)*.

Blair-Goldensohn, S., McKeown, K., & Schlaikjer, A. (2003). A hybrid approach for answering definitional questions. In *Processdings of the 26th ACM SIGIR Conference*. Toronto, Canada: ACM.

Chen, Y., Zhou, M., & Wang, S. (2006). Reranking answers for definitional QA using language modeling. In *Proceedings of COLING/AACL 2006*.

Document Understanding Conferences (DUC) (2002) Retrieved August 9, 2007 from http://duc.nist.gov/

Fleischman, M., Hovy, E., & Echihabi, A. (2003). Offline strategies for online question answering: Answering questions before they are asked. In *Proceedings of the ACL 2003* (pp. 1-7).

Hildebrandt, W., Katz, B., & Lin, J. (2004). Answering definition questions using multiple knowledge sources. In *Proceedings of HLT-NAACL 2004* (pp. 49-56).

Hirschman, L., & Gaizauskas, R. (Eds.). (2001). Special issue on question answering. *Journal of Natural Language Engineering, 7*(4).

Mani, I., & Maybury, M.T. (Eds.). (1999). *Advances in automatic text summarization*. The MIT Press.

Maybury, M.T. (Ed.). (2004). *New directions in question answering*. AAAI Press.

Phan. X.-H, Nguyen, L.-M., & Horiguchi, S. (2006). Personal name resolution crossover documents by a semantics-based approach. *IEICE Transactions on Information and Systems, E89-D*(2), 825-836.

Radev, D., Hovy, E., & McKeown K. (2002, December). Special issue on summarization. *Computational Linguistics, 8*(4).

Ravichandran, D., & Hovy, E. (2002). Learning surface text patterns for a question answering system. In *Proceedings of the 40th Annual Meeting of the Association for Computational Linguistics* (pp. 41-47).

Saggion, H. (2006). Text summarization resources and evaluation. LREC 2006 Tutorial Notes. Retrieved March 26, 2007, from http://www.dcs.shef.ac.uk/~saggion/sum-biblio.pdf

Sierra, G., Medina, A., Alarcón, R., & Aguilar, C. (2003). Towards the extraction of conceptual information from corpora. In D. Archer, P. Rayson, A. Wilson & T. McEnery (Eds). In *Proceedings of the Corpus Linguistics 2003 Conference* (pp. 691–697). University Centre for Computer Corpus Research on Language.

Text Retrieval Conferences—Question Answering Track (TREC/QA). Retrieved March 26, 2007, from *http://trec.nist.gov/data/qa.html*

Zhou, L., Chin-Yew Lin, C.Y., & Hovy, E. (2006). Summarizing answers for complicated questions. In *Proceedings of LREC 2006.*

ENDNOTE

1. http://www.dcs.shef.ac.uk/~saggion/summa/default.htm

Chapter V
Deriving Taxonomy from Documents at Sentence Level

Ying Liu
Hong Kong Polytechnic University, Hong Kong SAR, China

Han Tong Loh
National University of Singapore, Singapore

Wen Feng Lu
National University of Singapore, Singapore

ABSTRACT

This chapter introduces an approach of deriving taxonomy from documents using a novel document profile model that enables document representations with the semantic information systematically generated at the document sentence level. A frequent word sequence method is proposed to search for the salient semantic information and has been integrated into the document profile model. The experimental study of taxonomy generation using hierarchical agglomerative clustering has shown a significant improvement in terms of F_{score} based on the document profile model. A close examination reveals that the integration of semantic information has a clear contribution compared to the classic bag-of-words approach. This study encourages us to further investigate the possibility of applying document profile model over a wide range of text based mining tasks.

INTRODUCTION

A well-formed taxonomy, also known as concept hierarchy, provides a critical assistance in information browsing and navigation. There are many scenarios where the taxonomy generation is of great interest to be applied. For one instance in information retrieval, given a specific query and the set of documents retrieved, we are curious whether these documents actually share multiple topics and how they link to each other. For another example in enterprise intelligence and knowledge management, product designers are interested to find out, based on the service records, how customer complaints can be grouped to further understand product defects. The taxonomy derived from such text documents can offer a comprehensive but concise form to reveal

Figure 1. An example of articles from Google news and the taxonomy we expect

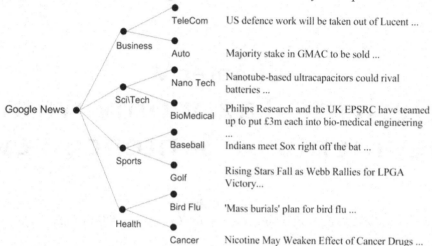

how the information is interwoven. Therefore, its importance has been well recognized in information retrieval and text mining. Figure 1 shows an example of articles from Google News and the taxonomy we expect.

Most existing studies on taxonomy generation are reported using a hierarchical clustering approach (Mirkin, 1996). Hierarchical clustering algorithms work by grouping data objects into a tree of clusters. The methods can be further classified into hierarchical agglomerative clustering (HAC) and hierarchical divisive clustering, depending on whether the hierarchy is formed in a bottom-up or top-down fashion (Jain, Murty & Flynn, 1999).

In hierarchical clustering, the similarity between any pair of clusters, for example, C_i and C_j, is usually calculated in a manner as single linkage, complete linkage, and group average linkage. For single linkage, the similarity is defined as the highest similarity between two objects, for example, O_a and O_b, in C_i and C_j respectively. For complete linkage, the similarity is defined as the smallest similarity between O_a and O_b in C_i and C_j. Lastly, for group average linkage, the similarity is defined as the averaged similarity between all pairs of members in C_i and C_j that are being considered.

In applying HAC to a textual dataset, cosine similarity is usually adopted as a similarity measure, and each document in the dataset is initially considered as a cluster. For a textual dataset with N documents, a $N \times N$ document similarity matrix is generated to compare the closeness of a document with every other document in the dataset. Cosine similarity is initially computed between the documents, and the similarity matrix is then updated with the values. The two most similar documents are merged to form a new cluster, and the cluster similarity is re-evaluated between the resulting set of (N-1) clusters, using the linkage method specified. The process of merging and re-evaluation of cluster similarity continues until some stopping criterion is achieved. In divisive hierarchical clustering, the process is reversed; all documents are initially grouped in one big cluster, and subsequently subdivided into smaller clusters based on dissimilarity among clusters, until some stopping criterion is achieved. For both methods, the stopping criterion can be a target number of clusters found or the similarity between the two closest clusters not exceeding a certain threshold.

In literature, various efforts have been reported. One origin says that text clustering starts with the cluster hypothesis formulated by van Rijsbergen, that is, comparing keyword based and document based clustering (Jardine & van Rijsbergen, 1971; van Rijsbergen, 1979). Salton integrates it into the SMART retrieval system as the cluster-based search (Salton, 1971). Willett has compared several linkage methods in measuring the similarity of documents, highlighted the higher demand of computational cost for complete linkage, and proposed a document clustering approach which is essentially a binary tree based hierarchical generation (Willett, 1988). Sanderson and Croft report their effort in deriving concept hierarchy based on the salient words and phrases extracted from documents (Sanderson & Croft, 1999). Their approach is formulated due to the observation of co-occurrence which tends to indicate the document association. While the aforementioned linkage methods are all term frequency based similarity measurement, Resnik (1999) presents a semantic similarity in an IS-A taxonomy based on the notion of information content and shows its effectiveness compared to the traditional edge counting approach. Muller, Dorre, Gerstl, and Seiffert (1999) have launched the Tax-Gen project using HAC. While it demonstrates that HAC is able to group rich text documents into coherent clusters, some open questions are left, such as the labeling of clusters at the higher level. Vaithyanathan and Dom (2000) propose a model based hierarchical clustering by formulating an objective function based on a Bayesian analysis. The key idea is based on the observation that some features may share a common distribution pattern across certain clusters while being differently distributed in others. However, the computational cost in generating the cluster model is more expensive. Assisted by a large corpus which defines the semantic neighborhood of a new word, Widdows (2003) reports how this unknown word can be placed correctly into an existing taxonomy by combining the merits of latent semantic analysis and POS tagging. This will be helpful in building an evolving taxonomy. The recent study from Chuang and Chien (2005) demonstrates how the concept taxonomy can be generated from a collection of text segments, short text forms such as search queries. The essential idea is to send text segments as the Web search queries, and extract extra features from the retrieved results to enrich the background information of segments. They also borrow the Min-Max idea of Ding, He, Zha, Gu, and Simon (2001) in generating the multi-way-tree, a wide but shallow taxonomy.

After the survey, we notice that while it is generally understood that word sequences, for example, "finite state machine," "machine learning," and "supply chain management," convey more semantic information in representing textual documents than single terms, they have seldom been explored in text clustering and are rarely integrated into the current study of taxonomy generation. In fact, it is lack of a systematic approach to generate such high quality word sequences automatically. As a matter of fact, most existing clustering studies only consider documents as bag-of-words (BoW), that is, each unique word in the document is considered as the smallest unit to convey information. The rich semantic information resident in word sequences has been ignored. In view of the status quo, we propose a novel document model which involves a systematic search and generation of word sequences at sentence level. The key idea behind our approach is to involve more semantic information in the document modeling. These semantic indexes are dynamically maintained and will provide more clues to link up documents in clustering.

In the rest of this chapter, we first introduce the concept of maximal frequent word sequence (MFS) and explain how to use MFS in soliciting high quality word sequences in a systematic way. A document model with more semantic information embodied by MFSs is then proposed. After a brief review of hierarchical agglomerative clustering, the experimental studies and results of taxonomy generation using HAC based on the proposed document model are reported. Finally, we have more discussion with respect to the proposed model and conclude.

DOCUMENT MODELING WITH SALIENT SEMANTIC FEATURES

borrow from information retrieval, the most widely accepted document model in both text clustering and classification is probably vector space model (Jurafsky & Martin, 2000; Manning & Schütze, 1999; Sebastiani, 2002), that is, a document d_i is represented as a vector of term weights $\vec{v}_i(w_{1i}, w_{2i}, ..., w_{|\Gamma|i})$, where Γ is the collection of terms that occur at least once in the document collection D. The term weights $w_{|\Gamma|i}$ is often computed in *tfidf* manner, that is, *term frequency* times *inverse documents frequency*, (Baeza-Yates & Ribeiro-Neto, 1999; Salton & Buckley, 1988; Salton & McGill, 1983; van Rijsbergen, 1979). The more popular "ltc" form (Baeza-Yates & Ribeiro-Neto; Salton & Buckley; Salton & McGill) is given by,

$$tfidf(t_i, d_j) = tf(t_i, d_j) \times \log(\frac{N}{N(t_i)}) \qquad (1)$$

and its normalized version is:

$$w_{i,j} = \frac{tfidf(t_i, d_j)}{\sqrt{\sum_{k=1}^{|\Gamma|} tfidf(t_k, d_j)^2}} \qquad (2)$$

where N and $|\Gamma|$ denote the total number of documents and unique terms contained in the collection respectively, and $N(t_i)$ represents the number of documents in the collection in which term t_i occurs at least once, and

$$tf(t_i, d_j) = \begin{cases} 1 + \log(n(t_i, d_j)), & \text{if } n(t_i, d_j) > 0 \\ 0, & \text{otherwise} \end{cases} \qquad (3)$$

where $n(t_i, d_j)$ is the number of times that term t_i occurs in document d_j. In practice, the summation in equation (2) is only concerned about the terms occurred in document d_j.

Besides the vector space model, some other commonly used models are the Boolean model, the probability model (Fuhr, 1985; Robertson, 1977), the inference network model (Turtle & Croft, 1989), and the statistical language model. Essentially, a statistical language model is concerned about the probabilities of word sequences, denoted as $P(S : w_1, w_2, ..., w_n)$ (Manning & Schütze, 1999). These sequences can be phrases, clauses, and sentences. Their probabilities are often estimated from a large text corpus. As reported, statistical language modeling has been successfully applied to many domains, such as its original application in speech recognition and part-of-speech tagging (Charniak, 1993), information retrieval (Hiemstra, 1998; Miller, Leek, & Schwartz, 1999; Ponte & Croft, 1998), and spoken language understanding (Zue, 1995). In practice, the most widely used statistical language model is N-gram model (Manning & Schütze, 1999), such as:

Unigram:

$$P(S : w_1, w_2, ..., w_n) = P(w_1)P(w_2)...P(w_n)$$

Bigram:

$$P(S : w_1, w_2, ..., w_n) = P(w_1)P(w_2|w_1)...P(w_n|w_{n-1})$$

Trigram:

$$P(S : w_1, w_2, ..., w_n) = P(w_1)P(w_2|w_1)P(w_3|w_{1,2})...P(w_n|w_{n-2,n-1})$$

The N-gram model is formed based on the observation that the occurrence of a specific word may be affected by its immediately preceding words. In unigram model, words are assumed to be independent. Hence, the probability of a word sequence S is approximated by the product of all individual words' probabilities. In bigram and trigram model, more context information has been taken into consideration, that is, the probability of word depends on its previous one word or two words respectively.

Most studies in both text clustering and classification adopt the vector space model, where the terms, often called features in the machine learning literature, are a set of single words occurred in the corpus, that is, BoW approach (Chuang & Chien, 2005; Jain et al., 1999; Lewis, Yang, Rose, & Li, 2004; Muller et al., 1999; Sebastiani, 2002; Seo & Sycara, 2004; Willett, 1988; Yang & Liu, 1999). In text classification, we have witnessed some recent efforts by transforming the term-based feature space into a concept-based feature space. These include the work to use n-grams, phrases, or co-occurred words as context information to enrich document representations (Dumais, Platt, Heckerman, & Sahami, 1998; Lewis, 1992; Sahlgren & Cöster, 2004), or to tackle the linguistic variation such as synonyms, vocabulary, and word choice by introducing techniques like synonym clusters and latent semantic analysis (LSA) to handle the overlapped meanings of different words (Baker & McCallum, 1998; Cai & Hofmann, 2003). We noted that some of these approaches are either expensive to compute or the results are not human readable. Moreover, the performance gained is neither consistent nor easy to tell whether the improvement is achieved due to the concept handling or other reasons such as boosting. Surprisingly, previous efforts in generating more sophisticated document representation have not shown significant improvement than those BoW based approaches (Sebastiani, 2002).

However, the limitation with BoW approach is apparent. Single words are not the only units to convey the thematic information. While we observe that sequences like "finite state machine," "machine learning," and "supply chain management" are surely in a better position to represent the content of sentences and documents, they are rarely integrated into the current study of taxonomy generation. As a matter of fact, these sequences are in a superior stand to supply the critical information that differentiates a cluster node from its siblings, parents, and children nodes. We have examined the previous work using

phrases or bigrams as the indexes. We repeated their procedures to generate phrases and bigrams in several datasets. Two major problems are noted. In the first place, we observed that there are many phrases irrelevant to the themes of documents. We suspect that using these irrelevant phrases as indexes does not give them a better presentation, and indeed confuses the learning algorithms. Secondly, the size of indexing terms, that is, the dimension of document features, has been dramatically expanded. The well-known problem of data sparsity in document vectors becomes even worse. This alerts us that the word sequences should be carefully selected. Furthermore, to our knowledge, we are lacking a systematic approach to automatically generate such fine word sequences as aforementioned. In summary, we are interested in venturing beyond the existing document models commonly used in hierarchical clustering for the purpose of taxonomy generation. We are concerned about whether we can explicitly generate the salient word sequences and integrate them in the taxonomy generation in chasing better performance.

Frequent Word Sequences

In deriving the taxonomy from documents, we are concerned about how to search for a fine set of word sequences which embody the salient content information of each document. In our work, we extend Ahonen's work in finding the maximal frequent word sequence (MFS) out of a textual dataset (Ahonen-Myka, 1999). An MFS is a sequence of words that is "frequent in the document collection and, moreover, that is not contained in any other longer frequent sequence. (p. 2)" A word sequence is frequent if it appears in at least σ documents, where σ is a prespecified support threshold. The goal of MFS algorithm is to find all maximal frequent phrases in the textual dataset.

The strength of MFS method is that it employs a versatile technique for finding sequential text phrases from full text, allowing, if desired, gaps between the words in a phrase. For example, the word sequence "product knowledge databases" can be extracted as a frequent phrase even if its occurrence is in the form of:

"...product management using knowledge databases..."

"...product data in knowledge databases..."

"...product specifications, knowledge databases..."

in the supporting documents of the document collection. The maximum gap allowed between words in a sequence is determined by the maximal word gap parameter g.

In its original application, the MFSs discovered acted as content descriptors of the documents in which they occurred (Ahonen-Myka, Heinonen, Klemettinen, & Verkamo, 1999; Yap, Loh, Shen, & Liu, 2006). These descriptors are compact but human-readable, and have the potential to be used in subsequent analysis of the documents.

Essentially, we are interested in applying the MFS method to a collection of documents and using the MFSs discovered as the key to render the documents' themes. Through adjusting the support σ and the gap g, our aim is to search an optimal set of MFSs to represent the most important content of the documents. We notice that when we increase the gap g resulting in longer word sequences, more MFS phrases are generated. While this may increase the coverage of topics, many of them are discovered as irrelevant to the category themes. This is alleviated by increasing the support threshold σ.

Previously, MFS has been applied to text classification and topic detection (Ahonen-Myka, 1999; Yap et al., 2006). The limitation with current MFS method and its application is that the MFSs must be generated and supported based on a group of documents which are assumed to be conceptually similar, for example, sharing the same category labels or thematic topics. This assumption is often weak in a clustering scenario. In order to exploit what an individual document really contains, we propose an extended approach to select frequent single words and generate MFSs simultaneously at the document sentence level. Our method aims to provide a uniform model primarily from the perspective of a document itself. We believe that the MFSs found at the sentence level within a document will provide more clues with respect to its thematic information.

Document Model

In order to facilitate our explanation in the following sections, we introduce a concept called document profile (DP). In essence, DP is concerned about how documents should be represented. In the BoW approach, documents are basically defined by all single words which have occurred at least once in the document collection. In our work, DPs are given by a set of single words and MFSs. The particular questions are how to search them and what should be included in documents' DPs.

Algorithm 1 gives the details how we generate the DP for a document. It starts with a set of sentences $S_j\{s_{j1}, s_{j2}, ..., s_{jn}\}$ of document d_i. Based on the sentence support threshold σ prespecified, a set of frequent single words $\Gamma_j\{t_{j1}, t_{j2}, ..., t_{jn}\}$ are selected. Given the prespecified word gap g, $\Gamma_j\{t_{j1}, t_{j2}, ..., t_{jn}\}$ is extended to a set of ordered word pairs. For instance, supposing $g = 1$ and the original sentence s_{jn} comprises the words "*ABCDEFGHI*." After the identification of frequent single words, only words "*ABCEFI*" are left for s_{jn}. Therefore, the ordered pairs arising out of s_{jn} would be "*AB*," "*AC*," "*BC*," "*CE*," and "*EF*." Pairs like "*BE*" and "*CF*" are not considered because the number of words between "*BE*" and "*CF*" exceed the g parameter. Each ordered pair is then stored into a hash data structure, along with its occurrence information, such as location and frequency. This is repeated for all sentences in d_j, with a

Algorithm 1. Generation of document profile (DP)

```
Input:    S_j{s_{j1}, s_{j2}, ..., s_{jn}}: a set of n pre-processed sentences in document d_j
          σ: sentence support
          g: maximal word gap

1.    for all sentences s ∈ S_j
              identify the frequent single words t, Γ_j ← t;
2.    expand Γ_j to Grams_2, frequent ordered word pairs
      //Discovery phase
3.    k = 2;
4.    MFS_j = null;
5.    while Grams_k not empty
6.        for all seq ∈ Grams_k
7.            if seq is frequent
8.                if seq is not a subsequence of some Seq ∈ MFS_j
                      // Expand phase: expand frequent seq
9.                    max = expand(seq);
10.                   MFS_j = MFS_j ∪ max;
11.                   if max = seq
12.                       remove seq from Grams_k
13.           else
14.               remove seq from Grams_k
          // Join phase: generate set of (k + 1)-seqs
15.       Grams_{k+1} = join(Grams_k);
16.       k = k + 1;
17.   DP_j ← Γ_j + MFS_j;
18.   return DP_j
```

corresponding update of the hash. Thereafter, each ordered pair in the hash is examined, and the pairs that are supported by at least σ sentences are considered frequent. This set of frequent pairs is named $Grams_2$.

The next phase, the *Discovery* phase, forms the main body of Algorithm 1. It is an iteration of gram expansion for the grams in the current $Grams_k$, and gram joining, to form $Grams_{k+1}$. Only grams that are frequent and not subsequences of the previously discovered MFSs are considered suitable for expansion. The latter condition is in place to avoid a rediscovery of MFSs that have already been found. This Expand-Join iteration continues until an empty gram-set is produced from a *Join* phase.

We further break the *Discovery* phase into the *Expand* phase and the *Join* phase. In the *Expand* phase, every possibility of expansion of an input word sequence *seq* form $Grams_k$ is explored. The expansion process continues, for that particular input word sequence *seq*, until the resulting sequence

is no longer frequent. The last frequent sequence achieved in the expansion, *seq'*, will be an MFS by definition, and it will be stored together with its occurrence information. This process of gram expansion and information recording continues, for every suitable gram in $Grams_k$. Subsequently, the *Join* phase follows, which consists of a simple join operation amongst the grams left in $Grams_k$, to form $Grams_{k+1}$, that is, the set of grams that are of length (*k*+1). When an empty gram set is produced from the *Join* phase, namely, no more grams are left for further expansion, the set of MFS_j and $Γ_j$ is returned for document d_j. In the end, the DP_j for document d_j is composed of $Γ_j$ plus MFS_j found. This process continues for the next document d_{j+1}.

Figure 2 illustrates how we generate the document DPs and index documents from the system point of view. Suppose we have generated $DP_{j+1}\{MFS_{j+1} + Γ_{j+1}\}$ for document d_{j+1}, the unification step will examine whether any MFSs in MFS_j is a subsequence of any MFSs in MFS_{j+1}

Figure 2. The general flowchart of Document Profile discovery for documents

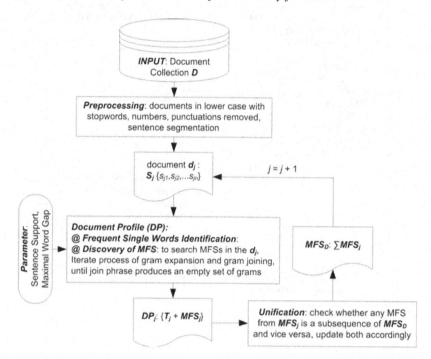

and vice versa. For instance, "wireless network" and "wireless network mobile computing" are two MFSs from MFS_j and MFS_{j+1} respectively. Apparently, "wireless network" is a subsequence of the latter, and hence, it will be replaced by the latter in MFS_j with its occurrence information being left intact. As a result, the system dynamically maintains an overall MFS list, MFS_D, which covers every single MFS found in the collection D. This examination and unification step is deemed as the key to provide more clues with regard to document thematic information and retain the dimension of feature space in a small size.

An Illustration Example

In this subsection we give an example to illustrate how the proposed document modeling can be accomplished. Given two documents d_j and d_{j+1} which are actually labeled under the same topic, Figure 3 lists their details.

Immediately, we preprocess the documents. These include various standard procedures that are commonly utilized in text processing, such as lexical analysis (also known as tokenization), stop word removal, number and punctuation removal, and word stemming (Porter, 1980). Please note that the sentence segmentation has been retained. Figure 4 shows the details of d_j and d_{j+1} after preprocessing. In the classic BoW approach, the document processing will generally stop here before the document is sent for term weighting, that is, to convert the document from its textual form to a numeric vector (Baeza-Yates & Ribeiro-Neto, 1999; Salton & McGill, 1983; Sebastiani, 2002).

Given the sentence support $\sigma = 2$ and the word gap $g = 1$, Figure 5 gives the details of DP_j and DP_{j+1}. After document profiling, the number of indexing terms has been reduced from 80 in BoW approach to 28 in DP model. The details are presented in Figure 6 and 7 respectively.

Figure 3. Two original documents, d_j and d_{j+1}

......

d_j: Characterization of surface fault patterns with application to a layered manufacturing process. Detection of faults is a continuing need in all manufacturing processes. This need is more pronounced in new manufacturing processes where continual product improvement is desired. A systematic approach is developed for addressing this need. Contemporary experimental and surface analysis techniques provide a basis for incrementally diagnosing the fault mechanisms leading to surface deviations. Based on this general approach, a maturing layered manufacturing process is investigated, notably, Selective Laser Sintering (SLS). First through experimental analysis it is shown that layer thickness and part orientation affect surface quality. Using these experimental results, random process analysis is carried out to determine the specific fault patterns. The quantification of these fault patterns leads to the identification of fault sources, providing a foundation for monitoring and control.

d_{j+1}: On the Integration of Layered Manufacturing and Material Removal Processes. In this paper, we develop methodologies for the integration of layered manufacturing and traditional material removal processes into an integrated manufacturing setup. The scenarios under which this integration would be beneficial are identified and algorithms for the integration developed. As examples, we consider two current layered manufacturing technologies that use material removal operations as a part of their process. The benefits of our procedure are demonstrated by examples. The exterior sculpting of layers transforming 2.5D layers into 3D layers was studied in this paper. Two different processes for sculpting the layer were considered NC milling and shaping the surface with trowels. Three different approaches for the integration of NC milling with LM were identified.

......

Figure 4. d_j and d_{j+1} after preprocessing

......

d_j: character surfac fault pattern applic layer manufactur process. detect fault continu manufactur process. pronounc manufactur process continu product improv desir. systemat approach develop address. contemporari experiment surfac analysi techniqu provid basi increment diagnos fault mechan lead surfac deviat. base approach matur layer manufactur process investig notabl select laser sinter sl experiment analysi shown layer thick orient affect surfac qualiti. us experiment result random process analysi carri determin specif fault pattern. quantif fault pattern lead identif fault sourc provid foundat monitor control.

d_{j+1}: integr layer manufactur materi remov process. paper develop methodolog integr layer manufactur tradit materi remov process integr manufactur setup. scenario integr benefici identifi algorithm integr develop. exampl consid current layer manufactur technolog materi remov oper process. benefit procedur demonstr exampl. exterior sculpt layer transform layer layer studi paper. process sculpt layer consid mill shape surfac trowel. approach integr mill identifi.

......

Figure 5. DP_j and DP_{j+1}, where sentence support is two and word gap is one

......

DP_j: analysi analysi analysi approach approach continu continu experiment experiment experiment experiment_analysi experiment_analysi fault fault fault fault fault fault_lead fault_lead ... layer_manufactur_process layer_manufactur_process ... process process process process process provid provid surfac surfac surfac

DP_{j+1}: consid consid develop develop exampl exampl identifi identifi integr integr integr integr ... integr_layer_manufactur_materi_remov_process integr_layer_manufactur_materi_remov_process layer layer layer layer layer ... remov remov remov sculpt sculpt sculpt_layer sculpt_layer

......

Figure 6. Indexing terms in DP modeling approach for d_j and d_{j+1}

analysi	experiment_analysi	integr_layer_manufactur_materi_remov_process	pattern
approach	fault	layer	process
consid	fault_lead	lead	provid
continu	fault_pattern	manufactur	remov
develop	identifi	materi	sculpt
exampl	integr	mill	sculpt_layer
experiment	integr_identifi	paper	surfac

Figure 7. Indexing terms in BoW modeling approach for d_j and d_{j+1}

address	current	increment	paper	shape
affect	demonstr	integr	pattern	shown
algorithm	desir	investig	procedur	sinter
analysi	detect	laser	process	sl
applic	determin	layer	product	sourc
approach	develop	lead	pronounc	specif
base	deviat	manufactur	provid	studi
basi	diagnos	materi	qualiti	surfac
benefici	exampl	matur	quantif	systemat
benefit	experiment	mechan	random	techniqu
carri	exterior	methodolog	remov	technolog
character	fault	mill	result	thick
consid	foundat	monitor	scenario	tradit
contemporari	identif	notabl	sculpt	transform
continu	identifi	oper	select	trowel
control	improv	orient	setup	us

Figure 8. Sentence frequence of terms in DP model and term frequence of terms in BoW model

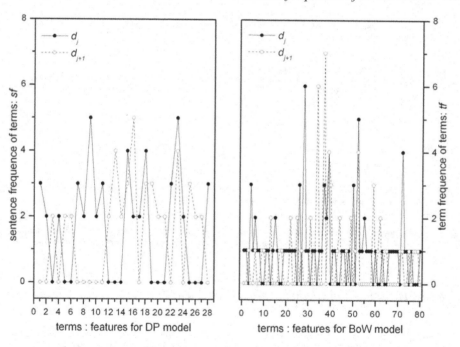

In DP_j, one of the MFSs found is *layer_manufactur_process*, which is a subsequence of another longer MFS *integr_layer_manufactur_materi_remov_process* discovered in DP_{j+1}. The latter will supersede *layer_manufactur_process* in DP_j. But the occurrence information of *layer_manufactur_process*, for example, sentence frequence, remains unchanged in DP_j.

Figure 8 illustrates the sentence frequence of indexing terms, that is, frequent single words plus MFSs, in our DP modeling approach and the term frequence of indexing terms, that is, single words, in BoW approach. Compared to BoW model, we note that given a smaller size of indexes in DP model, that is, 28 terms, both document vectors have actually become less sparse.

If we evaluate the similarity between d_j and d_{j+1} in terms of their cosine similarity, that is, the cosine value of the angle between two corresponding document vectors $\vec{v}_j$ and $\vec{v}_{j+1}$:

$$sim(d_j, d_{j+1}) = \cos(\vec{v}_j, \vec{v}_{j+1}) = \frac{\vec{v}_j \cdot \vec{v}_{j+1}}{\left\| \vec{v}_j \right\| \left\| \vec{v}_{j+1} \right\|} \quad (4)$$

then we have

$$sim(d_j, d_{j+1})_{DP} = 0.3818$$

$$sim(d_j, d_{j+1})_{BoW} = 0.3523$$

This illustration example helps to reveal that our proposed DP model is able to increase the similarity value of two similar documents.

HIERARCHICAL AGGLOMERATIVE CLUSTERING

A hierarchical agglomerative clustering (HAC) produces a binary tree hierarchy of clusters (Jain et al., 1999; Mirkin, 1996). It starts by assigning each object in the data set to its own cluster. Given a similarity function, it proceeds to search the pair of objects that are most similar and forms them as a new object, that is, a cluster. Subsequently, the similarity between the newly formed object and the rest will be computed and updated accordingly. It repeatedly performs this search and fusion until all objects have been joined as a single cluster, that is, the root of the hierarchy. Algorithm 2 gives the details of HAC.

Using HAC algorithm to derive the taxonomy from documents, the key is the function chosen to measure how similar the pair of document clusters is. In our work, we consider the most commonly used intercluster similarity schemes:

Algorithm 2. Hierarchical agglomerative clustering

Input:	$O : \{\vec{v}_1, \vec{v}_2, \ldots \vec{v}_n\}$: object vectors
	f_{sim} : similarity function
1.	for all $\vec{v}_i$, $1 \leq i \leq n$ do
2.	$C_i \leftarrow \vec{v}_i$;
3.	$\Im$: pairwise similarity matrix, $f_{sim}(C_k, C_l)$;
4.	for all C_l, $1 \leq i \leq n$ do
5.	$C_{n+i} \leftarrow C_k \cup C_l$, if $f_{sim}(C_k, C_l)$ is the highest in $\Im$;
6.	update $\Im$ with C_{n+i};
7.	return the agglomerative tree

Single linkage: $f_{simSL}(C_k, C_l) = \max sim(\vec{v}_i, \vec{v}_j)$, where $\vec{v}_i \in C_k, \vec{v}_j \in C_l$

Complete linkage: $f_{simCL}(C_k, C_l) = \min sim(\vec{v}_i, \vec{v}_j)$ where $\vec{v}_i \in C_k, \vec{v}_j \in C_l$

Average linkage: $f_{simAL}(C_k, C_l) = sim(C_k, C_l)$,

where $sim(C_k, C_l) = \frac{1}{|C_k||C_l|} \sum\sum sim(\vec{v}_i, \vec{v}_j)$

and $\vec{v}_i \in C_k, \vec{v}_j \in C_l$

The similarity function of two document vectors, that is, $sim(\vec{v}_i, \vec{v}_j)$, is still the cosine similarity defined in equation (4). In the case of single linkage scheme, the similarity of a document cluster pair is given by the highest similarity score between two documents in both clusters. In contrast, the complete linkage scheme adopts the lowest similarity score. The average linkage symbolizes a compromise between these two extremes.

In literature, these three linkage methods are useful in different types of applications. The group average method favors ball-shaped clusters (Kaufman & Rousseeuw, 1990), the single linkage method can delineate non-ellipsoidal clusters (Johnson & Wichern, 2002), and the complete linkage method is able to identify compact clusters that not well separated (Kaufman & Rousseeuw, 1990).

EXPERIMENTS AND RESULTS

Experimental studies have been carried out to test whether the taxonomy generation using HAC is able to perform better based on the proposed DP model. We used a real-world data collection, that is, Manufacturing Corpus Version 1 (MCV1) (Liu, Loh, & Tor, 2004). MCV1 is an archive of 1434 manufacturing related engineering papers which we have gathered from the Society of Manufacturing Engineers (SME). It combines all engineering technical papers from SME between year 1998 and year 2000. All documents have been manually classified. There are totally 18 major categories in MCV1.

Figure 9 gives the details of MCV1 used in the experiment and the number of documents in each category. Figure 10 reveals the profile of sentence frequence in MCV1's documents. On average, there are more than six sentences in each document. Only 12 documents possess two sentences each.

To measure the overall quality of different taxonomies derived, we adopted the F score as the performance evaluation metric (Larsen & Aone, 1999). The F_{score} of cluster C_i with respect to C_j is defined as:

$$F_{i,j} = \frac{2r_{i,j}p_{i,j}}{r_{i,j} + p_{i,j}}$$

where $r_{i,j}$ and $p_{i,j}$ are recall and precision. Suppose n_i and n_j are the number of documents in C_i and C_j respectively, then $r_{i,j}$ and $p_{i,j}$ are defined as $n_{i,j}$ / n_i and $n_{i,j}$ / n_j, where $n_{i,j}$ is the number of documents of C_i that has been grouped in C_j. The F_{score} shares exactly identical concerns as the F_β measure widely used in information retrieval (Baeza-Yates & Ribeiro-Neto, 1999; van Rijsbergen, 1979), where $\beta = 1$, that is, F_1 metric.

Figure 9. Category details and number of documents in MCV1

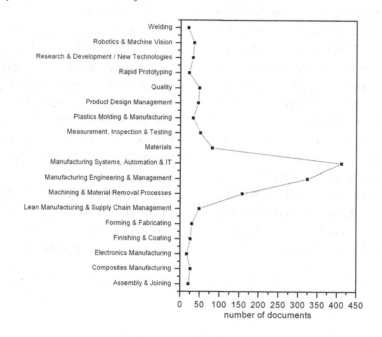

Figure 10. The profile of sentence frequence in MCV1's documents

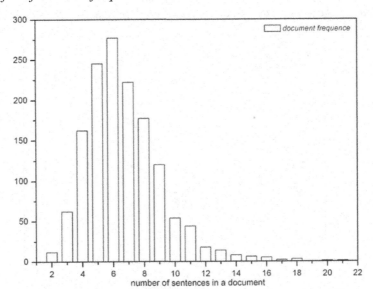

Table 1. Feature size (dimension) and the average size of document vector in BoW approach and the proposed DP model, where in "σ:X g:Y", σ is the sentence support and g is the word gap

	BoW	Document Profile					
		σ:2 g:0	σ:2 g:1	σ:2 g:2	σ:3 g:0	σ:3 g:1	σ:3 g:2
Dimension	7517	5553	6379	8177	3460	3876	4269
Average size of document vector, $\vec{v}_j$	52	21	27	32	7	8	8

The F_{score} of any category is its highest F_{score} value achieved at any node in the hierarchy. As for the entire taxonomy, the overall F_{score} is computed as the weighted F_{score} of each individual category, namely:

$$F = \sum_{i=1}^{c} \frac{n_i}{n} \max(F_{i,j})$$

where c is the total number of categories and n is the total number of documents. This is also known as macro-averaged F_1 measure in the information retrieval and text classification (Baeza-Yates & Ribeiro-Neto, 1999; Yang & Liu, 1999). In general, the higher the score, the better the taxonomy.

Table 1 shows the details of feature size (dimension) in both BoW approach and the proposed DP

model. Originally, MCV1 possesses 7517 unique words, and on average, each document has 52 words. We started to generate the DPs for MCV1 by varying the sentence support σ and the word gap g in the range of two to three and zero to two respectively. In theory, when the sentence support σ is equivalent to one, the MFSs of a document are its sentences themselves, regardless of the word gap. Due to the profile of sentence frequence in MCV1 shown in Figure 10, we did not search beyond three for support σ. From Table 1, we note that the DP model is able to provide a smaller feature space for MCV1. The average dimension of document vector has been shrunk to less than 50% of its original size. This demonstrates that the inclusion of MFSs won't necessarily enlarge the dimension of textual datasets.

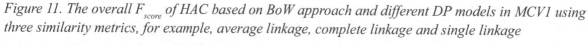

Figure 11. The overall F$_{score}$ of HAC based on BoW approach and different DP models in MCV1 using three similarity metrics, for example, average linkage, complete linkage and single linkage

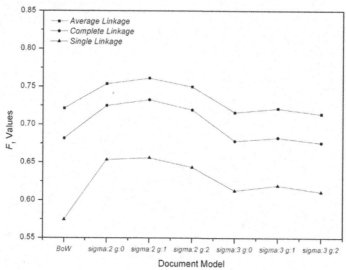

Figure 11 shows the overall performance of HAC based on BoW Approach and different DP models generated over MCV1. Since MCV1 is an imbalanced data set, the reported F_{score} is an average of 10 runs of experiments. From Figure 11, the most important observation is that DP models were able to deliver better performances than what BoW approach could achieve, in terms of F_{score} and when suitable parameter ranges were given, for example, σ = 2. The performance of DP model was largely affected by the value of sentence support σ than the word gap *g* did. When σ was three, DP models could only achieve a performance that was comparable to BoW's results. A close look of experiments shows that a higher sentence support had removed more single words than MFSs in DP models. These single words had their marginal contribution to the similarity comparison, and hence, a slight decrease in performance is noted. Meanwhile, HAC achieved the best performance when the word gap was one. We noted that a higher word gap, that is, two, has actually included more irrelevant MFSs which did not really improve the chance to group similar documents together, and as a result, slightly lowered the overall performance. In general, we

also found that the average linkage and complete linkage metrics performed much better than the single linkage did in terms of F_{score}. The average linkage method, which takes into consideration the similarity of every document pair in two clusters, took the lead in all experiments. Different from the case in BoW approach, the performance gap between the single linkage metric and the average linkage metric has been reduced in DP models. Our examination reveals the fact that incorporating more semantic information in DP models has a significant impact on the similarity computation. For instance, in BoW approach documents centered on "Forming & Fabricating," "Assembly & Joining," and "Welding" are usually dominated by a few frequent words, such as "process," "metal," "manufacturing," and so on. These words do not offer an effective means to represent the difference among documents. In contrast, the integration of MFSs, for example, "draw process," "assembly process," "laser cut process," "weld process," "sheet metal form process," and many others, in these documents' DPs have born more clues to link up similar ones. Figure 12 demonstrates some examples of MFS found from various categories in MCV1.

Figure 12. Some MFS examples for various categories in MCV1

Assembly and Joining	Robotics and Machine Vision
assembl line	ccd camera
assembl process	imag process
assembl sequenc	machin vision
assembl system	parallel manipul
genet algorithm	robot system
line balanc	six degree freedom
......	... ...
Forming and Fabricating	**Rapid Prototyping**
bend oper	comput aid design
die cast	layer manufactur
draw die	rapid prototyp technolog
draw process	revers engin
finit element method	select laser sinter sl
form sheet metal	solid freeform
heat transfer	stereolithographi apparatu sla
laser cut process	......
metal flow	
pressur die	**Welding**
process model	
process paramet	arc weld
process plan	ga metal
roll form	laser weld
sheet metal form process	weld paramet
trial error	weld process
......	......

DISCUSSION

A taxonomy offers insights with respect to the thematic relationship in textual documents. Its automatic generation using hierarchical agglomerative clustering algorithm is a challenging task. Documents may share various topics and the emphases of different topics in a single document are often unevenly stressed. In a strict manner, as an unsupervised learning method, the clustering approach cannot take into account the topical information or category membership. As a result, the performance varies and the final taxonomy generated may not reflect the domain's internal structure or users' interests.

Existing studies primarily focus on using different similarity metrics (Resnik, 1999; Willett, 1988); making use of the external sources, such as Web (Chuang & Chien, 2004), co-occurrence information of terms (Sanderson & Croft, 1999), and context information regarding users' searching patterns (Wen, Nie, & Zhang, 2002); exploiting existing taxonomies and employing explicit category memberships (Agrawal & Srikant, 2001; Chakrabarti, Dom, Agrawal & Raghavan, 1998) and further partitioning of the taxonomy generated

by HAC (Chuang & Chien, 2002). Different from current methods, the proposed DP modeling approach intends to model documents with enriched semantic information based on their generic profile shown at the sentence level. Our method aims to draw the essential profile of document content in a self centered manner, without the assistance of a large enterprise document collection or external knowledge base which is often demanded in classic modeling approaches, for example, probability based document model and statistical language model. The exploration of MFSs at sentence level has provided a systematic solution in searching more semantic information. Our experimental study shows a significant performance improvement when DP models are adopted.

To the best of the authors' knowledge, the generation of MFSs is conceptually similar to the well known Apriori algorithm (Agrawal, Imieliński, & Swami, 1993; Agrawal & Srikant, 1994, 1995). Although in Ahonen's initial work (Ahonen-Myka, 1999), she did not mention any links between MFS and Apriori, MFS is indeed dedicated to mine sequential textual patterns. However, different from Apriori, we do not cap the maximal length of word sequences and we need to

Table 2. The user test of using different number of MFSs as the names for clusters. The average score ranges from 1 to 5, where 1 means the MFSs used are completely irrelevant to the clusters' themes and 5 means completely relevant.

	# of MFS: 1	# of MFS: 2	# of MFS: 3	# of MFS: 4	# of MFS: 5
Avg. Accuracy	4.3	4.4	4.8	4.8	4.7

specify the word-gap-in-between in MFS. In the original proposal and its application of Apriori, for example, basket data mining, the gap-in-between may not play a significant role in identifying the shopping pattern of a customer. For example, the manager may not care about when or in what exact sequence the customer picks up beers and snacks. However, we are afraid that is not true in word sequences. A loose pattern, that is, a word sequence with a wide gap among its words, will reduce the effectiveness of using MFSs to represent the core content of documents. In fact, it has generated more meaningless sequences.

The development of DP model has given the textual documents some unique advantages. In the first place, it will be ideal if a concise name can be assigned to the clusters formed. This is often referred as cluster naming. We acknowledge that cluster naming is still a difficult task largely because of the nature of clustering approach, and, hence, very few researchers have reported their solutions to label the clusters, such as using frequent single words (Muller et al., 1999) and a type of co-occurrence known as subsumption (Lawrie, Croft & Rosenberg, 2001). In our DP model, the word sequences found by MFS search have demonstrated their nice quality in representing the essential contents of clusters as shown in Figure 12. Our evaluation shows that on average only 5-8% of MFSs found are completely irrelevant to the themes of clusters, for example, "paper discuss," and "figure show." We then conjectured that the longest MFSs of each cluster can be considered as the cluster name. We carried out a simple user test by asking four human subjects to rank the accuracy if MFSs are adopted as cluster names. Table 2 gives the averaged results of four

subjects when one to five MFSs are considered as the names of clusters generated in the top three level of the taxonomy.

We observe that in users' perception, using the three longest MFSs can almost cover all essential contents of top clusters, while the incremental contribution of additional MFSs is trivial. Our understanding from the test subjects reveals that the top longest MFSs have covered almost all frequent single words and the MFSs found are in a very readable manner. We believe that our approach has provided an alternative choice regarding cluster naming. Also, the exploration of MFSs without specifying the maximal length has demonstrated its merit.

Furthermore, the DP model can also be applied in other mining tasks such as topic detection, structure analysis for long documents, and concept based text classification, which need further exploration.

CONCLUSION

Taxonomy generation from documents is of great interest to researchers and professionals in the information retrieval and text mining communities. In this chapter, we propose a novel document profile model that enables document representations with the semantic information systematically generated from documents at the sentence level. Experimental studies of taxonomy generation using hierarchical agglomerative clustering have shown the significant improvement in terms of F_{score} based on the document profile model. A close examination reveals that the integration of semantic information has a clear contribution compared to the bag-of-words approach. Our DP model does not necessarily increase the feature size, and, as a matter of fact, a better performance is achieved in a smaller feature dimension. Moreover, the longest word sequences found in the DP model have indicated their potential to fulfill cluster naming. This study encourages us to further investigate the possibility of applying DP model over a wide range of text based tasks.

FUTURE RESEARCH DIRECTIONS

One immediate future research is the application of the DP model to different text processing tasks, for example, text classification and summarization. As noted that the DP model could significantly reduce the overall feature dimension, it would be nice to explore a classification algorithm based on the DP model. Meanwhile, we also plan to integrate POS tagging and mutual information as a means to further refine the semantic information found. While we currently search the semantic information mainly at the document sentence level, we intend to examine whether it is feasible to apply the DP model on text blocks, especially in long documents, to better understand the internal topic relations. We foresee this will be useful for several tasks, for example, topic detection and semantic mapping. Finally, the automated generation of quality taxonomy is always desirable for information processing and knowledge management purposes. In the last a few years, we have witnessed many applications based on taxonomy and ontology for the organization information and knowledge integration and management, and very recently, the enterprise application of Semantic Web. We believe our study is central to the aforementioned tasks.

REFERENCES

Agrawal, R., Imieliński, T., & Swami, A. (1993). *Mining association rules between sets of items in large databases.* Paper presented at the Proceedings of the 1993 ACM SIGMOD International Conference on Management of Data.

Agrawal, R., & Srikant, R. (1994). *Fast algorithms for mining association rules.* Paper presented at the Proceedings of the 20th Very Large Data Bases (VLDB) Conference, Santiago, Chile.

Agrawal, R., & Srikant, R. (1995). *Mining sequential patterns.* Paper presented at the Proceedings of the Eleventh International Conference on Data Engineering, Taipei, Taiwan.

Agrawal, R., & Srikant, R. (2001). *On integrating catalogs.* Paper presented at the Proceedings of the 10th International World Wide Web Conference (WWW10), Hong Kong, China.

Ahonen-Myka, H. (1999). *Finding all frequent maximal sequences in text.* Paper presented at the Proceedings of the 16th International Conference on Machine Learning ICML-99 Workshop on Machine Learning in Text Data Analysis, J. Stefan Institute, Ljubljana.

Ahonen-Myka, H., Heinonen, O., Klemettinen, M., & Verkamo, A. I. (1999). *Finding co-occurring text phrases by combining sequence and frequent set discovery.* Paper presented at the Proceedings of 16th International Joint Conference on Artificial Intelligence IJCAI-99 Workshop on Text Mining: Foundations, Techniques and Applications.

Baeza-Yates, R., & Ribeiro-Neto, B. (1999). *Modern information retrieval.* Boston: Addison-Wesley Longman Publishing.

Baker, L. D., & McCallum, A. K. (1998). *Distributional clustering of words for text classification.* Paper presented at the Proceedings of the 21st Annual International ACM SIGIR Conference on Research and Development in Information Retrieval, Melbourne, Australia.

Cai, L., & Hofmann, T. (2003). *Text categorization by boosting automatically extracted concepts.* Paper presented at the Proceedings of the 26th Annual International ACM SIGIR Conference on Research and Development in Information Retrieval, Toronto, Canada.

Chakrabarti, S., Dom, B., Agrawal, R., & Raghavan, P. (1998). Scalable feature selection, classification and signature generation for organizing large text databases into hierarchical topic taxonomies. *The VLDB Journal - The International Journal on Very Large Data Bases, 7*(3), 163-178.

Charniak, E. (1993). *Statistical language learning.* Cambridge, MA: MIT Press.

Chuang, S. L., & Chien, L. F. (2002). *Towards automatic generation of query taxonomy: A hierarchical term clustering approach.* Paper presented at the Proceedings of 2002 IEEE Conference on Data Mining (ICDM'2002).

Chuang, S.-L., & Chien, L.-F. (2004). *A practical Web-based approach to generating topic hierarchy for text segments.* Paper presented at the Proceedings of the Thirteenth ACM International Conference on Information and Knowledge Management, CIKM 2004, Washington, DC.

Chuang, S.-L., & Chien, L.-F. (2005). Taxonomy generation for text segments: A practical Web-based approach. *ACM Transactions on Information Systems (TOIS), 23*(4), 363-396.

Ding, C. H. Q., He, X., Zha, H., Gu, M., & Simon, H. D. (2001). *A min-max cut algorithm for graph partitioning and data clustering.* Paper presented at the Proceedings of the 2001 IEEE International Conference on Data Mining, ICDM.

Dumais, S., Platt, J., Heckerman, D., & Sahami, M. (1998). *Inductive learning algorithms and representations for text categorization.* Paper presented at the Proceedings of the Seventh International Conference on Information and Knowledge Management, Bethesda, Maryland.

Fuhr, N. (1985). *A probabilistic model of dictionary based automatic indexing.* Paper presented at the Proceedings of the Riao 85 (Recherche d' Informations Assistee par Ordinateur), Grenoble, France.

Hiemstra, D. (1998). *A linguistically motivated probabilistic model of information retrieval.* Paper presented at the Research and Advanced Technology for Digital Libraries, Second European Conference, ECDL 1998, Heraklion, Crete, Greece.

Jain, A. K., Murty, M. N., & Flynn, P. J. (1999). Data clustering: A review. *ACM Computing Surveys (CSUR), 31*(3), 264-323.

Jardine, N., & van Rijsbergen., C. J. (1971). The use of hierarchical clustering in information retrieval. *Information Storage and Retrieval, 7,* 217-240.

Johnson, R. A., & Wichern, D. W. (2002). *Applied multivariate statistical analysis* (5th ed.). Prentice Hall.

Jurafsky, D., & Martin, J. H. (2000). *Speech and language processing: An introduction to natural language processing, computational linguistics and speech recognition.* Prentice Hall.

Kaufman, L., & Rousseeuw, P. J. (1990). *Finding groups in data: An introduction to cluster analysis.* Wiley-Interscience.

Larsen, B., & Aone, C. (1999). *Fast and effective text mining using linear-time document clustering.* Paper presented at the Proceedings of the Fifth ACM SIGKDD International Conference on Knowledge Discovery and Data Mining, San Diego, California.

Lawrie, D., Croft, W. B., & Rosenberg, A. (2001). *Finding topic words for hierarchical summarization.* Paper presented at the Proceedings of the 24th Annual International ACM SIGIR Conference on Research and Development in Information Retrieval, New Orleans, Louisiana.

Lewis, D. D. (1992). *An evaluation of phrasal and clustered representations on a text categorization task.* Paper presented at the Proceedings of SIGIR-92, 15th ACM International Conference on Research and Development in Information Retrieval.

Lewis, D. D., Yang, Y., Rose, T. G., & Li, F. (2004). RCV1: A new benchmark collection for text categorization research. *Journal of Machine Learning Research, 5*, 361-397.

Liu, Y., Loh, H. T., & Tor, S. B. (2004). *Building a document corpus for manufacturing knowledge retrieval*. Paper presented at the Proceedings of the Singapore MIT Alliance Symposium, Singapore.

Manning, C. D., & Schütze, H. (1999). *Foundations of statistical natural language processing*. Boston: The MIT Press.

Miller, D. R. H., Leek, T., & Schwartz, R. M. (1999). *A hidden Markov model information retrieval system*. Paper presented at the Proceedings of SIGIR-99, 22nd ACM International Conference on Research and Development in Information Retrieval, Berkeley, California.

Mirkin, B. (1996). *Mathematical classification and clustering*. Springer.

Muller, A., Dorre, J., Gerstl, P., & Seiffert, R. (1999). *The taxgen framework: Automating the generation of a taxonomy for a large document collection*. Paper presented at the Proceedings of the 32nd Hawaii International Conference on System Sciences, Maui, Hawaii.

Ponte, J. M., & Croft, W. B. (1998). *A language modeling approach to information retrieval*. Paper presented at the Proceedings of the 21st Annual International ACM SIGIR Conference on Research and Development in Information Retrieval, Melbourne, Australia.

Porter, M. F. (1980). An algorithm for suffix stripping. *Program, 14*(3), 130-137.

Resnik, P. (1999). Semantic similarity in a taxonomy: An information-based measure and its application to problems of ambiguity in natural language. *Journal of Artificial Intelligence Research, 11*, 95-130.

Robertson, S. E. (1977). The probability ranking principle in IR. *Journal of Documentation, 33*(4), 294-304.

Sahlgren, M., & Cöster, R. (2004). *Using bag-of-concepts to improve the performance of support vector machines in text categorization*. Paper presented at the Proceedings of the 20th International Conference on Computational Linguistics (COLING 2004), Geneva.

Salton, G. (Ed.). (1971). *The SMART retrieval system: Experiments in automatic document processing*. Englewood Cliffs, NJ: Prentice Hall.

Salton, G., & Buckley, C. (1988). Term weighting approaches in automatic text retrieval. *Information Processing and Management, 24*(5), 513-523.

Salton, G., & McGill, M. J. (1983). *Introduction to modern information retrieval*. New York: McGraw-Hill.

Sanderson, M., & Croft, B. (1999). *Deriving concept hierarchies from text*. Paper presented at the Proceedings of SIGIR-99, the 22nd ACM Conference on Research and Development in Information Retrieval, Berkeley, California.

Sebastiani, F. (2002). Machine learning in automated text categorization. *ACM Computing Surveys (CSUR), 34*(1), 1-47.

Seo, Y.-W., & Sycara, K. (2004). *Text clustering for topic detection* (No. CMU-RI-TR-04-03). Robotics Institute, Carnegie Mellon University.

Turtle, H., & Croft, W. B. (1989). *Inference networks for document retrieval*. Paper presented at the Proceedings of the 13th Annual International ACM SIGIR Conference on Research and Development in Information Retrieval, Brussels, Belgium.

Vaithyanathan, S., & Dom, B. (2000). *Model-based hierarchical clustering*. Paper presented at the Proceedings of the Sixteenth Conference on Uncertainty in Artificial Intelligence, Stanford, California.

van Rijsbergen, C. J. (1979). *Information retrieval* (2nd ed.). London: Butterworths.

Wen, J.-R., Nie, J.-Y., & Zhang, H.-J. (2002). Query clustering using user logs. *ACM Transactions on Information Systems, 20*(1), 59-81.

Widdows, D. (2003). *Unsupervised methods for developing taxonomies by combining syntactic and statistical information.* Paper presented at the Proceedings of the 2003 Conference of the North American Chapter of the Association for Computational Linguistics on Human Language Technology, Edmonton, Canada.

Willett, P. (1988). Recent trends in hierarchic document clustering: A critical review. *Information Processing and Management, 24*(5), 577-597.

Yang, Y., & Liu, X. (1999). *A re-examination of text categorization methods.* Paper presented at the Proceedings of the 22nd Annual International ACM SIGIR Conference on Research and Development in Information Retrieval, Berkeley, California.

Yap, I., Loh, H. T., Shen, L., & Liu, Y. (2006). *Topic detection using MFSs.* Paper presented at the Proceedings of the 19th International Conference on Industrial & Engineering Applications of Artificial Intelligence & Expert Systems (IEA\AIE 2006), Annecy, France.

Zue, V. W. (1995). Navigating the information superhighway using spoken language interfaces. *IEEE Expert: Intelligent Systems and Their Applications, 10*(5), 39-43.

Additional Readings

Antoniou, G., & Harmelen, F. v. (2004). *A semantic Web primer.* The MIT Press.

Brachman, R., & Levesque, H. (2004). *Knowledge representation and reasoning.* Morgan Kaufmann.

Budanitsky, A., & Hirst, G. (2001). *Semantic distance in wordnet: An experimental, application-oriented evaluation of five measures.* Paper presented at the Workshop on WordNet and Other Lexical Resources, in the North American Chapter of the Association for Computational Linguistics (NAACL-2001), Pittsburgh. Pennsylvania.

Chakrabarti, S. (2002). *Mining the Web: Analysis of hypertext and semi structured data.* Morgan Kaufmann.

Christophides, V., Karvounarakis, G., Plexousakis, D., Scholl, M., & Tourtounis, S. (2004). Optimizing taxonomic semantic Web queries using labeling schemes. *Journal of Web Semantics, 1*(2), 207-228.

Ciaramita, M., Hofmann, T., & Johnson, M. (2003). *Hierarchical semantic classification: Word sense disambiguation with world knowledge.* Paper presented at the 18th International Joint Conference on Artificial Intelligence (IJCAI).

Dill, S., Eiron, N., Gibson, D., Gruhl, D., Guha, R., Jhingran, A., et al. (2003). A case for automated large scale semantic annotation. *Journal of Web Semantics, 1*(1), 115-132.

Doan, A., Madhavan, J., Domingos, P., & Halevy, A. (2002). *Learning to map between ontologies on the semantic Web.* Paper presented at the Proceedings of the 11th International World Wide Web Conference (WWW11), Hawaii.

Gauch, S., Chaffee, J., & Pretschner, A. (2003). Ontology-based personalized search and browsing. *Web Intelligence and Agent System, 1*(3-4), 219-234.

Gomez-Perez, A., Corcho, O., & Fernandez-Lopez, M. (2005). *Ontological engineering:* Springer.

Guha, R. V., McCool, R., & Miller, E. (2003). *Semantic search.* Paper presented at the Proceedings of the Twelfth International World Wide Web Conference, WWW2003, Budapest, Hungary.

Handschuh, S., Staab, S., & Ciravegna, F. (2002). *S-CREAM: Semi-automatic CREAtion of metadata.* Paper presented at the Proceedings of the 13th International Conference on Knowledge Engineering and Knowledge Management. Ontologies and the Semantic Web, Siguenza, Spain.

Hofmann, T., Cai, L., & Ciaramita, M. (2003). *Learning with taxonomies: Classifying documents and words.* Paper presented at the Workshop on Syntax, Semantics, and Statistics, Neural Information Processing (NIPS).

Jones, K. S., & Willett, P. (Eds.). (1997). *Readings in information retrieval.* San Francisco: Morgan Kaufmann.

Jonyer, I., Cook, D. J., & Holder, L. B. (2002). Graph-based hierarchical conceptual clustering. *The Journal of Machine Learning Research, 2,* 19-43.

Kamel, M. S., & Hammouda, K. M. (2004). Efficient phrase-based document indexing for Web document clustering. *IEEE Transactions on Knowledge and Data Engineering, 16*(10), 1279-1296.

Kandola, J., Shawe-Taylor, J., & Cristianini, N. (2002). *Learning semantic similarity.* Paper presented at the Advances in Neural Information Processing Systems 15.

Kiryakov, A., Popov, B., Terziev, I., Manov, D., & Ognyanoff, D. (2005). Semantic annotation, indexing, and retrieval. *Journal of Web Semantics, 2*(1), 49-79.

Rijsbergen, C. J. v. (2004). *The geometry of information retrieval.* Cambridge University Press.

Seo, Y.-W., & Sycara, K. (2004). *Text clustering for topic detection* (No. CMU-RI-TR-04-03). Robotics Institute, Carnegie Mellon University.

Zhang, D., & Lee, W. S. (2004). Learning to integrate Web taxonomies. *Journal of Web Semantics, 2*(2).

Zhuang, L., Jing, F., & Zhu, X.-Y. (2006). *Movie review mining and summarization.* Paper presented at the Proceedings of the 15th ACM International Conference on Information and Knowledge Management, Arlington, Virginia.

Chapter VI
Rule Discovery from Textual Data

Shigeaki Sakurai
Toshiba Corporation, Japan

ABSTRACT

This chapter introduces knowledge discovery methods based on a fuzzy decision tree from textual data. The author argues that the methods extract features of the textual data based on a key concept dictionary, which is a hierarchical thesaurus, and a key phrase pattern dictionary, which stores characteristic rows of both words and parts of speech, and generate knowledge in the format of a fuzzy decision tree. The author also discusses two application tasks. One is an analysis system for daily business reports and the other is an e-mail analysis system. The author hopes that the methods will provide new knowledge for researchers engaged in text mining studies, facilitating their understanding of the importance of the fuzzy decision tree in processing textual data.

INTRODUCTION

Large amounts of textual data, such as daily business reports, e-mail, and electronic newspapers, can be stored easily on computers, owing to the dramatic progress of computer environments and network environments. The textual data includes various kinds of knowledge. The knowledge can facilitate decision making in many situations; therefore, knowledge discovery from the textual data is significant. However, it is difficult to discover the knowledge because of the huge amounts of textual data and it is impracticable to thoroughly investigate all the textual data. Methods are needed that facilitate knowledge discovery. Thus, this chapter focuses on a method of knowledge discovery described by a rule set, that is, a rule discovery method. The rule set can classify the textual data based on viewpoints of the analysis. Also, it can reveal relationships between the features of the textual data, which constitute knowledge.

Rule discovery methods have been studied since the start of research into artificial intelligence in the field of machine learning. These studies have yielded many techniques, such as decision tree, neural network, genetic algorithm, and association rules, which acquire the rule set from the structured data. A decision tree can describe a rule set in the format of a tree structure. The tree is regarded as the set of IF-THEN rules. C4.5 (Quinlan, 1992) is one example of the algorithms that acquire a compact tree with high classification efficiency from the structured data. Each item of the data is composed of attribute values and a class. The algorithm uses an information criterion to effectively acquire the tree. A neural network can describe a rule set in the format of a network structure. The network stores the relationships between attributes and classes as weights of the arcs in the network. The weights are appropriately adjusted by the back propagation algorithm. A genetic algorithm inspired by the concept of evolution can acquire a rule set from structured data. The algorithm describes a rule or a rule set as a solution. The algorithm repeatedly improves a solution set to acquire the optimum solution by using three operations: cross-over, mutation, and selection. Association rules can describe relationships between items. If an item set is frequent, its subsets are frequent. This is called the apriori property. The association rules can be discovered by expanding small item sets to big item sets including small ones based on the property.

These techniques are important for the rule discovery, but they cannot directly deal with the textual data because the textual data is not structured. It is necessary to deal with the textual data by extracting its structured features to acquire a rule set from the textual data. A key point of the extraction is the ambiguity of textual data. That is, the same words and phrases can represent different meanings. Also, different words and phrases can represent similar meanings. In addition, even if the same textual data is given, its interpretation depends on a human. It is necessary to overcome the ambiguity. Thus, we employ fuzzy set theory,

because fuzzy set theory can describe ambiguity by defining appropriate membership functions. We introduce rule discovery methods based on fuzzy set theory.

On the other hand, we need to grasp the meaning of discovered rules in order to check their validity and to gain new knowledge from them. Rules described in a visible format are required. Thus, we employ a decision tree, because the tree is an IF-THEN rule set and we intuitively grasp the meaning of rules by looking through attribute values in the IF-part and classes in the THEN-part. We introduce rule discovery methods based on the decision tree.

As anticipated in the above introduction, this chapter focuses on rule discovery methods from textual data based on a fuzzy decision tree. The tree expands the concept of the previous decision tree by incorporating the concept of fuzzy set theory. In this chapter, first, we introduce the format of the textual data. Next, we introduce the format of the fuzzy decision tree, its inductive learning method, and the inference method using it. In addition, we introduce two methods of extracting features included in the textual data and the rule discovery methods based on the features. One method is based on a key concept dictionary and the other method is based on a key phrase pattern dictionary. Lastly, this chapter introduces two application tasks based on the methods. One is an analysis system for daily business reports and the other is an e-mail analysis system.

FORMAT OF TEXTUAL DATA

There are many kinds of textual data. One kind of data is composed of texts and their additional tags such as HTML and XML. Another kind of data is composed of texts and their mutual links such as a blog. However, this chapter focuses on the items of textual data composed of texts and their text classes. Here, the text classes correspond to a viewpoint that decides similarity of contents.

An item of the textual data can be classified in different text classes by using another viewpoint. For example, an item describes complaints of users of a refrigerator. Then, the item is classified into the text class "Refrigerator" when the viewpoint is based on home appliance products. The item is also classified into the text class "Complaints" when the viewpoint is based on evaluation by customers. These text classes reflect interests of users. The text mining techniques introduced in this chapter discover relationships between key features and text classes from items of textual data.

FUZZY DECISION TREE

Format of Fuzzy Decision Tree

A fuzzy decision tree is a set of fuzzy IF-THEN rules described by a tree structure. The tree is composed of branch nodes, leaf nodes, and branches, but the following explanation does not consider the case that the tree is composed of only one leaf node. The top branch node is called the root node. The root node is connected to lower branch nodes or leaf nodes. The remaining branch nodes are connected to both an upper branch node and lower nodes. Each branch node is assigned an attribute. Each attribute is composed of basic attribute values characterized by their corresponding membership functions. The leaf nodes are connected to an upper branch node. Each leaf node is assigned classes with certainty factors. The branches connect an upper node with a lower node. Each branch is assigned a basic attribute value that composes an attribute of an upper branch node. In the fuzzy decision tree, each path from the root node to a leaf node shows a fuzzy rule. Figure 1 shows an example of a fuzzy decision tree. In this figure, white circles are branch nodes, shaded circles are leaf nodes, and arrows between nodes are branches. The root node is assigned the attribute "Size." The attribute is characterized by three basic

Figure 1. An example of a fuzzy decision tree

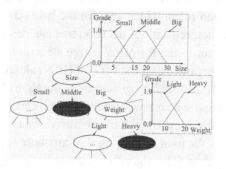

attribute values: "Small," "Middle," and "Big." These basic attribute values are characterized by corresponding membership functions as shown at upper right in this figure. The leaf node in the center is assigned the class "Bad" with certainty factor 0.8 and the class "Good" with certainty factor 0.2. The path at extreme right shows a fuzzy rule: "If Size = Big and Weight = Heavy, then Class = (Bad, 1.0)".

Inductive Learning Method

A fuzzy decision tree is automatically acquired from a set of training examples using a fuzzy inductive learning algorithm (Sakurai, Ichimura, Suyama, & Orihara, 2001b), where each training example is composed of an attribute value vector and a class. The learning algorithm is similar to C4.5. The algorithm is expanded by the fuzzy set theory (Zadeh, 1978) in order to thoroughly deal with discrete values, numerical values, and fuzzy values. Each training example is composed of attribute values and a class with a certainty factor. The certainty factor is normally set to 1.0 in the root node. The attribute values are discrete values, numerical values, or fuzzy values. In the selection phase, the algorithm assigns the training examples to a node. The learning algorithm calculates values of the attributes for the node according to formula (1)—formula (3).

$$gain(A_i, S) = I(S) - E(A_i, S) \qquad (1)$$

$$I(S) = -\sum_{c_n} p_{s,c_n} \times \log_2(p_{s,c_n}) \qquad (2)$$

$$E(A_i, S) = \sum_j \{ p_{s_{f_{ij}}} \times \sum_{c_n} p_{s_{f_{ij}},c_n} \times \log_2(p_{s_{f_{ij}},c_n}) \} \qquad (3)$$

Here, S is a set of training examples assigned to the node, A_i is i-th attribute, c_n is n-th class, f_{ij} is j-th basic attribute value of i-th attribute and $S_{f_{ij}}$ is a subset of S divided by f_{ij}. p_{s,c_n} is a probability that classes of training examples included in S are equal to c_n. $p_{s_{f_{ij}}}, c_n$ is a probability that classes of training examples included in $S_{f_{ij}}$ are equal to c_n. These probabilities are normally calculated by formula (4) and formula (5).

$$p_{s,c_n} = \frac{|S_{c_n}|_{cf}}{|S|_{cf}} \qquad (4)$$

$$p_{s_{f_{ij}},c_n} = \frac{|S_{f_{ij},c_n}|_{cf}}{|S_{f_{ij}}|_{cf}} \qquad (5)$$

Here, S_{c_n} is a subset in which classes of training examples included in S are equal to c_n. $S_{f_{ij}}, c_n$ is a subset in which classes of training examples included in $S_{f_{ij}}$ are equal to c_n. $|\cdot|cf$ is an operation that calculates the sum of certainty factors of training examples included in a set.

The algorithm selects an attribute whose evaluation value is the maximum. The algorithm divides the set according to basic attribute values of the selected attribute into subsets. That is, certainty factors of the training examples in the set are updated according to the basic attribute values and examples with updated certainty factors are assigned to corresponding subsets. For example, we consider the case that a training example with certainty factor 1.0 has attribute value 28 in the attribute "Size." The attribute value has grades 0.8 and 0.2 for two basic attribute values "Middle" and "Big," respectively. The algorithm divides

the training example into the example with certainty factor 0.8 and the example with certainty factor 0.2. Divided examples are assigned to the subsets corresponding to "Middle" and "Big," respectively. The update of the certainty factors is explained in the next section in detail. On the other hand, if the subsets corresponding to basic attribute values are empty sets, the subsets are omitted. The algorithm generates nodes that assign remaining subsets and it ties the node of the set to the nodes of the subsets with branches. The basic attribute values are assigned to the branches. Each generated node is judged as to whether or not it should be a leaf node by evaluating two stop conditions. One is the minimum occupation ratio of the maximum class and the other is the minimum existence ratio. These ratios are calculated by formula (6) and formula (7), respectively. If the former ratio is bigger than or equal to the predefined threshold or the latter ratio is smaller than or equal to the predefined threshold, the algorithm judges that the node should be a leaf node. Otherwise, the algorithm judges that the node should be a branch node.

$$\frac{\max_n(|S_{f_{max,j},c_n}|_{cf})}{|S_{f_{max,j}}|_{cf}} \qquad (6)$$

$$\frac{|S_{f_{max,j}}|_{cf}}{|S_0|_{cf}} \qquad (7)$$

Here, $S_{f_{max,j}}$ is j-th subset divided by A_{max}, which is the attribute with the maximum evaluation value in the upper branch node, and $S_{f_{max,j},c_n}$ is a subset in which classes of training examples included in $S_{f_{max,j}}$ are equal to c_n. S_0 is a set of training examples assigned to the root node. If the node is a leaf node, the algorithm assigns classes with certainty factors $|S_{f_{max,j},c_n}|_{cf} / |S_{f_{max,j}}|_{cf}$ to the node.

The algorithm recursively repeats the selection and the division until all nodes are leaf nodes. Table 1 shows a pseudo-code algorithm. In this

Table 1. Fuzzy inductive learning algorithm

```
setNode(S₀, N₀);
while((N=pickupNode())!=NULL){
    if(checkStopCondition(N)==TRUE){
        setLeafNode(N);
        continue;
    }
    for(i){
        calcEvalValue(N, A_i);
    }
    selectAttr(N, A_max);
    divideSet(N, A_max, S_{f_max,j});
    setBranchNode(N, A_max);
    for(j){
        setNode(S_{f_max,j}, N_{f_max,j});
        setBranch(N, N_{f_max,j}, f_max,j);
    }
}
exit(0);
```

algorithm, N_0 is the root node and $N_{f_{\max,j}}$ are the nodes corresponding to $f_{\max,j}$. setNode() generates an unprocessed node N and assigns the set S to the node. pickUpNode() picks up an unprocessed node. checkStopCondition() judges whether the set assigned to N satisfies the stop condition or not. setLeafNode() assigns classes with certainty factors to N. calcEvalValue() calculates an evaluation value of an attribute A_i for N. selectAttr() selects the attribute $A_{\max}$ with the maximum evaluation value in the attributes of N. divideSet() divides the set assigned to N into subsets $S_{f_{\max,j}}$ based on basic attribute values $f_{\max,j}$ of $A_{\max}$. setBranchNode() assigns $A_{\max}$ to N. setBranch() generates a branch that connects N to $N_{f_{\max,j}}$ and assigns $f_{\max,j}$ to the branch.

Inference Method

The inference using a fuzzy decision tree deals with an evaluation target composed of an attribute value vector as the input and outputs their classes with certainty factors. In each branch node, the inference compares membership functions of the node with the membership function of the attribute value of the evaluation target. The inference also calculates certainty factors that propagate to the lower nodes based on formula (8).

$$cf_{ikr} = \frac{\max_x \{\min(f_{ikr}(x), g_i(x))\}}{\sum_l \max_x \{\min(f_{ikl}(x), g_i(x))\}} \times cf_k \tag{8}$$

Here, $f_{ikr}(x)$ is a membership function corresponding to r-th basic attribute value in k-th branch node assigned i-th attribute, $g_i(x)$ is a membership function of an attribute value corresponding to i-th attribute of the evaluation target and cf_k is a certainty factor of the evaluation target in k-th branch node. But, the certainty factor 1.0 is assigned to the evaluation target in the root node.

The inference integrates results propagated to leaf nodes by gathering up certainty factors of the same classes. If it is necessary to select a class, the inference selects the class whose certainty factor is the maximum value. For example, the evaluation target has the attribute vectors in which "Size" is "28" and "Weight" is "20" and the fuzzy decision tree shown in Figure 1 is given. The grade of the attribute value "28" in the node B1 is 0.8 for the basic attribute value "Big" as shown at upper right in Figure 2. Similarly, its grade is 0.2 for the basic attribute value "Middle." On the other hand, its grade is 0.0 for the basic attribute value "Small." The evaluation target is divided into two evaluation targets. They are propagated to the lower nodes corresponding to "Big" and "Middle" with the certainty factors 0.8 (= 0.8/(0.8 + 0.2 + 0.0) × 1.0) and 0.2 (= 0.8/(0.8 + 0.2 + 0.0) × 1.0), respectively. The evaluation target does not propagate to the lower node of "Small," because the certainty factor of "Small" is 0.0. Also, the grade of the attribute value "20" in the node B2 is 1.0 for the basic attribute value "Heavy" and its grade is 0.0 for the basic attribute value "Light." The evaluation target with certainty factor 0.8 (= 0.8/(0.8 + 0.0) × 0.8) is propagated to the lower node of "Heavy." The evaluation target is not propagated to the lower node of "Light." Figure 2 shows the outline of its propagation. The infer-

Figure 2. An example of inference using a fuzzy decision tree

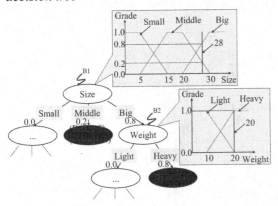

Figure 3. An example of a key concept dictionary

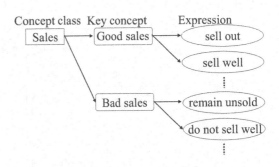

ence multiplies certainty factors of the evaluation targets with certainty factors of the propagated leaf nodes. The inference sums up the certainty factor for each class. Therefore, the certainty factor of the class "Bad" is 0.96 (=0.2 × 0.8 + 0.8 × 1.0) and that of the class "Good" is 0.04 (=0.2 × 0.2). If the inference selects a class, the inference outputs the class "Bad." The inference assigns the class "Bad" to the evaluation target.

RULE DISCOVERY BASED ON A KEY CONCEPT DICTIONARY

This section introduces the method that deals with textual data based on a key concept dictionary (Sakurai, Ichimura, & Suyama, 2002; Sakurai, Ichimura, Suyama, & Orihara, 2001a, 2001b; Sakurai, Suyama, & Fume, 2003; Sakurai & Suyama, 2005).

Format of a Key Concept Dictionary

A key concept dictionary is a thesaurus composed of three layers described with tree structure. The first layer is called the concept class and shows a set of concepts that have a common feature. The second layer is called the key concept and shows a set of expressions that have the same meaning. The third layer is called the expression and shows

important words and phrases concerning a target task. In this layer, the words and the phrases are described, taking the inflection into consideration. It is possible for the dictionary to deal with different expressions based on their meaning. Figure 3 shows an example of a key concept dictionary. The dictionary describes parts of key concepts for the concept class "Sales" including two key concepts "Good sales" and "Bad sales." The key concept "Good sales" includes two expressions "sell out" and "sell well," and the key concept "Bad sales" includes two expressions "remain unsold" and "do not sell well." We can also describe expressions by using the words and the phrases accompanied by their parts of speech and wild cards. That is, we can describe "sell<verb> * well<adverb>" instead of "sell well." Here, "*" is a wild card and means that one word can be inserted.

Creation of a Key Concept Dictionary

A key concept dictionary is manually created by human experts using a GUI-based support tool as shown in Figure 4.

First, the experts use the tool to apply the morphological analysis (Ichimura, Nakayama, Miyoshi, Akahane, Sekiguchi, & Fujiwara, 2001; Kupiec, 1992) to items of textual data. The tool

Figure 4. A GUI-based support tool of a key concept dictionary

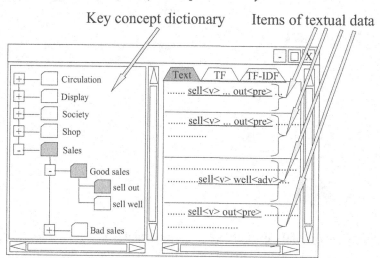

assigns parts of speech to the items and extracts stems of words. In the case of a language without word segmentation such as Japanese, the tool also decomposes rows of characters in the items into words. In addition, the tool calculates frequency of the words and the phrases, and their *TF-IDF* (term frequency - inverse document frequency) values (Salton & McGill, 1983). In this chapter, the values are defined by formula (9).

$$TF-IDF_i = \frac{1}{D} \times \log_2(\frac{D}{d_i}) \times \sum_j \frac{\log_2(t_{ij}+1)}{\log_2(w_j)} \quad (9)$$

Here, D is the number of items of textual data, d_i is the number of items including i-th word or phrase, w_j is the number of words and phrases included in j-th item, and t_{ij} is the number of i-th words or phrases included in j-th item. Each item includes at least 2 words. The value revises the frequencies of words and phrases by their numbers included in specific items. It is possible for the value to decrease the effect of common words and phrases such as "the," "it," and "is." It is possible to evaluate characteristics of words and phrases included in specific items.

The tool sorts the words and the phrases in ascending order based on their frequencies or their *TF-IDF* values. The experts select important words and phrases by referring to their sorted list and register them as expressions. The experts also create key concepts by gathering the expressions with the same meaning and create concept classes by gathering relevant key concepts. In addition, the experts apply the created key concept dictionary to the items. The tool shows the experts whether important words and phrases are extracted or not. In Figure 4, the tool underlines extracted phrases to be stand out. The experts check whether important expressions remain or not. If important expressions remain, the dictionary is revised to extract the expression. The revision of the dictionary is repeated with the aim of extracting all important expressions.

Acquisition of Rules

The method based on a key concept dictionary discovers rules that show relationships between key concepts and text classes. The method deals with training examples, each of which is composed of some key concepts and a text class. Each training example is generated from an item of textual data. A set of text classes is a viewpoint of analysis. Analysts read the item and give it a corresponding text class. We regard a concept class as an attribute, a key concept as a basic attribute value, and a text class as a class of a training example.

The method applies the morphological analysis to the item. The method compares the analyzed item with expressions included in a key concept dictionary. If the expressions correspond to the rows of words in the item, the method assigns key concepts including the expressions to the item. If all expressions are evaluated, the method gathers the extracted key concepts for the same concept class. The method assigns the gathered key concepts to the attribute corresponding to the concept class. But, in the case that a key concept included in a concept class is not extracted, a specific attribute value "unknown" is allocated to a corresponding attribute. The value means that the information corresponding to the concept class is unknown. For the concept class that does not have a key concept, it is necessary to consider all possibilities. Table 2 shows an example of training examples generated from three items of the textual data. Each training example is assigned one of three text classes: "Best practice," "Missed opportunity," and "Other." The third training example includes two key concepts "Complaint" and "Praise" in the attribute "Reputation." The description shows that the third item includes two key concepts of the attribute spontaneously.

Each basic attribute value of a training example has a membership function defined by formula (10). In this formula, a membership function corresponding to r-th basic attribute value in k-th

Table 2. Training examples based on a key concept dictionary

Attribute		Class
Sales	Reputation	
Good sales	Complaint	Best practice
Bad sales	Praise	Missed opportunity
unknown	{Complaint, Praise}	Other

branch node assigned i-th attribute is defined.

$$\left.\begin{array}{l} \text{If } l_{ikr} \in v_i, \text{ then } grade_{ikr} = \dfrac{1}{|v_i|} + \dfrac{1-\alpha}{|L_{ik}|} \\[3mm] \text{If } l_{ikr} \notin v_i, \text{ then } grade_{ikr} = \dfrac{1-\alpha}{|L_{ik}|} \\[3mm] \alpha = \dfrac{|v_i \cap L_{ik}|}{|v_i|} \end{array}\right\} \quad (10)$$

Here, v_i is a subset of key concepts included in i-th attribute of an example, L_{ik} is a subset of key concepts corresponding to k-th branch node assigned i-th attribute, and l_{ikr} is r-th element of L_{ik}. $|\cdot|$ is an operation that calculates the number of key concepts included in a set. We note that "unknown" does not correspond to all l_{ikr}. That is, if an example is divided by the value "unknown," the example propagates to all lower branches accompanied by the same certainty factor. Also, we note that different membership functions can be defined for the same attribute. This is because its branch nodes do not always have branches corresponding to all key concepts included in the attribute.

This formula has the following meaning. When a key concept included in i-th attribute of an example is equal to one of the key concepts corresponding to k-th branch node, the formulation gives a weight $1/|v_i|$ to a lower node connecting to the branch with the key concept. When the key concept in the attribute is not equal to any key concepts corresponding to the branch node, the formula gives an equal weight $(1-\alpha)/|L_{ik}|$ to all lower nodes connecting to the branch node. Then, we note that L_{ik} is composed of key concepts included in the attributes of examples, which are given to the branch node in the learning phase. That is, α is equal to 1 in the learning phase, because $v_i \cap L_{ik}$ is equal to v_i. On the other hand, $v_i \cap L_{ik}$ is not always equal to v_i in the inference phase, because there may be key concepts that occur only in the inference phase and the fuzzy inductive learning algorithm does not generate lower nodes corresponding to the key concepts. In this case, it is impossible to evaluate such attributes that the key concepts are included in their values. So, an equal weight is given to all lower nodes in order to inspect all possibilities.

For example, we consider the case shown in Figure 5 where "Sales" is i-th attribute and L_{ik} = {Bad sales, Good sales}. If an item of textual data has "Normal sales" as an attribute value of the attribute "Sales," v_i ={Normal sales}. That is, $|v_i \cap L_{ik}|$ = 0, $|v_i|$ = 1, $|L_{ik}|$ = 2, l_{ik1} = {Bad sales} $\notin v_i$, and l_{ik2} = {Good sales} $\notin v_i$. The membership functions of the "Sales" give 0.5 (= {(1 − 0/1)/2)}) to each branch. On the other hand, if an item of textual data has {Normal sales, Good sales} as an attribute value of the attribute "Sales," v_i = {"Normal sales," "Good sales"}. That is, $|v_i \cap L_{ik}|$ = 1, $|v_i|$ = 2, $|L_{ik}|$ = 2, $L_{ik1} \notin v_i$, and $L_{ik2} \in v_i$. The membership functions give 0.25 (={(1 −1/2)/2)}) and 0.75 (=1/2 + {(1 − 1/2)/2)}) to "Bad sales" and "Good sales," respectively.

We note that this generation of the training examples and the definition of the membership functions are not influenced by the frequency of key concepts. That is, even if an item of textual data includes an expression included in "Complaint" and two expressions included in "Praise," the attribute value "{Complaint, Praise}" is assigned to the item. We also note that the generation and the definition are not influenced by the similarity of expressions. That is, even if we can calculate the similarity by using an ontology that many people can use such as WordNet (Fellbaum, 1998), each expression is judged as to whether the expression

is included or not in a specific key concept. But we can deal with the frequency and the similarity by introducing certainty factors of key concepts, if it is necessary to deal with them.

Lastly, the method generates rules from the generated training examples by applying them to the fuzzy inductive learning algorithm. The rules are used to analyze textual data based on a viewpoint given by analysts.

RULE DISCOVERY BASED ON A KEY PHRASE PATTERN DICTIONARY

A key concept dictionary depends on target tasks. It is necessary to create the dictionary corresponding to them. The creation is a time-consuming task and the validity of the creation has a large impact on discovered rules. We cannot always create a sufficient key concept dictionary because of the lack of analysts. Thus, this section introduces a method based on a key phrase pattern dictionary (Sakurai, 2004). The dictionary does not depend on target tasks. We can easily apply the method to many target tasks.

Format of a Key Phrase Pattern Dictionary

A key phrase pattern dictionary is composed of key phrase patterns. Each pattern is a grammatical structure needed to describe the contents of textual data and composed of rows of both words and parts of speech. The pattern is described by using knowledge of the language describing the textual data. Table 3 shows an example of a key phrase pattern dictionary. In this table, the pattern R1 extracts a word set in which "auxiliary verb" and "verb" occur together in items of textual data. The pattern R3 also extracts a word set in which "noun," "of <preposition>," and "noun" occur together. The extracted word set is regarded as a key phrase.

Figure 5. Parts of rules based on a key concept dictionary

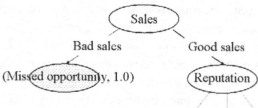

Table 3. An example of a key phrase pattern dictionary

ID	Key phrase pattern
R1	<auxiliary verb>+<verb>
R2	<numerical classifier>+<numerical classifier>
R3	<noun>+of<preposition>+<noun>

For example, the item of textual data, "He will sell shampoos at the supermarket." is given. The morphological analysis generates the analyzed item such as "he<pronoun>/ will<auxiliary verb>/ sell<verb>/ shampoo<noun>/ at<preposition>/ the<article>/ supermarket<noun>/ .<symbol>". The analyzed item includes the pattern "will<auxiliary verb>/ sell<verb>" corresponding to R1. R1 extracts a word set, "will sell," as a key phrase. Similarly, the item, "He displays a mascot of wood at the entrance." is given. The morphological analysis generates the analyzed item such as "he<pronoun>/ display<verb>/ a<article>/ mascot<noun>/ of<preposition>/ wood<noun>/ at<preposition>/ the<article>/ entrance<noun>/ .<symbol>". The analyzed item includes the pattern "mascot<noun>/ of<preposition>/ wood<noun>" corresponding to R3. R3 extracts a word set, "mascot of wood" as a key phrase.

Introduction of Center Word Sets

An item of textual data is characterized by sparse key phrases because textual data includes many kinds of expressions. If a key phrase is regarded as an attribute, the attribute is apt to have little robustness because textual data is characterized by having only a few parts of many key phrases. The attribute may not characterize the item appropriately. It is necessary to decrease the ratio of an attribute that does not have a key phrase. Thus, we gather key phrases with the common word set and generate a key phrase group. We call the word set a center word set in the following. We regard a center word set as an attribute and

regard key phrases included in the key phrase group as basic attribute values. But, in the case that key phrases corresponding to a key phrase group of a center word set are not extracted, a specific value "nothing" is assigned to the item. The value means that the center word set does not have a key phrase. The value is regarded as one of the key phrases.

For example, if "will sell," "must sell," and "do not sell" are given as key phrases and "sell" is given as a center word set, then "will sell," "must sell," and "do not sell" compose a key phrase group corresponding to "sell." The key phrases are regarded as basic attribute values. Therefore, the attribute values are composed of key phrase sets: "will sell," "must sell," "do not sell," "{will sell, do not sell}," "{will sell, must sell, do not sell}," and "nothing." That is, if the item of the textual data "He does not sell shampoo at the supermarket, but he will sell them," "{will sell, does not sell}" is given as an attribute value of the attribute "sell" of the item.

If we have to select specific word sets as center word sets, the sets are apt to depend on a specific target task. Thus, we point out words accompanied by important parts of speech, such as "verbs" and "adjectives," as center word sets, because they play important roles in describing the contents of the items. Center word sets are extracted from items of textual data using the parts of speech. It is possible for the extraction to select center word sets without depending on a specific target task.

Acquisition of Rules

The method based on a key phrase pattern dictionary discovers rules that show relationships between key phrases included in key phrase groups and text classes. The method deals with training examples, each of which is composed of some key phrases and a text class. But the method removes key phrases whose *TF-IDF* values are

Table 4. Training examples based on a key phrase pattern dictionary

	Attribute		Class
sell	supermarket	shampoo	
will sell	{cheerful supermarket, big supermarket}	shampoo	Best practice
do not sell	cheerful supermarket	nothing	Missed opportunity
must sell	big supermarket	shampoo	Other

Figure 6. Parts of rules based on a key phrase pattern dictionary

smaller than or equal to the predefined threshold. For example, six key phrases are given: will sell, must sell, do not sell, cheerful supermarket, big supermarket, and shampoo. Three center word sets are given: "sell," "supermarket," and "shampoo." Each training example is assigned one of three text classes: "Best practice," "Missed opportunity," and "Other." Table 4 shows an example of training examples based on key phrases.

The membership functions of attribute values are defined as shown in the case of key concepts. That is, key phrases including the specific attribute value "nothing" are defined by Formula (10). The method generates rules from the training examples by using the fuzzy inductive learning method. Figure 6 shows an example of rules. This figure shows that branches assigned "nothing" are included in the rules.

APPLICATION TASKS

This section introduces two application systems using the methods introduced in this chapter.

An Analysis System for Daily Business Reports

Many companies have adopted Sales Force Automation (SFA) systems in order to devise more rational sales strategies. The systems store many daily business reports described by sales workers. It is important for sales managers to promptly understand their outlines. However, it is difficult to understand them because of the large amount of reports. The systems are intended to support the managers. In this system, each report deals with a limited topic. We can describe characteristic concepts related to the topic. That is, we can describe a key concept dictionary of the topic. We can construct a system incorporating the method based on a key concept dictionary. The key concept dictionary is composed of 13 concept classes: "Circulation," "Display," "Society," "Shop," "Promotion," "Event," "Request," "Price," "Stock," "Reputation," "Trade," "Sales," and "Comments." Daily business reports are characterized by three text classes: Best practice, Missed opportunity, and Other. Figure 7 shows the outline of the system. The original system (Ichimura, 2001) was developed for the analysis of daily business reports in retailing. The system deals with reports written in Japanese. The system discovers rules between the key concepts and the text classes. The system sets the key concept, the date, and the store as analysis axes. The system calculates the number of reports related to selected axes by using discovered rules. In this figure, the key concept and the date are selected as the axes. Each value in the cells shows the number of reports. The managers can understand relationships among the key concept, the dates, and the text classes. The managers can also check reports in selected cells according to their interest. In this figure, the cell corresponding to "Sales," "Apr," and "Best practice" is selected.

In this application task, we compare the fuzzy decision tree with the decision tree. We use 780 daily business reports. But we select daily business

Figure 7. An analysis system for daily business reports

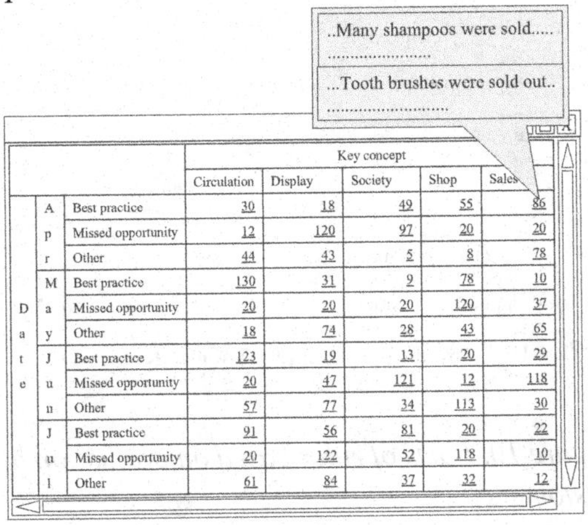

Date		Key concept: Circulation	Display	Society	Shop	Sales
Apr	Best practice	30	18	49	55	86
	Missed opportunity	12	120	97	20	20
	Other	44	43	5	8	78
May	Best practice	130	31	9	78	10
	Missed opportunity	20	20	20	120	37
	Other	18	74	28	43	65
Jun	Best practice	123	19	13	20	29
	Missed opportunity	20	47	121	12	118
	Other	57	77	34	113	30
Jul	Best practice	91	56	81	20	22
	Missed opportunity	20	122	52	118	10
	Other	61	84	37	32	12

reports such that only a key concept is included in a concept class, because C4.5 cannot process the reports with the multiple key concepts. Also, we deal with "unknown" as a missing value in C4.5. C4.5 predicts the missing value according to the probability distribution of attribute values in the attribute corresponding to the missing value. We perform experiments based on 10-fold cross-validation. That is, the reports are divided into 10 subsets. We learn a fuzzy decision tree or a decision tree from 9 subsets. Also, we evaluate the remaining subset based on the learned fuzzy decision tree or the learned decision tree, and calculate the respective correction ratio defined by formula (11).

$$\text{Correction ratio} = \frac{\text{Number of correctly classified examples}}{\text{Number of examples}} \quad (11)$$

The experiment is repeated 10 times by exchanging the evaluated subset. Table 5 shows average correction ratios and the size of the trees. Here, the size is the total number of branch nodes and leaf nodes. The results show that the fuzzy decision trees are more compact and more valid than the decision tree. In these experiments, each tree can correctly classify all examples used by the learning phase.

Table 5. Experimental results of the analysis system for daily business reports

	Fuzzy decision tree	Decision tree
Size	84.5	156.4
Correction ratio	97.18%	94.62%

An E-Mail Analysis System

It is important for companies and other organizations to improve customer satisfaction. Their customer centers, which are one point of customer access, play an important role. Nowadays, customers often communicate with them by e-mail. It is necessary for them to analyze the e-mails. Parts of the e-mails include images and programs, but the e-mails are mainly composed of textual data. The e-mails deal with various topics. It is impossible to describe expressions of all topics in advance and it is difficult to construct a key concept dictionary. Thus, we construct an e-mail analysis system (Sakurai, 2004) incorporating the method based on a key phrase pattern dictionary. This is because the method does not need a dictionary depending on a target task.

The system uses subjects and bodies of the e-mails. The system discovers rules based on two kinds of viewpoints given by operators of a customer center. One viewpoint analyzes e-mails in terms of home appliance products. The viewpoint includes five text classes: "Washing machine," "Vacuum cleaner," "Refrigerator," "Microwave oven," and "Other." Here, each e-mail assigned to any of the four first-mentioned text classes has a topic relating to the product. Each e-mail assigned to "Other" has a topic relating to a product other than the four products. In the case that multiple topics are described in an e-mail, the operator assigns the e-mail to a text class including the main topic. The other viewpoint analyzes e-mails in terms of evaluation by customers. The viewpoint includes five text classes: Question, Request, Suggestion, Complaint, and Other. Here, each e-mail assigned to any of the four first-mentioned text classes has a topic relating to one of the four kinds of voice of customer. Each e-mail assigned to "Other has a topic relating to another aspect of voice of customers, such as "Thanks" or "Comments." Also, the system can classify the e-mails into text classes by using the discovered rules. In addition, the system can present statistical information such as distribution of the key phrases and the number of e-mails included in each text class. The users can read only the e-mails classified into text classes corresponding to their interests. The users can directly understand the outline of characteristic key phrases included in the e-mails.

Figure 8 shows a view provided by the system. This view shows the distribution of key phrases in the text class "Suggestion." The users can check key phrases related to "Suggestion." Also, the users can check e-mails including the specific key phrase "energy consumption."

The system shows discovered decision trees to the users. Figure 9 and Figure 10 are parts of rules discovered by the system. In this figure, wave lines show that some branch nodes and their branches are omitted. Figure 9 shows that the products are related to their functions such as "refrigerating" and "washing." Also, this figure shows that they are related to their type codes such as "TA." Figure 10 shows that the phrase "energy consumption" is related to "Suggestion." The us-

Figure 9. Parts of rules based on home appliance products

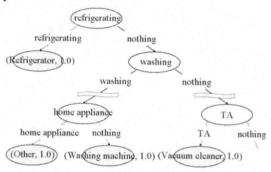

Figure 10. Parts of rules based on evaluation by customers

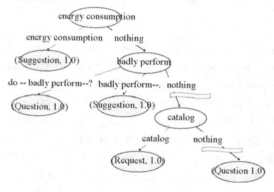

ers cannot predict what kinds of suggestions will be made by customers. The system can provide new knowledge to the users. Also, this figure shows that interrogative sentences such as "do - - badly perform - - ?" are related to "Question." The relationship corresponds to our intuition.

In this application task, we compare the fuzzy decision tree based on key phrases with the one based on words. In the case of words, we select word sets whose *TF-IDF* values are larger than or equal to a threshold. We use 466 e-mails. Each e-mail is assigned two kinds of text classes. One class is included in home appliance products and the other class is included in evaluation by customers. We perform experiments based on 10-fold cross-validation. Table 6 shows average correction ratios and the size of the trees. The

Figure 8. A view of an e-mail analysis system

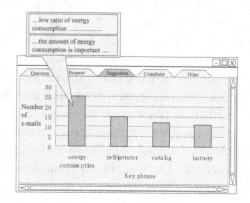

Table 6. Experimental results of the e-mail analysis system

		Key phrase	Word
Size	Products of home appliance	69.0	72.4
	Evaluation of customers	113.8	124.4
Correction ratio	Products of home appliance	80.00%	79.60%
	Evaluation of customers	64.40%	59.70%

results show that fuzzy decision trees based on key phrases are more compact and more valid than those based on words.

CONCLUSION

This chapter introduced methods that discover rules from items of textual data by using a fuzzy inductive learning method. Analysts can directly understand how specific key concepts and specific key phrases relate to their viewpoints by checking the discovered rules. The rules can also classify new items of textual data according to the viewpoints. The analysts can check only items corresponding to their interest and can understand the outline of the items. Here, we note the text classification, which is one of the advantages of text mining techniques. Some papers (Cardoso-Cachopo & Oliveria, 2003; Manevitz & Yousef, 2001) report that the method based on support vector machine (SVM) (Vapnik, 1995) gives higher classification efficiency than other learning methods. SVM may be more efficient than the fuzzy inductive learning method from the viewpoint of the classification efficiency; however, the method based on SVM inductively learns hyperplanes and the hyperplanes are not visualized easily. It is difficult for the method to directly understand the relationships; therefore, it is necessary to select the most valid method according to the aims of text mining.

On the other hand, there are various kinds of textual data this chapter does not deal with and text mining methods that deal with the data have been studied since the mid-1990s. For example,

Sakurai (2004) discovers frequent sequential patterns from items of textual data with time information. The patterns are composed of sequential rows of characteristic events, which are objects, actions, and evaluations described in the items. Analysts can understand the trend of the textual data and can predict future events by using the discovered patterns. Also, Sakurai and Orihara (2006) discover important discussions from bulletin board sites and extract characteristic expressions included in the discussions. The analysts can check discussions corresponding to their interest and can understand outlines of the discussions. In addition, Sakamoto, Arimura, and Arikawa (2001) discover parts of documents with frequent sub-tree structures from HTML documents. The method shows users how structures are included in the documents. The structures are also used as features that classify the HTML documents. Other textual mining techniques will be studied in order to deal with various kinds of textual data.

FUTURE RESEARCH DIRECTIONS

In the future, as the amount of textual data continues to increase, the analysis of textual data will become more important. In particular, two research directions are promising. One direction concerns Web data and the other direction concerns medical data. In the case of Web data, it will be desirable for text mining techniques to collaborate with Semantic Web technologies (Davies, Studer, & Warren, 2006). The latter technologies can intellectually combine various services and various data on the Web; however, it is necessary for the latter techniques to describe well-defined tags. The former technologies help to acquire them automatically or semi-automatically, and to situationally interpret their meanings. The collaboration of these technologies will lead to more effective and convenient support of human decision-making. Also, it is important for the text mining techniques to consider the validity of textual data in Web pages because all pages are not always valid and do not always describe correct information. In addition, it is necessary to deal with Web pages presented using various languages because specific information may be described only in a Web page offered in a specific language. The Web will come into its own as a huge knowledge base thanks to the progress of text mining techniques.

On the other hand, in the case of medical data, the United States National Library of Medicine (*http://www.nlm.nih.gov/*) has collected papers in medical fields since 1966. The number of these papers exceeds 9 million and it increases about 30,000 per year. The papers can be accessed freely. The text mining techniques try to acquire new knowledge from the results of the papers. However, the techniques are not always sufficient. For example, the papers are not described with the same technical terms because the main targets differ depending on the detailed medical fields and the technical term depends on the fields. It is necessary to generate ontologies of the medical fields and to use it in order to acquire new knowledge from the results of multiple papers. It is important for the techniques to generate the ontologies and to maintain them automatically or semi-automatically. Also, it is important for the techniques to situationally combine the ontologies. In addition, these papers include sequential data such as gene arrays and structural data such as chemical materials. It is important for the techniques to fuse them with sequential mining techniques and structural mining techniques. The progress of text miming techniques will contribute to the progress of human health.

I believe that the pace of the progress of text mining techniques in these directions will increase.

REFERENCES

Cardoso-Cachopo, A., & Oliveria, A. L. (2003). An empirical comparison of text categorization methods. In *Proceedings of the 10th International Symposium on String Processing and Information Retrieval* (pp. 183-196). Heidelberg: Springer-Verlag.

Davies, J., Studer, R., & Warren, P. (2006). *Semantic Web technologies: Trends and research in ontology-based systems.* John Wiley & Sons.

Fellbaum, C. (1998). *WordNet: An electronic lexical database.* MIT Press.

Ichimura, Y., Nakayama, Y., Miyoshi, M., Akahane, T., Sekiguchi, T., & Fujiwara, Y. (2001). Text mining systems for analysis of a salesperson's daily reports. In *Proceedings of the Pacific Association for Computational Linguistics 2001* (pp. 127-135).

Kupiec, J. (1992). Robust part-of-speech tagging using a hidden Markov model. *Computer Speech and Language, 6*(3), 225-242.

Manevitz, L. M., & Yousef, M. (2001). One-class SVMs for document classification. *Journal of Machine Learning Research, 2*, 139-154.

Quinlan, J. R. (1992). *C4.5: Programs for machine learning.* Morgan Kaufmann.

Sakamoto, H., Arimura, H., & Arikawa, S. (2001). Extracting partial structures from HTML documents. In *Proceedings of the 14th International FLAIRS Conference* (pp. 247-252).

Sakurai, S., Ichimura, Y., & Suyama, A. (2002). Acquisition of a knowledge dictionary from training examples including multiple values. In *Proceedings of the 12th International Symposium on Methodologies for Intelligent Systems* (pp. 103-113).

Sakurai, S., Ichimura, Y., Suyama, A., & Orihara, R. (2001a). Inductive learning of a knowledge dictionary for a text mining system. In *Proceedings of the 14th International Conference on Industrial, Engineering & Other Applications of Applied Intelligent Systems* (pp. 247-252).

Sakurai, S., Ichimura, Y., Suyama, A., & Orihara, R. (2001b). Acquisition of a knowledge dictionary for a text mining system using an inductive learning method. In *Proceedings of the IJCAI 2001 Workshop on Text Learning: Beyond Supervision* (pp. 45-52).

Sakurai, S., & Orihara, R. (2006). Discovery of important threads from bulletin board sites. *International Journal of Information Technology and Intelligent Computing, 1*(1), 217-228.

Sakurai, S., & Suyama, A. (2004). Rule discovery from textual data based on key phrase patterns. In *Proceedings of the 19th Annual ACM Symposium on Applied Computing* (pp. 606-612).

Sakurai, S., & Suyama, A. (2005). An e-mail analysis method based on text mining techniques. *Applied Soft Computing, 6*(1), 62-71.

Sakurai, S., Suyama, A., & Fume, K. (2003). Acquisition of a concepts relation dictionary for classifying e-mails. In *Proceedings of the IASTED International Conference on Artificial Intelligence and Applications (AIA03)* (pp. 13-19).

Sakurai, S., & Ueno, K. (2004). Analysis of daily business reports based on sequential text mining method. In *Proceedings of the International Conference on Systems, Man and Cybernetics 2004* (pp. 3278-3284).

Salton, G., & McGill, M. J. (1983). *Introduction to modern information retrieval*. McGraw-Hill.

Vapnik, V. N. (1995). *The nature of statistical learning theory*. Springer-Verlag.

Zadeh, L. A. (1978). Fuzzy sets as a basis for a theory of possibility. *Fuzzy Sets and Systems, 1*, 1762-1784.

Additional Reading

Agrawal, R., & Srikant, R. (1995). Mining sequential patterns. In *Proceedings of the 11th International Conference on Data Engineering* (pp. 3-14).

Agrawal, R., & Srikant, R. (1996). Mining sequential patterns: Generalizations and performance improvements. In *Proceedings of the 5th International Conference Extending Database Technology* (pp. 3-17).

Amarasiri, R., Alahakoon, D., Smith, K. A., & Premaratne, M. (2005). HDGSOMr: A high dimensional growing self-organizing map using randomness for efficient Web and text mining. In *Proceedings of the 2005 IEEE/WIC/ACM International Conference on Web Intelligence* (pp. 215-221).

Borges, J., & Levene, M. (1999). Data mining of user navigation patterns. In *Proceedings of the Workshop on Web Usage Analysis and User Profiling* (pp. 31-36).

Chi, E., Pirolli, P., & Pitkow, J. (2000). The scent of a site: A system for analyzing and predicting information scent, usage, and usability of a Web site. In *Proceedings of the Computer/Human Interaction 2000* (pp. 161-168).

Cohen, W., & Richman, J. (2002). Learning to match and cluster large high-dimensional data sets for data integration. In *Proceedings of the 8th ACM SIGKDD International Conference on Knowledge Discovery and Data Mining* (pp. 475-480).

Detyniecki, M., & Marsala, C. (2001). Fuzzy inductive learning for multimedia mining. In *Proceedings of the 2nd International Conference in Fuzzy Logic and Technology* (pp. 5-7).

Farzanyar, Z., Kangavari, M., & Hashemi, S. (2006). A new algorithm for mining fuzzy association rules in the large databases based on ontology. In *Proceedings of the ICDM 2006 Workshop on*

Ontology Mining and Knowledge Discovery from Semistructured Documents (pp. 65-69).

Faure, D., & Nédellec, C. (1998). ASIUM: Learning subcategorization frames and restrictions of selection. In *Proceedings of the 10th ECML Workshop on Text Mining*.

Fertig, C. S., Freitas, A. A., Arruda, L. V. R., & Kaestner, C. (1999). A fuzzy beam-search rule induction algorithm. In *Proceedings of the 3rd European Conference on Principles and Practice of Knowledge Discovery in Databases* (pp. 341-347).

Garofalakis, M., Rastogi, R., & Shim, K. (1999). SPIRIT: Sequential pattern mining with regular expression constraints. In *Proceedings of the 25th International Conference on Very Large Data Bases* (pp. 223-234).

Gomes, M. F., Jr., & Canuto, A. M. (2006). Carcara: A multi-agent system for Web mining using adjustable user profile and dynamic grouping. In *Proceedings of the 2006 IEEE/WIC/ACM International Conference on Intelligent Agent Technology* (pp. 187-190).

He, Y. C., Tang, Y. C., Zhang, Y-Q., & Sunderraman, R. (2006). Fuzzy-granular gene selection from microarray expression data. In *Proceedings of the 6th IEEE International Conference on Data Mining Workshops (ICDMW 2006)* (pp. 153-157).

Hu, Y., Carmona, J., & Murphy, R. F. (2006). Application of temporal texture features to automated analysis of protein subcellular locations in time series fluorescence microscope images. In *Proceedings of the 2006 IEEE International Symposium on Biomedical Imaging* (pp. 1028-1031).

Jain, A. K., Murty, M. N., & Flynn, P. J. (1999). Data clustering: A review. *ACM Computing Surveys, 31*(3), 264-323.

Janikow, C. (1996). Exemplar learning in fuzzy decision trees. In *Proceedings of the IEEE International Conference on Fuzzy Systems 1996* (pp. 1500-1505).

Kleinberg., J. (2002). Bursty and hierarchical structure in streams. In *Proceedings of the 8th ACM SIGKDD International Conference on Knowledge Discovery and Data Mining* (pp. 91-101).

Kou, Z., Cohen, W. W., & Murphy, R. F. (2003). Extracting information from text and images for location proteomics. In *Proceedings of the 3rd ACM SIGKDD Workshop on Data Mining in Bioinformatics* (pp. 2-9).

Laurent, A., Bouchon-Meunier, B., Doucet, A., Gancarski, S., & Marsala, C. (2000). Fuzzy data mining from multidimensional databases. *Proceedings of the International Symposium on Computational Intelligence, Studies in Fuzziness and Soft Computing, 54*, 278-283.

Lent, B., Agrawal, R., & Srikant, R. (1997). Discovering trends in text databases. In *Proceedings of the 3rd International Conference Knowledge Discovery and Data Mining* (pp. 227-230).

Lin, Y-F., Tsai, T.-H., Chou, W.-C., Wu, K.-P., Sung, T.-Y., & Hsu, W.-L. (2004). A maximum entropy approach to biomedical named entity recognition. In *Proceedings of the 4th ACM SIGKDD Workshop on Data Mining in Bioinformatics* (pp. 56-61).

Liu, B. (2007). *Web data mining: Exploring hyperlinks, contents, and usage data.* Springer-Verlag.

Motoda, H. (Eds.) (2002). *Active mining (Frontiers in artificial intelligence and applications).* IOS Press.

Orihara, R., Murakami, T., Sueda, N., & Sakurai, S. (2001). Information space optimization with real-coded genetic algorithm for inductive learning. In *Proceedings of the International Workshop on Hybrid Intelligent Systems (HIS 2001)* (pp. 415-430).

Pei, J., Han, J., Mortazavi-Asl, B., Pinto, H., Chen, Q., Dayal U., & Hsu, M-C. (2001). PrefixSpan: Mining sequential patterns efficiently by prefix-projected pattern growth. In *Proceedings of the 2001 International Conference Data Engineering* (pp. 215-226).

Sakurai, S., Goh, C., & Orihara, R. (2005). Analysis of textual data with multiple classes. In *Proceedings of the 16th International Symposium on Methodologies for Intelligent Systems* (pp. 112-120).

Sakurai, S., Kitahara, Y., & Orihara, R. (2006). Sequential mining method based on a new criterion. In *Proceedings of the 10th IASTED International Conference on Artificial Intelligence and Soft Computing* (pp. 544-545).

Sakurai, S., & Orihara, R. (2006). Discovery of important threads using thread analysis reports. *Proceedings of the IADIS International Conference WWW/Internet 2006, 2*, 253-258.

Sakurai, S., & Saito, Y. (2004). Text classification method using a named entity extractor. In *Proceedings of the Joint 2nd International Conference on Soft Computing and Intelligent Systems and 5th International Symposium on Advanced Intelligent Systems (TUE-3-4)*.

Sakurai, S., Ueno, K., & Orihara, R. (2005). Introduction of time constraints to a sequential mining method. *Proceedings of the IADIS International Conference WWW/Internet 2005, 2*, 328-332.

Silverstein, C., Brin, S., Motwani, R., & Ullman., J. (1998). Scalable techniques for mining causal structures. In *Proceedings of the 1998 International Conference Very Large Data Bases* (pp. 594-605).

Silverstein, C., Motwani, R., & Brin, S. (1997). Beyond market baskets: Generalizing association rules to dependence rules. In *Proceedings of the ACM SIGMOD International Conference on Management of Data (SIGMOD 1997)* (pp. 265-276).

Steinbach, M., Karypis, G., & Kumar, V. (2000). A comparison of document clustering techniques. In *Proceedings of the KDD 1999 Workshop on Text Mining*.

Su, Z., Yang, Q., Lu, Y., & Zhang, H. (2000). WhatNext: A prediction system for Web requests using n-gram sequence models. In *Proceedings of the 1st International Conference on Web Information System and Engineering Conference* (pp. 200-207).

Tan, A. (1999). Text mining: The state of the art and the challenges. In *Proceedings of the PAKDD 1999 Workshop on Knowledge Discovery from Advanced Databases* (pp. 65-70).

Weng, C., & Poon, J. (2006). A data complexity analysis on imbalanced datasets and an alternative imbalance recovering strategy. In *Proceedings of the 2006 IEEE/WIC/ACM International Conference on Web Intelligence* (pp. 270-276).

Wu, S-T., Li, Y., & Xu, Y. (2006). Deploying approaches for pattern refinement in text mining. In *Proceedings of the 6th IEEE International Conference on Data Mining* (pp. 1157-1161).

Yang, Y., Slattery, S., & Ghani, R. (2002). A study of approaches to hypertext categorization. *Journal of Intelligent Information Systems, 18*(2/3), 219-241.

Yi, L., & Liu, B. (2003). Eliminating noisy information in Web pages for data mining. In *Proceedings of the 9th ACM Conference on Knowledge Discovery and Data Mining* (pp. 595-607).

Zaki, M. J. (2001). SPADE: An efficient algorithm for mining frequent sequences. *Machine Learning, 4*(1/2), 31-60.

Zhou, X., Wu, S.-T., Li, Y., Xu, Y., Lau, R. Y. K., & Bruza, P. D. (2006). Utilizing search intent in topic ontology-based user profile for Web mining. In *Proceedings of the 2006 IEEE/WIC/ACM International Conference on Web Intelligence* (pp. 558-564).

Chapter VII
Exploring Unclassified Texts Using Multiview Semisupervised Learning

Edson Takashi Matsubara
University of São Paulo, Brazil

Maria Carolina Monard
University of São Paulo, Brazil

Ronaldo Cristiano Prati
University of São Paulo, Brazil

ABSTRACT

This chapter presents semisupervised multiview learning in the context of text mining. Semisupervised learning uses both labeled and unlabeled data to improve classification performance. It also presents several multiview semisupervised algorithms, such as CO-TRAINING, CO-EM, CO-TESTING, and CO-EMT, as well as reporting some experimental results using CO-TRAINING in text classification domains. Semisupervised learning could be very useful whenever there is much more unlabeled than labeled data. This is likely to occur in several text mining applications, where obtaining unlabeled data is inexpensive, although manual labeling the data is costly.

INTRODUCTION

A common task in text mining is text categorization, where we would like to classify texts according to some predefined categories. Its analogue task in data mining jargon is classification, where we would like to classify a given instance into a set of predefined classes. In both cases, the usual approach is to use a set of previously labeled texts or classified instances to learn a model, which can be used to classify new documents or instances. The labeled texts or classified instances are known as (labeled) examples, the model as a classifier and the learning process as supervised learning (Mitchell, 1997). The term supervised comes from the fact that an external agent (the supervisor) should provide the label of the texts or the class of the training instances.

Although supervised learning is widely used in data and text mining, the labeled examples used in this kind of learning are often expensive and difficult to obtain. On the other hand, unlabeled data is usually available in large quantities and is generally cheap and easy to collect. However, unsupervised learning (learning from unlabeled data) is only able to organize instances or texts in self-detected groups, not in predefined categories (Berry, 2003).

Semisupervised learning is the middle road between supervised and unsupervised learning. The semisupervised learning approach uses a set of examples of which only a few examples are labeled and the aim is to predict the labels of some of the remaining unlabeled examples. The main idea of semisupervised learning is to find ways whereby using unlabeled data it is possible to effectively improve classification performance, when compared with a classifier build only using a small set of labeled examples. In other words, semisupervised learning is an iterative process that in each step makes use of unlabeled data to refine the current model. Taking this into account, semisupervised learning should outperform supervised learning using a small training set by making use of unlabeled data in different ways.

Some characteristics of text mining applications make it suitable for semisupervised learning. In text mining, datasets having a small number of labeled examples and a large number of unlabeled ones can be easily obtained. For example, it is possible to construct a large set of unlabeled examples by collecting Web pages from the Internet and hand labeling some of them in order to construct a small set of labeled examples. Texts gathered from a source of digital texts can be transformed into the attribute-value representation using the so-called bag-of-words representation, where a feature vector represents each text and each feature value is given by its corresponding relevance in the text. By representing texts using this approach, it is possible to use semisupervised learning, as well as most standard learning algorithms.

Among semisupervised methods, multiview semisupervised learning is of special interest in text mining as it can incorporate several aspects of textual documents. This is due to the fact that multiview semisupervised learning algorithms use at least two independent sets of attributes to represent each example. For instance, a Web page classification task can be suitable for multiview learning where a page can be classified based on its content, as well as based on the anchor texts of its inbound hyperlinks. This work presents several multiview semisupervised algorithms and some applications for text mining.

After introducing semisupervised learning and presenting multiview semisupervised learning, we present some applications of multiview semisupervised learning in text classification domains. We report on experimental results followed by the conclusions.

SEMISUPERVISED LEARNING

Traditional supervised learning uses labeled examples to train a classifier. The goal of these algorithms is to learn a function (concept) that maps the set of attributes to one of the possible classes. On the other hand, semisupervised learning is the class of algorithms where the supervision information (the class associated to each example) is not available for all training examples.

In the design of semisupervised algorithms, the use of unlabeled data can be very useful. The main reason is that exploring unlabeled data may give rise to some evidence of the unknown distribution the examples are drawn from. To give an intuitive notion, consider a binary classification task presented in Figure 1 where just a few

Figure 1. Using unlabeled data to help parameter estimation (Zhu, 2005)

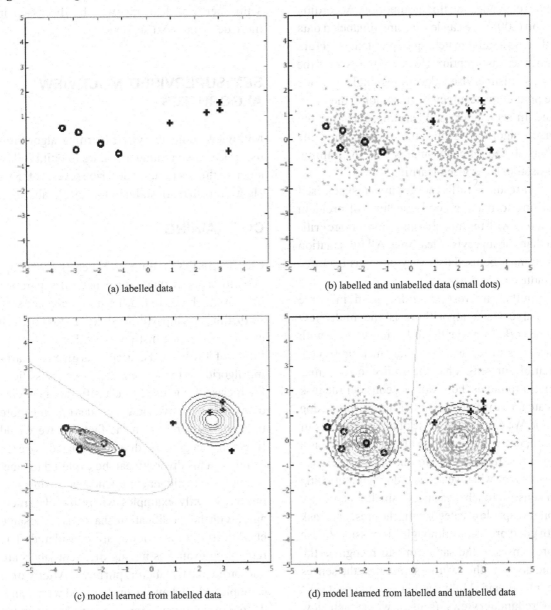

(a) labelled data

(b) labelled and unlabelled data (small dots)

(c) model learned from labelled data

(d) model learned from labelled and unlabelled data

labeled examples are given and each class has a Gaussian distribution. Depicting a few examples from this Gaussian distribution, Figure 1(a), it is difficult to discover the correct parameters of the Gaussian distributions, Figure 1(c). However, using both, labeled and unlabeled data, Figure 1(b),

the parameters of the model can be discovered, Figure 1(d).

There is an important assumption to work with semisupervised learning: the distribution of examples from which unlabeled data will help to learn the model should be appropriate to construct the classifier. Semisupervised learning is highly dependent on this assumption. According to Zhu (2005), we can learn using unlabeled data if there is a good matching of problem structure with model assumption. However, if this is not the case, semisupervised algorithms might degrade the prediction accuracy by misguiding the inference. In semisupervised learning, selecting the correct algorithm is much more complicated due to the labeled set being smaller than the training set used in supervised learning.

As a result, the effort needed in semisupervised learning to make a good matching of problem structure with the model assumption is more critical than for supervised learning. All information given must be used as a very precious resource to induce a classifier.

Another interesting notion used in some semisupervised algorithms is the multiview framework. Consider the following analogy with our senses: taste, vision, hearing, smell, and touch. Each of our senses has the ability to recognise things around us. For example, consider the task of categorise whether what is near from us is a dog or not. We can use the sense of touch without our vision, hearing, or smell to affirm whether it is a dog or not. It is the same for the other senses. We can say that what we see is a dog without using our sense of touch, hearing, or smell. Each sense alone is capable of categorizing the presented task with good precision, although it is possible to use more senses at the same time to recognise the same dog. In other words, sometimes the senses are "redundant". Multiview algorithms use at least two "redundant views" (senses), where each view is defined by mutually exclusive sets of features that can be used to learn the target concept.

Blum and Mitchell (1998) propose an interesting approach for semisupervised learning called CO-TRAINING which uses datasets that have a natural separation of their features into two disjoint sets, referred to as multiview semisupervised learning. In a multiview setting, the attributes are presented in subsets (views), which are sufficient

to learn the target concept. Other multiview semisupervised learning will be discussed in more details in next section.

SEMISUPERVISED MULTIVIEW ALGORITHMS

Multiview semisupervised learning algorithms use at least two redundant views to build a classifier. In this section, we describe several of these algorithms that are suitable for text databases.

CO-TRAINING

CO-TRAINING (Blum & Mitchell, 1998) applies to datasets that have a natural separation of their attributes into at least two disjoint sets, so that there is a partitioned description of each example into each distinct view. For each view, the set of few labeled examples is given to learning algorithms to induce independent classifiers. Each classifier is used to classify the unlabeled data in its respective view. The idea of using more than one view relies on the fact that we would like some degree of diversity related to each example. This diversity can be explored to label examples with higher confidence than using only one view. Only examples where the classifiers agree with the classification, that is, have the same classification in all views, are considered. The remaining examples having different labels are not considered for labeling purposes. Afterwards, examples which have been classified with a high degree of confidence for all views are included in the set of labeled examples and the process is repeated using the augmented labeled set until a stop criterion is met.

CO-TRAINING works as follows: Given a set of N examples $E = \{E_1, ..., E_N\}$ defined by a set of M attributes $\mathbf{X} = \{X_1, X_2, ..., X_M\}$ and the class attribute Y, where we only know the class attribute for a few examples, CO-TRAINING needs at least two disjoint and compatible views D_1 and

Figure 2. CO-TRAINING

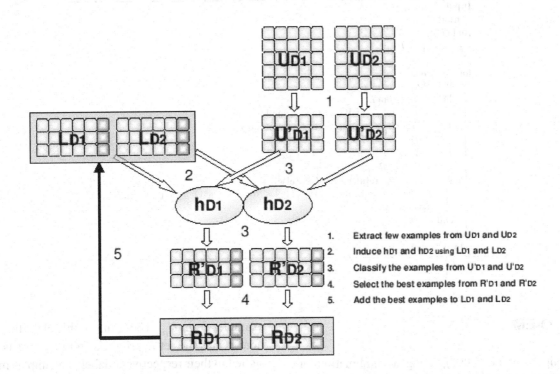

1. Extract few examples from U_D1 and U_D2
2. Induce h_D1 and h_D2 using L_D1 and L_D2
3. Classify the examples from U'_D1 and U'_D2
4. Select the best examples from R'_D1 and R'_D2
5. Add the best examples to L_D1 and L_D2

D_2 of the set of examples E to work with. In other words, for each example $j = 1, 2 \ldots N$ in D_1 we should have its j-th counterpart (compatible example) in D_2. We shall refer to these two views as $\mathbf{X}_{D1}$ and $\mathbf{X}_{D2}$ such that $\mathbf{X} = \mathbf{X}_{D1} \cup \mathbf{X}_{D2}$ and $\mathbf{X}_{D1} \cap \mathbf{X}_{D2} = \varnothing$. Furthermore, the set of labeled examples in each view should be adequate for learning.

Set E can be divided into two disjoint subsets L (Labeled) and U (Unlabeled) of examples. Both subsets L and U are further divided into two disjoint views respectively called, L_{D1}, L_{D2} and U_{D1}, U_{D2}. These four subsets L_{D1}, L_{D2}, U_{D1} and U_{D2}, illustrated in Figure 2, as well as the maximum number of iterations k, constitute the input of CO-TRAINING described by Algorithm 1.

Initially, two small pools U'_{D1} and U'_{D2} of compatible unlabeled examples, withdrawn from U_{D1} and U_{D2} respectively, are created, and the main loop of Algorithm 1 starts. First, the sets of training examples L_{D1} and L_{D2} are used to induce two classifiers h_{D1} and h_{D2}, respectively. Next, the set of examples U'_{D1} is labeled using h_{D1} and inserted into R'_{D1}, and the set of examples from U'_{D2} is labeled using h_{D2} and inserted into R'_{D2}. Both sets of labeled examples are given to the function *bestExamples* which is responsible for ranking compatible examples from R'_{D1} and R'_{D2} that have the same class label prediction, and selecting from them the "best" pairs of compatible examples to be inserted in L_{D1} and L_{D2} respectively. The process is repeated until a stop criterion is met: either the maximum number of iterations defined by the user or the set U_{D1} (or its counterpart U_{D2}) is empty.

Algorithm 1 describes the general idea of CO-TRAINING using the same base-learning algorithm (naïve Bayes in the original proposal) which makes it possible to construct a third classifier from h_{D1} and h_{D2} called combined classifier (Blum & Mitchell, 1998).

Algorithm 1. CO-TRAINING

Input: $L_{D1}, L_{D2}, U_{D2}, k$
Output: L_{D1}, L_{D2}
Build U'_{D1} and U'_{D2} as described;
$U_{D1} = U_{D1} - U'_{D1}$;
$U_{D2} = U_{D2} - U'_{D2}$;
for $i = 0$ *to* k **do**
$\quad$ Induce h_{D1} from L_{D1};
$\quad$ Induce h_{D2} from L_{D2};
$\quad$ $R'_{D1} = h_{D1}(U'_{D1})$ set of classified examples from U'_{D1};
$\quad$ $R'_{D2} = h_{D2}(U'_{D2})$ set of classified examples from U'_{D2};
$\quad$ $(R_{D1}, R_{D2}) = bestExamples(R'_{D1}, R'_{D2})$;
$\quad$ $L_{D1} = L_{D1} \cup R_{D1}$;
$\quad$ $L_{D2} = L_{D2} \cup R_{D2}$;
$\quad$ **if** $U_{D1} = \emptyset$ **then return**(L_{D1}, L_{D2}) **else**
$\quad\quad$ Randomly select compatible examples from U_{D1} and U_{D2} to replenish U'_{D1} and U'_{D2} respectively;
$\quad$ **end**
end
return(L_{D1}, L_{D2});

CO-EM

Nigam et al. (2000), using a combination of CO-TRAINING and expectation maximization (EM) (Dempster, Laird & Rubin, 1977), proposed CO-EM. The authors also used naïve Bayes as the base-learning algorithm to induce classifiers for both views. Algorithm 2 describes each step of CO-EM in detail. Initially, the labeled set L_{D1} is used to induce the classifier h_{D1}, which labels examples from U_{D1}. The result of this classification creates the set R_{D1}. Labels from R_{D1} are assigned to their respective unlabeled examples in the second view, U_{D2}, creating R_{D2}. The second classifier h_{D2} is induced using $L_{D2} \cup R_{D2}$. In this step h_{D2} labels the examples from U_{D2}. Similar to the previous step, the labels from U_{D2} are assigned to their respective examples in the first view, creating R_{D1}. Using L_{D1} U R_{D1}, the classifier h_{D1} is induced and the process is repeated until it

Algorithm 2. CO-EM

Input: $L_{D1}, L_{D2}, U_{D1}, U_{D2}, k$
induce the classifier h_{D1} from L_{D1};
for $it = 0$ *to* k **do**
$\quad$ $R_{D1} =$ label the examples from U_{D1} using the classifier h_{D1};
$\quad$ $R_{D2} =$ copy the labels from R_{D1} to U_{D2};
$\quad$ induce the classifier h_{D2} from $L_{D2} \cup R_{D2}$;
$\quad$ $R_{D2} =$ label the examples from U_{D2} using the classifier h_{D2};
$\quad$ $R_{D1} =$ copy the labels from R_{D2} to U_{D1};
$\quad$ induce the classifier h_{D1} from $L_{D1} \cup R_{D1}$;
end
Return $R_{D1}, R_{D2}, h_{D1}, h_{D2}$;

---

reaches a previously defined number of iterations k or until both classifiers converge.

As stated before, at the beginning of each iteration of the CO-TRAINING algorithm, two training datasets are used and two classifiers are induced in parallel. However, in CO-EM one classifier labels the training dataset to the other and they cannot be used at the same time as in CO-TRAINING. Another interesting difference from CO-TRAINING is that labels of the training set can be changed during the iterations of the algorithm. CO-TRAINING does not allow changes in the labels.

CO-TESTING and CO-EMT

Asking the domain expert to label the most informative unlabeled examples can reduce the cost of labeling training data; therefore, it is possible to induce better classifiers with fewer examples. This is the idea of selective sampling, which is a form of active learning (Cohn, Ghahramani & Jordan, 1996). In general terms, both active and semisupervised learning address the same problem, that is, scarcity of labeled and abundance of unlabeled data. Thus, it is natural to combine active and semisupervised learning to tackle the problem from both perspectives. CO-TESTING (Muslea, Minton & Knoblock, 2000) approaches this idea from the semisupervised multiview learning setting. The basic idea is to apply the induced classifiers for each view to the sets of unlabeled examples. Then, the examples with the greatest degree of disagreement, which can be considered as the most informative examples, are given to the human expert for manual labeling.

To clarify the concept of CO-TESTING, consider the toy task presented in Muslea's paper. The problem consists of classifying the employees of a computer science (CS) department into two categories: faculty (+) and non-faculty (−). The classification can be carried out either by using a person's salary (first view) or office number (second view). In both views the target concept has

two threshold values: \$65,000 for salary (faculty people have a salary above \$65,000), and 300 for the number of the office they work (faculties office numbers are below 300). To induce this concept we use a learning algorithm λ which identifies the pair of labeled examples that belong to different classes and have the closest attribute values; then λ sets the threshold to the mean of these two values.

CO-TESTING can be described as follows: first, the user provides two small sets of labeled examples L_{D1} and L_{D2}, one for each view, and their respective unlabeled set, U_{D1} and U_{D2}. In Figure 3(a) the unlabeled examples are denoted by points, while the labeled examples appear as (+) and (−). These symbols represent respectively the categories faculty and nonfaculty. The learner λ creates two classifiers, one for each view. The dotted and the dashed lines geometrically represent the two classifiers, one for the salary and the other for office number. Then, we apply the classifiers to all unlabeled examples and determine the contention points; the examples that are labeled differently by both classifiers. Note that the contention points are extremely informative (points within the gray areas) since whenever the two classifiers disagree, at least one of them must be wrong. If we select a point that is in the picture's white area, this point cannot give much information to improve the classifier. On the other hand, if we select a point that is in the picture's gray area and add it to the training set, the classifiers converge faster.

Another interesting point of CO-TESTING is the use of learners that can evaluate the confidence of its classification. In this case, it is possible to query the contention point in which both classifiers are most confident. In the toy task, the confident level is the distance between the point and the threshold: the larger the distance, the higher the confidence in the classification. In Figure 3(a), point Q1 is the contention point in which the sum of the distances to the two thresholds is maximal. This point has the greatest disagreement between the classifiers and maximally improves at least

Figure 3. CO-TESTING at work (Muslea et al., 2000)

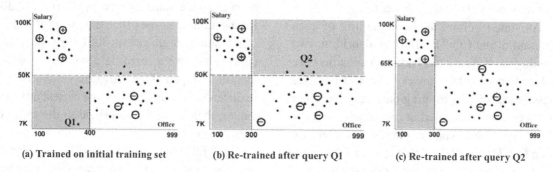

| (a) Trained on initial training set | (b) Re-trained after query Q1 | (c) Re-trained after query Q2 |

one of the hypotheses. Once the user labels the example, the classifiers are induced again with point Q1 within the training set. Then, CO-TESTING looks for a new contention point (Figure 3(b)), and re-trains again. Finally, as shown in Figure 3(c), the new classifiers agree on all unlabeled examples, and CO-TESTING stops.

Algorithm 3 presents CO-TESTING. Initially, classifiers h_{D1} and h_{D2} are induced using the base-learning algorithm and their respective training sets L_{D1} and L_{D2}. Afterwards, all unlabeled examples in U_{D1} and U_{D2} are labeled using h_{D1} and h_{D2} and a set of examples *ContentionPoints*, where the labels disagree on the views, is created. The function *Query* selects the most confidant examples from *ContentionPoints*, which will be hand labeled by the user. These examples should maximize the information given to the base-learners and they are inserted into the training set. The process is repeated until a stop criterion is met: either the *ContentionPoints* set is empty or the algorithm reaches k iterations.

Algorithm 3. CO-TESTING

Input: $L_{D1}, L_{D2}, U_{D1}, U_{D2}, k$
for $it = 0 \ to \ k$ **do**
  induce the classifier h_{D1} from L_{D1};
  induce the classifier h_{D2} from L_{D2};
  R_{D1} = label the examples from U_{D1} using the classifier h_{D1};
  R_{D2} = label the examples from U_{D2} using the classifier h_{D2};
  $ContentionPoints = \{(\mathbf{x}_{i_{D1}}, \mathbf{x}_{i_{D2}}) | h_{D1}(\mathbf{x}_{i_{D1}}) \neq$
  $h_{D2}(\mathbf{x}_{i_{D2}}) \wedge (\mathbf{x}_{i_{D1}}, h_{D1}(\mathbf{x}_{i_{D1}})) \in R_{D1} \wedge (\mathbf{x}_{i_{D2}}, h_{D2}(\mathbf{x}_{i_{D2}})) \in R_{D2}\}$;
  if $ContentionPoints = \emptyset$ **then Return**;
  $(\mathbf{x}_{i_{D1}}, \mathbf{x}_{i_{D2}}) = Query(ContentionPoints)$;
  r_i = ask the user to label some examples from $(\mathbf{x}_{i_{D1}}, \mathbf{x}_{i_{D2}})$;
  $L_{D1} = L_{D1} \cup \{(\mathbf{x}_{i_{D1}}, r_i)\}$;
  $L_{D2} = L_{D2} \cup \{(\mathbf{x}_{i_{D2}}, r_i)\}$;
  $U_{D1} = U_{D1} - \{\mathbf{x}_{i_{D1}}\}$;
  $U_{D2} = U_{D2} - \{\mathbf{x}_{i_{D2}}\}$;
end
Return $L_{D1}, L_{D2}, h_{D1}, h_{D2}$;

Algorithm 4. CO-EMT

Input: $L_{D1}, L_{D2}, U_{D1}, U_{D2}, k, k_{EM}$
for $it = 0 \; to \; k$ **do**

  $(R_{D1}, R_{D2}, h_{D1}, h_{D2}) = CO - EM(L_{D1}, L_{D2}, U_{D1}, U_{D2}, k_{EM})$
  $ContentionPoints = \{(\mathbf{x}_{i_{D1}}, \mathbf{x}_{i_{D2}}) | h_{D1}(\mathbf{x}_{i_{D1}}) \neq$
  $h_{D2}(\mathbf{x}_{i_{D2}}) \wedge (\mathbf{x}_{i_{D1}}, h_{D1}(\mathbf{x}_{i_{D1}})) \in R_{D1} \wedge (\mathbf{x}_{i_{D2}}, h_{D2}(\mathbf{x}_{i_{D2}})) \in R_{D2}\}$;
  if $ContentionPoints = \emptyset$ **then Return**;
  $(\mathbf{x}_{i_{D1}}, \mathbf{x}_{i_{D2}}) = Query(ContentionPoints)$;
  $r_i = $ ask the user to label the examples from $(\mathbf{x}_{i_{D1}}, \mathbf{x}_{i_{D2}})$;
  $L_{D1} = L_{D1} \cup \{(\mathbf{x}_{i_{D1}}, r_i)\}$;
  $L_{D2} = L_{D2} \cup \{(\mathbf{x}_{i_{D2}}, r_i)\}$;
  $U_{D1} = U_{D1} - \{\mathbf{x}_{i_{D1}}\}$;
  $U_{D2} = U_{D2} - \{\mathbf{x}_{i_{D2}}\}$;
end
Return $L_{D1}, L_{D2}, h_{D1}, h_{D2}$;

In CO-TESTING, incompatible examples can only be inserted into the labeled sets by manual labeling. This approach contrasts with CO-TRAINING, where only the most confident and compatible examples are labeled by the algorithm and inserted into the labeled sets.

It is worth noting that there is a variation of CO-TESTING which was designed to be used with any base-learning algorithm and not strictly with base-learners which evaluates the confidence of its classification. In case the base-algorithm does not supply such confidence, the function *Query* randomly queries the contention points. This algorithm is called naive CO-TESTING. Despite its simplicity, empirical results show that naive CO-TESTING is a powerful selective sampling algorithm (Muslea et al., 2000).

Another variation of CO-TESTING is CO-EMT (Muslea, Minton & Knoblock, 2002) described by Algorithm 4. As we can see, the algorithm is very similar to CO-TESTING. the main difference is the induction of h_{D1} and h_{D2}, which comes from CO-EM. The remaining steps are similar to CO-TESTING.

In order to put CO-EMT into a larger context, Figure 4 shows its relationship with the other algorithms considered in this study. On the one hand, CO-EMT is a semisupervised variant of CO-TESTING, which in turn was inspired by CO-TRAINING. On the other hand, CO-EMT builds on CO-EM, which is a semisupervised algorithm that combines the basic ideas from CO-TRAINING and EM.

Other Algorithms

CO-TRAINING has inspired several algorithms. In this section, we briefly describe some of them. Zhou and Li (2005a) propose a CO-TRAINING like semisupervised regression algorithm, known as COREG. The algorithm is based in two k-nearest neighbour regressors with different distance metrics. Each regressor labels the unlabeled data for the other regressor.

Another interesting algorithm, called TRI-TRAINING (Zhou & Li, 2005b), induces three classifiers from the original labeled data set. These classifiers are then refined using unlabeled

Figure 4. The lineage of the CO-EMT algorithm (Muslea et al., 2002)

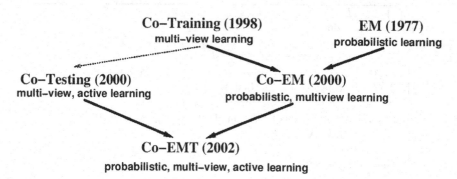

examples. The labeled dataset is split into three subsets. In each round of TRI-TRAINING, two different samples are used to induce two different classifiers. An unlabeled example is included in the other sample, if these two classifiers agree on the labeling. In the next iteration the process is repeated using a different pair of samples. Since tri-training neither requires the instance space to be described with sufficient and redundant views nor does it put any constraints on the supervised learning algorithm, its applicability is broader than that of previous CO-TRAINING style algorithms.

Brefeld and Scheffer (2004) proposed a version of CO-EM using support vector machines as the base-classifiers. It is worth mentioning that in their paper the authors conducted a broad range of experiments on text classification problems. For some problems, such as course Web page classification, they obtained the most accurate results reported so far.

APPLICATIONS OF CO-TRAINING TO TEXT CLASSIFICATION

Several research papers propose to apply multiview semisupervised learning in text mining, such as Web page classification (Blum and Mitchell, 1998), e-mail classification (Kiritchenko and Matwin, 2001; Kockelkorn, Lneburg & Scheffer, 2003), e-mail answering assistance (Scheffer, 2004), and text classification (Nigam, 2001). Nevertheless, the necessary views for multiview learning are highly dependent on the domain of application. In this section we describe some of these applications and how the multiviews are created.

Web Pages Classification

Blum and Mitchell (1998) applied CO-TRAINING in a Web pages classification task. In this application, the problem is related to classifying Web pages collected from computer science departments of various universities either as a course or not a course Web page. One of the views consists of words appearing on the page. The other view consists of the words from a link which points to a given Web page. For both views, the well-known bag-of-words approach was used to transform texts into the attribute-value table data format.

Although this approach is easy to apply and might produce good results, it has some drawbacks. One of them is that Web pages are also composed by images, animations, applets, and other components that do not provide any textual data. Thus, using only the texts in Web pages to generate the views will ignore this information. The second view may also have a similar problem. The underlined words from other pages which point to the Web page, in most of the cases, are key words, which provide a good indication of the pointed page's content. However, sometimes these words could be meaningless, such as "click here", "link", or a picture.

When one view cannot classify a Web page with good confidence the second view can be helpful. CO-TRAINING is based on the observation that the rate of disagreement between independent hypotheses upper bounds their individual error rate (Dasgupta, Littman & McAllester, 2002). Therefore, if one view cannot classify the page with good confidence and the other view is highly confident and the algorithm classifies the example, a correct classification can be very probable.

E-Mail Classification

Kiritchenko and Matwin (2001) used CO-TRAINING to classify e-mails using as the first view the subject and as the second the body of the messages. The authors selected the three largest folders from one of the authors' inbox and created three classification problems. For each problem, one of the folders was considered as interesting messages and the other two representing uninteresting e-mails. As in the previous section, the bag-of-words approach was used to transform texts into the attribute-value table data format.

However, for the e-mail domain, one of the assumptions of the original CO-TRAINING proposal is violated. CO-TRAINING needs two sets of attributes which have to be conditionally independent given the class. This condition is not always true for e-mail domain, as people often repeat words from the subject in the body of an e-mail message. To test whether the conditional independence affects the results, the authors removed from the body the words that appeared in

both the subject and the body of the messages and ran the experiment again. Although the original assumption of conditionally independent attributes was violated in the first experiment, the results in the latter experiment did not change much from the first one.

Another interesting result was obtained by applying an attribute subset selection method to the datasets. The authors used the correlation-based attribute subset selection implemented in the WEKA toolkit (Witten & Frank, 2000). For the e-mail classification problem which has the greatest disproportion between the classes, the improvement in accuracy was approximately 18%. For the more balanced problem, the improvement was approximately 4%.

Multigram Approach

As stated before, when identifying terms using the standard bag-of-words approach, each term (word) is used as an attribute of the dataset represented in the attribute-value format. This straightforward approach is usually called 1-gram bag-of-words (bag-of-words using single words, 1-gram, as attributes). However, a term can also be represented by composed words (2 and 3-gram) that occur in the document.

For text domains, a general way to construct the two views needed by CO-TRAINING is to use the multigram approach to construct the views (Matsubara, Monard & Batista, 2005). For example, one of the views can be constructed using 1-gram representation and a 2-gram representation for the other view. Note that this representation cannot guarantee complete independence among the views. However, the views are not completely correlated either. For example, consider the word *learning* and the composed word *machine learning*. They will have the same counts only in the case where all occurrences of *learning* in the text come from the composed word *machine learning*. Nevertheless, this situation seldom occurs in real texts.

This multigram approach for constructing views has been implemented in the PRETEXT system (Matsubara, Monard & Batista, 2003), available at http://www.icmc.usp.br/~edsontm/pretext/pretext.html, a text pre-processing computational tool to efficiently decompose text into words (stems) using the bag-of-words approach.

EXPERIMENTAL RESULTS

We conducted several experiments to evaluate CO-TRAINING in text databases. See Matsubara and Monard (2004) for more details. In this work we selected two experiments to give an overall idea of its performance.

Dataset Preprocessing

We carried out an experimental evaluation using three different text datasets: a subset of the UseNet news articles (20-NewsGroups) (Newman, Hettich, Blake & Merz, 1998), abstracts of academic papers, titles, and references collected from *Lecture Notes in Artificial Intelligence* (LNAI) (Melo, Secato & Lopes, 2003), and links and Web pages from the COURSE dataset (Blum & Mitchell, 1998), described as follows:

- **NEWS:** The NEWS dataset is a subset of the 20-newsgroups. We selected 100 texts from *sci.crypt, sci.electronics, sci.med, sci.space, talk.politics.guns, talk.politics.mideast, talk.politics.misc* and *talk.religion.misc*. All texts from the first four newsgroups were labeled as *sci* (400 - 50%) and texts from the remaining newsgroups were labeled as *talk* (400 - 50%).

- **LNAI:** The LNAI consists of academic papers collected from Lecture Notes in Artificial Intelligence. This dataset contains 396 papers from Case Based Reason (277 - 70%) and Inductive Logic Programming (119 - 30%).

- **COURSE:** The COURSE dataset (available at http://www.cs.cmu.edu/afs/cs/cmu.edu/project/theo-51/www/CO-TRAINING/data consists of 1,051 Web pages collected from various Computer Science department Web sites and divided into several categories. This dataset already provides the two views for each Web page example as explained in "Web pages classification" section. However, analysing the examples in the original dataset, we found 13 examples which are either empty (no text) or its compatible example in the counterpart view is missing. Thus, the original dataset was reduced to 1,038 examples. Similar to Blum and Mitchell (1998), Web pages were labeled as course (221 - 20%), and the remaining categories as non-course (817 - 80%).

To carry out the experiments, we used the PRETEXT systems (Matsubara et al., 2003). PRETEXT can handle texts written in Portuguese, Spanish, or English. Stemming is based on Porter's stemming algorithm for the English language (1980), which was adapted for Portuguese and Spanish. PRETEXT has several facilities, such as reducing the (inherent high) dimensionality of text representations using the bag-of-words approach by using Luhn cut-offs based on the Zipf's law, stemming and several normalization measures to represent the value of terms in the documents, stopwords, n-gram, inductive construction, graphics, and others.

Stemming is a process for removing the commoner morphological and inflexional endings from words. For instance, the words *learned, learning,* and *learns* are mapped to the stem *learn*. Zipf's law states that in natural language, the frequency of any word is roughly inversely proportional to its rank in the frequency table. Therefore, the most frequent word will occur approximately twice as often as the second most frequent word, which occurs twice as often as the fourth most frequent word, and so on. Luhn used

Table 1. Datasets description

Dataset	#Doc	View	#Stem	#Attr.	Class
NEWS	800	1-*gram*	15,711	8,668	sci talk
		2-*gram*	71,039	4,521	sci talk
LNAI	396	1-*gram*	5,627	2,914	ILP CBR
		2-*gram*	21,969	3,245	ILP CBR
COURSE	1,038	TEXTO	13,198	6,870	course non-course
		LINKS	1,604	1,067	course non-course

the Zipf's law to specify two cut-offs, an upper and a lower, as an attempt to exclude non-significant words. The general idea is that the words exceeding the upper cut-off can be considered to be common and those below the lower cut-off rare, and therefore not contributing significantly to the content of the text. Certain arbitrariness is involved to determine the Luhn cut-offs which have to be established by trial and error.

In our experiments, all text datasets were decomposed into the attribute value representation using the bag-of-words approach and stopwords. Stemming and Luhn cut-offs were also carried out.

For datasets NEWS and LNAI, the two views were constructed following the approach proposed in (Matsubara et al., 2005), using 1-gram representation as one view and 2-gram as the second view of the datasets. Initially, PRETEXT ignores the list of specified stopwords and constructs the stems of the remaining words. Afterwards, it constructs the 1-gram and 2-gram representation of the dataset. For example, in the 2-gram view, *artificial intelligence* will be mapped to *artifici_intellig* and *University of Cleveland* will be mapped to *univers_cleveland*. For the 2-gram view in the NEWS dataset, the minimum Luhn cut-off was set to 3. For the remaining views, the minimum Luhn cut-off was set to 2. The

Figure 5. 10-fold construction for CO-TRAINING evaluation

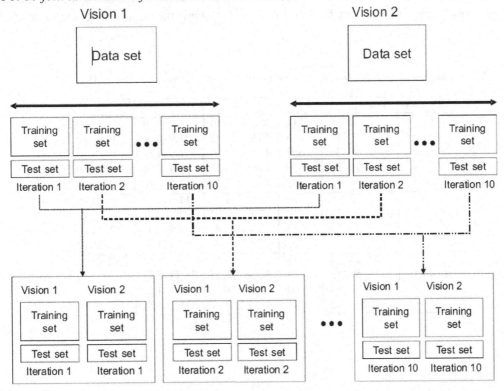

maximum Luhn cut-offs were left unbounded. For dataset COURSE 1-gram was used in both views, called TEXTO and LINKS. Table 1 summarises the datasets used in this work. It shows the dataset name (Dataset); number of documents in the dataset (#Doc); number of generated stems (#Stem); number of stems left after performing Luhn cut-offs in each view (#Attributes), and class distribution (%Class).

As all datasets are completely labeled, we can compare the labels assigned by CO-TRAINING in each iteration with the true labels of the datasets. In other words, we use CO-TRAINING in a simulated mode, in which the true labels are hidden from the algorithm and are only used to measure the number of examples wrongly labeled by CO-TRAINING. In our experiments, we used naïve Bayes (NB) as CO-TRAINING base-classifiers.

To assess the behavior of CO-TRAINING using cross-validation, we adapted the sampling method as shown in Figure 5. First, the examples in both views are paired and marked with an ID. Then, we sample the folds so that both train-

ing and test samples are compatible, that is, an example marked with a given ID appears only in the training or test sample in both views. All experiments described next were carried out using this adapted 10-fold cross-validation. Moreover, the minimum probability to label an example was always set to 0.6.

Experiment 1

As the main idea of semisupervised learning is to use a large unlabeled sample to improve the performance of supervised learning algorithms when only a small set of labeled examples is available, the aim of the first experiment is to observe the behaviour of CO-TRAINING using a different number of initial labeled examples. For this experiment, the number of examples of each class that may be inserted into L in each iteration was set to 2 for each class.

Table 2 shows the results obtained, where: $|L_{ini}|$ and $|U_{ini}|$ refer respectively to the initial number of labeled and unlabeled examples. After execution $|L_{end}|$ shows the mean number of examples labeled

Table 2. Mean number of CO-TRAINING incorrectly labeled examples varying $|L_{ini}|$

Dataset	% and $|L_{ini}|$	$|U_{ini}|$	$|L_{end}|$	#Errors	%Errors
NEWS	1% 6	714	402.0 (0.00)	2.4 (0.9)	0.6% (0.2)
	2% 14	706	409.3 (2.21)	1.9 (0.9)	0.5% (0.2)
	5% 36	684	432.0 (0.00)	1.9 (1.5)	0.5% (0.4)
	7% 50	670	446.0 (0.00)	2.4 (0.9)	0.6% (0.2)
	10% 72	648	468.0 (0.00)	2.6 (0.6)	0.7% (0.2)
LNAI	2% 6	350	275.7 (2.9)	11.0 (2.5)	4.1% (0.9)
	5% 17	339	276.8 (4.6)	9.5 (3.3)	3.7% (1.2)
	7% 24	332	276.0 (3.4)	3.5 (7.1)	2.8% (1.1)
	10% 34	322	279.8 (1.7)	7.4 (1.8)	3.0% (0.8)
COURSE	2% 17	917	273.5 (29.5)	57.3 (26.0)	23.1% (11.9)
	5% 45	888	327.6 (23.2)	21.3 (13.7)	7.5% (4.5)
	7% 64	869	338.6 (18.1)	21.9 (21.0)	7.9% (7.4)
	10% 92	841	372.2 (9.5)	11.1 (3.5)	4.0% (1.3)

Table 3. Mean error of NB and combined classifiers in the first and last iterations

Iteration	% de $|L_{ini}|$	h_{D_1}	h_{D_2}	h
NEWS		1-gram	2-gram	
first	1%	23.6 (9.8)	19.4 (9.2)	20.1 (11.1)
last		1.9 (1.9)	1.5 (1.0)	1.6 (1.4)
first	2%	13.9 (10.0)	15.0 (5.0)	12.4 (9.3)
last		2.0 (1.20)	1.5 (1.1)	1.4 (0.9)
first	5%	8.5 (4.6)	3.9 (2.7)	6.0 (3.8)
last		2.2 (1.3)	1.9 (1.2)	1.4 (1.2)
first	7%	5.4 (2.3)	2.7 (1.8)	2.7 (1.6)
last		2.0 (1.7)	1.9 (1.6)	1.4 (1.1)
first	10%	6.7 (4.0)	2.0 (2.0)	4.7 (2.7)
last		1.9 (1.2)	1.5 (1.3)	1.1 (0.9)
LNAI		1-gram	2-gram	
first	2%	13.4 (7.7)	20.0 (8.0)	11.1 (6.4)
last		5.3 (4.4)	4.0 (3.0)	3.0 (3.3)
first	5%	8.3 (4.9)	10.3 (4.3)	7.6 (4.6)
last		4.3 (3.4)	4.3 (2.9)	3.0 (2.3)
first	7%	6.6 (4.6)	8.3 (4.0)	5.8 (4.1)
last		4.0 (3.8)	3.5 (2.5)	3.0 (2.6)
first	10%	5.0 (3.9)	7.6 (2.9)	4.5 (3.7)
last		3.3 (4.5)	4.0 (3.3)	3.0 (3.3)
COURSE		TEXTO	LINKS	
first	2%	18.7 (4.5)	19.4 (6.5)	18.7 (4.6)
last		22.0 (8.6)	24.5 (5.8)	22.1 (7.9)
first	5%	12.8 (3.5)	16.0 (5.4)	11.4 (4.6)
last		12.9 (6.6)	18.0 (5.8)	12.6 (6.2)
first	7%	11.6 (2.3)	11.0 (3.6)	10.7 (2.3)
last		12.0 (7.5)	19.0 (5.8)	11.3 (7.2)
first	10%	10.3 (3.3)	14.7 (6.8)	8.4 (3.3)
last		9.8 (3.2)	18.0 (6.4)	8.1 (3.3)

by CO-TRAINING; #Errors and %Errors show the mean number and proportion of incorrectly labeled examples respectively where %Errors = #Errors / ($|L_{end}|$ - $|L_{ini}|$). Standard deviations are shown in brackets. In all cases the stop criteria was $U_{D1} = \varnothing$ — Algorithm 1 — for k near 70.

As can be observed, for NEWS and LNAI datasets, the performance of CO-TRAINING using the constructed views is very good for all $|L_{ini}|$ values, since few examples were labeled erroneously. However, results for COURSE using only 2% of labeled examples are poor, although they improve when the initial number of labeled examples grows. Moreover, using NB as the underlying classifier, it is possible to construct a combined classifier h which computes the probability $P(y_v, E_i)$ of class y_v given the instance $E_i =$ (x_{D1i}, x_{D2i}) by multiplying the class probabilities of h_{D1} and h_{D2}, that is, $P(y_v, E_i) = P(y_v|x_{D1i})P(y_v|x_{D2i})$ since both views are considered independent. Table 3 shows the mean error and standard deviation of the classifiers h_{D1}, h_{D2} and h on the first and last iteration of CO-TRAINING, and Figures 6, 7, and 8 illustrate the mean error of h in each iteration for NEWS, LNAI and COURSE datasets respectively.

For NEWS and LNAI datasets (Figures 6 and 7), it can be observed that the influence of the initial number of labeled examples ($|L_{ini}|$) on the error rate is intense at the beginning, causing a high variation on the error rate. However, this influence diminishes with the number of iterations. This does not hold for the COURSE dataset (Figure 8) where the error rate has less variation on all iterations. This can be explained due to the fact that the second view for the COURSE dataset is

less representative, as it only contains the words from a link which points to a given Web page and these words are generally short sentences containing a few representative words.

Experiment 2

The number of examples of each class which can be labeled in each iteration is a key factor for CO-TRAINING. To evaluate this impact, we use the same number of initial labeled examples (30 examples) evenly distributed by class (50% - 50%). In each iteration, up to the 10 "best" examples were allowed to be labeled and we varied the number of examples in each class (Matsubara, Monard & Prati, 2006).

Table 4 shows the mean value and standard deviation of the obtained results. The first line indicates the maximum number of examples by class that can be labeled in each iteration: sci/talk

Figure 6. Mean error of combined classifiers for different values of |Lini| for NEWS dataset

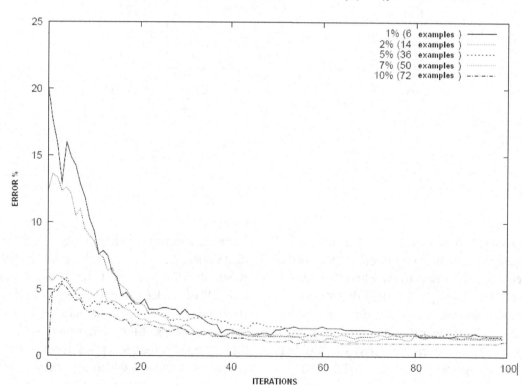

Figure 7. Mean error of combined classifiers for different values of |Lini| for LNAI dataset

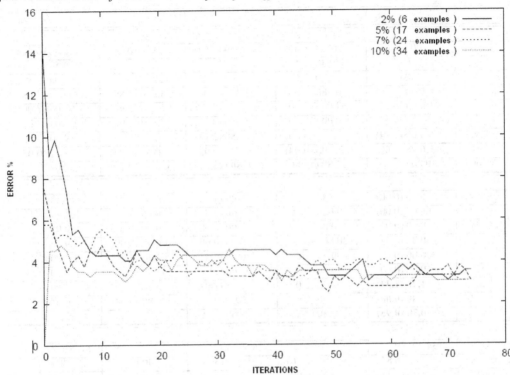

Figure 8. Mean error of combined classifiers for different values of |Lini| for COURSE dataset

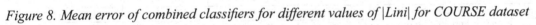

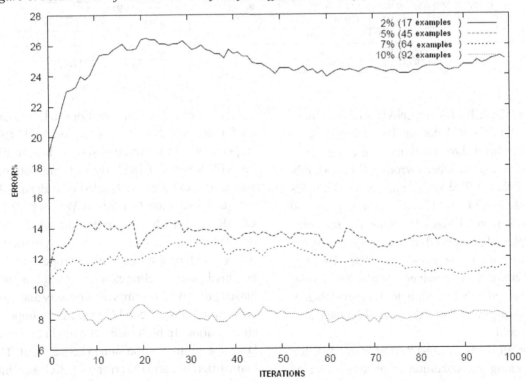

Table 4. CO-TRAINING results for NEWS, LNAI, and COURSE datasets

	2/8	3/7	5/5	7/3	8/2
			NEWS dataset		
sci(W)	18.00 (26.45)	10.60 (15.47)	1.10 (1.85)	0.40 (0.52)	0.80 (0.42)
sci(R)	344.50 (2.72)	339.40 (2.50)	325.70 (11.51)	203.60 (0.52)	139.50 (1.51)
talk(W)	1.60 (1.17)	2.20 (0.63)	5.70 (10.03)	42.50 (30.34)	131.00 (18.89)
talk(R)	139.40 (1.17)	201.80 (0.63)	324.30 (10.03)	345.70 (1.89)	347.80 (3.08)
LSize	503.50 (26.53)	554.00 (15.30)	656.80 (9.77)	592.20 (30.07)	619.10 (17.00)
U'Size	206.50 (26.53)	156.00 (15.30)	53.20 (9.77)	117.80 (30.07)	90.90 (17.00)
Error	3.00 (3.24)	2.38 (3.70)	**1.88 (2.14)**	6.25 (5.14)	19.00 (3.53)
AUC	0.98 (0.02)	0.98 (0.03)	**0.99 (0.02)**	0.97 (0.04)	0.92 (0.05)
Wrong	19.80 (26.96)	12.80 (15.80)	**6.80 (11.77)**	43.70 (30.29)	133.50 (19.31)
			LNAI dataset		
ilp(W)	0.00 (0.00)	1.30 (1.25)	5.40 (1.71)	9.30 (3.23)	12.30 (5.10)
ilp(R)	69.00 (0.00)	94.20 (2.20)	101.00 (1.49)	100.80 (1.14)	101.70 (1.57)
cbr(W)	0.70 (0.95)	0.00 (0.00)	0.00 (0.00)	0.00 (0.00)	0.00 (0.00)
cbr(R)	230.30 (0.95)	204.00 (0.00)	150.00 (0.00)	96.00 (0.00)	69.00 (0.00)
LSize	300.00 (0.00)	299.50 (1.08)	256.40 (2.41)	206.10 (3.54)	183.00 (5.10)
U'Size	50.00 (0.00)	50.50 (1.08)	93.60 (2.41)	143.90 (3.54)	167.00 (5.10)
Error	**1.26 (1.33)**	2.02 (2.00)	2.03 (1.07)	3.28 (1.69)	4.80 (3.03)
AUC	**1.00 (0.00)**	1.00 (0.01)	0.99 (0.01)	0.99 (0.01)	0.99 (0.01)
Wrong	**0.70 (0.95)**	1.30 (1.25)	5.60 (1.90)	9.30 (3.23)	12.50 (5.04)
			COURSE dataset		
course(W)	34.40 (29.73)	103.90 (66.05)	252.30 (72.89)	423.40 (27.35)	434.80 (112.58)
course(R)	146.00 (26.82)	132.80 (27.26)	155.50 (13.34)	175.40 (6.00)	179.30 (10.89)
ncourse(W)	5.30 (3.13)	7.20 (8.00)	4.20 (4.59)	1.50 (2.92)	2.40 (3.34)
ncourse(R)	505.20 (154.07)	307.10 (227.37)	146.80 (110.20)	81.60 (31.65)	81.30 (56.98)
LSize	690.90 (150.92)	551.00 (186.16)	558.80 (49.82)	681.90 (23.39)	697.80 (66.62)
U'Size	239.10 (150.92)	379.00 (186.16)	371.20 (49.82)	248.10 (23.39)	232.20 (66.62)
Error	**14.11 (13.26)**	32.65 (20.15)	49.43 (15.95)	61.91 (8.07)	60.29 (17.28)
AUC	**0.92 (0.08)**	0.82 (0.11)	0.71 (0.09)	0.68 (0.07)	0.67 (0.07)
Wrong	**40.20 (31.71)**	112.80 (67.28)	258.70 (72.08)	429.80 (25.59)	442.60 (111.98)

for NEWS, ILP/CBR for LNAI and course/non-course for COURSE dataset. For each dataset the first four lines show the number of examples in each class that have been wrongly (W) or rightly (R) labeled; LSize is the number of examples labeled by CO-TRAINING, including the 30 initial examples; USize is the number of unlabeled examples left; Error and AUC are respectively the error rate and the area under the ROC (Bradley, 1997) curve of the combined classifier and Wrong is the total number of examples wrongly labeled. The best mean results for these last three measures are in bold.

For all datasets CO-TRAINING ended due to reaching the condition of an empty set of unlabeled examples in iterations 64, 28, and 86 for datasets NEWS, LNAI, and COURSE, respectively. As it can be observed, best results for NEWS and COURSE datasets are obtained whenever examples are labeled considering the dataset distribution (5/5 for NEWS and 2/8 for COURSE). For LNAI dataset, although the best result is not obtained for its exact class proportion 3/7, it is obtained by its similar proportion 2/8. For this dataset, labeling examples using a slightly biased proportion towards the minority and most error-prone class (see Table 1) seems to improve classification. In both cases, the total number of labeled examples is the same (LSize' 300). The main difference is in the error of each class: while

3/7 proportion labels all CBR examples correctly, 2/8 proportion labels all ILP examples correctly. Moreover, for the best results the mean error rate of the combined classifiers are compatible with the one obtained using the labeled examples (Table 1), although the COURSE dataset presents a far greater variance.

Analyzing the behavior of CO-TRAINING when changing the class distribution of labeled examples shows an interesting pattern. For the balanced dataset NEWS, skewing the proportion of labeled examples towards the talk class (i.e., labeling more examples from the talk class: 7/2 and 8/2) does not diminish the performance significantly. The other way dramatically increases the error rate (from 1.88 in 5/5 labeling to 19.00 in 8/2 labeling) as well as in the number of examples incorrectly labeled (6.8% to 133.50%). For the imbalanced datasets the picture is clearer. Both the error rate and the number of incorrectly labeled examples increase as we go towards the opposite direction in terms of proportion of labeled examples.

Another interesting result is related to the AUC. For the datasets with high AUC values, NEWS and LNAI (near 1), the degradation in performance is weaker than for the COURSE dataset. This is because AUC values near 1 are a strong indication of a domain with a great separability, that is, domains in which the classes could be more easily separated from the others, and it is easy for the algorithm to construct accurate classifiers even if the proportion of examples in the training set is different from the natural one.

CONCLUSION

This chapter presented some applications of multiview semisupervised learning to text mining problems. Semisupervised learning uses a set of examples of which only a few examples are labeled and the aim is to predict the labels of some of the remaining unlabeled examples.

Multiview semisupervised learning uses two disjoint sets of attributes to label examples. This approach is suitable for domains where more than one natural representation (view) of examples is available. Various characteristics of texts can be explored to provide such multiple views.

Semisupervised learning algorithms described in this chapter include CO-TRAINING, in which examples classified with a high degree of confidence in both views are included in the labeled set of examples. We also described CO-EM, which is an Expectation Maximization version of CO-TRAINING. CO-TESTING and CO-EMT combine active and semisupervised learning to ease the process of labeling examples.

There are a significant number of text mining applications related to multiview semisupervised learning. However, how the views are created depends on the domain of application. Multigram is a general approach that can be used in most of the cases.

We also presented some experiments applied to text domains using CO-TRAINING. The aim of the first experiment was to observe the behaviour of CO-TRAINING using a different number of initial labeled examples. In the second experiment, we analyzed the relationship between the unknown class distribution of domains and the performance with respect to which proportion examples are labeled in each iteration. Results showed the suitability of CO-TRAINING in such experiments.

FUTURE RESEARCH DIRECTIONS

During the last years, semisupervised learning has emerged as an exciting new direction in machine learning, data, and text mining research. This is because dealing with the situation where relatively few labeled training data are available, although a large number of unlabeled data is given, is directly relevant to a broad range of practical applications, among them Web page classification, information retrieval, information extraction, question answering, entity recognition, and so forth. Adapting semisupervised learning algorithms to these tasks is still an open-ended problem and certainly a challenging and exciting research direction.

Another interesting research direction, especially when dealing with Web data, is to explore the relationship among documents. During the last couple of years, one of the most active areas of research in semisupervised learning has been in graph-based methods (see some references in the "Additional Reading" section). In these methods, data are represented by nodes in a graph and the edges represent the distances of the incident nodes. This formalism can be adapted to the multiview framework so that one of the views represents, for instance, the link structure or Web pages, and the other view the text of those pages. Thus, we can have a hybrid approach which puts together standard generative models (as presented in this chapter) and graph-based models.

Semisupervised learning is highly dependent on a good matching of problem structure with the model assumptions imposed by the learning algorithm. Inappropriate matching can lead to degradation in classifier performance. Selecting the best algorithm for a given task is one of the problems addressed by meta-learning. The combination of semisupervised learning and meta-learning might produce a good solution to overcome performance degradation and research in this direction would be welcome.

Another research direction is related to multiple classifier systems. Originally, this sort of systems was proposed for supervised classification tasks, and recently its use has been extended to unsupervised classification tasks. However, multiple classifier systems for semisupervised classification tasks have not received much attention in the machine learning literature although some results from semisupervised learning can be further exploited to promote research on semisupervised multiple classifier systems. Furthermore,

although some theoretical analysis have been carried out in order to show under what conditions unlabeled data can be used in learning to improve classification performance, these analysis refer to specific semisupervised learning methods. Thus, it is not known if other methods will exhibit the phenomenon of performance degradation as the ones already studied do.

Finally, another learning model related to semisupervised learning that is worth researching is called learning from positive and unlabeled examples (or PU learning). The difference here is that there are no labeled negative examples for learning. This kind of learning is useful in many situations. For example, if we have a set of documents (research papers, for example) and we want to identify other similar documents in a repository, the set of research papers we have can be treated as the positive data and the papers in the research repository can be treated as the unlabeled data.

ACKNOWLEDGMENT

The authors are grateful to the Brazilian research councils CAPES, FAPESP, CNPq e FPTI/Br.

REFERENCES

Berry, M.W. (Ed.). (2003). *Survey of text mining: Clustering, classification, and retrieval.* Springer-Verlag.

Blum, A., & Mitchell, T. (1998). Combining labeled and unlabeled data with CO-TRAINING. In *Proceedings of the 11th Annual Conference on Computational Learning Theory (COLT)* (pp. 92-100). ACM Press.

Bradley, A.P. (1997). The use of the area under the ROC curve in the evaluation of machine learning algorithms. *Pattern Recognition, 30*(7).

Brefeld, U., & Scheffer, T. (2004). CO-EM support vector learning. In *Proceedings of the 21st International Conference in Machine Learning (ICML)* (pp. 121-128). Morgan Kaufmann Publishers.

Cohn, D.A., Ghahramani, Z., & Jordan, M.I. (1996). Active learning with statistical models. *J. Artif. Intell. Res. (JAIR), 4,* 129-145.

Dasgupta, S., Littman, M.L., & McAllester, D. (2002). Pac generalization bounds for CO-TRAINING. In *Advances in Neural Information Processing Systems 14 (NIPS)* (pp. 375-382). MIT Press.

Dempster, A., Laird, N., & Rubin, D. (1997). Maximum likelihood from incomplete data via the EM algorithm. *Journal of the Royal Statistical Society, Series B, 39*(1), 1-38.

Kiritchenko, S., & Matwin, S. (2001). E-mail classification with CO-TRAINING. In *Conference of the Centre for Advanced Studies on Collaborative Research* (pp. 192-201). IBM Press.

Kockelkorn, M., Lneburg, A., & Scheffer, T. (2003). Using transduction and multiview learning to answer e-mails. In *Proceedings of the European Conference on Principle and Practice of Knowledge Discovery in Databases* (pp. 266-277). Springer-Verlag.

Matsubara, E.T., Martins, C.A., & Monard, M. C. (2003). *Pretext: A pre-processing text tool using the bag-of-words approach* (Tech. Rep. No. 209, ICMC-USP). Retrieved March 29, 2007, from ftp://ftp.icmc.sc.usp.br/pub/ BIBLIOTECA/rel tec/RT 209.zip

Matsubara, E.T., & Monard, M.C. (2004). *Experimental evaluation of the multiview semisupervised learning CO-TRAINING algorithm* (Tech. Rep. No. 235, ICMC-USP). Retrieved March 29, 2007, from ftp://ftp.icmc.usp.br/pub/ BIBLIOTECA/rel tec/RT 235.pdf

Matsubara, E.T., Monard, M.C., & Batista, G.E.A.P.A. (2005). Multiview semisupervised learning: An approach to obtain different views from text datasets. *Advances in Logic Based Intelligent Systems, 132,* 97-104.

Matsubara, E.T., Monard, M.C., & Prati, R.C. (2006). On the class distribution labeling step sensitivity of CO-TRAINING. In *Proceedings of IFIP Artificial Intelligence in Theory and Practice* (pp. 199-208).

Melo, V., Secato, M., & Lopes, A.A. (2003). Automatic extraction and identification of bibliographical information from scientific articles (in Portuguese). In *IV Workshop on Advances and Trends in AI* (pp. 1-10). Chile.

Mitchell, T.M. (1997). *Machine learning.* Mc-Graw-Hill.

Muslea, I., Minton, S., & Knoblock, C.A. (2000). Selective sampling with redundant views. In *Proceedings of the 15th National Conference on Artificial Intelligence (AAAI)* (pp. 621-626).

Muslea, I., Minton, S., & Knoblock, C. (2002). Active + semisupervised learning = robust multiview learning. In *Proceedings of the 19th International Conference on Machine Learning (ICML)* (pp. 435-432), Morgan Kaufmann Publishers.

Newman, D.J., Hettich, S., Blake, C.L., & Merz, C.J. (1998). UCI repository of machine learning databases. Retrieved March 29, 2007, from http://www.ics.uci.edu/~mlearn/MLRepository.html

Nigam, K. (2001). *Using unlabeled data to improve text classification* (Tech. Rep. No. CMU-CS-01-126). Doctoral dissertation, Carnegie Mellon University.

Nigam, K., McCallum, A.K., Thrun, S., & Mitchell, T.M. (2000). Text classification from labeled and unlabeled documents using EM. *Machine Learning, 39*(2/3), 103-134.

Porter, M. F., (1980) An algorithm for suffix stripping. *Program, 14*(3), 130-137.

Scheffer, T. (2004). Email answering assistance by semisupervised text classification. *Intelligence Data Analysis, 8*(5), 481-493.

Witten, I.H., & Frank, E. (2000). *Data mining, practical machine learning tools and techniques with Java implementations* (Vol. 1). Morgan Kaufmann Publishers. Retrieved March 29, 2007, from http://www.cs.waikato.ac.nz/ml/weka/index.html

Zhou, Z.H. & Li, M. (2005a). Semisupervised regression with CO-TRAINING. In *Proceedings of the International Joint Conference on Artificial Inteligence (IJCAI)* (pp. 908-916).

Zhou, Z.-H., & Li, M. (2005b). Tri-training: Exploiting unlabeled data using three classifiers. In *IEEE Transactions on Knowledge and Data Engineering* (Vols. 11-17, pp. 1529-1541).

Zhu, X. (2005). *Semisupervised learning literature survey* (Tech. Rep. No. 1530). University of Wisconsin-Madison, Computer Sciences. Retrieved March 29, 2007, from http://www.cs.wisc.edu/~jerryzhu/pub/ssl survey.pdf

Additional Reading

Abe, N., Zadrozny, B., & Langford. (2006). Outlier detection by active learning. In *Proceedings of the International Conference on Knowledge Discovery and Data Mining (KDD'2006)* (pp. 504-509).

Amini, R., & Gallinari, P. (2005). Semisupervised learning with an imperfect supervisor. *Knowl. Inf. Syst., 8*(4), 385-413.

Balcan, M.-F., & Blum, A. (2005). A PAC-style model for learning from labeled and unlabeled data. In *Proceedings of Conference on Learning Theory (COLT '2005)* (pp. 111-126).

Balcan, M.-F., Blum, A., Choi, P.P., Lafferty, J., Pantano, B., Rwebangira, M.R., & Zhu, X. (2005a). Person identification in Webcam images: An application of semisupervised learning. In *ICML2005 Workshop on Learning with Partially Classified Training Data* (pp. 1-9).

Brefeld, U., & Scheffer, T. (2006). SemiSupervised learning for structured output variables. In *Proceedings of the International Conference on Machine Learning (ICML'2006)* (pp. 145-152).

Chapelle, O., Schölkopf, B., & Zien, A.(2006). A continuation method for semi-supervised SVMs. In *Proceedings of the International Conference on Machine Learning (ICML'2006)* (pp. 185-192).

Cozman, F., & Cohen, I. (2006). Risks of semi-supervised learning: How unlabeled data can degrade performance of generative classifiers. In O. Chapelle, B. Schölkopf & A. Zien (Eds.), *Semisupervised learning* (pp. 57-72).

Ghahramani, Z., & Heller, K.A (2005). Bayesian sets. In *Advances in Neural Information Processing Systems (NIPS'2005)* (pp. 435-442).

Goldman, S., & Zhou, Y. (2000). Enhancing supervised learning with unlabeled data. In *Proceedings of International Conference on Machine Learning (ICML'2000)* (pp. 327-334).

Grira, N., Crucianu, M., & Boujemaa, N. (2004). Unsupervised and semisupervised clustering: A brief survey. In *A Review of Machine Learning Techniques for Processing Multimedia Content, Report of the MUSCLE European Network of Excellence (FP6)* (p. 11).

Joachims, T. (2003). Transductive learning via spectral graph partitioning. In *Proceedings of International Conference on Machine Learning (ICML'2003)* (pp. 290-297).

Krishnapuram,B., Williams, D., Xue, Y., Hartemink, A., Carin, L., & Figueiredo, M (2005). On semisupervised classification. In *Proceedings of Advances in Neural Information Processing System (NIPS'2005)* (pp. 721-728). MIT Press.

Lawrence, N.D., & Jordan, M.I. (2005). Semisupervised learning via Gaussian processes. In L.K. Saul, Y. Weiss & L. Bottou (Eds.), *Advances in neural information processing systems (NIPS'2005)* (pp. 753-760). MIT Press.

Leskes, B. (2005). The value of agreement, a new boosting algorithm. In *Proceedings of Conference on Learning Theory (COLT'2005)* (pp. 95-110).

Muslea, I. (2006). Active learning with multiple views. *Journal of Artificial Intelligence Research, 27,* 203-233.

Nigam, K., McCallum, A., & Mitchell, T. (2006). Semi-supervised text classification using EM. In O. Chapelle, B. Schölkopf & A. Zien (Eds.), *Semisupervised learning* (pp. 33-55). MIT Press.

Qi, Y., Missiuro, P.E., Kapoor, A., Hunter, C.P., Jaakkola, T.S., Gifford, D.K., & Ge, H. (2006). Semisupervised analysis of gene expression profiles for lineage-specific development in the *Caenorhabditis elegans embryo. Bioinformatics, 22,* 14.

Zhu, X (2007). SemiSupervised learning with graphs. Doctoral thesis, Carnegie Mellon University. Retrieved March 29, 2007, from http://www.cs.wisc.edu/~jerryzhu/pub/thesis.pdf

Zhu, X., Kandola, J., Ghahramani, Z., & Lafferty, J. (2005). Nonparametric transforms of graph kernels for semisupervised learning. In L.K. Saul, Y. Weiss & L. Bottou (Eds.), *Advances in neural information processing systems (NIPS'2005)* (pp. 1641-1648). MIT Press.

Chapter VIII
A Multi–Agent Neural Network System for Web Text Mining

Lean Yu
Chinese Academy of Sciences, China
City University of Hong Kong, China

Shouyang Wang
Chinese Academy of Sciences, China

Kin Keung Lai
City University of Hong Kong, China

ABSTRACT

With the rapid increase of the huge amount of online information, there is a strong demand for Web text mining which helps people discover some useful knowledge from Web documents. For this purpose, this chapter first proposes a back-propagation neural network (BPNN)-based Web text mining system for decision support. In the BPNN-based Web text mining system, four main processes, Web document search, Web text processing, text feature conversion, and BPNN-based knowledge discovery, are involved. Particularly, BPNN is used as an intelligent learning agent that learns about underlying Web documents. In order to scale the individual intelligent agent with the large number of Web documents, we then provide a multi-agent-based neural network system for Web text mining in a parallel way. For illustration purpose, a simulated experiment is performed. Experiment results reveal that the proposed multi-agent neural network system is an effective solution to large scale Web text mining.

INTRODUCTION

Web text mining is the process of using unstructured Web-type text documents and examining it in an attempt to find implicit patterns hidden in the Web text documents. With the amount of online Web text information growing rapidly, the need for a powerful Web text mining method that can analyze Web text information and infer useful patterns for prediction and decision purposes has increased. To be able to cope with the abundance of available Web text information,

Web users need assistance of some software tools and software agents (often called "softbots") for exploring, sorting, and filtering the available Web text information (Etzioni, 1996; Kozierok & Maes, 1993).

Much effort for Web text mining has been made and some important progresses are obtained. For example, Joachims (1996) utilized probabilistic TFIDF method and naïve Bayes method to perform text categorization task, one subtasks of the text mining. Feldman and Dagan (1998) proposed a keyword-frequency approach to explore unstructured text collections. Tan (1999) presented a two-phase text mining framework for knowledge discovery in text. Lee and Yang (1999) used a self-organizing map (SOM) method to perform Web text mining task. Chen and Nie (2000) proposed a parallel Web text mining approach for cross-language information retrieval. Choi and Yoo (2001) utilized a neural network approach to text database discovery on the Web. Recently, Yu, Wang, and Lai (2005) utilized rough set theory to refine text mining for prediction purpose. Generally speaking, existing research concentrated on the development of agents that are high level interfaces to the Web (Etzioni & Weld, 1994; Furnkranz, Holzbaur, & Temel, 2002), programs for filtering and sorting e-mail messages (Maes, 1994; Payne & Edwards, 1997), or usenet netnews categorization (Joachims, 1996; Lang, 1995; Lashkari, Metral, & Maes, 1994; Mock, 1996; Sheth & Maes, 1993). More examples about Web text mining can be found in two recent surveys (Chakrabarti, 2000; Kosala & Blockeel, 2000). In the meantime, a number of Web text mining systems, such as IBM Intelligent Miner (http://www-306.ibm.com/ software/data/ iminer/) and SAS Text Miner (http://www.sas. com/), have already been developed.

Although some progress in Web text mining has been made, there are still several important issues to be addressed. First of all, most text mining tasks focus on the text categorization/classification, text clustering, concept extraction, and docu-

ment summarization (Yu, Wang, & Lai, 2006). But the text content and entity relation modeling (i.e., the causality relationship between entities) is less explored in Web text documents; the essential goal of text mining is often neglected. As we know, the basic motivation of text mining is to find and explore some useful knowledge and hidden relationships from some unstructured text data to support decision-making, similar to data mining in structured data. In the existing literature, these text mining tasks little involved in hidden entity relationship modeling. For example, the main function of text categorization is to classify different documents into different prelabeled classes (e.g., Joachims, 1996), but how the different documents with different categories support decision-making is not clear. Differing in the previous Web text mining tasks, this chapter attempts to explore some implied knowledge hidden in Web text documents to support business prediction and decision-making (Yu et al., 2006).

Second, most text mining models usually utilize some well-known tools such as the vector space model (VSM) (e.g., TFIDF algorithm (Salton, 1971, 1991; Salton & Yang, 1973; Sparck Jones, 1972)) and some traditional statistical models, for example, naïve Bayes algorithm (Feldman & Dagan, 1998; Joachims, 1996; Katz, 1995)). Nevertheless, a distinct shortcoming of these models is that their extrapolation and generalization capabilities are often weak (Yu et al., 2006). To remedy this drawback, this chapter adopts an intelligent learning agent instead of traditional statistical models to perform the Web text mining tasks. Because the learning agent has good learning and flexible mapping capability between inputs and outputs, the generalization capability may be much stronger than the traditional models (Yu et al., 2006).

Third, even though some researchers have used some intelligent techniques such as self-organizing map (SOM) (Lee & Yang, 1999) and rough set (Yu et al., 2005) to perform Web text mining, an individual intelligent technique may come to have difficulty in training when the large numbers of available Web text documents exceeds a tolerable level. Furthermore, when new Web text documents are found, the single intelligent agent should be re-trained in order to learn from the new ones. Thus, the redundant training cost is quite burdensome when a designer scales up an existing intelligent agent into a large one with more Web text documents. In this chapter, we use a multi-agent technique to eliminate the redundant computational load.

Finally, most existing Web text mining methods focus on the traditional text clustering and categorization tasks rather than text knowledge discovery task, that is, their capability of knowledge discovery is worth improving further. In this chapter, the knowledge discovery from unstructured Web text documents is emphasized in addition to traditional text processing tasks, which is distinctly different from the previous studies (Yu et al., 2006).

In terms of the above issue, this chapter proposes a multi-agent neural network system to perform Web text mining for prediction and decision-making purpose. The generic framework of the multi-agent neural network system for Web text mining is composed of four main processes: Web document search, Web text processing, text feature conversion, and the BPNN-based knowledge discovery, which will be illustrated in the next section.

The main objective of this chapter is to develop a multi-agent intelligent Web text mining system that offers an effective and scalable Web text mining solution to support decision-making from Web text documents. The rest of this chapter is organized as follows. In the section on *The Framework of BPNN-based Intelligent Web Text Mining*, we present a generic framework of the BPNN-based intelligent learning agent for Web text mining, and then describe its main text mining processes and the limitation of the single intelligent agent approach. To overcome the inadequacy of single intelligent agent, a multi-agent-based intelligent

Web text mining system is proposed in the section on *Multi-Agent-Based Web Text Mining System*. For illustration, an experiment is performed in the section entitled *Experiment Study*. Finally, some concluding remarks and future directions are given in *Conclusions* and *Future Research Directions*.

THE FRAMEWORK OF THE BPNN-BASED INTELLIGENT WEB TEXT MINING

In this section, we first present a generic framework of the BPNN-based Web text mining system and then the main processes of the proposed text mining system are described. Finally, the limitation of the single intelligent agent approach to Web text mining is illustrated.

The Framework of BPNN-based Intelligent Web Text Mining

Web text mining, an emerging issue in the data mining and knowledge discovery research field, has evolved from text mining. According to Webster's online dictionary (http://www.Webster-dictionary.org), text mining, also known as intelligent text analysis (Gelbukh, 2002), text data mining (Hearst, 1999) or knowledge-discovery in text (KDT) (Feldman & Dagan, 1995; Karanikas & Theodoulidis, 2002), refers generally to the process of extracting interesting and non-trivial patterns and knowledge from unstructured text documents. Similarly, Web text mining utilizes Web-type textual documents and examines it in an attempt to discover inherent structure and implicit meanings "hidden" in the Web text documents using interdisciplinary techniques from data mining, machine learning, natural language processing (NLP), information retrieval (IR), information extraction (IE), and knowledge management (Karanikas & Theodoulidis, 2002; Yu et al, 2005, 2006). In this sense, Web text mining is only a subset of text mining. The unique difference is that the Web text mining focused on the knowledge discovery from the hypertext (e.g., HTML and XML) published on the Web while text mining includes broader text documents besides hypertext (e.g., Word file and ASCII text file). One main objective of Web text mining is to help people discover knowledge for decision support from large quantities of semi-structured or unstructured Web text documents.

Similar to data mining approaches, Web text mining also needs assistance of some intelligent software agent that can automatically analyze Web text data and extract some implied relationships or patterns from Web text documents. Therefore, it can be viewed as an extension of data mining or knowledge discovery from (structured) databases (Fayyad, Piatetsky-Shapiro, & Smyth, 1996). With the rapid increase of the number and diversity of distributed text sources on the Web, Web text mining has increasingly been one of the most potential research fields.

Actually, Web text mining consists of a series of tasks and procedures which involve many interdisciplinary fields such as data mining, machine learning, and NLP. Because the final goal of Web text mining is to support prediction and decision using explored knowledge discovered by Web text mining, the Web text mining must adapt the dynamic change over time as the Web text documents increase rapidly. Therefore, Web text mining must have learning and generalization capability. In this chapter, the BPNN is used as an intelligent computational agent for extrapolation and generalization purposes. In the environment of our proposed approach, the BPNN agent is first trained with the many related Web documents and then the trained BPNN agent can project to new documents for prediction and decision when new Web documents arrive. Figure 1 illustrates the main components of a BPNN agent for Web text mining and the control flows among them. Note that the control flows with thin arrow represent the training phase with in-sample data and

Figure 1. The generic framework of BPNN-based Web text mining system

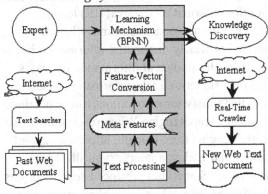

the control flows with thick arrow represent the out-of-sample testing phase of BPNN-based Web text mining agent.

As can be seen from Figure 1, the generic framework of the BPNN-based Web text mining system consists of four main components: Web document search, Web text processing, feature vector conversion, and BPNN-based learning mechanism, which is described in detail in the next section.

The Main Processes of the BPNN-Based Web Text Mining System

As previous subsection revealed, the BPNN-based Web text mining is composed of four main processes: Web document search, Web text processing, feature vector conversion, and BPNN-based learning mechanism.

Web Document Search

Clearly, the first step in Web text mining is to collect the Web text data (i.e., the relevant documents). The main work at this stage is to search text documents that a specified project needs. In general, the first task of document collection is to identify what documents are to be retrieved. When determining a subject, some keywords should be selected and then text documents can be searched and queried with search engines, Web crawlers, or other information retrieval (IR) tools.

The Internet contains enormous, hetero-structural, and widely distributed information bases in which the amount of information increases in a geometric series. In the information bases, text sets that satisfy some conditions can be obtained by using a search engine. When a user comes to the search engine (e.g., Google, http://www.google. com/) and makes a query, typically by giving keywords. Sometimes advanced search options such as boolean, relevancy-ranked search, fuzzy search, and concept search (Berry & Browne, 2002; Karanikas & Theodoulidis, 2002) are speci-

fied. The engine looks up the index and provides a listing of best-matching documents from internal file systems or the Internet according to its criteria, usually with a short summary containing the document's title and sometimes parts of the text. Thus, the large text documents can be obtained according to the specific project.

Web Text Processing

When Web text documents are collected, the collected text documents are mainly represented by Web pages, which are tagged by hypertext makeup language (HTML) or extensible markup language (XML). Thus collected documents or texts are

Figure 2. The three main procedures of Web text processing

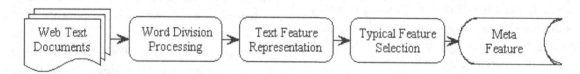

Figure 3. A typical word division processing example using a bag-of-words representation

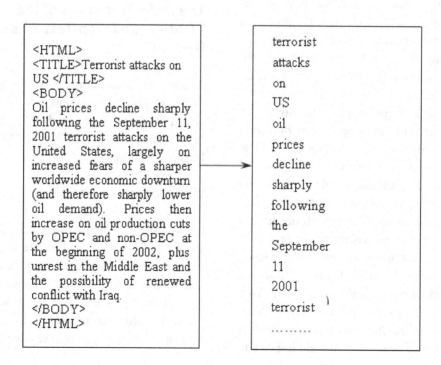

mostly semi- or non-structural information. Our aim of Web text processing is to extract some features that represent the text contents from these collected texts for further analysis. In this component, three important procedures, word division processing, text feature generation, and typical feature selection, as illustrated in Figure 2, are included here.

Word Division Processing

For word division processing, full text division approach is used. Actually, the full text division approach model acts by treating each document as a bag-of-words representation (Berry & Browne, 2002; Joachims, 1996). For example, "the price of oil rises" can be divided into word sets, that is, "the", "price", "of", "rises". More generally, we have the following definition of full text division for word division process (Yu et al., 2006).

[Full text division approach]: *Let $T = \{T_1, T_2, ..., T_m\}$ be a collection of documents. For each text document, assume that there are n words. Then each document T_i can be represented as a bag-of-words $W = \{W_1, ..., W_n\}$.*

Actually, word division processing is very simple because it only treats the text documents as a bag-of-words representation. A typical example is illustrated in Figure 3.

Text Feature Representation

Generally, the representation of a problem has a strong effect on the generalization accuracy of a learning system. For the Web text mining, a Web text document, which is typically a string of characters, has to be transformed into an appropriate representation, which is suitable for the learning algorithm and mining tasks. For process-

Figure 4. The attribute-value representation of the Web text documents

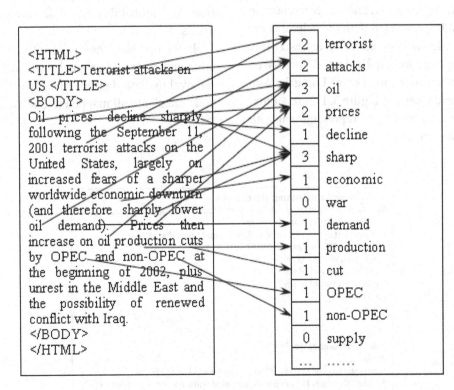

ing convenience of learning algorithms, a simple word division processing is not enough and the text feature representation is strongly required. In this chapter, we use an attribute-value style to format the text feature representation based on the previous bag-of-words representation. Particularly, we have the following definition for attribute-value feature representation. Note that the terms "feature" and "word" will be used interchangeably in the following.

[Attribute-value text feature representation]:
For a text document T with n words, its bag-of-words representation is $W = \{w_1, ..., w_n\}$ according to the word division processing. Suppose $I = \{I_1, I_2, ..., I_n\}$ is a set of interesting words appearing in T. Then the text document T can be represented as $W = \{w_j, V(w_j), ..., w_k, V(w_k)\}$, where $V(w_j)$ is the term frequency of word (w_j) and $1 <= j <= k <= n$.

With the above definition, the Web text documents can be represented by attribute-value format. In fact, the above text feature representation process can be completed with the help of some existing word statistical software, such as TMSK software package provided by Data-Miner's Web site (http://www.data-miner.com). Using the Web text document shown in Figure 3, Figure 4 illustrates a typical text feature representation with attribute-value style.

Typical Feature Selection

In the field of machine learning, many researchers have argued that the maximum performance is often not achieved by using all available features but by using a "good" subsets of those (Caruana & Freitag, 1994). Finding a "good" subset of features is actually a feature extraction process. Applied to text mining tasks, this means that we want to find a subset of words which can support decision-making. Usually, having too few features can make it impossible to formulate a good result. Nevertheless having some features which do not help improve performance may add some noise in the data; therefore selecting or extracting some typical features called metafeatures become very crucial for text mining analysis. The primary objective of the feature extraction is to extract some typical features that can identify facts and relations hidden in text documents (Yu et al., 2006).

In this chapter, a combination of the four feature selection methods (stem removal, infrequent words pruning, high frequency words elimination, and probability-based feature extraction) are used.

In the first step, the words with similar stems are mapping to one original word with the stem removal method. For example, "rises", "rising", and "risen" are all mapped to one original word "rise".

Box 1.

```
[Infrequent word pruning algorithm]
Input: W, all words in the document collection W = {w_1, ..., w_i, ..., w_m}
   K, the number of features desired
Output: FS(w_i, V(w_j)), a set of K features and times that occurs
1. Initialize HS = empty hashtable
2. For each word in W do
  If HS contains word then
   j = value of word in HS
   j = j + 1
  Else
   j = 1
  Endif
  Store j as value of word in HS
  Endfor
3. Sort the keys of V(w_j) in HS in descend way, denoted by SK.
4. Select the top K keys in SK as generated feature and output FS(w_i, V(w_j)).
```

In the second step, infrequent word pruning means the words will be removed if they occur less than a pre-specified times. Similarly, we can rank the word frequency to select the first k features thus pruning some infrequent words. In this chapter, the latter strategy is adopted. Concretely speaking, we use the following algorithm to prune the infrequent words in the text documents, as illustrated in Box 1.

With the above algorithm presented in the rectangle, k most frequent words can be obtained. But a deadly drawback of this algorithms is that the most frequent words may be some stop words and non-contents words like "the", "a/an", "of", "for". Thus the third method are used to eliminate these stop words and some non-content words. In this step, the b (a pre-specified cutoff), most frequently occurring words, are removed.

In the final step the remaining words are ranked according to their probability. Typically, a probability-based K-mixtures approach proposed by Katz (1995) is introduced for typical features extraction. In the K-mixture model, the probability $P_i(k)$ of the word w_i, appearing k times in a document, is given by:

$$P_i(k) = (1-a)\delta_{k,0} + \frac{a}{b+1} \times \frac{(b)^k}{(b+1)^k} \qquad (1)$$

where $\delta_{k,0} = 1$ if and only if $k = 0$; $\delta_{k,0} = 0$, otherwise. The parameters a and b can be fitted using the observed mean t and the observed inverse document frequency (IDF) as follows:

$$t = \frac{TF_i}{N}; IDF = \log\left(\frac{N}{DF_i(w_i)}\right); b = t \times 2^{IDF} - 1 = \frac{(TF_i - DF_i)}{DF_i}; a = \frac{t}{b}$$
$$(2)$$

where term frequency (TF_i) refers to the total number of occurrences of the ith term in the text collection; document frequency (DF_i) refers to the number of documents in the collection in which the ith term occurs; and N is the total number of documents on the collection. The parameter a used in the formula denotes the absolute frequency of the term, and b can be used to calculate the extra terms per document in which the terms occur (Katz, 1995; Salton, 1991; Salton & Yang, 1973; Sparck Jones, 1972).

Using the probability-based approach, some typical features with high probability are extracted as "meta-features". In view of these meta-features, we may explore some useful patterns using some knowledge discovery algorithms for decision-making.

Of course, some other text feature selection methods such as text weighting approach and semantic analysis based approach can be used. But conventional text weighting schemes do not reveal the text features in the related documents satisfactorily (Katz, 1995) and the semantic-based analysis often add some human interventions and must take a great deal of time.

Feature Vector Conversion

Before using knowledge discovery algorithm, text feature data must be transformed into numerical data by encoding. For example, assume that the metafeature data includes the following three features: profits, increase, and stock-price. Two documents include the following key information, that is, "profits increase lead to stock price rises up" and "profits decrease leads to stock price falls down". Obviously, the natural language representation is hard to be handled for large quantities of text documents analysis. Therefore, we try to transform the text data into numerical data, which is useful for later exploration and using some data mining and knowledge discovery techniques. Here we use a new algorithm proposed by Weiss, Indurkhya, Zhang, and Damerau (2005) to transform text data into a spreadsheet table in the sequel.

In the proposed algorithm, the meta features form the basis for creating a spreadsheet of numeric data corresponding to the document collec-

Box 2.

```
[Text data transformation algorithm]
Input: FS, a set of N features
    DC, a collection of M documents
Output: SS, a spreadsheet with m rows n columns
1. Initialize i = 1
2. For each document D in DC do
j = 1
    For each feature F in FS do
    K = number of occurrences of F in D
    If (K>0) then SS (row = i, col = j) = 1;
    Else SS (row = i, col = j) = 0
    Endif
    j = j +1
    Endfor
    i = i +1
    Endfor
3. Output SS.
```

tion. Each row is a document, and each column represents a feature. Thus a cell in the spreadsheet is a measurement of a feature (corresponding to the column) for a document (corresponding to a row). In the process of conversion, we simply check for the presence (1) or absence (0) of words by comparing with meta features, and the cell entries are binary entries corresponding to a document and a word. The document collection of words covers all the possibilities and corresponds to the number of columns in the spreadsheet. The cells in the spreadsheet will all have ones or zeros, depending on whether the words were encountered in the document. For instance, the two documents about oil price movement in the previous example can be represented by binary form, as illustrated in Table 1.

In such a way, the textual data are converted into numerical data. We will soon introduce some data mining techniques that learn from such data. From the representation of Table 1, the text knowledge discovery can be seen as a typical

supervised learning process if the "stock-price" and the "profit & increase" are considered as the dependent and independent variables respectively. In this chapter, we use BPNN as an intelligent agent to uncover the knowledge for prediction and decision-making purposes.

BPNN-Based Learning Mechanism

In this chapter, the BPNN is used as an intelligent learning agent to explore the hidden patterns that learn from the spreadsheet. The main reason of selecting BPNN as an intelligent learning agent is that the BPNN is often viewed as a "universal approximator" (Hornik, Stinchocombe, & White, 1989) and is widely used in many different fields. White (1990) found that a three-layer BPNN with an identity transfer function in the output unit and logistic functions in the middle-layer units can approximate any continuous function arbitrarily well given a sufficient amount of middle-layer units. That is, the BPNN has the ability to provide flexible mapping between inputs and outputs.

Actually, BPNN agent is a supervised learning mechanism in the form of the neural network associative memory as shown in Figure 5 as the shaded rectangle. Thus the BPNN agent acts in two phases: a training phase and a testing phase, as illustrated in Figure 5. Note that the top part of Figure 5 is a training phase (the control flows corresponds to thin arrow (the top part)) and the bottom part is testing phase (the control flows corresponds to thick arrow (the bottom part)).

During the training phase, the input and the output layer of the BPNN are set to represent a training pair (x, y) where x is the feature vector produced by the feature vector converter and y is the decision variable, which is determined by the truth or by the human expert's judgments. Commonly, $x \in R^n$ is an n-dimensional feature vector containing the independent variable or attributes, taking Table 1 as an example, the vector $(\ldots, 1, 1, \ldots)^T$ for Document 1 and $(\ldots, 1, 0, \ldots)^T$ for Document 2 can be seen as input vector or independent

Table 1. A simple example transformed from text to number

Document No.	...	Profits	Increase	...	Stock-price
Document 1	...	1 (yes)	1 (yes)	...	1 (up)
Document 2	...	1 (yes)	0 (no)	...	0 (down)

Figure 5. The learning mechanism of BPNN agent

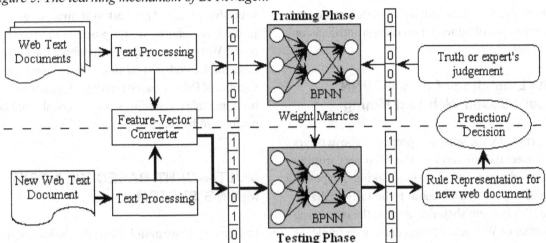

variables where "..." in the parentheses denotes some other text feature values contained in the text document, while y is the dependent variable.

Usually, the variable y can be output as a scalar or a high-dimensional vector, which is dependant on the problem. In the example presented in Table 1, the decision variable y is the stock price, which has two scalar values (0, 1). Naturally, the two scalar value can be represented as a two-dimension vector $(0\ 1)^T$ as an output of the neural network. In the text mining, the y values are determined either by the truth from the text contents or by human expert's judgment if the truth is not shown in the text documents. That is, if the text document does not show any truth about y value, expert judgment is needed to construct the training pair. In the example of Table 1, if Document 1 does not give the stock price information, the expert's judgment about stock price movement is required to formulate a full training pair (x, y).

Using the BPNN, we can construct a function or a model f, which can explore the relationships between the independent variable x and decision variable y, that is:

$$y = f(x) = f_\varphi(x) = f(x; \varphi),\ \varphi \in \psi, \qquad (3)$$

where $f = f_\varphi$ is defined by specifying parameters $\varphi \in \psi$ from an explicitly parameterized family of models ψ. There are well-known parameterizations for a wide variety of statistical models including various regression and classification models, and neural network models. To find the optimal parameters φ, the BPNN learning procedure (Freeman & Skapura, 1992; Hornik et al., 1989; White, 1990) is performed for all training pairs. The BPNN learning procedure repeatedly adjusts the link-weight matrices of BPNN in a way that minimizes the error for each training pair. When the average squared error computed over all training pairs is acceptably small, the BPNN learning procedure stops and produces the link-weight matrices, which is stored as the parameters for the use of testing phase.

During the testing phase, the input layer of the BPNN is activated by the feature vector produced by the feature-vector converter for a new Web text document. This activation of the BPNN spreads from the input layer to the output layer using the link-weight matrices stored during the training phase. That is, the model $f = f_\varphi$ determined by training phase is applied to previously unseen feature vectors x (i.e., feature vectors outside the training set) to produce the output of BPNN. Finally, the numerical vector obtained from the

BPNN can be converted into corresponding text representation. Accordingly, some rule representation can be obtained for prediction and decision purposes.

The Limitation of Single BPNN Agent-Based Web Text Mining

In principle, the approach proposed above offers the potential solution to the Web text mining for prediction and decision-making purposes. However, for that potential to be fully realized, the BPNN agent should scale with the increasing number of Web text documents. For example, as the number of available text documents increases over a tolerable limit, the BPNN agent may come to have difficulty in training its BPNN. Actually, for the larger number of Web text documents, the learning mechanism of the BPNN agent should extract the more features to train, and thus the computational task for training the BPNN increases in size and complexity. Tesauro and Janssens (1988) demonstrated that the training cost of the BPNN scales exponentially with the complexity of the computational task. It is therefore not feasible for a single BPNN agent to learn increasingly growing Web text documents.

Furthermore, if new Web text documents were added into the existing text documents, the BPNN agent should be re-trained for all the text documents because it needs to learn from the new ones. Thus, when a designer scales up an existing BPNN agent into a large one with more Web text documents, the redundant training cost is quite burdensome in practice.

To overcome these shortcomings, the multi-agent-based neural network system is suggested. In the next section, we propose the multi-agent-based Web text mining system where the knowledge for the Web text mining is distributed over a number of BPNN-based intelligent agents and the interoperable text mining system is collaboratively performed by those agents.

MULTI-AGENT BASED WEB TEXT MINING SYSTEM

In this section, we mainly describe the basic structure of the multi-agent-based Web text mining system consisting of a number of neural network agents and underlying Web text documents. At the same time, we also describe a detailed implementation process of the multi-agent-based Web text mining system in the distributed environment.

The Structure of Multi-Agent Based Web Text Mining System

Assume that there are a number of BPNN-based intelligent agents for Web text mining, each of which has its own available text documents as we described in the previous section. For handling the different Web text documents with different categories, a two-layer multi-agent Web text mining system is constructed, as illustrated in Figure 6.

As seen in Figure 6, the two-layer multi-agent-based Web text mining system includes one superordinate BPNN agent (i.e., A_1) and

Figure 6. The structure of multi-agent-based Web text mining system

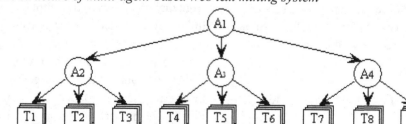

several subordinate BPNN agents (e.g., A_2 and A_3). Here the superordinate BPNN agent can treat the subordinate BPNN agents in the same way as the subordinate BPNN agents treat their available text documents. The main motivation for the multi-agent-based approach is to improve the text mining efficiency as the number of Web text documents increases rapidly.

Usually, the text documents in many cases can be categorized in terms of feature similarity; therefore, the Web text documents must be categorized before the multi-agent-based Web text mining system is performed. The main goal of text categorization is to dispatch similar Web text documents within the same category into a specific agent. In this chapter, a VSM-based text categorization algorithm (Salton, 1971) is used. The core idea of the algorithm is to judge the category of testing text by calculating similarity of eigenvectors of text features. The algorithm's basic process is divided into two stages.

The first stage is the sample training and learning stage. In this stage, a basic text feature set $W = \{w_1, w_2, ..., w_m\}$ and its attribute-values $V(w_i)$ are given as targets in advance. In order to verify the algorithm's classification capability, some training text document sets $S = \{s_1, s_2, ..., s_r\}$ and their values $V(s_i)$ are chosen. By calculating the similarity of texts, we can classify the category of training text documents. Here the similarity is calculated as:

$$Sim_{ik} = \frac{V_{si} * V_{wk}}{|V_{si}| * |V_{wk}|} \quad (1 \le i \le r, \; 1 \le k \le m) \quad (4)$$

where Sim_{ik} denotes the similarity between the ith category and the kth category, and V_{si} and V_{wk} represent the values of basic text feature and training text feature.

The second stage is the testing sample-identifying stage. Here we present some testing text sets $T = \{t_1, t_2, ..., t_n\}$ that are to be classified, a similarity matrix is used to tackle testing text sets, that is:

Similarity matrix =
$$[V_{t1}, V_{t2}, \cdots, V_{tn}]^T \otimes [V_{w1}, V_{w2}, \cdots, V_{wm}] =$$
$$\begin{bmatrix} Sim_{11} & Sim_{12} & \cdots & Sim_{1m} \\ Sim_{21} & Sim_{22} & \cdots & Sim_{2m} \\ \cdots & \cdots & Sim_{ij} & \cdots \\ Sim_{n1} & Sim_{n2} & \cdots & Sim_{nm} \end{bmatrix} \quad (5)$$

where $Sim_{ij} = \dfrac{V_{ti} * V_{wj}}{|V_{ti}| * |V_{wj}|}$ $(1 \le i \le n, 1 \le j \le m)$. In the matrix, the minimal value of every row can be obtained by, and then we can judge the t_i that is the most similar to w_j. So text t_i will be categorized into the class w_j.

As a result, the hierarchical multi-agent Web text mining system can utilize the hierarchical topic structure to efficiently perform the text mining task over a set of neural network agents, which will be illustrated later.

With such a multi-agent intelligent Web text mining system, the redundant training cost can also be solved. When a new Web text document arrives, we only need train one of BPNN agents to obtain the feature of the new Web text document while other BPNN agents need not be trained again.

The Implementation of Multi-Agent Web Text Mining System

In the multi-agent-based Web text mining system, the mining task of each subordinate BPNN agent is assigned by the superordinate BPNN agent (thus the superordinate agent of the root BPNN agent is human user). Therefore, each superordinate BPNN agent should provide some mining tasks to its subordinate BPNN agent in order to train them. In principle, the root BPNN agent receives some knowledge from the human experts for a given task and thus it can propagate the expert knowledge to the subordinate BPNN agents in order to let the training procedure apply to them. Actually, the BPNN agents in multi-agent Web text mining system can collaboratively explore useful patterns over the underlying text collections. The overall operation process including training and testing phase of the multi-agent-based Web text mining system is described as follows:

1. For a given mining task, some related Web text documents are collected and, in the meantime, collected Web text documents are categorized into different classes based on VSM text categorization algorithm (Salton, 1971) mentioned in a previous section.

2. The Web text documents with different categories are distributed in different agents.

3. The root BPNN agent sends a given mining task to the subordinate agents and the task proceeds top-down to the related Web text collections.

4. Many typical features are extracted from the related Web text documents and then these features proceed bottom-up to the root BPNN agent.

5. The root BPNN agent presents the union of all related features to the human experts.

6. The root BPNN agent receives the expert's judgment between the typical features.

7. The root BPNN agent propagates the expert's judgment to their associated subordinate BPNN agent and this propagation proceeds top-down to the subordinate BPNN agent.

8. Each related Web text documents are converted into a record in spreadsheet and then the final spreadsheet proceeds to the superordinate BPNN agent.

9. Each subordinate agent trains spreadsheet (i.e., some text features) in conjunction with expert's knowledge and finds some useful patterns in the new Web text documents, feedbacks them to the superordinate agents, and finally the feedback patterns or knowledge proceeds bottom-up to the root BPNN agent.

10. The root BPNN agent presents the union of all received patterns to the human user for prediction and decision.

11. Repeat 1. to 10. for all mining tasks given by the human user.

Each subordinate BPNN agent is trained with the training procedure of Figure 3 in terms of the mining task in Step (1) and the expert knowledge in Step (6), while the root BPNN agent is trained based upon the mining task and expert knowledge given by the human experts.

It is worth noting that the implementation of the multi-agent-based Web text mining system is collaboratively realized in a parallel way under the distributed environment. In other words, for a certain Web text mining task, every BPNN agent in Figure 6 will perform the mining process shown in Figure 1 based upon a parallel computing environment.

EXPERIMENT STUDY

In the experimental study, there are two main motivations: (1) to evaluate the performance of the proposed multi-agent Web text mining based on neural network technique; and (2) to evaluate the knowledge discovery function (e.g., prediction or decision capability) of the proposed Web text mining approach for practical applications. To perform the two motivations, a practical application for the crude oil price movement direction prediction using the proposed multi-agent-based Web text mining approach is presented. In this section, we first describe the experiment design and then some experimental results are reported.

Data Description and Experiment Design

The dataset used here is the Web text collection about crude oil price prediction, which has been used for a business decision-making experiment

(Yu et al., 2005, 2006). The text dataset was collected by the project team of crude oil price prediction in Chinese Academy of Sciences since 2002. According to the Web text processing and categorization presented in Sections *The Framework of BPNN-based Intelligent Web Text Mining* and *Multi-agent-based Web Text Mining System*, a corpus of 3552 Web text documents are classified into 32 categories, which is shown in Table 2. Obviously, the distribution of the Web documents in each of categories is very uneven. Each document can have multiple category labels and the class assignment was done manually. Note that the main aim of this dataset is to explore some decision rules from the meta-features affecting crude oil price movement hidden in the Web text documents so as to help improve the prediction performance of the crude oil price movement.

In this experiment, these Web documents with a total of 3552 documents are used to construct a hierarchically multi-agent text mining system for crude oil price movement direction prediction. For simplicity, the Web documents containing four categories are assigned to one BPNN agent. In this way, the multi-agent-based text mining system has nine BPNN agents (one superordinate agent and eight subordinate agents). The superordinate agent, which has eight subordinate agents, is used to dispatch mining tasks from user and collect the mining results to human user. Of the eight subordinate agents, each subordinate agent has four underlying Web document collections that have different number of Web text documents. The topology of the multi-agent-based text mining system is similar to Figure 6. To compare the efficiency of our proposed multi-agent Web text mining system, we also constructed a single-BPNN-agent-based text mining system that would operate on the above 3552 documents. Note that the text processing is performed by TMSK software package provided by Data-Miner's Web site (http://www.data-miner.com) and the BPNN is developed by Neural Network toolbox of Matlab software package.

In the multi-agent neural network system, each BPNN agent is assigned to different computers

Table 2. The summary of 32 categories and their related documents

Category	# of documents	Category	# of documents
1. Oil total demand	152	17. OPEC market share	89
2. Oil total supply	135	18. Market forward price	66
3. OPEC production	106	19. Environment and tax	128
4. OPEC production capacity	279	20. Oil Rumors	73
5. Core OPEC production	99	21. Oil future price	339
6. Non-OPEC production	67	22. OPEC oil embargo	32
7. Non-OPEC capacity	43	23. Oil worker strike	64
8. Capacity utilization ratio	111	24. Natural disasters	95
9. Oil inventory level	195	25. Wars in oil countries	102
10. Fuel switch capacity	55	26. Revolutions	21
11. Crude oil disposition	32	27. Political conflict	25
12. OPEC oil price	63	28. Economic sanction	78
13. Gasoline tax rate	93	29. Terrorist attack	164
14. Oil import fee	50	30. Hostage crisis	15
15. World economy growth	505	31. Oil company merger	57
16. Foreign exchange rate	113	32. Speculation	106

in the distributed environment. In our experiment, the distributed environment is created by using the PC computers of Key Laboratory of Management, Decision and Information Systems (MADIS), Chinese Academy of Sciences (CAS). The MADIS has two research rooms, which has a total of 25 PCs with Windows-XP on their office floor. Among them, we select a server and eight PCs with high system configuration to perform experiment, where all computers are on 100 Mbps Ethernet. The detailed system configuration is shown in Figure 7.

Usually, we use the front-end PC which is connected to the server to perform the text mining computation tasks. The server, acting as superordinate agent, distributes the Web text mining tasks to eight office PCs (e.g., eight subordinate agents). Upon completing the Web text mining job, each office PC returns to the results to the server, and then the server collects all the results for prediction and decision purposes, as illustrated in Figure 7.

In the meantime, the feature patterns or prediction rules discovered from Web text documents are ranked by chronology for prediction purpose. For example, in some specified period, if we can find an interesting feature in a Web text document, the corresponding rule can be used for predicting crude oil price movement direction, that is, up or down. In this experiment, since the rule representation is not suitable for level prediction,

the direction prediction or tendency prediction is used here. The feature patterns covered from January 1971 to December 2000 are used as training samples (300 cases), and the feature patterns between January 2001 and June 2005 are used as testing samples (54 cases). Such a processing way is similar to TEI@I methodology (Wang, Yu, & Lai, 2005) when dealing with irregular events. In this experiment, we only focus on monthly direction prediction of crude oil price movement as the final rule explored by the Web text mining system is only suitable for movement direction prediction. For verification, we use the monthly West Texas Intermediate (WTI) crude oil spot price (http://www.economagic.com/em-cgi/ data. exe/var/west-texas-crude-long) as the benchmark data. These data will be used to verify the prediction capability of the proposed intelligent Web text mining system. Using the benchmark data, we can easily calculate the movement direction (D_t) of the crude oil price using the following equations.

$$D_t = \begin{cases} 1, x_t - x_{t-1} \geq 0, \\ 0, otherwise. \end{cases} \qquad (6)$$

where x_t is crude oil price at t month, "1" and "0" denotes upward and downward trend of crude oil price movement respectively.

Figure 7. System configuration of the multi-agent Web text mining system

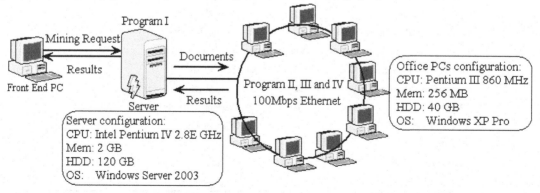

In addition, the experiment used a typical three-layer BP neural network model with a linear activation function in the output neuron and the logistic functions in the hidden nodes. The size of input nodes is determined by the selected meta-features of each Web text document. The output node is set to 1 (i.e., up (1) or down (0) of crude oil price) and hidden nodes are determined by trial and error. The learning rate and momentum rate is set to 0.1 and 0.15. The acceptable average squared error is 0.05 and the training epochs are set to 5000.

To compare the prediction performance of the proposed multi-agent Web text mining system, five text mining approaches: naïve Bayes based Web text mining (Joachims, 1996), keywords-based text mining (KBTM) (Feldman & Dagan, 1998), rough-set-refined text mining (RSTM) (Yu et al., 2005), SOM-based text mining (SOM) (Lee & Yang, 1999), and TEI@I methodology (TEI@I) (Wang et al., 2005), are also used for comparison purpose. It is worth noting that the SOM-based text mining model only provides some clustering features. Similarly, the naïve Bayes based text mining also provide some text categorization results. They are not suitable for exploring hidden rule from each document directly. The reported mining performance is made based on our further processing. That is, we utilize the clustered features and text categorization results to find some useful rules for prediction. In this sense, these two methods are not the strict text mining approaches. For comparison purpose, we still use them as the alternative methods. Because the predictions are based on some qualitative text information, the direction prediction of oil price movement is adopted. Thus hit ratio (%) is selected as a criterion of performance measurement, which is defined by:

$$\text{Hit ratio} = \frac{1}{N}\sum_{i=1}^{N} R_i \qquad (7)$$

where $R_i = 1$ if $IO_i = AO_i$ and $R_i = 0$ otherwise. IO_i is the prediction output from the text mining model, and AO_i is the actual output, N is the number of the testing examples. As earlier noted, we use the WTI crude oil price data x_t ($t = 1, 2, ..., n$) as benchmark data, then the actual output AO can be obtained using Equation (6). Then the hit ratio can be easily calculated.

Experimental Results

From the descriptions of the multi-agent-based Web text mining system in the previous sections, four main procedures: Web document research, Web text processing, feature vector conversion, BPNN-based learning, are performed.

In the single server environment (i.e., single BPNN agent), the total computation time took 7 hours and 17 minutes. The breakdown is as follows: 43 minutes for Web document research (Program I), 1 hour and 24 minutes for Web text processing (Program II), 28 minutes for feature vector conversion (Program III) and the remainder (4 hours and 42 minutes) for BPNN mining task (Program IV). Of course, the Web text mining task can be finished by a single PC environment, but the total computation time is 9 hours and 36 minutes.

For convenience, we can parallelize these procedures (i.e., the last three procedures) except Web document collection and categorization, because there are 3552 Web documents and thousands of BPNN learning iterations. These Web documents are assigned to eight subordinate agents to be handled and then BPNN is used to train the extracted feature vectors for knowledge discovery. The parallel procedures are run on different PCs on the distributed environment.

The speed-up obtained by our experiment is summarized in Figure 6. 3552 documents and thousands of BPNN learning iterations, which took 7 hours and 17 minutes on one single server environment indicated above, now take only 1 hour and 43 minutes, that is, the speed-up factor is over 4 times. It should be pointed out that the server is new and the CPU is Pentium IV with a clock rate of 2.8E GHz. While the CPU of office PCs is Pentium III, whose clock rate is 860 MHz; therefore, if the office PCs are replaced by some advanced PCs with high performance CPU and memory, the speed-up factor can arrive at six times or more. In addition, if the server is replaced by an office PC, the speed-up factor can also be smaller than that of the server because the performance of the office PC is worse than that of the server, as shown in Figure 8.

From Figure 8, it is not hard to find that the speed-up factor become larger and larger with the

increase of number of PCs. However, the speed-up factor is not limit. According to the Amdahl's law (Kleinrock & Huang, 1992) (i.e., (total computation time)/(nonparallelizable computation time)), the upper bound for the speed-up factors is 10.16 (= (437 minutes) / (43 minutes)) times.

For testing the prediction ability of the proposed Web text mining, we evaluate the prediction performance with five text mining approaches mentioned previously. Figure 9 illustrates the comparison results of crude oil price movement direction prediction.

As can be seen from Figure 9, we can see that (1) the proposed multi-agent-based Web text min-

Figure 8. The speed-up results for the multi-agent neural network system

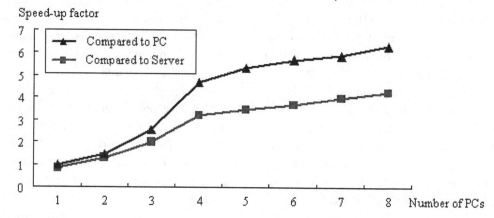

Figure 9. The oil price prediction results based on different text mining approach

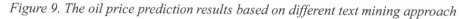
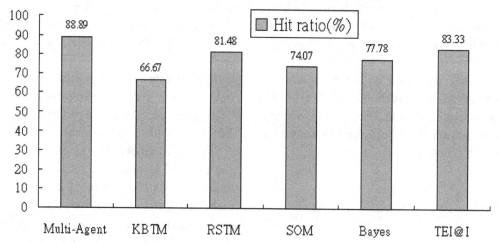

ing system outperforms the other five comparable text mining models listed in this chapter; (2) the keywords-based text mining performs the worst in the five text mining approaches, indicating that the performance of the statistical model (e.g., KBTM) seems to be worse than that of the intelligent model (e.g., SOM and BPNN); (3) of the six text mining methods, the proposed approach is the best, followed by TEI@I and RSTM, implying that the proposed approach is a feasible and potential solution to the crude oil price prediction. The main reason is that the proposed multi-agent intelligent text mining approach has a unique learning capability in a dynamical environment.

CONCLUSION

In this chapter, we proposed a multi-agent-based neural network system to solve the large scale Web text mining problem. The proposed multi-agent-based Web text mining system using neural network technique can discover some useful patterns or knowledge that can be used for prediction or decision from unstructured Web text documents. To evaluate the performance of the proposed text mining approach, an experiment about crude oil price prediction can be performed. From the experiment, we can find the following two main conclusions:

1. The multi-agent-based Web text mining system has a notable improvement of the computational performance as compared to single agent Web text mining approach; and
2. The multi-agent-based Web text mining system outperforms the other text mining models in prediction performance.

FUTURE RESEARCH DIRECTIONS

Although this chapter proposes a multi-agent-based neural network solution to Web text mining, there are still many issues to be addressed in the future. Currently, this chapter only provides a small-scale experiment with one server and eight PCs in a distributed computation environment. For large scale Web text mining problem, further speed-up of the Web text mining computation is required. For this purpose, we need to build a parallel computation environment with more than 100 PCs to solve the large scale text mining problem within the limit time.

Furthermore, the multi-agent-based Web text mining system over a distributed computational environment has at least one technical issue to be solved. This is the communication bottleneck or network loading problem. The current status of the Ethernet bandwidth in the officer floor is 100 Mbps. But the size of the total Web text documents for large scale Web text mining problems may be some hundreds megabytes. Therefore, even if we could construct a distributed computation environment with thousands of PCs, the time required to send the Web documents to different PCs in different sites becomes non-negligible, unless the gigabit Ethernet is implemented. There are several available technologies such as reliable multicast transport protocol (RMTP) using multicast to send the identical but large data very quickly to thousands of PCs. We plan to test and validate these technologies in near future.

Another important topic is the integrity of results. In this chapter, we use the simple majority voting principle to integrate the results. In the next stage, we try to use some new integration methods for this issue.

Finally, applying the emerging grid technology (Foster, Kesselman, & Tuecke, 2001) to construct a powerful supercomputing environment for multi-agent-based Web text mining is another promising research direction.

ACKNOWLEDGMENT

The authors would like to thank the editors and two anonymous referees for their valuable comments and suggestions. Their comments helped to improve the quality of the paper immensely. This work is supported by the grants from the National Natural Science Foundation of China (NSFC No. 70221001, 70601029), the Chinese Academy of Sciences (CAS No. 3547600), the Academy of Mathematics and Systems Science (AMSS No. 3543500) of CAS, and the Strategic Research Grant of City University of Hong Kong (SRG No. 7001677, 7001806).

REFERENCES

Berry, M.W., & Browne, M. (2002). *Understanding search engines: Mathematical modeling and text retrieval.* Philadelphia: SIAM Publisher.

Caruana, R., & Freitag, D. (1994). Greedy attribute selection. In *Proceedings of International Conference on Machine Learning* (pp. 28-36).

Chakrabarti, G. (2000). Data mining for hypertext: A tutorial survey. *SIGKDD Explorations, 1*(2), 1-11.

Chen, J., & Nie, J.Y. (2000). Parallel Web text mining for cross-language IR. *Algorithmica, 28*(2), 217-241.

Choi, Y.S., & Yoo, S.I. (2001). Text database discovery on the Web: Neural net based approach. *Journal of Information Systems, 16*, 5-20.

Etzioni, O. (1996). Moving up the information food chain: Deploying softbots on the World Wide Web. In *Proceedings of the 13th National Conference on Artificial Intelligence* (pp. 1322-1326).

Etzioni, O., & Weld, D. (1994). A softbot-based interface to the Internet. *Communications of the ACM, 37*(7), 72-76.

Fayyad, U., Piatetsky-Shapiro, G., & Smyth, P. (1996). From data mining to knowledge discovery: An Overview. In U. Fayyad, G. Piatetsky-Shapiro, P. Smyth, & R. Uthurusamy (Eds.), *Advances in knowledge discovery and data mining* (pp. 1-36). Cambridge, MA: MIT Press.

Feldman, R., & Dagan, I. (1995). Knowledge discovery in textual databases. In *Proceedings of the First International Conference on Knowledge Discovery and Data Mining (KDD'95)* (pp. 112-117).

Feldman, R., & Dagan, I. (1998). Mining text using keyword distributions. *Journal of Intelligent Information Systems, 10*, 281-300.

Foster, I., Kesselman, C., & Tuecke, S. (2001). The anatomy of the grid: Enabling scalable virtual organizations. *International Journal of High Performance Computing Applications, 15*(3), 200-223.

Freeman, J.A., & Skapura, D.M. (1992). *Neural networks algorithms, applications, and programming technique.* Boston: Addison-Wesley.

Furnkranz, J., Holzbaur, C., & Temel, R. (2002). User profiling for the Melvil knowledge retrieval system. *Applied Artificial Intelligence, 16*(4), 243-281.

Gelbukh, A. (2002). *Computational linguistics and intelligent text processing.* New York: Springer-Verlag, Lecture Notes in Computer Sciences.

Hearst, M.A. (1999). Untangling text data mining. *Proceedings of ACL'99: The 37th Annual Meeting of the Association for Computational Linguistics* (pp. 3-10).

Hornik, K., Stinchocombe, M., & White, H. (1989). Multilayer feedforward networks are universal approximators. *Neural Networks, 2*, 359-366.

IBM Intelligent Miner (2007). Retrieved August 9, 2007 from http://www-306.ibm.com/software/data/iminer/

Joachims, T. (1996). A probabilistic analysis of the Rocchio algorithm with TFIDF for text categorization. In *Proceedings of the 14th International Conference on Machine Learning (ICML-97)* (pp. 143-151). San Francisco: Morgan Kaufmann Publishers.

Karanikas, H., & Theodoulidis, B. (2002). *Knowledge discovery in text and text mining software* (Tech. Rep.). UMIST, Department of Computation.

Katz, S.M. (1995). Distribution of content words and phrases in text and language modeling. *Natural Language Engineering, 2*(1), 15-59.

Kleinrock, L., & Huang, J.H. (1992). On parallel processing systems: Amdahl's law generalized and some results on optimal design. *IEEE Transactions on Software Engineering, 18*(5), 434-447.

Kosala, R., & Blockeel, H. (2000). Web mining research: A survey. *SIGKDD Explorations, 2*(1), 1-15.

Kozierok, R., & Maes, P. (1993). Learning interface agents. In *Proceedings of the 11th National Conference on Artificial Intelligence* (pp. 459-465).

Lang, K. (1995). NewsWeeder: Learning to filter netnews. In *Proceedings of the 12th International Conference on Machine Learning* (pp. 331-339).

Lashkari, Y., Metral, M., & Maes, P. (1994). Collaborative interfaces agents. In *Proceedings of the 12th National Conference on Artificial Intelligence* (pp. 444-450).

Lee, C.H., & Yang, H.C. (1999). A Web text mining approach based on self-organizing map. In *Proceedings of the 2nd International Workshop on Web Information and Data Management* (pp. 59-62).

Maes, P. (1994). Agents that reduce work and information overload. *Communications of the ACM, 37*(7), 30-40.

Mock, K.J. (1996). Hybrid hill-climbing and knowledge-based methods for intelligent news filtering. In *Proceedings of the 13th National Conference on Artificial Intelligence* (pp. 48-53).

Payne, T.R., & Edwards, P. (1997). Interface agents that learn: An investigation of learning issues in a mail agent interface. *Applied Artificial Intelligence, 11*(1), 1-32.

Salton, G. (1971). *The SMART retrieval system: Experiments in automatic document processing.* Englewood Cliffs, NJ: Prentice Hall.

Salton, G. (1991). Developments in automatic text retrieval. *Science, 253,* 974-979.

Salton, G., & Yang, C.S. (1973). On the specification of term values in automatic indexing. *Journal of Documentation, 29*(4), 351-372.

SAS Text Miner. (2007). Retrieved August 9, 2007 from http://www.sas.com/technologies/analytics/datamining/textminer/

Sheth, B., & Maes, P. (1993). Evolving agents for personalized information filtering. In *Proceedings of the 9th Conference on Artificial Intelligence for Applications* (pp. 345-352).

Sparck Jones, K. (1972). A statistical interpretation of term specificity and its application to retrieval. *Journal of Documentation, 28*(1), 11-20.

Tan, A.H. (1999). Text mining: The state of the art and the challenges. In *Proceedings of the Pacific Asia Conference on Knowledge Discovery and Data Mining PAKDD'99 Workshop on Knowledge Discovery from Advanced Databases* (pp. 65-70).

Tesauro, G., & Janssens, R. (1988). Scaling relationships in back-propagation learning. *Complex Systems, 6,* 39-44.

Wang, S.Y., Yu, L., & Lai, K.K. (2005). Crude oil price forecasting with TEI@I methodology. *International Journal of Systems Science and Complexity, 18*(2), 145-166.

Webster's online dictionary (2004). retrieved August 9, 2007 from http://www.Webster-dictionary.org/.

Weiss, S.M., Indurkhya, N., Zhang, T., & Damerau, F.J. (2005). *Text mining: Predictive methods for analyzing unstructured information*. New York: Springer.

White, H. (1990). Connectionist nonparametric regression: Multilayer feedforward networks can learn arbitrary mappings. *Neural Networks, 3,* 535-549.

Yu, L., Wang, S.Y., & Lai, K.K. (2005). A rough-set-refined text mining approach for crude oil market tendency forecasting. *International Journal of Knowledge and Systems Sciences*, *2*(1), 33-46.

Yu, L., Wang, S.Y., & Lai, K.K. (2006). Intelligent Web text mining using neural networks. *International Journal of Computational Intelligence: Theory and Practice, 1*(2), 67-79.

Additional Reading

Berendt, B., Hotho, A., & Stumme, G. (2002). Towards semantic Web mining. In *Proceedings of the 1st International Semantic Web Conference* (pp. 264-278).

Brin, S., & Page, L. (1998). The anatomy of a large-scale hypertextual Web search engine. *Computer Networks*, *30*(1-7), 107-117.

Califf, M.E. (1999). *Machine learning for information extraction*. AAAI Press.

Califf. M.E. (2003). Bottom-up relational learning of pattern matching rules for information extraction. *Journal of Machine Learning Research*, *4*, 177-210.

Chakrabarti, S. (2002). *Mining the Web: Analysis of hypertext and semi structured data*. Morgan Kaufmann.

Chang, G., Healy, M.J., McHugh, J.A.M., & Wang, J.T.L. (2001). *Mining the World Wide Web: An information search approach*. Kluwer Academic Publishers.

Cooley, R., Mobasher, B., & Srivastava, J. (1999). Data preparation for mining World Wide Web browsing patterns. *Knowledge and Information Systems*, *1*(1), 5-32.

Craven, M., DiPasquo, D., Freitag, D., McCallum, A., Mitchell, T., & Nigam, K., et al. (2000). Learning to construct knowledge bases from the World Wide Web. *Artificial Intelligence*, *118*(1-2), 69-114.

Craven, M., & Slattery, S. (2001). Relational learning with statistical predicate invention: Better models for hypertext. *Machine Learning*, *43*(1-2), 97-119.

Craven, M., Slattery, S., & Nigam, K. (1998). First-order learning for Web mining. In *Proceedings of the 10th European Conference on Machine Learning (ECML-98)* (pp. 250-255).

Dean, J., & Henzinger, M.R. (1999). Finding related pages in the World Wide Web. In *Proceedings of the 8th International World Wide Web Conference (WWW-8)* (pp. 389-401).

Doorenbos, R.B., Etzioni, O., & Weld, D.S. (1997) A scalable comparison-shopping agent for the World-Wide Web. In *Proceedings of the 1st International Conference on Autonomous Agents* (pp. 39-48).

Eikvil, L. (1999). Information extraction from World Wide Web: A survey (Tech. Rep. No. 945). Norwegian Computing Center.

Freitag, D. (1998). Information extraction from HTML: Application of a general machine learning approach. In *Proceedings of the 15th National Conference on Artificial Intelligence (AAAI-98)*(pp. 517-523). AAAI Press.

Fürnkranz, J. (2002). Hyperlink ensembles: A case study in hypertext classification. *Information Fusion, 3*(4), 299-312.

Gordon, M., Lindsay, R., & Fan, W. (2002). Literature-based discovery on the WWW. *ACM Transactions on Internet Technology 2, 4,* 262-275.

Maes, P. (1994). Agents that reduce work and information overload. *Communications of the ACM, 37*(7), 30-40.

McCallum, A., & Nigam, K. (1998). A comparison of event models for naive bayes text classification. In *Proceedings of the 1998 AAAI/ICML Workshop* (pp. 41-48).

Mladenic, D. (1999). Text-learning and related intelligent agents: A survey. *IEEE Intelligent Systems, 14*(4), 44-54.

Mladenic, D., & Grobelnik, M. (1998). Word sequences as features in text learning. In *Proceedings of the 17th Electrotechnical and Computer Science Conference (ERK-98)* (pp. 145-148). Ljubljana, Slovenia, IEEE Section.

Mock, K.J. (1996). Hybrid hill-climbing and knowledge-based methods for intelligent news filtering. In *Proceedings of the 13th National Conference on Artificial Intelligence (AAAI-96)* (pp. 48-53).

Myllymaki, J. (2001). Effective Web data extraction with standard XML technologies (HTML). In *Proceedings of the 10th International World Wide Web Conference (WWW-01)* (pp. 689-696). Hong Kong, China.

Perkowitz, M., & Etzioni, O. (2000). Towards adaptive Web sites: Conceptual framework and case study. *Artificial Intelligence, 118,* 245-275.

Quinlan, J.R. (1990). Learning logical definitions from relations. *Machine Learning, 5,* 239-266.

Riloff, E. (1996a). Automatically generating extraction patterns from untagged text. In *Proceedings of the 13th National Conference on Artificial Intelligence (AAAI-96)* (pp. 1044-1049).

Riloff E. (1996b). An empirical study of automated dictionary construction for information extraction in three domains. *Artificial Intelligence, 85,* 101-134.

Salton, G. (1989). *Automatic text processing: The transformation, analysis, and retrieval of information by computer.* Reading, MA: Addison-Wesley.

Salton, G.., & Buckley, C. (1988). Term-weighting approaches in automatic text retrieval. *Information Processing and Management, 24* (5), 513-523.

Salton, G., Wong, A., & Yang. C. S. (1975). A vector space model for automatic indexing. *Communications of the ACM, 18*(11), 613-620.

Sebastiani, F. (2002). Machine learning in automated text categorization. *ACM Computing Surveys, 34*(1), 1-47.

Soderland, S. (1999). Learning information extraction rules for semi-structured and free text. *Machine Learning, 34*(1-3), 233-272.

Yang, Y., & Pedersen, J. (1997). A comparative study on feature selection in text categorization. In *Proceedings of the 14th International Conference on Machine Learning (ICML97)* (pp. 412-420).

Yang, Y., Slattery, S., & Ghani, R. (2002). A study of approaches to hypertext categorization. *Journal of Intelligent Information Systems, 18*(2-3), 219-241.

Chapter IX
Contextualized Clustering in Exploratory Web Search

Jon Atle Gulla
Norwegian University of Science and Technology

Hans Olaf Borch
Bekk Consulting AS, Norway

Jon Espen Ingvaldsen
Norwegian University of Science and Technology

ABSTRACT

Due to the large amount of information on the Web and the difficulties of relating users' expressed information needs to document content, large-scale Web search engines tend to return thousands of ranked documents. This chapter discusses the use of clustering to help users navigate through the result sets and explore the domain. A newly developed system, HOBSearch, makes use of suffix tree clustering to overcome many of the weaknesses of traditional clustering approaches. Using result snippets rather than full documents, HOBSearch both speeds up clustering substantially and manages to tailor the clustering to the topics indicated in a user's query. An inherent problem with clustering, though, is the choice of cluster labels. Our experiments with HOBSearch show that cluster labels of an acceptable quality can be generated with no supervision or predefined structures and within the constraints given by large-scale Web search.

INTRODUCTION

With the explosive growth of the Internet, Web search engines need to be able to handle billions of documents and deal with queries that may be very short, vague, or even ambiguous. As a con-sequence, a typical user query may easily result in millions of hits that are only partly related to each other. Overwhelmed by the number of results, many users investigate only the two or three top ranked documents. If nothing interesting shows up, most users reformulate their query rather than sift through numerous pages of search results. Studies of query logs from large commercial search engines reveal that users tend to type short queries and only look at the first results (Silverstein, Marais, Henzinger, & Moricz, 1999; Spink, Wolfram, Jansen, & Saracevic, 2001).

The idea behind *exploratory search* is to shift the focus from one-shot document retrieval to a multi-step learning and investigation process. This process is characteristic to situations in which users' information needs are imprecise or evolving or when their domain knowledge is limited (Kules, 2006). According to Rose and Levinson (2004), the exploratory queries constitute about 20-30% of all Web queries today. Traditional lists of ranked documents do not seem to be sufficient for these exploratory search tasks (White, Kules, Drucker & Schraefel, 2006), and we need additional techniques to help the users analyze the search results efficiently and drill down to the information they were looking for. We would like the users to explore the information relevant to them in a constructive manner, discovering new patterns, new entities, and knowledge they did not even realize they needed. Their initial queries set the stage for this exploration process, but other techniques are needed to extract the knowledge from the search results that will provide further insight into the domain.

A whole range of text mining techniques have been applied to extract additional patterns or knowledge from search result sets. These can be roughly classified according to function, resources, and content:

- **Function:** Whereas some techniques address the documents as a whole, others extract individual concepts or phrases from the documents. The techniques may either describe the content of each document or categorize and compare the documents according to some attributes or terms.
- **Resources:** The analysis may reflect the content of the result documents only, though

many techniques adapt the analysis to the user's information needs or context. Also, the techniques may involve some degree of supervision.
- **Content:** Whereas some techniques view words as incomprehensible tokens, other include linguistic analyses that take into account morphosyntactic or semantic aspects. For structuring the mining results, everything from incomprehensible tokens to well-defined concepts may be used.

One way of assisting users in finding the desired information quickly is to group the search results by topic. The user does not have to reformulate the query, but can merely click on the topic that most accurately describes his specific information need. The *function* here is the clustering of documents according to terms found in the documents, but the *resources* and *approach* used may differ depending on the way this grouping is implemented. The process of grouping documents is called *clustering* and was originally used for analyzing numerical data in the field of data mining. It has since been adapted to suit the needs in textual document collections.

The two main challenges with adapting clustering to the needs of Web search engines and textual data have been to find good descriptive labels to the clusters and to cluster documents on-the-fly in response to a particular user query. Traditional data mining approaches are not concerned with labeling clusters, but in return they are often very good at grouping data. Unfortunately, regardless of how good the document grouping is, users are not likely to use a clustering engine if the labels are poor. Clustering performance is also a major issue because Web users expect fast response times. To deal with this linear time, clustering algorithms that can cluster hundreds of documents per second have been developed.

Several commercial clustering engines have been introduced in recent years. Vivisimo, which was rewarded by SearchEngineWatch.com for best metasearch engine from 2001 to 2003, is well-known, but also large companies like Google and Microsoft have expressed interests in clustering for their future search platforms.

The objective of this chapter is to present a newly developed clustering component that both scales well for large-scale Web search and takes into consideration the user's expressed information needs. The component builds on the well-known suffix tree clustering (STC) algorithm, but addresses many issues not discussed in the original STC that heavily affect the quality of the clusters found. Experimenting with the prototype sheds new light on many of the choices made in STC, including the use of stemming, removal of stopwords, join criteria for clusters, and most importantly on labeling. Our main contribution lies in the way cluster labels may be selected in an STC context. We compare the STC approach to other text mining techniques used in exploratory search solutions and discuss some of the advantages and disadvantages of contextualized clustering.

SEARCH AND CLUSTERING

An information retrieval system processes a document collection to select a set of index terms and builds an index that allows searching the documents efficiently. Given a model for representing documents, the query can be matched against each document in the collection and a list of relevant documents is then ranked and returned to the user. The simplest strategy for selecting index terms is to use *all* words in all documents. Additional strategies aim at either reducing *index size* or improving *retrieval performance*. Strategies include removing stop words and stemming or lemmatizing the words before indexing.

In the vector space information retrieval model, each document is represented in the term space corresponding to the union of all index terms appearing in the document collection (Baeza-Yates & Ribeiro-Neto, 1999). A document collection of n documents $D = \{d_1, ..., d_n\}$ containing m unique words can be described by means of n document vectors $d_j = (w_{j1}, ..., w_{jm})$, where w_{ji} designates a weight for the term t_i in document d_j. The most widely adopted scheme for term weighting called *tf*idf* is defined as:

$$w_{i,j} = tf * idf = \frac{freq_{i,j}}{\max_l freq_{l,j}} * \log \frac{N}{n_i}$$

where $freq_{i,j}$ is the raw frequency of t_i in document d_j and the maximum frequency is computed over all words occurring in d_j. N is the number of documents in the collection and n_i is the number of documents containing the term t_i. The *tf*idf* measure tries to balance two effects: Words frequently occurring in a document are likely to be important (hence the *tf* or *term frequency* part), but words occurring in a large percentage of the document collection are less discriminating and thus less important for retrieval (hence the *idf* or *inverse document frequency* part). The denominator of the term frequency is a way of normalizing the term frequency according to the length of the document, so that long documents are not favored.

Although several alternatives have been proposed, some variants of *tf*idf* are often used for weighting. Several variations are described in Salton and Buckley (1988). For weighting query terms they suggest:

$$w_{i,q} = \left(0.5 + \frac{0.5\, freq_{i,q}}{\max_l freq_{l,q}}\right) * \log \frac{N}{n_i}$$

where w_{iq} is the weight for the term t_i in the query q, N is the number of documents in the collection and n_i is the number of documents containing the term t_i.

The similarity between two term vectors is determined by measuring their vector distance. A common measure is the *cosine-similarity* φ defined as:

$$\varphi(d_i, d_j) = \frac{\vec{d_i} \bullet \vec{d_j}}{|\vec{d_i}| * |\vec{d_j}|}$$

where $\vec{d_i}$ is the document vector for document d_i. The vector model is a simple and fast strategy that has the advantage of allowing partial matches and provides improved retrieval performance by ranking the results according to query similarity (Baeza-Yates & Ribeiro-Neto, 1999).

Clustering Search Results

In text mining, clustering is the process of grouping documents with similar contents. It has been used for browsing document collections (Cutting, Pedersen, Karger, & Tukey, 1992) and for automatically building taxonomies (Koller & Sahami, 1997), though in this work the focus is on using clustering to organize results from a search engine, like in Zamir, Etzioni, Madani, and Karp (1997).

Search results on the Web are traditionally presented as flat ranked lists of documents, frequently millions of documents long. The main use of clustering is not to improve the actual ranking, but to give the user a quick overview of the results. After the search engine has divided the result set into clusters, the user can quickly narrow down his search further by selecting a cluster. This resembles *query refinement*, but avoids the need to query the search engine for each step. Evaluations done using the Grouper system (Zamir & Etzioni, 1999) indicate that users tend to investigate more documents per query than in normal search engines. It is assumed that this is because the user clicks on the desired cluster rather than reformulate his query. The evaluation also indicates that once one interesting document has been found, the users often find other interesting documents in the same cluster.

Although it is possible to cluster documents before the user submits a query, the amount of information and variety of topics present on the Internet suggests that we need to come up with specialized categories in response to each user query. This has been referred to as *on-line* or *query-time* clustering, which obviously introduces major performance requirements. A typical Web user is not very patient and will be annoyed if he has to wait more than a couple of seconds at most for the results of his request; therefore, the performance of clustering is a major concern.

Document clustering shares several characteristics with the field of *text categorization* (Aas & Eikvil, 1999). The main difference is that categorization focuses on assigning documents to *predefined groups*, whereas document clustering tries to extract the groupings inherent in the documents. Many text categorization approaches build classifiers that are trained to categorize documents efficiently, but this would not work for clustering since the categories are not known in advance.

Document clustering essentially has two major challenges: to group similar documents into coherent clusters and to label these clusters with descriptive labels. The former challenge is often addressed by transforming the documents into vectors and then using well-tested data mining techniques for clustering numerical data. The labeling is more difficult, especially for the document vector approaches. While clustering has been researched for decades, only in the last decade has clustering algorithms specially tailored to unstructured textual data appeared.

Traditional Clustering Approaches

Traditional clustering techniques transform the documents into vectors and employ standard techniques for calculating differences between vectors to cluster the documents (Jain, Murty, & Flynn, 1999; Steinbach, Karypis, & Kumar, 2000).

Hierarchical Clustering

In general, there are two types of hierarchical clustering methods (Han et al., 2001):

- *Agglomerative* or bottom-up hierarchical methods create a cluster for each document and then merge the two most similar clusters until just one cluster remains or some termination condition is satisfied. Most hierarchical clustering methods fall into this category, and they only differ in their definition of intercluster similarity and termination conditions.
- *Divisive* or top-down hierarchical methods do the opposite, starting with all documents in one large cluster. The initial cluster is divided until some termination condition is satisfied.

Hierarchical methods are widely adopted but often struggle to meet the speed requirements of the Web. Since they usually operate on document vectors with a time complexity of $O(n^2)$ or more, clustering more than a few hundred snippets is often unfeasible. Another problem is that if two clusters are incorrectly merged in an early state there is no way of fixing this later in the process. Finding the best halting criterion that works well with all queries can also be very difficult.

K-Means Clustering

The iterative K-Means algorithm comes in many flavors and produces a fixed number (k) of flat clusters. The algorithms generally follow the following process: Random samples from the collection are drawn to serve as *centroids* for initial clusters. Based on document vector similarity, all documents are assigned to the closest centroid. New centroids are calculated for each cluster, and the process is repeated until nothing changes or some termination condition is satisfied (Lloyd, 1982).

The process can be speeded up by clustering a subset of the documents and later assigning all documents to the precomputed clusters. This strategy can however only produce a fixed number of clusters (k). It performs optimally when the clusters are spherical, but we have unfortunately no reason to assume that document clusters are spherical. Also, a "bad choice" in the random selection of initial clusters can severely degrade the performance of the system as a whole.

Buckshot and Fractation Algorithm

These linear time clustering algorithms were both introduced in Cutting et al. (1992) and are so-called *seed-based partitional* clustering techniques. Partitional clustering follows a three-step process: (1) Find k cluster centers; (2) Assign each document to the nearest cluster; and (3) refine the partitioning. Buckshot and Fractation are different strategies for generating the initial k cluster centers from n documents. The idea is to employ a slow (typically quadratic) but high-quality clustering technique on a subset of the data and then use the result to approximate the final clusters.

Buckshot selects $\sqrt{kn}$ of the documents and applies the clustering algorithm on this small selection. The technique is a non-deterministic but fast technique, as it runs in $O(nk)$ time. Fractation splits the document collection into m buckets *(m > k)* and clusters each bucket. These clusters are then treated as the individuals and the process is repeated until only k clusters remain. The process can be shown to run in $O(mn)$ time.

The rest of the documents are then assigned to their nearest cluster center based on some heuristics. In step three clusters are refined either by re-applying the nearest cluster center approach (resembling the k-means approach), or by splitting and/or joining clusters based on some heuristics of overlap/disjointness.

According to the authors, Buckshot achieves the higher performance and is better suited for *rough* clustering on-line, while fractation can be used to determine primary partitioning of an entire corpus. They propose a technique, Scatter/Gather (Cutting et al., 1992), that first uses Fractation to create an initial partitioning and then Buckshot to do on-the-fly clustering to tailor the results from the Fractation algorithm towards the specific user request at query time.

Suffix Tree Clustering

Text-oriented clustering approaches are characterized by their focus on words rather than document vectors. Instead of representing documents as vectors they typically focus on grouping documents that share sets of frequently occurring phrases. Fung, Wang, and Ester (2003) advocate the use of *frequent itemsets* from data mining to cluster documents. Frequent itemsets originate from *association rule mining* typically used in data warehouses. The idea is that documents that share a set of words that appear frequently are related and this is used to cluster documents. The article also presents a way to infer hierarchies of clusters. Ferragina and Gulli (2005) propose a similar method that mines for so-called *gapped sequences* that do not necessarily appear continuously in the text. They also cluster based on the occurrence of such frequent phrases and build hierarchical clusters. The QDC clustering algorithm (Crabtree, Andreae & Gao, 2006) is query-driven and makes use of the relationship between cluster descriptions and the query terms. A word semantic approach is used to merge clusters into document groups of a suitable size.

The most well-known text-oriented clustering technique is however the *suffix tree clustering (STC)* algorithm, which was introduced by Zamir et al. (1997) and further developed by a later work (Zamir & Etzioni, 1998). This algorithm focuses on clustering snippets faster than standard data mining approaches using a data structure called a suffix tree. Its time complexity is linear to the number of snippets, making it attractive when clustering a large number of documents.

The algorithm consists of three steps: (1) Document cleaning, (2) Identifying base clusters, and (3) combining base clusters into clusters. These steps are demonstrated running the algorithm on the following little document collection (resembling sample Web document titles):

Document 1: Jaguar car reviews—Review Centre
Document 2: ## PANTERA ONCA ##
Document 3: Jaguar reviews!
Document 4: Buy Pantera Onca Pictures

Cleaning Documents

A light stemming algorithm is applied on the text, sentence boundaries are marked, and non-word tokens are stripped. After the pre-processing, we are left with the following phrases for each of the documents:

Document 1: {jaguar car review, review centre}
Document 2: {pantera onca}
Document 3: {jaguar review}
Document 4: {buy pantera onca picture}

Identifying Base Clusters

The process of identifying base clusters resembles building an inverted index of phrases for the document collection. The data structure used is a *suffix tree* (Weiner, 1973), which can be built in time linear to the collection size (Ukkonen, 1992).

Formally, a suffix tree is a rooted, directed tree, and each internal node has at least two children. Each edge is labeled with a non-empty substring of the total set of phrases S (hence it is a *trie*). The label of a node is defined to be the concatenation of the edge-labels on the path from the root to that node. No two edges out of the same node can have edge-labels that begin with the same word (hence it is *compact*). For each suffix s of S, there exists a *suffix node* whose label equals s. Figure 1 illustrates the suffix tree built using the sentences identified in our sample document collection.

Figure 1. Suffix tree

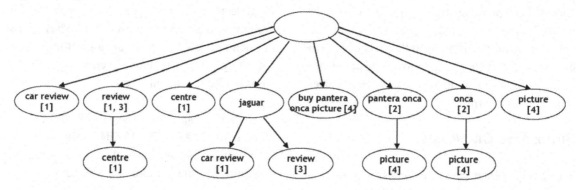

Each node represents a phrase and has a list of document IDs in which the phrase occurs.

Each node in the tree represents a group of documents (a *base cluster*) and is labeled with a phrase that is common to all of them. All groups containing two or more documents are selected to serve as the base clusters. Each of the base clusters are assigned a score according to the following formula:

$$s(B) = |B| \cdot f(|P|)$$

where $|B|$ is the number of documents in base cluster B, and $|P|$ is the number of words in the base cluster's phrase P that have a non-zero score (the *effective length* of the phrase). Words that appear in more than 40% of the collection or in less than three documents receive a score of zero. The

function f penalizes single word phrases, is linear for phrases of two to six words, and is constant for longer phrases.

The scored base clusters are shown in Table 1. Note that since there are only four documents in the sample collection, no words have been given a zero-score.

Combining Base Clusters

This step merges base clusters with highly over-lapping document sets. The similarity of base clusters B_n and B_m is a binary function ψ defined in equation 1.

In equation 1, $|B_m \cap B_n|$ is the number of documents shared by B_m and B_n. Calculating this similarity between all base clusters, we can create a *base cluster graph*, where nodes are base clusters, and two nodes are connected if the two base clusters have a similarity of 1. Using this graph a cluster is defined as a connected component in the graph.

The following algorithm is adapted from Cormen, Stein, Rivest, and Leiserson (2001) and presents a simple way of determining the connected components in a graph G, given a function $SET(v)$ that returns the set containing the vertex (base cluster) v.

Table 1. Base clusters

Phrase	Documents	Score
review	1, 3	2
jaguar	1, 3	2
pantera onca	2, 4	4
onca	2, 4	2

Equation 1.

$$\psi(B_m, B_n) = \begin{cases} 1 & \text{iff } |B_m \cap B_n| \, / \, |B_m| > 0.5 \text{ and } |B_m \cap B_n| \, / \, |B_n| > 0.5 \\ 0 & \text{otherwise} \end{cases}$$

Figure 2. Base cluster graph

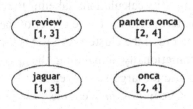

CONNECTED-COMPONENTS (*G*)
1.   **for** each vertex $v \in V[G]$
2.   **do** make new set containing v
3.   **for** each edge $(u, v) \in E[G]$
4.   **do if** SET $(u) \neq$ SET(v)
5.   **then** join sets u and v

Figure 2 shows the graph with its connected components.

Each connected component constitutes a cluster, and it consists of the union of the documents contained in each of its base clusters. In the original work on STC, Zamir and Etzioni (1998) state that "the final clusters are scored and sorted based on the scores of their base clusters and their overlap" without giving much detail as to how this is done.

Document Snippets

A common technique used by clustering engines is to cluster so-called *document snippets* rather than entire documents. Snippets are the small paragraphs often displayed along with Web search results to give the user an indication of the document contents. Figure 3 shows the first three results along with their snippets generated by the Google search engine.

Snippets are considerably smaller than the documents (typically only 100-200 characters), thereby drastically reducing the computational cost of clustering. This is very important since scalability and performance are major challenges for most clustering engines. When building clusters based only on short extracts from the documents, the quality of the snippets returned by the search engine naturally becomes very important. Snippet generation approaches vary from naive (e.g., first words in the document) to more sophisticated (e.g., display the passage containing the most words from the query or multiple passages containing all or most of the query keywords).

Figure 3. Snippets from Google

Web	Results 1 - 10 of about 21,200,000

Red Hot Chili Peppers Online
Red Hot Chili Peppers's official web site and fan club, featuring news, photos, concert tickets, merchandise, and more.
www.redhotchilipeppers.com/ - 18k - Cached - Similar pages

Red Hot Chili Peppers - Wikipedia, the free encyclopedia
Kiedis provides a range of vocal styles for **RHCP** songs, with his style of rapping and spoken verse (the latter being characteristic of his vocals up to ...
en.wikipedia.org/wiki/Red_Hot_Chili_Peppers - 58k - Cached - Similar pages

MTV - Music - Artist - **Red Hot Chili Peppers**
MTV Music is the ultimate destination for content on **Red Hot Chili Peppers**, including band info, music videos, live performances, news, albums and previews, ...
www.mtv.com/music/artist/ **red_hot_chili_peppers**/artist.jhtml - 60k -
Cached - Similar pages

Clustering algorithms differ in their sensitivity to document length but generally the qualitative effect of using snippets as opposed to entire documents is surprisingly small as demonstrated by Zamir and Etzioni (1998). Only about 15% average loss of precision for the clusters was found when using snippets rather than entire documents. The article suggests that this is caused by the search engines' efforts to extract meaningful snippets with respect to the user query, which reduces the noise present in the original document so much that the results do not deteriorate significantly. This further emphasises the importance of high quality snippet extraction for snippet clustering approaches.

Related Work on Search Result Clustering

Scatter/Gather (Cutting et al., 1992) was one of the first clustering approaches implemented on top of traditional search engines. It uses the non-hierarchical partitioning algorithms Buckshot and Fractionation to cluster documents in linear time based on the cosine similarity between documents.

Grouper (Zamir et al., 1999) was one of the early approaches to Web snippet clustering. It is a document clustering interface to the HuskySearch meta-search service, implementing the Suffix Tree Clustering algorithm. Heuristics based on word overlap and word coverage within each cluster are used to label the clusters with the best phrases identified by the STC algorithm. It is one of the best performing clustering engines, being able to cluster 500 clusters in only one second. The system is available through the open source project Carrot2.

The *Lingo* system (Osinski & Weiss, 2004) uses singular value decomposition (SVD) on the term-document matrix to find multiple word labels. It starts by identifying key phrases and represents them in the same vector space as the documents. Vectors are then transformed using

SVD, and clusters are identified through document similarity calculations, labeling the clusters with the terms closest to the center of the document vectors in the cluster. As SVD is known to be computationally demanding, the approach is problematic for large-scale Web search engines.

The *Clusty/Vivisimo* engine (www.clusty. com and www.vivisimo.com) is one of the best performing commercial clustering engines available. It produces high quality hierarchical clusters with multiple word or phrase labels. Clusty uses a meta-search approach drawing snippets from 10 other search engines, though little is known about the internals of their clustering approach.

SnakeT (Ferragina & Gulli, 2005) is a meta-search engine that draws results from 15 commodity search engines and builds hierarchical clusters based on snippets. It uses an on-line hierarchical clustering approach based on the notion of *frequent itemsets* from Data Mining. So-called *gapped-sentences* (related but not necessarily continuously appearing words) that form multiple-word labels are extracted, and it also employs two knowledge bases (the Dmoz hierarchy and "anchor texts'") to improve performance. The system produces clusters of quality comparable to that of Vivisimo, but fails when data sets grow large. Experiments show that the clustering of 200 snippets takes over 4 seconds, and 400 snippets takes about 9 seconds, which is too slow for the average Internet user.

ONLINE CLUSTERING IN HOBSearch

The objective of our search application, *HOBSearch*, was to be able to cluster Web search results efficiently while producing high-quality topical labels. The suffix tree clustering algorithm was chosen as the core of the approach. Snippets for Web documents are publicly available through common Web search engines. However, to increase the snippet quality, HOBSearch controls the snippet generation internally. It is important that the snippets are both representative for the document content and tailored to the user's information needs, but the snippets of most publicly available search engines are either not representative enough or too short for reliable clustering. Our clustering component is built on top of a standard vector space search engine.

The whole system operates in two separate phases. The first phase, Indexing, processes a document collection and builds an index to enable searching. This is done by tokenizing the documents, removing stopwords from the texts, and stemming the words. Stemming has been proposed as a means of reducing the index size and improving retrieval performance. Kraaij and Pohlmann (1996) conclude that stemming does improve recall, but an evaluation performed by Hull (1996) found little improvement in precision as compared to not using stemming. The Porter stemming algorithm (Porter, 1997) is applied to the text in order to reduce the index size. The indexing itself is done by parsing the tokenized documents, keeping a list of each unique word (called the vocabulary) and a list of occurrences (called postings) to keep track of how many times a word occurs in each of the documents in the collection. This gives us the classical *inverted index*, though words that only occur in a single document are removed before writing the index to disk. In addition to the vocabulary and postings, certain features are extracted and calculated from each of the documents and stored in a separate file.

The second phase, Retrieval, allows users to submit queries, uses the index to retrieve relevant documents, and clusters the documents on the user result page. Figure 4 shows the various steps involved in the retrieval phase. The search engine reads the necessary information from the index at the preparation stage. The user query is preprocessed using tokenization, stopword removal and stemming, before it is passed on to the search engine. At the retrieval stage, a vector space approach with the vocabulary and inverted index from the first phase is adopted. Term weights are calculated according to the well-known *td*idf* scheme, and term weights for queries are calculated using the measure suggested by Salton and Buckley (1998). Document similarity and ranking are based on standard cosine similarity calculations.

After ranking the result documents from the search engine, snippets from a number of the top resulting documents are generated. Using snippets instead of entire documents not only reduces the workload for the clustering algorithm drastically, it also takes load off the usually very busy search engine core. Relying only on snippets also allows clustering to be added on top of a regular search engine to create a *meta-search engine* that uses the results and snippets returned by the search engine for clustering. Our snippets were the 150

Figure 4. Document retrieval and clustering process

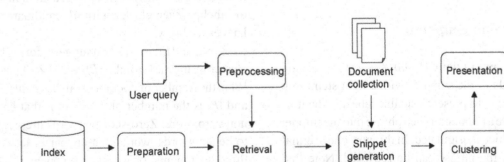

characters following the first occurrence of the first query term in each document. This ensured that the snippets are tailored to the user's information needs and context.

The results from the search engine were clustered using the suffix tree clustering algorithm described earlier. The algorithm takes as input the generated snippets and returns a list of labeled clusters of documents. Zamir and Etzioni (1998) list several key requirements for Web document clustering, including:

- **Relevance:** The clusters should be relevant to the user query and their labels easily understood by the user.
- **Overlap:** Because documents can have several topics, it is favorable to allow a document to appear in several clusters.
- **Snippet tolerance:** For deployment in large-scale applications, the algorithm should be able to produce high-quality clusters based only on the snippets returned by the search engine.
- **Speed:** The clusters should be generated in a matter of milliseconds to avoid user annoyance and scalability issues.

The standard STC algorithm has all these qualities, though there are many design decisions that may affect the performance of the technique. In the following section we discuss some of the choices we made to build a high-quality clustering component into a large-scale Web search architecture.

Stemming Snippets

Zamir and Etzioni (1998) suggest stemming all words in the snippets with a light stemming algorithm. To present readable labels to the user they save a pointer for each phrase into the snippet from which it originated. In this way one original form of the phrase can be retrieved. Note that several original phrases from different snippets

may belong to the same base cluster, but which of these original forms is chosen is not detailed in their work.

Our HOBSearch prototype only stems plurals to singular, using a very light stemming algorithm. The effects of stemming the snippets is further assessed in the evaluation section. Original snippets are stored to allow original phrases to be reconstructed after clustering.

Removing Stopwords in Snippets

The authors of STC suggest dealing with stopwords in phrases by allowing them as long as they are not the first or the last word in the phrase, for instance allowing "product of France" but not "product of". When testing the prototype without removing stopwords, it seemed that phrases containing stopwords are rarely selected as labels; therefore, our prototype simply skips stopwords and inserts phrase boundaries instead.

Labeling Clusters

The clustering algorithm outputs a set of labeled base clusters for each cluster In the Grouper system, clusters are labeled with all the labels from the base clusters. The STC algorithm assigns a score to each base cluster, but never utilizes it. The approach taken in HOBSearch is to treat the base cluster labels as *candidate labels* for the final cluster, and use the scoring to select the highest ranked candidate as the final label. It is assumed that having one or two phrases as a label instead of labeling each cluster with *all* candidates enhances usability.

Zamir and Etzioni (1998) suggest scoring base clusters using the formula $s(B) = |B| * f(|P|)$, where $|B|$ is the number of documents in base cluster B, and $|P|$ is the number of words in P that have a non-zero score. Zero-scoring words are defined to be stopwords, words that appear in less than three documents, or words that appear in more than 40% of the document collection. f is a function that penalizes single word phrases, is linear for two to six words long phrases and constant for longer phrases.

The scoring scheme used in HOBSearch closely resembles the suggested formula, as initial testing indicated that the formula worked very well. Our prototype does not include stopwords in the zero-scoring words since all stopwords are removed during preprocessing. The function f gives a score of 0.5 for single word phrases, 2 to 6 for two to six words phrases respectively, and 7 for longer phrases. If the two top ranked base clusters have the same score, the one with the largest document set is used as the label. This is because phrases occurring in many documents are assumed to represent more important categories.

Ranking Clusters

One of the best performing systems available, Clusty.com, seems to almost always present cluster lists sorted by the number of documents they contain. Minor deviations from this approach can be observed, indicating that they use some additional heuristics. This suggests that it might be a small trade-off between quality and performance, given that additional processing of the clusters can produce a slightly altered (and hopefully improved) ordering of clusters. In our prototype this extra processing is assumed to cost more time than it gains in quality. We assume that large clusters are more interesting, and clusters are thus simply ranked by the number of documents they contain.

The HOBSearch prototype shown in Figure 5 includes a Web front-end that allows users to submit queries and returns a list of matching documents and browsable clusters. The documents are presented with the document title, the generated snippet and a link to the corresponding Web page. The list to the left in Figure 5 shows the generated clusters for the query *Paris*.

Figure 5. The HOBSearch Web interface. The clusters are listed to the left.

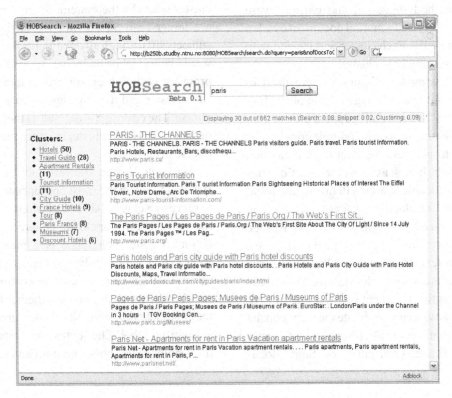

DISCUSSION

The standard STC algorithm, which lies at the core of our approach, has been evaluated against many other well known clustering algorithms by Zamir and Etzioni (1998). Our evaluation below goes more into the specifics of this particular implementation, focusing primarily on the cluster labels suggested by the approach. These labels are difficult to evaluate, as it ideally involves the investigation of the contents of thousands of documents in each cluster.

Evaluation Method

HOBSearch was set up according to the approach described above. This involved removing stopwords and stemming the words in the index, and removing all words that appear in only one document. The snippets were generated by reading 150 characters from the first appearing query word in the original file onwards. Stopwords were removed from the snippets and trailing s's in plural forms are removed. Candidates were scored using the standard method suggested and clusters were joined when they had a mutual document overlap of more than 40%. Each cluster was labeled with its highest scoring base cluster.

The following set of queries were used in the evaluation: "paris", "jaguar", "apple", "hollywood", and "red hot chili peppers".

For evaluation purposes, a simple crawler was developed to generate the document collection from the Web. It took as input the set of queries and used the Google Search API to download and store the top 1000 documents for each query. The documents varied in length but were on average about 5 kilobytes after stripping the HTML codes. For English text, this is about 800-1000 words. All documents containing less than twice as many characters as the document title were discarded. This is because many Web sites simply consist of flash animations or splash screens that are not interesting for retrieval purposes. Some docu-

ments were not retrieved because of technical issues such as Web servers not responding, and so forth. A total of about 3900 documents constitute the final document collection, and they were all in English.

In essence, the STC algorithm outputs a number of clusters that contain base clusters, whose labels can be used as candidate labels for the cluster. A crucial step in the algorithm is the selection of one or more of the base clusters to serve as cluster labels, since this greatly impacts the user experience. Given a set of candidate labels, this test evaluates whether the system correctly selects the best candidate to serve as a label for each cluster.

The test was performed individually by four persons without any particular domain knowledge related to the queries. After running the five queries, the system clustered the first 200 resulting documents for each of the queries. The test subjects were presented with all candidate phrases (in random order) of the top ten ranked clusters for each query, and they did not know which of the candidates that were selected as the cluster labels by the system. Since some clusters are larger than 50 documents, having the test subjects sift through all documents for all clusters would be too labor intensive. Instead, they were provided with five example document titles for each cluster and the coverage of each candidate phrase. The coverage is defined as the percentage of documents in the cluster in which the candidate phrase occurs.

For each cluster, the test subjects were instructed to select the most appropriate candidate to serve as a cluster label (precision). In addition, they gave a score for cluster coherence and label quality. Cluster coherence is a measure of to what extent the candidate phrases and example document titles seem to describe a common topic. Label quality was defined as whether they think the candidate they chose as cluster label is a suitable cluster label. The scores were given using a three point scale (poor, medium and good).

Overall Evaluation Results

Figure 6(a) shows the average score given for each query. Note that precision ranges from 0-1 while cluster coherence and label quality range from 0-2. Precision is defined to be 1 if the subject selected the same candidate as the prototype and 0 if another candidate was selected. Some of the test subjects often selected a candidate equal to the one selected by the prototype, but prefixed by the query (for instance selecting Paris Hotels instead of Hotels for the query "paris"). In these cases a score of 0.5 was assigned.

As seen from Figure 6(a), the candidate phrases were considered to be quite representative for the documents' content. However, except for the *apple* query, the users are less satisfied with the quality of the labels as cluster labels. The precision values are consistently high, indicating that the system is good at picking out the most appropriate cluster label from the set of candidate labels. There is some variation between the queries, though the approach seems equally attractive for multi-word queries as for single-word queries. Since only four test subjects were used, variability in the results was expected. It is interesting to see which of the dimensions (precision, coherence, quality) that vary the most. Figure 6(b) shows the total number of points assigned by each of the subjects for the three dimensions. Whereas

there is some disagreement about label quality, they all tend to agree with the system's choice of cluster labels.

The average number of times where the prototype selected the same label as the test subjects is close to 80%, which is quite impressive. It indicates that the prototype in most cases succeeds in selecting the same label as human users. However, this does not mean that it necessarily selects the *correct* label, but merely the same as a small sample of test users. The average score for the coherence of each cluster is 1.6 out of 2 points, which means that they on average are closer to "good" than "medium". This indicates that the clustering algorithm is good at grouping documents, and it confirms the original assumption that documents that share phrases often address the same topic. Results were less promising when it comes to label quality, averaging at only 1.3 out of 2 points. Looking at the results from each test subject, we discover that label clustering is very subjective, and more extensive testing has to be carried out before any conclusions can be made.

It is interesting to look at what causes low precision for some of the clusters. When clusters have many overlapping candidates and when they have little coherence, the precision scores tend to be particularly low. Having many similar candidates naturally makes it difficult to choose

Figure 6. (a) Results for each query, (b) average results for each test person

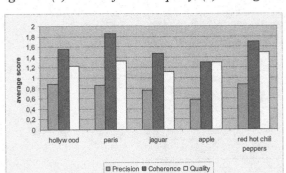

(a)

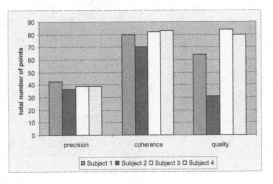

(b)

the correct label because users might find several labels equally good. The low precision is therefore to be expected.

Two of the test subjects repeatedly marked the same candidate as the prototype but prefixed with the query (for instance marking *Red Hot Chili Peppers Concert Tickets* rather than *Concert Tickets* for the query *red hot chili peppers*). We argue that in most cases labels should not be prefixed by the query. It is assumed that if the test subjects were shown a list of only the final cluster labels along with the query (much like in the Web interface) they would recognize the redundancy in prefixing each cluster with the query.

Clustering Performance

The performance test showed that up to 500 documents can be clustered in under a second. When clustering only 200 documents, the application spent on the average only 160 milliseconds to generate the necessary clusters. Moreover, the clustering can be built outside the search engine core (a metasearch approach) without impacting the performance of the search engine.

Whereas the original STC implementation was tested on a Pentium 200MHz, our application ran on an AMD Athlon 1700+ (1.47 GHz) with 512MB RAM. A comparison of execution times is given in Figure 7, though it should be added that the two curves should not be compared directly. It is however interesting to see that while the original implementation seems more or less linear to the collection size, the curve for HOBSearch forms a parabola. It is difficult to say exactly what separates the two, though one reason may be that the suffix tree construction in our system is not entirely linear.

Base Cluster Similarity

In the original work on STC base clusters that have more than 50% mutually overlapping documents are joined. Through manual inspection of the base clusters contained in each of the final clusters for several queries, it seems that many clusters are so similar that they should have been joined. A solution might be to lower the threshold to increase the number of base clusters joined, thus creating fewer and larger clusters. Figure 8(a) shows the clusters with all base clusters for the query "*paris*" when clustering 200 documents and using a 50% threshold.

Figure 7. Clustering performance

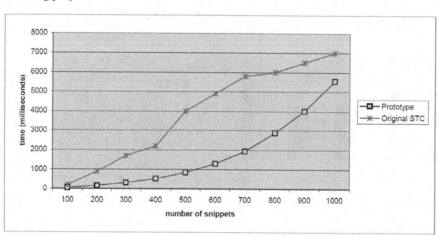

Figure 8. (a) Base clusters with 50% threshold; (b) base clusters with 40% threshold

Cluster	Phrases
1	{France}
2	{Hotels, Paris Hotels}
3	{Travel}
4	{Guide]
5	{Hotels Paris}
6	{Pages}
7	{Tour}
8	{City}
9	{Paris Apartment Rentals, Apartment Rentals, Apartments, Rentals, Paris Apartments}
10	{Travel Guide, Paris Travel Guide, Paris Travel, Restaurants}

(a)

Cluster	Phrases
1	{France}
2	{Hotels, Paris Hotels, Hotels Paris}
3	{Travel Guide, Paris Travel Guide, Travel, Guide, Paris Travel, Restaurants}
4	{Pages}
5	{Tour}
6	{Paris Apartment Rentals, Apartment Rentals, Apartments, Rentals, Rent}
7	{City}
8	{Information}
9	{Paris France}
10	{Hotel Reservation, Paris Hotel Reservation, Reservation}

(b)

Experiments with the prototype indicate that 40% might be a better threshold. Contrary to the findings by Zamir and Etzioni (1998), it seems that this factor impacts clustering performance a great deal. A mere 10% change from 50% to 40% resulted in a reduction from 136 to 96 clusters (30% fewer) when clustering results from the query "*paris*" using 200 snippets. Figure 8(b) shows the results with a 40% threshold enforced. It is difficult to quantitatively measure any improved quality resulting from this, but the average number of base clusters in the top 20 ranked clusters increased from 1.6 to 2.6 when lowering the threshold. Of the final clusters, "Travel" and "Guide" are joined into the cluster "Travel Guide", and "Hotels" and "Hotels Paris" are joined into the cluster "Hotels". Both of these changes seem attractive. In general, having a 40% threshold results in more clusters with only one base cluster.

Stemming and Tagging Snippets

The authors of the STC algorithm suggest stemming the snippets in the pre-processing stage. Perhaps the most popular stemmer available is the Porter stemming algorithm (Porter, 1997). Since we are mostly interested in nouns, Porter's algorithm is a bit cumbersome. Experimenting with our prototype revealed that stemming takes about 200 milliseconds when clustering 100 snippets, and it grows approximately linearly with larger numbers of snippets.

It is natural to assume that the additional cost of stemming would to some degree be made up for by the reduced size of the suffix tree and thus faster computation of clusters. A test done with 200 snippets from the query "paris" showed that 2058 tree nodes where created without stemming and as much as 2025 nodes with stemming. Surprisingly, it seems that stemming has little effect on the size of the tree.

This supports the idea of using only a very light stemming algorithm. In the first attempt, plural endings for nouns (such as -*s* and -*ies*) were stripped. Testing revealed that as much as 99% of the endings stripped were trailing s'es. To further increase the speed of the stemming algorithm, it was therefore reduced to simply stripping the *s* if it is at the end of a word and the second last character is not an s. In general, stemming does not seem to influence the clustering significantly. Several tests indicate only minor changes in the top 10 cluster labels and about 10% reduction in the total number of clusters.

For descriptive phrases, we are generally most interested in nouns and adjectives. To achieve this, one might use a part-of-speech tagger and then select only specific parts of speech to serve as label candidates. Unfortunately, part-of-speech tagging is generally very expensive. It is therefore interesting to observe that despite not using any part-of-speech detection, the resulting cluster labels are almost always nouns, sometimes adjectives, but rarely verbs or any other parts of speech. It seems that analyzing parts of speech is a waste of time when using the STC algorithm.

Label Overlap

Because all suffixes of each phrase is generated, it is common that clusters contain several very similar phrases (e.g., *jaguar car reviews*, *car reviews* and *reviews* for the query "jaguar"). Often the phrases start with the query itself, but it seems that the final labels seldom contain the query. This is because the query terms get zero score since they appear in more than 40% of the collection. This is a good thing, since we are usually not interested in having all clusters prefixed by the query.

However, in some cases we do want the query to appear in the label, like for instance when *Apple Macintosh* appears while searching for *apple*. A solution could be to use *Named Entity Recognition* (Bikel et al., 1999) to detect trademarks and people, and so forth. One could then say that the word *apple* in a phrase does not receive a zero score if the entire phrase is a *named entity* (e.g., when the next word is *macintosh*). That way, the phrase *apple macintosh* would receive a greater total score than *macintosh* and thus be selected as the label.

Additional Sources for Cluster Generation

Since extracting good cluster labels is so difficult, it has been suggested to make use of external sources that more accurately reflect the user's own vocabulary. One approach is to extract the labels from large logs of search queries submitted by users. The assumption is that users describe their information needs using their perception of a domain rather than the contents of the documents describing the domain. If we cluster based on log terms rather than snippet words, we may hope that the cluster labels better match the way users would label the clusters themselves. Another approach is to use the Open Directory Project (ODP) hierarchy or other pre-defined domain descriptions to work out appropriate cluster labels. The ODP category labels are likely to be good labels for clusters, since they often represent concepts that are shared and understood by a larger community.

However, tests with STC do not indicate much improvement when query logs or ODP categories are included. This may not mean that these sources are not useful, but it seems difficult to incorporate external sources like that into the STC algorithm properly. Because STC generates rather few candidate labels for each cluster, it is unlikely that ODP data or query log terms can improve the labeling substantially.

TEXT MINING IN WEB SEARCH

Text mining applications today draw on a wide range of techniques and serve many purposes in information management and business intelligence. Rooted in data mining and linguistics, they now also make use of semantic approaches, conceptual modelling, and artificial intelligence.

Figure 9. FRC characterization of suffix tree clustering in Web search

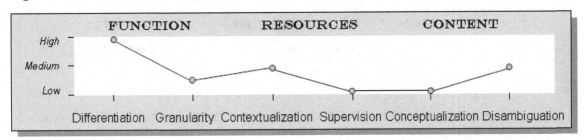

To better understand the similarities and differences between text mining techniques, it is useful to analyze them with respect to a common framework. The *function-resources-content (FRC)* framework, shown in Figure 9, provides a characterization of text mining techniques in terms of six features. Each feature is given a value of low, medium, or high, signalling to what extent the feature is addressed by the technique. Our clustering component can be given the following FRC characterization:

- **Differentiation** refers to the way documents or concepts are described with respect to each other. Whereas simple summarization techniques try to describe document content isolated from other documents, text categorization makes use of dictionaries that are partly differentiating. Clustering techniques display a high degree of differentiation, as the goal is to describe hierarchically how groups of documents differ from other groups of documents.
- **Granularity** tells us what the object of the analysis is. The object is usually the document, as in our component, but some text mining techniques are describing, for example, entities like persons or companies rather than documents.
- **Contextualization** denotes to what extent the context is taken into account. The context may be anything from user preferences to location and ongoing user tasks. Our component is partly contextualized, in the sense

that the query is used to pull out the relevant document sentences for the clustering.
- **Supervision** spans from no supervision at all to full supervision with extensive training sets. Text categorization is supervised in the form of precompiled dictionaries, while clustering is unsupervised.
- **Conceptualization** has to do with the degree of semantic content associated with the building blocks used in the analysis. Ontology-driven text mining utilizes highly conceptualized structures or ontology classes. Our clustering component's building blocks are document terms that do not carry any understood meaning.
- **Disambiguation** reflects the linguistic sophistication of the technique. A purely syntactic approach does not look into the internal structure or meaning of document words. A morphosyntactic approach uses stemming or lemmatization to merge conjugations of the same word, but without understanding what the words mean. A semantic approach may use WordNet or semantic grammars like Minimal Recursion Semantics to understand semantic relationships between words and disambiguate words or phrases.

Suffix tree clustering is attractive in current Web search engines as it supports contextualization and requires no supervision or deep semantic/conceptual processing. As seen from Figure 10, *text categorization* is similar to clustering in many ways but needs supervision and cannot contextual-

Figure 10. FRC characterization of text mining techniques

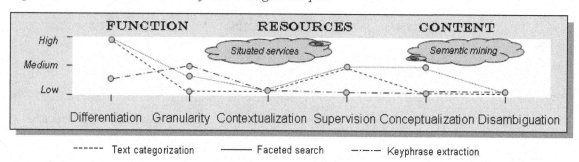

ize the categories (Gulla, Auran, & Risvik, 2002). An interesting alternative to clustering is *faceted search* (Hearst, 2006). Using multi-dimensional categories to describe (groups of) documents, faceted search systems can provide descriptions that are richer than the categories in text categorization. Since the categories in faceted search are defined manually, they tend to reflect concepts rather than words and be easier to understand to users. However, it is expensive to develop these categories beforehand, and so far it has been difficult to contextualize the descriptions or relate the document texts to the pre-defined concepts in a reliable manner. Unsupervised keyphrase extraction (Gulla, Borch, & Ingvaldsen, 2006), which is also shown in Figure 10, provides summary information for each document but is not very suitable for differentiating between (groups of) documents.

The curves in Figure 10 also tell us that most text mining techniques in search engines today are semantically poor and rarely contextualized. Linguistic analysis of text or well-defined conceptual descriptions are not used much, as they do not scale as well as purely statistical techniques. The research on the Semantic Web may, however, provide new and more efficient technologies, and we already see work on *semantic mining* that may be relevant in future search engines (Stumme, Hotho, & Berendt, 2006). Ontology-driven search solutions are now under development, even though it will still take some time before their performance is sufficiently close to traditional search

engines. The concept of *situated search services* is placing more emphasis on the contextualization of search results. This includes personalization with respect to profiles and preferences but also localization and task-orientation of the information available.

CONCLUSION

Clustering in a data mining setting has been researched for decades, but we are now witnessing an increased interest in employing the technique in a Web search context as well. This work has shown how an exploratory search engine with clustering capabilities can be developed. The approach described has been implemented as a working application that allows searching and browsing clusters of documents through a Web interface. The use of small snippets that are made up of the text surrounding the query terms in the documents both speeds up the algorithm and makes the clusters more adapted to the query context established by the user.

The evaluation indicates that the resulting clusters are coherent and that clustering several hundred documents on-the-fly is feasible. On the other hand, the quality of the cluster labels was found to be quite moderate by the test subjects. More fine-tuning and larger test groups are needed to verify whether this is an inherent weakness of the approach or not.

As part of an exploratory search environment, the clusters may prove useful in narrowing down the search for the desired information. Selecting the labels that most appropriately describe the users' needs, the system can present shorter, possibly clustered, lists of documents that are slightly more relevant than the original result set. The users can select subclusters, thereby continuing the navigation through the result set without knowing the full terminology or structure of the domain beforehand.

Although commercial clustering engines exist, clustering is yet to be deployed in major search engines like Google or FAST ESP. This is presumably because of the computational overhead and because it is so difficult to consistently produce high-quality labels for clusters in the noise world of the Web. The technique does, however, add value to Web search engines in ways that are appreciated by users and not addressed by other text mining techniques. The quality of cluster labels, which is so important to the usefulness of the approach, may also benefit from ongoing and future research on faceted search and ontology-driven search.

FUTURE RESEARCH DIRECTIONS

A crucial part of suffix tree clustering is the construction of snippets that are both representative to the content of the document and tailored to the needs of the user. In our prototype we search for the first occurrence of the first query term in the document and use the next 150 characters as the snippet for the document. This is a fast and simple approach to snippet construction and the snippets will to some extent be tailored to the first search term in the user's query. However, if there are several terms in the query, this tailoring is not necessarily a very good one. There may also be other parts of the document that are more representative to the content of the document as a whole. At the same time, we know that quality of the snippets is so important to the quality of the clusters and the cluster labels chosen by the system.

Future research need to address more sophisticated ways of constructing representative snippets. Ideally these snippets should be summaries of documents, as perceived by the user in his particular retrieval context. This calls for more comprehensive user models or user profiles that reflect the retrieval sessions and users' information needs. Generating proper summaries on-the-fly from whole documents is probably not feasible within the time constraints in Web search, but it may be possible to do some of these tasks during indexing. Maybe the indexing process can be modified to accommodate some of the information needed later for efficient clustering.

As far as user profiles are concerned, we need to relate the user queries to more high-level goals or information needs. In general we cannot require the users to indicate beforehand what they are interested in or why they are posting particular queries. The query log, with the whole list of queries posted by the users, may, however, allow us to reason about their real intentions. Their roles, background knowledge, or linguistic characteristics may help us clarify further how clusters and cluster labels should be tailored to the situation at hand.

Finally, there is now research on how ontologies can be combined with document clustering. A major weakness with current clustering techniques is their reliance on term vectors that are, by definition, incomprehensible and do not lend themselves to any reasoning or inspection. There is no transparency that helps the users understand why the clusters are the way they are. And the cluster labels, although real parts of the document text, may not be meaningful to the users, as the labels are only the result of standard statistical tests. An interesting idea would be to use ontological concepts and relationships to cluster documents and create appropriate cluster labels. We would be sure that the labels make sense to the users and the clustering itself can be inspected and verified by the users as well.

REFERENCES

Aas, K., & Eikvil, L. (1999). *Text categorization: A survey* (Technical Report). Norwegian Computing Center.

Araújo, M., Navarro, G., & Ziviani, N. (1997). Large text searching allowing errors. In *Proceedings of the Fourth South American Workshop on String Processing (WSP'97)* (pp. 2-20). Carleton University Press.

Baeza-Yates, R. A., & Ribeiro-Neto, B. A. (1999). *Modern information retrieval*. ACM Press/Addison-Wesley.

Bikel, D. M., Schwartz, R., & Weischedel. (1999). An algorithm that learns what's in a name [Special issue on natural language learning]. *Machine Learning, 34* (1-3), 211-231.

Brin, S., & Page, L. (1998). The anatomy of a large-scale hypertextual Web search engine. In *Proceedings of the Seventh International Conference on World Wide Web* (pp. 107-117).

Cormen, T. H., Stein, C., Rivest, R. L., & Leiserson, C. E. (2001). *Introduction to algorithms*. McGraw-Hill Higher Education.

Crabtree, D., Andreae, P., & Gao, X. (2006, December). Query directed Web page clustering. In *Proceedings of the 2006 IEEE/WIC/ACM International Conference on Web Intelligence* (pp. 202-210). Hong Kong, China. IEEE Computer Society.

Cutting, C. R., Pedersen, J. O., Karger, D., & Tukey, J. W. (1992). Scatter/Gather: A cluster-based approach to browsing large document collections. In *Proceedings of the Fifteenth Annual International ACM SIGIR Conference on Research and Development in Information Retrieval* (pp. 318-329).

Ding, L., Finin, T. Joshi, A., Peng, Y., Pan, R., & Reddivari, P. (2005, October). Search on the semantic Web. *Communications of the ACM,* 62-69.

Ferragina, P., & Gulli, A. (2005). A personalized search engine based on Web-snippet hierarchical clustering. In *WWW '05: Special Interest Tracks and Posters of the 14th International Conference on World Wide Web* (pp. 801-810). New York: ACM Press.

Fung, B. C. M., Wang, K., & Ester, M. (2003). Hierarchical document clustering using frequent item-sets. In *Proceedings of the SIAM International Conference on Data Mining (SDM'03)*.

Giannotti, F., Nanni, M., & Pedreschi, D. (2003). Webcat: Automatic categorization of Web search results. In *Proceedings of the Eleventh Italian Symposium on Advanced Database Systems (SEBD'03)* (pp. 507-518).

Gulla, J. A., Auran, P. G., & Risvik, K. M. (2002). Linguistics in large-scale Web search. In *Proceedings of the 7th International Conference on Applications of Natural Language to Information Systems (NLDB'2002)* (pp. 218-222).

Gulla, J. A., Borch, H. O., & Ingvaldsen, J. E. (2006). Unsupervised keyphrase extraction for search ontologies. In *Proceedings of 11th International Conference on Applications of Natural Language to Information Systems (NLDB'2006)*.

Han, J., & Kamber, M. (2001). *Data mining: Concepts and techniques*. Academic Press.

Heaps, H. S. (1978). *Information retrieval: Computational and theoretical aspects*. Academic Press.

Hearst, M. A. (2006, April). Clustering vs. faceted categories for information exploration. *Communications of the ACM,* 59-62.

Hearst, M. A., & Pedersen, J. O. (1996). Reexamining the cluster hypothesis: Scatter/gather on retrieval results. In *Proceedings of the 19th Annual International ACM SIGIR Conference on Research and Development in Information Retrieval (SIGIR'96)* (pp. 76-84).

Hull, D. A. (1996). Stemming algorithms: A case study for detailed evaluation. *JASIS, 47*(1), 70-84.

Jain, A. K., Murty, M. N., & Flynn, P. J. (1999). Data clustering: A review. *ACM Computing Surveys (CSUR), 31*(3), 264-323.

Koller, D., & Sahami, M. (1997). Hierarchically classifying documents using very few words. In *Proceedings of ICML-97, 14th International Conference on Machine Learning* (pp. 170-178). San Fransisco: Morgan Kaufmann Publishers.

Kraaij, W., & Pohlmann, R. (1996). Viewing stemming as recall enhancement. In *Proceedings of the 19th Annual International ACM SIGIR Conference on Research and Development in Information Retrieval (SIGIR'96)* (pp. 40-48).

Kules, W. M. (2006). *Supporting exploratory Web search with meaningful and stable categorized overviews*. Doctoral thesis, University of Maryland, College Park.

Lloyd, S. (1982). Least squares quantization in PCM. *IEEE Transactions on Information Theory, 28*(2), 129-137.

Marchionini, G. (2006, April). Exploratory search: From finding to understanding. *Communications of the ACM, 41-46.*

Osinski, S., & Weiss, D. (2004). Conceptual clustering using lingo algorithm: Evaluation on open directory project data. In *Advances in Soft Computing, Intelligent Information Processing and Web Mining, Proceedings of the International IIS (IIPWM'04)*.

Porter, M. F. (1997). An algorithm for suffix stripping. In *Readings in Information Retrieval* (pp. 313-316).

Porter, M. F. (2006). Porter stemmer in Java. Retrieved April 1, 2007, from http://www.tartarus.org/~martin/PorterStemmer

Rose, D. E., & Levinson, D. (2004). Understanding user goals in Web search. In *Proceedings of the 13th International Conference on World Wide Web* (pp. 13-19). ACM Press.

Salton, G., & Buckley, C. (1988). Term-weighting approaches in automatic text retrieval. *Information Processing Management, 24*(5), 513-523.

Silverstein, C., Marais, H., Henzinger, M., & Moricz, M. (1999). Analysis of a very large Web search engine query log. *SIGIR Forum, 33*(1), 6-12.

Spink, A., Wolfram, D., Jansen, M., & Saracevic, T. (2001). Searching the Web: The public and their queries. *Journal of the American Society for Information Science and Technology, 52*(3), 226-234.

Steinbach, M., Karypis, G., & Kumar, V. (2000). A comparison of document clustering techniques. In *KDD Workshop on Text Mining*.

Stumme, G., Hotho. A., & Berendt, B (2006, June). Semantic Web mining: State of the art and future directions. *Journal of Web Semantics, 4*(2), 124-143.

Ukkonen, E. (1992). Constructing suffix trees on-line in linear time. In *Proceedings of the IFIP 12th World Computer Congress on Algorithms, Software, Architecture - Information Processing '92* (Vol. 1, pp. 484-492). North-Holland.

Weiner, P. (1973). Linear pattern matching algorithms. In *Proceedings of the 14th IEEE Symposium on Switching and Automata Theory* (pp. 1-11).

Weiss, D., & Stefanowski, J. (2004). Web search results clustering in polish: Experimental evaluation of Carrot. *Advances in Soft Computing, Intelligent Information Processing and Web Mining, Proceedings of the International IIS (IIPWM'03)*.

White, R. W., Kules, B., Drucker, S. M., & Schraefel, M. C. (2006). Supporting exploratory search. *ACM Communications of the ACM, 49*(4), 36-39.

Zamir, O., & Etzioni, O. (1998). Web document clustering: A feasibility demonstration. In *Proceedings of the 21st Annual International ACM SIGIR Conference on Research and Development in Information Retrieval (SIGIR'98)* (pp. 46-54).

Zamir, O., & Etzioni, O. (1999). Grouper: A dynamic clustering interface to Web search results. *Computer Networks, 31*(11-16), 1361-1374.

Zamir, O., Etzioni, O., Madani, O., & Karp, R. (1997). Fast and intuitive clustering of Web documents. In *Proceedings of the 3rd International Conference on Knowledge Discovery and Data Mining* (pp. 287-290).

Zhang, D., & Dong, Y. (2001). Semantic, hierarchical, online clustering of Web search results. *Advanced Web Technologies and Applications.* Lecture Notes in Computer Science, 69-78.

Additional Reading

Bade, K., & Nürnberger, A. (2006, December). Personalized hierarchical clustering. In *Proceedings of the 2006 IEEE/WIC/ACM International Conference on Web Intelligence (WI 2006)*. Hong Kong, China. IEEE Computer Society.

Berry, M. W. (Ed.). (2004). *Survey of text mining: Clustering, classification, and retrieval.* Springer.

Berkhin, P. (2002). *Survey of clustering data mining techniques.* San Jose, CA: Accrue Software.

Bhatia, S.K., & Deogun, J.S. (1998). Conceptual clustering in information retrieval. *IEEE Transactions on Systems, Man and Cybernetics, Part B*, 427-436.

Cadez, I., Heckerman, D., Meek, C., Smyth, P., & White, S. (2003). Model-Based clustering and visualization of navigation patterns on a Web site. *Data Mining and Knowledge Discovery, 7*(4), 399-424.

Chakrabarti, S. (2003). *Mining the Web: Discovering knowledge from hypertext data.* Morgan Kaufmann.

Chen, Y., Qui, L., Chen, W., Nguyen, L., & Katz, R. H. (2002). Clustering Web content for efficient replication. In *Proceedings of the 10th IEEE International Conference on Network Protocols* (pp. 165-174).

Crabtree, D., Andreae, P., & Gao, X. (2006, December). Query directed Web page clustering. In *Proceedings of the 2006 IEEE/WIC/ACM International Conference on Web Intelligence (WI 2006)*. Hong Kong, China. IEEE Computer Society.

Dhillon, I., Kogan, J., & Nicholas, C. (2004). Feature selection and document clustering. In M. W. Berry (Ed.), *Survey of text mining: Clustering, classification, and retrieval* (pp. 73-100). Springer.

Fraley, C., & Raftery, A.E. (1998). How many clusters? Which clustering methods? Answers via model-based cluster analysis. *Computer Journal, 41*, 578-588.

Frigui, H., & Nasraoui, O. (2004). Simultaneous clustering and dynamic keyword weighting for text documents. In M. W. Berry (Ed.), *Survey of text mining: Clustering, classification, and retrieval* (pp. 45-72). Springer.

Geraci, F., Pellegrini, M., Maggini, M., & Sebastiani, F. (2006). Cluster generation and cluster labelling for Web snippets: A fast and accurate hierarchical solution. In *Proceedings of the 13th International Conference on String Processing and Information Retrieval (SPIRE)* (pp. 25-36).

Hearst, M. A. (1999). The use of categories and clusters for organizing retrieval results. In T. Strzalkowski (Ed.), *Natural language information retrieval* (pp. 333-370). Kluwer Academic Publishers.

Hearst, M., Pedersen, J. O., Pirolli, P., Schuetze, H., Grefenstette, G., & Hull, D. (1996). Four TREC-4 tracks: The Xerox site report. In *Proceedings of the Fourth Text REtrieval Conference (TREC-4)*.

Hotho, A., Maedche, A, & Staab, S. (2001). Ontology-Based text clustering. In *Proceedings of the IJCAI-2001 Workshop on Text Learning: Beyond Supervision*.

Khan, L., & Luo, F. (2002). Ontology construction for information selection. In *Proceedings of the 14th IEEE International Conference on Tools with Artificial Intelligence (ICTAI 2002)* (pp. 122-130). Washington. IEEE Computer Society.

Khan, L., & Luo, F. (2005). Hierarchical clustering for complex data. *International Journal on Artificial Intelligence Tools, 14*(5), 791-810.

Kleiboemer, A. J., Lazear, M. B., & Pedersen, J. O. (1996). Tailoring a retrieval system for naive users. In *Proceedings of the Fifth Annual Symposium on Document Analysis and Information Retrieval (SDAIR)*, Las Vegas, Nevada.

Levine, M., & Loizou, G. (1999). *Computing the entropy of user navigation in the Web*. Research Note RN/99/42, University College London, Department of Computer Science.

Lin, T. Y., Sutojo, A., & Hsu, J.-D. (2006). Concept analysis and Web clustering using combinatorial topology. In *Workshops Proceedings of the 6th IEEE International Conference on Data Mining (ICDM 2006), Foundation of Data Mining and Novel Techniques in High Dimensional Structural and Unstructured Data* (pp. 412-416).

Manning, C. D., & Schütze, H. (1999). *Foundations of statistical natural language processing*. The MIT Press.

Savaresi, S. M., & Boley, D. (2004). A comparative analysis on the bisecting K-means and the PDDP clustering algorithms. *Intelligent Data Analysis, 8*(4), 345-362.

Sen, R., & Hansen, M. H. (2003). Predicting a Web user's next access based on Log data. *Journal of Computational Graphics and Statistics, 12*(1), 143-155

Song, M. (1998). BiblioMapper: A cluster-based information visualization technique. In *Proceedings of the IEEE Symposium on Information Visualization* (pp. 130-136).

Strzalkowski, T., (Ed.). (1999). *Natural language information retrieval*. Kluwer Academic Publishers.

Su, Z., Ynag, Q., Zhang, H., Xu, X., & Hu, Y. (2001). Correlation-based document clustering using Web logs. In *34th Annual Hawaii International Conference on System Sciences (HICSS)*. IEEE Computer Society.

Willett, P. (1988). Recent trends in hierarchical document clustering: A critical review. *Information Processing & Management, 24*(5), 577-597.

Ypma, A., & Heskes, T. (2002). Automatic categorization of Web pages and user clustering with mixtures of hidden Markov models. In *Proceedings of the 4th International Workshop on Mining Web Data for Discovering Usage Patterns and Profiles (WEBKDD)* (pp. 35-49).

Chapter X
AntWeb—Web Search Based on Ant Behavior:
Approach and Implementation in Case of Interlegis

Li Weigang
University of Brasília, Brazil

Wu Man Qi
Federal Court of Accounts, Brazil

ABSTRACT

This chapter presents a study of ant colony optimization (ACO) to Interlegis Web portal, Brazilian legislation Web site. The approach of AntWeb is inspired by ant colonies foraging behavior to adaptively mark the most significant link by means of the shortest route to arrive at the target pages. The system considers the users in the Web portal as artificial ants and the links among the pages of the Web as the researching network. To identify the group of the visitors, Web mining is applied to extract knowledge based on preprocessing Web log files. The chapter describes the theory, model, main utilities, and implementation of AntWeb prototype in Interlegis Web portal. The case study shows off-line Web mining, simulations without and with the use of AntWeb, and testing by modification of the parameters. The result demonstrates the sensibility and accessibility of AntWeb and the benefits for the Interlegis Web users.

INTRODUCTION

The World Wide Web today is considered the biggest information and knowledge source in every field. These Web pages are accessed daily by a great quantity of people with different interests. However, they are heterogeneously constructed both in available information and quality and majorities are presented in HTML language. This manner limits and makes it difficult to extract useful information and knowledge using simple search by Internet.

The process of surfing the Web is similar to ant colonies foraging (Beckers, Deneubourg &

Gross, 1992; Heylighen, 1999). Ants' physical characteristics do not allow them to have a global vision of the environment, but their important and interesting foraging behavior help them to find shortest paths between food sources and their nest (Dorigo, Caro & Gambardella, 1999; Dorigo, Maniezzo & Colorni, 1996). With this insight, it is observed that the users visit the Web as a metaphor to ant colonies' foraging process. Sometimes, they may lose their way in the immense cyberspace without knowing where the information sources are.

Ants are efficient at foraging and finding the shortest route. Also, any one of them deposits a substance called pheromone on the ground, while walking from food sources to the nest and vice versa, forming a pheromone trail. Ants can smell the pheromone left in pheromone trails and when choosing their way they tend to choose paths marked by strong pheromone concentrations (Dorigo et al., 1996).

Different from ants, visitors to the Web do not have any way to communicate among them. Each one obtains their own route to find the objective page without having the association and assistance from other users that may have previously passed through the same path. Suppose that one implements an extended Web server within the Web site, this server can record the visited path on that Web site and put information on the visited links as ants put the pheromone. In such a way, the visitors can count on teamwork to guide them establishing an indirect communication. Thus, using ant searching mechanisms, laterally, a single user can find the objective page easier with this communication and increase the possibility of surfing faster by using the best path.

The application of collective intelligence on Web search has been studied by Heylighen (1999). His work is considered an initial research on the topic. A system inspired by the ants' foraging behavior to Web, AntWeb was proposed in the researches of Weigang, Dib, Teles, de Andrade, de Melo, and Cariolano (2002), Teles, Weigant,

and Ralha (2003), and Weigang and Wu (2005). In their study, AntWeb was developed as an adaptive Web system working as a metaphor of ants' foraging behavior in the following way: when a user visits a Web site, the system records some information of his route as the pheromone trail left by ants; other users with common objectives may be attracted by the pheromone trail using techniques from adaptive hypermedia technology and Web mining. AntWeb has been modified in two generations with the following three main utilities: the first one is to use it to evaluate the efficiency of the structure of Website (Weigang et al., 2002); the second one is to arrange a manner to assistant the new user to search his objective page with the help from the experience from the other users on the same Website (Teles et al., 2003); and the third one is to extend the Web site to have an adaptive capacity, which extracts information from the user's sequential path to change link strengths or to create new links between the entrance point to the target page or to create a significant mark in the entrance page (Teles et al., 2003; Weigang & Wu, 2005). Other manners to use artificial life behavior in Web search have also been reported in the research of Revel (2003). Chen, Park, and Yu (1996) explored data mining capability which involves mining path traversal patterns in a distributed information providing environment like WWW. To identify the group of visitors and target pages of their visit, Web mining is introduced. There are a lot of researches in Web mining. We adapted the methods from the references of Gamma, Helm, Vlissides, and Johnson (1994), Srivastava, Cooley, Deshpande, and Tan (2000), Srikant and Yang (2001), Yao, Hamilton, and Wang (2002), Han and Chang (2002), Mobasher (2004), and so forth.

The chapter presents the second generation model, an extension version of AntWeb, with the technology of the Web mining and the implementation in Interlegis Web portal, the Brazilian legislation Web site (Weigang & Wu, 2005). The case studies show some examples such as: (1)

Identifying the possible groups of visitors using offline data-mining modules by preprocessing the log file of accessing the Web server; (2) Demonstrating the visitors navigation processing using the extended model of AntWeb in a prototype of Interlegis Web portal; (3) Modification of the main parameters in AntWeb to verify of the efficiency of the system. The analysis result illustrates the sensibility of AntWeb and the benefits for the users in Interlegis Web portal. It also demonstrates that AntWeb improves the accessibility of the users in the portal to extract the necessary information and knowledge.

The following sections are organized in seven parts. The first section section presents the basic information about Interlegis web portal. In AntWeb's approach section, *Ant Colony Optimization* in Web is described such as algorithms and processes. The section of Implementation of AntWeb in Interlegis Portal shows the technique application of AntWeb. The simulation results from three situations are reported in the section of Case Study of AntWeb in Interlegis. And finally, the final sections show the conclusions, future research directions, and additional reading.

INTERLEGIS: INTEGRATION AND PARTICIPATION FOR BRAZILIAN LEGISLATIVE SOCIETY

Interlegis Program is the first large project using Web technology to implant a virtual legislative community in Brazil. Considering economic, social, and technological impacts, the main objective of this program is to establish the integration relationship with lower cost among the federal, state, and municipal legislative houses to achieve their missions.

This community is formed by two kinds of members: institutional and individual. The first one includes the Federal Senate and Chamber of Deputies, State Legislative Assemblies, City Councils, and Courts. The second includes the federal senators and deputies, state deputies, city councilmen, and others. Figure 1 shows the modified homepage of the Interlegis Program. It is different from real portal because of the implantation of AntWeb prototype.

Currently, a great quantity of information (legislation, education, community, administration, and so forth) is available in Interlegis

Figure 1. The AntWeb prototype in Interlegis Web portal

Web portal. Almost all of the Web pages in this portal are developed in HTML documents. The HTML mechanism organizes documents without semantic manner. It is difficult to get the useful information and knowledge from the portal by new users. In this environment, the users cannot get the correct orientation in the navigation and sometimes may lose their way in the site. In the attempt to find information, the user may get lost, confused, or overloaded with many inexact options because of the ill structure in HTML (Brusilovsky, 1996; Fensel, 2002; Joachims, Freitag & Mitchell 1997; Liu & Zhong, 2002; Palazzo, 2000). This is the main motivation in using the AntWeb approach to try to solve the problem for a real Web portal.

ANTWEB'S APPROACH

The name and basic approach of AntWeb were proposed by Weigang et al. (2002) and Teles et al. (2003) using the reference of the research by Heylighen (1999).

Basic Theory of AntWeb

Real ants are capable of finding the shortest path from a food source to their nest (Beckers et al., 1992) without using visual cues. They are also capable of adapting to environment changes, for example, finding a new shortest path once the old one is no longer feasible due to a new obstacle. While walking from the food sources to the nest and vice versa, ants deposit on the ground pheromone, forming a pheromone trail. Ants choose their way by the strong pheromone concentrations left on pheromone trails (Dorigo et al., 1999).

The approach used in AntWeb is a metaphor to the presented biological model. The developed system records information about every visit, such as the sequence of pages of the Web users, and the visitors putting the information as ants depositing pheromone in their trails. The amount of deposited

pheromone available is used for formatting the visual presentation of links in the Web pages. As more users visit the pages, more pheromone is deposited along the links. The strongest links, in terms of pheromone concentration, may help other users to visit common objective pages. Also the pheromone evaporation on links is considered in our approach. This section describes the combination of ant theory to Web technology to develop AntWeb.

The model is adapted from *Ant Colony Optimization (ACO)* presented in (Dorigo et al., 1996). In Ant System, the amount of pheromone $\tau_{ij}(t)$ associated to a link (i,j) is intended to represent the learned desirability of the choosing node j when in node i (Weigang et al., 2002; Teles et al., 2003). Ants deposit an amount of pheromone proportional to the quality of the solutions, the more number of links visited in the tour by the artificial ants, the greater the amount of pheromone is deposited on the links. If the initial amount of pheromone is noted as $\tau_{ij}(0)$, at iteration $t = 0$, it is set to a small positive constant value or zero for all links. In our case, the initial probability with which an artificial ant(k) chooses to go from page i to page $j \in N_i$, where N_i is the set of neighbors of pages i.

In the routing table, a probability value p_{ij}^d is used to express the goodness of choosing j as next page when the target page is d, where the constraint is proposed as:

$$\sum p_{ij}^d = 1, j \in N_i, N_i = \{neighbors(i)\} \qquad (1)$$

The modification of the routing table $A_i = [a_{ij}^d(t)]_{|Ni|}$ of the page i is obtained by the composition of the local pheromone trail values with the local heuristic values as follows:

$$a_{ij}^d(t) = [\tau_j^d(t)]^\alpha [\eta_j(t)]^\beta / \sum\{[\tau_l^d(t)]^\alpha [\eta_l(t)]^\beta\}, j \in N_i, l \in N_i \qquad (2)$$

where $\tau_j^d(t)$ is the amount of pheromone trail on the page j at the iteration t for destination d. α

and β are with both parameters that control the relative weights of pheromone trail and heuristic value. $\eta_j = 1/wt_j$ is the heuristic value of moving to page j:

$$wt_j = lt_j + vt_j \qquad (3)$$

where, wt_j is the estimated *staying* time for a visitor at the page j; it includes lt_j, the estimated time to get all of information of the page j to the browser at some velocity of the process; and vt_j is the estimated *reading (or downloading)* time to visit the page j.

The probability with which any ant chooses to go from the page i to page $j \in N_i$ considering destination d while building its route at the t-th algorithm iteration is:

$$p_{ij}^d = a_{ij}^d(t) / \sum a_{il}^d(t), l \in Ni \qquad (4)$$

After an ant has completed his tour, pheromone evaporation on all links is triggered, and then the ant(k) deposits a quantity of pheromone $\Delta\tau_i^{d,k}(t)$ on each link between related pages:

$$\Delta\tau_i^{d,k}(t) = \begin{cases} 1/[(nl_i^{d,k}(t) + 1)\sigma] & \text{if } i \in T^{d,k}(t) \\ 0 & \text{if } i \notin T^{d,k}(t) \end{cases} \qquad (5)$$

where $T^{d,k}(t)$ is the tour done by ant(k) at iteration t to get to object page d, and $nl_i^{d,k}(t)$ is the distance of i to d in the $T^{d,k}(t)$. σ is a parameter that represents how the distance of the page i until d in a $T^{d,k}(t)$ affects decreasing of $\Delta\tau_i^{d,k}(t)$.

$$\Delta\tau_i^d(t) = \sum \Delta\tau_i^{d,k}(t) \text{ for } k = 1, ..., m, i \in T^{d,k}(t) \qquad (6)$$

The addition of the new pheromone by ants and pheromone evaporation is implemented by the following rule applied to all links.

$$\tau_i^d(t) \leftarrow (1-\rho) \tau_i^d(t) + \rho\Delta\tau_i^d(t) \qquad (7)$$

where $\rho \in [0, 1]$ is the pheromone trail decay coefficient.

Goodness: The Mean Value of Access to Page

Related to adaptive hypermedia systems, the approach of AntWeb's implementation can be classified as a direct indication technique to the users (Liu & Zhong, 2002). Considering that all content pages of the site are included in the set of target pages represented by d, the mean value of access to each page, *goodness*, was adopted to set g^d as showing bellow:

$$g^d = \text{mean value of access to page } d \qquad (8)$$

The higher the value of g^d, the stronger the smell of that page comparing to other pages. By doing that, AntWeb is able to take the users to the most popular pages of the site through the shortest path. The objective is to orient the users to the page with highest probability to be the one that he is looking for, without having asked himself any information.

Related Processes and Algorithms of AntWeb

Model to Search More Than One Target Page

AntWeb is designed for the user to visit two or more destinations. Thus, the same as the manner in the ant system, the target pages are also exhaling the same special smell simultaneously to attract visitors in the site. As the target pages are with the same smell, the pages of these destinations with the short distance to the users will get priority.

The probability of visiting these pages is calculated as:

$$p_{ij}^{D} = \sum[a_{ij}^{d}(t)\ g^{d}]\ /\ \sum[\ a_{il}^{d}(t)\ g^{d}],\ l \in N_{i}\ ,\ d \in D \tag{9}$$

where D is the set of user's target pages; g^{d} is a coefficient that indicates the interesting level of page d for users as defined in equation (8).

Identification of the Target Pages

To identify the target pages of the visitors, in AntWeb, the Web mining methods from Srikant and Yang (2001) and Yao et al. (2002) are used. For some Web sites there is a clear separation between content and index pages; product pages on these Websites are content pages; and category pages are index or navigation pages. In such cases, the target pages for a visitor are considered to be exactly the set of content pages requested. Other Web sites, such as information portals, or corporate Web sites may not have a clear separation between content and index pages. In this case, a time threshold is used to distinguish whether or not a page is a target page. Thus, pages where the visitors spent more time than the threshold are considered as target pages.

The Algorithm for Updating Pheromone

To update the pheromone, a table of log is used to analyze the visitor's behavior and get the related information. In this table, the visitor's information is stored as the address of the accessed page, the ID of the user, and the time that the page was accessed. The detail algorithm for this procedure is as following (Teles et al., 2003).

1. Partition Web log by visitor:
   - Sort the log by visitor ID, as the primary key, and time, as the secondary key;
   - Partition the log by hashing on visitor ID and sort each partition separately;
   - Scan web log and extract sequence of pages for each visitor ID, passing them to 2;

2. Sort each partition for the hour where each page was accessed;
3. For each visitor, partition the log in a way that each partition finishes with a target page;
4. For each partition created by step 3, update the pheromone of the pages using equations 5, 6, and 7.

The Adaptive Process to Present the Pages

The adaptive AntWeb system considers that ants are influenced to follow paths that have significant amount of pheromone through the techniques of adaptive navigation support. These techniques consist of adapting the page at link level (Teles et al., 2003). The following is an algorithm using for this purpose: for each page i to be adapted:

- To calculate the probability of each neighboring page of i to be good to help the user considering the set of target pages.
- To use the technique of adaptive navigation support to guide the user to the page(s) with the highest probability value.

IMPLEMENTATION OF AntWeb IN INTERLEGIS PORTAL

AntWeb model is extended and implemented in a Web site prototype (Weigang & Wu, 2005) within Interlegis Web Portal (see Figure 1). The basic approach is based on the work of Teles et al. (2003), but the Web mining approach was introduced in the model to identify the group of visitors. In the extended AntWeb model, the platform of development is all based on free software. Web applications use the Zope as the server. The relation database is implemented using PostgreSQL and the Python is the programming language. Figure 2 shows the architecture of adaptive AntWeb with main modules.

Architecture of AntWeb

AntWeb consists of four modules (see Figure 2): the pheromone updating module, the adaptation page module, online Web mining module and off-line Web mining module. The pheromone updating module is being executed in second plan in the server and is responsible for keeping the taxes of pheromone of the pages brought up to date. The adaptation page module is executed each time and the user makes a request to AntWeb. It is responsible for presenting the page with links marked by artificial ants. The working sequence is as following:

Defining the Category Subset of Visitors

Using the technique of clustering, the off-line data-mining module was developed to identify the possible categories of existing users in the Web site. The process consists of the preprocessing the log file of access of the Web server and in the posterior extraction of categories, where each category resultant was formed to a represent section by a subset of visited pages or requested for the pertaining users to this category. Thus, these pages are considered of interest for these users, and are also considered as a subset of the interesting items for Web site.

Classifying a Visitor to a Category

When the active user looking a page to the Web server, this information is kept in the session of the user. The system in turn executes the online module dynamically to classify this user to a category already identified by last step; in case that this user is part of some category, the system will use the registered information in data base, or either, the amounts of pheromone contained in links among pages for the category in question.

Upgrade the Pheromone for the Identified Visitor

The amount of pheromone associated with one link (i, j) represents how much it is desirable for the users of this category to choose page j, when in i, at certain moment. The system will make the adaptation the pages in the form that is detached links contends a reasonable amount of pheromone and that interesting pages which are still not visited by these users.

The System Returns the Page Adapted for the User and the Cycle is Initiated Again

Once the user already has been classified to its category. The classification algorithm is not more

Figure 2. Architecture of AntWeb

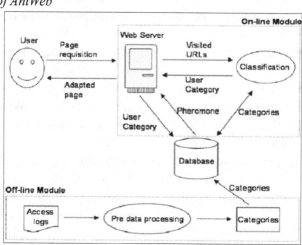

executed and any access made for the user is recorded in log of access stored in the data base. This information will serve for the process of update of the pheromone.

Database of AntWeb

Four tables have been developed to form the database of AntWeb. Log table keeps tracking of the access data in AntWeb. At each time that a user makes a request to AntWeb, it is included a register in this table. Pages table serves to keep information of the site pages where AntWeb is being used. These Information are the time of visit, the type of page (content or index), and if necessary the corresponding g^d value. Pheromone table is developed for keeping the amounts of pheromone of each page. If a page does not have its URL, it means that the amount of pheromone in this page with zero. Updates table is used to store data corresponding to the updates of pheromone in the Pheromone table. The table also consists of the date and hour of the updating, the values of the used parameters, such as the coefficient of evaporation and time of iteration.

The Pheromone Updating Module

The pheromone updating module is developed for keeping the rate of the pheromone of the pages brought for update. The system follows an object-oriented approach and consists of the following classes:

- **Configuration:** This class is responsible for controlling related parameters in the update of pheromone, such as the co-efficient of evaporation and the time of iteration.
- **MySqlConection:** This class is responsible for managing the connection between the application and the Data base server.
- **PheromoneIncreaser:** This class is responsible for the adding the information of pheromone to the links. Using this class, it

is possible to add the information the pheromone without any change to the system.
- **PheromoneUpdater:** This class is responsible for the update of the pheromone. The update process corresponds the verification if some users have arrived to their destinations. When a user arrived, he put the information of pheromone in the link to the pages.
- **PheromoneUpdaterTrigger:** This class is responsible for starting all the update process, which keeps in a loop style, pausing before restarting each system cycle.
- **QueryManager:** This class is responsible for managing the transactions made in the database.
- **UpdateRecorder:** This class is responsible for recording, in the Updates table, the corresponding data of each update.

The Adaptation Page Module

The adaptation page module is developed for presenting the page with links marked by users, that is, artificial ants. This module is also developed by object-oriented approach. The main classes are defined as following:

- **InternalLinksProcessor:** This class is used for transforming the relative paths of links into absolute ones.
- **LinksGuider:** The class is developed for altering all the links of the page making them a point to AntWeb and adding the information of parameter to the corresponding URL.
- **LinksHighlighter:** The class is used for marking selected links.
- **LinksSelector:** the class is responsible for selecting links that will be marked based on the tax of pheromone of each one of them and for getting the values of parameters of configuration.

- **Log:** The class is used for making the register of log in the corresponding table logs.
- **PageLoader:** The class is used to get the HTML code of the page to be adapted.
- **PheromoneSetter:** The class is used for getting the tax of pheromone of all links of the pages.
- **Sender:** The Class is used for sending the HTML code of the adapted page to the user's browser.
- **TagExtractor:** The Class is responsible for extracting the HTML code tag.
- **URL:** This is used for dealing with the URL of the page to be adapted.

Off-Line Web Mining Module and Online Web Mining Module

In offline Web mining module, the leader algorithm (Hartigan, 1975) was chosen to use in the AntWeb, as well as in the PagePrompter (Yao et al., 2002), due to its efficiency in the processing of great amount of entrances in the log file.

In online Web mining module, the method of Srikant and Yang (2001) was used as described in a previous section.

CASE STUDY OF AntWeb IN INTERLEGIS

The case study concerns three situations: off-line Web mining to identify the group of visitors, visiting simulation in Interlegis Web portal using AntWeb, and AntWeb simulation with the modification of the parameters (Weigang & Wu, 2005).

Off-Line Web Mining

To identify the group of visitors, a log file was collected from the Interlegis web with 1,724,881 visits during one week, from June 1, 2004 to June 7, 2004. Using preprocessing algorithm, 26,537

sessions were defined, considering every section with 30 minutes. In this case, approximately 40% (10,826 sessions were accessed 2 pages or more), about 26% (6,932 sessions) with 3 pages or more, and less than 4% (970 sessions) with 10 pages or more. Based on this analysis, NumMinPag (Number of Minimum Pages) was defined as 2 and the average of the accessed pages of the sessions was defined as 3 and for DistanciaMax (Maximum Distance) was also 3.

We observed the following results which were classified as three groups: Group 1 is with large number of visitors from 1307 sessions, which consists of the pages related to the legislative information and inspection; Group 2 is with 751 sessions which consists of the pages related to the elaboration of the public budget and the available courses on the public budget; Group 3 is with 385 sessions, related to the information about Interlegis and the available products and services, and so forth.

Visiting Simulation Using AntWeb

Visiting simulation using AntWeb in Interlegis Web Portal is to show where AntWeb system is helpful for guiding the visitors through the web site. Basically, the process of simulation is defined as:

- To correctly identify a visitor to a group according to its patterns during navigation if its behavior is similar to other visitors of this group.
- To suggest the visitor the pages of common interest of the visitors of this group by means of the cooperation among these users and based on his behavior in the first 2-3 visited pages. This is important for a web site to have this capacity to advise the visitor of a more related direction of the visit.
- To upgrade the pheromones on the links, which lead to the interesting pages that are still not visited by the visitors.

- To keep the preference on the shorter links that lead the visitor to the interesting pages of the group. This property was already established as a part of the basic model of AntWeb.
- Finally, the system returns the page adapted for the user and the cycle is initiated again.

Figure 3 shows the partial structure of the Web site of the prototype of Interlegis and the localization of the interesting pages of two groups of the visitors on the site. In the figure, the numbers are the codes of the pages. Table 1 is a relation of URLs corresponding some pages and nodes of Figure 3.

During the simulation, the system identified that two visitors are in the web site based on their trials. First visitor 10.1.10.119 Mozilla/4.0 (compatible; MSIE 6.0; Windows NT 5.1; SV1; NET CLR 1.1.4322) is similar the behavior of Group 1 and Second visitor 200.252.9.210 Mozilla/4.0 (compatible; MSIE 6.0; Windows NT 5.0) is similar the behavior of Group 2.

Figure 4 shows the possible next link for visitor 1. In this case, page 120, Law of Fiscal Responsibility (see table 1 and figure 4), with *goodness* 0.65, and page 126, Constitution of Brazil, with *goodness* 0.35. This preference reflects the in-

teresting of visitors of Group 1 and adapted by proper AntWeb system.

With this experiment, AntWeb shows the capability to present suitable interface and preference next link for visitor without extra information from the visitor. The knowledge from the previous visitors gotten from off-line Web mining and from actual visitor's experience makes the system with this possibility.

Simulation with the Modification of the Parameters

The simulation results presented in this section are divided in two parts: first, not using AntWeb; and second, using AntWeb, with change of those parameters (α, β and ρ) that affect directly or indirectly the computation of probability of the direction of the visitors in the Web site. An index *throughput* was defined to measure the efficiency of the system. For evaluation of the developed model, *throughput* is defined as an index to measure the performance of the accessibility in the Web site. It means the number of visitors to reach their target page per time unit related to the total number of the visitors.

To test the efficiency of AntWeb, the *throughput* gotten by means of logs generated in the navigations carried through the site with AntWeb should

Figure 3. Partial structure of Interlegis portal

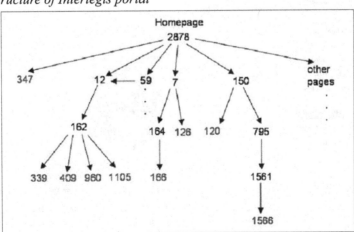

Table 1. Relation of URLs between some pages and nodes

Page code	Name of Web page	URL
2878	Homepage	./AntWeb
12	Education	./produtos_servicos/educação
162	Available courses	./produtos_servicos/educação/20020121101346
120	Law of Fiscal Responsibility	./fiscalizacao/20041227122456/view
59	Products and Services	./produtos_servicos
126	Constitution of Brazil	./processo_legislativo/20041227145212/view
339	Introduction of the public budget I	./produtos_servicos/educacao/20020121101346/20050107150039/view
1105	Introduction of the public budget II	./produtos_servicos/educacao/20020121101346/20050107152233/view
409	Introduction of the public budget III	./produtos_servicos/educacao/20020121101346/20050107151009/view
960	Introduction of the public budget IV	./produtos_servicos/educacao/20020121101346/20050107151318/view
164	Civil code	/processo_legislativo/20040204124657
166	New civil code	/processo_legislativo/20040204124657/20041227130626/view
795	Public Budget	./fiscalizacao/20040130112419
1561	Elaboration of the Public Budget	./fiscalizacao/20040130112419/20040415161133
1566	Public Budget in the Constitution	./fiscalizacao/20040130112419/20040415161133/20040415162834/view
...	...	...

Figure 4. The possible next link for visitor one

be larger than the *throughput* without AntWeb. In this sense, the prototype of AntWeb was placed available to the public users in the Internet from January 5, 2005 to January 20, 2005. Even though there were a few accesses, the invited visitors got a satisfactory experience with AntWeb.

The simulation condition is predefined as that the duration of each simulation is 160 seconds and a visitor is generated by each 5 seconds. Each simulation involves 32 iterations. When a visitor is generated, it is classified in one of the preexisting groups in accordance with random variable. When it reaches one of its destination pages, the simulation stops.

Simulation Without AntWeb

The simulation shows that in average 33% (*throughput*) of the total of 32 visitors arrived at their destination pages (see Table 2), under the outlined conditions. The higher valor of *throughput* means better accessibility for the users in the Web site. In the table, the category means that the group of visitors is with the same property or interesting of the visit destination.

Simulation With AntWeb

Six cases were simulated in the research according to the modification of the parameters α, β and ρ. As an example, Table 3 shows the simulation results of the case $\alpha = 1$, $\beta = 0$, $\rho = 0.1$.

The table shows that the average *throughput* from three simulations is 0.91. This means that almost 91% of visitors arrived at their destination pages.

As a summary from six cases in Table 4, generally, the index *throughput* from the simulation with AntWeb is lager than without AntWeb (0.33). It also shows the sensitivity of the system depending on the combination of the parameters. The best one (0.93) is from the case of $\alpha = 1$, $\beta = 1$, and $\rho = 0.1$. When $\alpha = 0$, this means no influence of pheromone of ant to the system, the simulation is

Table 2. Simulation of the system without AntWeb

Simulation ($\Delta t = 160$ seg.; Total N° of visitors = 32)	N° of visitors that arrive the interesting pages		Throughput
	Category 1	Category 2	
1ª	6	4	0.31
2ª	9	3	0.38
3ª	5	5	0.31
		Average Throughput	0.33

Table 3. Simulation of the system with AntWeb, Case of $\alpha = 1$, $\beta = 0$, $\rho = 0.1$

Simulation ($\Delta t = 160$ seg.; Total N° of visitors = 32)	N° of visitors that arrive the interesting pages		Throughput
	Category 2	Category 2	
1ª	13	15	0.88
2ª	16	14	0.94
3ª	15	14	0.91
		Average Throughput	0.91

Table 4. Throughput from simulation

	α	β	ρ	1ˢᵗ time	2ⁿᵈ time	3ʳᵈ time	Average
1	1	0	0.1	0.88	0.94	0.91	0.91
2	1	1	0.1	0.91	0.91	0.97	0.93
3	0	1	0.1	0.44	0.28	0.41	0.38
4	1	0	0.5	0.91	0.88	0.88	0.89
5	1	1	0.5	0.88	0.88	0.84	0.87

the same as without AntWeb: *throughput* is also lesser than 0.4.

CONCLUSION

AntWeb was developed as an adaptive Web model in this chapter. The potential application of AntWeb in Brazilian Legislative Web portal—Interlegis shows the social benefit of this research.

The chapter presents state of the art development of the adaptive AntWeb system. Compared to other existing approaches of adaptive Web, AntWeb completes its functions connecting to the target pages with optimized routes by means of finding the shortest distance. The initial experiment demonstrated that AntWeb for the legislative user to access Web portal is sensitive, which means that the accessibility of Interlegis portal may be improved. More importantly, the knowledge from Web log mining in both offline and online in AntWeb is suitable to help the identification of the visitor's group and further to upgrade pheromones between links. With the modification of the pheromones, the system has the potential to indicate the preference steps for the visitor in web site. The simulation of access Interlegis Web portal using the index *throughput* shows satisfactory results: significant profit with the use of AntWeb and consistent with the modification of the parameters.

FUTURE RESEARCH DIRECTIONS

Further research may improve the accessibility of AntWeb in the sense of the processing speed and to reduce extra processes in AntWeb model implementation. It is interesting to study the criteria to evaluate the efficiency of the artificial ant performance in the Web. The method of the estimation of the target Web paper for the visitors in the Web is still not well adapted online. It should be concentrated to introduce the new Web mining or ontology methods for the identification of the group and target pages. AntWeb can also be implemented in commercial applications in future studies referring to some developed Web mining tools such as oen market web reporter, Webtrends, net.Genesis, and so forth.

ACKNOWLEDGMENT

The authors would like to thank the colleagues from the University of Brasilia, especially Mr. Wesley M. Teles, Dr. Celia G. Ralha, and undergraduate students Tadeu, Paulo Henrique, and Rommell for their contribution in the development of the first generation of AntWeb. The authors also appreciate the cooperation with Dr. Hércules Antonio do Prado and Dr. Edilson Ferneda for the modification of this chapter.

REFERENCES

Beckers, R., Deneubourg, J. L., & Goss, S. (1992). Trails and u-turns in the selection of the shortest path by the ant Lasius niger. *Journal of Theoretical Biology, 159,* 397-415.

Brusilovsky, P. (1996). Methods and techniques of adaptive hyermedia. *User Modeling and User Adapted Interaction, 6*(2-3), 87-129.

Chen, M. S., Park, J. S., & Yu, P. S. (1996). Data mining for path traversal patterns in a Web environment. In *Proceedings of the 16th International Conference on Distributed Computing Systems* (pp. 385-392). Fort Lauderdale, Florida.

Dorigo, M., Caro, D. G., & Gambardella, L. M. (1999). Ant algorithms for discrete optimization. *Artificial Life, 5*(2), 137-172.

Dorigo, M., Caro, D. G., & Sampels, M. (Eds.). (2002, September 12-14). Ant algorithms. In *Proceedings of the ANTS 2002 Third International Workshop,* (LNCS 2463, pp. V-VII). Brussels, Belgium. Springer.

Dorigo, M., Maniezzo, V., & Colorni, A. (1996). The ant system: Optimization by a colony of cooperating agents. *IEEE Transactions on Systems, Man, and Cybernetics-Part B, 26*(1), 29-41.

Dorigo, M., & Stützle, T. (2004). *Ant colony optimization.* Cambridge: The MIT Press.

Fensel, D. (2002). Ontology-based knowledge management. *IEEE Web Intelligence, 35*(11), 56-59.

Gamma, E., Helm, R., Vlissides, J., & Johnson, R. (1994). *Design patterns.* Addison-Wesley Longman.

Han, J., & Chang, K. (2002). Data mining for Web intelligence. *IEEE Web Intelligence, 35*(11), 64-70.

Hartigan, J. (1975). *Clustering algorithms.* New York: John Wiley & Sons.

Heylighen, F. (1999). Collective intelligence and its implementation on the Web: Algorithms to develop a collective mental map. *Computational and Mathematical Theory of Organizations, 5*(3), 253-280.

Joachims, T., Freitag, D., & Mitchell, T. (1997). Webwatcher: A tour guide for the World Wide Web. In *Proceedings of the 15th International Joint Conference on Artificial Intelligence (IJCAI-97)* (Vol. 1, pp. 770-777). Nagoya, Japan.

Liu, J., Yao, Y., & Zhong, N., (2002). In search of the wisdom Web. *IEEE Web Intelligence, 35*(11), 27-31.

Mobasher, B. (2004). Web mining and personalization. In M. P. Singh (Ed.) *The practical handbook of internet computing.* CRC Press.

Netgen Analysis Desktop (1996). Retrieved April 2, 2007, from http://www.netgen.com

Open Market Inc. (1996). Open market Web reporter. Retrieved April 2, 2007, from http://www.openmarket.com

Palazzo, L. A. M.(2000). *Modelos proativos para hipermídia adaptativa.* Tese (Ciência da Computação) - Universidade Federal do Rio Grande do Sul, Brazil.

Revel, A. (2003). Web-agents inspired by ethology: A population of ant-like agents to help finding user-oriented information. In *Proceedings of IEEE Web Intelligence Consortium (WIC)* (pp. 482-485). Halifax, Canada.

Srikant, R., & Yang, Y. (2001). Mining Web logs to improve Website organization. In *Proceedings of the Tenth International World Wide Web Conference* (pp. 430-437). Hong Kong, China.

Srivastava, J., Cooley, R., Deshpande, M., & Tan, P.-N. (2000). Web mining: Discovery and applications of usage patterns from Web data. *SIGKDD Explorations 2000, 2*(1), 12-23.

Teles, W. M., Weigang, L., & Ralha, C. G. (2003). AntWeb—The adaptive Web server based on the ants' behavior. In *Proceedings of IEEE Web Intelligence Consortium (WIC)* (pp. 558-561). Halifax, Canada.

WebTrends Inc. (1995). Webtrends. Retrieved April 2, 2007, from http://www.webtrends.com

Weigang, L., Dib, M. V. P., Teles, de Andrade, W. M., V. M., de Melo, A. C. M. A., & Cariolano, J. T. (2002). Using ants' behavior based simulation model AntWeb to improve Website organization.

Proceedings of SPIE's Aerospace/Defense Sensing and Controls Symposium: Data Mining, 4730 (pp. 229-240).

Weigang, L., & Wu, M. Q. (2005). Web search based on ant behavior: Approach and implementation in case of Interlegis. *Proceedings of the 17th International Conference on Software Engineering & Knowledge Engineering (SEKE 2005), 1,* 572-577, Taipei, Taiwan.

Yao, Y. Y., Hamilton, H. J., & Wang, X. (2002). PagePrompter: An intelligent Web agent created using data mining techniques. *Proceedings of International Conference on Rough Sets and Current Trends in Computing, 2475,* 506-513. Malvern, Pennsylvania.

Additional Reading

The book *Ant Colony Optimization,* by Marco Dorigo and Thomas Stützle (2004) is interesting for a reader who wants to know more about ant colony optimization (ACO). This book describes the translation of observed ant behavior into working optimization algorithms, all major ACO algorithms, and a report on current theoretical findings. It surveys ACO applications including routing, assignment, scheduling, subset, machine learning, and bioinformatics problems. The reader can also find the progress in the field and outlining future research directions.

Chapter XI
Conceptual Clustering of Textual Documents and Some Insights for Knowledge Discovery

Leandro Krug Wives
Federal University of Rio Grande do Sul, Brazil

José Palazzo Moreira de Oliveira
Federal University of Rio Grande do Sul, Brazil

Stanley Loh
Catholic University of Pelotas, Brazil
Lutheran University of Brazil, Brazil

ABSTRACT

This chapter introduces a technique to cluster textual documents using concepts. Document clustering is a technique capable of organizing large amounts of documents in clusters of related information, which helps the localization of relevant information. Traditional document clustering techniques use words to represent the contents of the documents and the use of words may cause semantic mistakes. Concepts, instead, represent real world events and objects, and people employ them to express ideas, thoughts, opinions, and intentions. Thus, concepts are more appropriate to represent the contents of a document and its use helps the comprehension of large document collections, since it is possible to summarize each cluster and rapidly identify its contents (i.e., concepts). To perform this task, the chapter presents a methodology to cluster documents using concepts and presents some practical experiments in a case study to demonstrate that the proposed approach achieves better results than the use of words.

INTRODUCTION

Organizations are producing, collecting, and storing more and more documents, most of them containing texts. According to Tan (1999), about 80% of the documents an organization has are in textual format. This huge volume of unstructured or semi-structured data turns the act of finding relevant information harder to accomplish, generating a problem known as the information overload problem (Chen, 1996).

Techniques and tools from knowledge discovery in texts(KDT) (Feldman & Dagan, 1995) or simply text mining (Tan, 1999) are being developed to cope with this problem. One of these techniques is clustering (i.e., cluster analysis), a technique used to group similar documents of a given collection, helping the comprehension of its contents (Jain, Murty, & Flynn, 1999; Lu, Motoda, & Liu, 1997; Willet, 1988). One of its goals is to put similar documents in the same cluster and to place dissimilar documents in different clusters. The hypothesis is that, through a clustering process, similar objects will remain in the same group according to the attributes they have in common. This hypothesis is known as the cluster hypothesis, and it is appropriately described by Rijsbergen (1979).

It is important to analyze the difference between clustering and classification processes. The two activities have different purposes and are different in essence: the clustering process generates clusters without previous knowledge about document contents or about which classes exist, while classification (or categorization) is a process that starts with a predefined set of categories and tries to identify to which class a document belongs (Willet, 1988). Thus, clustering helps people identify classes and build taxonomies.

Some benefits of the clustering process are:

- **Capacity to cluster large amounts of documents:** Humans cannot analyze many aspects (characteristics) of documents;

- **Impartiality in the process:** Humans have background knowledge that tends to bias the personal clustering process;
- **Identification of common characteristics among documents (patterns such as words or concepts):** They can be used to understand or explain why the documents, within a cluster, are similar and to understand a whole collection of documents and its contents;
- **Organization of unstructured documents:** Clustering minimizes the information overload (incapacity to analyze excessive amounts of information) in information retrieval, automatically grouping similar information (splitting a set of documents), summarizing its common characteristics, thus helping the user to visualize the results of a query or search, and aiding the user to navigate in a set of documents.

The clustering of textual documents, specifically Web pages, is one of the current research challenges. This task is comparable to the clustering of structured records in a database. In both cases, elements are compared by means of a similarity function, which analyzes the elements' characteristics. However, when dealing with textual documents as elements, there is the need of an additional (previous) step to identify the characteristics of the documents, since these characteristics are not as clear as in structured data. Traditional textual clustering approaches use words or keywords, extracted automatically from the text, to represent the elements. However, words can lead to semantic mistakes, known as the vocabulary problem (Chen, 1994). It happens, for example, when people use subjective language facets, as synonymy (different words for the same meaning), polysemy (the same word with many meanings), lemmas (words with the same radical, like the verb "to marry" and the noun "marriage") and quasisynonymy (semantically related words).

In this chapter, we introduce a conceptual approach to cluster textual documents. The idea is to use concepts instead of words to represent the elements. Concepts, in this case, are entities that represent the content of a textual document in a higher level, minimizing the vocabulary problem.

To explain our approach, we start giving in the background section an overview of the cluster analysis technique and explaining how it can be used to cluster textual data. After, we elucidate the use of concepts to represent documents and show how they can be used to aid the clustering process. We also provide some experiments comparing the two approaches (words vs. concepts) to demonstrate the benefits of the concept-based one. At the end of the chapter, we discuss some insights to use the conceptual clustering approach for knowledge discovery in a textual collection, showing some practical experiments and some future trends in the field.

BACKGROUND

According to Mizzaro (1996), "knowledge" is the portion of the world that is perceived and represented by an agent (i.e., person), and can be more or less correct and complete. Thus, knowledge can be understood as the experience acquired by a person when he/she interacts with the world (identification of patterns). Moreover, it is a potential to execute certain types of actions (Kochen, 1974), such as the ones involved in the decision-making process, and to solve problems.

In this context, to discover knowledge (i.e., knowledge discovery) means to receive and identify relevant information and know how to compute and aggregate it to our previous knowledge, changing its state in a manner that it could be used to solve a problem. As we have so much information at our disposal and the manual analysis of this amount of data would take so much time, the process is usually computer supported to speed it up.

Thus, the (computer aided) knowledge discovery from data (KDD) process is "the nontrivial extraction of implicit, previously unknown, and potentially useful information from given data" (Feldman & Dagan, 1995, p. 112). Once it is extracted, it may become a potential to solve problems and to aid the decision taking process (i.e., knowledge, as stated before). Consequently, knowledge discovery from texts (KDT) is the process of discovering nontrivial and implicit information from textual documents. KDD and KDT have many useful applications and techniques. See Fayyard, Piatetsky-Shapiro, and Smyth (1996) for an overview. Clustering is one of them.

Clustering[1] or cluster analysis is an approach to explore and understand relationship among data. It is an unsupervised process that can be performed by a computer to identify the common characteristics of a given set of data and, based on its similarities, the relationship among data items itself. Consequently, similar objects are arranged in groups of relatively homogeneous elements—the clusters.

According to Jain et al. (1999), the clustering process can be divided in the following steps: (1) pattern representation, optionally including feature extraction and/or selection, (2) definition of a pattern proximity measure appropriate to the domain, (3) clustering or grouping of the elements, (4) data abstraction (if necessary), and (5) assessment of output (if necessary). These steps are detailed in the following sections. The idea is to present an overview of the process used to cluster any type of data (i.e., object), but we try to focus and give details on the specificities of textual data whenever as possible.

Pattern Representation

The pattern representation step is concerned with identifying or deciding which characteristics will represent each object (in our case, documents). The characteristics should be descriptive (to aid the process of understanding groups), minimal (to the process be as fast as possible), and should aggregate semantic to minimize the (vocabulary) differences.

The characteristics are identified in a process known as feature selection. Feature selection is the process of identifying the most effective subset of the original features (characteristics) to use in clustering or the transformation of the input features to produce new salient features. When we work with documents, usually their words are the features used to represent them.

The most simple textual feature selection technique is based on a list of *stop words* that must be eliminated or ignored because they appear in almost all existing documents or texts. Thus, they have a low discriminating factor and cannot be used to represent and distinguish one document from another (Korfhage, 1997; Salton & McGill, 1983). Prepositions, conjunctions, and other similar words or terms used to aid the syntactical construction of phrases are included in this list. Fox (1992) states that some words that are specific to the context of the collection being manipulated can also be considered *stop words*, and ignored.

Another way to select the most relevant words or features of the documents is to look for the "weight" of each word or term. This is done, basically, by analyzing the frequency of the words in the documents. The most frequent words of one document, which are not so frequent on other documents, are selected, since they are strongly related to this specific document and discriminate it from the others. It is important to state that this process can be used to find new stop words, since they are the most frequent words on many (i.e., most) of the documents.

There are many ways to identify or calculate the term weight. Most of them are based on the frequency of the word in a document or document collection. According to Salton and McGill (1983), a writer is used to repeat the same terms when is writing, since the inclusion of new terms causes an effort bigger than the necessary to explain one subject (law of the least effort). Thus, words do not occur eventually in a document and this fact can be used to evaluate the significance of a word or term in a text. Consequently, most techniques encountered in the literature are based on the frequency of a word in the documents.

The simplest technique is the *absolute term frequency*, which is the number of times a specific word appears in a document. It is not so usual because it is not normalized to the size of the document (the sum of the absolute frequency of all its words). Thus, if the term "medic" appears one time in a document containing 10 words and one time in a document containing 1000 words, they will have the same weight, but it is clear that in the first it has a stronger influence than in the last. So, the *relative term frequency* can be used to measure the weight of a word in a document considering the size of the document (relative term frequency is the absolute frequency of the term divided by the size of the document).

The absolute or relative term frequency does not take in account the number of documents a word appears. It can be an important factor to decide the selection of a feature or not. Therefore, the *inverse document frequency* was defined to analyze both the term frequency and the document frequency of a word to find the most relevant terms to represent a document.

There are many combinations and variations of the above frequencies, like the term-selection algorithm used by Wiener, Pedersen, and Weigend (1995), the correlation coefficient of Schutze (1995) or of Ng, Goh, and Low (1997), and so on. Some methods include also the structure of the document (see Cowie & Lehnert, 1996) or the statistical correlations among words, like LSI (see Deerwester, Dumais, & Harshman, 1990, for more details). Some of them are very useful and produce impressive results (like the former), but sometimes the time they need to perform is so high and one should take it in consideration.

Independently of the method chosen, we need to consider that the features being analyzed are usually the words contained in the documents, and words can have different meanings or are subject for the vocabulary problem listed before.

Rajaraman and Pan (2000) sustain that similarity functions based on richer document representations can improve performance in clustering processes. Alternatives include the use of pairs of terms or syntactic relations between terms (e.g., noun-verb-noun) (Jain et al., 1999). They also present experiments comparing 1-tuple (unique terms), 2-tuple (pairs) and 3-tuple of terms. In Reuters' collection, this approach results in better performances with methods that use 3-tuple. However, the synonymy problem is not solved.

Jain et al. (1999) discusses the alternative of incorporating domain constraints in the clustering process. The idea is to use explicitly available domain knowledge to constrain or guide the clustering process.

Chen (1994), for example, uses concepts to identify the content of comments in a brainstorm discussion. In information retrieval, concepts are used with success to index and retrieve documents. Lin and Chen (1999) comment that the concept-based retrieval capability has been considered by many researchers and practitioners to be an effective complement to the prevailing keyword search or user browsing.

Thus, we suggest the use of concepts instead of words alone. Concepts, as we will see, are structures used by people to express ideas, ideologies, thoughts, opinions and intentions, and represent real-world entities (objects and events). Later in this chapter, we refine this idea and demonstrate how concepts can be identified and used to represent the contents of documents in the clustering process.

Pattern Proximity

Pattern proximity evaluation is the task of estimating the similarity among the elements to be clustered. Usually, similarity (or proximity) is measured by a distance function defined on pairs of patterns. Different distance measures are in use in many communities (Jain et al., 1999). In the context of textual data, a simple distance measure like Euclidean distance (Salton & McGill, 1983), which within its variants is the most popular, can often be used to reflect dissimilarity between two patterns, whereas other similarity measures can be used to characterize the conceptual similarity between patterns (Michalski & Stepp, 1983). The most important aspect to considerate is that the user must know which method is being used, what are its side effects and if it is appropriated to the data he wants to manipulate. For a list of the existing proximity evaluation techniques of different types, see Aldenderfer and Blashfield (1984) and Everit, Landau, and Leese (2001).

Clustering or Grouping

The clustering or grouping step can be performed in a number of ways and its results may vary depending on the algorithm applied. The *clustering output* can be *hard*, when its data is partitioned into groups where no data element belongs to more than one cluster, or *fuzzy*, where each pattern has a variable degree of membership in each of the output clusters. In the first case, the clustering algorithm allocates each pattern to a single cluster, thus its decision is hard and it is named a hard algorithm. In the second case, the method assigns membership degrees (i.e., similarity) in several clusters to each input pattern and the algorithm is said to be fuzzy (as the choice it takes). A fuzzy clustering can be converted to a hard one by assigning each pattern to the cluster with the largest measure of membership.

According to its *topology*, the clustering can be *flat* or *hierarchical*. In the flat partition, the objects (documents) are distributed to distinct groups (sometimes one object can be assigned to more than one cluster, in a fuzzy way). In the hierarchical partition, the identification of groups is applied recursively, initially using documents as inputs, and then the groups identified in the previous steps. Hierarchical clustering algorithms produce a nested series of partitions based on some criteria for merging or splitting clusters based on similarity. Partitional clustering algorithms identify the partition that optimizes (locally, usually) clustering criteria. The result is a tree of groups.

Jain et al. (1999) describe the algorithmic structure and the *operational aspect* of clustering and states that it can also be *agglomerative* or *divisive*. An agglomerative approach begins with each pattern in a distinct cluster and successively merges clusters together until a stopping criterion is satisfied. A divisive method begins with all patterns in a single cluster and performs splitting until a stopping criterion is met.

In this context, the clustering algorithm can also be *monothetic* or *polythetic*. This aspect relates to the sequential or simultaneous use of features in the clustering process. Most algorithms are polythetic; that is, all features enter into the computation of distances between patterns, and decisions are based on those distances. When a monothetic approach is applied, one single feature is chosen and data is divided into two groups according to this characteristic. Then, each of these groups is further divided independently using another feature and the process goes on until the last feature is used to separate the elements.

In relation to its *complexity and processing time*, the clustering process can be *constant* (Silverstein & Pedersen, 1997), *linear,* or *exponential* of quadratic order.

The first are those in which the time to process each element is constant (does not change with the time). At each element, the time it would take to process is known *a priori.* Thus, knowing the number of comparisons to be made, one can estimate the overall (maximum) processing time. Currently, there is no known algorithm of this type. They are all linear or exponential.

According to Cutting, Karger, Pedersen and Tukey (1992), the ones that are said linear grow its processing time according to the number of elements to process. This time, however, grows slightly and gradually, since not all elements need to be compared. The quadratic algorithms grow exponentially, and each time an element is added it has to be compared with all the others.

Finally, the clustering process can be *incremental* or *non-incremental.* This issue arises when the pattern set to be clustered is large, and constraints on the execution time or memory space affect the algorithm. The early history of clustering methodology does not contain many examples of clustering algorithms designed to work with large data sets. The introduction of data mining has fostered the development of clustering algorithms that minimize the number of scans through the pattern set, reduce the number of patterns examined during execution, or reduce the size of data structures used in the algorithm's operations.

Due to this diversity of factors, there are many types or families of clustering algorithms. Some of them require that the user guess how many clusters can better represent the collection of documents (k-means family). Others require that the user guess the minimum or maximum threshold of similarity that a document must have to be or not in some cluster (graph theoretic family). Most approaches found in the text-mining field use the k-means algorithm or one of its variations. The problem with them is the definition of the best k (number of clusters) for a given collection of documents. We designed a variation of an existing algorithm from the graph theoretic family, which identifies relevant clusters without the need of a specific k (see details in the appropriate section).

Data Abstraction

Data abstraction is the process of extracting a simple and compact representation of a set of data (documents). Simplicity is perceived from the perspective of automatic analysis (with the intention that a machine can perform further processing efficiently) or from a human-oriented perspective (the representation obtained is easy to understand and intuitively appealing). In the clustering context, a typical data abstraction is a compact description of each cluster, usually in terms of cluster prototypes or representative patterns such as a centroid (Diday & Simon, 1976; Salton & McGill, 1983).

Centroid is a term originated in the field of physics and can be defined as the center of mass of a set of objects (i.e., particles) represented as vector of forces. Since documents are represented as vectors of words or concepts, representing the dimensions, and have weights associated to them (the forces), the term is used.

The term *prototype* (Cutting, Kardger, & Oederson, 1993) is a more abstract concept that includes the centroid and others representation forms. In the literature, it is usual to observe that both terms are used as synonyms.

All techniques described in the previous sections (term frequency, etc.) can be used to identify the more relevant features of a cluster of documents, thus creating the centroids or prototypes. However, others are more specific to this context, such as the *relevance score* described by Wiener et al. (1995). It was designed to build prototypes to represent categories of documents and is often used on classification or categorization systems. For each category or cluster, it analyzes its words and for each of them it identifies the number of documents inside and out of the category that the word appears. Taking it all in account, the words that are exclusive or more frequent on the documents of a specific category receive positive points and the others receive negative points. In the end, words that appear on many categories became with a low score and are excluded from the prototypes.

This is the method that we recommend and use for the conceptual clustering of textual documents described in this chapter.

Assessment of Output

Once the clustering process is finished, a very important and subjective task begins—the analysis of the resulting clusters. As so, it is also important to make sure that the clusters are generated appropriately and in a valid manner.

Since the clustering process is of exploratory origin, that is, nothing about the data being analyzed is known a priori, it is very difficult to evaluate if the resulting clusters are correct. In this context, what is correct and valid means is subjective. Usually, to valididate some process it is necessary to compare the resulting data with an expected one. Another form is to verify if it complies or conforms to some established patterns. Both ways need a metric to evaluate the result.

The first case, based on comparison, is usually disregarded since in clustering we do not have information about what should result from a given data set. The idea is to explore, to know a bit of it after or during the process. In the literature, few works conduct experiments using specific pre-processed data or corpus (in the case of documents), like Reuters,[2] whose elements are manually classified in specific categories, and these are used as the expected clusters to be found. Then, after the clustering process, the result is compared to the pre-existing categories using recall, precision and its variations such as macro or micro recall. See Lewis (1991) for information about these metrics. This kind of evaluation is more usual in the field of classification or categorization of documents.

The second is more applicable and is found in some works related to clustering. According to Halkidi, Batistakis and Vazirgiannis (2000a, 2000b), it is possible, for example, to test if the result was influenced by the clustering method or

Figure 1. Original vs. clustering result configuration

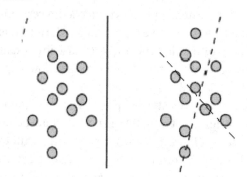

(a) Original configuration   (b) Clustering result

if the configuration found is due to some natural relation among the objects themselves. It is an aspect very important to know, because some relations cannot be valid or possible among the elements—they may not be disposed in a way that constitutes any cluster at all (see Figure 1).

This figure shows that the elements have physically a configuration that is not the one found by the clustering process. It can be seen that the automated clustering process has found divisions that do not exist in the original data. It also shows that humans can sometimes easily see and understand what is right or wrong in the resulting set of clusters if it is disposed visually. However, when we process a huge volume of elements and use many different features (dimensions in the case showed) it becomes more difficult to analyze the result.

Therefore, it would be better if there were an automated (computational) form of evaluating the influence or correctness of some clustering process. Jain et al. (1999) states that the idea is to find that the data has what they call cluster tendency, and the optimal result would be the one that better approximates to the inherent partitions of the data set. It is not an easy task, and Halkidi et al. present two works related to this problem (2002a, 2002b). We also recommend the readings of Aldenderfer et al. (1984) and Everitt et al. (2001) for more information about validating and evaluating clustering results.

CONCEPTUAL CLUSTERING OF TEXTUAL DOCUMENTS

The clustering process seems to have two problems not well covered. The first is to evaluate and validate the resulting sets of elements, determining useful subsets of elements or objects. The second is characterizing and representing the elements or objects. This second problem is the subject of this chapter.

In traditional clustering processes, performed on structured databases, a vector of attribute-value pairs easily represents elements or objects. However, when dealing with textual documents, the first step of the clustering process (pattern representation) must identify textual characteristics in the documents. These characteristics may be external (about the document, as authors, date of publication, format, etc.) or internal (about the content of the document). To use clustering for knowledge discovery, it is more important to deal with the internal characteristics approach. Explicitly, texts are composed only by words; however, words represent certain meanings, that is, part of the real world.

Most approaches to textual clustering use words extracted from texts to represent the documents. This implies that the similarity function, used in the pattern proximity step, must compare words present in the documents. According to Steinbach, Karypis and Kumar (2000), this approach, in which the similarity is based on common words, is not well suited since only part of the document matter is evaluated since the words are taken isolated.

The use of words as a bag of independent terms to represent document content can lead to semantic mistakes due to the vocabulary problem (Chen, 1994, 1996; Furnas, Landauer, Gomez, & Dumais, 1987). In this problem, different people tend to use different words to express the same objects or use the same word to express different ideas, since the language is inherently ambiguous. Thus, the vocabulary problem may cause poor clustering results. For example, clusters with nonrelated documents may be generated because one word is common to these documents (but this word may have different meanings in each document—polysemy problem). Other situation happens when similar documents are put in different clusters only for the reason that they do not share common words (but they deal with the same subject using different words—synonymy problem). Furthermore, other problems that can occur with the use of negative words (i.e., *stop words* like "not") are usually not considered. The general problem is not taking into consideration the context of words.

Since the use of words alone (without context) are not appropriate to represent the content of textual documents due to the vocabulary problem, our approach is the use of concepts instead of words to represent the content of the textual documents in the clustering process. Concepts are in a higher level of abstraction and represent real world events and objects, and people use them to express ideas, ideologies, thoughts, opinions, and intentions through the language.

In previous works (Loh, Wives, & Oliveira, 2000; Loh, Oliveira, & Gastal, 2001), concepts

were used with success in the mining processes of textual documents. The hypothesis here is that, using concepts, clustering will generate better results than using sets of isolated words. The methods used in the conceptual clustering process are described in the next section.

Pattern Representation

The first step of the conceptual clustering process (pattern representation) is the extraction of concepts from texts in order to characterize documents. The fundamental idea consists on preprocessing phase that analysis the documents in order to find (i.e., identify) concepts and use them instead of the words to represent the documents; however, documents do not have concepts explicitly stated. Concepts are expressed through word associations or constructions present in the language; consequently, it is possible to identify concepts in texts analyzing their phrases in the search of these associations. Moreover, a knowledge base containing concepts and its definitions (i.e., identification rules) must exist. Figure 1 illustrates this process.

Figure 1. Concept identification process

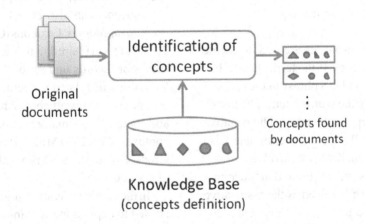

231

In this figure, a tool analyzes the original documents looking for the concepts definitions in a knowledge base that contains rules that specify how they can be found. Once a concept is found, it is used to represent the contents of the document analyzed. Our hypothesis is that concepts minimize the vocabulary problem and better identify the contents of the documents.

In our case, the identification rules are very simple and combine positive and negative words. The element of analysis for the identification of concepts is every phrase of the text, one at a time. Each phrase is individually analyzed based on the hypothesis that they represent one specific idea and one document may have different ideas on different phrases. Besides, we have found that the concept identification rules work better when the granularity of analysis is a phrase and not the whole text.

To identify a concept in a phrase, all the positive words of a concept rule must be present but no negative word. If one of the concept rules is true, the concept is considered present in the phrase and, consequently, in the text. For example, in a medical domain, "headache" (a symptom) may be defined as a concept using the following rules (negative words are identified by a "-" sign before them):

1. headache -deny -denies -not
2. head pain -deny -denies -not.

In this example, two rules are used to define the "Headache" concept. If the term "headache" or "head pain" is found in a phrase of the text and it does not contains the words "deny", "denies", or "not", the concept is identified. The negative terms (e.g., "denies") are used to eliminate false hints like "the patient denies headache").

If the concept is present more than once in a text, the total counting is used as the associative degree between the text and the concept. This degree may be used to indicate how strong a concept in a text is.

The knowledge base may be generated in different ways. We suggest a combination of automatic tools and human decision. Automatic tools may help people having an insight of the language used in the texts (different terms and meanings). Humans can augment this vocabulary using general or technical dictionaries. Software tools can also be useful to analyze textual samples verifying if the defined rules perform correctly. False hits may help defining negative words. The final decision about the rules in each concept definition should be the responsibility of humans. A more detailed discussion of how to define concepts can be found in the paper of Loh et al. (2000).

In the experiments presented in this chapter, the concepts base used in the conceptual clustering process had 65 concepts, all of them defined by experts in the domain of medicine with help of technical dictionaries, the ICD-10 (EDUSP, 1993), and analyses of sample textual records. Concepts correspond to symptoms, signals, and social characteristics (for example, *inappetence, insomnia, aggressiveness, tobacco use, living alone)* or reference events, person, or objects (for example, *marriage, husband, wife, children, neighbors, knife, weapon, hanging).* We have carried out formal evaluation of the concept extraction step. An error lower than 10% was reached showing the extraction step process quality.

Concepts can also be defined in *lexicons* or *domain ontologies.* Lexicons (Chalendar & Grau, 2000) are very similar to dictionaries because they store words and its definitions, which are lists of words related to them. Each relationship may contain many attributes that indicate its type and context. Lexicons are usually built to specific contexts. WordNet (Miller, Beckwith, Fellbaum, Gross, & Miller, 1993) is a well known example of lexicon.

In the context of computing, the term ontology is used to express many things. Guarino and Giaretta (1995) made a survey of the many different forms it can be found in this field and indicates that one of them is to represent a taxonomy of words. Similarly, Wagner (2000) used the expression "linguistic ontology" to define a structure that offers useful information to the disambiguation of the words senses and, consequently, a lexicon can be a kind of ontology.

Pattern Proximity

Equation 1 gives the degree of similarity between two documents. It calculates the degree of similarity summing the degree of equality among the common concepts of the documents being compared, dividing it by the number of concepts found on each document.

$$gs(X,Y) = \frac{\sum_{h=1}^{k} gi_{h}(a,b)}{n} \quad (1)$$

In this equation, *gs* is the degree of similarity between documents *X* and *Y*; *gi* is the equality degree between weights of the term *h* on each document (*a* in *X* and *b* in *Y*); *h* is an index for the terms that are common to *X* and *Y*; *k* is the number of terms that are common to *X* and *Y*; and *n* is the number of terms in both documents. The equality degree among the weights is measured by the next Equation (2).

$$gi(a,b) = \frac{1}{2}\left[(a \to b) \wedge (b \to a) + (\bar{a} \to \bar{b}) \wedge (\bar{b} \to \bar{a})\right] \quad (2)$$

In this equation, $\bar{x} = 1-x$; a➜b=max{c∈[0,1]|a*c <= b}; and ^ = min. It takes account on the fact that the term may have different degrees of importance on each document. Instead of calculating the average between both degrees, the function determines the degree of equality between them. Let us see an example: if a term h (that is common to both documents being analyzed) has a weight of 0.9 in one document and 0.3 in the other, the average would be 0.6. However, the same is true

if the weights were, respectively, 0.6 and 0.6. In the second case, the weights are more similar than the first case and the standard calculation of the average does not take this fact in account, which is not the case in our approach.

Clustering Algorithm

The next step consists in the identification of clusters, which is performed by a clustering algorithm that takes the results given by the similarity function (described in the patter proximity section) and tries to find similar elements and put them together.

As stated earlier in this chapter, there are many types or families of clustering algorithms. One of these families is the graph theoretical, which is based in the graph theory. These algorithms create graphs of different types with different connections to represent the similarity among the elements. The Stars is one of the algorithms of this family of clustering. It is responsible for identifying clusters that have one central element and many points or node elements linked to it, constituting a figure that is very similar to a star on the nightly sky. In this method, one document is selected as the center of the star. Then, elements are added or linked to this center if they have a similarity value greater than a prespecified threshold.

Usually, the user should guess the minimum or maximum threshold of similarity that a document must have to be or not in some cluster, which is a subjective task. Thus, we refined the Stars algorithm and implemented the Best Star method, in which the elements are rearranged to the star (cluster) to which it is more similar. Therefore, elements already assigned to a group (and that are not centers of the existing stars) can be reassigned if its degree of similarity to another center is greater than the previous one. In this case, the user does not need to establish a threshold and the best configuration of stars tend to be found. A drawback in this case is that many clusters can be created and it could be very difficult to understand and analyze them, since humans have problems analyzing many concepts; this limitation is known as the cognitive limit of rationality (Simon, 1954). One solution is to generate clusters in a recursive manner, creating hierarchies that establish relationships among them.

In order to demonstrate the practical application of this type of clustering, we have conducted some experiments that are described in the next section.

Case Study

We have conducted some experiments in a particular context to show how the conceptual clustering of documents should be performed in practice to allow the knowledge discovery from texts. They are also used to compare the clustering process using concepts with the traditional approach that uses bag of words as representatives of the textual documents.

One problem that was already discussed in this chapter is that the evaluation step is subjective in nature, mainly because the clustering result is valid only if it cannot occur accidentally or by influence of the algorithm chosen. Another point is that the same collection may be partitioned differently, for different purposes. Different algorithms may present different results or the same algorithm, depending on the starting options, may present different clusters. Thus, it is difficult to determine which features have a good clustering result. Validity assessments should be objective and are performed to determine whether the output is meaningful (Jain et al., 1999). One way to accomplish this validation is to compare the resulting structure of clusters to an a priori structure. This examination of validity tries to determine if the structure is appropriate for the purpose. A relative test compares two structures and measures their relative merit (Jain et al., 1999).

Under this hypothesis, we have chosen the information gain measure, explained in details by

Bradley and Reina (1998). This measure compares the resulting clusters to pre-existing ones. The reasoning is that the clustering result is "good" if it can separate the elements in clusters similarly to the structure known *a priori*. The objective is to obtain pure clusters, with little mixture of elements, according to the pre-existing classes.

One concept related to the information gain is Entropy, which is used to measure the degree of disorder, that is, the degree of mixture of elements from different classes (the greater the disorder, the greater the entropy). Information gain measures the difference between the entropy of the original structure and the entropy of the resulting one.

In the experimental case chosen, we assumed that the original entropy is zero, since there is no mixture of classes. The formulas of these measures are presented below:

- **Information gain** = Total Entropy—Process Weighted Entropy.
- **Total entropy** = $-(p_1 \log_2 p_1)-\ldots-(p_N \log_2 p_N)$ where, p is the number of documents within the class (in the original collection) divided by the total number of documents in the original collection, and N is the number of existing classes in the original collection.
- **Process weighted entropy** = sum of the weighted entropies of all resulting clusters.
- **Cluster weighted entropy** = (total number of documents in the cluster/total number of documents in the original collection) * Cluster Entropy.
- **Cluster entropy** = $-(p_1 \log_2 p_1)-\ldots-(p_N \log_2 p_N)$ where, p is the number of documents of the class in the cluster/total number of documents in the cluster, and N is the number of classes present in the cluster.

The experiments were carried out on a collection of medical records from a psychiatric hospital (our case study). The first medical record of patients, created in the patient admission, was used. Physicians generated the texts after interviewing the patient and his/her relatives. These records include the patient history and do not have explicitly stated the final diagnosis. Information about the patient concerns the diary activities, social, and familiar behavior and past medical history if readmitted. The records also contain symptoms and signals identified by the physician during the interview.

The collection was divided into four subcollections, each one representing a unique class, identified by one psychiatric disease, and containing only texts (medical records) corresponding to patients associated with the related disease. The class (i.e., the disease) of each text was previously determined by the physicians in a real diagnosis process. Each text was formatted in a separated text file and all files vary from one Kbytes to seven Kbytes.

We used the four major classes in Psychiatry, corresponding to diseases of the International Classification of Diseases, 10th revision (ICD-10) (EDUSP, 1993). The classes are:

- *Organic* mental disturbances (due to brain damage), including codes F00 to F09 of the ICD-10;
- Mental and conduct disturbances due to psychoactive *substances*, including codes F10 to F19;
- *Schizophrenia*, schizoid disorders and delirious disturbances, including codes F20 to F29;
- *Affective* and mood disturbances, including codes F30 to F39.

Three methods were compared. The conceptual method presented in the previous section was represented by two variations: one using the associative degree between texts and concepts, to indicate how much a concept is referred by a text (conceptual method with weights), and one disregarding this degree, presuming that all concepts have equal importance within a text (conceptual method without weights).

To represent the approach based on words, we used a term vector, with only significant words (i.e., no *stop words*), each of them associated to its relative frequency in the text, as suggested by Salton and McGill (1983).

In the end, five experiments were carried out with five different test collections, as described below:

- **Experiment 1:** A test collection with 12 texts in each class (total of 48 texts);
- **Experiment 2:** A test collection with 48 different texts (12 in each class) to confirm or not the previous result;
- **Experiment 3:** A test collection with a greater volume of texts (total of 155), with similar distributions among the classes (40 texts in each one, but organic class with 35);
- **Experiment 4:** A test collection with 200 texts with the following distribution: organics = 18 (9%), substances = 52 (26%), schizophrenia = 103 (51.5%), affective = 27 (13.5%);
- **Experiment 5:** A test collection with 201 texts different from the previous experiment, with the following distribution: organics = 17 (8.4%), substances = 53 (26.3%), schizophrenia = 106 (52.7%), affective = 25 (12.4%).

The number of documents appears to be small to the field of Computer Science, but in the field of Psychiatry (like others in the Human and Social Sciences), the data set is large enough and representative in relation to the existing population. As we are not trying to evaluate the complexity of the algorithm (memory usage, time, etc.) but to evaluate its gain in relation to the metrics above, the experiment is well enough, and the results were evaluated and validated by the Medical staff.

Table 1 presents the results of the five experiments. The total time of the clustering process was greater using the method by word. In the conceptual clustering, the time included 1 hour

Table 1. Experimental results

	Number of Clusters	Grouping time	Total Entropy	Total Weighted Entropy	Information Gain (IG)	Difference (%) to the better IG
Experiment 1 (48 documents)						
Method by word	17	03:37:22	2.000	0.944	1.056	12.51%
Conceptual method with weight	17	01:21:40	2.000	0.793	1.207	
Conceptual method without weight	17	01:21:39	2.000	0.862	1.138	5.72%
Experiment 2 (48 documents)						
Method by word	14	03:45:11	2.000	1.111	0.889	37.31%
Conceptual method with weight	15	01:21:29	2.000	0.792	1.208	14.81%
Conceptual method without weight	17	01:21:28	2.000	0.582	1.418	
Experiment 3 (155 documents)						
Method by word	38	21:22:52	1.998	1.067	0.931	34.53%
Conceptual method with weight	48 + 3 alone	01:32:00	1.998	0.576	1.422	
Conceptual method without weight	42 + 3 alone	01:32:11	1.998	0.749	1.249	12.17%
Experiment 4 (200 documents)						
Method by word	60	28:39:50	1.701	0.722	0.979	12.20%
Conceptual method with weight	56 + 4 alone	01:38:52	1.701	0.588	1.113	0.18%
Conceptual method without weight	59 + 4 alone	01:38:52	1.701	0.586	1.115	
Experiment 5 (201 documents)						
Method by word	56 + 2 alone	30:36:59	1.669	0.816	0.853	23.63%
Conceptual method with weight	63 + 7 alone	01:38:24	1.669	0.552	1.117	
Conceptual method without weight	61 + 7 alone	01:37:54	1.669	0.752	0.917	17.91%

and 20 minutes for the extraction of concepts (the time for the definition of the concepts base was not computed and depends on several factors).

Some clustering processes produced isolated elements that could not be classified in any cluster. These elements were disregarded for the entropy calculus. However, analyzing them in details, we found that no concept was identified on them. For this reason, the two conceptual methods left them alone (i.e., isolated), while the method by word grouped them. Our conclusion is that the conceptual method does better than the method by word, since it evaluates the content of the texts. The isolated elements indicate that the conceptual method does not identified significant content while the method by word tried, wrongly, to put these elements in clusters due to their common words (and disregarding the corresponding context).

In all experiments, the best information gain was obtained by the conceptual methods. These results confirm the initial hypothesis that concepts can represent better than words the content of documents for clustering purposes.

The conceptual method with weights produced better results than the method without in three experiments (experiments 1, 3, and 5 against experiments 2 and 4). As the difference was not significant, it is difficult to say which one produces the best clustering results.

An interesting finding is that some clusters generated by the conceptual method with weights are identical (have the same elements) to the clusters generated by the method without weights. This raises a trend of similar grouping results between the two methods (but this hypothesis must be better evaluated).

After the experiments, a process of analysis was performed to identify reasons or causes for the results. The hypothesis is that clustering textual documents can help discovering new knowledge, which is implicit in the written language. The cluster analysis technique looks for common characteristics in the elements present in each resulting cluster. These characteristics are concepts, according to the defined concepts base. In the case of medical records, we presume that common concepts inside a cluster may represent the profile (description model) of a special group of patients. Only the concepts present in all texts of a cluster were considered.

One kind of interesting cluster is the one that have a dominant disease/class among its texts. In this case, the common concepts may indicate a profile for a specialized group of patients of that disease. An example is one cluster having "organic" as the dominant class and "autism" and "injuries" as common concepts, leading to the hypothesis that there is a significant group of patients with that disease and those symptoms.

Other category of analysis is performed when there are many common concepts in a cluster. In this case, we can presume that these concepts may compose a prediction model. Thus, the presence of some of them in one patient record could be used to predict or evaluate the presence of the others.

An interesting analysis is to compare clusters with different dominant disease but having similar common concepts. For example, one cluster had the same concepts as other, except for "injuries". The former (with "injuries") had "organic" as dominant class and the latter had the "substances" as the dominant class. The hypothesis is that "injuries" can make the difference when diagnosing a patient with symptoms similar to both diseases.

An interesting case was the presence of three symptoms in many clusters: autism, dromomania (mania of walking) and mania. A special statistical analysis (conditional probability) produced the following result:

a. If autism and dromomania are present, mania is present in 100% of the cases;

b. If autism and mania are present, dromomania is present in 85.7% Of the cases;

c. If mania and dromomania are present, autism is present in 42.9% of the cases.

This comes up with the hypothesis that the symptoms "autism" and "dromomania" condition the presence of the symptom "mania" (95.8% of the cases with the three symptoms are of schizophrenic patients).

An interesting discover occurred when we performed again the experiments but having as original structure groups of texts written by the same physician. In this case, the results pointed to a better information gain with the method by word, as following:

•   Method by word: 1.901
•   Conceptual method with weights: 1.547
•   Conceptual method without weights: 1.523

This result confirms that physicians have unique writing styles, since texts written by the same person were grouped together.

FUTURE TRENDS

In this section, we present some applications for the conceptual clustering approach and some future trends in the field.

A promising application of clustering is to find the structure of a domain ontology. Domain ontologies are composed by concepts and relations between concepts. These relations can generate a hierarchy. Clustering may separate elements in a way that each resulting cluster may represent a concept of the ontology. If a divisive clustering process is used, the hierarchical structure of the clusters may represent the hierarchy of concepts in the domain ontology. Initial experiments using an algorithm based on k-means with an extension to discover automatically the best k showed that it is possible to generate a hierarchical structure of concepts to represent a domain. Future works will reveal the quality of the resulting structure.

Another interesting application is the use of clustering techniques for helping the organization of the results given by a search engine. An example can be found at http://www.vivissimo.com. This company implemented a cluster engine and a tool that searches the Web using traditional search engines and presents the results in a clustered manner. Thus, the user can navigate though the clusters found; instead of looking for the most relevant information in a linear list of links that does not show its relationships. One problem is that it still uses words instead of concepts. In the future, this kind of application may use concepts or similar structures to help identifying better clusters and to aid the interpretation of them.

We can preview that in the near future clustering and other text mining technologies will be integrated in the existing search engines providing new and extra functionalities, aiding the user finding the most relevant information to satisfy its needs. These technologies will also be integrated in its desktop environment, since basic search engines are already in the market (such as Google Desktop Search[3], Windows Desktop Search[4], Yahoo Desktop Search[5] and Copernic Desktop Search[6]) to be integrated in the existing Operating Systems.

Finally, there is the need for more sophisticated background knowledge to support the mining process. Techniques based in Concepts, as presented here, and more specifically in domain ontologies should be integrated in the tools to come. The meta-information, the information about the information itself, is also important. The path opened for the semantic Web, once it is established and of common practice, must be followed for all types of information and systems, allowing the creation and use of more intelligent tools for mining and processing any kind of data and information.

CONCLUSION

This chapter presented a conceptual approach for clustering textual documents. Instead of using words to represent documents, the approach uses concepts. Concepts are high-level structures and allow capturing more meaning than isolated words. While words lose contextual information, concepts express real world happenings in a broader way.

Experiments show that the conceptual approach has advantages over methods based on words. This advantage is accomplished because concepts minimize the vocabulary problem, generating clusters with more cohesion among their elements. Furthermore, the conceptual approach reduces the total time of the clustering process and helps the health professionals finding useful information about their patients, proceedings, treatments and relationship among them, aiding the knowledge discovery process.

Other advantage of the conceptual approach is in the cluster validity step. The analysis of the resulting clusters, when based on words, may lead to semantic mistakes, since only words represent the cluster. For example, the word "visual", very common in some texts of the experiment, leads to a doubt whether it refers to "visual illusions" or to "visual deficit". In the conceptual approach, concepts (high-level structures) represent the clusters in a way closer to the reality, helping people to identify common characteristics in elements within a cluster.

On the other hand, one advantage of the method based on words is that it obtained better results when clustering texts by authors. This is because people (at least, the experts who wrote the texts) tend to use a particular language (same words for the same meanings).

The work also investigated the use of the conceptual clustering approach for knowledge discovery in texts. Some findings of the discovery process were validated by physicians (psychiatrists) and others deserve deeper studies. That leads us to believe that is feasible to use the approach to discover new knowledge in textual collections.

Although the results were good, some cautions remain. For example, the ontology must be generated with certain accuracy; otherwise, concepts erroneously extracted may lead to wrong results. The discussion about the grouping algorithm used in the experiments (Best-Star) and its advantage over other algorithms are a theme for another work.

FUTURE RESEARCH DIRECTIONS

We believe that the future research on clustering should be focused on three main topics: cluster visualization and understanding, parallel algorithms, and semantic Web. The first has to do with the development of methods and tools to provide better visualization and comprehension of the clustering results, since they are not easy to see and understand, especially when dealing with textual data. Textual clustering deals with many dimensions, due to the nature of the features used to characterize the objects (i.e., its words, which are many). The identification and analysis of how the objects are clustered in one or another way are based on the features they have in common, and, as they tend to be so many, it is very difficult to visualize such relations in a two dimensional space. Thus, new forms of visualization of the clusters, their elements, links, and features are needed to provide a better understanding of the resulting clusters and its contents.

In terms of parallel algorithms, it is correct to state that, traditionally, clustering is a complex and time-consuming task and some tasks of the process may be distributed over different processors. With the advent of the multi-core processor technologies currently provided by Intel and AMD, all the field of programming and design of software may be affected. This technology is relatively cheap and every computer will be capable of parallel computing in a few years. It allows the study and development of new algorithms to cluster large amounts of data in lower or constant times.

Finally, the semantic that can be added to the existing content on the Web may aid the process of identification of relevant features of the objects before they are clustered. One of the current challenges of any text mining or processing software is the correct identification and understanding of the contents of a document. If the future Web tools provide a way to add semantic information in a computer readable manner, many of the problems described in the beginning of this chapter would be minimized and the tools would have a more correct and rich information to use and perform better processing.

REFERENCES

Aldenderfer, M. S., & Blashfield, R. K. (1984) *Cluster analysis* (p. 88). Beverly Hills, CA: Sage.

Bradley, P., & Fayyad, U. M., & Reina, C. (1998). Scaling clustering algorithms to large databases. In *International Conference on Knowledge Discovery & Data Mining, IV*, New York (pp. 9-15). Menlo Park: AAAI Press.

Chalendar, G. D., & Grau, B. (2000). SVETLAN: A system to classify nouns in context. In *International Conference on Knowledge Engineering and Knowledge Management (OL-2000) in conjunction with the 14th European Conference on Arti-*

ficial Intelligence, ECAI (p. 6). Berlin, Germany. Retrieved August 15, 2007 from http://sunsite.informatik.rwth-aachen.de/Publications/CEUR-WS/Vol-31/GChalendar_12.pdf

Chen, H. (1994). The vocabulary problem in collaboration [Special Issue on CSCW]. *IEEE Computer Society, 27,* 2-10.

Chen, H. (1996). A concept space approach to addressing the vocabulary problem in scientific information retrieval: An experiment on the worm community system. *Journal of the American Society for Information Science, 47,* 8.

Cowie, J., & Lehnert, W. (1996) Information extraction. *Communications of the ACM, 1*(39), 80-91.

Cutting, D., Karger, D. R., Pedersen, J. O., & Tukey, J. W. (1992). Scatter/Gather: A cluster-based approach to browsing large document collections. In *Conference on Research and Development in Information Retrieval* (pp. 318-329). New York: ACM Press.

Cutting, D., Kardger, D., & Oederson, J. (1993). Constant interaction-time scatter/gatter browsing of very large document collections. In *Conference on Research and Development in Information Retrieval* (pp. 126-134). New York: ACM Press.

Deerwester, S., Dumais S. T., & Harshman, R. (1990). Indexing by latent semantic analysis. *Journal of the Society for Information Science, 41*(6).

Diday, E., & Simon, J. C. (Eds.). (1976). *Clustering analysis: Digital pattern recognition.* Secaucus, NJ: Springer-Verlag.

EDUSP. (1993). *International classification of diseases and health related problems in Portuguese* (10th rev.). São Paulo: EDUSP (in collaboration with the World Health Organization).

Everitt, B. S., Landau, S., & Leese, M. (2001). *Cluster analysis* (p. 237, 4th ed.). New York: Oxford University Press.

Fayyad, U. M. (1996). *Advances in knowledge discovery and data mining.* Menlo Park: AAAI Press.

Feldman, R., & Dagan, I. (1995). Knowledge discovery in textual databases (KDT). In *International Conference on Knowledge Discovery* (pp. 112-117). Montreal, Canada.

Fox, C. (1992). Lexical analysis and stoplists. In W. B. Frakes & R. A. Baeza-Yates (Eds.), *Information retrieval: Data structures & algorithms* (pp. 102-130). Upper Saddle River, NJ: Prentice Hall PTR.

Furnas, G. W., Landauer, T. K., Gomez, L. M., & Dumais, S. T. (1987). The vocabulary problem in human-system communication. *Communications of the ACM, 30,* 964-970.

Guarino, N., & Giaretta, N. (1995). Ontologies and knowledge bases: Towards a terminological clarification. In N. Mars (Ed.), *Towards very large knowledge bases: Knowledge building and knowledge sharing* (pp. 25-32). Amsterdam: IOS Press.

Halkidi, M., Batistakis, Y., & Vazirgiannis, M. (2002a). Cluster validity checking methods: Part I. *ACM SIGMOD Record, 31*(2), 40-45.

Halkidi, M., Batistakis, Y., & Vazirgiannis, M. (2002b). Cluster validity checking methods: Part II. *ACM SIGMOD Record, 31*(3), 19-27.

Jain, A. K., Murty, M. N., & Flynn, P. J. (1999). Data clustering: A review. *ACM Computing Surveys, 31*(3), 264-323.

Kochen, M. (1974). *Principles of information retrieval* (p. 203). New York: John Wiley & Sons.

Korfhage, R. R. (1997). *Information retrieval and storage* (p. 349). New York: John Wiley & Sons.

Lewis, D. D. (1991). Evaluating text categorization. In *Speech and Natural Language Workshop* (pp. 312-318). San Mateo: Morgan Kaufmann.

Lin, C.-h., & Chen, H. (1999). An automated indexing and neural network approach to concept retrieval and classification of multilingual (Chinese-English) documents. *IEEE Transactions on Systems, Man and Cybernetics, 26*(1), 1-14.

Loh, S., Wives, L. K., & Oliveira, J. P. M. de. (2000). Concept-based knowledge discovery in texts extracted from the Web. *ACM SIGKDD Explorations, 2*(1), 29-39.

Loh, S. (2001). Knowledge discovery in textual documentation: Qualitative and quantitative analysis. *Journal of Documentation, 57*(5), 577-590.

Lu, H., Motoda, H., & Liu, H. (Eds.). (1997). *KDD: Techniques and applications.* Singapore: World Scientific.

Michalski, R., & Stepp, R. (1983). Automated construction of classifications: Conceptual clustering vs. numerical taxonomy. *IEEE Transactions on Pattern Analysis and Machine Intelligence (PAMI), 5*(5), 396-409.

Miller, G. A., Beckwith, R., Fellbaum, C., Gross, D., & Miller, K. (1993). *Five papers on WordNet.* Cognitive Science Laboratory, Princeton University.

Mizzaro, S. A. (1996). Cognitive analysis of information retrieval. In *Information Science: Integration in Perspective, CoLIS2* (pp. 233-250). The Royal School of Librarianship.

Ng, H. T., Goh, W. B., & Low, K. L. (1997). Feature selection, perceptron learning, and a usability case study for text categorization. In *Conference on Research and Development in Information Retrieval* (pp. 67-73). New York: ACM Press.

Rajaraman, K., & Pan, H. (2000). Document clustering using 3-tuples. In *The Sixth Pacific RIM International Conference on Artificial Intelligence (PRICAI'2000)*, Melbourne, Australia.

Rijsbergen, C. v. (1979). *Information retrieval.* London: Butterworths.

Salton, G., & McGill M. J. (1983). *Introduction to modern information retrieval.* New York: McGraw-Hill.

Schutze, H., Hull, D. A., & Pedersen, J. O. (1995). A comparison of classifiers and document representations for the routing problem. In *Conference on Research and Development in Information Retrieval* (pp. 229-238). New York: ACM Press.

Simon, H. A. (1954). A behavioural model of rational choice. *The Quarterly Journal of Economics, 69*(1), 99-118.

Silverstein, C., & Pedersen, J. (1997). Almost-constant-time clustering of arbitrary corpus subsets. In *Conference on Research and Development in Information Retrieval* (pp. 60-67). New York: ACM Press.

Steinbach, M., Karypis, G., & Kumar, V. (2000). A comparison of document clustering techniques. In *Mining Workshop; Proceedings of the Sixth ACM SIGKDD International Conference on Knowledge Discovery and Data Mining* (KDD 2000) (pp. 109-110). Boston.

Tan, A.-H. (1999). Text mining: The state of the art and the challenges. In *Workshop on Knowledge Discovery From Advanced Databases - PAKDD'99* (pp. 65-70). Beijing, China.

Wagner, A. (2000). Enriching a lexical semantic net with selectional preferences by means of statistical corpus analysis. In *Workshop on Ontology and Learning, ECAI* (pp. 37-42). CEUR Workshop Proceedings.

Wiener, E. D., Pedersen, J. O., & Weigend, A. S. (1995). A neural network approach to topic spotting. In *Annual Symposium on Document Analysis and Information Retrieval, SDAIR, 4* (pp. 317-332).

Willet, P. (1988). Recent trends in hierarchic document clustering: A critical review. *Information Processing & Management, 24*, 577-597.

Additional Reading

Aggarwal, C., Gates, S., & Yu, P. (1999). On the merits of building categorization systems by supervised clustering. In *Fifth ACM SIGKDD International Conference on Knowledge Discovery and Data Mining* (pp. 352-356). New York: ACM Press.

Anderberg, M. R. (1973). *Cluster analysis for applications*. New York: Academic Press.

Bradley, P., & Fayyad, U. (1998). Refining initial points for k-means clustering. In *Proceedings of the Fifteenth International Conference on Machine Learning* (pp. 91-99). San Francisco: Morgan Kaufmann.

Brailovsky, v. L. (1991). A probabilistic approach to clustering. *Pattern Recognition Letters, 12*(4), 193-198.

Brito, M. R., Chavez, E., Quiroz, A., & Yurich, J. (1997). Connectivity of the mutual k-nearest-neighbor graph in clustering and outlier detection. *Statistics & Probability Letters, 35*, 33-42.

Buckland, M. K. (1997). What is a "document"? *Journal of the American Society for Information Science, 48*(9), 804-809.

Cheng, C., Fu, A. W., & Zhang, Y. (1999). Entropy-based subspace clustering for mining numerical data. In *Proceedings of Internationl Conference on Knowledge Discovery and Data Mining* (pp. 84-93). New York: ACM Press.

Cohen, W. W. (2000). Automatically extracting features for concept entities. In *International Conference on Machine Learning, ICML* (vol. 17, pp. 159-166).

Dhillon, I., Fan, J., & Guan, Y. (2001). Efficient clustering of very large document collections. In R. Grossman, G. Kamath & R. Naburu (Eds.), *Data mining for scientific and engineering applications* (p. 25). Kluwer Academic Publishers.

Dixon, M. (1997). An overview of document mining technology. Retrieved April 3, 2007, from http://citeseer.ist.psu.edu/dixon97overview.html

Dubes, R. C., & Jain, A. K. (1988). *Algorithms for clustering data*. Prentice Hall.

Fayyad, U. M., Piatetsky-Shapiro, G., & Smyth, P. (1996). From data mining to knowledge discovery: An overview. In U. M. Fayyad (Ed.), *Advances in knowledge discovery and data mining* (pp. 1-34). Menlo Park: AAAI Press.

Glover, F., & Laguna, M. (2000). Fundamentals of scatter search and path relinking. *Control and Cybernetics, 29*(3), 653-684.

Goebel, M., & Gruenwald, L. (1999). A survey of data mining and knowledge discovery software tools. *SIGKDD Explorations, 1*(1), 20-33.

Guha, S., Rastogi, R., & Shim, K. (2000). Rock: A robust clustering algorithm for categorical attributes. *Information Systems, 25*(5), 345-366.

Larsen, B., & Aone, C. (1999). Fast and effective text mining using linear-time document clustering. In *Proceedings of the Conference on Knowledge Discovery and Data Mining, KDD '99* (pp. 16-22). New York: ACM Press.

Leuski, A. (2001). Evaluating document clustering for interactive information retrieval. In *Proceedings of the Conference on Information and Knowledge Management* (pp. 33-40). New York: ACM Press.

Lorena, L. A. N., & Furtado, J. C. (2001). Constructive genetic algorithm for clustering problems. *Evolutionary Computation, 9*(3), 309-327.

Mizzaro, S. (1997). Relevance: The whole history. *Journal of the American Society for Information Science, 48*(9), 810-832.

Oliveira, J. P. M. de, Loh, S., Wives, L. K., Scarinci, R. G., Musa, D. L., & Silva, L., (2004). Applying text mining on electronic messages for competitive intelligence. In *Electronic Commerce and Web*

Technologies (LNCS 3182, pp. 277-286). New York: Springer-Verlag.

Rasmussen, E. (1992). Clustering algorithms. In W. B. Frakes & R. A. Baeza-Yates (Eds.), *Information retrieval: Data structures & algorithms* (pp. 419-442). Upper Saddle River, NJ: Prentice Hall PTR.

Scarinci, R. G., Wives, L. K., Loh, S., Zabenedetti, C., & Oliveira, J. P. M. de. (2002). Managing unstructured e-commerce information. In *ER-Workshops, Lecture Notes in Computer Science 3182* (pp. 414-426). New York: Springer-Verlag.

Schütze, H., & Silverstein, C. (1997). Projections for efficient document clustering. In *Conference on Research and Development in Information Retrieval, SIGIR* (pp. 60-66). New York: ACM Press.

Silberschatz, A., & Tuzhilin, A. (1996). What makes patterns interesting in knowledge discovery systems. *IEEE Transactions on Knowledge and Data Engineering, 8*, 970-974.

Zamir, O., Etzioni, O., Madani, O., & Karp, R. M. (1997). Fast and intuitive clustering of Web documents. In *Proceedings of the 3rd International Conference on Knowledge Discovery and Data Mining* (pp. 287-290).

ENDNOTES

[1] Clustering can be seen as just the process (action) of identification of clusters (or groups) of objects, and thus cluster analysis can be understood as the overall process, including the understanding of how and why the clusters were formed and what to do with them.

[2] The Reuters collection can be found at http://about.reuters.com/researchandstandards/corpus.

[3] http://desktop.google.com

[4] http://desktop.msn.com.

[5] http://desktop.yahoo.com.

[6] http://www.copernic.com.

Chapter XII
A Hierarchical Online Classifier for Patent Categorization

Domonkos Tikk
Budapest University of Technology and Economics, Hungary

György Biró
TextMiner Ltd., Hungary

Attila Törcsvári
Arcanum Development Ltd., Hungary

ABSTRACT

Patent categorization (PC) is a typical application area of text categorization (TC). TC can be applied in different scenarios at the work of patent offices depending on at what stage the categorization is needed. This is a challenging field for TC algorithms, since the applications have to deal simultaneously with a large number of categories (in the magnitude of 1,000–10,000) organized in hierarchy, large number of long documents with huge vocabularies at training, and they are required to work fast and accurate at on-the-fly categorization. In this chapter we present a hierarchicalonline classifier, called HITEC, which meets the above requirements. The novelty of the method lies in the taxonomy dependent architecture of the classifier, the applied weight updating scheme, and in the relaxed category selection method. We evaluate the method on two large English patent application databases, the WIPO-alpha and the Espace A/B corpora.[1] We also compare the presented method to other TC algorithms on these collections and show that it outperforms them significantly.

INTRODUCTION

The immense growth in the number of electronic documents necessitates powerful algorithms and tools that are able to manage data of such quantity. An obvious way to handle the vast number of documents is organizing them according to their topic into hierarchicalcategory systems (taxonomies), which eases the search, retrieval, insertion, and storage. In general, the set-up of such document-management systems from scratch requires considerable time and cost, both at the time when the taxonomy is created and when it is filled up. In this chapter, we concentrate on the field of patent categorization where these initial steps can be skipped, because various taxonomies and patent databases are already available.

The rapid growth of data can also be observed in this field: the number of patent applications[2] is increasing every year, demanding higher and higher level of computer support for categorization-related tasks. Let us now briefly mention some properties of patent categorization (PC) problems that are challenging for text categorization (TC) algorithms.

Patent offices organize patent applications into very large topic taxonomies. The most important among them is the international patent classification (IPC),[3] which is a standard taxonomy developed and maintained by the World Intellectual Property Organization (WIPO), but other national taxonomies are also in use, such us the US patent Classification (UPC), the Canadian Patent Classification (CPC), and others. The IPC consists of about 80,000 categories that cover the whole range of industrial technologies. There are 8 sections at the highest level of the hierarchy, then 128 classes, 648 subclasses, about 7,200 main groups, and about 72,000 subgroups at lower levels. From the total 80,000 categories, the top four levels are mostly used in automated patent categorization systems.

Documents are also quite large compared to usual benchmark domains of TC such as, for example, business news (Reuters-21578 and its variants, Reuters Corpus Volume 1), and short communications (20 Newsgroups data). An average document contains more than 3,000 words. A patent application document consists of several fields, annotated by metadata, a feature which may be partly or fully taken into account at categorization.

The vocabulary of patent applications is quite diverse, which leads to an extremely large dictionary. Many vague or general terms are often used in order to avoid narrowing the scope of the invention (Fall, Torcsvari, Benzineb & Karetka, 2003). Combinations of general terms often have a special meaning that also has to be captured. Patent documents also include acronyms and much new terminology (Kando, 2000). Moreover, unlike news stories, patents are necessarily all different at a semantic level, as each must describe a new invention. This may complicate the training of a classifier. Furthermore, IPC categories often cover large and disparate areas, resulting in large vocabularies in even in single categories.

The patent applications are usually assigned to one primary category and several secondary categories. At the evaluation of TC approaches, this characteristic has to be also taken into account. For this task, particular evaluation functions were proposed (Fall, Torcsvari, Benzineb et al., 2003; see also the experimental section).

Therefore TC approaches for PC problems have to manage simultaneously:

- A very large size of taxonomy,
- Large documents,
- A huge feature set,
- Multilabeled documents.

Finally, another often occurring phenomenon of patent classification is that capturing the semantics of a document statistically is not sufficient for proper categorization. This can be explained by the nature of how the primary categories are assigned to documents: the primary category is that particular topic in which the patent application contains the novelty. It often happens that the document is about an application of a known technique in a new field. The patent application thoroughly specifies the new application area but also describes the known technique in details and then it is extremely difficult to determine the real category of the document: even qualified humans often err.

In this chapter we propose a hierarchical online classifier that is able to manage the above difficulties of PC and generates significantly better categorization results than other approaches proposed and tested in the literature.

The chapter is organized as follows. The first section presents the various types of classification tasks in patent offices. In what follows we give an overview of approaches related to automated patent classification. Finally, the proposed hierarchical online classifier (HITEC—hierarchical text classifier) is described in detail. In this case it is compared to other methods on two patent corpora in the subsequent section.

TYPICAL SCENARIOS FOR PATENT CLASSIFICATION TASKS

There are different PC problems that patent offices have to face and that could facilitate the use of patent database; those can be distinguished depending on the human assistance necessary at the categorization stage and on the expertise of the users.

Preclassification

Large intellectual property offices receive hundreds of patent applications a day. By "preclassification" is meant a first stage of routing, for purposes of internal handling, whereby the subject of the claimed invention (or the invention first claimed, if there is more than one) is broadly identified by means of the appropriate classification symbols (GUIEX, 2005, Part B, Chapter V, 1).

The incoming document is precategorized by an expert of the classification system with a general knowledge about all technology fields. The expert then redirects the document to the respective department related to the supposed technical field of the invention. If the redirection fails (GUIEX, 2005, Part B, Chapter V, 3) because the precategorizer expert missed the subject matter where the application contains presumed novelty, the classification experts of the receiving department redirect the document.

This process could be potentially replaced by an information broker application that receives the document in electronic form, performs precategorization, and passes the document to the electronic desktop of the respective department.

Patent Categorization in Small Offices

"By »official classification« is meant the assigning of the appropriate classification symbols identifying the technical subject of the claimed invention" (GUIEX, 2005, Part B, Chapter V, p. 1).

Small intellectual property offices have limited expert staff. These experts are responsible for the classification of patent applications that cover relatively broad areas of technology in comparison to large offices where classification experts work on very narrow technical areas.

The classification experts generally must use the same detailed category system and, therefore, the likelihood of errors. Even more important is that, during substantive examination, checking of the state-of-the-art in a certain field is more problematic since the expert cannot hold in mind all recent developments in all areas and may not recognize the lack of novelty of certain claims of the application, especially those that are on the borderline of the knowledge of the classification expert.

The work of classification experts could be potentially supported by systems which suggest categories suspiciously close to the semantic range expressed by the text of the patent application.

Eventual Inventors

There are certain patent information users who have no or very limited knowledge about patent classification systems; potential inventors are experts in their own field but not necessarily in patent databases for state-of-the-art technology.

In order to support the inventors getting an overview of patents, a hint is to be given to them, based on the text of their invention indicating which are the categories where similar granted patents or applications were categorized by classification experts. The inventor could check in public patent databases how inventive his/her idea is or —since the bibliographic data of patents contain the applicant information as well—who are the potential competitors or cooperating partners for the invention.

Patent Information Providers

Patent information providers must build profiles of their users, on which they submit filtered patent information to their customers.

During building or extending this profile they could benefit from category codes provided by an autocategorization system, which uses free text provided by their customers.

Evaluation of PC Tasks

Here, we define text categorization problems and possible evaluation guidelines based on the above listed tasks:

- **Autocategorization:** The best guess of the categorizer is matched against the primary category

- **Precategorization:** The best guess must hit one of the categories (either primary or any secondary)
- **Flat categorization assistance:** Among the first three guessed section (class, subclass, maingroup) there must be the most relevant section (class, subclass, maingroup)
- **Hierarchical categorization assistance:**[4] Knowing a correct intermediate or parent category in the hierarchy, the best guess of the categorizer on the next level is matched against the correct primary category at the given level.

The scenario of the last task appears when the user browses hierarchicalally the categorization results and first opens the correct intermediate category and then tries to determine the most relevant among its children (at the subsequent level).

STATE-OF-THE-ART OF PATENT CATEGORIZATION

Automating the attribution of patent classification categories to patent application by using machine learning techniques received increasing attention in the research community of information retrieval and knowledge engineering from the late 1990s.[5] Managing the hierarchicalstructure of a patent classification scheme can be performed in two ways. An algorithm can either flatten the taxonomy and consider it as a system of independent categories or can incorporate the hierarchy in the categorization algorithm. Early patent categorizers chose the former solution but these were outperformed by real hierarchicalclassifiers. The first hierarchicalclassifier was developed by Chakrabarti, Dom, Agrawal, and Raghavan (1997, 1998), who implemented Bayesian hierarchicalclassification system where they applied the Fisher's discriminant—a well-known technique from statistical pattern recognition—to distinguish efficiently feature terms from noise terms. They tested the approach on a small-scale subtree of a patent classification consisting of 12 subclasses organized in three levels. Here they found that by using already-known classifications of cited patents in the application, the effectiveness of the categorization could be much improved (Chakrabarti, Dom & Indyk, 1998). Larkey (1998, 1999) has created a tool for attributing U.S. patent codes based on a k-Nearest Neighbor (k-NN) approach. The inclusion of phrases (multiword terms) during indexing is reported to have increased the system's precision for patent searching but not for categorization (Larkey, 1998), though, the overall system precision is not specified. Kohonen, Kaski, Lagus, Salojarvi, Honkela, Paatero et al. (2000) developed a self-organizing map based PC system with a back-propagation network based categorization approach. Their baseline solution achieved a precision of 60.6% when classifying patents into 21 categories. This could be raised to 64% when different feature selection techniques have been applied. A comprehensive set of patent categorization tests is reported in Krier and Zaccà (2002). These authors organized a competitive evaluation of various academic and commercial categorizers, but have not disclosed detailed results. The participant with the best results has published his findings separately (Koster, Seutter & Beney, 2001). They implemented a variant of the Balanced Winnow, an online classifier with perceptron algorithm and multiplicative weight updating schema. Categorization is performed at the level of 44 or 549 categories specific to the internal administration of the European Patent Office, with around 78% and 68% precision, respectively, when measured with a customized success criterion. The above listed approaches are difficult to compare given the lack of a benchmark patent application collection and a standard patent taxonomy.

This lack has been at least partly alleviated with the disclosure of the WIPO document col-

lections: first, the WIPO-alpha English collection was published in 2002 (Fall, Torcsvari & Karetka, 2002), and shortly after the WIPO-de German patent application corpus became publicly available (Fall, Torcsvari, Fievet & Karetka, 2003). See more details in the experimental section. The creators of the WIPO-alpha collection (Fall, Torcsvari, Benzineb et al., 2003) performed a comparative study with four state-of-the-art classifiers (naïve Bayes (NB); support vector machine (SVM); k-NN and a variant of Winnow) and evaluated them by means of performance measures customized to typical PC scenarios. The author found that at the class level NB and SVM were the best (55%), while at the subclass level SVM outperformed other methods at most evaluation aspects (41%).

Since then, several works have been reported tests results on WIPO-alpha. Unfortunately, most authors scaled-down the problem by working only on a subset of the whole corpus. Hofmann et al. (2003) experimented on the D section (Textile) with 160 leaf level category and obtained 71.9% accuracy. Rousu, Saunders, Szedmak, and Shawe-Taylor (2005) evaluated their SVM-like maximum margin Markov network approach also on the D section of the hierarchy, and achieved 76.7% averaged overall F_1-measure value. Cai and Hofmann (2004) tested their hierarchical SVM-like categorization engine on each section of WIPO-alpha, and obtained 32.4-42.9% accuracy at the maingroup level. Godbole and Sarawagi (2004) presented another SVM variant that has been evaluated on the entire hierarchy and specifically on the F subtree (mechanical engineering, lighting, heating, weapons, blasting) of the corpus. They achieved 44.1 and 68.8% accuracy, respectively.

A patent application oriented knowledge management system has been developed by Trappey, Hsu, Trappey, and Lin (2006), which incorporates patent organization, classification and search methodology based on back-propagation neural network (BPNN) technology. This approach focuses on the improvement of the patent document management system in terms of both usability and accuracy. The authors compared their method with a statistical and a Bayesian model and found some improvement in accuracy when tested again a small-scale two-level subset of WIPO-alpha collection (a part of B25; power hand tools) with 9 leaf level categories. The chapter put special emphasis on the extraction of key phrases from the document set, which are then used as inputs of the BPNN classifier.

Other hierarchical categorization algorithms such as Dekel, Kesher, and Singer (2004), Ruiz and Srinivasan (2002), or Dumais and Chen (2000), have not been evaluated on patent categorization benchmarks and therefore will not be compared to HITEC here.

HIERARCHICAL ONLINE CLASSIFIER

Notation

Text classifiers usually represent a document in the vector space model as a set of features $d = \{f_1, f_2, ..., f_m\}$, where m denotes the number of *active features*, that is, those that occur in the document. Features typically represent a word, or a sequence of words (phrase). The relevance of a feature f in document d is given by a weight $w(f, d)$, that depends on the number of times f occurs in the document $w(f, d) = o(f, d)$, and can also reflect other characteristics of the document and the given feature with respect to the document or a document set. When determining the relevance of a document d related to a category c, the text classifier calculates a function $\Phi_c(d)$. Based on this value the classifier can work according to the following scenarios. The document d can be assigned to category c if this score exceeds a category-dependent threshold (category-pivoted categorization). Alternatively, when evaluating this function on a set of categories, C, the document d is assigned to class(es) producing the best score(s).

A *linear* text classifier uses analogous representation for categories as for documents. A category is represented as a weight vector of features $c = \langle w(f_1, c), ..., w(f_n, c) \rangle = \langle w_1, ..., w_n \rangle$, where n is the total number of features in the document collection, and $w(f, c)$ represent the importance feature f for category c. The vector can be interpreted as the prototype document of the category. Therefore, linear classifiers can evaluate the similarity of a document to a category by calculating the dot-product of the corresponding document and category vectors:

$$\Phi_c(d) = \sum_{f \in d} w(f, d) \cdot w(f, c) := \sum_{j=1}^{m} w_{i_j} \cdot v_{i_j},$$

here i_j denotes the index set of active features of a document d. For brevity, we denote by w_k and v_k the weight corresponding to term k in the document and in the category, respectively. The text classifier learns the characteristics of each category by means of training samples. A training sample d is labeled with $y(d,c)$ being 1 or 0 depending on if d is a positive or a negative example for a given category. The training algorithm of a linear classifier aims at finding the best weight vector for each category to classify correctly new documents. It means that a linear classifier works as a linear separator for each category in the vector space spanned by the set of features, $f_1, ..., f_n$.

Schema of Online Classifiers

Online (or *incremental*) categorization methods create a classifier based on a sequence of trials on the training documents. At each trial the classifier makes a guess, and then it gets the feedback about the success of the guess, which may be used to update the classifier. This process can be repeated several times on the training data to obtain the incrementally built model that works sufficiently well on the set of training documents. This methodology is useful when the entire set of training documents is not available at once, or

Figure 1. Weight updating of online mistake-driven classifiers

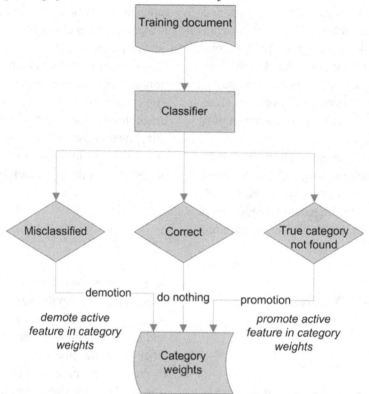

when the semantic of the category may change in time after the arrival of new samples (Sebastiani, 2002). This is also pertinent in such applications in which the user may provide feedback on the success of test document categorization, which can be later exploited in a subsequent training phase of the classifier. Some PC scenarios (e.g., precategorization, hierarchical categorization assistance) typically in this class.

The core idea of the proposed algorithm is the mistake-driven online learning model, first proposed in the seminal paper of Littlestone (1988). Mistake-driven algorithms change category weights $\langle w_1, ..., w_n \rangle$ only when a mistake is made at guessing. Online mistake driven algorithms have typically three parameters: a threshold θ, a promotion parameter α, and a demotion parameter β. After initializing the category weights, Littlestone's *Positive Winnow* assigns a document

to a category iff: $\sum_{j=1}^{m} w_{i_j} \cdot v_{i_j} > \theta$. The algorithm performs multiplicative weight updating on active features with $\alpha > 1$ and $0 < \beta < 1$. Positive Winnow updates the category weights w_i in the following two cases of mistakes (see also Figure 1.):

1. **True label is not found:** If the algorithm guesses 0 and the true label is 1 then all active weights are promoted by multiplying them with α.

2. **Misclassification:** If the algorithm guesses 1 but the true label is 0 then all active weights are demoted by multiplying them with β.

In both cases the other, non-active weights remain unchanged. A classifier may often commit both types of mistake simultaneously.

A very similar weight updating algorithm is used in the *Perceptron* algorithm (Rosenblatt, 1958), which differs from Positive Winnow in that an additive schema is applied with a single $\alpha > 0$ parameter: at promotion it is added to, while at demotion it is subtracted from the weight of active features; non-active weight are unchanged. This algorithm is commonly applied to TC: see Dagan, Karov, and Roth (1997); Schütze, Hull, and Pedersen (1995); Liere and Tadepalli (1997); Ng, Goh, and Low (1997).

The *Balanced Winnow* (Littlestone, 1988) also uses a multiplicative weight updating schema. It keeps two weights for each feature, w^+ and w^-, and the overall weight is their difference. So, a guess is deemed 1, iff $\sum_{j=1}^{m}(w_{i_j}^+ - w_{i_j}^-) \cdot v_{i_j} > \theta$. The active weights are updated as follows when a mistake is made:

1. True label is not found: the positive part of active weights are promoted by multiplying them with α: $w_{i_j}^+ := \alpha \cdot w_{i_j}^+$; the negative part of the active weights is demoted by multiplying them by β: $w_{i_j}^- := \beta \cdot w_{i_j}^-$. The overall weight of active features increases.

2. Misclassification: the negative part of active weights are promoted by multiplying them with α: $w_{i_j}^- := \alpha \cdot w_{i_j}^-$; the positive part of the active weights is demoted by multiplying them by β: $w_{i_j}^+ := \beta \cdot w_{i_j}^+$. The overall weight of active features decreases.

In Balanced Winnow, features may have negative weight as well, which improves the efficiency of the algorithm considerably (Dagan et al., 1997). In this work a good comparison of the above three online mistake-driven algorithms is given with some modification that improves the balanced version. They show that Balanced Winnow outperforms the other two algorithms in all tests.

Theoretical analyses of Winnow and its versions (e.g., Blum, 1995; Golding & Roth, 1996; Littlestone, 1988, 1995) show that they are very effective; they are able to learn any linear threshold function. It is guaranteed that they find the prefect separator if it exists, and the scheme works quite well in cases when such separators do not exist. The Algorithm is tolerant to the presence of noise, irrelevant features, and target function changes in time. A key feature of Winnow is that its mistake bound grows linearly with the number of active features and only logarithmically with the entire set of features (e.g., Dagan et al., 1997). The noise tolerance is attributed to being mistake-driven. Intuitively, it raises some important and relevant features, while it makes the algorithm resistant to the presence of noise features.

Other uses of online classifier algorithms are exponentiated gradient (Lewis, Schapier, Callan & Papka, 1996) and sleeping experts (Coen & Singer, 1999), which differs from Perceptron and Winnow in that:

1. They update the classifier also when a document is categorized correctly;
2. They update all weights, not only those of active features.

For patent categorization tasks, Koster et al. (2001) reported remarkable results with Balanced Winnow using the *thick threshold heuristic*, and they achieved improved convergence by using *normalized feature weight initialization*.

In the next section we present our mistake-driven online classifier algorithm that is particularly devoted to categorization into hierarchicaltaxonomies. Key differences from the previously described algorithms are that our proposed method:

•   Is adapted to hierarchicalcategory systems;
•   Applies a novel weight updating method;

Figure 2. Architecture of the categorization network

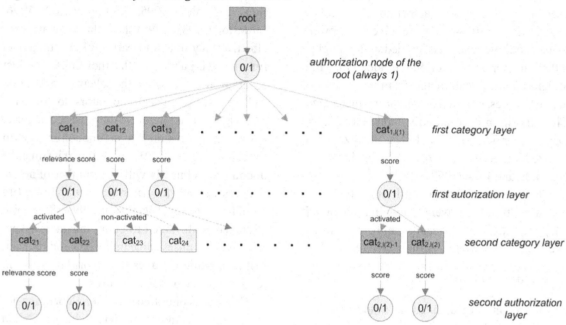

- Allows relaxed category selection, in order to avoid high level mistakes in the taxonomy.

In what follows the classifier will be presented in detail, with special emphasis on the above three features.

The Proposed Algorithm of HITEC

Taxonomy Driven Architecture

One of the main drawbacks of categorization algorithms applied to PC is that they do not take into account the hierarchical structure of the taxonomy but flatten the category system as if the individual categories at various levels of the taxonomy would be independent. Our solution applies a neural network to overcome this problem. The network copies the structure of the taxonomy, which is assumed to have a tree structure. Each node in the network represents a category. Branches of the taxonomy are connected under a single root category. Nodes are organized in layers with

respect to their level in the taxonomy; these are called *category layers*.

An additional *authorization layer* is placed between each category layer in the network. It controls the number of propagated categories at each level, that is, acts as a parameterized threshold. An authorization layer node receives its input from a parent node of the upper category layer, and its binary output is connected to those nodes in the next category layer that represent the categories of the parent node's descendants in the original taxonomy. An authorization layer node simultaneously sets all its child nodes *active* (i.e., their activation score is 1) if its input is "large enough". The threshold of activation is determined on the basis of the *relaxed greedy algorithm* described later. The architecture of the categorization network is depicted in Figure 2.

During the categorization of a document, only *active category nodes* are evaluated. The categorization of a document is performed downward in the hierarchy starting from the root. The root node is always set active. The algorithm calculates the relevance score of the document for the *active category nodes* at the given level. Based on the score, the authorization layer nodes set the activation score and propagate the active category nodes to the next category layer. The relevance score of the parent category is not propagated to its children categories. Therefore, a child category can only have a high relevance score if its own profile is similar to the given document. For the reasoning behind this selection strategy see the description of relaxed greedy strategy.

Calculation of Relevance Score and Weight Updated Schema

The *relevance score* of a document *d* for a category *c* is calculated as follows:

$$\Phi_c(d) = (1 + \eta) \cdot \tanh \left(\sum_{j=1}^{m} w_{i_j} \cdot v_{i_j} - \theta \right)$$

where η and θ are threshold parameters. The function $\tanh(\circ)$ is applied as a smoothing function to alleviate the oscillating behavior of training (as in control theory). It can be substituted with an arbitrary monotone increasing smoothing function f that satisfies $\lim_{x \to 0} f(x) = 0$ and $\lim_{x \to \infty} f(x) = 1$. The relevance score can be converted to a binary value with a threshold; however, the real valued relevance score gives more information about the classifier. It can be considered a *confidence value* of the categorization that may be exploited when the result of the categorization is processed; for instance, it can be readily used to rank categories. The algorithm evaluates its own guesses by the confidence values and gives hints to the field expert or to the user for the reliability and interpretation of the results.

The categorization error is calculated as the difference of the required output and the relevance score:

$$e(d, c) = y(d, c) - \Phi_c(d)$$

The error can take either positive or negative value. Category weights are updated if a mistake is made by means of the following additive weight updating schema:

1. **True label is not found:** If the error $e(d, c)$ is positive, that is the algorithm's guess is lower than the required output then all active weights are promoted by changing them: $w_{i_j} := w_{i_j} + e(d,c) \cdot \alpha \cdot v_{i_j}$, where α is the promotional learning rate.
2. **Misclassification:** If the error $e(d, c)$ is negative, that is the algorithm's guess is higher than the required output then all active weights are demoted by changing them: $w_{i_j} := w_{i_j} + e(d,c) \cdot \beta \cdot v_{i_j}$, where β is the demotional learning rate.

The weights of category vectors are initialized uniformly to zero. The number of nonzero weights, however, increases as the training procedure goes on repeatedly. In order to avoid the proliferation of insignificantly small, nonzero weights, which increases calculation time but has no effect on efficiency, we apply a cut-off strategy and set zero weights being under a certain threshold.

Relaxed Greedy Algorithm for Category Activation

The activated categories at each level should be determined carefully because they may seriously affect the performance of the classifier. The most trivial solution is the greedy selection strategy that activates the category with the best relevance score at each level. From the point of view of computational efficiency it is very advantageous compared to flattened taxonomy: only a fraction of total category nodes are evaluated during the categorization of a document, drastically decreasing the time requirement for training and on-the-fly categorization, as well. This speed-up makes it possible to manage significantly larger PC related tasks than the regular TC benchmark problems.

As, McCallum, Rosenfeld, Mitchell, and Ng (1998) pointed out, the greedy algorithm requires high accuracy at intermediate nodes, since if an error is committed there, the leaf-level category cannot be found. To alleviate this problem while maintaining the computational efficiency of the greedy strategy we propose the following *relaxed greedy strategy* for category activation.

The relaxed greedy strategy has two parameters: maximum variance ($0 < v_{max} \leq 1$) that controls the number of activated categories from above, and a minimal threshold parameter ($0 \leq \vartheta < 1$) that sets minimal allowable relevance score. By maximum variance v_{max} one can specify the maximal allowed deviation (ratio) in relevance score from the maximal relevance score at the given category layer to set a node as activated. By threshold ϑ, one can set the minimal relevance score of a node to be activated. A node is activated if it satisfies both criteria. Let $\Phi_{\ell}(d) = \max_{c\ in\ level\ \ell} \Phi_c(d)$ be the maximal relevance score of d at level hierarchy level ℓ. Then the greedy strategy sets the activation score of a category node c in level ℓ to 1 iff its relevance score fulfills:

$$\Phi_c(d) \geq \max(\vartheta, \Phi_{\ell}(d) \cdot v_{max})$$

This strategy is called relaxed greedy because instead of keeping track of a category path of width one, it widens the category path—that is the search space of the algorithm. In case of a high level mistake at the selection of the best category, the algorithm is able to correct this at lower level, if other meaningful alternatives exist at the level of mistake.

With the help of the two parameters of relaxed greedy strategy, one can make a trade-off between recall and precision. Setting v_{max} and ϑ low—typically ($0.3 \sim 0.6$) and ($0.05 \sim 0.15$), respectively—results in numerous activated categories, which improves recall and decreases precision. Setting them high—typically (≥ 0.8) and (≥ 0.5), respectively—yield fewer activated categories with higher precision and lower recall.

The relaxed greedy strategy works well only if there is no information propagated from the parent category to the child category at the evaluation (e.g., as scaling factor). Such a factor would emphasize and propagate a possible incorrect selection downward in the hierarchy during the entire selection, and, therefore, it contradicts the purpose of the relaxed greedy strategy.

Training with Primary and Secondary Categories

One particular feature of PC is that patent applications usually have a single primary category and numerous secondary categories. This feature has to be taken into account when training a patent application classifier because (see also the experimental section) it is more important for the user to find the primary category than the secondary ones. To adapt our algorithm to this challenge, we modified the weight updating schema as follows. We keep two sets of weights at each category, one for primary and another for secondary ones. The weight updating works analogously for the two types of categories, except in the following cases. When training for primary categories and a secondary category is found the demotion effect is less than otherwise:

Misclassification, but a secondary category label is found. The negative error $e(d, c)$ is added a positive parameter $\varepsilon \geq 0$, and all active weights are demoted as: $w_{i_j} := w_{i_j} + (e(d,c)+\varepsilon) \cdot \beta \cdot v_{i_j}$, where β is the demotional learning rate.

An analogous technique is applied when a primary category is found instead of a secondary one.

Summary of the Algorithm

Let us now put together the tiles of the proposed algorithm and see the picture in whole! The skeleton of the algorithm follows the previously described online mistake driven methodology. Training documents are categorized downward in the hierarchy activating a variable size category path. A categorization pass normally outputs a relevance score based ranked list of leaf-level categories. A categorization pass can also terminate at an intermediate category layer if there is no category whose relevance score is above the minimal threshold ϑ. After each categorization pass, category weights are updated for the mistakes. A training cycle consists of training with all training documents. The number of training cycles is controlled by an upper bound for maximal iteration (in PC with large training corpra the typical value is 10-20) and a training evaluation function:

$$Q = \sum_{k=1}^{N} Q(d_k)/N \text{ where } Q(d_k) = \frac{TP}{\sum_{c \in C} y(c, d_k)} \cdot \frac{1}{1+FP}$$

where C is the set of all categories, TP is the number of correctly assigned categories (true positive), and FP is the number of incorrectly assigned categories (false positive). Training terminates if Q drops below $q \cdot Q_{best}$, where q is a learning parameter (typically 0.95~1.0) and Q_{best} is the best achieved value of Q during the training.

At testing the algorithm determines a ranked list of categories after searching in the category path of activated categories.

EXPERIMENTS

Corpora of Patent Applications

As a courtesy of WIPO, we could experiment with the English WIPO-alpha and Espace EP-A and EP-B (Espace A/B) patent application corpora issued in late 2002 and 2005, respectively.[6] WIPO-alpha is a large collection (3 GB) of about 75,000 patent application distributed over 5,000 categories in four levels (the top four levels of IPC). Espace A/B is an even larger collection of about 600,000 documents defined on the same

taxonomy (IPC). At WIPO, they experimented with several text categorization techniques on the WIPO-alpha collection (Fall et al., 2003); those results serves as the basis of comparison. We decided to test our algorithm on the much larger Espace A/B dataset as well, because we intended to verify the empirical observation that classifier trained with larger training set perform better (Fall et al., 2003, p. 22). The other goal of our Espace A/B experiments was to create the best possible classifier on IPC taxonomy from available data that can be equally useful for practitioners and researchers.

The WIPO-alpha collection is provided with a train/test split (46324 and 28926 documents.) For Espace A/B we created the split of 302,088 train and 304,870 test documents after removing extremely sparse subclasses. Documents are assigned one main category, and additional secondary categories (0 or more), since WIPO-alpha was designated to have even distribution across the taxonomy it does not include all top-four level IPC categories and the same holds for Espace A/B dataset. The documents of WIPO-alpha are distributed in 8 sections, 114 classes, 451 subclasses and 4427 main groups, and these numbers are 8, 119, 578 and 6,094 for Espace A/B, respectively.

Training collections consist of documents roughly evenly spread across the IPC main groups, subject to the restriction that each subclass contains between 20 and 2,000 documents. Test collections consist of documents distributed roughly according to the frequency of a typical year's patent applications, subject to the restriction that each subclass contains between 10 and 1,000 documents. All documents in test collections also have attributed IPC symbols, so there is no blind data.

In both corpora, documents are provided in XML format consisting of the following text fields: title, list of inventors, list of applicant companies or individuals, abstract, claims section, and long description. For Espace A/B dataset we did not use the long description field.

Figure 3. Explanation to the three evaluation measures Top, Top 3, Any (Fall et al., 2002)

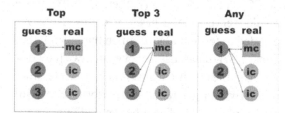

Performance Measures

We have adopted three heuristic evaluation measures for categorization success proposed by the provider of the WIPO collections (Fall et al., 2002). Let us suppose that the method returns a confidence ranked list of predicted IPC codes. Then we can define the following measures (see Figure 3):

- **Top prediction (Top):** The top category predicted by the classifier is compared with the main IPC class, shown as (mc) in Figure 3.

- **Three guesses (Top 3):** The top three categories predicted by the classifier are compared with the main IPC class. If a single match is found, the categorization is deemed successful. This measure is adapted to evaluate categorization assistance task, where a user ultimately makes the decision. In this case, it is tolerable that the correct guess appears second or third in the list of suggestions.

- **All classes (Any):** We compare the top prediction of the classifier with all classes associated with the document: the main IPC symbol and additional IPC symbols, shown as (ic) in Figure 3. If a single match is found, the categorization is deemed successful.

One can observe that "Top" is the most appropriate to evaluate the autocategorization task, "Top3" is good for the flat assisted categorization task, and "Any" fits the precategorization task.

Details of Implementation

Feature Weights

Feature weights of documents should reflect not only the occurrence or frequency of features in the document itself, but the relevance of the feature for the entire training set. Let us assume that we have N training documents $d_k (1 \leq k \leq N)$. We experimented with two well-known weighting schemes for determining feature weights: tf-idf and entropy weighting. The former sets weights to:

$$v_{ik} = a_{ik} \cdot \left(\frac{N}{n_i} \right),$$

while the latter specifies them as

$$v_{ik} = \log(1 + a_{ik}) \cdot \left(1 + \frac{1}{\log N} \sum_{j=1}^{N} \frac{a_{ij}}{n_i} \log\left(\frac{a_{ij}}{n_i} \right) \right),$$

where $a_{ik} = o(f_i, d_k)/N_k$ is the relative frequency of feature f_i in document d_k, N_k being the number of features in document d_k; and n_i is the number of documents where feature f_i occurs at least once in the training set.

Dimensionality Reduction

When dealing with a huge document collection, the large number of feature can cause problem in document processing, indexing, and also in categorization. Therefore, before indexing documents it is a common step to apply some *dimensionality reduction* (DR) method to reduce the size of the feature set. This can speed up the training and categorization, and increase the performance of the classifier by a few percent (e.g., Koller & Sahami, 1997; Wibowo & Williams, 2002).

In our previous experiments on smaller corpora (Tikk, Yang, & Bang, 2003) we also found that performance can be increased slightly (less than 1%) if rare terms are disregarded, but the effect of DR on time efficiency is more significant. We applied a simple and popular filtering type feature selection technique (Sebastiani, 2002) by removing all features that occur:

1. Less than d_1 times in the entire training corpus, or
2. In more than d_2 proportion of all training documents.

By the former filtering we disregard features that are not significant in the categorization, while by the later filtering we ignore features that are not discriminative enough between categories. The typical values are $d_1 \in [1, ..., 10]$, and $d_2 \in [0.05, ..., 1.0]$.

The construction of patent documents provides another way of DR as well. One may select certain XML fields as the basis of the feature set, and index the other parts of the documents using this dictionary. For instance, the long description part can be ignored for feature set creation because it may contain lot of dummy words. Fall et al. (2003) reported that they achieved the best performance when the basis of the feature set was the aggregation of first 300 different words of "long description" field in each document. In our experiments we also applied XML field based selection and determined which set of fields provides the best performance. We handled each field uniformly, give no extra weight to words appearing in particular fields.

The fact that features represent text elements offers other obvious techniques to perform DR: stop-word filtering and lemmatization. On the former, it is meant the removal of topic-independent words, such as articles, prepositions, adverbs, and so forth, while lemmatization is the substitution of words with their canonical, that is, stemmed form. While stop-word filtering is almost always applied in TC, the effect of lemmatization is more controversial (see Sebastiani,

2002, p. 12) when used. In our experiments we applied stop-word removal based on a list of 598 words for English. The Porter stemmer was used for lemmatization.

Results

WIPO-Alpha Corpus

We present the results obtained by HITEC on WIPO-alpha in Figure 4 and the summarizing table (Table 1). Interpreting relevance score as *confidence level*, we differentiate results based on this value. A confidence cutoff of 0.0 means that all guesses are considered, while 0.8 means that only those decisions are considered where the value of confidence level is not less than 0.8. Obviously, the higher is the confidence level the lower is the number of predicted documents. Therefore the two diagrams of Figure 4 can be evaluated only simultaneously. The figures show all the three performance measures at class, subclass, and main group levels by increasing confidence levels in 0.1 steps. Table 1 compares some significant values for each parameter setting.

The best results have been achieved after seven iterations when only text of the XML fields *inventors, applicants, title, abstract* and *claims* served as the basis of dictionary ("iptac" setting) and the entropy weighting scheme is employed to calculate feature weights (see Figure 4). The value of the other parameters are: $d_1 = 2$, $d_2 = 0.25$, $\eta = 0.1$, $\theta = 0.2$, $\varepsilon = 0.2$, $\vartheta = 0.05$, and $v_{max} = 0.8$. We get a bit lower values for evaluation measures when the text of claim field is not used for the dictionary ("ipta" setting); see Table 1.

We also tested other settings and hypotheses with HITEC on WIPO-alpha. When applying tf-idf weighting scheme for feature weights somewhat worse results are obtained, but the time requirement for indexing the collection is decreased by about 30%, because this scheme requires one pass less for indexing. The inferiority of the results is also due to the $v_{max} = 0.5$

Figure 4. Results of the best setting ("iptac"): (a) Precision by confidence levels. (b) Comparisons of precisions, extrapolated to 100\% recall—The upper diagram shows the percentage of correct guesses from all guess at a given confidence level. A high value here only indicates the quality of such guesses whose confidence level exceeds the threshold. In other words, this diagram justifies the self-evaluation mechanism performed by relevance score of the algorithm. The lower diagram depicts the precision in terms of the proportion of recalled documents.

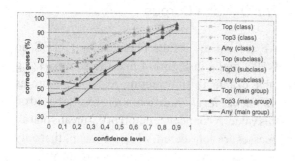 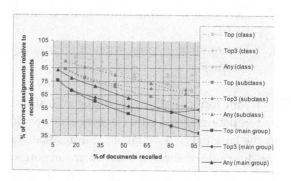

Table 1. Summary of results on WIPO-alpha corpus with HITEC. For comparison the best result from Fall et al. (2003) is also given

Evaluation measure	Setting	IPC level/confidence level			
		class/0.0	class/0.8	subclass/0.0	main group/0.0
Top	iptac	**65.75**	**92.93**	**53.25**	**36.89**
	ipta	65.50	**92.93**	53.14	36.78
	main	62.81	84.37	49.41	32.28
	tf-idf	64.04	83.56	50.76	33.75
	Fall et al (2003a)	55.00 NB, SVM	—	41.00 SVM	—
	difference	10.75		12.25	
Top3	iptac	**85.56**	**92.93**	**75.05**	55.44
	ipta	85.51	**92.93**	75.00	**55.58**
	main	83.61	84.37	70.89	48.98
	tf-idf	70.71	84.11	56.57	37.05
	Fall et al (2003a)	79.00 NB	—	62.00 k-NN	—
	difference	6.56		13.05	
Any	iptac	**73.68**	**95.83**	62.45	46.46
	ipta	73.41	95.64	62.28	46.38
	main	71.32	94.97	58.97	41.51
	tf-idf	72.22	90.38	60.18	42.71
	Fall et al (2003a)	63.00 NB	—	48.00 SVM	—
	difference	10.68		14.45	

value applied. As a consequence, the number of predicted documents increases at high confidence levels significantly, and this decreases evaluation scores. Applying a higher value, however, would lead to too few predicted documents at high confidence levels.

We investigated the effect of using only the main category of each document for training. This experiment was suggested in Fall, Torcsvari, and Benzineb et al. (2003a), and it can be argued that by this filtering since no ambiguous documents are used for training, ambiguity may decrease. The obtained results did not support the hypothesis, as they were inferior to the ones with regular setting as can be seen in Table 1.

Table 1 also contains reference results from Fall et al. (2003) for IPC class and subclass levels. That paper does not contain results for main group level. We assumed that their results refer to the 0.0 confidence level (the most difficult setting), although it is not indicated explicitly. One can observe that HITEC outperforms the best technique experimented with in Fall et al. significantly at each confidence level and performance measure, and with going deeper in the IPC taxonomy the difference increases.

It is worth noting that the graph of Top3 measure drops at confidence levels 0.1-0.3 compared to the 0.0 value. The reason is that at a lower confidence levels more categories are predicted, and in some cases the one returned with lower confidence level is actually the correct one, which is left out at higher confidence levels. When the consistency level goes higher than 0.4, fewer and fewer documents are predicted, and then the Top3 values increase again. (This does not apply to the tf-idf setting with low variance, because there the number of predicted documents is low even at low consistency levels.)

One can observe that the relationship between evaluation measures is Top < Any < Top3 except when tf-idf is applied in which case "Any" provides the best values. Naturally, the lower we go in the taxonomy the more imprecise predictions

are obtained. At IPC class level the Top3 measure of HITEC at the lowest confidence level (i.e., when basically all documents are considered) is 85.56% with the best setting, a quite significant result. indicating that the algorithm can be used for large document corpora in real-world applications. Because of the very large taxonomy and range of documents, the results on the main group level seems to be quite weak. However, if we consider that human experts can do this categorization work with about 64% accuracy then this result turns out to be much more significant.

Espace A/B Corpus

Our second test ran on the Espace A/B dataset. The results are obtained with the same settings as in case of WIPO-alpha: 7 iterations, "iptac" fields for feature set creation, and the above listed values of parameters. First, we analyzed the reliability of categorization for autocategorization ("Top" measure), precategorization ("Any" measure), flat assisted categorization ("Top3" measure), and hierarchical assisted categorization. The latter is calculated as a conditional categorization: knowing the parent category of a document how well the same classifier can predict its next level category. The results are given as a function of the ratio of predicted document at reliability level (Figure 5). The results are summarized in Table 2. The hierarchical assisted categorization is meaningless at section level since there is no parent category in that case. In Figure 5d we indicated the Top 3 measure for section level for comparison, while the related cell in Table 2 is empty.

In Figure 6 the confidence level vs. reliability is depicted. It can be observed that if documents with higher confidence levels are selected, the classifier achieves higher precision—we conclude that users can rely on the quality of the returned confidence level.

It can be also observed that larger amount of training data resulted in significant improvement in all three evaluation measure.

Figure 5. Reliability of HITEC on Espace A/B data for various PC tasks: (a) Autocategorization, (b) precategorization, (c) flat assisted categorization, (d) hierarchical assisted categorization

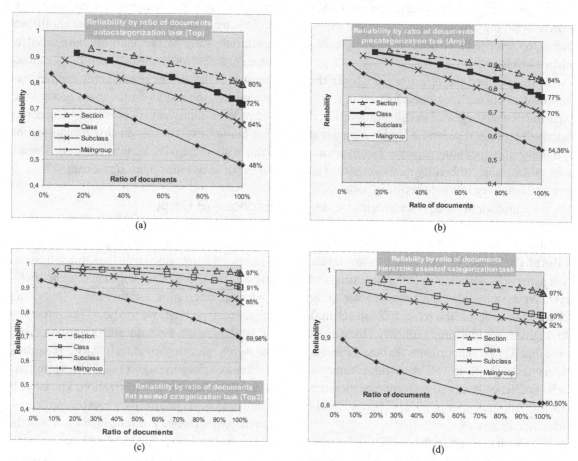

Figure 6. Reliability vs. confidence level on Espace A/B data for various PC tasks: (a) Autocategorization, (b) precategorization, (c) flat assisted categorization, (d) hierarchical assisted categorization

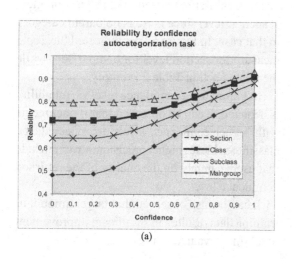

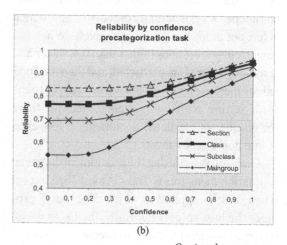

Continued on next page

Figure 6. Continued

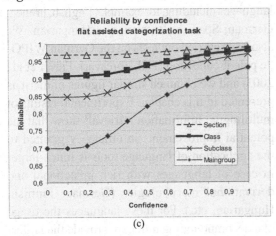

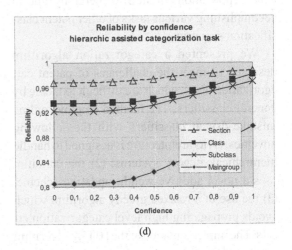

(c)   (d)

Table 2. Summary of results on Espace A/B data with HITEC

Categorization task	IPC level			
	Section	Class	Subclass	Main group
Autocategorization	79.67	71.75	64.04	48.34
Precategorization	83.54	76.42	69.46	54.33
Flat assisted categorization	96.78	90.75	84.77	69.94
Hierarchical assisted categorization		93.48	92.17	80.50

Time Requirement and Availability

Let us shortly describe the time efficiency of the HITEC. Our experiments were executed on a regular PC (Linux OS, 2 GHz processor, 1 GB RAM). The indexing of the entire WIPO-entire training set took around 55 minutes with entropy weighting and just over 40 minutes with tf-idf weighting. Note, that the average number of active features/document due to the inclusion of long description field is 468.63. The training algorithm (7 iterations) required about 2 hours with each setting. Increasing the number of iterations did not improve results significantly.

In case of Espace A/B data, indexing took 46 minutes with entropy weighting, but here the average number of active features/document was only 51, due to the exclusion of long description field. The training algorithm (7 iterations) required about 1.5 hours.

The HITEC classifier trained on WIPO-alpha is publicly available for tests online[7].

CONCLUSION

We presented a hierarchicalonline classifier and demonstrated its application for patent categorization tasks using the IPC taxonomy. IPC covers all areas of technology and is widely used by the intellectual property offices of many countries. Patent categorization is indispensable for the retrieval of patent documents in the search for prior art. Such retrieval is crucial to patent-issuing authorities, potential inventors, research and development units, and others concerned with the application or development of technology. An efficient automated patent classifier is a crucial component in providing an automated classification assistance system for categorizing patent applications in the IPC hierarchy, and to accomplishing various tasks of other patent classification scenarios.

We presented a categorization algorithm designed to meet the challenges of patent categorization tasks, which are difficult to tackle by general classifiers. The method employs online mistake-driven classifiers with the following novelties: (1) its architecture is designed to handle hierarchicalcategory systems; (2) the classifier uses a novel additive weight updating scheme, (3) the use of a relaxed greedy algorithm which avoids propagating high level categorization errors. The implementation of the HITEC algorithm was tested to published results on two large patent application corpora, the entire WIPO-alpha, and Espace EP-A and EP-B collections. We compared the proposed algorithm on the former and showed that our solution outperforms other state-of-the art classifiers significantly (by 6.5~14.5%). The results show that HITEC is a prominent candidate to be a core component of a patent categorization system.

FUTURE RESEARCH DIRECTIONS

The presented approach and the problem of patent classification itself offer numerous potential directions for future research. First, let us investigate the possible improvements of the algorithm. Supposing further high quality data becomes available, we shall verify whether efficiency can be further improved using the boosting algorithms (Schapire, 2001); however, for proper evaluation of these, we need at least two times more data. We shall also analyze whether the efficiency can be improved by the usage of more sophisticated language-specific tools, such as part-of-speech (POS) tagger, named entity recognizer, morphological parser, decompounding unit, and so forth. This issue also brings into the picture the application of the algorithm on patent corpora of different languages. The HITEC engine

is endowed with language support of 13 European languages including, for example, English, French, German, Spanish, Russian, and Hungarian. We also have carried out tests on the German WIPO-de patent collection (Fall, Torcsvari, Fievet et al., 2003) and we obtained similar figures of merit as presented in this chapter. Experimental results of multilingual information retrieval[8] show that the potential improvements in efficiency granted to the application of language tools is much larger in case of languages with rich inflectional and derivational morphologies (German, Finnish, Hungarian, etc.). For those languages the usage of a decompounding unit may provide the largest improvement (Halácsy, 2005).

Another direction of future research is the application of the learning technique of HITEC on other, possibly language-independent domains. This is a rather undiscovered area, and the first results suggest promising outcomes. Reskó, Tikk, Hashimoto, Baranyi (2006) applied HITEC for polygon shape recognition. The core algorithm of HITEC was used as the major component of a classifier committee that has won the prestigious KDD Cup in 2006[9] on a difficult medical diagnostic problem being very sensitive to false positive prediction. In this regard, the winning solution (Tikk, Kardkovács & Szidarovszky, 2006) benefited the self evaluation feature of HITEC's; the confidence value could be effectively employed to set up parametrical threshold limits for the false positive rate. The research of classifier committee can be investigated in different set-ups. First, committees comprised of HITEC instances with different setting should be evaluated and, alternatively, inclusion of other classifier (SVM, linear regression based models, etc.) should also be analyzed. In order to support research of this field, we will shortly make HITEC's source code publicly available for educational and research purpose. Finally, a thorough mathematical analysis of HITEC's efficiency should also be carried out.

ACKNOWLEDGMENT

Domonkos Tikk was supported by the János Bolyai Research Scholarship of the Hungarian Academy of Science.

REFERENCES

Blum, A. (1995). Empirical support for Winnow and weighted-majority based algorithms: Results on a calendar scheduling domain. In *Proceedings of the 12th International Conference on Machine Learning* (pp. 64-72). San Francisco: Morgan Kaufmann.

Cai, L., & Hofmann, T., (2004). Hierarchical document categorization with support vector machines. In *Proceedings. of the 13th ACM International Conference on Information and Knowledge Management (CIKM'04)*, Washington, DC (pp. 78-87). New York: ACM Press.

Chakrabarti, S., Dom, B., Agrawal, R., & Raghavan P. (1997). Using taxonomy, discriminants, and signatures for navigating in text databases. In *Proceedings of the 23rd Very Large Date Bases Conference* (pp. 446-455). Athens, Greece: Morgan Kaufmann.

Chakrabarti, S., Dom, B., Agrawal, R., & Raghavan P. (1998). Scalable feature selection, classification and signature generation for organizing large text databases into hierarchical topic taxonomies. *Very Large Date Bases Journal, 7*(3), 163-178.

Chakrabarti, S., Dom B., & Indyk, P. (1998). Enhanced hypertext categorization using hyperlinks. In *Proceedings SIGMOD98, ACM International Conference on Management of Data*, Seattle, Washington (pp. 307-318). New York: ACM Press.

Cohen, W.W., & Singer, Y. (1999). Context sensitive learning methods for text categorization. *ACM Transactions on Information Systems, 17*(2), 141-173.

Dagan, I., Karov, Y., & Roth, D. (1997). Mistake-driven learning in text categorization. In C. Cardie & R. Weischedel (Eds.), *Proceedings of the 2nd Conference on Empirical Methods in Natural Language Processing (EMNLP 97)*, Providence, Rhode Island (pp. 55-63). Somerset, NJ: Association for Computational Linguistics.

Dekel, O., Keshet J., & Singer Y (2004). Large margin hierarchical classification. In *Proceedings of the 3rd International Conference on Machine Learning and Cybernetics (ICML'04)* (pp. 209-216), Banff, AB, Canada. Morgan Kaufmann.

Dumais S.T., & Chen, H. (2000). Hierarchical classification of Web content. In *Proceedings of 23rd ACM International Conference on Research and Development in Information Retrieval (SIGIR'00)*, Athens, Greece (pp. 256-263). New York: ACM Press.

Fall, C.J., Törcsvári, A., Benzineb, K., & Karetka, G. (2003). Automated categorization in the international patent classification. *ACM SIGIR Forum Archive, 37*(1), 10-25.

Fall, C.J., Törcsvári, A., Fievét, P., & Karetka, G. (2003). Additional readme information for WIPO-de autocategorization data set. Retrieved April 5, 2007, from http://www.wipo.int/ibis/datasets/wipo-de-readme.html

Fall, C.J., Törcsvári, A., & Karetka, G. (2002). Readme information for WIPO-alpha autocategorization training set. Retrieved April 5, 2007, from http://www.wipo.int/ibis/datasets/wipo-alpha-readme.html

Godbole, S., & Sarawagi, S., (2004). Discriminative methods for multi-labeled classification. In H. Dai, R. Srikant & C. Zhang (Eds.), *Proceedings of the 8th Pacific-Asia Conference on Knowledge Discovery and Data Mining (PAKDD'04)*, Sydney, Australia (LNAI 3056, pp. 22-30). Berlin/Heidelberg, Germany: Springer-Verlag.

Golding, A.R., & Roth, D., (1996). Applying Winnow to context-sensitive spelling correction. In *Proceedings of 13th International Conference on Machine Learning* (pp. 182-190), Bari, Italy: Morgan Kaufmann.

GUIEX (2005). *Guidelines for examination in the European patent office.* Published by the European Patent Office Directorate Patent Law 5.2.1. Munich: European Patent Office. ISBN 3-89605-074-5.

Halácsy, P. (2005). Benefits of deep NLP-based lemmatization for information retrieval. In *Working Notes for the CLEF 2006 Workshop*, Alicante, Spain.

Hofmann, T., Cai, L., & Ciaramita, M., (2003). Learning with taxonomies: Classifying documents and words. In *Workshop on Syntax, Semantics, and Statistics (NIPS'03)*, Whistler, BC, Canada.

Kando, N. (2000). What shall we evaluate? Preliminary discussion for the NTCIR Patent IR Challenge based on the brainstorming with the specialized intermediaries in patent searching and patent attorneys. In *ACM-SIGIR Workshop on Patent Retrieval*, Athens, Greece (pp. 37-42). New York: ACM Press.

Kohonen, T., Kaski, S., Lagus, K., Salojärvi, J., Honkela, J., Paatero, V., et al. (2000). Self organization of a massive document collection. *IEEE Transactions on Neural Networks, 11*(3), 574-585.

Koller, D., & Sahami, M. (1997). Hierarchicalally classifying documents using a very few words. *Proceedings of the 14th International Conference on Machine Learning, 14,* (pp. 170-178). Nashville, Tennessee: Morgan-Kaufmann.

Koster, C.H.A., Seutter M., & Beney, J. (2001). Classifying patent applications with Winnow. In *Proceedings of Benelearn 2001 Conference* (pp. 19-26). Antwerpen, Belgium.

Krier, M., & Zaccà, F. (2002). Automatic categorization applications at the European Patent Office. *World Patent Information, 24,* 187-196.

Larkey, L.S. (1998). Some issues in the automatic classification of US patents. In *Working Notes for the Workshop on Learning for Text Categorization, 15th National Conference on Artificial Intelligence (AAAI-98)*. Madison, Wisconsin.

Larkey, L.S. (1999). A patent search and classification system. In *Proceedings of DL-99, the 4th ACM Conference on Digital Libraries*, Berkeley, California (pp. 179-187). New York: ACM Press.

Lewis, D.D., Schapire, R.E., Callan, J.P., & Papka, R., (1996). Training algorithms for linear text classifiers. In *Proceedings of SIGIR-96, 19th ACM International Conference on Research and Development in Information Retrieval*, Zürich, Switzerland (pp. 298-306). New York: ACM Press.

Liere, R., & Tadepalli, P. (1997). Active learning with committees for text categorization. In *Proceedings of AAAI-97, the 14th National Conference of Artificial Intelligence* (pp. 591-496). Providence, Rhode Island: AAAI Press.

Littlestone, N. (1988). Learning quickly when irrelevant attributes around: A new linear-threshold algorithm. *Machine Learning, 2,* 285-318.

Littlestone, N. (1995). Comparing sereval linear-threshold learning algorithm on tasks involving superfluous attributes. In *Proceedings of 12th International Conference on Machine Learning*, San Francisco (pp. 353-361). Morgan Kaufmann.

McCallum, A., Rosenfeld, R., Mitchell, T., & Ng, A. (1998). Improving text classification by shrinkage in a hierarchy of classes. In *Proceedings of 15th International Conference of Machine Learning* (pp. 359-367). Madison, Wisconsin: Morgan Kaufmann.

Ng, H.T., Goh, W.B., & Low, K.L. (1997). Feature selection, perceptron learning, and a usability case study for text categorization. In N.J. Belkin, A.D. Narasimhalu & P. Willett (Eds.), *Proceedings of SIGIR-97, 20ʰ ACM International Conference on Research and Development in Information Retrieval*, Philadelphia (pp. 67-73). New York: ACM Press.

Reskó, B., Tikk, D., Hashimoto, H., & Baranyi, P. (2006). Visual feature array based cognitive polygon recognition using UFEX text categorizer. In *Proceedings of the IEEE 3ʳᵈ International Conference on Mechatronics* (pp. 539-544). Budapest, Hungary.

Rosenblatt, F. (1958). The perceptron: A probabilistic model for information storage and organization in brain. *Psychological Review, 65*, 386-407. (Reprinted in *Neurocomputing*. MIT Press, 1988).

Rousu, J., Saunders, C., Szedmak, S., & Shawe-Taylor, J. (2005). Learning hierarchical multi-category text classification models. In *Proceedings of the 22ⁿᵈ International Conference on Machine Learning* (pp. 745-752). Bonn, Germany: Omnipress.

Ruiz, M.E., & Srinivasan, P. (2002). Hierarchical text categorization using neural networks. *Information Retrieval, 5*(1), 87-118.

Schapire, R. (2001). The boosting approach to machine learning: An overview. In *MSRI Workshop on Nonlinear Estimation and Classification*, Berkeley, California.

Schütze, H., Hull, D.A., & Pedersen, J.O. (1995). A comparison of classifiers and document representations for the routing problem. In *Proceedings of SIGIR-95, 18ʰ ACM International Conference on Research and Development in Information Retrieval*, Seattle, Washington (pp. 229-237). New York: ACM Press.

Sebastiani, F. (2002). Machine learning in automated text categorization. *ACM Computing Surveys, 34*(1), 1-47.

Tikk, D., Kardkovács, Zs.T., & Szidarovszky, F.P., (2006). Voting with a parameterized veto strategy: Solving the KDD Cup 2006 problem by means of a classifier committee. *Special Interest Group on Knowledge Discovery and Data Mining Explorations Exploration Newsletter, 8*(2), 53-62.

Tikk, D., Yang, J.D., & Bang, S.L. (2003). Hierarchical text categorization using fuzzy relational thesaurus. *Kybernetika, 39*(5), 583-600.

Trappey, A.J.C., Hsu, F.-C., Trappey, C.V., & Lin C.-I., (2006). Development of a patent document classification and search platform using a back-propagation network. *Expert Systems with Applications, 31*(4), 755-765.

Wibovo, W., & Williams, H.E. (2002). Simple and accurate feature selection for hierarchical categorisation. In *Proceedings of the 2ⁿᵈ ACM Symposium on Document Engineering*, McLean, Virginia (pp. 111-118). New York: ACM Press.

Additional Reading

Aas, L., & Eikvil, L. (1999). *Text categorisation: A survey* (Report NR 941). Norwegian Computing Center.

Adams, S., (2000). Using the international patent classification in an online environment. *World Patent Information, 22*(4), 291–300.

Apte, C., Damerau, F.J., & Weiss, S.M., (1994). Automated learning of decision rules for text categorization. *ACM Transaction on Information Systems, 12*(3), 233-251.

Bacchin, M., Ferro, N., & Melucci, M., (2002). University of Padua at CLEF 2002: Experiments to evaluate a statistical stemming algorithm. In *Working Notes for the CLEF 2002 Workshop*, Roma, Italy.

Baeza-Yates, R., & Riveiro-Nieto, B. (1999). *Modern information retrieval*. Reading, MA: Addison-Wesley.

Breiman, L. (1996). Bagging predictors. *Machine Learning, 24*, 123-140.

Canvar, W.B., & Trenkle, J.M. (1994). N-gram based text categorization. In *Symposium on Document Analysis and Information Retrieval* (pp. 161-176). Las Vegas, Nevada.

Dumas, S., Platt, J., Heckerman, D., & Sahami, M., (1998). Inductive learning algorithms and representations for text categorization. In *Proceedings of 7th ACM International Conference on Information and Knowledge Management* (pp.148-155). Bethesda, Maryland.

Fall, C.J., Törcsvári, A., Fievét, P., & Karetka, G. (2004). Automated categorization of German-language patent documents. *Expert Systems with Applications, 26*(2), 269-277.

Fattori, M., Pedrazzi, G., & Turra, R. (2003). Text mining applied to patent mapping: A practical business case. *World Patent Information, 25*, 335-342.

Fujii, A., Iwayama, M., & Kando, N. (2006). Test collections for patent retrieval and patent classification in the fifth NTCIR Workshop. In *Proceedings of the 5th International Conference on Language Resources and Evaluation* (pp. 671-674). Tokyo, Japan.

Hooper, R. (2004). *The design and optimization of stemming algorithms*. (Master's thesis). Bailrigg, Lancaster, UK: University of Lancaster, Department of Advanced Computing.

Joachims, T. (1997). *Text categorization with support vector machines: Learning with many relevant features* (Tech. Rep.). Dortmund, Germany: University of Dortmund, Department of Informatics.

Kardkovács, Zs.T., Tikk, D., & Bánsághi, Z. (2005). The Ferrety algorithm for the KDD cup 2005 problem. *Special Interest Group on Knowledge Discovery and Data Mining Explorations Newsletter, 7*(2), 111-116.

Koster, C.H.A., & Seutter, M. (2003). Taming wild phrases. In *Proceedings of the 25th European Conference on Information Retrieval Research* (pp. 161-176).

Lyon, M. (1999). Language related problems in the IPC and search systems using natural language. *World Patent Information, 21*, 89-95.

Manning, C.D., & Schütze, H., (1999). *Foundations of statistical natural language processing*. Cambridge, MA: MIT Press.

Mitchell, T.M. (1996). *Machine learning*. New York: McGraw-Hill.

Paice, C.D. (1996). Method for evaluation of stemming algorithms based on error counting. *Journal of the American Society for Information Science, 47*(8), 632-649.

Porter, M.F. (1980). An algorithm for suffix stripping. *Program, 14*(3), 130-137.

Shen, D., Pan, R., Sun, J.-T., Pan, J.J., Wu, K., Yin, J., et al. (2005). Q2C@UST: Our winning solution to query classification in KDDCUP 2005. *Special Interest Group on Knowledge Discovery and Data Mining Explorations Newsletter, 7*(2), 100-110.

Smith, H. (2002). Automation of patent classification. *World Patent Information, 24*(4), 269-271.

Tomlinson, S. (2004). Finnish, Portugese and Russian Retrieval with hummingbird searchserver at CLEF 2004. In *Working Notes for the CLEF 2004 Workshop*. Bath, United Kingdom.

Trón, V., Németh, L., Halácsy, P., Kornai, A., Gyepesi, G., & Varga D. (2005). Hunmorph: Open source word analysis. In *Proceedings of ACL Workshop on Software at the 43rd Annual Meeting of ACL*.

Weiss, S.M., Apte, C., Damerau, F.J., Johnson, D.E., Oles, F.J., Goetz, T., et al. (1999). Maximizing text-mining performance. *IEEE Intelligent Systems, 14*(4), 2-8.

Yang, Y. (1999). An evaluation of statistical approaches to text categorization. *Information Retrieval, 1*(1-2), 69-90.

Yang, Y., & Liu, X. (1999). A re-examination of text categorization methods. In *Proceedings of SIGIR-99, 22nd ACM International Conference on Research and Development in Information Retrieval*, Berkeley, California (pp. 42-49). New York: ACM Press.

Yang Y., & Pedersen, J.P. (1997). Feature selection in statistical learning of text categorization. In *Proceedings of the 14th International Conference on Machine Learning* (pp. 412-420), Nashville, Tennessee: Morgan Kaufmann.

Yoon, B.-G., & Park, Y.-T., (2004). A text-mining-based patent network: Analytical tool for high-technology trend. *Journal of High Technology Management Research, 15*, 37-50.

ENDNOTES

[1] Courtesy of WIPO, World Intellectual Property Organization, Geneva, Switzerland, 2002

[2] In patent related terminology a document is termed *patent application*.

[3] Classification means taxonomy in patent related terminology

[4] Also called conditional categorization

[5] A good collection of patent processing publications can be found here: http://www.slis.tsukuba.ac.jp/~fujii/pat_proc_pub.html

[6] WIPO-alpha is available at http://www.wipo.int/ibis/datasets/index.html after registration, Espace EP-A and EP-B can be purchased from European Patent Office, see more info at: http://www.european-patent-office.org/patinfopro/cdrom/key/epo/espace_ep.shtml

[7] http://categorizer.tmit.bme.hu/ipc-en-form.php

[8] See the Web page of Cross Language Evaluation Forum (CLEF): http://www.clef-campaign.org/

[9] http://www.cs.unm.edu/kdd_cup_2006

Chapter XIII
Text Mining to Define a Validated Model of Hospital Rankings

Patricia Bintzler Cerrito
University of Louisville, USA

ABSTRACT

The purpose of this chapter is to demonstrate how text mining can be used to reduce the number of levels in a categorical variable to then use the variable in a predictive model. The method works particularly well when several levels of the variable have the same identifier so that they can be combined into a text string of variables. The stemming property of the linked words is used to create clusters of these strings. In this chapter, we validate the technique through kernel density estimation, and we compare this technique to other techniques used to reduce the levels of categorical data.

INTRODUCTION

Nominal data of any type usually require some accommodation before it can be used in comparison studies, particularly if there is a large number of levels in the nominal field. At the same time, nominal data frequently consist of nouns only so that such variables are not normally analyzed using text mining. However, if there is also an identifier field such that multiple items of the nominal field can be linked to one identifier code, then it is possible to use text mining to group and rank clusters of levels in the nominal data field. Once the levels are clustered, an outcome variable can be used to rank the clusters.

The process generally involves the following steps:

1. Transpose the data so that the observational unit is the identifier and all nominal values are defined in the observational unit.

2. Tokenize the nominal data so that each nominal value is defined as one token.

3. Concatenate the nominal tokens into a text string such that there is one text string per identifier. Each text string is a collection of tokens; each token represents a noun.

4. Use text mining to cluster the text strings so that each identifier belongs to one cluster.

5. Use other statistical methods to define a natural ranking in the clusters.

6. Use the clusters defined by text mining in other statistical analyses.

In this chapter, we will demonstrate steps 1-6 to show how nominal data related to patient medical conditions can be used to define a patient severity index needed to model the quality of health care providers. We will first define the problems associated with determining health care provider quality using existing methods (Background into Patient Severity Indices) followed by the application of text mining (Solutions Using Text Analysis). The section, Predictive Modeling with Text Clusters, in this chapter will show how the text clusters defined by text mining can be used in other applications that are relevant to health care.

BACKGROUND INTO PATIENT SEVERITY INDICES

Problems with Terminology Definitions

In many cases, the analysis of a set of data depends almost entirely upon data definitions used during data entry. If entities rely on different definitions and comparisons are made in entity performance, then it is possible to "game" the system to receive a favorable ranking. For example, consider the issue of infant mortality. It seems a relatively simple expression, one with a fairly concrete definition. However, is infancy one year or two? Does infancy begin at birth regardless of the gestational age

of the infant? The definition of the World Health Organization is any death that occurs from the moment of the birth of a living child through the first year of life. It is the definition used in the United States. However, many European nations do not count infants less than 500 grams, or less than 28 weeks gestational age in the infant mortality numbers (Buitendijk & Nijhuis, 2004; Cardlidge & Stewart, 1995; Gourbin & Masuy-Stroobant, 1995; Graafmans, Richardus, Macfarlane, Rebagliato, Blondel, & Verloove-Vanhorick, 2001; Joseph, Allen, Kramer, Cyr, & Fair, 1999). By eliminating infants at highest risk of death, the numbers will look more favorable compared to nations that do count those infants. By using a more stringent definition, the United States ranks lower compared to European nations that do not count similar deaths.

An even more difficult term is that of "health". A recent study published in JAMA indicated that men in the United Kingdom are healthier compared to men in the United States (Banks, Marmot, Oldfield, & Smith, 2006). The definition of "health" was determined to be whatever health factors could be examined using self-report studies that are readily available. For example, the study looked at self-reported rates of cancer and concluded that American men have a higher rate of occurrence, and used that occurrence as an indication of poorer health. However, British men have a higher rate of cancer mortality, which suggests that cancers may not be detected for early treatment. In other words, cancer occurrence must be considered in relationship to cancer screening and early detection. Moreover, the study did not differentiate between types of cancer. British men report a higher rate of smoking and obesity compared to American men. These lifestyle factors were discounted in the authors' conclusions.

In addition, the study reports the results of an HbA_{1c} test as a method for screening for diabetes. This test gives the average blood sugar level over time. However, this test is not the most common screening tool for diabetes, and most men will not be given this test without a previous, positive fasting glucose test first (Appleby, 1997; Ellison, Elliott, & Moyes, 2005; Wiener & Roberts, 1998). Therefore, those men with an HbA_{1c} available are already at high risk for diabetes, so it is not the general population that is being tested. Nevertheless, this study generalizes the results to the population at large. While the HbA_{1c} test is both specific and objective, what is variable is the population of men who are given the test. If the populations in Britain and the United States differ, then different results will not be surprising. It is the difficulty of ranking the severity of a patient's condition that creates problems in ranking the quality of health care providers.

The World Health Organization defines the term *health* as complete physical, mental, and social well-being, which is more inclusive than just the absence of disease. However, the definition is somewhat circular. Just what is physical well-being? Because the definition is so vague, any paper that performs a statistical analysis comparing states of health should clearly define the term and how they are using it to make comparisons.

Modeling the Quality of Healthcare Providers

Most statistical methods, especially linear models, make assumptions concerning the population under study. In particular, there is an assumption as to the uniformity of data entry. That means that different entities must use standard definitions of terms and that the standards are used across all entities for data entry. Therefore, any statistical model used to compare infant mortality across nations will not be valid because the governmental definition of infant mortality changes for the nations supplying numbers, and the data entry is not uniform. However, the lack of validity of the statistical measure does not prevent the measure from being used (Buitendijk & Nijhuis, 2004; Graafmans et al., 2001). It is, of course, much easier to change the definition to improve the ranking of

a nation than it is to actually improve the level of infant mortality. Because most statistical models require the basic assumption of the uniformity of data entry, the fact that uniformity does not exist tends to be overlooked or ignored.

There have been many attempts to rank the quality of health care providers, particularly hospitals. The definition of quality must take into consideration the severity of a patient's condition. Sicker patients will be more at risk for complications and mortality. A hospital that treats a greater proportion of high risk patients will have a lower rate of favorable outcomes compared to a hospital that treats only low risk patients. Without considering patient severity, hospitals might only admit low risk patients to improve quality rankings, while transferring their more severe patients to another provider. The problem is to define what patient severity really means. Providers will have greater incentive to report on patient severity as insurance reimbursements become linked to the defined level of quality (Archer & Macario, 2006).

As an example, Healthgrades.com uses Medicare data available through Medpar reporting (Hospital Report Cards, 2001). The company uses logistic regression to define a predicted value of mortality based upon patient risk factors. There are thousands of possible risk factors; only a small proportion is used in the logistic regression. The primary limitation of the modeling as discussed by Healthgrades.com is that not all hospitals document all possible patient risk factors; hospitals that do not document the risk factors that are used in the logistic regression will be penalized. The hospital ranking is then defined by comparing the predicted mortality rate to the actual mortality rate. There are two ways to improve a hospital's ranking. The first is to lower the actual mortality rate. The second is to increase the predicted mortality rate. The predicted rate can be increased by more documentation of patient risk factors. Other severity indices are defined similarly (Epps, 2004).

A model that can define patient severity without assuming the uniformity of data entry will improve the ability to compare the quality of care across health care providers.

Patient Condition Coding

Patient severity is determined by the patient's entire health status as determined by all patient illnesses, both chronic and acute. The patient condition is defined by a list of ICD9 (ICD10) codes developed by the World Health Organization. The codes are a series of 5-digit numbers with the first 3 digits representing the main condition and the last 2 digits representing specifics of the condition. For example, "401" represents hypertension and "4019" represents unspecified essential hypertension. Similarly, "250" codes diabetes, and 25003 codes Type I diabetes without mention of complications, uncontrolled.

Usually, the codes are manually entered into billing records from information in the patient record. The physician must clearly document the patient's conditions. If the physician treats a patient problem (for example, prescribing insulin) while failing to record specific details of a patient's condition (diabetes or uncontrolled diabetes), then that condition cannot be entered into the billing record. Clearly, then, the definition of a patient's condition can only be as good as the quality of the documentation.

The reason that the assumption of uniform data entry is not valid is that there can easily be differing levels of detail. For example, there are 51 ICD-9 codes related to diabetes. Consider just the following five:

1. 250 Diabetes Mellitus without mention of complications
2. 25000 Type II diabetes mellitus without mention of complications
3. 25001 Type I diabetes mellitus without mention of complications
4. 25002 Type II diabetes mellitus without mention of complications uncontrolled
5. 25003 Type I diabetes mellitus without mention of complications uncontrolled

A physician has sole discretion in documenting "uncontrolled diabetes" with very few guidelines, although one provider has posted a definition to be used for charting patient conditions (Coding & DRG notes: Diabetes mellitus, 2002; Johnson, Gordon, Peterson, Wray, Shroyer, & Grover, 2002).

1. Symptomatic hyperglycemia
2. Fasting blood glucose level above 300 mg/dl
3. Hgb A1-C two times the usual limit of normal
4. Frequent swings between hyperglycemia and hypoglycemia

If a physician is more in the habit of adjusting insulin treatment without documenting "uncontrolled", then one hospital will have fewer patients with a more severe condition than another hospital where the physician continually documents "uncontrolled" after one measurement above 300. Therefore, since uniform data entry depends upon uniform physician documentation, the assumption of the uniformity of that data entry cannot be valid. Also, some providers can document using only the first 3 digits of the ICD9 codes while other providers can detail all 5 digits.

There are thousands of possible ICD9 codes. Since multiple codes can apply to each patient (usually up to a total of 9 or 10), the number of code combinations climbs exponentially. Moreover, different code combinations are more likely to occur than others, so that different codes cannot be considered independent. With these problems, we need to compress the code combinations into a severity ranking of no more than 4-10 levels.

More recently, the use of electronic medical records allows the physician to define a patient's condition through a menu list of check boxes that are more directly related to these ICD9 codes. However, only a small proportion of health care providers are using such a system. In addition, physicians can use these menus differently, so that the lack of uniformity of coding will remain a problem for quite some time.

Compressing Large Numbers of Categorical Variables

There are some simple methods to reduce a complex categorical variable. Probably the easiest is to define a level called "other". All but the most populated levels can be rolled into the "other" level. This method has the advantage of allowing the investigator to define the number of levels, and to immediately reduce the number to a manageable set. For example, in a study of medications for diabetes, there were a total of 358 different medications prescribed. Table 1 gives the most commonly used medications, reduced to a total of 10.

By combining the least-used categories, the total number of levels is reduced from 351 to 11. Using domain knowledge, it is possible to reduce the levels even more. The terms, Novolin, Insulin, and Humulin are all types of insulin, so that these three levels can be combined into one. The levels

Table 1. Most commonly prescribed diabetes medications

Medication	Frequency
Glucophage	3040
Softclix	2526
Novolin	2210
Insulin	2047
Glyburide	1604
Humulin	1452
Glucatrol	1154
Avandia	730
Amaryl	695
Glipizide	606

that were combined into the "other" level are all relatively homogeneous, since every drug in the "other" category is used to treat diabetes.

Another method is called target-based enumeration. In this method, the levels are quantified by using the average of the outcome variable within each level. The level with the smallest outcome is recoded with a 1, the next smallest with a 2, and so on. A modification of this technique is to use the actual outcome average for each level. Levels with identical expected outcomes are merged. This modification is called weight-of-evidence recoding (Smith, Lipkovich, & Ye, 2002).

The weight-of-evidence technique works well when the number of observations per level is sufficiently large to get a stable outcome variable average (Smith et al., 2002). It does not generalize well to fresh data if the number of levels is large and the number of observations per level is small. In addition, there must be one clearly defined target variable since the levels are defined in terms of that target. In a situation where there are multiple targets, the recoding of categories is not stable. In addition, the target variable is assumed to be interval so that the average value has meaning. If there are only two outcome levels (for example, mortality), the weight-of-evidence would be reduced to defining a level by the number of observations in that level with an outcome value of "death".

Consider a selected list of patient conditions with corresponding mortality rates and length of stay. The weight-of-evidence (WOE) compression for the two outcome variables (length of stay (LOS) and mortality) is given in Table 2.

As Table 2 indicates, the weight-of-evidence ranks these levels differently, depending upon the definition of the outcome variable. For example, #41041 is ranked ninth by mortality but fifth by length of stay. The definition of patient severity, then, is not stable.

Neither of these methods is currently used to compress thousands of patient condition codes into a patient severity index. The thousands of patient

Table 2. Selected weight-of-evidence values

Condition Code	Code Label	Number of Patients	Mortality WOE	Mortality WOE Rank	LOS WOE	LOS WOE Rank
4271	Paroxysmal ventricular tachy-cardia	347	1.44	1	5.31	1
41400	Congestive heart failure	209	1.91	2	7.47	2
41401	Coronary atherosclerosis of native coronary artery	8289	2.17	3	7.76	3
4241	Aortic valve disorders	524	4.01	4	9.37	8
41402	Coronary atherosclerosis of autologous biological bypass graft	223	4.48	5	8.96	6
4414	Abdominal aneurysm without mention of rupture	652	4.75	6	8.08	4
41071	Subendocardial infarction	1551	5.22	7	10.06	10
4240	Mitral valve disorders	324	6.17	8	9.99	9
41041	Infarction of other inferior wall	655	7.02	9	8.52	5
41011	Infarction of other anterior wall	503	9.54	10	9.25	7
4280	Congestive heart failure	204	13.73	11	15.56	11

conditions are usually condensed into an index of 4-6 levels, and those levels are used to examine the relationship to different target variables of mortality, length of stay, and cost factors. Because there are multiple targets, weight-of-evidence will not find a unique index. Similarly, some patient conditions that are rarely used can require extraordinary costs and should not be rolled into a general "other" category. An example of this is a patient who requires a heart transplant and one who has a ventricular assist device inserted prior to transplant. There are few such patients, but they are extremely costly.

Standard Model to Define Patient Severity

The standard procedure for examining hospital quality and cost effectiveness has been to use a stepwise logistic regression equation for mortality (or linear regression for cost or length of stay). The model uses the form:

$$y = B_0 + B_1 x_1 + ... + B_k x_k + e$$

where y = dependent variable (variable to be modeled—sometimes called the response variable), $x_1, x_2, ..., x_k$ = independent variable (variable used as a predictor of y), e = random error, and B_i determines the contribution of the independent variable x_i (Iazzoni, 1997; O'Keefe, 1998). The variable y can be continuous (such as length of stay or costs), or discrete (such as mortality). Each x variable denotes the presence or absence of a risk factor for a particular patient. Therefore, y is equal to the sum of the weights B_i for each factor x_i that is positive for that patient. If y is a continuous variable such as length of stay, then the predicted LOS is the linear combination of weights. If y is a discrete variable such as mortality, an optimum threshold value is found, and mortality is predicted if the sum of the weights exceeds that threshold.

To determine a ranking, the value Expected [y (difference)]=Expected [y (predicted)-y(actual)] is computed. If Expected [y(difference)] is positive then the outcome is good; if it is negative then the outcome is poor. The providers are listed by the greatest expected difference. The higher the expected difference, the higher the ranking. The higher a negative expected difference, the lower the ranking.

Although the p-values in the standard regression models tend to be highly statistically significant, the r² (for linear regression) and c-statistic (for logistic regression) tend to be very low. Because the datasets are usually large, the effect size approaches zero, explaining the significant p-values. However, the small effect sizes tend to make the results meaningless with too much of the variability unexplained.

Because there are so many possible risk factors that can be included (the entire set of ICD9 codes), many are initially eliminated because they lack statistical significance in a pairwise comparison. Given a sufficiently large set of patients, almost any factor can become significant. Therefore, a stepwise procedure is used to find the most important significant predictors of risk in the model. Because there are so many possible risk factors to choose from, this procedure can result in many different models, and each commercial organization that has developed a model can use one that has different risk factors compared to other models. However, each of these models will have similar problems with model assumptions.

In order to create the model, an assumption has to be made that patient risk factors are uniformly entered across all providers. If one hospital regularly under-reports on risk factors, then y (predicted) will have fewer weights compared to other hospitals, and will be lower compared to other hospitals. A low predicted y will result in a low ranking. Therefore, the process rewards hospitals that tend to over-report on risk factors (McKee, Coles, & James, 1999).

Once models are created, they should be validated. Validation requires an examination of the model assumptions to determine their reliability. It also requires consistent results when new data are entered. However, consistency will occur if hospitals do not change reporting practices from one year to the next. A model can be validated

by comparing its outcomes to that of another model. However, if both models hold the same faulty assumptions, then neither is valid. In this chapter, a model will be proposed and validated for examining health care quality.

Examining Lack of Uniformity in Data Entry

The issue of patient severity was investigated using one dataset consisting of 14,700+ patient records across 13 different hospitals, and a second dataset consisting of 7000+ records with 8 different hospitals. The datasets were limited to an investigation of patients with heart DRGs (104-110). The datasets were from the years 1998 and 2001 respectively. DRG stands for diagnostic related group, and is the coding used by Medicare for billing purposes. Medicare billing data are available publicly for a charge. The total number of patients by provider for the first dataset is given in Table 3.

A hospital that can successfully shift its patients from the least rank of severity to the highest rank of severity will benefit by the standard logistic regression methods. For example, hospital

Table 3. Number of patients by hospital

Hospital Number	Number of Patients
1	889
2	2745
3	3230
4	946
5	417
6	1143
7	400
8	386
9	2379
10	638
11	478
12	462
13	750

#4 has only 3% of its patients in the lowest severity category, while hospital #7 has 12% there (Table 4). Similarly, hospitals #4, 6, and 12 have approximately 40% of their patients in the most severe risk category. Hospitals #4, 6, and 12 will have high predicted values for length of stay and total charges while hospitals #5 and 13 will have low predicted values. In order for hospitals #5 and 13 to rank high in quality, they will have to have extremely low actual values. The health care providers can improve their rankings by shifting patients into higher risk categories through improved coding.

Hospitals #3, 6, and 11, in particular, will suffer from the use of standard logistic regression methodology. They have a much higher proportion of patients in the first two classes, suggesting that they are not coding patient conditions that are included in the logistic model.

Consider the average length of stay of these patients by class and by hospital using standard methodology (Figure 1). If it is assumed that patients with a higher level of severity will require more provider services and higher cost, the shift to higher severity categories is clearly demonstrated.

The average length of stay is fairly consistent for classes 1-3 with a considerable increase for all but Hospital #2. Hospital #12 has an average length of stay of 13 days with over 40% of patients in Class 4 indicating higher expenses compared to other hospitals. The question is whether hospital #12 has more critical patients, or is able to make them appear to be more critical. Also, hospital #3 has higher charges compared all other hospitals. We would need to examine actual reimbursements to find out whether the charges are reasonable.

It could be that hospital #3 greatly inflates charges in order to increase reimbursements. The charges should be examined in greater detail. Notice that once the charges have been established for Class 1 that the pattern across all hospitals through classes 2-4 are nearly identical (Figure 2).

Another thing to consider as well is that an average value for charges or for length of stay, while susceptible to the influence of outliers, does not reflect the variability of individuals. Ultimately, we would need to consider the entire population distribution of outcomes and to look at confidence intervals instead of just using the averages. This aspect of the study will be exam-

Figure 1. Average length of stay by standard method to define patient severity

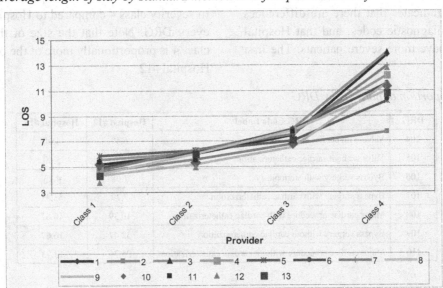

Figure 2. Average total charges by provider and patient severity class

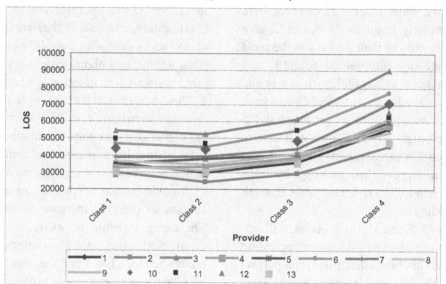

ined in the section entitled Predictive Modeling with Text Clusters.

We consider hospitals #12 and #13 in more detail since they represent extremes. Hospital #12 has the greatest proportion in Class 4; #13 has the least. Table 5 gives the proportion of patients by each of the DRGs 104-110. These are the DRG codes used in 2000 when the data were collected; the codes have subsequently been updated and changed.

Table 5 indicates that there are differences across the diagnostic codes, and that Hospital #12 might have more severe patients. The first two DRG codes, 104 and 105 include heart valve replacement and have higher risk compared to the other procedures. DRG codes 106, 107, and 109 are for standard bypass surgery with and without cardiac catheterization; codes 108 and 110 are for other major cardiac procedures.

Figure 3 compares just 2 of the hospitals, #12 and 13, since they have such different proportions of patients in severity class 4. It indicates that Hospital #12 has a higher proportion of patients in severity class 4 compared to Hospital #13 for every DRG. Note that the size of the box for class 4 is proportionally more of the bar area for Hospital #12.

Table 5. Proportion of patients by DRG

DRG	DRG Code Label	Hospital #12	Hospital #13
104	Valve with cardiac catheterization	6.49	4.00
105	Valve without cardiac catheterization	16.02	5.60
106	Bypass surgery with angioplasty	1.08	4.13
107	Bypass surgery with cardiac catheterization	7.79	53.33
108	Major cardiac procedure with cardiac catheterization	10.39	16.67
109	Bypass surgery without cardiac catheterization	32.47	16.67
110	Major cardiac procedure without cardiac catheterization	25.76	13.73

Figure 3. Comparison of severity class by DRG for hospitals #12 and #13

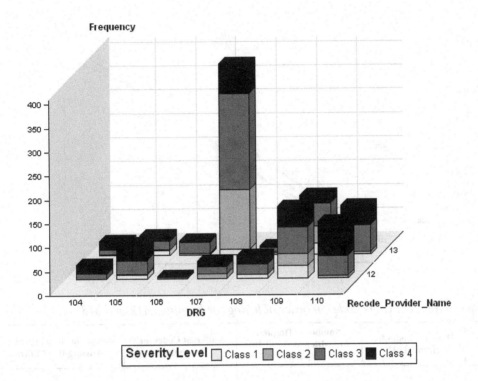

The data allow for a total of nine different ICD9 codes for each patient in order to define the patient's health status. Not all patients have every data column with a code listing; some patients have only one code while others have two or three. Table 6 gives the proportion of patients in each class with a ninth ICD9 code (and correspondingly, codes in the first 8 columns as well), regardless of what the code represents. The table indicates that 60% of patients in class

Table 6. Proportion of patients with a ninth ICD9 code by severity class

Severity Class	Proportion with a Ninth Code
1	1.76
2	6.77
3	24.79
4	60.28

4 have values in all 9 columns for ICD9 codes. The proportion increases to 71% of the patients in class 4 who have an eighth ICD9 code listed (includes all patients with a ninth code), and 86% with a fifth ICD9 code. Therefore, it appears that just being able to document enough patient factors will increase the patient's severity class. It suggests that overdocumenting will benefit the provider by increasing the appearance that it is treating "sicker" patients.

Since Figure 4 shows that there is a difference across hospitals concerning the number of coded ICD9 values that are typically listed, there is an obvious disparity in the level of documentation. The hospital with the highest proportion of patients in class 4 has the lowest drop-off from the ninth code. Other hospitals (#5, 11) with a high proportion of patients in class 4 have a higher proportion of patients with 4-6 ICD9 codes, but then have a higher drop-off at codes 7-9.

Figure 4. Proportion of patients by number code for selected hospitals

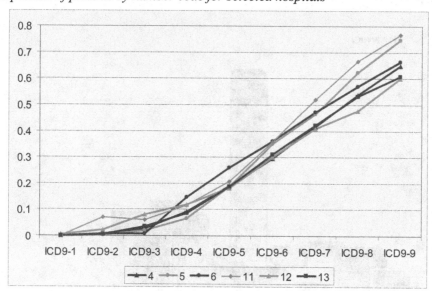

Table 7. Number of different ICD9 codes in order of listing for hospitals #12 and #13

Order of ICD9 Code	Different Codes for Hospital #12	Number in Hospital #12 with Missing ICD9 Entries	Different Codes for Hospital #13	Number in Hospital #13 with Missing ICD9 Entries
1	92	2	55	0
2	137	10	113	4
3	124	37	172	26
4	156	'55	163	65
5	167	84	157	140

Table 7 gives the number of different codes for Hospitals #12 and #13. We list the number of different ICD9 codes in columns 1-5 in order to compare the depth of documentation of the two hospitals. Also, given that Hospital #13 has a total of 750 patients and that there are only two codes with a frequency of more than 50, combining all small codes into an "other" category will lose considerable information.

Initially, Hospital #12 has more variability in their coding; Hospital #13 surpasses it by the ordered third code. The first code is supposed to be the most important factor of the patient's condition. Hospital #12 has 186/462 = 40% with a ninth code listed, hospital #13 has 293/750=39%

with a ninth code, so in that respect, the two hospitals are similar.

SOLUTIONS USING TEXT ANALYSIS

Expectation Maximization Clustering of Patient Condition Codes

For each patient, all ICD codes are combined into one text string using preprocessing techniques. The codes are concatenated into the text string after being transposed if necessary. An example of such a string is "4271 42731 42781 4019 41401

412 2724". This patient suffers from unspecified paroxysmal tachycardia, atrial fibrillation, cardiac dysrhythmia, unspecified essential hypertension, coronary atherosclerosis, old myocardial infarction, and lipoid metabolism disorder. Note the stem of "427" used in the first three patient codes. A second patient has "4271 412 4280 2724 4019 27800" or unspecified paroxysmal tachycardia, old myocardial infarction, congestive heart failure, lipoid metabolism disorder, unspecified essential hypertension, and obesity. These two examples demonstrate that certain ICD9 codes tend to be associated. Because of the manner in which the codes are defined, it becomes possible to examine these defined text strings for patterns using text mining (Fischer, 2000).

We treat the ICD-9 codes as text rather than as levels of a categorical variable. In that way, similarities between codes can be related to similarities in patient conditions, taking full advantage of the stemming properties contained within the codes. It is also possible to translate the ICD9 codes into their corresponding language description. However, it is the experience of the author that the number codes provide better results by reducing the amount of noise in the system.

The basics of text analysis are, according to Martens (2002):

- **Coding** (involves simply determining the basic unit of analysis, and counting how many time each word appears).
- **Categorizing** (involves creating meaningful categories to define the unit of analysis. For example, terms signifying "cooperation" and terms signifying "competition" can be assigned.
- **Classifying** (involves verifying that the units of analysis can be easily and unambiguously assigned to the appropriate categories).
- **Comparing** (involves comparing the categories in terms of numbers of members in each category).

- **Concluding** (involves drawing theoretical conclusions about the content in its context).

These are exactly the same steps that are required for defining a patient severity index. Coding has already been done before the information is acquired for analysis; categorizing is important to convert the text strings of ICD9 codes into a collection of severity clusters. The conclusion is reached by ranking the defined clusters of ICD9 codes to patient outcomes.

The first step in analyzing text data is to define a term by document matrix. Each document forms a row of the matrix; each term forms a column. The resulting matrix will be extremely large, but very sparse with most of the cells containing zeros. The matrix can be compressed using the technique of singular value decomposition with the matrix restricted to a maximum of N dimensions. In our example, the document consists of a text string of ICD9 codes, and each of the codes forms a column.

Singular value decomposition is based upon an assignment of weights to each term in the dataset. Terms that are common and appear frequently, such as *of*, *and*, and *the* are given low or zero weight while terms that appear in only a handful of documents are given a high weight (entropy). Other weighting schemes take into consideration target or outcome variables (information gain, chi-square). In our example, we initially use the standard entropy weighting method so that the most common ICD9 codes (hypertension, disorder of lipid metabolism or high cholesterol) will be given low weights while less common (uncontrolled Type I diabetes with complications) will be given higher weights.

Clustering was performed using the expectation maximization algorithm listed below. It is a relatively new, iterative clustering technique that works well with nominal data in comparison to the K-means and hierarchical methods that are more standard.

$$Z_i^n = \begin{cases} 1 & \text{if pattern } t^n \text{ is generated by expert } i \\ 0 & \text{Otherwise} \end{cases}$$

$$p(t, Z \mid X) = \sum_{i=1}^{m} Z_i \left(g_i(x) \phi_i(t \mid x) \right)$$

$$= \prod \left(g_i(x) \phi_i(t \mid x) \right)^{z_i}$$

with error function

$$E_c = -\sum_n \sum_{i=1}^{m} z_i^n \ln \left(g_i(x^n) \phi_i(t^n \mid x^n) \right)$$

Differences between clusters were then examined using the general linear model and kernel density estimation (Devroye & Gyorfi, 1985; Silverman, 1986). A kernel density provides the entire population distribution without requiring the assumption that the distribution is from a normal population. It can also be thought of as a smoothed histogram. It has a considerable advantage over a histogram in that kernel density curves can be overlaid to compare different subgroups within the population. The estimate is given below:

$$f(x) = \frac{1}{na_n} \sum_{i=1}^{n} K \left(\frac{x - X_i}{a_n} \right)$$

The statistical software (SAS) (SAS Institute, Cary, NC) was used to perform both the preprocessing and the text mining. A total of nine text clusters were identified (Table 8). Once the clusters are defined, it is important to label them. In our example, a domain expert was given the terms in the clusters and asked to provide labels. The defined text clusters created from the ICD9 code text strings are labeled:

- Mild general risk factors
- More severe general risk
- Complications after surgery
- Unrelated risk factors and aortic problems

- IDDM Diabetes with complications
- Moderate risk with specific factors
- Severe risk and severe complication after surgery
- Very severe complications after surgery
- Severe complications after surgery

Table 8 gives the codes and their corresponding medical terminology used to define the cluster labels.

There are only small differences between some of the clusters that can lead to natural groupings. The clusters 2, 4, 6 can be grouped together as can 8, 9. Then 3 and 7 can be grouped leaving 1, 5 to create four categories of risk, A(2,4,6)<B(1,5)<C(3,7)<D(8,9). Once A-D have been identified, an outcome variable can be compared by category to determine whether a natural ranking in outcomes can be discerned. For this, kernel density is used. The overall relationship of rank to outcome is given in Figure 5 for length of stay and Figure 6 for hospital charges.

Note that as the rank increases, the probability that the length of stay goes beyond 9 days is greater. Similarly, the probability that total charges exceed $60,000 increases as the rank increases. In addition, the upper tail of the distribution is relatively large, indicating the presence of many outliers in the population. In fact, it seems more likely that the distribution of costs and length of stay will resemble an exponential or gamma distribution rather than the normal distribution that is usually assumed in linear modeling.

It would seem reasonable that patients at higher risk will stay longer at increased cost. This is not true for standardized rankings (RDRG category) defined via logistic regression that are provided with the original dataset (Figure 7 for length of stay and Figure 8 for average total charges).

In this case, it is more likely that class 2 patients will have lower total charges compared to class 1 patients; moreover, rank 1 patients have almost the same total charges as class 3 patients beyond the $55,000 threshold.

Table 8. Text clusters defined by expectation maximization

Cluster Number	ICD-9 Codes	ICD-9 Risk Factors	Frequency	Label
1	3051, 2724, 4111, 4439, 4019, 4140, 5990, 496	Tobacco abuse, hypergammaglobinemia, intermediate coronary syndrome, unspecified peripheral vascular disease, coronary atherosclerosis, urinary tract infection, other chronic airway obstruction	1682	Mild general risk factors
2	4271, 4139, 9971, 2500, 4019, 5180, 4107, 2724, 2859	Tachycardia, supraventricular paroxysmal, unspecified angina, surgical cardiac complication, uncomplicated diabetes, essential hypertension, pulmonary collapse, acute myocardial infarction, unspecified anemia	3187	More severe general risk
3	5849, 4104, 4280, 4273, 7855, 9975, 3940, 4260, 3051	Acute renal failure, acute myocardial infarction, congestive heart failure, atrial fibrillation, cardiogenic shock, surgical urinary complication, endocarditis, complete atrioventricular shock, tobacco abuse	1139	Complications after surgery
4	5533, 2449, 5308, 4241, 2780, 4412, 4939, 1464, 3000	Diaphogmatic hernia, hypothyroidism, esophageal reflux, endocardium disease, obesity, ruptured aortic aneurysm, asthma, congenital aortic valve insufficiency	1133	Unrelated risk factors and aortic problems
5	25001, 2780, 2766, 5939, 4101, 2768, 7855, 3620, 25050, 25060	IDDM diabetes, obesity, fluid disorder, kidney disease, acute myocardial infarction, unspecified shock, retinopathy, ophthalmic manifestations of diabetes, neurological manifestations of diabetes	1469	IDDM Diabetes with complications
6	7159, 5121, 4139, 2500, 2780, 4140, 4019, 4294, 4111	Osteoarthrosis, iatrogenic pneumothorax, unspecified angina, diabetes, obesity, chronic ischemic heart disease, unspecified hypertension, functional heart disturbance, intermediate coronary syndrome	907	Moderate risk with specific factors
7	5121, 4140, 2768, 2506, 4294, 9981, 4273, 4148, 4278	Iatrogenic pneumothorax, chronic ischemic heart disease, Fluid disorder, neurological manifestations of diabetes, functional heart disturbance, hemorrhage, atrial fibrillation, heart ischemia, cardiac dysrhythmia	4159	Severe risk and severe complication after surgery
8	5180, 5119, 9973, 6826, 4242, 4240, 4239, 9981, 4410	Pulmonary collapse, pleural effusion, respiratory surgical complications, cellulites and abscess, endocardium disease, hemopericardium, hemorrhage, aneurysm and dissection	586	Very severe complications after surgery
9	4448, 4440, 2875, 389, 4442, 5185, 4402, 5601, 486, 9974	Arteriol embolism and thrombosis (aorta abdominal, extremities, other artery), unspecified thrombocytopenia, hearing loss, pulmonary insufficiency following surgery, atherosclerosis, paralytic Ileus, unspecified pneumonia, digestive system complication	1856	Severe complications after surgery

Figure 5. Kernel density estimate for length of stay by defined severity rank

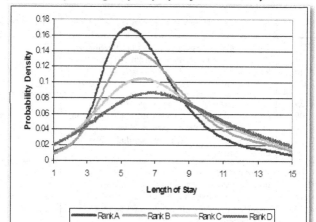

Figure 6. Kernel density estimate for average total charges by defined severity rank

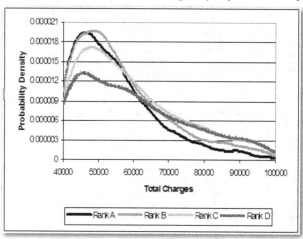

Figure 7. Kernel density estimate for length of stay by standard severity class defined by logistic regression

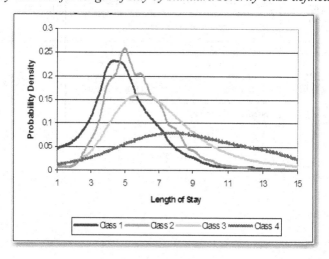

Figure 8. Kernel density estimate for average total charges by standard severity class defined by logistic regression

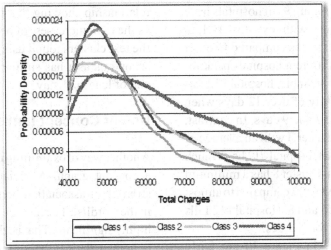

Figure 9. Length of stay by provider and by text cluster

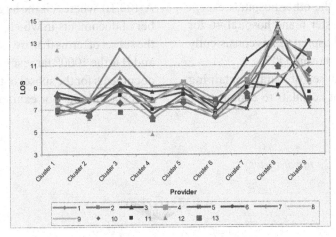

Figure 10. Total charges by provider and text cluster

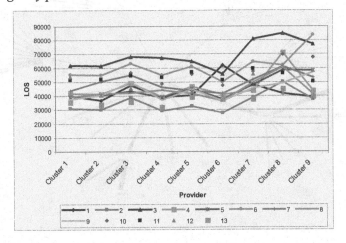

Figures 9 and 10 compare average length of stay and average total charges by cluster and by hospital. As shown in Figure 9, all hospitals have the same general pattern with text clusters 1, 3, 8, and 9 having higher peaks compared to other clusters. In addition, different hospitals peak for different clusters. For example, hospital #12 has an average length of stay of over 12 days when the average is between 7 and 9 days. In contrast, hospital #1 peaks for cluster 3 with an average of over 12 days. In contrast, hospital #12 has a much lower stay for cluster 4. Cluster 8 has a minimum of 8+ days also for hospital #12 compared to almost 16 days for hospitals #5 and 8. Hospital #12 falls roughly in the middle for charges.

While the patterns in Figure 10 are fairly regular, hospital #3 is consistently higher in charges compared to the other hospitals except for hospital #1 for cluster 6 and hospital #6 for cluster 9. In contrast, hospital #2 has consistently lower charges as does hospital #13.

Using the second set of data, containing 7,081 patients in eight hospitals to demonstrate the effectiveness of the text mining process, the four ranks defined through text mining yielded a relationship showing that total charges increase as the rank increases. In other words, by scoring the text clusters found using the first dataset, the second dataset has similar distributions of cost and of length of stay.

Use of Concept Links

Another way of examining the data is to construct a concept graph. Association rules define the strength of association between different terms in the wordlist. The relationship between terms is highly significant. That is, the chi-square statistic is greater than 12. Both terms occur in at least n documents. The default value of n is MAX(4, A/100, B), where A is the largest value of the number of documents in which that term appears for the subset of terms that are used in concept linking and B is the 1000th largest value of the number of documents for the subset of terms that are used in concept linking. For example, for 13,000 docu-

Figure 11. Concept links for diabetes

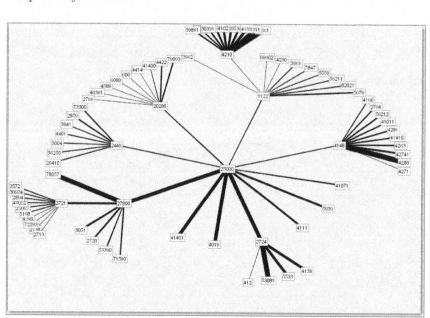

Figure 12. Concept links for nervous system complication

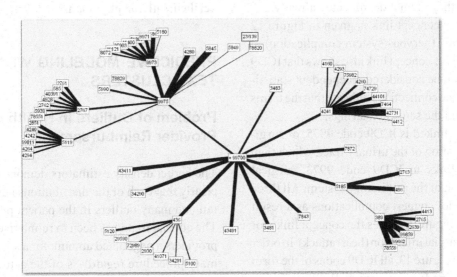

ments, every term in the term set must occur in at least 130 documents. Text Miner in SAS was again used to define the concept links.

Using concept links, we can examine the connections between ICD9 codes to see if the relationships are reasonable. Consider Figure 11 showing the ICD9 codes that are linked to the diabetes code, "25000". Some of the direct links

are for 4111, or intermediate coronary syndrome. Also directly linked are codes for 414 (coronary artery syndrome). The value, 410 is another direct link for acute myocardial infarction. Obesity (2780) is directly linked with hyperclyceridemia (2721, high level of triglycerides) and is indirectly linked to 2720, high cholesterol. These two are both linked to obesity. It suggests that in the pres-

Figure 13. Concept links for heart attack

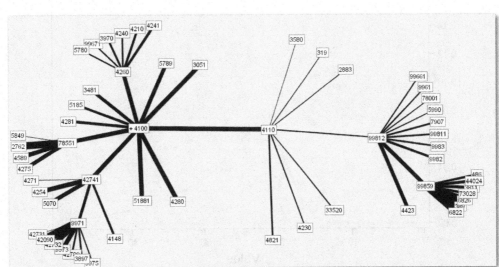

ence of obesity, these two conditions should be checked if they are not documented already.

A similar concept link is given in Figure 12 with "99700" (nervous system complication) at the center. This concept link also shows that ICD9 terms cannot be considered independent statistically since the connections indicate that the terms occur within the same text strings.

Directly linked is ICD9 code 9975, or surgical complication of the urinary tract, which then indirectly links to ICD9 code 9973, surgical complication of the respiratory system. All three of these codes suggest complications as a result of surgery. Figure 3.9 gives the concept links for acute myocardial infarction (heart attack). In order to complete Figure 13, all ICD9 codes of the form 410xx were made equivalent to 41000.

One of the direct connections to acute myocardial infarction is to other acute ischemic heart disease (4110) with indirect connections to surgical complications of 99812 (hemorrhage) and then to 9983 (disruption of operation wound) and 99859 (postoperative infection). If these combinations are not already present in the patient documen-

tation, the documentation should probably be verified with the physician.

PREDICTIVE MODELING WITH TEXT CLUSTERS

Problem of Outliers in Health Care Provider Reimbursements

The kernel density estimators demonstrate very clearly that each of the distributions has a heavy tail and many outliers in the patient population. The current trend has been to reimburse hospital providers a negotiated amount for a specific, primary procedure regardless of the actual cost of the treatment and care. As a result, the provider will not be reimbursed for those patients who require extraordinary treatment and extra days in the hospital (Pine, 2001).

There is considerable concern that the practice of reimbursing hospitals by diagnosis code requires the providers to operate at a loss. There is also concern that some health care providers can

Figure 14. Length of stay comparing outlier patients to non-outlier patients

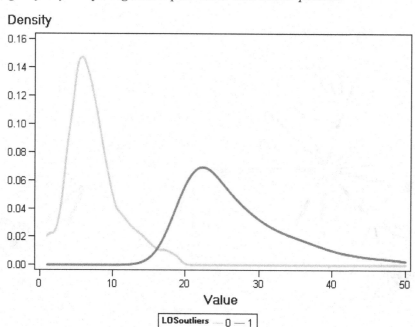

"game" the system through a routine practice of cost-shifting (London, Rosengart, Jurkovich, & Nathens, 2006; Taheri, Butz, & Greenfield, 1999). In addition, while patient severity and cost can increase substantially, payer reimbursements do not increase at a similar rate (Rutledge, Shaffer, & Ridky, 1996). Therefore, new reimbursement models are under consideration (Neumann, Rosen, & Weinstein, 2005). There is also the issue of treating the outlier patients differently in reimbursements(Bodenheimer & Fernandez, 2005; McCanne, 2003; Thurkettle & Noji, 2003; Weintraub & Shine, 2004).

The distribution of length of stay overall is given in Figure 14, comparing the results for patients who are outliers vs. non-outliers. Note that the distribution is exponential rather than normal. If providers are paid based on average cost under an assumption that costs are normally distributed when they are actually exponential, the providers will suffer a loss of revenue because of the higher cost of outliers (which only occur on one side of the cost distribution). In other words, a normal distribution assumes that the level of loss

for high cost patients will be approximately equal to the gain for lower cost patients. However, in an exponential distribution, there is almost no gain because the average is very close to the minimum cost for any one patient; that gain can not offset the loss caused by high cost patients.

The average length of stay for the non-outlier patients is approximately 22 days compared to an average length of stay of 8 days for the non-outlier patients. If the payer (government or private insurance) only pays a set amount based upon an average stay, then the hospital has to make up the difference. A hospital that has more critical patients with a high risk of becoming an outlier will lose money. How much money they lose is somewhat demonstrated in Figure 15.

The average charges for the non-outlier patients is approximately $40,000 with the average for the outlier patients at $100,000. The overall average is skewed when including outliers, increasing to 8.53 days and $49,582 for charges; these averages are nowhere near the cost of the outlier patients. Therefore, there is a need to be able to predict which patients become outliers in order to ad-

Figure 15. Total charges comparing outlier patients to non-outlier patients

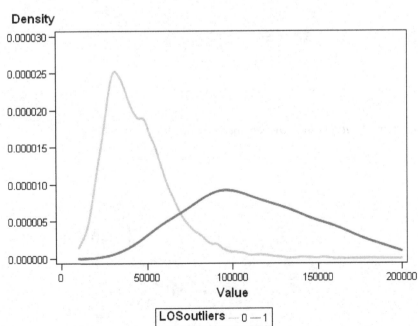

equately pay for their care. Using the standard logistic regression with the standard classes 1-4 of patient severity, the accuracy level is 83% with a c-statistic of 0.837. However, because the outliers represent only 5% of the population, the predictability is poor. In order to get a better result, the outlier patients need to be over-sampled. In addition, we are interested in the actual accuracy of prediction.

Predictive Modeling Using Text Clusters for Outlier Reimbursements

One of the extensions of using text mining to define patient severity is the ability to use the values in predictive modeling to determine the likelihood that the patient will require extraordinary care, giving health care providers the ability to negotiate for a rate based on patient needs rather than on specific treatment codes. Different target variables are used to examine the existence of outliers; the first target is the length of stay. An outlier patient is defined as one with length of stay beyond three standard deviations of the mean. The proportion of outliers by class (and rank) is given in Figures 5-8. With the standard severity class defined by logistic regression, there is consistency, and only a small proportion of outliers in Classes 1-3 (Figures 16-17). However, class 4 has a considerable proportion of outliers, almost 30% for Hospital #3.

However, we first modify our text clusters by changing the weight to mutual gain, which uses the target value of patient outlier to modify the clusters. Table 9 gives the revised clusters. The use of the target results in clustering based upon the more severe patient conditions.

Figure 16. Proportion of outliers by provider and standard patient severity index

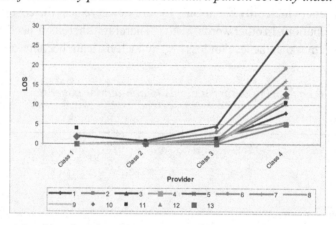

Figure 17. Proportion of outliers by provider and text cluster

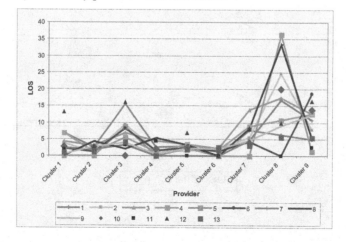

Table 9. Revised text clusters defined by expectation maximization and mutual information gain

Cluster Number	ICD-9 Codes	ICD-9 Risk Factors	Frequency	Label
1	2875, 4260, 4160, 2761, 4101, 3970, 4140, 3989, 7803	Hearing loss, congestive heart failure, pulmonary hypertension, hyperosmolality, acute myocardial infarction, tricuspid valve disease, atherosclerosis, unspecified rheumatic heart disease, convulsions	1711	Severe
2	5185, 4260, 5939, 4241, 4107, 4101, 4039, 4148, 5308	Paralytic Ileus, congestive heart failure, kidney disease, endocardium disease, pulmonary collapse, acute myocardial infection, unspecified hypertensive renal disease, heart ischemia, Nodular lymphoma	1352	Severe
3	5188, 5185, 7855, 488, 389, 9985, 5991, 5849, 2762	Hypertension, Surgical urinary complication, Pneumonia, Pulmonary insufficiency, Hypostatic pneumonia, Urinary tract infection, acute renal failure, fluid disorder	1816	Moderate
4	5070, 4274, 9981, 2765, 4210, 4254, 4275, 9971, 2768	Aspiration pneumonia, Atrial fibrillation, Respiratory conditions, Fluid disorder, Bacterial endocarditis, Endocardium disease, Unspecified angina, Kidney disease	828	Severe
5	9970, 5601, 4349, 9983, 9974, 9981, 436, 78820, 9973	Surgical urinary complication, Paralytic Ileus, Cerebral artery occlusion, Hemorrhage, Acute, ill-defined cerebrovascular disease, Urine retention	1092	Severe
6	2780, 2720, 2449, 3051, 4111, 2724, 5308, 2500, 7159	Obesity, Acute myocardial infarction, Hypothyroidism, Tobacco abuse, Intermediate coronary syndrome, Esophageal reflux, diabetes, Osteoarthrosis	6141	Moderate
7	9970, 5185, 4280, 389, 9981, 2762, 5849, 9975, 5188	Nervous system complication, Atherosclerosis, Cardiogenic shock, Pulmonary insufficiency, Hemorrhage, Fluid disorder, Acute renal failure, Pneumonitis due to Other Solids and Liquids, Hypertension	1351	Severe
8	7855, 4101, 4104, 4103, 4274, 4275, 4589, 4260, 4100	Endocardium disease, Chronic ischemic heart disease, Primary cardiomyopathy, Tachycardia, Congestive heart failure, Tricuspid valve disease, Old myocardial infarction, Atrial fibrillation	289	Mild
9	4240, 4148, 4254, 4271, 4280, 3970, 412, 4273, 5849	Cardiogenic shock, Acute myocardial infarction, Ventricular Fibrillation, Cardiac arrest, Hypotension	1538	Severe

Figure 18. Kernel density estimation for total charges

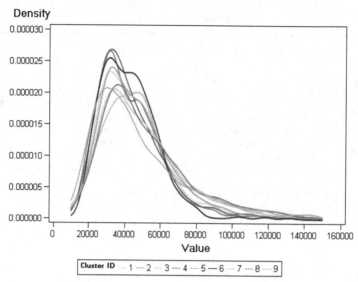

Figure 19. Kernel density estimation for length of stay

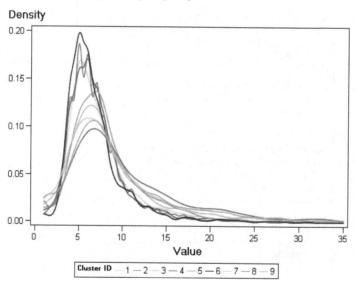

To see if these newly defined text clusters have a natural ranking in terms of patient severity, kernel density estimation was performed for both length of stay and charges for all nine clusters (Figures 18-19). Figure 18 clearly shows this hierarchy, with clusters 4 and 6 having the lowest charges and clusters 8 and 9 having the highest charges. Note that the curves have decreasing heights and areas around the $40,000 mark indicating a peak at lower cost with a crossover starting at about the $70,000 value with the curves reversed for the outlier costs.

The hierarchy is even more pronounced for length of stay, with clusters 2 and 6 having the highest probability of a shorter stay (at the value 5). Cluster 8 has the highest probability of a length

Figure 20. ROC curve comparing predictive models

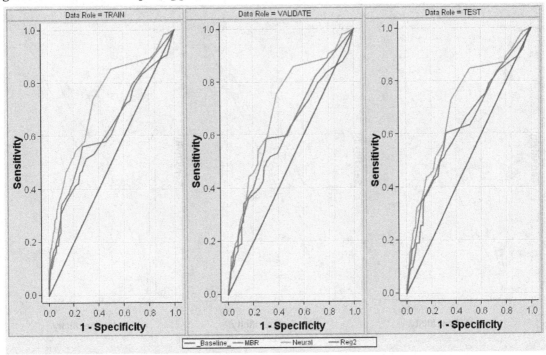

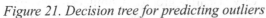

Figure 21. Decision tree for predicting outliers

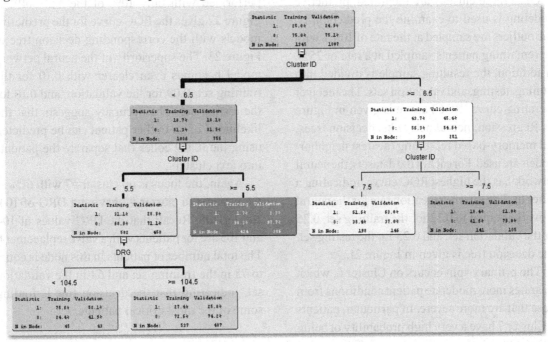

Figure 22. ROC curves for predict models using 10% of the non-outliers

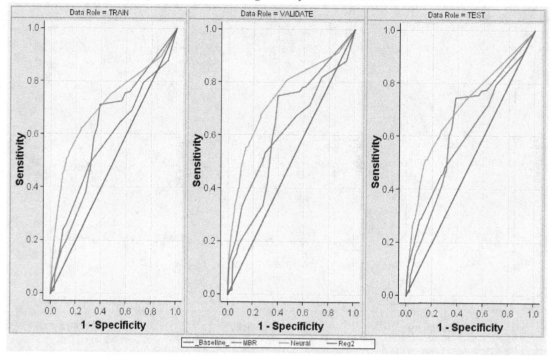

of stay exceeding 15 days. Again, clusters 8 and 9 have the lowest probability of a short length of stay.

Once these clusters are identified, predictive modeling is used to examine the predictability. The outliers are sampled at the rate of 100% with the remaining patients sampled at a rate of 25%. In addition, the resulting sample is divided into training, testing, and validation sets. The receiver operating curve (ROC) curve is given in Figure 20. Regression, neural networks, decision trees, and memory-based reasoning (nearest neighbor) models are used. For each of the datasets, the neural network has the highest ROC curve, indicating a better fit. The misclassification rate for the neural network is equal to 0.22 for the training set, 0.25 for the validation set, and 0.23 for the testing set. The decision tree is given in Figure 21.

The primary split occurs on Cluster 6, which separates more moderate patient conditions from those that are more severe. In particular, patients in Cluster 7 have a very high probability of being in the outlier group as do patients in Clusters 1-4 who require valve surgery.

Since the outliers represented only 5% of the dataset, using 25% of the non-outliers still results in very disparate groups. A similar analysis was performed with only 10% of the non-outliers. Figure 22 gives the ROC curve for the predictive models with the corresponding decision tree in Figure 23. The superiority of the neural network model becomes even clearer with 0.10 for the training set, 0.09 for the validation, and 0.10 for the testing set. The accuracy suggests that the likelihood of an outlier patient can be predicted using the ICD9 codes that separate the patients into text clusters.

Again, the focus is on cluster #7 with 61% of the patients in cluster #7 having a DRG of 104, 105, or 106. Recall that the DRG values of 104 and 105 are for patients with a valve replacement. The total number of patients in this node is equal to 75 in the training set and 64 in the validation set, indicating that the decision tree is finding some of the most critical patients.

Figure 23. Decision tree for modified data sample

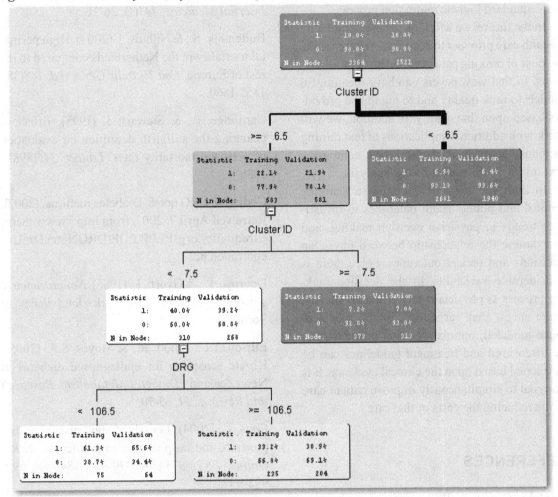

FUTURE RESEARCH DIRECTIONS

It is possible to develop a model to rank the quality of care so that the model does not assume uniformity of data entry. The model can also be validated by the examination of additional data. The means of developing the model is to use the stemming properties of the ICD9 codes where the first three digits of the code represent the primary category while the remaining two digits represent a refinement of the diagnosis. The model compares well to those developed through the standard logistic regression technique.

Hospitals that rank low should compare their coding using text analysis to determine where the coding can be improved by shifting ranks from low to high. Text analysis provides means for hospitals to examine their own coding practices. It also allows us to define a patient severity grouping without relying on patient outcomes; then, we can use outcomes to validate the grouping and to use the grouping in predictive modeling to define hospital quality.

The use of text analysis also allows us to predict outliers in the patient population so that their care can be adequately compensated. The use of text clusters makes it easier to extract the outliers for prediction purposes compared to the more standard logistic regression process.

In the future, we will look to collaborate with a health care provider to develop software for the purpose of ranking patients upon hospital admissions. In that way, payers can have meaningful models to rank quality and to reimburse providers based upon that quality. In addition, we will work with additional applications of text mining to reduce levels in categorical data, combining text mining with market basket analysis.

In addition, we will continue to examine clinical and public health databases to investigate trends in physician decision making, and to examine the relationship between physician decisions and patient outcomes. Since there is considerable variability in the decision making process as physicians rely primarily on past experiences, that variability can be modeled. Once modeled, optimal decision pathways can be discovered and treatment guidelines can be developed based upon the clinical evidence. It is our goal to simultaneously improve patient care while reducing the costs of that care.

REFERENCES

Appleby, C. (1997). Will plans follow the new diabetes screening guidelines? Managed Care. Retrieved April 7, 2007, from http://www.man-agedcaremag.com/archives/9712/9712.diabetes.shtml

Archer, T., & Macario, A. (2006). The drive for operating room efficiency will increase quality of care. *Current Opinion in Anaesthesiology, 19*(2), 171-176.

Banks, J., Marmot, M., Oldfield, Z., & Smith, J.P. (2006). Disease and disadvantage in the United States and England. *JAMA, 295*(17), 2037-2045.

Bodenheimer, T., & Fernandez, A. (2005). High and rising health care costs. Part 4: Can costs be controlled while preserving quality? *Annals of Internal Medicine, 143*(1), 26-31.

Buitendijk, S., & Nijhuis, J. (2004). High perinatal mortality in the Netherlands compared to the rest of Europe. *Ned Tijdschr Geneeskd, 148*(38), 1855-1860.

Cardlidge, P., & Stewart, J. (1995). Effect of changing the stillbirth definition on evaluation of perinatal mortality rates. *Lancet, 346*(8981), 1038.

Coding & DRG notes: Diabetes mellitus. (2002). Retrieved April 7, 2007, from http://www.medi-carequality.org/PEPP/PDF/DRGNotesDmUn-controlled.pdf

Devroye, L., & Gyorfi, L. (1985). *Nonparametric density estimation.* New York: John Wiley & Sons.

Ellison, T.L., Elliott, R., & Moyes, S.A. (2005). HbA1c screening for undiagnosed diabetes in New Zealand. *Diabetes/Metabolism Research and Reviews, 21*, 65-70.

Epps, C. (2004). Length of stay, discharge disposition, and hospital charge predictors. *APRN Online, 79*(5), 975-976, 979-981, 984-988, 990, 992-997.

Fischer, W. (2000). A comparison of PCS construction principles of the American DRGs, the Austrial LDF system, and the German FP/S E system. *Casemix, 2*(1), 12-20.

Gourbin, G., & Masuy-Stroobant, G. (1995). Registration of vital data: Are live births and stillbirths comparable all over Europe? *Bulletin of the World Health Organization, 73*(4), 449-460.

Graafmans, W., Richardus, J., Macfarlane, A., Rebagliato, H., Blondel, B., & Verloove-Van-horick, S., et al. (2001). Comparability of published perinatal mortality rates in Western Europe: The quantitative impact of differences in gestational age and birthweight criteria. *International*

Journal of Obstetrics & Gynaecology, 108(12), 1237-1245.

Hospital Report Cards Methodology. (2001). Healthgrades.com. Retrieved April 7, 2007, from http://www.healthgrades.com/public/index.cfm?fuseaction=mod&modtype=content&modact=Hrc_Methodology

Iazzoni, L. (1997). *Risk adjustment for measuring health care outcomes* (2nd ed.). Chicago: Healthcare Administration Press.

Johnson, M.L., Gordon, H.S., Peterson, N.J., Wray, N.P., Shroyer, L.A., Grover, F.L., et al. (2002). Effect of definition of mortality on hospital profiles. *Medical Care, 40*(1), 7-16.

Joseph, K., Allen, A., Kramer, M., Cyr, M., & Fair, M. (1999). Changes in the registration of stillbirths<500 g in Canada, 1985-1995. Fetal-infant mortality study group of the Canadian perinatal surveillance system. *Paediatric Perinatal Epidemiology, 13*(3), 278-287.

London, J.A., Rosengart, M.R., Jurkovich, G.J., & Nathens, A.B. (2006). Prospective payments in a regional trauma center: The case for recognition of the transfer patient in diagnostic related groups. *Injury Infection & Critical Care, 60*(2), 390-5.

Martens, B.V. d.V. (2002). IST 501: Research techniques for information management. Retrieved April 7, 2007, from http://web.syr.edu/~bvmarten/index.html

McCanne, D. (2003). Why incremental reforms will not solve the health care crisis. *Journal of the American Board of Family Medicine, 16*, 257-261.

McKee, M., Coles, M., & James, P. (1999). Failure to rescue as a measure of quality of hospital care: The limitations of secondary diagnosis coding in English hospital data. *Journal of Public Health Medicine, 21*(4), 453-458.

Neumann, P.J., Rosen, A.B., & Weinstein, M. (2005). Medicare and cost-effectiveness analysis. *The New England Journal of Medicine, 353*(14), 1516-1522.

O'Keefe, K. (1998). Accounting for severity of illness in acutely hospitalized patients: A framework for clinical decision support using DYNAMO. General Electric Medical Systems. Retrieved April 7, 2007, from http://www.gemedicalsystems.com/inen/prod_sol/hcare/resources/library/article07.html

Pine, M. (2001). Episodes in action: Linking the cost and quality of nonsurgical coronary revascularization. *Managed Care Quarterly, 9*(3), 25-33.

Rutledge, R., Shaffer, V.D., & Ridky, J. (1996). Trauma care reimbursement in rural hospitals: Implications for triage and trauma system design. *The Journal of Trauma, 40*(6), 1002-1008.

Silverman, B. (1986). *Density estimation for statistics and data analysis*. Boca Raton, FL: CRC Press.

Smith, E.P., Lipkovich, I., & Ye, K. (2002). *Weight of evidence (WOE): Quantitative estimation of probability of impact*. Blacksburg, VA: Virginia Tech, Department of Statistics.

Taheri, P., Butz, D.A., & Greenfield, L.J. (1999). Paying a premium: How patient complexity affects costs and profit margins. *Annals of Surgery, 229*(6), 807.

Thurkettle, M.A., & Noji, A. (2003). Shifting the healthcare paradigm: The case manager's opportunity and responsibility. *Case Management, 8*(4), 160-165.

Weintraub, W.S., & Shine, K. (2004). Is a paradigm shift in US healthcare reimbursement inevitable? *Circulation, 109*(12), 1448-1455.

Wiener, K., & Roberts, N. (1998). The relative merits of haemoglobin A1c and fasting plasma glucose as first-line diagnostic tests for diabetes mellitus in non-pregnant subjects. *Diabetic Medicine, 15*(7), 558-563.

Additional Reading

Text and Data Mining

Costa, R., & Kristbergsson, K. (2007). Predictive modeling and risk assessment. *Integrating safety and environmental knowledge into food studies towards European sustainable development.* Berlin: Springer.

Feldman, R., & Sanger, J. (2006). *The text mining handbook: Advanced approaches in analyzing unstructured data.* Cambridge: Cambridge University Press.

SanJuan, E., & SanJuan, F.I. (2006) *Text mining without document context.* Atlanta, GA: Elsevier, Ltd.

Weiss, S., Indurkhya, N., & Zhang, T. (2007). *Text mining: Predictive methods for analyzing unstructured information.* Berlin:Springer.

Definition of Health Care Quality

Diugacz, Y.D. (2006). *Measuring health care: Using quality data for operational, financial, and clinical improvement.* San Francisco: Jossey-Bass.

Kerr, E.A. (2000). *Quality of care for cardio-pulmonary conditions: A review of the literature and quality indicators.* Santa Monica, CA: Rand Corporation.

Pearson, M. (1997). *An implicit review method for measuring the quality of in-hospital nursing care of elderly congestive heart failure patients.* Santa Monica, CA: Rand Corporation.

Chapter XIV
An Interpretation Process for Clustering Analysis Based on the Ontology of Language

Wagner Francisco Castilho
Federal University of Rio Grande do Sul (UFRGS), Brazil
Federal Savings Bank (CEF), Brazil

Gentil José de Lucena Filho
Catholic University of Brasília, Brazil

Hércules Antonio do Prado
Catholic University of Brasilia, Brazil
Embrapa Food Technology, Brazil

Edilson Ferneda
Catholic University of Brasilia, Brazil

ABSTRACT

Clustering analysis (CA) techniques consist of, given a set of objects, estimating dense regions of points separated by sparse regions, according to the dimensions that describe these objects. Independently from the data nature, structured or nonstructured, we look for homogenous clouds of points that define clusters from which we want to extract some meaning. In other words, when doing CA, the analyst is searching for underlying structures in a multidimensional space for what one could assign some meaning. To carry a CA application, two main activities are involved: generating clusters configurations by means of an algorithm and interpreting these configurations in order to approximate a solution that could contribute with the CA application objective. Generating a clusters configuration is typically a computational task, while the interpretation task brings a strong burden of subjectivity. Many approaches are presented in the literature for generating clusters configuration. Unfortunately, the interpretation task has not received so much attention, possibly due to the difficulty in modeling something that is subjective in nature. In this chapter a method to guide the interpretation of a clusters configuration is proposed. The inherent subjectivity is approached directly by describing the process with the apparatus of the Ontology of Language. The main contribution of this chapter is to provide a sound conceptual basis to guide the analyst in extracting meaning from the patterns found in a set of data, no matter whether we are talking about data bases, a set of free texts, or a set of Web pages.

INTRODUCTION

According to Fayyad, Piatetsky-Shapiro, and Smyth (1996), knowledge discovery in databases (KDD) is "the non-trivial process of identifying valid, new, potentially useful and ultimately understandable patterns in data." In other words, KDD refers to the general process of discovering useful knowledge from data. Each stage of the KDD process is complex and involves decisions by analysts and specialists in that domain. The analysts' previous knowledge heavily influences the KDD process, which involves a series of decisions at each stage, including interpretation and evaluation of results. These decisions are also influenced by the database used, the domain, and the anticipated use of the acquired knowledge. The analysts' decisions also involve preexisting knowledge structures associated with their experience and knowledge of the domains and database.

All processes of knowledge generation taken from data and information cannot ignore the very phenomenon of interpretation done by human beings that correspond to the result of assessments made by a group of individuals associated with the process. KDD cannot disregard the effect of previous knowledge that permeates the entire process within the perspective of those involved.

Besides the assessments and decisions taken by those involved in the KDD process, it is of special importance to consider the manner these people communicate in the elaboration of these assessments and interpretations and how they coordinate themselves in making decisions and executing actions and procedures. This has a decisive influence on the planning cycle, execution, and evaluation of the results from knowledge creation process.

Regarding the interpretations and communication involved in the knowledge creation process, there are interesting contributions developed based on the philosophy of a language model known as the ontology of language.

This chapter presents the contributions that ontology of language can offer to an interpretation model of KDD results, specifically in clustering analysis (CA). To this end, some fundamentals of the Ontology of Language will be presented in the next section. Later, the CA model will be discussed, taking into consideration the decision making process and the knowledge creation from clusters, its stages and the action coordination cycle, and the methodology of result interpretation in CA. It is also discusses the challenge to aggregate more semantics to the CA process, specifically the influence of previous knowledge and the communication phenomenon that permeates the knowledge creation process.

Usually, KDD refers to databases organized in relational structures. For the sake of simplicity and considering that, for our aim, it does not matter if the data are structured or not, we consider in this chapter a broader definition of KDD that includes the knowledge discovery from nonstructured data, including free texts and Web pages. By doing so, we are emphasizing the generality of our method without losing a clear comprehension of the interpretation task.

ONTOLOGY OF LANGUAGE

Within classical philosophy, ontology is the branch of metaphysics dedicated to the study of being while. Metaphysics, according to Aristotle, means *beyond the physical,* or rather, beyond what we can perceive with our senses.

Echeverría (1997, pp. 27-28, 37-45) uses a new, nonmetaphysical perspective of the term ontology to support his use based on the tradition established by the German philosopher Martin Heidegger. In this tradition, ontology encompasses the idea he denominates as *dasein,* which refers to the particular way of existing as human beings. So, ontology refers to the generic comprehension or the interpretation of what it means to be human. This comprehension is the cornerstone of all that is done. As a primary interpretation, this precedes any other postulate about being anything else.

Thus, ontology refers to the interpretation made from the constituent dimensions that are shared by human beings and that offer them a particular way of being. It is a postmodern metaphysics perspective (Echeverría, 1997, p. 28).

The main presuppositions of Ontology of Language, according to Echeverría (1997, pp. 31-37), can be summarized as follows:

1.   Human beings are linguistic beings. Therefore, it is language that makes humans be the particular way they are.
2.   Language possesses a creative character. It does not only describes but also creates realities. Language is, therefore, action, shaping the future, the identity, and the world which we live in.
3.   Humans construct themselves in the dynamics of language. The human being is not, therefore, a determined and permanent form of being: it is a space of possibilities that creates and recreates itself by means of language.

Talking about the organizations, Echeverría (1997, pp. 259-260) and Flores (1989, p. 14; 1996, p. 79) propounded the following ideas which define the role of conversations in the structure of organizations, not only to social microcosms, but also to families and teams and large corporations:

*   Organizations are linguistic phenomenon, developed from specific conversations which are based on the capacity of human beings to make mutual agreements when they communicate amongst themselves.
*   An organization is a dynamic web of conversations. As such, it generates an identity in the world that transcends its individual members.
*   Everything in an organization can be understood and improved based on conversations.

Its directors, managers, and collaborators are conversational agents, where the management of the organization is a conversational game.

KDD, including the CA process, have been increasingly adopted in the organizational context, making the ontological approach to language a relevant alternative to improve dialog, not only in the interpretation of results, but in any other process.

The assessments and decisions of the people involved in the process and the way they communicate in the creation of these assessments and how they coordinate themselves to make decisions, execute actions and procedures, is a decisive influence in the planning cycle, execution and evaluation of the CA results. So, an important contribution of the ontology of language is in remembering that interpretation is generated by one observer and that discovered knowledge cannot exist independently from this observer. This is one of the first aspects that will be studied: the observer, his mental models, his previous knowledge, and his influence on the entire process of the creation of knowledge.

THE KNOWLEDGE BASED ON THE OBSERVER

According to Maturana and Varela (1992), as cited by Kofman (2002, vol. I, p. 31), "everything said is said by someone," which highlights that it is an illusion to try to present an object independently from the subject.

Kofman (2002, vol. I, p. 47), alluding to Kant's critique of reason and his theory of knowledge, recognizes that this conception of knowledge in the perspective of the observer is not new and that observation is conditioned by the "previous knowledge" of the observer. "Over 200 years ago, Kant proved without a doubt that what we call *objective perception* is conditioned by our cognitive categories."

We can, therefore, consider, paraphrasing Maturana, as cited by Kofman (2002, vol. I, p. 31), that if "everything said is said by someone," then everything known is known by someone, emphasizing the role of the observer in the process of the conception of knowledge.

The conception of knowledge as an absolute truth, an objective and independent reflection from reality, is displaced, therefore, to a relativistic conception of knowledge depending on the observer.

Echeverría (1997, p. 40) said that "it is not possible to know how things are, but only how we observe and interpret them, since we live in interpretative worlds." Later, he associates the origin of knowledge to the process of making interpretations by the observer.

Knowledge is always an assessment made by a particular observer when observing determined behaviors. If knowledge resides anywhere, it is in the assessment that an observer makes as behaviors are observed. However, knowledge arises precisely as a means to qualify (judge) the observed behavior. (Echeverría, 1997, p. 51)

In the same way, Davenport and Prusak (1998) define knowledge and highlight its origin and application in the mind of those who know:

Knowledge is a fluid mixture of condensed experience, values, contextual information and experienced insight, which provides a structure for evaluation and incorporation of new experiences and information. It has its origin and is applied in the mind of those who know. In organizations, it is usually contained not only in documents or repositories, but also in organizational routines, processes, practices and principles. Knowledge may be defined as the most valuable information—the raw material essential to any organization—and because it moves so rapidly, without respecting physical limits, it is very difficult to manage. However, it is a strategic tool for organizational

survival and growth, which allows competition and guarantees the survival of the organization. (Davenport & Prusak, 1998, p. 6)

Any transformation of information into knowledge cannot be done without human intervention expressed by an interpretation that is the product of certain observers.

Nonaka and Takeuchi (1995) advocate that an organization depends strictly on individuals to create knowledge. An organization cannot create knowledge without individuals." In the same way, a discussion on KDD and CA avoid to approach the knowledge that permeates the entire process under the perspective of the people involved. Bearing this in mind, a study will be developed regarding the influence of previous knowledge and mental models on the process of knowledge generation.

MENTAL MODELS AND GENERATION OF KNOWLEDGE

Mental Models and Previous Knowledge

According to Hanson (1990), an analyst's previous knowledge influences the CA process, which involves a series of complex decisions, among which the following are noted: definition of the objects to be analyzed, selection of relevant and discriminant variables in the area studied, definition of the number of groups, selection of the clustering algorithm or technique, standardization of variables, decision regarding how satisfactory the clustering achieved is. The analyst's decisions take into consideration, therefore, pre-existing knowledge structures.

Although, in the clustering process, the structure of the groups cannot be determined *a priori,* the KDD analyst can have a certain quota of previous knowledge in relation to the desirable and undesirable characteristics for a clustering plan.

He has enough previous knowledge to choose an acceptable clustering structure among the different means of segmenting a population. What makes this practice not feasible, even with the high computational power available, is the vast number of alternative groups that would have to be evaluated to find the optimal solution.

On the other hand, in a general sense, there is, in the analysis of any phenomenon, some undeniable dependency on the mechanism of its interpretation in relation to the personal history of the subject, his beliefs, values, and knowledge.

Senge (1990, 1994) named this previous knowledge as *mental models* which are characterized, among other things, as being strongly rooted assumptions, pictures, figures, images or a narrative that influence our lives and our behavior.

This mental context is, thus, a complex of experiences, knowledge, rules of rationale, inferences, among others, which influence the interpretation made in any situation where the mind is challenged to assess and act in the most

diverse situations. Kofman (2002, vol. I, p. 250) said that these mental models also operate in a subconscious way, permeating all dimensions of the person's life, being responsible for the synthesis of understanding.

Mental models, therefore, condition all of a person's interpretations and actions, including in the technical, professional and scientific realms. From this comes the importance of studying them and being conscious of their influence. Next, a learning model will be presented that considers the influence of the mental model. This scheme will then be applied to a decision making model and the creation of knowledge in CA in the section entitled Clustering Analysis Model.

Mental Models and Learning

Figure 1 presents a learning model with a simple, double, and triple loop, drawn by Kofman (2002, vol. I, p. 316). The drawing has as its starting point the environment, which is interpreted by each

Figure 1. Learning model (Adapted from Kofman, 2002, vol. I, p. 316)

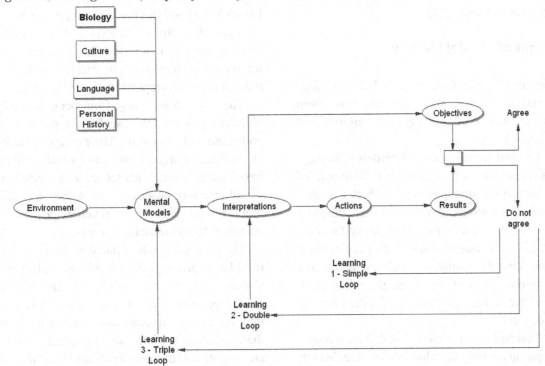

person's mental model, composed of its constitutive biological, cultural, linguistic, and personal factors. When something relevant draws our attention from the environment, a representation of it is created based on the mental model.

An array of possible actions is seen from the evaluation of a situation. Results are anticipated and the one that will most probably generate the desired results is chosen. If the achieved results coincide with the established objectives, the individual does not need to modify his action. If, on the other hand, the results do not match the objectives, the person is impelled to change.

This change is characterized by learning based on experience, which can assume three learning levels or loops. Simple loop learning is a *feedback* process, in which only the actions are changed in order to obtain the desired results. Double loop learning is a change in the interpretation of the problem, which can open new solution opportunities. It represents a change in the set of possible actions as well as in the objectives. Triple loop learning corresponds to a new means of production of interpretations, or, if you will, a change in the very mental model.

Origin of Mental Models

Kofman (2002, vol. I, pp. 254-263) describes mental models as reality filters that arise from four sources: biology, language, culture, and personal history.

The first source of mental models is biology. It is connected to the physiological limitations of the human sensorial perception, which is understood to be within a certain spectrum defined by the limits of human senses. Nervous systems are not, however, exactly alike in all people, since some have more highly developed perceptive capabilities than others or, on the other hand, may have anomalies which restrict their area of perception.

A second source of mental models is language. People do not only say what they see, but, in fact,

see only what they are able to express. Language, as a descriptive system to label and classify things, is what defines the cognitive space in which we can reflect, generating understanding, and which defines the ambit where we can share concepts with other people. Consequently, language contributes in determining each person's field of distinctions.

The third source of mental models is culture, which is a type of collective mental model, constituting a standard of shared basic assumptions.

The fourth source of mental models is formed by personal history: race, sex, nationality, ethnic origin, family influences, social and economic conditions, beliefs, values, and life experiences, among others. Experiences and concepts acquired are placed in the conscience substrata, creating an automatic predisposition to interpret and act.

We have now arrived at a point where we can attempt to define with greater comprehension what is understood as previous knowledge from within the context of this chapter. Kofman (2002) denominates mental models the previous knowledge (tacit or explicit), referring to what human beings bring inside themselves, originated, as we have seen, in personal histories, biology, culture, and language. Mental models can be considered interpretative filters that can somehow influence the process of concept formation and action.

The CA is a long way from being a purely objective process that can be compared to a computational algorithm. The process contains an enormous margin of subjectivity that is solved based on previous knowledge, as expected. It would therefore be satisfactory to consider this previous knowledge in, as much as possible, a coordinated and conscious process.

Thus, the knowledge related to this approach includes the presuppositions which are indispensable to change the type of observer involved in the CA process, and that allow the observer to improve dialog and create more knowledge from the consideration of previous knowledge. There are cognitive and linguistic distinctions that are indispensable for this proposal that can guide a *coordination of actions* and a management of effective conversations in the clustering process. Maturana and Varela (1992) say that knowledge is effective action. Bearing this in mind, some of the theoretical fundamentals related to the linguistic aspects that permeate the decision making process and interpretation of results, which are also present in the CA, will be introduced. Next, some aspects related to fundamental linguistic acts, with emphasis on assessment, the core of the interpretation process, will be studied.

FUNDAMENTAL LINGUISTIC ACTS

In conversations, there are two fundamental linguistic acts: affirmations and statements. Each of these linguistic acts will be studied based on Echeverría's considerations (1997, pp. 69-137), Flores, Graves, Hartfield, and Winograd (1988), Flores (1989, 1996), and Kofman (2002, Vol. II, pp. 185-200).

Affirmations

Affirmations are made regarding the state of the world in which people report what is observed based on the distinctions that they possess. It can be said that words follow the world, because they speak of an existing world.

When an affirmation is made, there is an implicit commitment with the veracity of this affirmation. Nevertheless, from the same area of distinctions in a field of shared observations, affirmations can be true or false based on a social consensus of the evidence that proves it. Not all affirmations can be confirmed or refuted due to the fact that descriptive facts may be inaccessible for confirmation. An example given by Echeverría (1997, p. 74) is, "It snowed in Bariloche on April 10th, 1945."

Statements

Statements change the state of the world. To make a statement is to say how the world should conform itself—adapt itself to what has been said, and thereby create new contexts by means of speaking. We could say, consequently, that the world follows words, because speaking creates a different reality.

When a statement is made, there is an implicit obligation regarding its authenticity. Nonetheless, statements can be either valid or not valid based on the power of the person who makes them. Statements are therefore sustained by power. This power can derive either from authority or strength. Authority can be instituted by someone or established by the person who declared it. When a statement is made, there is an obligation on the declarer's part to have the authority to make it and that the declarer's actions will be coherent with what was declared.

Assessments

Assessments are a type of statement. However, even if each assessment is a statement, not all statements are assessments. Assessments, just like statements, can be either valid or not valid according to the authority of the person making them. To have social effectiveness, they cannot be declared without the existence of the authority given to formulate them.

People usually make assessments even when they do not have the authority to do it, which invalidates the opinion, even with social support. When an assessment is made, besides the commitment to have authority, people assume that the opinion is based on observations of actions in the past.

The authority to make assessments is not always formally given, as in the case of a judge, a professor, a referee or a manager. This concession can be informal, as with children and their parents, for instance.

Assessments are like verdicts and inherit the ability from statements to change the world in relation to all of the actors involved: the one who makes the assessment, the object of the assessment, and those who accept the assessment. They constitute a new reality that resides in the interpretation that they carry and have, therefore, existing only in the realm of language. The assessment always exists in the person that makes it and not in the object of the assessment. Assessments are made nearly every moment and almost automatically every time something new is faced.

Assessments are either founded or unfounded based on the past actions, what is not required for other types of statements. Next, some assessments validation aspects will be studied in the context of the CA.

PROCESS OF SUBSTANTIATING ASSESSMENTS

Model of Validation of Assessments

As we have seen, assessments can either be valid or not valid after checking the authority of the person who formulated them. They can be founded or unfounded based on the affirmations or observations that back them up. The assessment validation activity is crucial for the correlation of the actions in life and for living in society, particularly for the effective coordination of actions. Knowledge itself, whether common or scientific, is built based on assessments and affirmations.

People's actions unfold starting from assessments, which are an interpretation of the context of a situation being faced. It happens, therefore, that a model which effectively describes the process of assessment validation is essential, not only for the CA process but also to handle all the complexities of life.

According to Echeverría (1997), what makes assessments different from affirmations, that is, what makes them different actions, are the social

obligations that both entail. When we make an affirmation, we commit ourselves to providing evidence. This means to provide a witness, a person (or other type of proof) that can testify in favor (or not) of what we have said. When we make an assessment, we first commit ourselves to having the authority that allows us to make that assessment and secondly, to provide support for the assessment.

The suggested steps for the validation of assessments, based on the five phases presented by Echeverría (1997, pp. 119-125), with the added phase of fundamental expansion of a shared social space, are the following:

1. Identify the reason why an assessment was formulated. There is always a reason for making an assessment;
2. Identify the standards under which the assessment is being formulated. Assessment standards are constituted by the set of behaviors or conceptions carried out, from a historical, cultural, moral, and social point of view. These are mental model components shared in a consensual way by a certain social group;
3. Identify the particular observation domain from which the assessment was created;
4. Identify the support actions and events (affirmations) that favor this assessment. These support affirmations may or may not support the assessments;
5. Perform the validation of the divergent, opposite assessment, verifying if it is unfounded;
6. Substantiate the assessment with other people, opening the previous cycle into a wider spiral, sharing the assessment validation process, seeking to find a consensual area for the knowledge building.

According to Echeverría (1997, p. 125), when speaking on the five steps that precede the expansion of shared assessment with other people: "the assessments that do not satisfy these five conditions are called *unfounded* assessments."

This sixth step of the assessment substantiation cycle was included in order to endow the process with a spiral opening of expansion. This last step is, therefore, nothing more than the development of a process going from an individual dimension to a collective dimension. This way, we go from a closed cycle to an open one, in spiral, that considers the creation of knowledge to be a consensual, socially built process, but keeping the decision making process that characterizes current strategic management.

In the CA process, it is interesting that the decision making process be a team effort, sharing assessments and the coordination of actions. This is particularly important in the following CA process steps: understanding the domain and the

data structure, definition of objectives, evaluation of results, and the knowledge building.

Figure 2 illustrates the five phases of assessment validation with a spiral expansion step to a space of progressive sharing in an action coordination cycle.

ACTION COORDINATION MODEL

Commitments and Conversation

As we studied in the section *Ontology of Language*, organizations are linguistic phenomena, built upon specific conversations, which are based on the human capacity to form commitments. Kofman (2002, Vol. II, p. 186) said that "the capacity to accept and make commitments

Figure 2. Assessment validation spiral

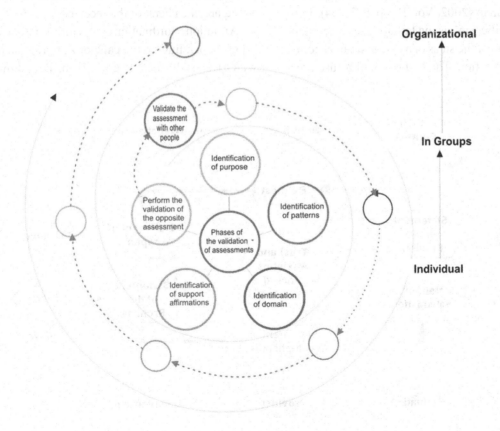

is one of the characteristics that define a person." Commitments are also a key to the coordination of actions. An extensive and complex net of commitments is at the base of any production system as well as in the construction and dissemination of knowledge.

Also from Kofman (2002, Vol. II, p. 187), "there are three paths that lead to commitments: a promise, an offer and a request." Moving on, a commitment management or action coordination model will be depicted, in only a few of its traces, which can be applied to several domains of human action, including the CA process, as will be suggested in the section Clustering Analysis Model.

Commitment Cycle: Its Types, Steps, and Phases

This item is based, in a more general way, on Echeverría (1997) and Flores (1996, 1998), as well as on Kofman (2002, Vol. II, pp. 223-244), in a more specific way, as the latter makes a detailed explanation of the steps of a conversational commitment in action. The first two will be used for

drawing a general picture whose details will be drawn based on this last one. An effort will be made to juxtapose the ideas of the latter and the former ones in a mixture that will be the action coordination model to be considered for the goals of this method.

A promise consists of a request or an offer along with a declaration of acceptance. A promise includes some indispensable factors: a request or an offer, the action to be performed, the satisfaction conditions, and the deadline for its fulfillment.

The action coordination cycle or the promise cycle is made up of two steps: constitution of the promise and the fulfillment of the promise. The first stage can be divided into two steps: the creation of the context and the negotiation. The second stage can also be divided into two: the implementation and the evaluation. In the action coordination cycle, there are two poles or agents around which the game or the dance evolves: the provider, or the issuing agent, and the client, or the receiver.

An action coordination cycle can be one of two types, depending on the category of promise on which it is established. There is, then, the commit-

Figure 3. Request cycle

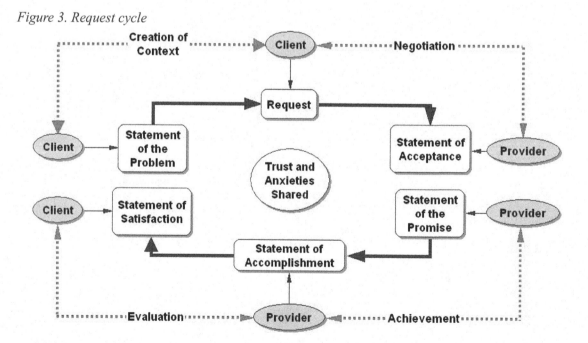

ment cycle based on a request and a commitment cycle based on an offer. In either case, both the provider and the client share common interests and mutual commitments that are built based on the expected reciprocal benefits, which are based on assessments that presuppose a minimum of reciprocal confidence.

Figures 3 and 4 present illustrative drawings of the request cycle and the offer cycle, respectively, so that both can be explained in a descriptive way. Both cycles, request and offer, begin with the announcement of a problem, starting a context creation phase. The difference between them is that, in the case of the request, this announcement of the problem is made by the client, who, recursively reflects about his own necessities, for which he needs help to satisfy. In the case of the offer, this analysis of necessities is made from the contemplation, made by the provider, concerning which can be the client's needs.

Next is the negotiation phase. In Figures 3 and 4, the negotiation phase begins with the formulation of a request and an offer, respectively, and ends with the declaration of acceptance. The difference is that with a request, the person making

the declaration is the provider, whereas with the offer it is the client.

After this comes the declaration of promise, which is always made by the service provider, just as in the development of the implementation phase and the declaration of accomplishment.

The beginning of the evaluation phase is characterized by the declaration of accomplishment. This is followed by the evaluation phase that ends with a declaration of satisfaction, which is always made by the client. It is worth mentioning that this cycle does not always end in an effective way. The client with the closing of the conversation phase may even express dissatisfaction.

Highlighting the differences between the cycles, which begin with either a request or an offer, it can be noticed that they only happen in the upper quadrants of the cycle, more specifically in the first one.

In the cycle that begins with a request, the first quadrant marks the client's recursive reflection regarding his needs; in the offer, it marks the provider's reflection concerning that one's needs. The client appears, thus, in the request, occupying both poles that delimit the context creation phase.

Figure 4. Offer cycle

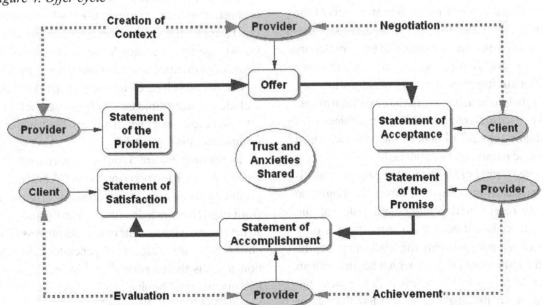

He is the agent of the announcement of the problem and of the formulation of the linguistic act, which can result in a promise—a request.

In contrast, in the cycle that begins with an offer, the provider appears as an agent that occupies both poles that define the context creation phase, as an agent of the announcement of the problem and of the formulation of the linguistic act that can propitiate a promise—an offer. This is the only difference between the action coordination cycle starting from a request or from an offer.

Between the third and fourth quadrants of the coordination of actions image, there are not any significant differences between the cycle that begins with a request and the one that begins with an offer. The same agents, at the same phase delimitation poles, trigger the same linguistic acts, which signal the end of a phase and, consequently, the beginning of the following one. Both the cycle that starts from a request and the cycle that begins from an offer have the same development, in a clock-wise direction, going through a series of linguistic acts that characterize the commitment and the action coordination cycle.

The negotiation and evaluation phases are characterized by client-provider bipolarity in a process of assessment sharing, seeking for creating a consensual space in relation to the parameters of the promise: the action to be performed, the satisfaction conditions, and the deadline for completion. In the negotiation phase, this consensual space is built aiming at establishing these parameters, with goals to be achieved. In the evaluation phase, this consensual space is used with the objective of evaluating the fulfillment of the promise, based on these parameters established.

The context creation and the promise fulfillment phases are unipolar, since the linguistic agents represented occupy both poles of the border. As has already been seen, there is only one difference between the cycle that begins with a request and the one which begins with an offer. In the cycle that begins with a request, the client is the linguistic agent that has the role of beginning the action coordination cycle, making the first statements that constitute it. In the cycle that begins with an offer, the provider is the agent who triggers the process, starting it, making the first statements.

In each one of the phases of the action coordination cycle, it may be necessary to trigger new cycles in the net of commitments making, for example, a request to the others providers. This is what we tried to demonstrate through the series of overlapped and intertwined circles shown in Figures 3 and 4.

In the heart of the action coordination cycles, occupying the central position in the illustrations, are the shared trust and anxieties, with bases that sustain the cohesion of the process, without which the process can fragment at any moment.

CLUSTERING ANALYSIS MODEL

Decision Making and Creation of Knowledge in Clustering Analysis

Based on the triple loop model of learning, presented by Kofman (2002, vol. I, p. 316), we will present a CA model that encompasses the phases of continuous data-information-knowledge, bearing in mind the interaction between previous knowledge and the knowledge discovered. The knowledge creation and decision making process in CA is comprised of learning loops that also include the three dimensions of changes: actions, interpretations, and mental models. Figures 5 and 6 illustrate this CA model.

Explaining Figure 5, one can start from the database, which is worked on by the CA process to produce information. The information originated from explicit knowledge of the domain and data structures can also feed the clustering process. The object aggregation algorithm generates information, and it is also capable of working conditioned by information. The phases of the CA process will be detailed in the following item.

Figure 5. CA model

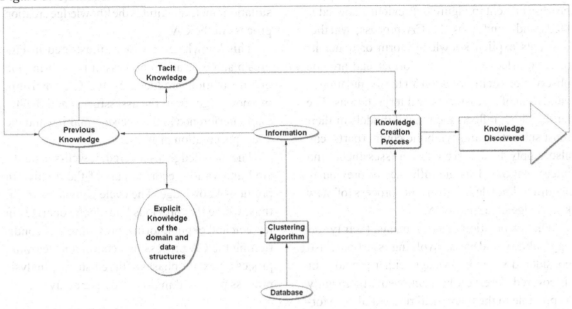

Figure 6. Knowledge creation process in the CA model

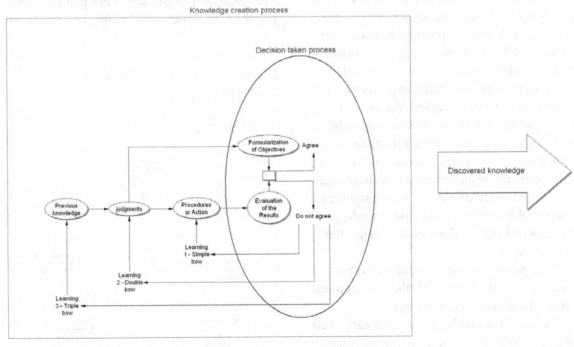

Figure 5 shows in detail the knowledge creation process present in Figure 6. Previous knowledge feeds and conditions the CA process, whether under its explicit knowledge form or under its tacit knowledge form. The former can provide observations or information for the formulation or validation of assessments or interpretations. The latter, which reflects the mental models in their most subjective and symbolic counterparts, can also supply, feed, and condition assessments and interpretations. It is the influence of previously acquired knowledge over the process of new knowledge creation in CA.

The formulation of assessments, their typology, validity, and basis, involving assertions, also considered while knowledge, either previous or discovered, deserve to be mentioned as thoroughly as possible in the theoretical referential. The formulation of assessments and their validation are in the center of the decision making and, also, of the knowledge creation or learning process in CA.

According to the learning model of Kofman (2002, vol. I, p. 316), the actions or procedures in CA come from interpretations or assessments, which launch actions into the future, translating themselves into objectives and boosting actions in the present towards what had been prospected. The assessments or interpretations also compare the results achieved with the objectives formulated, producing adjustments in the actions in a feedback process. In a deeper learning mechanism, the assessments or interpretations can be changed into second-order learning. In a more significant and complex change, the previous knowledge or the mental models can be transformed into third-order learning.

This process works as rehearsal-error, regarding a situation for which there is not much accumulated previous knowledge.

The decision making process appears in all phases of the clustering process with assessments and knowledge associated with each decision. This decision making process and the resulting actions or procedures in the context of a game between previous knowledge and the formula-

tion and validation of assessments, regarding the situations met, constitutes the knowledge creation process in the CA.

This knowledge creation, illustrated in Figures 5 and 6, is also a process of transformation of information produced by the CA algorithm in knowledge, from the assessments and the human interference in the decision making and the concepts creation process.

The knowledge discovered, if well-substantiated and valid, becomes part of the archive of previous knowledge. The cycle completes itself, thus, where this previous knowledge operates in its tacit and explicit forms, providing and conditioning the CA process in a continuous learning process. Next the phases of the clustering analysis process proposed in this study are analyzed.

Phases of the Clustering Analysis Process

The CA model, according to our point of view, has the nine phases listed below, also shown in

Figure 7. Stages of the CA process

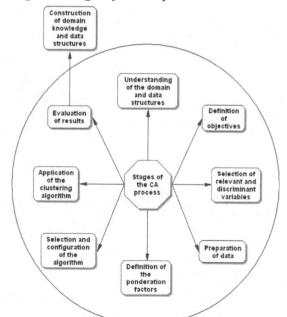

Figure 7: (a) understanding the domain and the data structures; (b) definition of objectives; (c) selection of relevant and discriminant variables; (d) preparation of the data; (e) definition of the weighting factors (if that is the case); (f) selection and configuration of the algorithm; (g) application of the aggregation algorithm; (h) evaluation of the results; and (i) construction of domain knowledge and data structures.

In the first phase, we tried to create a shared space for the understanding of the domain and of the data structures between the two main actors of the CA process: the domain specialist and the analyst. The former is the person involved in the business or in the field of knowledge or action in which we intend to apply the CA. The latter is the one who manages the CA in a more effective way, being responsible, in a general way, for the execution of all phases. While the domain specialist has got more knowledge of the business, the analyst has got more knowledge of KDD and CA techniques. The first one is expected to get as close as possible to an understanding, in general terms, of the CA process. The second one should build an understanding of the business and a view on how data are structured and organized.

In the second phase, starting from the space of shared understanding, the definition of objectives is made. The objectives must translate the expectations that we have in relation to the possible knowledge that may improve the understanding of the business.

In the third phase, due to the objectives determined, one tries to select the variables that are relevant and discriminant to the solution for the problem proposed. In a database, it is common to have controlled data redundancy and a big set of aspects observations translated as objects attributes. Not all of these descriptive attributes or variables of the objects can be relevant for the problem in question. To aid the assessment regarding the discriminance of a variable, the Main Component Analysis or the Factorial Analysis can be applied. Simplifying, nondiscriminant variables are those whose values change very little from one object to the other and that, therefore, will have very little effect on the clustering process.

In the fourth phase, the data must be prepared for the CA. The data need to be selected within a convenient sampling space. The data need to be cleansed of any kind of noise, as, for example, HTML commands in a Web page. The CA process must only operate with trustworthy data. This phase refers, thus, mainly to the condition of trust, quality and significant extension of the space of the data.

In the fifth phase, the weighting components of the object aggregation algorithm are defined. The algorithm must be prepared to receive a matrix of information that reflects the relevant previous knowledge of the business and data. In this phase it is also interesting to determine a relationship map or implication of the variables to assist in the creation process of the information matrix that will act as a weighting agent in the execution of the aggregation algorithm. This problem of the weighting of the algorithm from previous knowledge was developed by Castilho, Prado, and Ladeira (2003, 2004) and is not the focus of this chapter.

In the sixth phase, a clustering technique is chosen, considering the analysis objectives and the characteristics of the data space. The aggregation algorithm also needs to be configured adequately for the execution of the aggregation process, according to the characteristics of the data. It may be necessary to define the number of groups in which the data sample will have to be partitioned, depending on the algorithm used. It may also be necessary, depending on the size of the space of the data worked on, to define the maximum number of interactions in the cycles of calculation of combinations of the aggregation algorithm. It is necessary to avoid very long times processing the data set, although this restriction could diminish the rate of trust in the results. Finally, there are many necessary configurations in the clustering

Figure 8. Spiral of knowledge creation in the CA

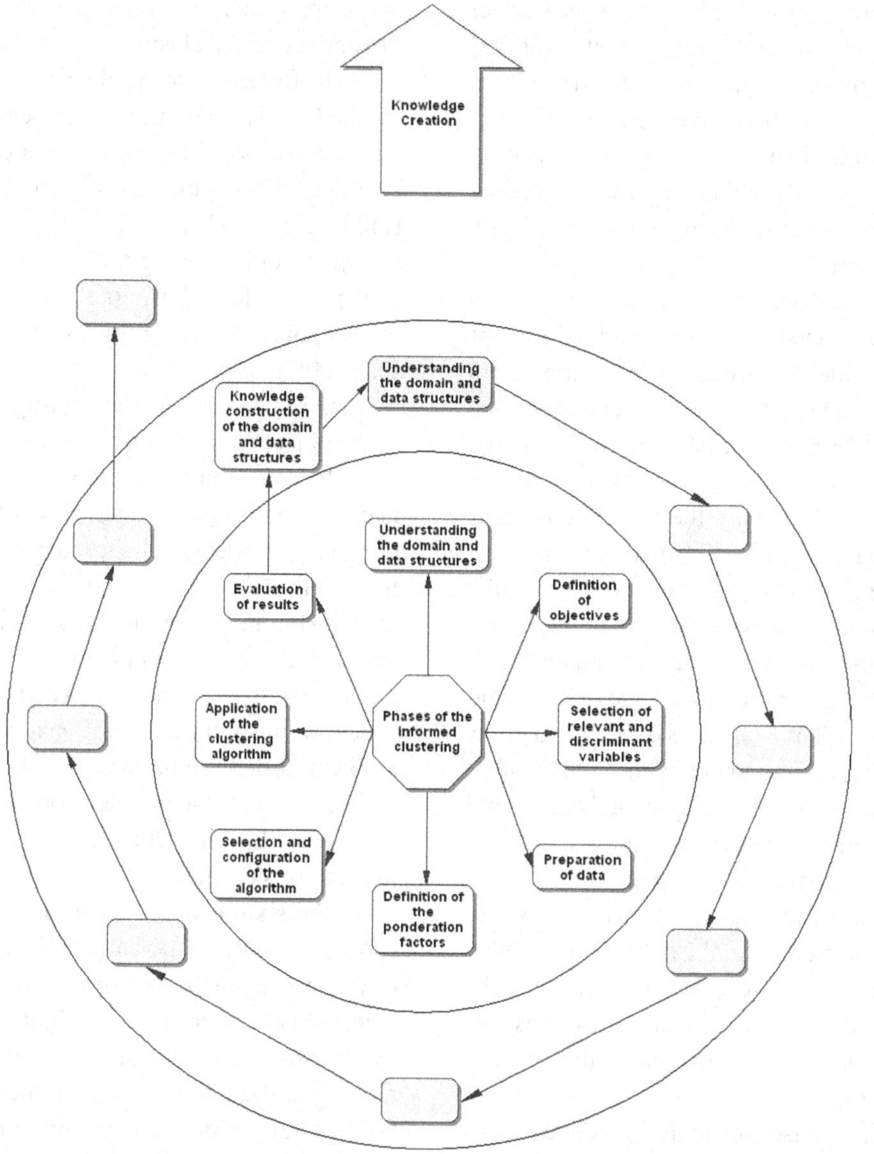

process, depending on the characteristics of the data space, on the specification of the partition technique used, as well as on the peculiarities of the computational tool employed for the clustering process.

In the seventh phase, we apply the aggregation algorithm to the selected space of objects and their characteristics so as to partition these observations into a group configuration, with maximum internal similarity among objects and minimum external similarity among groups. This phase is normally very interactive, with recurrence to the preceding phases. The knowledge creation process also has a rehearsal-error component, in which we return to the previous steps, making adjustments in a first-order learning process that can evolve to learning processes of second and third orders.

In the eighth phase, the results of the CA process are evaluated. There are, according to Cormack (1971), several techniques that can be used to assess the quality of the groupings generated. There are two types of evaluation techniques of clustering results: the quantitative and the qualitative ones. The importance of the latter cannot be ignored. We recommend, therefore, a combined application of both approaches. It is interesting to use mathematical techniques, "objective," to evaluate the clustering results, but these must be complemented by qualitative approaches and, thus, more "subjective," with the participation of the people involved. It is, for example, important for the domain specialist to declare his satisfaction, as one of the criteria of this subjective evaluation.

In the ninth phase, we try to build knowledge of the domain and data structures from the analysis and interpretation of the results in the CA process as a whole. This phase comprises the interpretation work that can result in more knowledge of the business structure. In Figure 7, this phase is beyond the circle that comprises the previous phases. This tries to illustrate that we are seeking for knowledge expansion.

Figure 8 shows these ideas by presenting a spiral of knowledge creation in the CA, where at each complete cycle of the process, the understanding of the domain and data structures expands itself into a bigger diameter, representing the creation of knowledge.

CYCLE OF ACTION COORDINATION IN CLUSTERING ANALYSIS

An action coordination model, according to Echeverría (1997) and Flores (1996, 1998), was presented in the section Action Coordination Model. Based on these studies, Figure 9 shows an application of the cycle of action coordination in the CA model.

The cycle of action coordination in CA corresponds to the generic cycle of the offer. The analyst and the domain specialist are instances, respectively, of the provider and the client. The analyst is considered a provider of knowledge creation service. The context creation phase corresponds to the phase of understanding the domain and the data structures, as a preparation of the analyst to interact with the domain specialist in the following phase, the definition of objectives. The analyst makes a first offer based on the analysis of the domain specialist's needs and on the knowledge of the business he tried to acquire. This phase begins with the announcement of the problem to the analyst, and ends with the first offer that he makes based on the study of the business and the organization of the data.

In the phase of definition of objectives, one tries to create a space of shared knowledge between the analyst and the domain specialist. This phase corresponds to the negotiation phase, in which the object of the negotiation is the definition of the desired objectives with the CA. The phase of definition of objectives ends with an acceptance declaration, made by the domain specialist, related to the objectives defined with the help of the analyst.

In the configuration and application phase, which corresponds to the operation phase, the analyst promotes the selection of variables or texts, the preparation of data, the definition of weighting factors, the choosing and configuration of the algorithm, as well as the application or execution of this aggregation algorithm. This execution phase, however, is characterized by the integration between analyst and domain specialist. As illustrated by the circle in the center of Figure 9, a space of trust and sharing of anxieties must be kept between them. This configuration and application phase completes itself with the presentation of the clustering results for evaluation, corresponding, on the part of the analyst, to a declaration of having kept a promise.

Figure 9. Cycle of action coordination in clustering

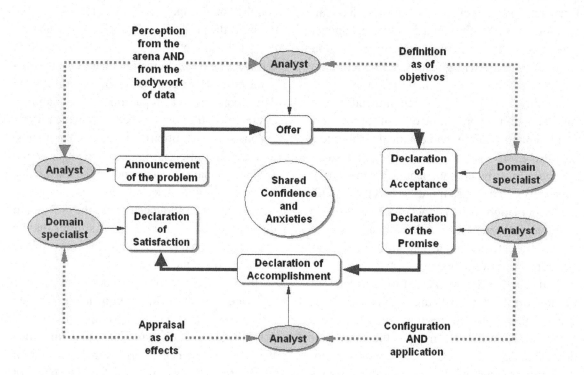

In the result evaluation phase, which corresponds to the evaluation phase in the generic cycle of the action coordination, the products of the CA need to be worked on by the assessments of the domain specialist and the analyst. An effective interaction between them, permeated also by the shared space of cognitive and conversational competencies, must exist. This phase also comprises the phase of the CA in which we try to build progressive knowledge of the domain and data structures.

The action coordination cycle in CA can continue being operated several times with redefinition of objectives or renegotiation, with new configurations and executions of the aggregation algorithm, with reassessments and a new effort of knowledge creation. This process would repeat until the domain analyst stated being totally satisfied or any other of the closure situations of the generic cycle mentioned in the section *Action Coordination Model*.

RESULTS INTERPRETATION IN CLUSTERING ANALYSIS

Model of Assessment Validation in CA

In the section *Process of Substantiating Assessments*, we studied the model of assessment validation presented by Echeverría (1997, pp. 119-125) that comprises five steps, to which one more step was added: sharing assessments with other people.

The results reached in a clustering process may not have any meaning by themselves. It is necessary to deduct or create knowledge from these results. So, we also recommend seeking the evaluation and interpretation of results, according to the following steps:

1. Select the results generated by the data mining algorithms;

2. Make assessments based on the results selected;

3. Substantiate the assessments made:
   - Define for what purpose the assessment is being made;
   - Define in which domain it is being judged;
   - Define with which patterns it is being judged;
   - Define which actions and events (assertions) corroborate this assessment;
   - Validate assessments with other people;

4. Incorporate the results as organizational knowledge.

Description of the Assessment Validation Phases

This item will be developed based on Echeverría's ideas (1997, pp. 119-125), by detailing each phase of the assessment validation process.

1. **Identification of purpose:** An assessment is always originated for a reason. We always have a future in mind in which the assessment will open or close possibilities, making some actions possible and others not. When we make behavior assessments, it is useful to figure out an action that could be anticipated in the future. In the assessment "John speaks well", it is important to identify the future action related to the assessment made. The assessment will be much different if this future action is to interact with small work team or during an international conference presented in a foreign language. As you can see, the purpose of the assessment can be connected to a more detailed drawing of the future action, which is the reason or objective of making the assessment.

2. **Identification of patterns:** An assessment is made based on a number of patterns. When we make an assessment, we assume a number of patterns with which things or individuals, that are being judged, will be confronted. Assessments are not only social, because they reflect the patterns of a community and its traditions, but they are also historical, since the patterns used to create them can change over time. An interesting example is given by Echeverría (1997, pp. 120-121) with the following assessment: "we found ourselves in front of huge mountains." This assessment will, possibly, be different for people who are used to finding themselves surrounded by mountains and for those who are not, because their assessment patterns will probably be different.

3. **Identification of the domain:** Upon making an assessment, we normally render a verdict, based on certain observations. This assessment is, therefore, limited to the private domain of these observations. An assessment is generally made inside a specific domain of observation: family, health, work, relationships, financial, entertainment, the private domain of science or technique, a variety of actions, among others. So, they can be substantiated strictly in the domain of observations with respect to which they were made. One cannot generalize assessments to different domains. We cannot necessarily infer from, for instance, the following assessment: "Peter is very democratic at work" that Peter is also democratic in the scope of his family relationships.

4. **Identification of support assertions:** The affirmations related to a specific observation domain, based on a certain pattern, are the ones that can substantiate a correlated assessment. To validate assessments it is, thus, necessary to enumerate affirmations related to the object of assessment. Assertions are, therefore, indispensable to the assessment validation process. Echeverría (1997, p. 123) gives us the following example of assessment: "Catherine is very competent in

running meetings." The assertions that he presents as the validation support are the following: "since she started running these meetings, her department has been spending less time in meetings and receiving a smaller number of complaints from its clients".

5. **Substantiate the contrary assessment:** A certain amount of support assertions are not always enough to guarantee that an assessment is well substantiated. It is possible that we may find a much bigger quantity of assertions regarding a contrary or opposite assessment. We frequently consider an assessment to be substantiated starting from observations made in a certain number of instances, but after checking the foundation of the opposite assessment we verify that there are many more instances pointing at the divergent assessment.

As an example, we present the following assessment: "Professor Carlos was rejected by the students". We observed that five students went to the dean's office to complain about him. Although a certain number of affirmations exist, which support the assessment made, it is not enough to consider it as being substantiated. We verify that the opposite assessment has many more support assertions: upon finding out what had happened 20 students, among the 25 of the whole class, went to the dean's office to testify that Professor Carlos is an excellent Professor. As we can see, the previous assessment cannot be substantiated. The opposite assessment would be this: "Professor Carlos was not rejected by the class." Therefore, an assessment can only be considered as being validated, if a sufficient number of assertions to support the opposite assessment have not been found.

6. **Substantiating the assessment with other people:** Substantiating assessments made in groups is a theme of extreme modernity, as an example of this is the growing approach in

collaborative work. Typically, this sharing of assessments with other people corresponds to a change in the types of the observers involved, from an observer with only one approach, to an observer with multiple approaches. As a result, we suggest that, in the sharing of assessments with other people, the following steps should be taken:

1. Share with the others the anxieties that led you to make the assessment: what is the purpose of the assessment that you are making? Ask them if they share your anxieties or if they have different ones. If they have different anxieties, what are the consequences of these differences? Explore the possibility of making an agreement.

2. Share the domain with them starting from with what your assessment is made. Ask them if they share the notion that this is the adequate domain. If not, investigate what are the consequences of these differences. Explore the possibility of making an agreement.

3. Share with them the patterns used to make your assessment. Explain why such patterns seem adequate to you. Ask if they have different patterns and if so, why did they choose them? Explore the consequences that result from these differences. Explore the possibility of making an agreement.

4. Describe the actions or events (assertions) that support your assessment. Ask the others if they describe the facts in a different way or if they can point out other facts to be considered. Examine the consequences of what they say. Explore the possibility of making an agreement.

5. Explain the inferences (narratives) made to create other assertions or assessments. Ask the others if they would make distinct inferences. Examine the

differences and consequences that they bring. Explore the possibility of making an agreement.

6. If the differences persist, explore with them the possible actions or events that allow you to solve these differences and avoid increasing them.

7. Throughout the whole process, try to understand other peoples' points of view, and also try to let yours to be known. Combine questioning and proposition. Be willing to change your points of view according to what you hear (that is, try to act as an observer of multiple focuses).

CONCLUSION

According to what was studied, previous knowledge comprises all the archives of abilities, attitudes, values, beliefs, conceptions, experience, explicit knowledge, and tacit knowledge that were acquired by the individual throughout his life. This previous knowledge influences the process of opinion formation, as well as the creation of new knowledge. Any process of knowledge discovery needs, therefore, to consider the influence of this knowledge, especially in the evaluation and results interpretation phases.

This chapter is centered in the notion that the tasks of (data, text, etc.) mining, comprising its techniques and algorithms, can provide excellent tips, starting from the data, for producing a new dimension of information that was formerly implicit or hidden. Nevertheless, only these techniques and algorithms are unable to create knowledge by themselves. The information generated must be interpreted by the human beings involved in the process and in the business of the application.

The presented study considers that the CA process can be better conducted based on a domain theory, which represents the knowledge of the organization of the data, and the relation between its attributes. In the CA process, taking previous knowledge into consideration, whether in its explicit or in its tacit form (mental models), can contribute to the aggregation of more semantics to the CA process. The use of Ontology of Language can be important to produce greater effectiveness in the knowledge creation process in CA.

Finally, we reaffirm the hypothesis that, from the development of the research in CA, the importance of taking previous knowledge into consideration as a provider and a condition of the discovered knowledge has to be more and more emphasized. Without approaching the CA problem in an integrated way, which also involves, in addition to the technological and the computational aspects involved, the ontological and the epistemological aspects related to the discovery of knowledge by means of these techniques, we leave out the main meaning aggregation factor, the creation of semantics, the production of knowledge: the subjects who observe, the people involved in the process. The main factor in considering the previous knowledge is, finally, the individual himself that knows about the domain. As we tried to demonstrate in most of this chapter, there is no knowledge independent from the observer, from the individual who knows.

FUTURE RESEARCH DIRECTIONS

A model of clustering analysis (CA) that proposes to aggregate more semantics to the process of knowledge discovery, starting from data of a certain domain, needs to seek the improvement of the techniques and algorithms, to consider the influence of previous knowledge, in its explicit and tacit forms (mental models), and also the communication and coordination of actions between the people involved in the process.

In this case, it is not only about measuring and representing the relation between variables of the clustering problem, but another phase of the process of knowledge transformation, in the context of the continuous data-information-knowledge, is attacked. This phase is the knowledge creation one that starts from the human interpretation of the information generated by the data mining techniques and algorithms. Since, according to Weil and Snapper (1989), as well as to Berger and Luckmann (2001), knowledge creation is a social and historical process, more than heeding the relation between variables in a domain theory, we worry about the conditions and structure of the coordination of actions between the people involved in the CA process.

From this also arises the preoccupation with the study of Ontology of Language, especially with the mental models, the linguistic acts, the validation of assessments, and the coordination of actions. The assessments are in the core of the knowledge creation process; communication and coordination of actions permeate the whole knowledge creation process in data mining.

To aggregate more semantics to the clustering process, it is necessary, thus, to use an approach that considers previous knowledge, the communication, and the coordination of the actions of the team involved. Some analysts of KDD believe that their work comprises only the configuration and the application of data mining algorithms or techniques. They believe that once the information generated by these techniques and algorithms is delivered to the domain specialist, their work is finished. They do not think that they are also responsible for the follow-up process of interpretation of this information in a social process of knowledge creation.

This research suggests a cycle of coordination of actions in CA that involves analyst and specialist in a coordinated knowledge creation process, based on the conversational competences that comprise the differences between linguistic acts and the conscious handling of the dynamics of conversations. The domain knowledge creation and data structure phases, which happen right after the clustering results evaluation phase, are therefore carried out with the active participation of the CA analyst as well.

We open, thus, an encouraging field of research aiming at advancing studies of Ontology of Language in order to improve the action coordination model, validation of assessments, and management of conversations in CA so as to aggregate more semantics to the process of clustering generation.

REFERENCES

Berger, P.L., & Luckmann, T. (1966) *The social construction of reality: A treatise in the sociology of knowledge.* Garden City, NY: Anchor Books.

Castilho, W.F., Prado, H.A., & Ladeira, M. (2003) Introducing prior knowledge into the clustering process. In *Proceedings of the Fourth International Conference on Data Mining* (pp. 171-181).

Castilho, W.F., Prado, H.A., & Ladeira, M. (2004) Informed k-means: A clustering process biased by prior knowledge. In *Proceedings of the 6th International Conference on Enterprise Information Systems (ICEIS)* (pp. 469-475).

Cormack, R.M. (1971). A review of classifications. *Journal of the Royal Statistical Society [Series A] (General), 134*(3), 321-367.

Davenport, T.H., & Prusak, L. (1998). *Working knowledge: How organizations manage what they know.* Cambridge, MA: Harvard Business School Press.

Echeverría, R. (1997). *Ontologia del Lenguaje* (4ª ed.). Santiago, Chile: Dolmen Ediciones.

Fayyad, U.M., Piatetsky-Shapiro, G., & Smyth, P. (1996). From data mining to knowledge discovery: Overview. In U.M. Fallad et al. (Eds.), *Advances in knowledge discovery and data mining.* MIT Press.

Flores, F. (1989). *Inventando la empresa del siglo XXI.* Hachette.

Flores, F. (1996). *Creando organizaciones para el futuro.* Santiago, Chile: Dólmen.

Flores, F., Graves, M., Hartfield, B., & Winograd, T. (1988). Computer systems and the design of organizational interaction. *ACM Transactions on Office Information Systems, 6*(2), 157-172.

Hanson, S.J. (1990). Conceptual clustering and categorization: Bridging the gap between induction and causal models. In Y. Kodratoff & R. Michalski (Eds.), *Machine learning: An artificial intelligence approach* (vol. III, pp.235-268). San Mateo, CA: Morgan.

Kofman, F. (2002). *Metamanagement* (in Portuguese). São Paulo, Brazil: Antakarana Cultura Arte Ciência.

Maturana, H.R., & Varela, F.J. (1992). *The tree of knowledge: The biological roots of human understanding* (Rev. Sub. ed). Boston: Shambhala.

Nonaka, I., & Takeuchi, H. (1995). *The knowledge-creating company: How Japanese companies create the dynamics of innovation.* Oxford University Press.

Senge, P. (1990). *The fifth discipline: The art and practice of the learning organization.* New York: Doubleday.

Senge, P., Kleiner, A., Roberts, C., Ross, R., & Smith, B. (1994). *The fifth discipline fieldbook: Strategies for building a learning organization.* New York: Doubleday/Currency.

Weil, V., & Snapper, J. (Eds.). (1989). *Owning scientific and technical information: Value and ethical issues.* New Brunswick, NJ: Rutgers University Press.

Additional Reading

Anderberg, M.R. (1973). *Cluster analysis for applications.* London: Academic Press.

Béjar, J., Cortés, U., & Poch, M. (1992). LINNEO+: Herramienta para la adquisición de conocimiento y generación de reglas de clasificación en dominios poco estruturados. In *Proceedings of the 3rd Congresso Iberoamericano de Inteligencia Artificial (IBERAMIA 92)* (pp. 471-478). La Habana, Cuba.

Burt, C. (1937). Correlation between persons. *Brit. J. Psychol., 28,* 59-96.

Hartigan, J. (1975). *Clustering algorithms.* New York: John Wiley & Sons.

Kuhn, T.S. (1962). *The structure of scientific revolutions.* Chicago: University of Chicago Press.

Martins, C.A., Monard, M.C., & Halembeck, G.C. (2002). A computational framework for interpreting clusters through inductive learning: A case study (Tech. Rep. No. ICMC-USP). São Carlos(Brazil): ICMC.

Pearson, K. (1901). On links and planes of closest fit to a systems of points in space (Series 557-572). *Phil. Mag., 2,* 6.

Siponen, M., Vesanto, J., Simula, O., & Vasara, P. (2001). An approach to automated interpretation of SOM. In N. Allinson, H. Yin, L. Allinson & J. Slack (Eds.), *Advances in self-organizing maps* (pp. 89-94). Springer.

Sokal, R.R., & Sneath, P. (1963). *Principles of numerical taxonomy.* San Francisco: W.H. Freeman and Company.

Spearman, C. (1904). General intelligence objectively determined and measured. *Am. J. Psychol., 15,* 201-293.

Stephenson, W. (1935, September). Correlating persons instead of tests. *Character and Personality, 4*(1), 17-24

Sveiby, K.E. (2001) Knowledge management: Lessons from the pioneers. Retrieved April 9, 2007, from www.kmadvantage.com/km_articles.htm

Tryon, R.C. (1935). A theory of psychological components: An alternative to mathematical factors. *Psychol. Rev., 42,* 425-454.

Wrobel, S. (1994). *Concept formation and knowledge revision* (p. 240). Dordrecht, The Netherlands: Kluwer.

Compilation of References

Aas, K., & Eikvil, L. (1999). *Text categorization: A survey* (Technical Report). Norwegian Computing Center.

Abney, S. (1991). Parsing by chunks. In R. Berwick, S. Abney, & C. Tenny (Eds.), *Principle-based parsing: Computation and psycholinguistics* (pp. 257-278). Boston: Kluwer Academic Publishers.

Agrawal, R., & Srikant, R. (1994). *Fast algorithms for mining association rules*. Paper presented at the Proceedings of the 20th Very Large Data Bases (VLDB) Conference, Santiago, Chile.

Agrawal, R., & Srikant, R. (1995). *Mining sequential patterns*. Paper presented at the Proceedings of the Eleventh International Conference on Data Engineering, Taipei, Taiwan.

Agrawal, R., & Srikant, R. (2001). *On integrating catalogs*. Paper presented at the Proceedings of the 10th International World Wide Web Conference (WWW10), Hong Kong, China.

Agrawal, R., Imieliński, T., & Swami, A. (1993). *Mining association rules between sets of items in large databases*. Paper presented at the Proceedings of the 1993 ACM SIGMOD International Conference on Management of Data.

Ahonen-Myka, H. (1999). *Finding all frequent maximal sequences in text*. Paper presented at the Proceedings of the 16th International Conference on Machine Learning ICML-99 Workshop on Machine Learning in Text Data Analysis, J. Stefan Institute, Ljubljana.

Ahonen-Myka, H., Heinonen, O., Klemettinen, M., & Verkamo, A. I. (1999). *Finding co-occurring text phrases by combining sequence and frequent set discovery*. Paper presented at the Proceedings of 16th International Joint Conference on Artificial Intelligence IJCAI-99 Workshop on Text Mining: Foundations, Techniques and Applications.

Aldenderfer, M. S., & Blashfield, R. K. (1984) *Cluster analysis* (p. 88). Beverly Hills, CA: Sage.

Appleby, C. (1997). Will plans follow the new diabetes screening guidelines? Managed Care. Retrieved April 7, 2007, from http://www.managedcaremag.com/archives/9712/9712.diabetes.shtml

Araújo, M., Navarro, G., & Ziviani, N. (1997). Large text searching allowing errors. In *Proceedings of the Fourth South American Workshop on String Processing (WSP'97)* (pp. 2-20). Carleton University Press.

Archer, T., & Macario, A. (2006). The drive for operating room efficiency will increase quality of care. *Current Opinion in Anaesthesiology, 19*(2), 171-176.

Baeza-Yates, B. & Ribeiro Neto, B. (1999). *Modern information retrieval*. Addison Wesley.

Baker, L. D., & McCallum, A. K. (1998). *Distributional clustering of words for text classification*. Paper presented at the Proceedings of the 21st Annual International ACM SIGIR Conference on Research and Development in Information Retrieval, Melbourne, Australia.

Balaj, S. T. (2005, September). Telemar boots sales and satisfaction with powerful performance if informatica powercenter. *DM Review Magazine.* Retrieved March 25, 2007, from http://www.dmreview.com/article_sub.cfm?articleID=1035576

Balaj, S. T. (2005, October). *Telemar Projeto Business Intelligence em DW.* Paper presented at the Symposium Inteligência Organizacional 2005 Rio de Janeiro. Rio de Janeiro, RJ.

Banks, J., Marmot, M., Oldfield, Z., & Smith, J.P. (2006). Disease and disadvantage in the United States and England. *JAMA, 295*(17), 2037-2045.

Barnbrook, G. (2002). *Defining language. A local grammar of definition sentences.* John Benjamins Publishing Company.

Beckers, R., Deneubourg, J. L., & Goss, S. (1992). Trails and u-turns in the selection of the shortest path by the ant Lasius niger. *Journal of Theoretical Biology, 159,* 397-415.

Berger, A. L., Della Pietra, S. A., & Della Pietra, V. J. (1996). A maximum entropy approach to natural language processing. *Computational Linguistics, 22,* 39-71.

Berger, P. L., & Luckmann, T. (1966) *The social construction of reality: A treatise in the sociology of knowledge.* Garden City, NY: Anchor Books.

Berry, M. W. (Ed.). (2003). *Survey of text mining: Clustering, classification, and retrieval.* Springer-Verlag.

Berry, M. W., & Browne, M. (2002). *Understanding search engines: Mathematical modeling and text retrieval.* Philadelphia: SIAM Publisher.

Bikel, D. M., Schwartz, R., & Weischedel. (1999). An algorithm that learns what's in a name [Special issue on natural language learning]. *Machine Learning, 34* (1-3), 211-231.

Blair-Goldensohn, S., McKeown, K., & Schlaikjer, A. H. (2004). Answering definitional questions: A hybrid approach. In M. T. Maybury (Ed.) *New directions in question answering* (pp 47-58). MIT Press.

Blum, A. (1995). Empirical support for Winnow and weighted-majority based algorithms: Results on a calendar scheduling domain. In *Proceedings of the 12th International Conference on Machine Learning* (pp. 64-72). San Francisco: Morgan Kaufmann.

Blum, A., & Mitchell, T. (1998). Combining labeled and unlabeled data with CO-TRAINING. In *Proceedings of the 11th Annual Conference on Computational Learning Theory (COLT)* (pp. 92-100). ACM Press.

Bodenheimer, T., & Fernandez, A. (2005). High and rising health care costs. Part 4: Can costs be controlled while preserving quality? *Annals of Internal Medicine, 143*(1), 26-31.

Boser, B. E., Guyon, I. M., & Vapnik, V. N. (1992). A training algorithm for optimal margin classifiers. In D. Haussler (Ed.), *5th Annual ACM Workshop on COLT* (pp. 144-152). Pittsburgh, PA: ACM Press.

Boutin, E. (1999). *Le traitement d'une information massive par l'analyse réseau: Méthode, outils et applications.* Unpublished doctoral dissertation, Université Aix-Marseille III. Marseilles.

Boutin, E. (2001, December). *A cadeia de tratamento da informação do CRRM.* Paper presented at the Seminar Tecnologias para Tratamento da Informação na Embrapa. Brasilia, DF.

Boutin, E., & Quoniam, L. (2006, May—June). *Thésaurus et clusterisation automatique de données Web: Deux outils au service de la détection de signaux faibles.* Paper presented at the 3rd CONTECSI International Conference on Information Systems and Technology Management. São Paulo, SP.

Bradley, A.P. (1997). The use of the area under the ROC curve in the evaluation of machine learning algorithms. *Pattern Recognition, 30*(7).

Bradley, P., & Fayyad, U. M., & Reina, C. (1998). Scaling clustering algorithms to large databases. In *International Conference on Knowledge Discovery & Data Mining, IV*, New York (pp. 9-15). Menlo Park: AAAI Press.

Brefeld, U., & Scheffer, T. (2004). CO-EM support vector learning. In *Proceedings of the 21st International Conference in Machine Learning (ICML)* (pp. 121-128). Morgan Kaufmann Publishers.

Brill, E. (1992) A simple rule-based part of speech tagger. In *Proceedings of the Third ACL Applied NLP*, Trento, Italy.

Brill, E. (1995, December). Transformation-Based error-driven learning and natural language processing: A case study in part of speech tagging. *Computational Linguistics, 21*(4), 543-565.

Brin, S., & Page, L. (1998). The anatomy of a large-scale hypertextual Web search engine. In *Proceedings of the Seventh International Conference on World Wide Web* (pp. 107-117).

Brusilovsky, P. (1996). Methods and techniques of adaptive hyermedia. *User Modeling and User Adapted Interaction, 6*(2-3), 87-129.

Buitendijk, S., & Nijhuis, J. (2004). High perinatal mortality in the Netherlands compared to the rest of Europe. *Ned Tijdschr Geneeskd, 148*(38), 1855-1860.

Bunescu, R., & Mooney, R. J. (2005). Statistical relational learning for natural language information extraction. In L. Getoor & B. Taskar (Eds.), *Statistical relational learning*, forthcoming.

Bunescu, R., Ge, R., Kate, R. J., Marcotte, E. M., Mooney, R. J., Ramani, A. K., et al. (2005). Comparative experiments on learning information extractors for proteins and their interactions. *Artificial Intelligence in Medicine [special issue on Summarization and Information Extraction from Medical Documents], 33*(2), 139-155.

Burges, C.J.C. (1998). A tutorial on support vector machines for pattern recognition. *Data Mining and Knowledge Discovery, 2*(2)955-974.

Cai, L., & Hofmann, T. (2003). *Text categorization by boosting automatically extracted concepts.* Paper presented at the Proceedings of the 26th Annual International ACM SIGIR Conference on Research and Development in Information Retrieval, Toronto, Canada.

Cai, L., & Hofmann, T., (2004). Hierarchical document categorization with support vector machines. In *Proceedings. of the 13th ACM International Conference on Information and Knowledge Management (CIKM'04)*, Washington, DC (pp. 78-87). New York: ACM Press.

Califf, M. E., & Mooney, R. J. (1998). Relational learning of pattern-match rules for information extraction. In *Working Notes of AAAI Spring Symposium on Applying Machine Learning to Discourse Processing* (pp. 6-11).

Califf, M. E., & Mooney, R. J. (2003). Bottom-up relational learning of pattern matching rules for information extraction. *Journal of Machine Learning Research, 4*, 177-210.

Cardlidge, P., & Stewart, J. (1995). Effect of changing the stillbirth definition on evaluation of perinatal mortality rates. *Lancet, 346*(8981), 1038.

Cardoso-Cachopo, A., & Oliveria, A. L. (2003). An empirical comparison of text categorization methods. In *Proceedings of the 10th International Symposium on String Processing and Information Retrieval* (pp. 183-196). Heidelberg: Springer-Verlag.

Caruana, R., & Freitag, D. (1994). Greedy attribute selection. In *Proceedings of International Conference on Machine Learning* (pp. 28-36).

Castilho, W.F., Prado, H.A., & Ladeira, M. (2003) Introducing prior knowledge into the clustering process. In *Proceedings of the Fourth International Conference on Data Mining* (pp. 171-181).

Castilho, W.F., Prado, H.A., & Ladeira, M. (2004) Informed k-means: A clustering process biased by prior knowledge. In *Proceedings of the 6th International Conference on Enterprise Information Systems (ICEIS)* (pp. 469-475).

Chakrabarti, G. (2000). Data mining for hypertext: A tutorial survey. *SIGKDD Explorations, 1*(2), 1-11.

Chakrabarti, S., Dom B., & Indyk, P. (1998). Enhanced hypertext categorization using hyperlinks. In *Proceedings SIGMOD98, ACM International Conference on Management of Data*, Seattle, Washington (pp. 307-318). New York: ACM Press.

Chakrabarti, S., Dom, B., Agrawal, R., & Raghavan P. (1997). Using taxonomy, discriminants, and signatures for navigating in text databases. In *Proceedings of the 23rd Very Large Date Bases Conference* (pp. 446-455). Athens, Greece: Morgan Kaufmann.

Chakrabarti, S., Dom, B., Agrawal, R., & Raghavan, P. (1998). Scalable feature selection, classification and signature generation for organizing large text databases into hierarchical topic taxonomies. *The VLDB Journal - The International Journal on Very Large Data Bases, 7*(3), 163-178.

Chalendar, G. D., & Grau, B. (2000). SVETLAN: A system to classify nouns in context. In *International Conference on Knowledge Engineering and Knowledge Management (OL-2000) in conjunction with the 14th European Conference on Artificial Intelligence, ECAI* (p. 6). Berlin, Germany. Retrieved August 15, 2007 from http://sunsite.informatik.rwth-aachen.de/Publications/CEUR-WS/Vol-31/GChalendar_12.pdf

Charniak, E. (1993). *Statistical language learning*. Cambridge, MA: MIT Press.

Chen, H. (1994). The vocabulary problem in collaboration [Special Issue on CSCW]. *IEEE Computer Society, 27*, 2-10.

Chen, H. (1996). A concept space approach to addressing the vocabulary problem in scientific information retrieval: An experiment on the worm community system. *Journal of the American Society for Information Science, 47*, 8.

Chen, J., & Nie, J.Y. (2000). Parallel Web text mining for cross-language IR. *Algorithmica, 28*(2), 217-241.

Chen, M. S., Park, J. S., & Yu, P. S. (1996). Data mining for path traversal patterns in a Web environment. In *Proceedings of the 16th International Conference on Distributed Computing Systems* (pp. 385-392). Fort Lauderdale, Florida.

Chen, S. F., & Rosenfeld, R. (1999). *A Gaussian prior for smoothing maximum entropy models* (Tech. Rep. No. CMU-CS-99-108). Carnegie Mellon University.

Choi, Y. S., & Yoo, S.I. (2001). Text database discovery on the Web: Neural net based approach. *Journal of Information Systems, 16*, 5-20.

Chuang, S. -L., & Chien, L. F. (2002). *Towards automatic generation of query taxonomy: A hierarchical term clustering approach*. Paper presented at the Proceedings of 2002 IEEE Conference on Data Mining (ICDM'2002).

Chuang, S.-L., & Chien, L.-F. (2004). *A practical Web-based approach to generating topic hierarchy for text segments*. Paper presented at the Proceedings of the Thirteenth ACM International Conference on Information and Knowledge Management, CIKM 2004, Washington, DC.

Chuang, S.-L., & Chien, L.-F. (2005). Taxonomy generation for text segments: A practical Web-based approach. *ACM Transactions on Information Systems (TOIS), 23*(4), 363-396.

Ciravegna, F. (2001). (LP)2 An adaptive algorithm for information extraction from Web-related texts. In *Proceedings of the IJCAI-2001 Workshop on Adaptive Text Extraction and Mining held in conjunction with 17th International Joint Conference on Artificial Intelligence (IJCAI)*, Seattle, Washington.

Coding & DRG notes: Diabetes mellitus. (2002). Retrieved April 7, 2007, from http://www.medicarequality.org/PEPP/PDF/DRGNotesDmUncontrolled.pdf

Cohen, W. W., & Singer, Y. (1999). Context sensitive learning methods for text categorization. *ACM Transactions on Information Systems, 17*(2), 141-173.

Cohn, D. A., Ghahramani, Z., & Jordan, M.I. (1996). Active learning with statistical models. *J. Artif. Intell. Res. (JAIR), 4,* 129-145.

Collins, M. (2002). Discriminative training methods for hidden Markov models: Theory and experiments with perceptron algorithms. In *Proceedings of the Conference on Empirical Methods in NLP (EMNLP'02)* (pp. 1-8).

Cormack, R. M. (1971). A review of classifications. *Journal of the Royal Statistical Society [Series A] (General), 134*(3), 321-367.

Cormen, T. H., Stein, C., Rivest, R. L., & Leiserson, C. E. (2001). *Introduction to algorithms.* McGraw-Hill Higher Education.

Cowie, J., & Lehnert, W. (1996) Information extraction. *Communications of the ACM, 1*(39), 80-91.

Crabtree, D., Andreae, P., & Gao, X. (2006, December). Query directed Web page clustering. In *Proceedings of the 2006 IEEE/WIC/ACM International Conference on Web Intelligence* (pp. 202-210). Hong Kong, China. IEEE Computer Society.

Craven, M., & Kumlien, J. (1999). Constructing biological knowledge bases by extracting information from text sources. In *Proceedings of the 7th International Conference on Intelligent Systems for Molecular Biology (ISMB-1999)* (pp. 77-86).

Cucerzan, S. & Brill, E. (2004). Spelling correction as an iterative process that exploits the collective knowledge of web users. *Proceedings of EMNLP 2004* (pp. 293-300).

Cunningham, H., Maynard, D., Bontcheva, K., & Tablan, V. (2002). GATE: A framework and graphical development environment for robust NLP tools and applications. In *ACL 2002.*

Cutting, D., Kardger, D., & Oederson, J. (1993). Constant interaction-time scatter/gatter browsing of very large document collections. In *Conference on Research and Development in Information Retrieval* (pp. 126-134). New York: ACM Press.

Cutting, D., Karger, D. R., Pedersen, J. O., & Tukey, J. W. (1992). Scatter/Gather: A cluster-based approach to browsing large document collections. In *Conference on Research and Development in Information Retrieval* (pp. 318-329). New York: ACM Press.

Dagan, I., Karov, Y., & Roth, D. (1997). Mistake-driven learning in text categorization. In C. Cardie & R. Weischedel (Eds.), *Proceedings of the 2nd Conference on Empirical Methods in Natural Language Processing (EMNLP 97)*, Providence, Rhode Island (pp. 55-63). Somerset, NJ: Association for Computational Linguistics.

Damerau, F. J., (1964) Technique for computer detection and correction of spelling errors. *Communications of the ACM, 7*(3), 171-176.

Darroch, J. N., & Ratcliff, D. (1972). Generalized iterative scaling for log-linear models. *The Annals of Mathematical Statistics, 43*(5), 1470-1480.

Dasgupta, S., Littman, M.L., & McAllester, D. (2002). Pac generalization bounds for CO-

TRAINING. In *Advances in Neural Information Processing Systems 14 (NIPS)* (pp. 375-382). MIT Press.

Davenport, T. H., & Prusak, L. (1998). *Working knowledge: How organizations manage what they know.* Cambridge, MA: Harvard Business School Press.

Davies, J., Studer, R., & Warren, P. (2006). *Semantic Web technologies: Trends and research in ontology-based systems.* John Wiley & Sons.

Dedijer, S. (2003, September). *Development & intelligence 2003-2053.* Paper presented at the Infoforum Business Intelligence Conference, Zagreb (Working Paper Series 10, Kund: Lund Institute of Economic Research).

Deerwester, S., Dumais S. T., & Harshman, R. (1990). Indexing by latent semantic analysis. *Journal of the Society for Information Science, 41*(6).

Dekel, O., Keshet J., & Singer Y (2004). Large margin hierarchical classification. In *Proceedings of the 3rd International Conference on Machine Learning and Cybernetics (ICML'04)* (pp. 209-216), Banff, AB, Canada. Morgan Kaufmann.

Dempster, A., Laird, N., & Rubin, D. (1997). Maximum likelihood from incomplete data via the EM algorithm. *Journal of the Royal Statistical Society, Series B, 39*(1), 1-38.

Devroye, L., & Gyorfi, L. (1985). *Nonparametric density estimation.* New York: John Wiley & Sons.

Diday, E., & Simon, J. C. (Eds.). (1976). *Clustering analysis: Digital pattern recognition.* Secaucus, NJ: Springer-Verlag.

Dimitrov, M., Bontcheva, K., Cunningham, H., & Maynard, D. (2004). A light-weight approach to coreference resolution for named entities in text. In A. Branco, T.M., & R. Mitkov (Eds.), *Anaphora processing: Linguistic, cognitive and computational modelling.* John Benjamins Publishing Company.

Ding, C. H. Q., He, X., Zha, H., Gu, M., & Simon, H. D. (2001). *A min-max cut algorithm for graph partitioning and data clustering.* Paper presented at the Proceedings of the 2001 IEEE International Conference on Data Mining, ICDM.

Ding, L., Finin, T. Joshi, A., Peng, Y., Pan, R., & Reddivari, P. (2005, October). Search on the semantic Web. *Communications of the ACM,* 62-69.

Dorigo, M., & Stützle, T. (2004). *Ant colony optimization.* Cambridge: The MIT Press.

Dorigo, M., Caro, D. G., & Gambardella, L. M. (1999). Ant algorithms for discrete optimization. *Artificial Life, 5*(2), 137-172.

Dorigo, M., Caro, D. G., & Sampels, M. (Eds.). (2002, September 12-14). Ant algorithms. In *Proceedings of the ANTS 2002 Third International Workshop,* (LNCS 2463, pp. V-VII). Brussels, Belgium. Springer.

Dorigo, M., Maniezzo, V., & Colorni, A. (1996). The ant system: Optimization by a colony of cooperating agents. *IEEE Transactions on Systems, Man, and Cybernetics-Part B, 26*(1), 29-41.

Dou, H. (1989). Quelques indicateurs bibliométriques en science et technique. *La Tribune des Mémoires et Thèses, 3,* 25-28.

Dou, H. (1995). *Veille technologique et compétitivité.* Paris: Dunod.

Dou, H. (2003, September—October). *Competitive intelligence, trends, methodologies and tools.* Paper presented at the I Seminario Internacional Ferramentas para Inteligencia Competitiva. Brasília, DF.

Ducheneaut, N., & Bellotti, V. (2001). E-mail as habitat: An exploration of embedded personal information management. *Interactions, 8,* 30-38.

Dumais S. T., & Chen, H. (2000). Hierarchical-classification of Web content. In *Proceedings of 23rd ACM International Conference on Research and Development in Information Retrieval (SIGIR'00)*, Athens, Greece (pp. 256-263). New York: ACM Press.

Dumais, S., Platt, J., Heckerman, D., & Sahami, M. (1998). *Inductive learning algorithms and representations for text categorization.* Paper presented at the Proceedings of the Seventh International Conference on Information and Knowledge Management, Bethesda, Maryland.

Echeverría, R. (1997). *Ontologia del Lenguaje* (4ª ed.). Santiago, Chile: Dolmen Ediciones.

EDUSP. (1993). *International classification of diseases and health related problems in Portuguese* (10th rev.). São Paulo: EDUSP (in collaboration with the World Health Organization).

Ellison, T. L., Elliott, R., & Moyes, S.A. (2005). HbA1c screening for undiagnosed diabetes in New Zealand. *Diabetes/Metabolism Research and Reviews, 21*, 65-70.

Epps, C. (2004). Length of stay, discharge disposition, and hospital charge predictors. *APRN Online, 79*(5), 975-976, 979-981, 984-988, 990, 992-997.

Etzioni, O. (1996). Moving up the information food chain: Deploying softbots on the World Wide Web. In *Proceedings of the 13th National Conference on Artificial Intelligence* (pp. 1322-1326).

Etzioni, O., & Weld, D. (1994). A softbot-based interface to the Internet. *Communications of the ACM, 37*(7), 72-76.

Everitt, B. S., Landau, S., & Leese, M. (2001). *Cluster analysis* (p. 237, 4th ed.). New York: Oxford University Press.

Fall, C. J., Törcsvári, A., & Karetka, G. (2002). Readme information for WIPO-alpha autocategorization training set. Retrieved April 5, 2007, from http://www.wipo.int/ibis/datasets/wipo-alpha-readme.html

Fall, C. J., Törcsvári, A., Benzineb, K., & Karetka, G. (2003). Automated categorization in the international patent classification. *ACM SIGIR Forum Archive, 37*(1), 10-25.

Fall, C. J., Törcsvári, A., Fievét, P., & Karetka, G. (2003). Additional readme information for WIPO-de autocategorization data set. Retrieved April 5, 2007, from http://www.wipo.int/ibis/datasets/wipo-de-readme.html

Fayyad, U. M. (1996). *Advances in knowledge discovery and data mining.* Menlo Park: AAAI Press.

Fayyad, U., Piatetsky-Shapiro, G., & Smyth, P. (1996). From data mining to knowledge discovery: An Overview. In U. Fayyad, G. Piatetsky-Shapiro, P. Smyth, & R. Uthurusamy (Eds.), *Advances in knowledge discovery and data mining* (pp. 1-36). Cambridge, MA: MIT Press.

Feldman, R., & Dagan, I. (1995). Knowledge discovery in textual databases. In *Proceedings of the First International Conference on Knowledge Discovery and Data Mining (KDD'95)* (pp. 112-117).

Feldman, R., & Dagan, I. (1998). Mining text using keyword distributions. *Journal of Intelligent Information Systems, 10,* 281-300.

Fellbaum, C. (1998). *WordNet: An electronic lexical database.* MIT Press.

Fensel, D. (2002). Ontology-based knowledge management. *IEEE Web Intelligence, 35*(11), 56-59.

Ferragina, P., & Gulli, A. (2005). A personalized search engine based on Web-snippet hierarchical clustering. In *WWW '05: Special Interest Tracks and Posters of the 14th International Conference on World Wide Web* (pp. 801-810). New York: ACM Press.

Finkel, J. R., Grenager, T., & Manning, C. D. (2005). Incorporating nonlocal information into information extraction systems by Gibbs sampling. In *Proceedings of the 43rd Annual Meeting of the Association for Computational Linguistics (ACL-2005)* (pp. 363-370).

Finn, A. (2006). *A multi-level boundary classification approach to information extraction.* Doctoral thesis, University College Dublin.

Finn, A., & Kushmerick, N. (2004). Information extraction by convergent boundary classification. In *AAAI-04 Workshop on Adaptive Text Extraction and Mining* (pp. 1-6). San Jose, CA.

Fischer, W. (2000). A comparison of PCS construction principles of the American DRGs, the Austrial LDF system, and the German FP/S E system. *Casemix, 2*(1), 12-20.

Fleischman, Hovy, & Echihabi. (2003). Offline strategies for online question answering: Answering questions before they are asked. In *Proceedings of the ACL 2003* (pp. 1-7).

Flores, F. (1989). *Inventando la empresa del siglo XXI*. Hachette.

Flores, F. (1996). *Creando organizaciones para el futuro*. Santiago, Chile: Dólmen.

Flores, F., Graves, M., Hartfield, B., & Winograd, T. (1988). Computer systems and the design of organizational interaction. *ACM Transactions on Office Information Systems, 6*(2), 157-172.

Foster, I., Kesselman, C., & Tuecke, S. (2001). The anatomy of the grid: Enabling scalable virtual organizations. *International Journal of High Performance Computing Applications, 15*(3), 200-223.

Fox, C. (1992). Lexical analysis and stoplists. In W. B. Frakes & R. A. Baeza-Yates (Eds.), *Information retrieval: Data structures & algorithms* (pp. 102-130). Upper Saddle River, NJ: Prentice Hall PTR.

Freeman, J.A., & Skapura, D.M. (1992). *Neural networks algorithms, applications, and programming technique.* Boston: Addison-Wesley.

Freitag, D. (1998). Information extraction from HTML: Application of a general machine learning approach. In *Proceedings of the 15th Conference on Artificial Intelligence (AAAI'98)* (pp. 517-523).

Freitag, D., & Kushmerick, N. (2000). Boosted wrapper induction. In *Proceedings of 17th National Conference on Artificial Intelligence* (pp. 577-583).

Fuhr, N. (1985). *A probabilistic model of dictionary based automatic indexing.* Paper presented at the Proceedings of the Riao 85 (Recherche d' Informations Assistee par Ordinateur), Grenoble, France.

Fuld, L. M. (1995). *The new competitor intelligence: the complete resource for finding, analyzing and using information about competitors.* New York: Wiley & Sons.

Fung, B. C. M., Wang, K., & Ester, M. (2003). Hierarchical document clustering using frequent item-sets. In *Proceedings of the SIAM International Conference on Data Mining (SDM'03)*.

Furnas, G. W., Landauer, T. K., Gomez, L. M., & Dumais, S. T. (1987). The vocabulary problem in human-system communication. *Communications of the ACM, 30*, 964-970.

Furnkranz, J., Holzbaur, C., & Temel, R. (2002). User profiling for the Melvil knowledge retrieval system. *Applied Artificial Intelligence, 16*(4), 243-281.

Gaizauskas, R, Greenwood, M., Hepple, M, Roberts, T, Saggion, H., & Sargaison, M. (2004). In *Proceedings of TREC 2004*. The University of Sheffield's TREC 2004 Q&A.

Gaizauskas, R., Hepple, M., Saggion, H., Greenwood, M., & Humpreys, K. (2005). SUPPLE: A practical parser for natural language engineering applications. In *Proceedings of the International Workshop on Parsing Technologies.*

Gamma, E., Helm, R., Vlissides, J., & Johnson, R. (1994). *Design patterns.* Addison-Wesley Longman.

Ge, N., Hale, J., & Charniak, E. (1998). A statistical approach to anaphora resolution. In *Proceedings of the Sixth Workshop on Very Large Corpora.* (pp. 161-170). Montreal, Canada.

Gelbukh, A. (2002). *Computational linguistics and intelligent text processing.* New York: Springer-Verlag, Lecture Notes in Computer Sciences.

Ghahramani, Z., & Jordan, M. I. (1997). Factorial hidden Markov models. *Machine Learning, 29,* 245-273.

Giannotti, F., Nanni, M., & Pedreschi, D. (2003). Webcat: Automatic categorization of Web search results. In *Proceedings of the Eleventh Italian Symposium on Advanced Database Systems (SEBD'03)* (pp. 507-518).

Godbole, S., & Sarawagi, S., (2004). Discriminative methods for multi-labeled classification. In H. Dai, R. Srikant & C. Zhang (Eds.), *Proceedings of the 8th Pacific-Asia Conference on Knowledge Discovery and Data Mining (PAKDD'04),* Sydney, Australia (LNAI 3056, pp. 22-30). Berlin/Heidelberg, Germany: Springer-Verlag.

Golding, A. R., & Roth, D., (1996). Applying Winnow to context-sensitive spelling correction. In *Proceedings of 13th International Conference on Machine Learning* (pp. 182-190), Bari, Italy: Morgan Kaufmann.

Gourbin, G., & Masuy-Stroobant, G. (1995). Registration of vital data: Are live births and stillbirths comparable all over Europe? *Bulletin of the World Health Organization, 73*(4), 449-460.

Graafmans, W., Richardus, J., Macfarlane, A., Rebagliato, H., Blondel, B., & Verloove-Vanhorick, S., et al. (2001). Comparability of published perinatal mortality rates in Western Europe: The quantitative impact of differences in gestational age and birthweight criteria. *International Journal of Obstetrics & Gynaecology, 108*(12), 1237-1245.

Gruber, T. R. (1993). A translation approach to portable ontologies. *Knowledge Acquisition, 5*(2), 199-220.

Grune, D. & Jacobs, C. J. H. (1991). *Parsing techniques: A practical guide.* Ellis Horwood Ltd.

Guarino, N. (1998). Formal ontology and information systems. In N. Guarino (Ed), *Proceedings of the 1st International Conference on Formal Ontology and Information Systems, (FOIS'98)* (pp. 3-15). Trento, Italy: IOS Press.

Guarino, N., & Giaretta, N. (1995). Ontologies and knowledge bases: Towards a terminological clarification. In N. Mars (Ed.), *Towards very large knowledge bases: Knowledge building and knowledge sharing* (pp. 25-32). Amsterdam: IOS Press.

GUIEX (2005). *Guidelines for examination in the European patent office.* Published by the European Patent Office Directorate Patent Law 5.2.1. Munich: European Patent Office. ISBN 3-89605-074-5.

Gulla, J. A., Auran, P. G., & Risvik, K. M. (2002). Linguistics in large-scale Web search. In *Proceedings of the 7th International Conference on Applications of Natural Language to Information Systems (NLDB'2002)* (pp. 218-222).

Gulla, J. A., Borch, H. O., & Ingvaldsen, J. E. (2006). Unsupervised keyphrase extraction for search ontologies. In *Proceedings of 11th International Conference on Applications of Natural Language to Information Systems (NLDB'2006).*

Halácsy, P. (2005). Benefits of deep NLP-based lemmatization for information retrieval. In *Working Notes for the CLEF 2006 Workshop*, Alicante, Spain.

Halkidi, M., Batistakis, Y., & Vazirgiannis, M. (2002). Cluster validity checking methods: Part I. *ACM SIGMOD Record, 31*(2), 40-45.

Halkidi, M.,Batistakis, Y., & Vazirgiannis, M. (2002). Cluster validity checking methods: Part II. *ACM SIGMOD Record, 31*(3), 19-27.

Hammersley, J., & Clifford, P. (1971). *Markov fields on finite graphs and lattices*. Unpublished manuscript.

Han, H., Giles, L., Manavoglu, E., Zha, H., Zhang, Z., & Fox, E. A. (2003). Automatic document metadata extraction using support vector machines. In *Proceedings of 2003 Joint Conference on Digital Libraries (JCDL'03)* (pp. 37-48).

Han, J., & Chang, K. (2002). Data mining for Web intelligence. *IEEE Web Intelligence, 35*(11), 64-70.

Han, J., & Kamber, M. (2001). *Data mining: Concepts and techniques*. Academic Press.

Hanson, S. J. (1990). Conceptual clustering and categorization: Bridging the gap between induction and causal models. In Y. Kodratoff & R. Michalski (Eds.), *Machine learning: An artificial intelligence approach* (vol. III, pp.235-268). San Mateo, CA: Morgan.

Harabagiu, S., Moldovan, D., Clark, M., Bowden, J., Williams, & Bensley, J. (2003). Answer mining by combining extraction techniques with abductive reasoning. In *Proceedings of TREC-2003* (pp. 375-382).

Hartigan, J. (1975). *Clustering algorithms*. New York: John Wiley & Sons.

Heaps, H. S. (1978). *Information retrieval: Computational and theoretical aspects*. Academic Press.

Hearst, M. A. (1992). Automatic acquisition of hyponyms from large text corpora. In *Proceedings of the Fourteenth International Conference on Computational Linguistics*. Nantes, France.

Hearst, M. A. (2006, April). Clustering vs. faceted categories for information exploration. *Communications of the ACM*, 59-62.

Hearst, M. A., & Pedersen, J. O. (1996). Reexamining the cluster hypothesis: Scatter/gather on retrieval results. In *Proceedings of the 19th Annual International ACM SIGIR Conference on Research and Development in Information Retrieval (SIGIR'96)* (pp. 76-84).

Hearst, M.A. (1999). Untangling text data mining. *Proceedings of ACL'99: The 37th Annual Meeting of the Association for Computational Linguistics* (pp. 3-10).

Heylighen, F. (1999). Collective intelligence and its implementation on the Web: Algorithms to develop a collective mental map. *Computational and Mathematical Theory of Organizations, 5*(3), 253-280.

Hiemstra, D. (1998). *A linguistically motivated probabilistic model of information retrieval*. Paper presented at the Research and Advanced Technology for Digital Libraries, Second European Conference, ECDL 1998, Heraklion, Crete, Greece.

Hofmann, T., Cai, L., & Ciaramita, M., (2003). Learning with taxonomies: Classifying documents and words. In *Workshop on Syntax, Semantics, and Statistics (NIPS'03)*, Whistler, BC, Canada.

Hood, W. W., & Wilson, C. S. (2003). Informetric studies using databases: Opportunities and challenges. *Scientometrics, 58*(3), 587-608.

Hornik, K., Stinchocombe, M., & White, H. (1989). Multilayer feedforward networks are universal approximators. *Neural Networks, 2*, 359-366.

Hospital Report Cards Methodology. (2001). Healthgrades.com. Retrieved April 7, 2007, from http://www.healthgrades.com/public/index.cfm?fuseaction=mod&modtype=content&modact=Hrc_Methodology

Hull, D. A. (1996). Stemming algorithms: A case study for detailed evaluation. *JASIS, 47*(1), 70-84.

Iazzoni, L. (1997). *Risk adjustment for measuring health care outcomes* (2nd ed.). Chicago: Healthcare Administration Press.

IBM Intelligent Miner (2007). Retrieved August 9, 2007 from http://www-306.ibm.com/software/data/iminer/

Ichimura, Y., Nakayama, Y., Miyoshi, M., Akahane, T., Sekiguchi, T., & Fujiwara, Y. (2001). Text mining systems for analysis of a salesperson's daily reports. In *Proceedings of the Pacific Association for Computational Linguistics 2001* (pp. 127-135).

Ide, N. & Véronis, J. (1995). *Corpus encoding standard.* Document MUL/EAG CES1 Annex 10.Retrieved from http://www.lpl.univ-aix.fr/projects/multext/CES/CES1.html

Jacsó, P. (1993). Searching for skeletons in the database cupboard Part I; Errors of omission. *Database, 16*(1), 38-49.

Jacsó, P. (1993). Searching for skeletons in the database cupboard Part II; Errors of comission. *Database, 16*(2), 38-49.

Jacsó, P. (1997). Content evaluation of databases. In M. E. Williams (Ed.), *Annual review of information science and technology (ARIST), 32,* (pp. 231-267). Medford, NJ: American Society for Information Science (ASIS).

Jain, A. K., Murty, M. N., & Flynn, P. J. (1999). Data clustering: A review. *ACM Computing Surveys, 31*(3), 264-323.

Jambu, M. (2000). *Introduction au data mining: Analyse intelligente des donnees.* Paris: Editions Eyrolles.

Jardine, N., & van Rijsbergen., C. J. (1971). The use of hierarchical clustering in information retrieval. *Information Storage and Retrieval, 7,* 217-240.

Jizba, R., (2000). *Measuring search effectiveness,* Retrieved March 9, 2006 from http://www.hsl.creighton.edu/hsl/Searching/Recall-Precision.html

Joachims, T. (1996). A probabilistic analysis of the Rocchio algorithm with TFIDF for text categorization. In *Proceedings of the 14th International Conference on Machine Learning (ICML-97)* (pp. 143-151). San Francisco: Morgan Kaufmann Publishers.

Joachims, T. (2002), *Learning to classify text using support vector machines, methods, theory and algorithms,* Kluwer Academic Publishers.

Joachims, T., Freitag, D., & Mitchell, T. (1997). Webwatcher: A tour guide for the World Wide Web. In *Proceedings of the 15th International Joint Conference on Artificial Intelligence (IJCAI-97)* (Vol. 1, pp. 770-777). Nagoya, Japan.

Johnson, F. C., Paice, C. D., Black, W. J., & Neal, A. (1993). The application of linguistic processing to automatic abstract generation. *Journal of Document & Text Management, 1,* 215-241.

Johnson, M. L., Gordon, H. S., Peterson, N. J., Wray, N. P., Shroyer, L. A., Grover, F.L., et al. (2002). Effect of definition of mortality on hospital profiles. *Medical Care, 40*(1), 7-16.

Johnson, R. A., & Wichern, D. W. (2002). *Applied multivariate statistical analysis* (5th ed.). Prentice Hall.

Joho, H., & Sanderson, M. (2000). Retrieving descriptive phrases from large amounts of free text. In *Proceedings of Conference on Information and Knowledge Management* (pp. 180-186). ACM.

Joseph, K., Allen, A., Kramer, M., Cyr, M., & Fair, M. (1999). Changes in the registration of stillbirths<500 g in Canada, 1985-1995. Fetal-infant mortality study group of the Canadian perinatal surveillance system. *Paediatric Perinatal Epidemiology, 13*(3), 278-287.

Jurafsky, D., & Martin, J. H. (2000). *Speech and language processing: An introduction to natural language processing, computational linguistics and speech recognition.* Prentice Hall.

Kando, N. (2000). What shall we evaluate? Preliminary discussion for the NTCIR Patent IR Challenge based on the brainstorming with the specialized intermediaries in patent searching and patent attorneys. In *ACM-SIGIR Workshop on Patent Retrieval*, Athens, Greece (pp. 37-42). New York: ACM Press.

Kantrowitz, M., Mohit, B., & Mittal, V. O. (2000). Stemming and its effects on TFIDF ranking. In *Proceedings of SIGIR 2000* (pp. 357-359).

Karanikas, H., & Theodoulidis, B. (2002). *Knowledge discovery in text and text mining software* (Tech. Rep.). UMIST, Department of Computation.

Katz, S. M. (1995). Distribution of content words and phrases in text and language modeling. *Natural Language Engineering, 2*(1), 15-59.

Kauchak, D., Smarr, J., & Elkan, C. (2004). Sources of success for boosted wrapper induction. *The Journal of Machine Learning Research, 5*, 499-527.

Kaufman, L., & Rousseeuw, P. J. (1990). *Finding groups in data: An introduction to cluster analysis.* Wiley-Interscience.

Keith, S., Kaser, O. & Lemire, D. (2005). *Analyzing large collections of electronic text using OLAP.* arXiv:cs.DB/0605127 v1.

Kiritchenko, S., & Matwin, S. (2001). E-mail classification with CO-TRAINING. In *Conference of*

the Centre for Advanced Studies on Collaborative Research (pp. 192-201). IBM Press.

Kleinrock, L., & Huang, J. H. (1992). On parallel processing systems: Amdahl's law generalized and some results on optimal design. *IEEE Transactions on Software Engineering, 18*(5), 434-447.

Kochen, M. (1974). *Principles of information retrieval* (p. 203). New York: John Wiley & Sons.

Kockelkorn, M., Lneburg, A., & Scheffer, T. (2003). Using transduction and multiview learning to answer e-mails. In *Proceedings of the European Conference on Principle and Practice of Knowledge Discovery in Databases* (pp. 266-277). Springer-Verlag.

Kofman, F. (2002). *Metamanagement* (in Portuguese). São Paulo, Brazil: Antakarana Cultura Arte Ciência.

Kohonen, T., Kaski, S., Lagus, K., Salojärvi, J., Honkela, J., Paatero, V., et al. (2000). Self organization of a massive document collection. *IEEE Transactions on Neural Networks, 11*(3), 574-585.

Koller, D., & Sahami, M. (1997). Hierarchicalally classifying documents using a very few words. *Proceedings of the 14th International Conference on Machine Learning, 14*, (pp. 170-178). Nashville, Tennessee: Morgan-Kaufmann.

Konchady M., (2006), *Text mining applications programming*, Boston: Charles River Media.

Korfhage, R. R. (1997). *Information retrieval and storage* (p. 349). New York: John Wiley & Sons.

Kosala, R., & Blockeel, H. (2000). Web mining research: A survey. *SIGKDD Explorations, 2*(1), 1-15.

Koster, C.H.A., Seutter M., & Beney, J. (2001). Classifying patent applications with Winnow. In *Proceedings of Benelearn 2001 Conference* (pp. 19-26). Antwerpen, Belgium.

Kouylekov, M., Magnini, B., Negri, M., & Tanev, H (2003). ITC-irst at TREC-2003: The DIOGENE QA system. In *Proceedings of TREC-2003*.

Kozierok, R., & Maes, P. (1993). Learning interface agents. In *Proceedings of the 11th National Conference on Artificial Intelligence* (pp. 459-465).

Kraaij, W., & Pohlmann, R. (1996). Viewing stemming as recall enhancement. In *Proceedings of the 19th Annual International ACM SIGIR Conference on Research and Development in Information Retrieval (SIGIR'96)* (pp. 40-48).

Krier, M., & Zaccà, F. (2002). Automatic categorization applications at the European Patent Office. *World Patent Information, 24*, 187-196.

Kristjansson, T. T., Culotta, A., Viola, P. A., & McCallum, A. (2004). Interactive information extraction with constrained conditional random fields. In *Proceedings of AAAI'04* (pp. 412-418).

Kules, W. M. (2006). *Supporting exploratory Web search with meaningful and stable categorized overviews.* Doctoral thesis, University of Maryland, College Park.

Kupiec, J. (1992). Robust part-of-speech tagging using a hidden Markov model. *Computer Speech and Language, 6*(3), 225-242.

Kushmerick, N. (2000). Wrapper induction: Efficiency and expressiveness. *Artificial Intelligence, 118*, 15-68.

Kushmerick, N., Weld, D. S., & Doorenbos, R. (1997). Wrapper induction for information extraction. In *Proceedings of the International Joint Conference on Artificial Intelligence (IJCAI'97)* (pp. 729-737).

Lacatusu, F., Hick, L., Harabagiu, S., & Nezd, L. (2004). Lite-GISTexter at DUC2004. In *Proceedings of DUC 2004*. NIST.

Lafferty, J., McCallum, A., & Pereira, F. (2001). Conditional random fields: Probabilistic models for segmenting and labeling sequence data. In *Proceedings of the 18th International Conference on Machine Learning (ICML'01)* (pp. 282-289).

Landauer, T. K., Foltz, P. W., & Laham, D. (1998) Introduction to latent semantic analysis. *Discourse Processes, 25*, 259-284.

Lang, K. (1995). NewsWeeder: Learning to filter netnews. In *Proceedings of the 12th International Conference on Machine Learning* (pp. 331-339).

Lappin, S. & Leass, H. (1995). An algorithm for pronominal anaphora resolution. *Computational Linguistics, 20*(4), 535-561

Larkey, L. S. (1998). Some issues in the automatic classification of US patents. In *Working Notes for the Workshop on Learning for Text Categorization, 15th National Conference on Artificial Intelligence (AAAI-98)*. Madison, Wisconsin.

Larkey, L. S. (1999). A patent search and classification system. In *Proceedings of DL-99, the 4th ACM Conference on Digital Libraries*, Berkeley, California (pp. 179-187). New York: ACM Press.

Larsen, B., & Aone, C. (1999). *Fast and effective text mining using linear-time document clustering*. Paper presented at the Proceedings of the Fifth ACM SIGKDD International Conference on Knowledge Discovery and Data Mining, San Diego, California.

Lashkari, Y., Metral, M., & Maes, P. (1994). Collaborative interfaces agents. In *Proceedings of the 12th National Conference on Artificial Intelligence* (pp. 444-450).

Lawrence, S., Giles, C. L., & Bollacker K. (1999). Digital libraries and autonomous citation indexing. *IEEE Computer, 32*(6), 67-71.

Lawrie, D., Croft, W. B., & Rosenberg, A. (2001). *Finding topic words for hierarchical summarization*. Paper presented at the Proceedings of the 24th

Annual International ACM SIGIR Conference on Research and Development in Information Retrieval, New Orleans, Louisiana.

Le Coadic, Y. F. (2003). Mathématique et statistique en science de l'information: Infométrie mathématique et infométrie statistique. *Information Sciences for Decision Making, 6*(03).

Lee, C. H., & Yang, H. C. (1999). A Web text mining approach based on self-organizing map. In *Proceedings of the 2nd International Workshop on Web Information and Data Management* (pp. 59-62).

Leeds, S. (2000, January). Data mining: Beware of the shaft. *Direct Marketing.* Retrieved March 25, 2007, from http://www.tmiassoc.com/articles/shaft.htm

Levet, J. L. (2001). *L'Intelligence Economique— Mode de pensée, mode d'action.* Paris: Economica.

Lewis, D. D. (1991). Evaluating text categorization. In *Speech and Natural Language Workshop* (pp. 312-318). San Mateo: Morgan Kaufmann.

Lewis, D. D. (1992). *An evaluation of phrasal and clustered representations on a text categorization task.* Paper presented at the Proceedings of SIGIR-92, 15th ACM International Conference on Research and Development in Information Retrieval.

Lewis, D. D., Yang, Y., Rose, T. G., & Li, F. (2004). RCV1: A new benchmark collection for text categorization research. *Journal of Machine Learning Research, 5*, 361-397.

Lewis, D.D., Schapire, R.E., Callan, J.P., & Papka, R., (1996). Training algorithms for linear text classifiers. In *Proceedings of SIGIR-96, 19th ACM International Conference on Research and Development in Information Retrieval*, Zürich, Switzerland (pp. 298-306). New York: ACM Press.

Li, X., & Liu, B. (2003). Learning to classify texts using positive and unlabeled data. In *Proceedings of International Joint Conference on Artificial Intelligence (IJCAI'2003)* (pp. 587-592).

Liere, R., & Tadepalli, P. (1997). Active learning with committees for text categorization. In *Proceedings of AAAI-97, the 14th National Conference of Artificial Intelligence* (pp. 591-496). Providence, Rhode Island: AAAI Press.

Lin, C.-h., & Chen, H. (1999). An automated indexing and neural network approach to concept retrieval and classification of multilingual (Chinese-English) documents. *IEEE Transactions on Systems, Man and Cybernetics, 26*(1), 1-14.

Lin, C.-Y. (2004). ROUGE: A package for automatic evaluation of summaries. In *Proceedings of the Workshop on Text Summarization*. Barcelona, ACL.

Littlestone, N. (1988). Learning quickly when irrelevant attributes around: A new linear-threshold algorithm. *Machine Learning, 2*, 285-318.

Littlestone, N. (1995). Comparing sereval linear-threshold learning algorithm on tasks involving superfluous attributes. In *Proceedings of 12th International Conference on Machine Learning*, San Francisco (pp. 353-361). Morgan Kaufmann.

Liu, J., Yao, Y., & Zhong, N., (2002). In search of the wisdom Web. *IEEE Web Intelligence, 35*(11), 27-31.

Liu, Y., Loh, H. T., & Tor, S. B. (2004). *Building a document corpus for manufacturing knowledge retrieval.* Paper presented at the Proceedings of the Singapore MIT Alliance Symposium, Singapore.

Lloyd, S. (1982). Least squares quantization in PCM. *IEEE Transactions on Information Theory, 28*(2), 129-137.

Loh, S. (2001). Knowledge discovery in textual documentation: Qualitative and quantitative analysis. *Journal of Documentation, 57*(5), 577-590.

Loh, S., Wives, L. K., & Oliveira, J. P. M. de. (2000). Concept-based knowledge discovery in texts extracted from the Web. *ACM SIGKDD Explorations, 2*(1), 29-39.

London, J. A., Rosengart, M. R., Jurkovich, G. J., & Nathens, A. B. (2006). Prospective payments in a regional trauma center: The case for recognition of the transfer patient in diagnostic related groups. *Injury Infection & Critical Care, 60*(2), 390-5.

Lu, H., Motoda, H., & Liu, H. (Eds.). (1997). *KDD: Techniques and applications*. Singapore: World Scientific.

Maes, P. (1994). Agents that reduce work and information overload. *Communications of the ACM, 37*(7), 30-40.

Manevitz, L. M., & Yousef, M. (2001). One-class SVMs for document classification. *Journal of Machine Learning Research, 2*, 139-154.

Mani, I. (2001). *Automatic text summarization*. John Benjamins Publishing Company.

Mani, I., Klein, G., House, D., Hirschman, L., Firmin, T., & Sundheim, B. (2002). SUMMAC: A text summarization evaluation. *Nat. Lang. Eng., 8*(1), 43-68.

Manning, C. D., & Schütze, H. (1999). *Foundations of statistical natural language processing*. Boston: The MIT Press.

Marchionini, G. (2006, April). Exploratory search: From finding to understanding. *Communications of the ACM,* 41-46.

Marcu, D. (1999). The automatic construction of large-scale corpora for summarization research. In M. Hearst, F., G., Tong, R. (Eds.), *Proceedings of SIGIR'99 22nd International Conference on Research and Development in Information Retrieval* (pp. 137-144). University of California, Berkeley.

Martens, B.V. d.V. (2002). IST 501: Research techniques for information management. Retrieved April 7, 2007, from http://web.syr.edu/~bvmarten/index.html

Martins, B. & Silva, M. J. (2004). Spelling correction for search engine queries. *EsTAL—España for Natural Language Processing* (pp. 372-383). Alicante, Spain.

Masson, H. (2001). *Les fondements politiques de l'intelligence économique*. Unpublished doctoral dissertation, Faculté Jean Monnet à Sceaux, Droit, Economie, Gestion—Université Paris Sud XI. Paris.

Matsubara, E. T., & Monard, M.C. (2004). *Experimental evaluation of the multiview semisupervised learning CO-TRAINING algorithm* (Tech. Rep. No. 235, ICMC-USP). Retrieved March 29, 2007, from ftp://ftp.icmc.usp.br/pub/ BIBLIOTECA/rel tec/RT 235.pdf

Matsubara, E. T., Martins, C.A., & Monard, M. C. (2003). *Pretext: A pre-processing text tool using the bag-of-words approach* (Tech. Rep. No. 209, ICMC-USP). Retrieved March 29, 2007, from ftp://ftp.icmc.sc.usp.br/pub/ BIBLIOTECA/rel tec/RT 209.zip

Matsubara, E. T., Monard, M.C., & Batista, G.E.A.P.A. (2005). Multiview semisupervised learning: An approach to obtain different views from text datasets. *Advances in Logic Based Intelligent Systems, 132*, 97-104.

Matsubara, E. T., Monard, M.C., & Prati, R.C. (2006). On the class distribution labeling step sensitivity of CO-TRAINING. In *Proceedings of IFIP Artificial Intelligence in Theory and Practice* (pp. 199-208).

Maturana, H. R., & Varela, F.J. (1992). *The tree of knowledge: The biological roots of human understanding* (Rev. Sub. ed). Boston: Shambhala.

Maynard, D., Bontcheva, K., & Cunningham, H. (2003). Towards a semantic extraction of named entities. In *Proceedings Recent Advances in Natural*, Borovets, Bulgaria.

McCallum, A. (2003). Efficiently inducing features of conditional random fields. In *Proceedings of the 19th Conference in Uncertainty in Artificial Intelligence* (pp. 403-410).

McCallum, A., Freitag, D., & Pereira, F. (2000). Maximum entropy Markov models for information extraction and segmentation. In *Proceedings of the 17th International Conference on Machine Learning (ICML'00)* (pp. 591-598).

McCallum, A., Rosenfeld, R., Mitchell, T., & Ng, A. (1998). Improving text classification by shrinkage in a hierarchy of classes. In *Proceedings of 15th International Conference of Machine Learning* (pp. 359-367). Madison, Wisconsin: Morgan Kaufmann.

McCanne, D. (2003). Why incremental reforms will not solve the health care crisis. *Journal of the American Board of Family Medicine, 16*, 257-261.

McKee, M., Coles, M., & James, P. (1999). Failure to rescue as a measure of quality of hospital care: The limitations of secondary diagnosis coding in English hospital data. *Journal of Public Health Medicine, 21*(4), 453-458.

Medawar, K. (1995). Database quality: A literature review of the past and a plan for the future. *News of Computers in Libraries, 29*(3), 257-272.

Melo, V., Secato, M., & Lopes, A. A. (2003). Automatic extraction and identification of bibliographical information from scientific articles (in Portuguese). In *IV Workshop on Advances and Trends in AI* (pp. 1-10). Chile.

Michalski, R., & Stepp, R. (1983). Automated construction of classifications: Conceptual clustering vs. numerical taxonomy. *IEEE Transactions on Pattern Analysis and Machine Intelligence (PAMI), 5*(5), 396-409.

Miller, D. R. H., Leek, T., & Schwartz, R. M. (1999). *A hidden Markov model information retrieval system.* Paper presented at the Proceedings of SIGIR-99, 22nd ACM International Conference on Research and Development in Information Retrieval, Berkeley, California.

Miller, G. A., Beckwith, R., Fellbaum, C., Gross, D., & Miller, K. (1993). *Five papers on WordNet.* Cognitive Science Laboratory, Princeton University.

Miller, G. A. (1995, November). WordNet: A lexical database. *Communications of the ACM, 38*(11), 39-41.

Mirkin, B. (1996). *Mathematical classification and clustering.* Springer.

Mitchell, T. M. (1997). *Machine learning.* McGraw-Hill.

Mitkov, R. (1999). *Anaphora resolution: The state of the art.* University of Wolverhampton, Wolverhampton.

Mizzaro, S. A. (1996). Cognitive analysis of information retrieval. In *Information Science: Integration in Perspective, CoLIS2* (pp. 233-250). The Royal School of Librarianship.

Mobasher, B. (2004). Web mining and personalization. In M. P. Singh (Ed.) *The practical handbook of internet computing.* CRC Press.

Mock, K. J. (1996). Hybrid hill-climbing and knowledge-based methods for intelligent news filtering. In *Proceedings of the 13th National Conference on Artificial Intelligence* (pp. 48-53).

Mogee, M. E. (1997). Patents and technology intelligence. In W. B. Ashton & R. A. Klavans (Eds.), *Keeping abreast of science and technology: Technical intelligence for business.* New York: Battelle Press.

Morik, K., Brockhausen, P., & Joachims, T. (1999). Combining statistical learning with a knowledge-based approach: A case study in intensive care monitoring. In *Proceedings of International Conference on Machine Learning (ICML'99)* (pp. 268-277).

Muller, A., Dorre, J., Gerstl, P., & Seiffert, R. (1999). *The taxgen framework: Automating the generation of a taxonomy for a large document collection.* Paper presented at the Proceedings of the 32nd Hawaii International Conference on System Sciences, Maui, Hawaii.

Muslea, I. (1999). Extraction patterns for information extraction tasks: A survey. In *Proceedings of AAAI-99: Workshop on Machine Learning for Information Extraction.*

Muslea, I., Minton, S., & Knoblock, C. (1998). STALKER: Learning extraction rules for semistructured, Web-based information sources. In *the AAAI Workshop on AI and Information Integration* (pp. 74-81).

Muslea, I., Minton, S., & Knoblock, C. (1999). Hierarchical wrapper induction for semistructured information sources. *Autonomous Agents and Multi-Agent Systems, 4,* 93-114.

Muslea, I., Minton, S., & Knoblock, C. (2002). Active+semisupervised learning=robust multiview learning. In *Proceedings of the 19th International Conference on Machine Learning (ICML)* (pp. 435-432), Morgan Kaufmann Publishers.

Muslea, I., Minton, S., & Knoblock, C. A. (2003). Active learning with strong and weak views: A case study on wrapper induction. In *Proceedings of the International Joint Conference on Artificial Intelligence (IJCAI)* (pp. 415-420).

Muslea, I., Minton, S., & Knoblock, C.A. (2000). Selective sampling with redundant views. In *Proceedings of the 15th National Conference on Artificial Intelligence (AAAI)* (pp. 621-626).

Naisbitt, J. (1996). *Megatrends 2000.* New York: Smithmark Publishers.

Netgen Analysis Desktop (1996). Retrieved April 2, 2007, from http://www.netgen.com

Neumann, P.J., Rosen, A. B., & Weinstein, M. (2005). Medicare and cost-effectiveness analysis. *The New England Journal of Medicine, 353*(14), 1516-1522.

Newman, D. J., Hettich, S., Blake, C. L., & Merz, C.J. (1998). UCI repository of machine learning databases. Retrieved March 29, 2007, from http://www.ics.uci.edu/~mlearn/MLRepository.html

Ng, H. T., Lim, C. Y., & Koo, J. L. T. (1999). Learning to recognize tables in free text. In *Proceedings of the 37th Annual Meeting of the Association for Computational Linguistics on Computational Linguistics (ACL'99)* (pp. 443-450).

Ng, H. T., Goh, W. B., & Low, K. L. (1997). Feature selection, perceptron learning, and a usability case study for text categorization. In N.J. Belkin, A.D. Narasimhalu & P. Willett (Eds.), *Proceedings of SIGIR-97, 20th ACM International Conference on Research and Development in Information Retrieval*, Philadelphia (pp. 67-73). New York: ACM Press.

Nigam, K. (2001). *Using unlabeled data to improve text classification* (Tech. Rep. No. CMU-CS-01-126). Doctoral dissertation, Carnegie Mellon University.

Nigam, K., McCallum, A. K., Thrun, S., & Mitchell, T.M. (2000). Text classification from labeled and unlabeled documents using EM. *Machine Learning, 39*(2/3), 103-134.

Nobrega, R. G. (2001). Data warehousing. In K. Tarapanoff (Ed.), *Inteligência organizacional e competitiva* (pp. 285-302). Brasília: Editora Universidade de Brasília.

Nocedal, J., & Wright, S. J. (1999). *Numerical optimization.* New York: Springer Press.

Nonaka, I., & Takeuchi, H. (1995). *The knowledge-creating company: How Japanese compa-*

nies create the dynamics of innovation. Oxford University Press.

O'Keefe, K. (1998). Accounting for severity of illness in acutely hospitalized patients: A framework for clinical decision support using DYNAMO. General Electric Medical Systems. Retrieved April 7, 2007, from http://www.gemedicalsystems. com/inen/prod_sol/hcare/resources/library/article07.html

O'Neill, E. T., & Vizine-Goetz, D. (1988). Quality control in online databases. In M. E. Williams (Ed.), *Annual review of information science and technology (ARIST), 23*, (pp. 125-156). Amsterdam: Elsevier Science Publishers, American Society for Information Science (ASIS).

O'Neill, E. T., Rogers, S. A., & Oskins, M. W. (1993). Characteristics of duplicate records in OCLC's online union catalog. *Library Resources and Technical Services, 37*(1), 59-71.

Open Market Inc. (1996). Open market Web reporter. Retrieved April 2, 2007, from http://www.openmarket.com

Osinski, S., & Weiss, D. (2004). Conceptual clustering using lingo algorithm: Evaluation on open directory project data. In *Advances in Soft Computing, Intelligent Information Processing and Web Mining, Proceedings of the International IIS (IIPWM'04)*.

Palazzo, L. A. M.(2000). *Modelos proativos para hipermídia adaptativa.* Tese (Ciência da Computação) - Universidade Federal do Rio Grande do Sul, Brazil.

Pao, M. L. (1989, May). Importance of quality data for bibliometric research. In M. E. Williams (Ed.), *Proceedings of the 10th national online meeting* (pp. 321-327). Medford, NY: Learned Information Inc.

Payne, T. R., & Edwards, P. (1997). Interface agents that learn: An investigation of learning issues in a mail agent interface. *Applied Artificial Intelligence, 11*(1), 1-32.

Pearson, J. (1998). Terms in context. *Studies in corpus linguistics: Vol. 1.* John Benjamins Publishing Company.

Peng, F. (2001). *Models for information extraction* (Technique Report).

Peng, F., & McCallum, A. (2004). Accurate information extraction from research papers using conditional random fields. In *Proceedings of HLT-NAACL* (pp. 329-336).

Penteado, R. (2006). *Création de systèmes d'intelligence dans une organisation de recherche et développement avec la scientométrie et la médiamétrie.* Unpublished doctoral dissertation, Université du Sud Toulon Var, Toulon.

Penteado, R., & Quoniam, L. (2001, October). Aplicação da bibliometria na análise estratégica das competências da Embrapa. In *Proceedings of the 2º Workshop Brasileiro de Inteligência Competitiva e Gestão do Conhecimento.* Florianópolis, SC.

Penteado, R., Dou, H., Boutin, E., & Quoniam, L. (2003). De la création des bases de données au développement de systèmes d'intelligence pour l'entreprise. *Information Sciences for Decision Making, 8,* 67-105. Retrieved March 25, 2007, from http://isdm.univ-tln.fr/articles/num_archives.htm#isdm8

Pereira, J. J. de O. (2005, June). *Data mining—Trazendo poder ao business intelligence.* Paper presented at the Symposium Inteligência Organizacional 2005 Brasília. Brasília, DF.

Perez, C. (2006). Open source full text search engines written in java. *Manageability Blog.* Retrieved January 9, 2007, from www.manageability.org/blog/stuff/full-text-lucene-jxta-search-engine-java-xml

Pierret, J. D. (2006). *Méthodologie et structuration d'un outil de découverte de connaissances basé sur la littérature biomédicale: Une application basée sur l'exploitation du MeSH.* Unpublished doctoral dissertation, Université du Sud Toulon Var, Toulon.

Pierret, J. D., & Boutin, E. (2004). Découverte de connaissances dans les bases de données bibliographiques. Le travail de Don Swanson: de l'idée au modèle. *Information Sciences for Decision Making, 12,* 109. Retrieved March 25, 2007, from http://isdm.univ-tln.fr/PDF/isdm12/isdm12a109_pierret.pdf

Pine, M. (2001). Episodes in action: Linking the cost and quality of nonsurgical coronary revascularization. *Managed Care Quarterly, 9*(3), 25-33.

Pinto, D., McCallum, A., Wei, X., & Croft, W. B. (2003). Table extraction using conditional random fields. In *Proceedings of the 26th Annual International ACM SIGIR Conference on Research and Development in Information Retrieval (SIGIR'03)* (pp. 235-242).

Polity, Y., & Rostaing, H. (1997, June). Cartographie d'un champ de recherche à partir du corpus des thèses de doctorat soutenues pendant 20 ans: Les sciences de l'information et de la communication en France: 1974-94. *Actes du Colloque: Les systèmes d'informations élaborées (SFBA).* Ile Rousse.

Pollock, J., & Zamora, A. (1975). Automatic abstracting research at chemical abstracts service. *Journal of Chemical Information and Computer Sciences, 15*(4), 226-232.

Ponte, J. M., & Croft, W. B. (1998). *A language modeling approach to information retrieval.* Paper presented at the Proceedings of the 21st Annual International ACM SIGIR Conference on Research and Development in Information Retrieval, Melbourne, Australia.

Porter, A. L. (2003). Text mining for technology foresight. In *Futures Research Methodology-V2.0, The Millennium Project.* New York: American Council for the United Nations University.

Porter, A. L., & Cunningham, S. W. (2005). *Tech mining: Exploiting new technologies for competitive advantage.* New Jersey: John Wiley and Sons.

Porter, M. F. (1980). An algorithm for suffix stripping. *Program, 14*(3), 130-137.

Porter, M. F. (1997). An algorithm for suffix stripping. In *Readings in Information Retrieval* (pp. 313-316).

Porter, M. F. (2006). Porter stemmer in Java. Retrieved April 1, 2007, from http://www.tartarus.org/~martin/PorterStemmer

Quinlan, J. R. (1992). *C4.5: Programs for machine learning.* Morgan Kaufmann.

Quoniam, L. (1996). *Les productions scientifiques en bibliométrie.* Unpublished Habilitation à diriger des recherches, Université Aix Marseille III, Marseilles.

Quoniam, L. (2001, December). *Data mining, teoria e prática.* Paper presented at the Seminar Tecnologias para Tratamento da Informação na Embrapa. Brasilia, DF.

Quoniam, L., Hassanaly, P., Baldit. P., Rostaing, H., & Dou, H. (1993). Bibliometric analysis of patent documents for R&D management. *Research Evaluation, 3*(1), 13-18.

Rabiner L. R., (1989, February). A tutorial on hidden markov models and selected applications in speech recognition. In *Proceedings of the IEEE,* 77 (2), 257-286.

Radev, D., Allison, T., Blair-Goldensohn, S., Blitzer, S., Çelebi, A., Dimitrov, S., et al. (2004, May). MEAD: A platform for multidocument multilingual text summarization. In *Proceedings of LREC 2004*, Lisbon, Portugal.

Radev, D. R., & McKeown, K. R. (1998). Generating natural language summaries from multiple on-line sources. *Computational Linguistics, 24*, 469-500.

Rajaraman, K., & Pan, H. (2000). Document clustering using 3-tuples. In *The Sixth Pacific RIM International Conference on Artificial Intelligence (PRICAI'2000)*, Melbourne, Australia.

Ramshaw, L. A., & Marcus, M. P. (1995). Text chunking using transformation-based learning. In *Proceedings of Third Workshop on Very Large Corpora, ACL* (pp. 67-73).

Ratnaparkhi, A. (1998). Unsupervised statistical models for prepositional phrase attachment. In *Proceedings of COLING ACL'98* (pp. 1079-1085). Montreal, Canada.

Reskó, B., Tikk, D., Hashimoto, H., & Baranyi, P. (2006). Visual feature array based cognitive polygon recognition using UFEX text categorizer. In *Proceedings of the IEEE 3rd International Conference on Mechatronics* (pp. 539-544). Budapest, Hungary.

Resnik, P. (1999). Semantic similarity in a taxonomy: An information-based measure and its application to problems of ambiguity in natural language. *Journal of Artificial Intelligence Research, 11*, 95-130.

Revel, A. (2003). Web-agents inspired by ethology: A population of ant-like agents to help finding user-oriented information. In *Proceedings of IEEE Web Intelligence Consortium (WIC)* (pp. 482-485). Halifax, Canada.

Reynolds, G. W. (1992). *Information systems for managers*. St. Paul, MN: West Publishing Co.

Rijsbergen, C. v. (1979). *Information retrieval*. London: Butterworths.

Riloff, E. (1993). Automatically constructing a dictionary for information extraction tasks. In *Proceedings of the Eleventh National Conference on Artificial Intelligence* (pp. 811-816).

Riloff, E. (1996). Automatically generating extraction patterns from untagged text. In *Proceedings of the Thirteenth National Conference on Artificial Intelligence* (pp. 1044-1049).

Riloff, E., & Jones, R. (1999). Learning dictionaries for information extraction by multi-level bootstrapping. In *Proceedings of the Sixteenth National Conference on Artificial Intelligence* (pp. 474-479).

Robertson, S. E. (1977). The probability ranking principle in IR. *Journal of Documentation, 33*(4), 294-304.

Rose, D. E., & Levinson, D. (2004). Understanding user goals in Web search. In *Proceedings of the 13th International Conference on World Wide Web* (pp. 13-19). ACM Press.

Rosenblatt, F. (1958). The perceptron: A probabilistic model for information storage and organization in brain. *Psychological Review, 65*, 386-407. (Reprinted in *Neurocomputing*. MIT Press, 1988).

Roth, D., & Yih, W. (2004). A linear programming formulation for global inference in natural language tasks. In *Proceedings of the Eighth Conference on Computational Natural Language Learning (CoNLL-2004)* (pp. 1-8). Boston.

Rouach, D. (1999). *La veille technologique et l'intelligence économique*. Paris: Collection Que sais-je? PUF.

Rousu, J., Saunders, C., Szedmak, S., & Shawe-Taylor, J. (2005). Learning hierarchical multi-category text classification models. In *Proceedings of the 22nd International Conference on Machine Learning* (pp. 745-752). Bonn, Germany: Omnipress.

Ruiz, M. E., & Srinivasan, P. (2002). Hierarchicaltext categorization using neural networks. *Information Retrieval, 5*(1), 87-118.

Rutledge, R., Shaffer, V. D., & Ridky, J. (1996). Trauma care reimbursement in rural hospitals: Implications for triage and trauma system design. *The Journal of Trauma, 40*(6), 1002-1008.

Saeed, J. L. (1997). *Semantics*. Oxford: Blackwell

Sag, I. A., Baldwin, T., Bond, F., Copestake, A. & Flickinger, D. (2002). Multiword expressions: A pain in the neck for NLP, In *Proceedings of the Third International Conference on Intelligent Text Processing and Computational Linguistics (CICLING 2002)*, Mexico City, Mexico.

Saggion, H. (2002). Shallow-based robust summarization. In *ATALA Workshop,* Paris.

Saggion, H., & Gaizauskas, R. (2004). Mining on-line sources for defnition knowledge. In *Proceedings of the 17th FLAIRS 2004*, Miami Beach, Florida. AAAI.

Saggion, H., & Gaizauskas, R. (2004). Multi-document summarization by cluster/profile relevance and redundancy removal. In *Proceedings of the Document Understanding Conference 2004.* NIST.

Saggion, H., & Lapalme, G. (2002). Generating indicative-informative summaries with SumUM. *Computational Linguistics, 28*(4), 497-526.

Saggion, H., Radev, D., Teufel, S., & Lam, W. (2002). Meta-evaluation of summaries in a cross-lingual environment using content-based metrics. In *Proceedings of COLING 2002* (pp. 849-855). Taipei, Taiwan.

Sahlgren, M., & Cöster, R. (2004). *Using bag-of-concepts to improve the performance of support vector machines in text categorization*. Paper presented at the Proceedings of the 20th International Conference on Computational Linguistics (COLING 2004), Geneva.

Sakamoto, H., Arimura, H., & Arikawa, S. (2001). Extracting partial structures from HTML documents. In *Proceedings of the 14th International FLAIRS Conference* (pp. 247-252).

Sakurai, S., & Orihara, R. (2006). Discovery of important threads from bulletin board sites. *International Journal of Information Technology and Intelligent Computing, 1*(1), 217-228.

Sakurai, S., & Suyama, A. (2004). Rule discovery from textual data based on key phrase patterns. In *Proceedings of the 19th Annual ACM Symposium on Applied Computing* (pp. 606-612).

Sakurai, S., & Suyama, A. (2005). An e-mail analysis method based on text mining techniques. *Applied Soft Computing, 6*(1), 62-71.

Sakurai, S., & Ueno, K. (2004). Analysis of daily business reports based on sequential text mining method. In *Proceedings of the International Conference on Systems, Man and Cybernetics 2004* (pp. 3278-3284).

Sakurai, S., Ichimura, Y., & Suyama, A. (2002). Acquisition of a knowledge dictionary from training examples including multiple values. In *Proceedings of the 12th International Symposium on Methodologies for Intelligent Systems* (pp. 103-113).

Sakurai, S., Ichimura, Y., Suyama, A., & Orihara, R. (2001). Inductive learning of a knowledge dictionary for a text mining system. In *Proceedings of the 14th International Conference on Industrial, Engineering & Other Applications of Applied Intelligent Systems* (pp. 247-252).

Sakurai, S., Ichimura, Y., Suyama, A., & Orihara, R. (2001). Acquisition of a knowledge dictionary for a text mining system using an inductive learning method. In *Proceedings of the IJCAI 2001 Workshop on Text Learning: Beyond Supervision* (pp. 45-52).

Sakurai, S., Suyama, A., & Fume, K. (2003). Acquisition of a concepts relation dictionary for classifying e-mails. In *Proceedings of the IASTED International Conference on Artificial Intelligence and Applications (AIA03)* (pp. 13-19).

Salton, G. (1971). *The SMART retrieval system: Experiments in automatic document processing.* Englewood Cliffs, NJ: Prentice Hall.

Salton, G. (1991). Developments in automatic text retrieval. *Science, 253,* 974-979.

Salton, G., & Buckley, C. (1988). Term weighting approaches in automatic text retrieval. *Information Processing and Management, 24*(5), 513-523.

Salton, G., & McGill M. J. (1983). *Introduction to modern information retrieval.* New York: McGraw-Hill.

Salton, G., & Yang, C.S. (1973). On the specification of term values in automatic indexing. *Journal of Documentation, 29*(4), 351-372.

Sanderson, M., & Croft, B. (1999). *Deriving concept hierarchies from text.* Paper presented at the Proceedings of SIGIR-99, the 22nd ACM Conference on Research and Development in Information Retrieval, Berkeley, California.

SAS Text Miner. (2007). Retrieved August 9, 2007 from http://www.sas.com/technologies/analytics/datamining/textminer/

Schapire, R. (2001). The boosting approach to machine learning: An overview. In *MSRI Workshop on Nonlinear Estimation and Classification,* Berkeley, California.

Scheffer, T. (2004). Email answering assistance by semisupervised text classification. *Intelligence Data Analysis, 8*(5), 481-493.

Schiffman, B., Mani, I., & Concepcion, K. (2001). Producing biographical summaries: Combining linguistic knowledge with corpus statistics. In *Proceedings of EACL/ACL.*

Schölkopf B., Burges, C. J. C., & Smola A. J. (1999). *Advances in kernel methods: Support vector learning.* MA: MIT Press.

Schütze, H., Hull, D. A., & Pedersen, J. O. (1995). A comparison of classifiers and document representations for the routing problem. In *Proceedings of SIGIR-95, 18th ACM International Conference on Research and Development in Information Retrieval,* Seattle, Washington (pp. 229-237). New York: ACM Press.

Sebastiani, F. (2002). Machine learning in automated text categorization. *ACM Computing Surveys, 34*(1), 1-47.

Senge, P. (1990). *The fifth discipline: The art and practice of the learning organization.* New York: Doubleday.

Senge, P., Kleiner, A., Roberts, C., Ross, R., & Smith, B. (1994). *The fifth discipline fieldbook: Strategies for building a learning organization.* New York: Doubleday/Currency.

Seo, Y.-W., & Sycara, K. (2004). *Text clustering for topic detection* (No. CMU-RI-TR-04-03). Robotics Institute, Carnegie Mellon University.

Sha, F., & Pereira, F. (2003). Shallow parsing with conditional random fields. In *Proceedings of Human Language Technology, NAACL* (pp. 188-191).

Shapire, R. E. (1999). A brief introduction to boosting. In *Proceedings of the 16th International Joint Conference on Artificial Intelligence (IJCAI-1999)* (pp. 1401-1405).

Shapiro, C. & Varian, H. R. (1998). *Information rules: a strategic guide to the network economy.* Boston: Harvard Business School Press.

Sheth, B., & Maes, P. (1993). Evolving agents for personalized information filtering. In *Proceedings of the 9th Conference on Artificial Intelligence for Applications* (pp. 345-352).

Shewchuk, J. R. (1994). *An introduction to the conjugate gradient method without the agonizing pain*. Retrieved March 22, 2007, from http://www-2.cs.cmu.edu/.jrs/jrspapers.html#cg

Siefkes, C., & Siniakov, P. (2005). An overview and classification of adaptive approaches to information extraction. *Journal on Data Semantics, 4*, 172-212.

Silverman, B. (1986). *Density estimation for statistics and data analysis*. Boca Raton, FL: CRC Press.

Silverstein, C., & Pedersen, J. (1997). Almost-constant-time clustering of arbitrary corpus subsets. In *Conference on Research and Development in Information Retrieval* (pp. 60-67). New York: ACM Press.

Silverstein, C., Marais, H., Henzinger, M., & Moricz, M. (1999). Analysis of a very large Web search engine query log. *SIGIR Forum, 33*(1), 6-12.

Simon, H. A. (1954). A behavioural model of rational choice. *The Quarterly Journal of Economics, 69*(1), 99-118.

Smith, E. P., Lipkovich, I., & Ye, K. (2002). *Weight of evidence (WOE): Quantitative estimation of probability of impact*. Blacksburg, VA: Virginia Tech, Department of Statistics.

Soderland, S. (1999). Learning information extraction rules for semi-structured and free text. *Machine Learning, 34*(1-3), 299-272.

Soderland, S., Fisher, D., Aseltine, J., & Lehnert, W. (1995). CRYSTAL: Inducing a conceptual dictionary. In *Proceedings of the Fourteenth International Joint Conference on Artificial Intelligence (IJCAI'95)* (pp. 1314-1319).

Sparck Jones, K. (1972). A statistical interpretation of term specificity and its application to retrieval. *Journal of Documentation, 28*(1), 11-20.

Spink, A., Wolfram, D., Jansen, M., & Saracevic, T. (2001). Searching the Web: The public and their queries. *Journal of the American Society for Information Science and Technology, 52*(3), 226-234.

Srikant, R., & Yang, Y. (2001). Mining Web logs to improve Website organization. In *Proceedings of the Tenth International World Wide Web Conference* (pp. 430-437). Hong Kong, China.

Srivastava, J., Cooley, R., Deshpande, M., & Tan, P.-N. (2000). Web mining: Discovery and applications of usage patterns from Web data. *SIGKDD Explorations 2000, 2*(1), 12-23.

Steele, R. D. (2005, August). The future of intelligence: Not federal, not secret, not expensive. In *Speech to DHS Intelligence*, Washington. Retrieved March 25, 2007, from http://www.oss.net/extra/news/?module_instance=1&id=2633

Steinbach, M., Karypis, G., & Kumar, V. (2000). A comparison of document clustering techniques. In *Mining Workshop; Proceedings of the Sixth ACM SIGKDD International Conference on Knowledge Discovery and Data Mining* (KDD 2000) (pp. 109-110). Boston.

Stumme, G., Hotho. A., & Berendt, B (2006, June). Semantic Web mining: State of the art and future directions. *Journal of Web Semantics, 4*(2), 124-143.

Sulaiman, A., & Souza, J. M. (2001). Data mining mineração de dados. In K. Tarapanoff (Ed.), *Inteligência Organizacional e Competitiva* (pp. 265-278). Brasília: Editora Universidade de Brasília.

Sutton, C., & McCallum, A. (2005). An introduction to conditional random fields for relational learning. In L. Getoor & B. Taskar (Eds.), *Statistical relational learning*, forthcoming.

Sutton, C., Rohanimanesh, K., & McCallum, A. (2004). Dynamic conditional random fields: Factorized probabilistic models for labeling and segmenting sequence data. In *Proceedings of ICML'2004* (pp. 783-790).

Swanson, D. R. (1986). Fish oil, Raynaud's syndrome, and undiscovered public knowledge. *Perspectives in Biology and Medicine, 30*(1), 7-18.

Swanson, D. R. (2001). ASIST award of merit acceptance speech: On fragmentation of knowledge, the connection explosion, and assembling other people's ideas. *Bulletin of the American Society for Information Science and Technology, 27*(3).

Taheri, P., Butz, D. A., & Greenfield, L. J. (1999). Paying a premium: How patient complexity affects costs and profit margins. *Annals of Surgery, 229*(6), 807.

Tan, A.-H. (1999). Text mining: The state of the art and the challenges. In *Proceedings of the Pacific Asia Conference on Knowledge Discovery and Data Mining PAKDD'99 Workshop on Knowledge Discovery from Advanced Databases* (pp. 65-70).

Tang, J., Hong, M., Li, J., & Liang, B. (2006). Tree-structured conditional random fields for semantic annotation. In *Proceedings of 5th International Conference of Semantic Web (ISWC'2006)* (pp. 640-653).

Tang, J., Li, H., Cao, Y., & Tang, Z. (2005). E-mail data cleaning. In *Proceedings of SIGKDD'2005* (pp. 489-499). Chicago.

Tang, J., Li, J., Lu, H., Liang, B., & Wang, K. (2005). iASA: Learning to annotate the semantic Web. *Journal on Data Semantic, 4*, 110-145.

Tang. J., Hong, M., Zhang, J., Liang, B., & Li, J. (2006). A new approach to personal network search based on information extraction. In *Proceedings of the first International Conference of Asian Semantic Web (ASWC)*. To appear.

Taskar, B., Guestrin, C., & Koller, D. (2003). Max-margin markov networks. In Proceedings of Advances in *Neural Information Processing Systems* (NIPS'03). Cambridge, MA: MIT Press.

Teles, W. M., Weigang, L., & Ralha, C. G. (2003). AntWeb—The adaptive Web server based on the ants' behavior. In *Proceedings of IEEE Web Intelligence Consortium (WIC)* (pp. 558-561). Halifax, Canada.

Tesauro, G., & Janssens, R. (1988). Scaling relationships in back-propagation learning. *Complex Systems, 6,* 39-44.

Tetko, I. V., Livingstone, D. J., & Luik, A. I. (1995). Neural network studies. 1. Comparison of overfitting and overtraining. *Journal of Chemical Information and Computer Sciences, 35,* 826-833.

Thurkettle, M. A., & Noji, A. (2003). Shifting the healthcare paradigm: The case manager's opportunity and responsibility. *Case Management, 8*(4), 160-165.

Tikk, D., Kardkovács, Zs.T., & Szidarovszky, F. P., (2006). Voting with a parameterized veto strategy: Solving the KDD Cup 2006 problem by means of a classifier committee. *Special Interest Group on Knowledge Discovery and Data Mining Explorations Exploration Newsletter, 8*(2), 53-62.

Tikk, D., Yang, J. D., & Bang, S. L. (2003). Hierarchical text categorization using fuzzy relational thesaurus. *Kybernetika, 39*(5), 583-600.

Tjong Kim Sang, E. F., & Buchholz, S. (2000). Introduction to the CoNLL-2000 shared task: Chunking. In *Proceedings of CoNLL-2000* (pp. 127-132).

Trappey, A. J. C., Hsu, F. -C., Trappey, C. V., & Lin C. -I., (2006). Development of a patent document classification and search platform using a back-propagation network. *Expert Systems with Applications, 31*(4), 755-765.

Turtle, H., & Croft, W. B. (1989). *Inference networks for document retrieval.* Paper presented at the Proceedings of the 13th Annual International ACM SIGIR Conference on Research and Development in Information Retrieval, Brussels, Belgium.

Ukkonen, E. (1992). Constructing suffix trees on-line in linear time. In *Proceedings of the IFIP 12th World Computer Congress on Algorithms, Software, Architecture - Information Processing '92* (Vol. 1, pp. 484-492). North-Holland.

Vaithyanathan, S., & Dom, B. (2000). *Model-based hierarchical clustering.* Paper presented at the Proceedings of the Sixteenth Conference on Uncertainty in Artificial Intelligence, Stanford, California.

van Rijsbergen, C. J. (1979). *Information retrieval* (2nd ed.). London: Butterworths.

Vapnik V. (1999). *The nature of statistical learning theory.* NY: Springer-Verlag.

Vapnik, V. (1998). *Statistical learning theory.* NY: Springer-Verlag.

Vapnik, V. N. (1995). *The nature of statistical learning theory.* Springer-Verlag.

Wagner, A. (2000). Enriching a lexical semantic net with selectional preferences by means of statistical corpus analysis. In *Workshop on Ontology and Learning, ECAI* (pp. 37-42). CEUR Workshop Proceedings.

Wainwright, M., Jaakkola, T., & Willsky, A. (2001). Tree-based reparameterization for approximate estimation on graphs with cycles. In *Proceedings of Advances in Neural Information Processing Systems (NIPS'2001)* (pp. 1001-1008).

Wallach, H. (2002). *Efficient training of conditional random fields.* Unpublished master's thesis, University of Edinburgh, USA.

Wang, S. Y., Yu, L., & Lai, K. K. (2005). Crude oil price forecasting with TEI@I methodology. *International Journal of Systems Science and Complexity, 18*(2), 145-166.

Wang, T., Li, Y., Bontcheva, K., Cunningham, H., & Wang, J. (2006). Automatic extraction of hierarchical relations from text. In *Proceedings of the Third European Semantic Web Conference (ESWC 2006).* Lecture Notes in Computer Science 4011. Springer.

Wang, Y., & Hu, J. (2002). A machine learning based approach for table detection on the Web. In *Proceedings of the 11th International World Wide Web Conference (WWW'02)* (pp. 242-250). Honolulu, Hawaii.

Webster's online dictionary (2004). retrieved August 9, 2007 from http://www.Webster-dictionary.org/.

WebTrends Inc. (1995). Webtrends. Retrieved April 2, 2007, from http://www.webtrends.com

Weigang, L., & Wu, M. Q. (2005). Web search based on ant behavior: Approach and implementation in case of Interlegis. *Proceedings of the 17th International Conference on Software Engineering & Knowledge Engineering (SEKE 2005), 1,* 572-577, Taipei, Taiwan.

Weigang, L., Dib, M. V. P., Teles, de Andrade, W. M., V. M., de Melo, A. C. M. A., & Cariolano, J. T. (2002). Using ants' behavior based simulation model AntWeb to improve Website organization. *Proceedings of SPIE's Aerospace/Defense Sensing and Controls Symposium: Data Mining, 4730* (pp. 229-240).

Weil, V., & Snapper, J. (Eds.). (1989). *Owning scientific and technical information: Value and ethical issues.* New Brunswick, NJ: Rutgers University Press.

Weiner, P. (1973). Linear pattern matching algorithms. In *Proceedings of the 14th IEEE Symposium on Switching and Automata Theory* (pp. 1-11).

Weintraub, W. S., & Shine, K. (2004). Is a paradigm shift in US healthcare reimbursement inevitable? *Circulation, 109*(12), 1448-1455.

Weiss, D., & Stefanowski, J. (2004). Web search results clustering in polish: Experimental evaluation of Carrot. *Advances in Soft Computing,*

Intelligent Information Processing and Web Mining, Proceedings of the International IIS (IIPWM'03).

Weiss, S. M., Indurkhya, N., Zhang, T., & Damerau, F. J. (2005). *Text mining: Predictive methods for analyzing unstructured information*. New York: Springer.

Wen, J. -R., Nie, J. -Y., & Zhang, H. -J. (2002). Query clustering using user logs. *ACM Transactions on Information Systems, 20*(1), 59-81.

White, C. (2005). Consolidating, accessing and analyzing unstructured data. *B-eye Business Intelligence Network*. Retrieved March 25, 2007, from http://www.b-eye-network.com/view/2098

White, H. (1990). Connectionist nonparametric regression: Multilayer feedforward networks can learn arbitrary mappings. *Neural Networks, 3*, 535-549.

White, R. W., Kules, B., Drucker, S. M., & Schraefel, M. C. (2006). Supporting exploratory search. *ACM Communications of the ACM, 49*(4), 36-39.

Wibovo, W., & Williams, H. E. (2002). Simple and accurate feature selection for hierarchical categorisation. In *Proceedings of the 2nd ACM Symposium on Document Engineering*, McLean, Virginia (pp. 111-118). New York: ACM Press.

Widdows, D. (2003). *Unsupervised methods for developing taxonomies by combining syntactic and statistical information*. Paper presented at the Proceedings of the 2003 Conference of the North American Chapter of the Association for Computational Linguistics on Human Language Technology, Edmonton, Canada.

Wiener, E. D., Pedersen, J. O., & Weigend, A. S. (1995). A neural network approach to topic spotting. In *Annual Symposium on Document Analysis and Information Retrieval, SDAIR, 4* (pp. 317-332).

Wiener, K., & Roberts, N. (1998). The relative merits of haemoglobin A1c and fasting plasma glucose as first-line diagnostic tests for diabetes mellitus in non-pregnant subjects. *Diabetic Medicine, 15*(7), 558-563.

Willett, P. (1988). Recent trends in hierarchic document clustering: A critical review. *Information Processing and Management, 24*(5), 577-597.

Witten, I. H., & Frank, E. (2000). *Data mining, practical machine learning tools and techniques with Java implementations* (Vol. 1). Morgan Kaufmann Publishers. Retrieved March 29, 2007, from http://www.cs.waikato.ac.nz/ml/weka/index.html

Xu, J., Licuanan, A., & Weischedel, R. (2003). TREC2003 QA at BBN: Answering definitional questions. In *Proceedings of TREC-2003*.

Yang, H., Cui, H., Maslennikov, M., Qiu, L., Kan, M.-Y., & Chua, T.-S. (2003). QUALIFIER in TREC-12 QA main task. In *Proceedings of TREC-2003*.

Yang, Y., & Liu, X. (1999). *A re-examination of text categorization methods*. Paper presented at the Proceedings of the 22nd Annual International ACM SIGIR Conference on Research and Development in Information Retrieval, Berkeley, California.

Yao, Y. Y., Hamilton, H. J., & Wang, X. (2002). PagePrompter: An intelligent Web agent created using data mining techniques. *Proceedings of International Conference on Rough Sets and Current Trends in Computing, 2475*, 506-513. Malvern, Pennsylvania.

Yap, I., Loh, H. T., Shen, L., & Liu, Y. (2006). *Topic detection using MFSs*. Paper presented at the Proceedings of the 19th International Conference on Industrial & Engineering Applications of Artificial Intelligence & Expert Systems (IEA\AIE 2006), Annecy, France.

Yu, L., Wang, S. Y., & Lai, K. K. (2005). A rough-set-refined text mining approach for crude oil market tendency forecasting. *International Journal of Knowledge and Systems Sciences, 2*(1), 33-46.

Yu, L., Wang, S. Y., & Lai, K. K. (2006). Intelligent Web text mining using neural networks. *International Journal of Computational Intelligence: Theory and Practice, 1*(2), 67-79.

Zadeh, L. A. (1978). Fuzzy sets as a basis for a theory of possibility. *Fuzzy Sets and Systems, 1,* 1762-1784.

Zamir, O., & Etzioni, O. (1998). Web document clustering: A feasibility demonstration. In *Proceedings of the 21st Annual International ACM SIGIR Conference on Research and Development in Information Retrieval (SIGIR'98)* (pp. 46-54).

Zamir, O., & Etzioni, O. (1999). Grouper: A dynamic clustering interface to Web search results. *Computer Networks, 31*(11-16), 1361-1374.

Zamir, O., Etzioni, O., Madani, O., & Karp, R. (1997). Fast and intuitive clustering of Web documents. In *Proceedings of the 3rd International Conference on Knowledge Discovery and Data Mining* (pp. 287-290).

Zanasi, A. (2005). Text mining and its applications to intelligence, CRM and knowledge management *Advances in management information, 2,* 131-143.

Zelenko, D., Aone, C., & Richardella, A. (2003). Kernel methods for relation extraction. *Journal of Machine Learning Research, 3,* 1083-1106.

Zhang, D., & Dong, Y. (2001). Semantic, hierarchical, online clustering of Web search results. *Advanced Web Technologies and Applications.* Lecture Notes in Computer Science, 69-78.

Zhang, L., Pan, Y., & Zhang, T. (2004). Recognizing and using named entities: Focused named entity recognition using machine learning. In *Proceedings of the 27th Annual International ACM SIGIR Conference on Research and Development in Information Retrieval (SIGIR'04)* (pp. 281-288).

Zhou, L., Ticrea, M., & Hovy, E. (2004). Multi-document biography summarization. In *Proceedings of Empirical Methods in Natural Language Processing.*

Zhou, Z. -H. & Li, M. (2005). Semisupervised regression with CO-TRAINING. In *Proceedings of the International Joint Conference on Artificial Inteligence (IJCAI)* (pp. 908-916).

Zhou, Z. -H., & Li, M. (2005). Tri-training: Exploiting unlabeled data using three classifiers. In *IEEE Transactions on Knowledge and Data Engineering* (Vols. 11-17, pp. 1529-1541).

Zhu, J., Nie, Z., Wen, J., Zhang, B., & Ma, W. (2005). 2D conditional random fields for Web information extraction. In *Proceedings of 22nd International Conference on Machine Learning (ICML2005)* (pp. 1044-1051). Bonn, Germany.

Zhu, X. (2005). *Semisupervised learning literature survey* (Tech. Rep. No. 1530). University of Wisconsin-Madison, Computer Sciences. Retrieved March 29, 2007, from http://www. cs.wisc. edu/~jerryzhu/pub/ssl survey.pdf

Zue, V. W. (1995). Navigating the information superhighway using spoken language interfaces. *IEEE Expert: Intelligent Systems and Their Applications, 10*(5), 39-43.

About the Contributors

Hércules Antonio do Prado is a researcher in computer science at the Brazilian Agricultural Research Corporation (Embrapa Food Technology) and an assistant professor at the Catholic University of Brasília. He received his DSc in computer science at the Federal University of Rio Grande do Sul, Brazil (2001) and his MS in systems engineering from the Federal University of Rio de Janeiro (1989). In 1999 he joined the Information Sciences Department of University of Pittsburgh as a visitor scholar, developing research for his doctoral program. He did his undergraduate work in computer systems at the Federal University of São Carlos, Brazil (1976). His research interest includes data/text mining, neural networks, knowledge-based systems, and knowledge management.

Edilson Ferneda is a full professor at the Catholic University of Brasília. He has a DSc in computer science from University of Montpellier, France (1992), an MS in computer science from Federal University of Paraíba, Brazil (1988) and did his undergraduate work in computer systems at The Aeronautics Technological Institute, Brazil (1979). His research interests include data/text mining, machine learning, knowledge acquisition, knowledge-based systems, CSCL/CSCW, knowledge management, and e-learning.

* * * * *

Christian Aranha was born in 1975 in São Paulo, Brazil. He is an electrical engineer with emphasis on decision support systems, has an MS in statistics and a PhD in text mining by Pontifical Catholic University of Rio de Janeiro. He has also a BA degree in psychology with emphasis on cognitive science and artificial intelligence. He became a member of the Computational Linguistics Center at PUC-Rio (2002). He won the national prize of innovation for an automatic NLP system for competitive intelligence (2004). In 2006 he won the HAREM competition for Portuguese Named Entity Recognition.

György Biró was born in Hungary in 1973. He received the MS in electrical engineering from the Technical University of Budapest, Hungary, in 1999. He was research assistant at the Computer Automation Research Institute, Budapest, Hungary (1998 to 2001). He has been the owner and general manager of Textminer Ltd, where he has been working on different text mining products, including hierarchical text categorizer (since 2002). He has been working on medical devices at GE Healthcare (since 2004). His research interests include data mining with fuzzy and neural network techniques. He was a member of KDD cup winner team(2006).

Hans Olaf Borch received his MS in information systems at the Norwegian University of Science and Technology (2006). His master's thesis focused on clustering and text mining in search engines. Borch is currently a consultant at BEKK Consulting in Norway, working with enterprise Java applications. His research interests are search engines and text mining.

Eric Boutin is a former student of the National Superior School of Education of Cachan, France, and holds a PhD of information and communication sciences. He is currently a senior associate professor at the Ingemedia Institute of the University du Sud Toulon Var and is fully accredited to manage research work for doctorate/PhD students. An expert in information technology, he notably specializes in cybermetrics, competitive intelligence, and lectures to graduate students in competitive intelligence. His activities on knowledge management and cybermetrics are regularly published or disseminated throughout the world, through printed media and conferences or lectures.

Wagner Francisco Castilho holds an MS in knowledge and data management from the Catholic University of Brasilia. He is a DSc candidate in computer science and education in the Federal University of Rio Grande do Sul, Brazil. Certified as an ontological coach, he develops research in the CSCL and CSCW areas. His research interests include the following areas: knowledge management, e-learning, organizational learning, KDD, text mining, and project development. He is also a specialist in project financing and projects in operations that are structured on infra-structure, sustainable development, and energy, concerning urban development, in general, environmental sanitation, solid residue, hydrography, highways, bridges, road paving, biomass energy facilities, hydroelectric, wind energy, thermoelectric, and other energy generating alternatives.

Patricia Cerrito has made considerable strides in the development of data mining techniques to investigate large, complex data, primarily related to physician decision making. She has recently completed a book on data mining, published by SAS Press, Inc. In particular, she has developed a method to automate the reduction of the number of levels in a nominal data field to a manageable number that can then be analyzed using other data mining techniques. She is currently developing a text on the data mining of public health and clinical databases. Another innovation of the author is to combine text analysis with association rules to examine nominal data. She has received funding from the National Science Foundation to combine geographic information systems and data mining techniques to train graduate students to examine public health data.

Jon Atle Gulla is professor of information systems at the Norwegian University of Science and Technology since 2002. He received his MS and his PhD (1988 and 1993, respectively), both in information systems, at the Norwegian Institute of Technology. Gulla also has an MS in linguistics from the University of Trondheim and an MS of management (Sloan fellow) from London Business School. He has previously worked as a manager in fast search and transfer in Munich and as a project leader for Norsk Hydro in Brussels. Gulla's research interests include text mining, semantic search, ontologies, and large-scale enterprise systems.

Mingcai Hong is a master's candidate in the Department of Computer Science and Technology, Tsinghua University, China. He got his BS from the same department (2004). His research interests cover information extraction, semantic annotation, and information retrieval. He participated in the internship program in Intel China Research Center and Microsoft ATC, where he focused his work on named entity extraction and name origin classification, respectively.

Jon Espen Ingvaldsen is a PhD student at the Norwegian University of Science and Technology. He received his MS in information systems at the Norwegian University of Science and Technology (2003). Ingvaldsen is also working as a software developer at Businesscape AS. His research interest includes text mining and business process monitoring.

Kin Keung Lai is the chair professor of management science at City University of Hong Kong and he is also the associate dean of the Faculty of Business. Currently, he is acting as the dean of the College of Business Administration at Hunan University, China. Prior to his current post, he was a senior operational research analyst at Cathay Pacific Airways and the area manager on marketing information systems at Union Carbide Eastern. Professor Lai received his PhD at Michigan State University, USA. Professor Lai's main research interests include logistics and operations management, computational intelligence, and business decision modeling.

Juanzi Li is an associate professor in the Department of Computer Science and Technology (DCST), Tsinghua University, China. She received her PhD from DCST, Tsinghua (2000), and became a post doctor in the Department of Electronic Engineering, Tsinghua. Her research interests include Semantic Web, natural language processing, and knowledge discovery on the Internet. She is now in charge of several research work/projects funded by Nation 863 Plan, National Science Foundation China, and so on. She is also the course lecturer of data mining and knowledge engineering in the department.

Bangyong Liang is an associate researcher in NEC Laboratories, China. He received his BS and PhD from the Department of Computer Science and Technology, Tsinghua University (2001 and 2006, respectively). His research interests include knowledge base system, data mining, XML technology, information retrieval and Semantic Web content management. His homepage is http://keg.cs.tsinghua.edu.cn/persons/lby.

Ying Liu is presently a lecturer with the Department of Industrial and Systems Engineering at the Hong Kong Polytechnic University. He obtained his PhD from the Singapore MIT Alliance (SMA) at the National University of Singapore (2006). His current research interests focus on data mining and text mining, information processing and management, machine learning, design informatics and their joint applications in design, and manufacturing for knowledge management purposes.

Han Tong Loh is an associate professor and deputy head in the Department of Mechanical Engineering at the National University of Singapore (NUS). He obtained his BS of engineering from the University of Adelaide, an MS of engineering from NUS, and an MS and PhD of philosophy from the University of Michigan (Ann Arbor). He is also a fellow of the Singapore-MIT Alliance, which is an innovative global engineering education and research collaboration between MIT, NUS, and the Nanyang Technological University. Dr. Loh's research interests are in the areas of data mining, rapid prototyping, robust design, and computer aided design and he has published widely in these fields.

Stanley Loh is a professor at the Catholic University of Pelotas (UCPEL) and at the Lutheran University of Brazil (ULBRA), in Brazil. He has a PhD in computer science, obtained at the Federal University of Rio Grande do Sul (UFRGS) (2001). His research interests include recommender systems, information retrieval, data-text-Web mining, and technology applied to knowledge management and business intelligence.

Wen Feng Lu is currently the deputy director of the Centre for Design Technology as well as an associate professor of the Department of Mechanical Engineering at National University of Singapore (NUS). He received his PhD in mechanical engineering from the University of Minnesota, USA. He was with the University of Missouri-Rolla and Singapore Institute of Manufacturing Technology before joining NUS. His research interests include design methodologies, IT in product design, product life-cycle management, knowledge discovery and intelligent manufacturing. He is the recipient of Society of Automotive Engineers Ralph R. Teetor Educational Award (1997).

Gentil José de Lucena Filho is an associate professor at the Catholic University of Brasília. He has a PhD in systems design from the University of Waterloo, Canada (1978). He holds an MS in computer science from Federal University of Paraíba, Brazil (1974), where he also finished his graduate studies (BSc) in physics (1971). In 1988 he joined, as a postdoctoral fellow, the Logic Programming Group, Informatics Deparment, at the Universidade Nova de Lisboa, Lisbon, Portugal. Dr. Lucena was also the adjoint coordinator of the Brazilian Information Society Programme of the Ministry of Science and Technology, (2001-2002) and has been assigned director of the Master's Programme in Knowledge Management and Information Technology of the Catholic University of Brasília (2003-2006). His present research interests include the areas of knowledge management, organizational learning, coaching, conversational skills/ontology of language, e-learning, knowledge acquisition, and CSCL/CSCW.

Edson Takashi Matsubara was awarded an MS from the University of São Paulo, Brazil (2004). Currently he is a full time PhD student at the Institute of Mathematics and Computer Science of the University of São Paulo, Campus Sao Carlos, and a research student visitor at the University of Bristol, UK.

Maria Carolina Monard was awarded an MS from Southampton University, UK, and a PhD from Pontificia Universidade Católica do Rio de Janeiro, Brazil, (1968 and 1980, respectively). She is currently a full professor in computer science at São Paulo University, Campus São Carlos, Institute of Mathematics and Computer Science. Her research interests in the field of artificial intelligence including machine learning, and data and text mining.

José Palazzo Moreira de Oliveira is full professor of computer science at the Federal University of Rio Grande do Sul-UFRGS. He has a PhD in computer science from the Institut National Politechnique-IMAG (1984), Grenoble, France; an MS in computer science from PPGC-UFRGS (1976), and a BS in electronic engineering (1968). His research interests include information systems, e-learning, database systems and applications, conceptual modeling and ontology, applications of database technology, and distributed systems. He has published about 160 papers, has been advisor of 10 PhD and 47 MS students. For a full official curriculum see http://buscatextual.cnpq.br/buscatextual/visualizacv.jsp?id=K4783549P2.

Emmanuel Passos is a pioneer in Brazil for artificial intelligence. He has a mathematics degree from the Federal University Brazil; an MS in computer science from PUC-Rio; and a PhD in computer science from the Federal University Brazil and a postdoctoral degree from Purdue University, USA. From 1973 to 1977 he headed the project "Software for the First Brazilian Computer - G10". Currently he holds a position as visiting scholar at the Department of Electrical Engineering at Pontifical Catholic University of Rio de Janeiro, where he is a research advisor on data mining and text mining. He has also authored five books in computer science.

Roberto Penteado is a professional journalist and has worked since 1990 at the Brazilian Agricultural Research Corporation-Embrapa. He concluded in October of 2006 a PhD of information and communication sciences at the University du Sud Toulon Var, Toulon, France. His expertise is in the areas of information and communication sciences, with emphasis in quantitative methods and bibliometry, text and data analyses, competitive intelligence, SC&T indicators, knowledge management, strategical management, organizational communication, communication management, public relations, and social responsibility.

Ronaldo Cristiano Prati was awarded both the MS and PhD in computer science from the University of São Paulo, Brazil (2003 and 2006, respectively). His reseach interests include machine learning for data and text mining. Currently he holds a postdoctoral research position at the Laboratory of Computational Intelligence at the Institute of Mathematics and Computer Science of the University of São Paulo, Campus Sao Carlos.

Wu Man Qi has a MS in informatics in artificial intelligence from the University of Brasilia, Brazil (2005) and currently is a specialist in technology of information at the Federal Court of Accounts, Brazil. She worked at Interlgis as a consultant of the United Nations Development Program (2000-2004) and is also a collaborator in research of the application of collective intelligence on Web search in the University of Brasilia.

Horacio Saggion is a research fellow in the Natural Language Processing Group in the Department of Computer Science, University of Sheffield. His area of expertise is text summarization. He works on information extraction, question answering, and text summarization. He obtained his PhD (2000) from Université de Montréal, Département d'Informatique et de Recherche Operationnelle. He has published over 40 works in conferences, workshops, and journal papers as well as written two book chapters. From 1987 until 1996, he was assistant professor and researcher at the Universidad de Buenos Aires, Argentina. He has been a member of several scientific program committees in natural language processing and artificial intelligence and organized several scientific events in his field of expertise. He was researcher for a number of European and UK projects. He has received a number of awards including Ministério de Cultura y Educación de la Nación Award (Argentina), Fundación Antorchas Award (Argentina), and Agence Canadienne de Développement International Award (Canada).

Shigeaki Sakurai was born on April 11, 1966, in Japan. He received both the MS and PhD from the Science University of Tokyo (1991 and 2001, respectively). He joined Toshiba Corporation (1991), where he is a research scientist at the System Engineering Laboratory. His research interests are text mining techniques and sequential mining techniques, and he develops systems employing these techniques. Dr.

Sakurai is a PEJp in the field of information engineering, is a director of the Japan Society for Fuzzy Theory and Intelligent Informatics, and served as financial chair of the international conference SCIS & ISIS 2006.

Jie Tang is now an associate professor in Department of Computer Science and Technology (DCST), Tsinghua University. He was born in 1977 and got the PhD from DCST, Tsinghua (2006). His research directions are information extraction, text mining, Semantic Web, ontology interoperability, and machine learning. He has published more than 30 research papers in conferences/journals, such as SIGKDD, ISWC, and WWW. He has participated in several research projects funded by NSFC. More information can be found on his homepage: http://keg.cs.tsinghua.edu.cn/persons/tj.

Domonkos Tikk is a senior researcher at Budapest University of Technology and Economics (BUTE). He has received his PhD (2000) from the same institution in fuzzy systems. His research covers text and data mining, natural language processing (NLP), Internet search engines, fuzzy systems, and soft computing techniques. Recently he has been focusing on classification problems, particularly hierarchical text categorization, and NLP related problems. The team led by D. Tikk won the prestigious ACM Knowledge Discovery and Data Mining (KDD) cup (2006), and achieved three runner-up awards at the same competition (2005 and 2006).

Attila Törcsvári, owner and general manager of Arcanum Development Ltd, received his MS in computer science from the Eötvös Lorand University (1990). He was awarded with the Pro Sciencia medal of the Hungarian Academy of Sciences (1989) in the field of computational geometry. His company has worked for international organizations since 1994. Its main interest areas are categorizations of intellectual property, taxonomy building and management, legal text management, and publication.

Shouyang Wang received the PhD in operations research from Institute of Systems Science, Chinese Academy of Sciences (CAS), Beijing (1986). He is currently a Bairen distinguished professor of management science at Academy of Mathematics and Systems Sciences of CAS and a Lotus chair professor of Hunan University, Changsha. He is the editor-in-chief or a co-editor of 12 journals. He has published 18 books and over 150 journal papers. His current research interests include financial engineering, e-auctions, knowledge management, and decision analysis.

Li Weigang has a PhD in computer science and operation research from the Technological Institute of Aeronautics, Brazil (1994) and currently is an associate professor at the Department of Computer Science of the University of Brasilia and vice-president of the Brazilian Air Transportation Research Society (SBTA). He is also a researcher of the Brazilian Science and Technology Committee (CNPq) and leader of some research projects. His research interests include artificial intelligent in Web and transportation application.

Leandro Krug Wives is associate professor of computer science at the Federal University of Rio Grande do Sul (UFRGS). He has a PhD in computer science from PPGC-UFRGS (2004); an MS in computer science from PPGC-UFRGS (1999), and a BS in computer science (1996) at the Catholic University of Pelotas (UCPEL). His research interests include text mining, clustering, recommender systems, information retrieval, information extraction, and digital libraries.

Lean Yu received the PhD in management sciences and engineering from the Institute of Systems Science, Academy of Mathematics and Systems Sciences, Chinese Academy of Sciences (2005). He is currently a research fellow at Department of Management Sciences of City University of Hong Kong. He has published about 20 papers in journals including *IEEE Transactions on Knowledge and Data Engineering, European Journal of Operational Research, International Journal of Intelligent Systems,* and *Computers & Operations Research.* His research interests include artificial neural networks, Web text mining, multi-agent technology, decision support systems, and financial forecasting.

Duo Zhang is now a MS student in the Knowledge Engineering Group (KEG), Department of Computer Science at Tsinghua University. He received his BS from Department of Computer Science at Tsinghua University (2005), and expects to receive his MS from the same department in (2007). He started his research in KEG from (2005), and his research interests include information extraction, data mining, information retrieval, and statistical machine learning. From December 2004 to March 2006, he was a visiting student in Microsoft Research Asia, and his research work there focused on topic word extraction from data streams. Currently, he is working with Jie Tang, Mingcai Hong, and Juanzi Li on social network research. He has published three academic papers. For more details, please refer to Mr. Zhang's home page: http://keg.cs.tsinghua.edu.cn/persons/duozhang.

Index